Also by Diane Solway

A DANCE AGAINST TIME:
THE BRIEF, BRILLIANT LIFE OF
A JOFFREY DANCER

Nureyev: His Life

NUREYEV:

HIS LIFE

Diane Solway

William Morrow and Company, Inc.

NEW YORK

It is the policy of William Morrow and Company, Inc., and its imprints
and affiliates, recognizing the importance of preserving what has been
written, to print the books we publish on acid-free paper, and we exert
our best efforts to that end.

Library of Congress Cataloging-in-Publication Data
Solway, Diane.
    Nureyev, his life / Diane Solway.
    p.   cm.
    Includes bibliographical references and index.
    ISBN 0-688-12873-4
    1. Nureyev, Rudolf, 1938–1993.   2. Ballet dancers—Russia
(Federation)—Biography.   I. Title.
GV1785.N8S66   1998
792.8'028'092—dc21
[B]   98-13483
                                                                    CIP

Printed in the United States of America

First Edition

1   2   3   4   5   6   7   8   9   10

Frontispiece photograph by Snowdon.

For David

ACKNOWLEDGMENTS

Given that Rudolf Nureyev was the most traveled dancer in history, his life comprised many lives in countless cities large and small, and populated by a seeming cast of thousands. In pursuing Nureyev from Russia to the West and back again, I interviewed more than two hundred firsthand participants, many of them repeatedly, over five years. The biographer, wrote Virginia Woolf, must go "ahead of the rest of us, like the miner's canary, testing the atmosphere, detecting falsity, unreality, and the presence of obsolete conventions." To that end I have revisited scenes and stories, all the while intent on conveying the sweep of Nureyev's life and the complexity of the man at its center.

The quest for Nureyev has been an absorbing adventure, one I could not have undertaken or completed without the support, humor, and insight of my husband and soulmate David Resnicow, to whom this book is dedicated. He has read every word many times over, challenged easy assumptions, and made invaluable suggestions and improvements at every turn. No writer could have a more dedicated editor.

I am also extremely grateful to Lisa Queen for nurturing this book into print, and to Susan Halligan, my original editor, for her enthusiasm and advocacy during the book's earliest and most challenging stages. Ann Shortell, with her usual generosity and keen judgment, not only read and commented on the original manuscript but provided immeasurable assistance and care during its preparation. Dennis Freedman pointed me toward some wonderful sources and generously lent his unparalleled expertise in the selection of photographs; Laura Coverson read portions of the manuscript and made helpful suggestions. Mark von Hagen of the Harriman Institute at Columbia University gave a number of chapters a close reading and helped to clarify the fine points of Soviet politics.

I am particularly indebted to Natasha Gerasimova, my principal Russian translator, whose skill, compassion, and ability to convey the subtlest nuances contributed enormously to my understanding of Nureyev's early years. I would also like to thank Nureyev's sister Razida Yevgrafova and niece Alfia Rafikova for their trust and not least their patience in fielding hundreds of questions over the last five years. They also shared with me family documents, letters and photographs, many of which are published here for the first time.

In Ufa, the Nureyevs' longtime neighbor Inna Guskova gave me a tour of the neighborhood and, as curator of the Rudolf Nureyev Museum, organized several interviews at the Ufa Opera House. Aza Kuchumova, another neighbor and childhood friend, opened her home to me, while Albert Arslanov spent many hours recalling his closest boyhood friend.

In St. Petersburg, Tamara Zakrzhevskaya and Liuba Myasnikova gave extensive interviews, as did Menia Martinez in Brussels; Clara Saint, Charles Jude, the late Igor Eisner, the late Genya Polyakov and Michel Canesi in Paris; Joan Thring, John Lanchbery, Keith Money, Antoinette Sibley and Lynn Seymour in London; Rudi van Dantzig in Amsterdam; Luigi Pignotti in Milan; Carla Fracci in Florence; Marika Besobrasova in Monte Carlo; Susse Wold in Copenhagen; the late Wilhelm Hübner in Vienna; Linda Maybarduk, Karen Kain and Sergiu Stefanschi in Toronto; Alla Osipenko in Hartford, Connecticut; Sonia Arova in Birmingham, Alabama; Patricia Neary in Los Angeles; and Jane Hermann, Irina Kolpakova and Mikhail Baryshnikov in New York.

Lola Fisher dug into long-forgotten boxes to retrieve fascinating photographs and a program, the first Nureyev inscribed in English. Val Golovitser and Yevgenya Tykotski, the Bolshoi and Kirov of balletomanes, led me to key sources in their respective home cities and arranged interviews. Sergei Mironenko helped open doors to a number of Russian archives, including the Russian State Military Archive, the Archive of the Ministry of Defense and the Center for Storing Contemporary Documentation (formerly the Archive of the Central Committee of the CPSU). Millicent Hodson and Kenneth Archer also offered leads in the book's early stages, as did André Larquié and Hélène Traïline, formerly of the Paris Opéra Ballet. Bernard Spitz and Isabelle LeBret were my generous hosts in Paris. I am also grateful to Phyllis Wyeth for giving me permission to publish photographs from her family album and to Suzanne Weil for her enthusiastic support.

Hugo Vickers, too, deserves special thanks, not only for opening his biographer's dream of a library to me, but for leading me to Michael Wishart and to Wishart's letter to Stephen Tennant, and for generously sharing with me Cecil Beaton's voluminous unpublished diaries. I thank him both for allowing me to quote from them and for his steadfast encouragement.

In addition to those already cited, I conducted interviews with the following, many of whom gave me hours of their time or other significant assistance. My thanks to them and my apologies to anyone I have inadvertently overlooked.

Edward Albee, Lucette Aldous, Gregory Alexinsky, Gerd Andersson, Querube Arias, Giovanna Augusta, Frank Augustyn, Armen Bali, Charles Barker, Patrice Bart, Keith Baxter, Pierre Bergé, Michael Birkmeyer, Mario Bois, Vladimir Brovkin, Joy Brown, Michael Brown, Betty Cage, Yvette Chauviré, Theodora Christon, Sybil Christopher, Colette Clark, Florence Clerc, Elizabeth Cooper, David Cronin, Nikita Dolgushin, Anthony Dowell, Senta Driver, Gilles Dufour, Natalia Dudinskaya, Janet Eilber, Wendy Ellis, Mica Ertegün, Eva Evdokimova, Marianne Faithfull, HRH Princess Firyal, Flemming Flindt, Vivi Flindt, Charles France, Ezio Frigerio, Christopher Gable, Giuliana Gargiulo, Patrick Garland, Farid Gilfanov, Ingrid Glindemann, Alexander Grant, Kenneth Greve, Andrew Grossman, Marit Gruson, Isabelle Guérin, Jean Guizerix, Natasha Harley, Vanessa Harwood, Melissa Hayden, Susan Hendl, Rosella Hightower, Laurent Hilaire, Marat Hismatullin, Barbara Horgan, Lydia Hübner, Elisabeth Hübner, Derek Jarman, Zizi Jeanmaire, Martin Kamer, Rosemarie Kanzler, Hiram Keller, Patrick Kinmoth, Ninel Kurgapkina, Pierre Lacotte, Robert La Fosse, André Larquié, Gerd Larsen, Tatiana Legat, Manuel Legris, David Lewellyn, Silva Lon, Monique Loudières, François Loussasa, Roch-Olivier Maistre, Askold Makarov, HRH The Princess Margaret, Peter Martins, Monica Mason, Boaz Mazor, Aileen Mehle, Beppe Menegatti, Zaitouna Nazretdinova, Joanne Nisbet, Gouzel Nureyeva, Patrick O'Connor, Betty Oliphant, Elisabeth Platel, Maya Plisetskaya, Ron Protas, Baron Alexis de Redé, Vicomtesse Jacqueline de Ribes, Liz Robertson, Simon "Blue" Robinson, Gerald Rosenberg, Herbert Ross, the late Baronne Marie-Hélène de Rothschild, Patricia Ruanne, Anthony Russell-Roberts, Lady Sainsbury, David Scott, Vladilen Semonov, Alla Sizova, Earl of Snowdon, the late Michael Somes, the late Sergei Sorokin, Peter Sparling, Franca Squarciapino, Pamira Suleimanova, Thor Sutowski, John Taras, Paul Taylor, Elena Tchernichova, Veronica Tennant, Glen Tetley, James Toback, Sir John Tooley, Jeremiah Tower, Hélène Traïline, Dame Ninette de Valois, Monique van Vooren, Vladimir Vasiliev, Gloria Venturi, Violette Verdy, Elizabeth Vickers, Marina Vivien, Catherine Walrafen, Lord Weidenfeld, Sam Welsh, Valerie Wilder, the late Michael Wishart, Jamie Wyeth, and Loretta Young.

In my research, I was fortunate to have such tireless assistants as Donald Thumim of the Davis Center for Russian Studies at Harvard University and Nancy Sifton, who also transcribed numerous tapes, chased down facts, and delved into her own considerable collection of Nureyev clippings, photographs and programs. Nancy also braved the enormous task of compiling a list of Nureyev's performances in the West. Robert Greskovic supplied a chronology of Nureyev's key roles in the West, Lynne and Sandy Perry turned over volumes of press clippings, and Peter Cunningham tracked down Rudolf Nureyev Dance Foundation records. Gerard Raymond conducted an interview with the late Derek Jarman on my behalf and transcribed a number of interviews. Pamela Wain helped with fact-checking and Rachel Leyshon tracked down photographs and information.

In addition, I would like to acknowledge the assistance of the following curators, archives and resources: the Rudolf Nureyev Museum, Ufa; Marina Vivien, curator of the Vaganova Ballet Academy; Marina Ilichova, administrator of the Kirov Ballet; the Center for Storing Contemporary Documentation in Moscow; Francesca Franchi, Royal Ballet Archives; Janet Jempson; Sarah Woodcock, Theatre Museum; Pierre Vidal, Sophie Feldmann and Claire Tréhou, Bibliothèque-Musée de l'Opéra; Irina Klyagin, the Dance Collection, New York Public Library at Lincoln Center; Elena Gordon and Bob Pontarelli, American Ballet Theatre.

Translators also played a significant role, and I'd like to record my debt to Aaron Betsky (Dutch), Denis Bellocq (French), Alexander Storozhuk and Anna Thumim (Russian) and Melly Resnicow (German).

For their loving encouragement at various crossroads and their unflagging interest in the progress of this book, I am also grateful to my parents, Elaine Solway and Herb Solway, my brothers, Gary and Michael, my grandmother Sophia Bassin, my late father-in-law, Herb Resnicow, the Moore family, Carole Solway, Sylvia Schwartz and the late Pamela Allen. And for their friendship, moral support and other assistance, my thanks to Laura Coverson, Dennis Freedman, John Carrafa, Jennifer Fischer, Gabrielle Glaser, Andrew Farber, Isabel Bassett, Steve Engelberg, Sharon Messitte and Margaret Hornick.

My gratitude also extends to Harvey Ginsberg, my sharp-eyed editor at William Morrow, for his intelligent direction; to Richard Aquan for his cover design; and to Patrick Dillon for his close reading of the manuscript in its final stages. No less essential has been the gentle care and astute counsel of my agent, Barney Karpfinger, and the optimism of Weidenfeld and Nicholson's Ion Trewin, whose enthusiasm for this project proved invigorating.

My final thanks must go to my son, Nicholas, who waited until the day his mother finished writing this life story before beginning his own.

CONTENTS

Nureyev: His Life

Prologue

THE LINE BEGAN FORMING hours before the event itself, stretching well down Fifty-ninth Street. By 7 P.M. there wasn't a seat to be had in either the main room or the gallery that had been added for the overflow crowd. The standing room was packed with television crews and reporters. It was yet another opening night, and even posthumously, the most celebrated dancer of the century exerted his seductive pull.

The sale of Rudolf Nureyev's artworks, costumes and personal belongings at Christie's New York had all the elements that make an auction something more than the sum of its parts: abundant publicity, intrigue and a flamboyant superstar at its center. Simply titled "Nureyev," Christie's biggest celebrity sale yet was launched with a six-day preview which began, curiously, on the second anniversary of the great dancer's death from AIDS on January 6, 1993. He was fifty-four years old. In its aggressive marketing campaign, the auction house produced a lavish catalogue, stuffed with photographs by Snowdon, and sleek black shopping bags inked with bold red letters that read "Nureyev, Join us in January, Christie's."

A record crowd of fifty thousand fans, collectors and the merely curious thronged the auction house that week in the hopes of edging close to the man behind the luxurious, if eclectic, contents of his New York home, a six-room apartment at the landmark Dakota building overlooking Central Park. Here Nureyev perched for more than a decade during his stays in the city, entertaining a battalion of friends and acquaintances, everyone from Jacqueline Onassis, Dame Margot Fonteyn, Leonard Bernstein and Jerome Robbins to fledgling dancers and musicians to call-service hustlers and one-night stands.

Over a lifetime of impassioned acquiring he had gathered antique maps, Old Master paintings, academic studies of male nudes, bundles of kilim carpets, antique musical instruments, books and sheet music. There was a Roman white marble torso; a carved Elizabethan four-poster bed; an eight-foot rococo Murano glass chandelier; eighteenth-century hand-painted Chinese wallpaper panels; a Russian birchwood settee on winged gilded feet.

These were but a portion of Nureyev's possessions, the markers of a nomadic life, their sheer range and volume as much a testament to his impoverished beginnings as to his taste for the exotic and erotic. It was not surprising that a man who was famously slow to trust, one who spent much of his life dodging taxes and the KGB, should have preferred to invest his earnings in the tangible, in real estate and objets d'art, in things he could see and touch and admire. So addicted was he to collecting that he not only amassed seven homes—in London, Paris, Monte Carlo, New York, St.-Bart's, a farm in Virginia and an island in Italy—but filled many of them with his burgeoning collections. "Everything I have," he proudly acknowledged toward the end of his life, "the legs have danced for."

There were also the items touched by celebrity: the snakeskin Nehru jacket with matching pants and boots that Nureyev had worn on a much-talked-of television interview, the costumes he had worn in such ballets as *Giselle*, *Le Corsaire*, *Don Quixote* and two matching mustard velvet sofas that had once belonged to Maria Callas, another of the vanishing breed known as *monstre sacré*, as Nureyev was often called.

In its Park Avenue galleries, Christie's had attempted to re-create Nureyev's grandly theatrical stage set of an apartment. But without Nureyev's commanding presence to animate them, the furniture looked worn, and the rooms felt somehow vacant, dismantled. More than the beautiful objets, paintings, and fin-de-siècle grandeur, however, what drew many to Christie's was the chance to walk off with a piece of the Nureyev legend. Or as Christie's more crudely put it in a full-page advertisement in *The New York Times*: "Dance home with something Nureyev loved!"

"NEVER LOOK BACK," Nureyev liked to say, "that way, you fall downstairs." Over a glass of wine late at night in the company of close friends, he might offer up a shard from the past, but most who knew him trod warily when asking him about his youth or ruled it unwise to ask at all. Schooled from birth in the art of survival, Nureyev had little interest in his own past and neither the time nor inclination for nostalgia. And yet many of his characteristic traits took root in early childhood: his remarkable resilience, his unwavering self-assurance, his bracing candor, his appetite for knowledge and, not least, his innate sense that boundaries were meant to be crossed. He spent the better part of his youth trying to move out of the remote Ural village where he had grown up and into Leningrad's hallowed Kirov Ballet. Upon arriving at his destination, he was reluctant to retrace his steps. He never stopped moving forward, eager for the freedom to go where he wanted to go, to perform what he wanted to perform, to become whatever he wanted to make of himself. After his defection to the West, he became, overnight, an international star and political symbol, and he disliked revisiting even that momentous event, particularly with the Parisian friends who had witnessed it. "It's finished," Nureyev said curtly when one of them brought it up. "Why talk about it?" In later years, when another friend suggested that Nureyev missed his family, friends and roots, Nureyev was quick to correct him: "Don't put things in my mind that are not mine. These are your ideas. I am perfectly happy here. I don't miss anybody or anything. Life here has given me everything I want, all possibilities."

By assuming that anything was possible, Nureyev redefined his art as no other dancer had done before or done since. Within months of his defection, he had created a whole new audience for ballet. He not only restored the male dancer to a place of prominence, he brought sex to an art form long associated with the effete, stirring women and men alike. He reignited the fading career of Margot Fonteyn and together they became the most charismatic duo in ballet. Traversing the globe on his own, he became the most traveled dancer in history, an evangelist for the dance.

Offstage, he shrewdly orchestrated his role as an elite member of the emerging celebrity culture. If he possessed the haughty grandeur of the great star, he was not without the earthy cunning of his Tatar forebears. Having burst upon the Western world with a mere thirty francs to his name, he quickly set about amassing a fortune estimated to be about twenty-five to thirty million dollars at the time of his death. He set a marathon schedule for himself, determined to feel all of life's textures. He swathed himself in Missoni shawls, wore thigh-high boots and leathers. Though stinting when sharing his money with others, he was the most generous of artists, giving endlessly of himself to audiences. Through his teaching, coaching and directing, he inspired generations of dancers and dance lovers.

To the end, Nureyev projected his prodigious energy forward, filling his calendar with performances even in the final stages of AIDS. Repose was neither considered nor planned for.

THE MOOD WAS HIGH the first night of the auction on January 12, 1995. Of all the items on the block, it was the seventeen lots of worn, soiled and tattered ballet slippers that created the most excitement. Nureyev was loath to part with favorite shoes, and these crusty scraps of leather, many of them glued, stitched and reglued hundreds of times over, still retained the perfume of performance, the sweat of effort expended. The slippers linked spectator to performer in a way no other memento could, their totemic power drawing many inside the auction house for the first time, just as Nureyev's dancing had once drawn scores of newcomers to the ballet. In the process, he had become ballet's first pop star, an international celebrity known as much for his high living as for his vaulting leaps on the world's stages.

The presale estimates for the shoes were surprisingly low—just $40–$60 for the most worn and, even more curious, $150–$200 for the barely used ("Apart from some very slight soiling in very good condition"). During the preview, Christie's mounted the shoes for display using double-sided tape on the soles, damaging the patina of performance. The first set of shoes offered for sale were four white slippers estimated at $150–$200. When auctioneer Christopher Burge started the bidding at $1,000, an audible groan went up. By the end of the night, one pair of pale pink slippers, worn, soiled and estimated at $40–$60, brought a record $9,200 as well as shrieks, tears and rounds of applause from the astonished crowd. Christie's had miscalculated in valuing the objects over the life that had informed them.

Nureyev had predicted that the dispersal of his estate would have its own backstage intrigue. Christie's had originally planned to sell the contents of both his New York and Paris apartments in back-to-back auctions in New York and London, but the auctions had to be postponed after one of Nureyev's sisters and his niece contested his will in court. The proceeds of the sales were to go to the two foundations Nureyev had created, largely for tax reasons, one in Europe, the other in America. However, Nureyev's relatives disputed whether Nureyev really intended to give these foundations control of his assets. When Nureyev's friends accused them of being greedy, especially since he had left them money, they countered that he intended for his possessions to be housed in a museum. In his will, Nureyev specified that a museum should be created in his memory in Paris, but just what should be included was a matter of confusion and contention. Only after the two foundations agreed to buy back a number of costumes and photographs at the sale, and to reserve many of those in Paris for some future exhibition, among other concessions, did his sister Rosa and niece Gouzel agree not to block the New York auction. Hours before the New York auction began, Gouzel, her lawyers, the foundations' lawyers and Christie's lawyers met just a few blocks from Christie's to select items from the catalogue to be withdrawn. Having already settled a claim filed by one of Nureyev's many former lovers, the American foundation, headed by Nureyev's longtime tax lawyer, was eager to avoid any further delay or embarrassment. Though the London sale would go ahead the following November, the accusations and legal entanglements would continue well beyond both auctions.

In the end the possessions that mattered most to Nureyev were in the traveling case he always kept with him: the shoes, costumes and other tools of his life on the stage, the only place, he claimed, he felt truly at home. As Mikhail Baryshnikov eloquently observed after his death, "He was serious about being on the stage in any capacity—dancer, choreographer, conductor. That is what he lived for. He couldn't imagine his life without it."

1

The Season of Bad Roads

IN MARCH 1938, Farida Nureyeva packed up her belongings and together with her three young daughters, Rosa, eight, Lilya, seven, and Razida, three, boarded the Trans-Siberian Express near her home in Kushnarenkovo, a small Ural village halfway between Leningrad and Siberia. Her husband, Hamet, a political officer in the Red Army, was stationed on Russia's easternmost border, just outside the Pacific port city of Vladivostok.

Farida had only reluctantly agreed to make the six-day journey across Siberia and the Russian Far East. At thirty-three, she was eight and a half months pregnant and worried that she might go into labor on the train. She would have three small girls to mind and the railway cars were sure to be crowded with soldiers and refugees. There would be little room for her to lie down and rest, and few diversions for the children. The train made two brief stops a day, but the March winds were so severe they made her ears ache, making it impossible to spend more than a few minutes out of doors. She feared there would be no one to help her and little in the way of medical assistance should anything go awry. This she dreaded most of all.

And yet Farida was anxious to be reunited with her husband and didn't want to delay the trip until after the baby's birth, when travel might prove even more taxing. After her neighbors reassured her that two military doctors and another family from their village would be traveling on the same train, Farida proceeded with the thirty-nine-hundred-mile journey. A small, pretty woman with doleful brown eyes, Farida Nureyeva was not in the least frail or fainthearted. Her black hair, parted severely in the center and wrapped neatly around her ears, framed a wide, proud face, its complexion dulled by hardship. In the ten years she and Hamet had been married, their lives had been irrevocably altered by the turbulent social and political currents sweeping the country. For generations, Hamet's family had worked in the fields, a pattern only recently broken by the Revolution. In the new social order, the ambitious Hamet had been able to reinvent himself and he had gladly exchanged the mantle of poor Tatar peasant for the more promising one of *politruk*. His advance through the ranks had brought a steady change of postings, which required him to be perpetually on the move. Often, Farida was left alone for weeks on end to look after their small children. But uprooted as their life had been, they had lived among their own people and in familiar surroundings in whichever Tatar village Hamet happened to be sent.

This trip to the Far East, however, marked a departure from the patterns of their past, and as Farida boarded the train, she couldn't dispel her nagging fears, despite all the reassurances she had been given. She had never taken such a long journey before and she was moving her children from the relatively safe haven of the Ural Mountains to a potentially dangerous port of call. She wondered what kind of life she could make there for her children, especially for the infant she now awaited with anticipation and concern.

As the Trans-Siberian snaked its way across the undulating Urals and into Siberia, past hundreds of identical small towns and gaily painted wooden bungalows, Farida passed the time gazing out at the snow-blanketed steppes, the monotony of white broken now and then by ghostly forests of pine and silver birch. Meanwhile, Rosa, Lilya and Razida took delight in this new adventure and passed the time running up and down the corridors, exploring the train with great excitement, only dimly aware of just how soon their new sibling would arrive.

On March 17, Farida went into labor. She was still nineteen hundred miles from Vladivostok. As promised, her neighbors sent for the doctors, and clean white sheets were spread about the carriage. Sometime that afternoon, Farida gave birth to a boy. Upon hearing his first cries, his sister Rosa became so enraptured that she neglected to pay attention to the comings and goings of other passengers in the corridor and caught her fingers in a closing door, her sobs mingling with those of her newborn brother. Following a Muslim custom that children's names should begin with the same letter as that of the first child, Farida named her son Rudolf.* She picked the name for its sonorous rhythms and not in honor of Rudolph Valentino, as has sometimes been presumed.†

*The second Nureyev daughter, Lilya, was the exception, though the reason for it is a mystery even Lilya's daughter cannot unravel.

†According to her daughter Razida, the silent screen star and the glamour of 1920s Hollywood he came to represent were utterly unknown to her mother at the time.

Carried in his mother's arms, the Nureyevs' only son was at the beginning of a journey that would take him from one end of the country to the other, and nearly halfway back again—some seven thousand miles over the next five years. The upheaval of those first years would leave him with a permanent sense of rootlessness. He would always be a gypsy, never a native. "It seems to me very symbolic and revealing that I should have been born en route, in between two places. It makes me feel that it was my destiny to be cosmopolitan. Ever since I was born, I have had no real sense of 'belonging'; no real country or house to call my own. My existence had none of the usual, normal limitations which make for a feeling of permanence and this has always left me with a strong sensation of having been born stateless."

Beginning with the time and place of his birth, Nureyev's life was fraught with uncertainty. Unfortunately neither his birth records nor relatives' recollections provide any conclusive answers, a problem that dogs anyone trying to piece together the details of a life that began in the darkest hours of the Stalinist era. Even Nureyev himself came up short when, late in his life, he tried to divine the precise moment of his birth in order to have his astrological chart done. While the family story has it that he was born in the afternoon, neither Nureyev's sister Razida nor his niece Alfia—both of whom lived with Farida Nureyeva—recall ever hearing her mention where he was born along the Trans-Siberian route. Rudolf, however, claimed not to have any doubts: In his memoir, which has served as the basis for preceding accounts of his life, he notes that the train was "dashing along the banks of the Baikal Lake, not far from Irkutsk" and that his sister Rosa, then eight, got off the train at Irkutsk to wire their father with the good news. But geography rules his account impossible: On the Trans-Siberian route, one arrives at Irkutsk prior to rounding Lake Baikal, the world's largest and deepest freshwater lake.* Rudolf—or his mother—may have simply chosen Baikal as the spot to mark his birth because it was the only natural wonder along the dreary route. His ghostwritten memoir, it should be remembered, was published in the West in 1962, at a time when eyewitnesses could not be consulted, and when much was unknown to even Nureyev, particularly regarding the early history of his family.

Nureyev's birth was registered on April 4, 1938, eighteen days after it took place, in Razdolnoye, the town nearest Hamet's army base. Farida, exhausted after reaching the Far East, needed to regain her strength before traveling into town to register his birth, which, by law, she had

---

*If we accept that Rosa wired their father from Irkutsk, then Rudolf would have had to have been born at some point west of Baikal or along the Angara River, Baikal's only outlet. If Rosa didn't disembark at Irkutsk but farther east, then it's possible that he was born either on Baikal's southern shores or at some other point along the route, closer to Vladivostok.

one month to do. Rudolf's birth certificate lists Razdolnoye as the place of both his birth and registration. This may have been a clerical error or perhaps Farida's convenient way of dealing with officialdom.

Regardless of the precise details, Rudolf's birth could not have come at a more volatile or violent moment: The nation was in the final convulsions of the Great Terror and the world was heading toward war. That same month Germany annexed Austria and the third of the infamous show trials was under way in Moscow, at the end of which seventeen leading Bolsheviks, including the party theoretician Nikolai Bukharin, would be executed. Looming ominously over the proceedings was Joseph Stalin, who by 1938 was consolidating his absolute power through terror, intimidation and wholesale purges. Stalin's purge of the party had begun in 1934 with the murder of Sergei Kirov, the popular Leningrad party boss whose name would be given to the ballet company where Rudolf would make his mark years later.

The Kirov assassination pitched the country into a state of mass hysteria. Where preceding campaigns of repression had aimed at specific social classes, the Great Terror opened fire on the entire population, eliminating not only party members, but just about anyone else who "might still show some initiative, have faith in moral values, believe in revolution or in anything other than Stalin." In 1936, at the first of the Moscow show trials, the old Bolsheviks Grigori Zinoviev and Lev Kamenev "confessed" to murdering Kirov and plotting to kill Stalin, and were executed. Their confessions were filmed and distributed widely.

"Everywhere and in everything [Stalin] saw 'enemies,' 'two-facers' and spies," observed Nikita Khrushchev. Children were turned against their parents; friends and relatives against one another. Informing was the order of the day. Denunciations were not only taken as proof of guilt, but seen as an act of patriotism, though the charges were almost always entirely false, prompted as they were by fear, torture, envy or spite. Throughout the *yezhovshchina*,* as the nightmare years 1936 through 1938 were known, the NKVD's "black raven" sedans took victims from their homes at night; most were never heard from again. Many disappeared off sidewalks; others from railway cars. No one, writes a historian of the period, "save Stalin himself, could be certain of not being woken in the small hours of the night by a knock at the door, dragged out of bed and snatched away from family and friends . . . no one could be sure of not attracting the next accusation in the capricious chain. Many people, in fact, lived with a small suitcase permanently packed with a few essentials, just in case." Among the victims was a man who removed a portrait of Stalin while painting a wall and a seventy-year-old school-

---

*Nikolai Yezhov, to whom the term refers, was then head of the NKVD, the forerunner to the KGB.

teacher using an old textbook which still had a picture of Trotsky. An estimated one thousand people per day were executed in 1937.

By the time Farida Nureyeva boarded the train for Vladivostok, millions had been sent to their deaths and millions more to prisons and camps in Siberia and the far north, where few survived. "If I had the vast spaces of Siberia," Hitler remarked, "I wouldn't need concentration camps." In March 1938, the population of the Gulag was nearly eight million; in one labor camp alone, more prisoners were shot in 1938 than in the entire previous century under the czars.

Prominent cultural figures were also persecuted, killed and dispatched to labor camps. The bold experiments of the 1920s had been rejected in favor of Socialist Realism and the party had become the sole authority and censor in all spheres of the arts. Artists were reduced to little more than propagandists for the state. Stalin personally revised Sergei Eisenstein's screenplay for *Alexander Nevsky*, released in 1938, editing out the scene of Alexander's death. "Such a good prince must not die!" Great poets were another matter. The year Nureyev was born, Osip Mandelstam died in a labor camp, following his arrest a few months earlier. His widow, Nadezhda, was convinced that terror had made the Russian people "slightly unbalanced mentally — not exactly ill, but not normal either." Still, slogans reminded the Soviet people daily that "life has become better. Life is more joyful."

Such was the apocalypse into which Nureyev was born, a period when one of the most popular songs in the country proclaimed: "I know of no other country where people breathe so freely."

EVEN IF they weren't exactly thriving during the terror years, Nureyev's parents still believed that they were helping to create a brighter future for their children than their own parents had bequeathed to them. Certainly life in 1938 held more possibilities for peasants such as Hamet and Farida than it had in 1903, the year Hamet Nureyev had been born in Asanovo, a small Ural village. Little more than a generation away from serfdom, his parents were poor peasants, Muslim Tatars who tilled their narrow strip of land and struggled through near famine to provide for their two sons, Hamet and Nurislam, and three daughters, Saima, Fatima and Jamila. To step inside their *izba*, a log cabin on the bank of the Karmazan River, was to experience traditional, patriarchal rural life, one bound by religion and custom and cut off from the country's political debates.

The family name was originally Fasliyev, not Nureyev. At birth, Rudolf's father was named Hamet Nuriakhmetovich Fasliyev, after his own father, Nuriakhmet Fasliyevich Fasliyev. However, surnames were never firmly fixed in Russian villages until the first decades of this century and boys were often known by their patronymics. Thus, in Asanovo,

Rudolf's father was known as Nuriakhmetovich, or Nuri's son. (*Nuri* is
a Tatar word meaning "beam of light.") It was a common Tatar practice
for boys to take their father's given names as their surnames, which is
how Hamet Fasliyev became Hamet Fasliyevich Nuriyev when he left
his village for the city of Kazan in the 1920s.* Hamet was the only member of his family to change his surname; today, his relatives still carry
the Fasliyev name.†

Hamet's Fasliyev relatives traced their lineage back to Genghis Khan
and the Mongol hordes who conquered Russia in the thirteenth century.
Ice and snow, which had previously safeguarded Russia's borders against
invaders, failed to repel these warriors, known as Mongols or Tatars, who
were said to be "inured to Siberian cold." (So feared were the Mongols
that in Europe it was believed that they were called Tatars because they
had come from Tartarus, the region below Hades where the Titans were
interned.)

Hamet's son, Rudolf, would take great pride in those bloodlines,
which would contribute to his sense of self much more keenly than his
connection to a particular place. He was Tatar and not Russian and, like
his conquering forebears, a nomad. If the indomitable character of his
adulthood owed anything to his past, it was, as *he* later described it, to
his Tatar roots, or rather, to his romanticized sense of them.

Our Tatar blood runs faster somehow, is always ready to boil. And yet it seems
to me we are more languid than the Russian, more sensuous; we have a certain
Asiatic softness in us, yet also the *fougue* of our ancestors, those lean superb
cavaliers. We are a curious mixture of tenderness and brutality—a blend which
rarely exists in the Russian. . . . Tatars are quick to catch fire, quick to get into
a fight, unassuming, yet at the same time passionate and sometimes cunning as
a fox. The Tatar is in fact a pretty complex animal: and that's what I am.

As a young boy growing up in an observant Muslim family,
Rudolf's father had dreamed of becoming a priest. Following local custom, he and his brother Nurislam had attended the village *mekteb*, the
Tatar school, which until the early years of this century had prepared
students solely for clerical life. There Hamet and his brother learned to
read and write in Arabic, Tatar and Russian. Hamet's literacy and early

*When Hamit had his own children, the authorities registered *their* surname and Farida's
surname as Nureyev (the women as Nureyeva), evidently thinking Nureyev easier to pronounce
than Nuriyev. According to Rudolf's sister Razida, Hamit didn't notice that their surnames were
spelled differently in official records until she pointed it out to him after reviewing some of his
papers, when it was already too late to do much about it.
†It has been widely presumed that the Nureyev name came about as a result of a clerical
error; however, it was Hamet Nureyev himself who changed his surname.

lessons in Russian would serve him well when he reached manhood, by which time his ambitions had shifted from the priesthood to the party.

In 1920, when Hamet was seventeen, his family, like all their Ural neighbors, found themselves caught in the crossfire between the Red Army and counterrevolutionary Whites, both of whom were battling for control of the area. Neighbors, and even members of the same family, were divided against one another. Where the Whites urged Russian solidarity, the Bolsheviks won the support of the Tatars and poor peasants by promising them autonomy and by convincing them that the counterrevolutionaries were out to exploit them. After claiming victory, the Reds made good on their promise, at least in part: Without allowing the Tatars any real autonomy, Lenin gave them their own republic and declared the ancient Mongol city of Kazan its capital.

Five years later, twenty-two-year-old Hamet had moved to Kazan to pursue a career in the military. Mixing with the Russians in Kazan was frowned upon by his family, who believed sons ought to stay in their own village. But like a great many young men from peasant origins, Hamet saw the army as his avenue of upward mobility, leading to important party jobs. With a view to one day joining the party, Hamet presented himself to the local party cadres, who sent him for political training at the Soviet party school. When they saw what an ideal candidate he was — reliable, pliant and literate — they dispatched him at once to the cavalry academy.

Hamet graduated in 1927 and soon after joined the party. Like most new recruits at the time, he knew only the buzzwords of early Communism. He had little idea how the party was structured and could hardly have differentiated among Lenin, Trotsky and Marx. Still, he relished all that the Bolsheviks promised him: a radiant future of urban, industrial prosperity, and opportunities for education and advancement. Like Hamet, the Georgian-born Stalin also came from humble origins and spoke a heavily accented Russian. And, like Hamet, Stalin, a onetime seminarian, had also dreamed of the clergy before converting to Bolshevism and changing his name.*

The Bolsheviks were happy to open up admission. With no foothold in the countryside, they needed to strengthen the party's control over the undisciplined Russian peasant and to penetrate the vast expanse of tradition-bound rural villages. The quickest way to do it was by gaining allegiance from the people who lived in them. (At the time, nine out of ten Russians were peasants.) In an early version of affirmative action, the party made a big push to sign up national minorities.†

---

*His real name was Dzhugashvili. *Stalin* means "man of steel."

†By the end of the 1920s, Tatars were one of the groups who were actually overrepresented in the Communist Party.

It was in Kazan that Hamet met his future wife, Farida, a shy, striking woman. The daughter of Tatar peasants from the nearby village of Tugulban, twenty-three-year-old Farida Agilivulyevna had known only a fleeting childhood: At the age of seven, she lost both her parents to typhoid fever. Farida, the youngest child, was sent to Kazan to live with her oldest brother, who worked in a bakery and sent her to the local Islamic school, where she learned to read and write in Arabic. Though she spoke Tatar at home and later learned to speak Russian, Farida would insist on writing in Arabic for the rest of her life. Eventually her brother married and Farida became a maid in his home and took care of his son. The arrangement was not a happy one. Her sister-in-law disliked her and made no effort to conceal her contempt. Farida never forgot the day she was drawing water from the local well when there was a loud explosion at the nearby power plant. In her panic, she had rushed home, leaving the brand-new buckets at the well. Her sister-in-law was furious and ordered Farida to go back and retrieve them. Farida was so distressed that she soon left her brother's house.

Farida had hoped to take teacher's training courses in Kazan, but put her plans on hold soon after meeting twenty-four-year-old Hamet Nureyev in 1927. By turns reserved, kind and resolute, Hamet was a handsome, broad-shouldered young man with the pronounced Tatar cheekbones, thick black eyebrows, full lips and fierce demeanor his son would inherit. He had a muscular, sturdy build and wore his wavy black hair very short on the sides and brushed back high off his face, accentuating his widow's peak. Perhaps equally appealing to Farida, Hamet had prospects: As a party member and student at the cavalry school, he seemed poised for important assignments sure to bring him privileges. Years later, Hamet would reveal to his daughter Razida just what had drawn him to the young Farida. "Do you know why I liked your mother?" Hamet had tendered, in a rare display of candor. "Because she was a good singer and dancer." The admission came as a surprise to the Nureyevs' daughter, who, like the rest of her siblings, wasn't accustomed to declarations of affection from her parents and knew little about their early life.

Hamet and Farida were married in Kazan in 1928, the year Stalin introduced the first of his Five-Year Plans, a massive campaign to build Soviet industry and lift Russia "from backwardness up to superpower status." By then Farida had also joined the party. Their Tatar culture naturally bound them—both had grown up in observant Muslim households—but Hamet and Farida shared something more urgent: a fervent belief in the promises of Communism.* "For them the Revolution was a miracle," their son, Rudolf, later acknowledged. "At last there was a possi-

---

*The year they were wed, the Communist party had 1,360,000 members, of which 198,000 were peasants—roughly 1 Communist peasant per 125 peasant households.

bility of sending their children to school—even to the universities. . . ."
Hamet had told his new wife that if she worked until he finished
his training at the cavalry school, then he would support them while she
studied to become a teacher. Their bargain was only half realized. By the
fall of 1929, a year into their marriage, Farida was pregnant with their first
child. "He finished his schooling all right," Farida would lament to her
granddaughter. "But I never got to go to school because of the children."

That December Stalin announced the start of a new revolution, one
that would destroy forever the traditional Russian village and wipe out
the most productive peasant households. While Lenin had permitted
private farming, Stalin ordered an all-out drive to collectivize peasant
agriculture. Not only were the peasants denied the right to sell their
grain, they were deprived of their land, livestock and machinery, all of
which was to be concentrated in collective farms under party control.
The richest peasants, the so-called kulaks, were singled out as enemies
of the regime. (*Kulak* is the Russian word for "fist.") "We must smash
the kulaks," Stalin commanded, "eliminate them as a class." In theory,
a kulak was anyone who hired labor or owned a cow, plot of land or
house, but in practice, the term was so slippery that anyone who was
simply unpopular in the village or disliked by the authorities was branded
a kulak, whether they had property or not. By the spring of 1930 the party
claimed that half of all peasant households had been collectivized. The
results were ruinous. Many peasants killed their own livestock and destroyed their own fields rather than let the state have them. A quarter of
the country's livestock and 80 percent of the horses were slaughtered,
grain production slumped disastrously, and the most enterprising peasants were executed or deported to Siberia, the Urals and the far north.*

As the tempo of collectivization gained momentum, junior officers
were urgently dispatched to the countryside to quell the protests. Among
them was Hamet Nureyev. In early 1931, Hamet, Farida and their infant
daughter, Rosa, left Kazan for Kushnarenkovo, a village near Hamet's
hometown of Asanovo. There Lilya, the second Nureyev daughter, was
born that November, following her sister Rosa by seventeen months.

The Nureyevs were assigned to a house commandeered from an
exiled kulak, only to find the kulak's wife and two daughters still living
there when they arrived. Hamet's granddaughter recalls being told that
Hamet took pity on them and allowed them to stay on, a noble, if some-

*Through 1931, the country's 130 million peasants were forced into collectives, with Stalin
maintaining the pretense that this was a voluntary movement. By 1932, 62 percent of peasant
households had been collectivized; by 1937, that number had jumped to 93 percent. Each year,
Stalin increased his demands for grain, and soon starvation was widespread. Experts estimate
that between 1929 and 1937, 5 to 7 million peasants lost their lives as a result of dekulakization
and famine.

what improbable, course of action given the climate of the time and Hamet's subsequent promotion.* Just what Hamet's private feelings were about the kulaks is unknown, though it is safe to assume that he would have regarded them as parasites, as did most party members. Typically he would have opened village meetings by asking, "Who is against the collective farm and the Soviet government?" leaving no doubt about the options open to those who considered resisting. Nevertheless, many kulaks *did* resist, setting fire to Soviet buildings and beating and murdering scores of party officals. According to family legend, Hamet himself barely escaped with his life after a group of kulaks pushed him into an icy lake in the middle of winter.

Since Hamet's duties took him away from home, sometimes for weeks at a time, Farida was frequently left alone with their two infant daughters. During one of his long absences in 1932, when the country was gripped by famine, Farida went to the well for water, leaving her daughters at home so that she could carry the buckets. When she returned, five-month-old Lilya was outside in the chilly spring air. Two of the little girls in their communal house had taken her out to play, "as if she were a little doll," recalls Lilya's only daughter, Alfia. Soon after, Lilya developed meningitis. Frightened and bereft, Farida had no one to help her. The nearest hospital was twenty-four miles away in Ufa, and travel was particularly difficult, for it was April, "the season of bad roads," as it was known. Melting snow and spring rains made village streets treacherously muddy. By the time Farida managed to get her daughter to the hospital, Lilya was permanently deaf. "My grandmother always blamed my grandfather for what happened to my mother," says Lilya's daughter. "She felt that if he hadn't been away, she could have taken my mother to the hospital in time."

In 1935, Farida returned to Ufa's hospital, this time to give birth to her third daughter, Razida. Farida knew her husband would be disappointed, since boys were most prized in Muslim families. Hamet was away, so Farida wrote to him that she had given birth to a boy. He rushed home as soon as he could, only to discover to his great dismay that there was no son after all.

But finally on March 17, 1938, days away from her destination, their son, Rudolf Hametovich, arrived. When Farida and the children pulled into Vladivostok, Hamet was waiting for them at the station, a grand

---

*Hamet may have allowed the kulak family to stay on in the house for a brief spell, but in all likelihood, they were forced out before he could be accused of not being vigilant enough. Perhaps in recounting this period to his grandchildren, Hamet altered the story to placate his guilty conscience. For according to Red Army expert Mark von Hagen, former poor peasants like Hamet Nureyev were often among the most militant "depeasantizers," a term of the period used to describe those with a violent dislike of anything backward or rural.

nineteenth-century marble building overlooking the harbor. Now Hamet could see with his own eyes that indeed this was a boy, and he gathered his infant son into the folds of his overcoat, shielding him from the wind.

Such unfettered moments between father and son seldom would be repeated.

2

A Friend, a Religion,

a Way to Good Fortune

RUDOLF'S EARLIEST sights and sounds were of men preparing for battle. He spent the first sixteen months of life on an artillery base in Razdolnoye, which was just sixty miles northwest of Vladivostok, whose ice-free harbor was of crucial strategic importance to the Russian navy. Korea lay directly south, China immediately east, and the tip of Japan was only four hundred miles from its shores. In 1938, Vladivostok was also home to a growing number of troops; war with Japan was expected and several armed skirmishes had already taken place. That July, four months after Farida and the children arrived, Hamet's platoon fought the Japanese in a major campaign at nearby Lake Khasan.

Against this backdrop of war and international unrest, Rudolf's parents resumed family life, with soldiers filling in as playmates for their children. Razida remembers how she and her siblings would scream with laughter as the soldiers swung them around by their arms. Once, Hamet had to rush four-year-old Razida to the hospital after a soldier swung her with a little too much vigor and twisted her wrists.

As a senior *politruk* in the Red Army, Hamet was entrusted with the soldiers' political education, which was considered as important as their military training. Hamet spread the gospel of Communism: the history and goals of the Revolution, the party, the army and the state. With Stalin as the country's historian-in-chief, Hamet's textbook was the *Short Course* history of the Communist Party, "the bible of High Stalinism," published that fall and meant to be followed to the letter. Anyone who put his own interpretation on events — or, worse, restored or deleted "facts" — was sure to be exiled or jailed.

In the wake of the purges then cutting a wide swath through the military, Hamet's job assumed a more sinister dimension: He was one of the regime's watchdogs, the role political commissars were originally assigned to play when Trotsky created the position following the Revolution.* As war commissar, Trotsky had insisted on bolstering the ranks of the new Red Army with former officers of the czarist army. To ensure their loyalty, he made certain they were supervised and spied on by political commissars; no order was valid unless signed by both. Regular officers' relationship with the political commissars was tainted from the start by the aura of suspicion that defined it. (While the officers reported to the Commissariat of Defense, the commissars reported directly to the Central Committee of the Communist Party.)

In the panic of the Great Terror of 1937, the commissars' ranks were increased. Apart from his lessons, Hamet was expected to boost troop morale and participate in any military operations in the area. Although only a low-ranking commissar, Hamet enjoyed all the perks accorded army officers: a wage roughly twice as high as the average citizen's — about five hundred rubles a month — as well as superior housing, access to medical care, schooling and special stores, providing him with hard-to-come-by luxuries and services.

And yet, at a time when suspicion alone was tantamount to conviction, no one, not even a political commissar, was immune from persecution. "I have fired 215 political workers of whom a substantial number have been arrested, " Lev Mekhlis, the Red Army's chief political commissar and hatchet man, cabled Stalin in July 1937. "But I am far from finishing the purge of the political apparatus, especially the lower ranks. . . ." Indeed, the month Rudolf was born, the purge of the military was at its peak, particularly in the district where his father was stationed — and to which Mekhlis himself was soon dispatched. Between 1937 and 1938, at least 45 percent of the command and political staff of the army and navy perished, crippling the officer corps just before the eve of World War II. Stalin, in fact, murdered more of his own senior officers (colonel and above) than Hitler's troops were to kill during the war.

In such circumstances, it seems unlikely that Hamet Nureyev could have kept his hands clean. Even if he himself were not shooting other officers, Hamet would have been expected to expose alleged traitors to the secret police and to inform the party of any discontent within the ranks. In the view of Red Army historian Mark von Hagen, Hamet was probably sent to the Far East to restore some stability to the shaken post-Terror army, a rather serious assignment indicative of the kind of trust Hamet had earned.

A fuller picture of Hamet's role in the purges is difficult to deter-

---

*At that time, the regime had so few of its own officers that it had to accept the services of many former czarist officers in order to battle the counterrevolutionary White forces.

mine, because Hamet's family would never have been privy to those details and the army only began to open its archives in the 1990s, and even then reluctantly, at best. To have become a *politruk* and *remained* a *politruk*, Hamet would have had to display unfailing devotion to the party, as well as blind adherence to the ever-changing orders of the day. When the time came for decisive action, Hamet could be counted on to suppress whatever misgivings he may have had. Though he had little choice but to conform in order to survive, he nevertheless prevailed despite terrible events and terrible odds; in this respect, perhaps only in this respect, would his son take after him.

RUDOLF WAS sixteen months old when his father was transferred to Moscow in July 1939. Once again, the family boarded the Trans-Siberian, this time stopping off at a military camp in Alkino in the Urals for a few weeks. Alkino was not far from Asanovo, giving Hamet and Farida a chance to show off Rudolf—Rudik as they called him—to his Fasliyev relatives.

The family's life improved in Moscow, the seat of the Soviet government* and the headquarters of PUR, the Political Administration of the Revolutionary Military Council of the Workers-Peasants Red Army, to which Hamet belonged. Hamet went to work at the leading artillery school and managed to find quarters for his family just across the street, in a two-story wooden building overlooking a railway line on the western outskirts of the city. The small room on the top floor was their first real home since Rudolf's birth. Beyond the back fence, the children could see the railway cars rattling by. At night the whistling of oncoming trains punctuated the quiet, perhaps sparking young Rudik's childhood obsession with trains.

One of the few surviving family photographs from this period shows the Nureyev children lined up in a row according to height, their worn clothes and wary expressions revealing the hardship of their early childhood. Dressed in a sailor's suit, chubby, round-faced Rudik, his blond hair just sprouting, stares hard at the camera, unsmiling, his slanting eyes wide apart and questioning. Nevertheless, it was a time of relative security and domesticity such as the Nureyevs were not to know again for many years. During the day, Rudik went to kindergarten with five-year-old Razida, who remembers being taught how to eat with a spoon "because I didn't hold it in the right way." Ten-year-old Rosa took up gymnastics at her school, while Lilya learned to lip-read at a special school for the deaf, though her siblings continued to speak to her in the sign language they invented.

*The capital was transferred from Petrograd to Moscow in 1918.

With the artillery school just across the boulevard, the children still counted soldiers among their playmates. Hiding Rudik and Razida beneath their overcoats, the soldiers would sneak them into the nearby cinema house, where small children were not permitted. Though too young to understand what he was seeing, Rudik was mesmerized by the strange images on the screen, his first glimpse of a world different from his own. But happy memories—indeed, any memories—of that period are few, dimmed as they were by the upheaval of war.

In the predawn hours of June 22, 1941, Germany invaded the Soviet Union, catching the Russian forces off guard. Heavy bombers of the German Luftwaffe thundered over the country's western borders while, on the ground below, German tanks opened fire on every village and town within range. Despite numerous warnings, Stalin had refused to believe that Hitler would violate their nonaggression pact. When he did, the Soviet leader went into shock and retreated to his dacha outside Moscow, leaving his commanders and the Russian people to fend for themselves. It would be another two weeks before he finally addressed the nation.

Rudolf and Razida were on an excursion with their kindergarten class outside Moscow when news of the German advance crackled over the airwaves. Farida rushed out at once to bring them home. A week later, Minsk had fallen and Hamet had left for the western front, where he was to serve as both soldier and *politruk* in an artillery unit. Hamet, who would not return for several years, gradually became a stranger to his children, forever remaining at the edge of their lives, a shadowy, intimidating figure.

Alone with their four children in Moscow, Farida lived in fear of the German bombers. Night after night, she would have to keep the children awake long enough to hustle them to the air-raid shelter in the nearby metro station.

Six weeks into the war, Farida and the children were evacuated to Chelyabinsk along with the families of other military men. Believing Stalin's promise that the war would be over quickly, they decamped with only a wheelbarrow full of belongings, among these the family radio, which would soon serve as their only link to the world outside. Rudolf's sister Razida recalls that they packed in a hurry. "I don't think we even took winter clothes, because we assumed we were coming back soon." Chelyabinsk, about 850 miles east of Moscow, was a sixteen-hour journey under normal conditions. The Nureyevs spent two days traveling there after bombing in the region forced their train to make several unscheduled stops. On their arrival, they had to register at the local collective. Standing in line with them was a manicurist, who was carrying so many hats with her that Farida Nureyeva assumed she must be the wife of a party boss. Just how far they had traveled from the city soon became apparent when the soldier registering the evacuees asked the manicurist to describe her occupation. "Manicurist" meant nothing to him, so the soldier insisted on asking her the same question again and again. Finally, he gave up. "Just put down 'prostitute,'" he instructed his clerk.

The dark, drafty izba where the family was sent to live in nearby Shuchye was Rudolf's third home in as many years of life. Built of mud bricks, with a roof made of lime bark, it had no running water, no indoor plumbing and only a floor of bare earth. There was a large stove, a clay oven, benches along the walls and a table. During the winter months, Farida took her turn sleeping on the stove, while the children lay bundled on old mattresses on the floor. The family shared their single room with assorted strangers, for, as Rudik quickly learned, "everything of value was automatically subscribed to the communal life" and a young boy "stood no chance of development without the backing of the group." Razida still recalls the preferential treatment shown the families of the higher-ranking officers. "My mother told me that the Muscovites we traveled with were given much better housing than we were offered." Farida felt this injustice sharply. Thirty-four years later, she was standing in a queue in Ufa with her grandaughter when she found herself face-to-face with one of the women with whom she had been evacuated from Moscow. "[Farida] refused to stand next to her in line," her granddaughter Alfia recalls, "because she remembered that when they had been evacuated to the Ural village, they had been treated as second-rate because they were 'local.' This woman who came from Moscow—a big-city dweller—was given a house with a stove right away, while they had to live in a hut which was not heated."

Wartime life in that distant Bashkirian village proved lonely and difficult and it was here that Nureyev formed most of his earliest impressions of the world. "Icy, dark, and, above all, hungry," he would recall. Winter lasted from October to April and the winter of 1941 was one of the coldest on record. In those "ice months," as one historian has written, "the blank whiteness of the steppe appeared to reach into the villages, for there were no hedges or fences to break its monotony." To young Rudik, the tremendous snowdrifts on either side of the only road looked "like dirty mountains on each side of a narrow, frightening path." He remembered playing alone on that road, "without ever striking up a mutual friendship," and sailing in a boat "in the middle of a green lake, crying and shouting with fear." But hunger was the most terrible and persistent fact of life: Potatoes were the only staple, and meat and fruit were nonexistent, prompting Nureyev to refer to this grim childhood chapter as his Potato Period. It took so long to boil the potatoes on their feeble stove that Rudik was often fast asleep by dinnertime and Farida would have to spoon-feed her sleeping son. With no memory of having eaten, he would awaken the next morning convinced he'd gone without supper. Her daughters rarely grumbled, but Rudik, she said later, "cried all the time." That fierce deprivation bred in him an unerring instinct for survival, which he would never lose. Sharing their room was an old Russian peasant couple, devout Christians, who decorated their tiny corner with icons, lit on holy days by a little oil lamp. Each morning they would wake Rudik and entice him to join them in prayer by offering him bits of goat cheese and sweet potato as a reward. The sleepy boy would comply, until his mother awoke and put a stop to their proselytizing. To a Communist and atheist like Farida, religious practice was backward, a relic of Old Russia and not to be encouraged. To her headstrong, hungry son, however, the "strange words" meant extra food and were well worth muttering, even if they stirred his mother's anger.*

Photographs of Farida reveal her hard, worn features and broad, rounded figure, but what remains imperceptible is the unyielding strength she conveyed to her children. She never complained, Rudolf later said of her, and yet "without raising her voice she could be extremely severe." It was the rare occasion when she smiled, and never once could her son recall hearing her laugh "out loud." Even today, neighbors remember her as solemn and overburdened. She also was not given to displays of affection. "It wasn't our habit to be very close and tender or to kiss and hug one another," explains Razida. "To show our feelings is not the Tatar way. We are a somewhat restrained people. It's in the blood."

Farida's emotional resiliency may have had more to do with the extreme austerity of her own childhood, one spent first as an orphan and then as an outsider in her brother's home. Having faced shortages, malnutrition and poor housing for virtually all of her life, she was accustomed to hardship and certainly steeled for the further privations brought on by the war. Still, the reports from the front were terrifying and death haunted their daily lives. "Almost every family around us was mourning a son, a brother, a husband lost in the war," Rudolf remembered. At least in this respect, the Nureyevs were spared.

Ignoring his mother's advice that he would feel his hunger less the less he moved about, Rudik couldn't remain still for long. Once, he had to be taken to the hospital in Chelyabinsk after he upset their tiny Primus stove and a pot of boiling water—containing the half-cooked potatoes that were to be their dinner—spilled on him, scalding his stomach. In his excitement about traveling to the big town, Rudik soon forgot about his pain, especially when he saw what a fuss everyone made over him. His mother brought him colored pencils and paper cows to color,

*Religious practice, though strongly discouraged, had never been officially outlawed by the Soviet government. During the war, it was not only tolerated but tacitly encouraged by the party only because Stalin believed it helped fuel patriotic feeling.

the first present he had ever received, and the doctors and nurses showered him with concern. "That feeling of doctors and nurses taking care of me as if I were the only person in the whole hospital was my first strong childish delight."

Rudik was his mother's favorite, and the tacit affection that sprang up between mother and son endured throughout his life. Much more patient with Rudik, Farida was also quicker to indulge him, never once slapping him, as she did her daughters. Indeed he seemed to coax from her whatever tenderness and humor she possessed. Years later he fondly remembered every line of the folktale she told him night after night to distract him from his hunger, a fable he "adored" and "which still makes me smile today."*

Four-year-old Rudik relied on the radio to escape the bracing solitude of village life. For hours he would sit, enraptured, listening to whatever happened to be playing. Music was his first passion and it led, invariably, to his second. But it was always music he counted on to provide solace in lonely moments. Throughout his life, Nureyev would make sure that he was never without the records or musical instruments he began to collect as soon as he could afford them. "I looked upon music, from my earliest days, as a friend, a religion, a way to good fortune." So apparently did his sister Lilya, who, though deaf, liked to sing and occasionally responded to some distant sounds on the radio. Every now and then the family would catch her in the act of listening, which led Farida to conclude that Lilya might have become a singer, for she had "good vocal cords" and seemed to possess an affinity for music even without fully hearing a note.

---

*The folktale was about two brothers who go into the woods to chop trees. After one of the brothers mistakenly chops the head off the other, he brings his brother's body to the izba of his widowed sister and asks her, "Maria, I can't remember, did he have a head when he was alive?" She tells him she can't remember. "But I *do* know," she says, "that I gave him some pancakes before he went into the wood with you. And while he was eating them, his beard quivered slightly."

3

Epiphany

LESS THAN ONE YEAR after leaving Moscow, the Nureyevs relocated yet again, this time to nearby Ufa, the capital of the Bashkir Soviet Republic. Hamet's brother, Nurislam, lived there with his family, though like most young men at the time, Nurislam was away at the front. The Nureyevs moved in with his wife and young son, sharing a tiny room on the top floor of a two-story wooden house on Sverdlov Street. Situated on the right bank of the Belaya River, Ufa lay on a sloping hill behind the town square, its street names a lesson in Russian history: Pushkin, Communist and October Revolution streets led into the main thoroughfare of Lenin; running parallel was Karl Marx, just one street over to the left.

The town's roads ran straight and unpaved, and one traveled by tram or foot to the local bakery or shop. When it rained, the ground turned to mud. In the eighteenth century, Ufa was known as the Devil's Inkpot because of its dirty streets; even the usually eloquent Maxim Gorky was at a loss to describe Ufa's charms after a visit there in the 1920s. "The town was somehow very low," he observed. "It really seemed to be sitting down instead of standing on the ground." No more than two stories high, Ufa's simple, rough-hewn wooden houses, some with ornately carved eaves known as wooden lace, dotted the roadways. In the yard, one found a patchwork of vegetable gardens in summer and the outhouse year-round. Clumps of birch trees and apple trees ran down to the river and later rowan ash trees were planted, many of them by Rudolf, his sisters and the other neighborhood children. The dreariness of the town was offset by the forests, hills and two looping rivers that composed the surrounding landscape.

Today many of Ufa's wooden houses have been replaced by concrete Soviet apartment blocks or painted over in a dingy brown, though the residential streets are still unpaved and continue to look wild and neglected. Sverdlov Street and Zentsov Street, in the heart of the Nureyevs' former neighborhood, are ramshackle, unpaved and muddy when wet. Even downtown Ufa, with its brick buildings, paved streets and tram wires, feels overlooked by time, suggesting perhaps a midwestern American town of the 1930s. The Western influences now so omnipresent in Moscow are rarely glimpsed in Ufa, a town hazy with industrial exhaust. Statues of Lenin still loom large and menacing, fruit and vegetables are not easily obtained, and business—in this city of 1.1 million people—is conducted only in rubles, for the American dollar has yet to become the preferred currency it is in the country's other major cities. Even well-placed government ministers live in apartment buildings that Westerners might hesitate to enter; the stench and ruin of their lobbies call to mind the tenements of American inner cities.

The Soviet Ufa of Nureyev's boyhood is readily brought home in other ways as well. Visitors are treated to traditional fare, meatballs wrapped in dough, for example, and expected to join in the repeated rounds of toasts over *kumys*, a supposed cure-all drink made from fermented mare's milk that has long been a Bashkirian specialty.* Communication with the rest of the country often requires hours of waiting while a central operator places the call, and in 1996 communication with the West was virtually nonexistent. In the room that now houses the Rudolf Nureyev Museum at the Ufa Opera House, there is a VCR, but no videotapes of any Nureyev performances in the West. "If you could get even one to us, we would be so grateful," pleaded the museum's curator, Inna Guskova. She once lived across the street from the Nureyevs and today still lives on that same street, a few houses down from where she grew up, as do many of the people who populated Nureyev's early life.

BY THE TIME the Nureyevs arrived in 1942, Ufa was overrun by industry and playing a important role in the war effort.† Under Stalin's industrial drive during the 1930s, critical industries had been evacuated to the Urals and a number of new factories built, many of them in Ufa. As Stalin saw it, the mineral-rich Urals made an ideal center for heavy industry: Pro-

---

*Tolstoy, another celebrated visitor to Ufa, came in 1862 especially to sample the local kumys. Tolstoy is said to have bought property in Ufa, but never settled there.
†By then Ufa's population was 250,000, of which 175,400 were Russian, 39,100 Tatar and 15,400 Bashkir. Despite having a republic of their own, the Bashkirs made up only 25 percent of its total population.

tected by the mountains, they were at a safe remove from Russia's frontiers and capable of supplying the country with the arms, machines and oil necessary to keep its divisions in the field. Home to a major gasoline plant, an oil refinery and one of the largest internal-combustion engine plants in the Soviet Union, Ufa was a "closed"* city and soon disappeared from maps.

The local authorities kept promising Farida her own room, but each time she checked on her assigned lodgings, she found someone else living there. As a result, the family had no choice but to live with their relatives. Rudolf despaired and his own descriptions of their cramped living conditions paint a dire picture: "I can't find words to describe the psychic upheaval that set up in me. . . . We must have achieved a miracle in sharing that nightmarish existence without getting to the point where we couldn't bear the sight of each other."

Their sense of dislocation was only heightened after Farida received word from Hamet that their Moscow apartment house had been hit by a bomb. (While the bomb didn't explode, the force of its impact caused serious damage to the building.) He had gone to check on their flat, he wrote, and found it completely emptied. All that remained were two photographs — one of himself, the other of Farida — which had clung to the wall. He enclosed the photographs in his letter.

By August 1942, Hamet had been promoted to the rank of major and was serving on the western front. He was clearly pained about missing out on the first years of his son's life: He addressed one of the few letters he managed to send home during the war to Rudolf, care of his mother. That month he wrote:

> Hello, my beloved son Rudik! Best regards to all: Rosa, Razida, Lilya and mama. I am alive and in good health.
>
> > Your father, Nureyev

With the end of the war nowhere in sight, Farida had little choice but to exchange Hamet's civilian clothes and boots for food. "Daddy's gray suit was really quite tender," the children would joke, referring to their meals by the bartered goods they had paid for them. For Farida, the emotional cost must have been high; selling her husband's clothes no doubt reminded her that she might never see him again.

Many of Hamet's relatives still lived in Asanovo, which was twenty-four miles from Ufa, and sometimes Farida would travel there on foot in search of food. She usually took Rosa with her on these two-day expeditions, but once, in the middle of winter, she decided to go alone.

*Foreigners were banned from visiting.

Emerging from the woods at nightfall, she saw flashes of light, which she assumed to be fireflies, but which proved to be the eyes of watching wolves. Alone, exhausted and bitterly cold, she quickly set fire to the blanket she was wearing as a shawl and scared off the hungry wolves. The stoicism she often showed her children belied the lengths she traveled to protect them. She didn't tell them about the wolves until many years later, because she didn't want to frighten them. When Nureyev related this story in a documentary about his life, he paid tribute to his mother's fortitude: "Ballsy lady!"

SINCE HIS MOTHER was away at work all day—first in a bakery and later on an assembly line in a refinery—Rudolf and his sisters were regularly left to themselves. Rosa was nearly twelve when they moved to Ufa and played with older children, but Razida, Lilya and Rudolf were close enough in age to play together with the children who gathered in their communal courtyard. Rudolf began life as a weak and frail boy, whose utter lack of physical power made him the object of scorn. A highly sensitive child, small for his age, he didn't go in for roughhousing like other boys. When threatened or provoked, he would fling himself to the ground and cry until his tormentors left him alone. He preferred the company of women, usually his sisters and their friends, although they, too, considered him a weakling and picked on him. His sole protector was his neighbor Kostya Slovookhotov, who, while only a year or two his senior, took pity and came to his aid whenever he saw the other children bullying little Rudik.

One of the few games Rudik liked to play was hide-and-seek, but much to his displeasure, he mostly had to play the seeker. Aza Kuchumova, one of the little girls who made sure of that, is now a full-figured soprano with the Ufa Opera. "Why do I always have to be the one to find you?" she remembers Rudik complaining. "Why don't I ever get to hide?" Come summer, they would follow the serpentine path to the nearby Belaya River to bathe and swim. In the colder months, they skated on the frozen lake on homemade skates.

Domestic rituals set the pace of family life. Each Sunday, Rudolf and his sisters dutifully accompanied their mother to the local steam bath, taking with them their broom of birch twigs with which to invigorate their skin. In the evenings, they gathered in the communal kitchen down the hall from their room. Most Ufa kitchens had a stove heated with wood or charcoal, some with electricity, but no running water; in winter, food was stored in cloth bags on the windowsill to keep it fresh. As the wife of a soldier, Farida had been able to shop at special stores in Moscow, but in Ufa, there were none. To pass the time while waiting for their supper, Rudik and Razida liked to play checkers. "When he won, everything went well," Razida remembers. "But when he lost, he would say, 'You won with all the wrong moves and I don't want to play anymore!' "

It was during the after-dinner hour that the Nureyev children felt the pull of family as they sat with their mother drinking tea, sewing or reading a book by the light of the Primus lamp. "That was the most tender time," says Razida. The children borrowed their books from the library and read them together, huddled beneath the bedcover. They loved the stories of Jules Verne most of all. Rosa and Razida would read Rudik to sleep, feeding his emerging sense of wonder with these tales of travel, adventure and romance.

When the time came for Rudolf to go to the local kindergarten, a converted army barracks across the street from the Nureyevs' home, his mother dressed him in his sister Lilya's overcoat and carried him there on her back because he had no shoes. The other children laughed at him, leaving him humiliated and hurt. He would later insist that he heard the children call him a *bump*—Tatar for "beggar"—on that first day of school; however, two of his classmates take issue with the details of his recollection. They laughed at him, they say, because they thought he looked silly in girl's clothes and not for the more profound reason Nureyev supposed. Even so, he was an outsider, derided before he'd had a chance to join the group. "We were all poor then," explains his childhood neighbor Inna Guskova. "During those years, no one had anything, so we wouldn't have mocked anyone else's poverty. My mother would give me two potatoes to take to school and tell me to share them with the children who were hungry." To young Rudik, however, a child who had food to share was wealthy indeed. "It was on that first day that I became aware of class differences. I realized with a shock that many children at school were much better off than I was, better dressed, and above all, better fed." Even by the standards of the time, the Nureyev family *was* less well off than others, says another classmate. "But I never heard anyone call Rudik a beggar." The fortunes of many local families hadn't changed as dramatically during the war as they had for evacuees like the Nureyevs, who had been forced to leave their possessions behind in Moscow.

Afraid that he might go without dinner on any given night, Rudolf would make sure to eat breakfast before going to school, where he was then given a second breakfast. When his teacher demanded to know why he came late to class, he tried to explain that he was at home eating breakfast. "She'll never understand, I thought, that now I have the chance to eat twice in the morning, I simply can't let that chance pass me by."

If kindergarten had its share of humiliating moments, it was not without its lasting pleasures. That first year Rudolf was introduced to simple Bashkirian and Tatar folk dances. He had only to see a step performed once before he had it mastered and memorized, a facility helped along by his ear for music. Returning home, he would practice the day's lesson, singing and dancing until bedtime. His neighbor Albert Arslanov shared his love of dancing and quickly became his one close friend. A small, black-haired Tatar boy with velvety black eyes, Albert was the first person with whom Rudik could share his dreams and ideas. When their teachers saw the ardor they brought to their performances, they invited them to take part in the children's ensemble, which had developed a local following. Rudolf's first concerts took place in Ufa's hospitals, where the children were sent to entertain wounded soldiers back from the front. Rudolf and Albert were even filmed for a newsreel and later taken to October, the cinema house in town, so that they could see themselves on the screen. But "when the shot appeared I had been cut out," Nureyev remembered. "I expect I didn't look enough like a typical Tatar; I was a blond boy and most Tatars are dark." Nevertheless, his talent was soon the talk of the neighborhood. "You must send him for training in Leningrad!" the neighbors exhorted Farida, who would quietly acknowledge their compliments and say nothing. What was the point of encouraging him? Leningrad was a thousand miles away and they were in the middle of a war. It wasn't until many years later, in fact, long after Rudolf had left home, that she finally let on just how proud of him she had been. Her Rudik, she told her granddaughter, "was the best dancer in the kindergarten."

Rudolf's academic studies began in earnest at the age of seven. At School Number Two, the local all-boys school, a portrait of the schoolboy Lenin hung in every classroom. Russian was the dominant language of instruction, although some subjects were offered in Tatar, and each day began with the singing of the Soviet national anthem and "Song of the Fatherland."

> *Soviet land so dear to every toiler*
> *Peace and progress build their hope on thee*
> *There is no other land in the whole world over*
> *Where man walks the earth so proud and free.*

Rudolf and Albert—or Rudka and Alka, as they nicknamed one another—shared one desk, but were often separated for talking during the lesson. They lived only a block apart, making it easy for them to call to each other from the street. The neighborhood boys all played mock war games, using homemade wooden sabers. Though Rudolf had grown bolder, he was still singled out from the pack. "Hey, Adolf!" the boys teased, not only because the names sounded similar, but because his blond hair, rarely combed, stuck out in all directions, as Hitler's did when he was particularly irate. The only way out was to go along with the joke. Whenever the boys cried "Adolf," Rudolf would pull a stern face and stick his comb under his nose to mimic Hitler's mustache. But his efforts fell flat, Albert remembers. "The other boys didn't take him seriously."

By all surviving accounts, Albert understood Rudolf as almost no one else in Ufa ever did. Yet while family members, former schoolmates and Albert himself describe the boys as inseparable, Rudolf never once mentions Albert in his autobiography. Possibly he meant to protect Albert, since the book was published in 1962, though it's more likely that in looking back on his boyhood, Nureyev saw himself only in a solitary light. Classmates from that period have painted him as insular and separate, and Rudolf himself wrote movingly of the isolation of his Ufa childhood. Inna Guskova, a friend of all the Nureyev children, remembers that he "had difficulty making friends and being close to others." Albert, on the other hand, describes Rudolf as an outgoing little boy, though he also recalls moments when Rudolf would become "pensive and quiet and withdraw into himself." Certainly Rudolf's own descriptions of those years leave the impression that he relied more on his imagination for companionship than on any single individual. "I spent all my leisure time either listening to the music endlessly poured out by our radio . . . or climbing up to my private observation point." His favorite perch overlooked Ufa's marble railway station, a two-mile hike from home. There he would sit for hours, watching the trains. He loved imagining the places they were traveling to, not the cold dark villages he had already seen, but the more exotic lands he had read about in Jules Verne's adventures. "In my mind," he would say long afterward, "I traveled with those trains."

THE SECOND WORLD WAR ended in Europe on May 9, 1945, and news soon reached the Nureyevs that a military transport train was bound for Ufa. The town anxiously awaited its fathers, sons and husbands. On the appointed day, Rudolf accompanied his mother and sisters to the station to welcome Hamet Nureyev back from the front. They waited and waited, recalls Razida, "but our father never came," so they trooped back home, disappointed and concerned. "Then we got a letter saying that he would stay in Germany for another year. He even said he might bring us to Germany, though he never did. Our permit to return to Moscow was still valid and my mother wanted to go back there, but my father was against it." Hamet had fought on the Second Byelorussian front and participated in the forced crossing of the river Oder, which had led to the capture of Berlin. He was then stationed just outside Berlin, where he was serving as a political instructor in the Soviet occupation army.

As 1945 drew to a close, the Nureyevs had been living in Ufa for nearly two years and had finally begun to put down roots. The end of the war made travel easier, but with vast distances, long winters, internal passports and residence permits to contend with, Ufa's citizens remained cut off from the major cities of the Soviet empire. By train, Moscow was two days away, Leningrad farther still, and few had the spare rubles for excursions.* Yet despite its isolation, Ufa was not a cultural backwater. In the wake of the Revolution, many among the Moscow–St. Petersburg intelligentsia, newly defined as "undesirables," had been exiled to the Urals and other points east and north. Uprooted from their cosmopolitan milieus, they were scattered among provincial towns, resulting in a kind of cultural pollination. By the 1940s, Ufa boasted a former dancer with the Maryinsky Theater (then known as the Kirov) and a former dancer with Diaghilev's Ballets Russes, each determined to pass on her cultural inheritance to a new generation.

There were other developments from which young Nureyev would benefit: In 1938, the year he was born, Ufa had opened the doors of its new opera house,† and in 1941, the year before his family moved there, the city's first ballet company was founded. The Ufa Ballet had strong ties to Leningrad's fabled ballet school, where a number of the company's soloists had been sent for training by the Bashkirian government. During the war years, the Ufa Ballet's ranks were further bolstered by a number of evacuees from Moscow's Bolshoi and Leningrad's Kirov companies.

Rudolf first stepped inside the opera house on New Year's Eve 1945 at the age of seven, and from that moment forward, his aspirations were never in doubt. Although his mother had purchased only one ticket for the performance, she somehow managed to sneak the whole family in with her amid the crush of the crowd at the entrance. Once he was inside, the world was transformed for Rudik, as if by magic. To his eyes, the theater was a fun house of visual wonders, a place "you could only hope to encounter in the most enchanted fairy tale." Everywhere he looked, there was something to pique his curiosity. As he sat for the first time in a chair of red velvet, he could see beautiful ladies gazing down at him from the painting on the ceiling. A lyre, molded in plaster, decorated a band across the top of the stage. Colored lights played against the curtain as the music began.

*Even with the advent of air travel, Ufa is not easily reached. Visas are still required, and from downtown Moscow it takes two hours to reach the national airport, where one boards an Aeroflot plane, albeit tentatively, given the airline's safety rating. Once aboard, one has to contend with broken tray tables and shabby seats, piled with luggage.
†The great Russian basso Fedor Chaliapin had made his professional debut in Ufa in 1890. Born in Farida Nureyeva's hometown of Kazan in 1873, Chaliapin died the year Nureyev was born. He first performed as an extra in Kazan, but it was while singing with a local troupe in Ufa that he graduated from the chorus to the role of soloist.

The ballet on the program was *The Song of the Cranes*, a Soviet-era morality tale created to honor the founding of the Bashkirian republic.* The story of an innocent shepherd who outwits a cunning landowner to win the love of a young girl, the ballet starred Zaitouna Nazretdinova,† Ufa's reigning ballerina, whose powerful technique and stage presence had come of her schooling in Leningrad. More than the dancing, it was the alchemy of the experience itself that transported Rudolf: "Something was happening to me which was taking me far from my sordid world and bearing me right up to the skies. From the moment I entered that magic place I felt I had really left the world, borne far away from everything I knew by a dream staged for me alone . . . I was speechless."

Many children have been mesmerized by such encounters, only to put them aside when distracted or blocked. It was lucky for Rudolf that his father hadn't returned home directly after the war, for it's unlikely that the family would have gone to the ballet that New Year's Eve or indeed any other evening. Hamet had never been to the theater and took a dim view of artists, calling them idlers and drunkards. But by the time he returned to family life, Rudolf was already obsessed with dancing and well beyond his reach.

---

*Legend had it that when the Bashkirs were at war with their enemies, a flock of cranes suddenly covered the sky during a critical battle and helped the Bashkirs to victory. To this day, the Bashkirian people believe that their relationship to the natural world is so strong that in difficult times, nature will come to their aid.

†Nureyev would later tell John Percival, an early biographer, that he thought Nazretdinova had studied under Agrippina Vaganova, the legendary Soviet ballet teacher; however, according to Nazretdinova, she never did.

4

Hamet

ONE DAY IN AUGUST 1946 "a shadow appeared" in the open doorway and Rudolf looked up to see "this great big man wearing a dirty gray coat." His mother rushed to the man and threw her arms around him and only then did Rudolf realize it was his father. At that moment, he would say later, he felt he had lost his mother. Having been the lone male in the household, he was suddenly supplanted without warning. To eight-year-old Rudolf, the change was cataclysmic.

As completely as he felt coddled and understood by his mother, Rudolf felt intimidated by his father, who was more adept at commanding soldiers than at responding to the needs of young children. Hamet's stern mien and gruff manner made his son wary of him, as did his fondness for fishing and hunting, activities his young son found "all very uncomfortable." His sisters found the adjustment equally discomfiting. The Nureyev children had always called their mother *enny*, the Tatar word for "mother," and addressed her in the familiar form of "you." With their father, however, they felt awkward, so instead of addressing him in their native language as *etiy*, they used the more formal Russian name of "papa" and the more formal form of "you." Hamet Nureyev had returned home to find himself a stranger in his own family.

"We couldn't get used to him as the father," recalls Razida. "He was upset that I didn't address him in Tatar and complained to my mother. 'Why are the children more formal with me than with you?' It was difficult for us to develop a feeling of closeness as a family." Even Palma, the chocolate-brown cocker spaniel Hamet brought home one day, was considered Hamet's hunting dog, never the family pet.

Even as she tried to ease the way for her husband's reentry into civilian life, Farida Nureyeva was making some adjustments of her own. She hadn't lived with her husband for over five years and had rarely enjoyed any prolonged periods of domesticity with him during their sixteen years of marriage. Though Hamet arrived home a much-decorated major in the army and never appeared without his medals in family photographs, he decided to quit military life and turned down the job of deputy political commissar in Ufa's Internal Ministry.* The work was demanding, he told his daughter Razida, and despite, or perhaps even because of, his alienation from them, he wanted to spend more time with his family. He soon went to work as an assistant manager at a vocational school, which was situated on the hill overlooking the railway station, near Rudolf's lookout perch. Sometimes Rudolf and Razida would visit him there, and on these occasions, Hamet, a camera buff, liked to snap pictures of them.

One of the more positive changes prompted by their father's return was the improvement in their domestic quarters. After years of living with others, the Nureyevs were finally assigned to a two-room flat of their own at number 37 Zentsov Street, a one-story wooden house near the corner of Sverdlov Street. But when they got there, they found the second room occupied by a woman intending to relocate to Leningrad. When she eventually moved out, another tenant replaced her, so all six Nureyevs were crammed into one room of fourteen square meters, which was to remain Rudolf's home for the rest of his Ufa boyhood. With its "old" wooden furniture, their room, remembers a neighbor, "looked squalid." Compared with the homes Rudolf had known, however, it was bright and relatively spacious. It had a stove and electricity, but running water had to be retrieved from the water pump behind the house. A wood-burning stove heated the room in winter; in spring and summer, natural light spilled through its four windows. A large wooden table covered with an oilcloth sat in the middle of the room, a wooden chest occupied a corner, and two metal beds were pushed against opposite walls. Hamet and Farida Nureyev slept in one bed, while Rudolf and his sisters shared the second, larger bed, sleeping head to foot to create more space. No one could stir, let alone dance, without disturbing the others.† Their situation was hardly unusual. Typically, two or three generations shared a single room and sexual relations took place under less than private circumstances. (The Russian language has no word for "privacy.") Not

---

*His decorations included the Order of the Red Star (1944), the Order of the Great Patriotic War (1944) and medals for the Defense of Moscow (1945) and for the victory over Germany (1945). He was also given an official letter of thanks for excellent military operations during the forced crossing over the river Oder.

†Hamet's youngest sister, Jamila, had died the year he returned, and he had hoped to take in her four children, but with six people already crowded into their one room, he decided against it and the children were sent to a nearby orphanage.

until Rudolf was twenty-three and living in the West would he have a room to himself. "To go to the toilet," he recalled, "you have to go to the street in a severe winter and be ventilated by hurricane or snow storm." Out in the yard, near the outhouse they shared with their neighbors, was the garden in which Rudolf and his sisters planted flowers. Hamet, an avid gardener himself, was eventually allotted a tiny piece of land, some thirty minutes away from home by tram, where he grew potatoes and onions.

In an effort to forge some kind of link with his son, Hamet taught Rudolf how to make lead shot for his shotguns. Cutting the lead into pieces, he would have Rudolf roll them into small balls with the help of a hand mill. In this way, he hoped to initiate Rudolf into his world and make a man of his overmothered son. To Rudolf, however, the assignment was not some manly rite of passage but a tiresome chore he tried to be done with as quickly as possible. Whenever he could, he enlisted Albert to help him. Hamet, recalls Albert, "never sat idle. He was always doing something. He was a strict father, but at the same time, he could be kind. But he never showed his affection for his son. I never once saw him embrace or kiss Rudik." Another neighbor remembers Hamet as "reserved and solitary." In Rudolf's eyes, he was "a severe, very powerful man with a strong chin and a heavy jaw-line—an unknown force that rarely smiled, rarely spoke and who scared me." On one of their few hunting trips together, Hamet went off in search of game and left Rudolf alone in the forest, parked in his rucksack and hanging from a tree. "I suddenly saw a woodpecker who scared me and ducks flying in and out," he still remembered forty years later. But Hamet only laughed when he returned to find his son wailing in fear. "My mother," he said, "never could forgive him this incident."

It was Hamet who now took Rudolf for his weekly steam bath, something his mother had always done. During one of these visits, as his father was scrubbing him, Rudolf got an erection, which so angered Hamet that he beat him when they got home. Recalling this episode long afterward, Rudolf would tell Kenneth Greve, a young dancer with whom he became deeply infatuated late in life, that it was one of his most painful childhood memories. Only rarely, however, did he talk about his father at all.

A man of few words, Hamet had little patience, and crying only irritated him further. "Our father hated tears," says Razida. "He would just look at you and all your tears dried." Lilya's daughter, Alfia, would later come to share their child's-eye view of his temper: "Once I said something wrong—maybe it was about the food I didn't like—and my grandfather flew into a rage. My grandmother grabbed me and took me into the bedroom to hide me." Despite an explosive temper, Hamet rarely fought with his wife in front of the children, at least as far as his daughter Razida recalls. "I never heard him shout at her. Most of the time, he kept his feelings to himself. When he was angry, he would just go out fishing and hunting."

One of Rudolf's first excursions outside Ufa was an overnight visit with his father to nearby Krasni Yar and Asanovo to see his Fasliyev aunts, Saima and Fatima. Rosa had always been the one to join their mother on expeditions, and Rudolf and Razida were excited when their father decided to take them instead. On the way, Hamet stopped to hunt, relying on his trusted "hunting" dog, Palma, for companionship.* Palma, however, failed to live up to his billing and "Father usually ended up going into the water himself to retrieve the ducks he shot," recalls Razida. At night, they slept in a haystack. Unlike their father, their aunts Saima and Fatima held fast to the traditional ways and insisted on speaking to the children in Tatar. When the children answered in Russian, they would press them to use their native tongue. But while Hamet and Farida spoke Tatar to one another, they insisted that their children speak Russian. "Our mother was a modern woman," says Razida. "She would say, 'You should speak Tatar only when you really need to.' "

Hamet had high expectations of his only son, seeing in him the potential to become an engineer, doctor or officer. He also granted him special privileges, as he still honored certain Muslim traditions. Rudolf was, after all, the only other man in the household and therefore not expected to undertake domestic chores, not even jobs usually considered "men's work." In wintertime, when wood was needed to heat their stove, Hamet relied on Razida to help him chop it because Rudolf never wanted to do it. Farida worked at a kefir factory bottling milk, and rushed home each day to make lunch for her children without stopping to eat herself. Rosa, Lilya and Razida took turns cleaning the flat, doing the shopping, and helping their mother make supper. They also prepared the table whenever their parents entertained neighbors, although they were forbidden to join the gathering as long as they remained unmarried. Rudolf's only chores were to plant and dig potatoes with Razida, get kerosene for the stove, and buy the bread each day for supper. "Why do you send a boy to buy bread?" Hamet would complain to his wife, thinking even this duty inappropriate. "There are three girls and none of them can go to the shop?" By that time the ration card system had been abolished and shopping meant hours of waiting on line—for everyone except Rudolf and Albert, who figured out how to crawl through the columns of legs to reach the front. Stuffing the bread into their string bags, they would run off to the Tatar cemetery, where they would happily pass the day, climbing over rocks and into caves.

---

*The scar on Rudolf's lip came after Rudolf was bitten by a neighbor's dog, not by Palma, as is commonly believed. Palma did, however, bite Razida.

Dinner in the Nureyev household was always at seven o'clock, the hour when Hamet returned from work. Neighbors remember Farida Nureyeva as an accomplished cook and baker, whose specialty was a thick Bashkirian soup made with meat, potatoes, carrots, onion, cabbage and homemade noodles.

Outside of the daily routine of meals and chores, there was little contact between father and son. Occasionally, Rudolf tried to draw his father into his own life, but Hamet never responded to him in the way he hoped. When Rudolf confessed that he longed to study the piano, Hamet objected that its unwieldy size and complexity put it out of the question. It was too difficult to learn, he advised, and Rudik wouldn't be able to carry it on his back, the way he would an accordion, which, to his mind, was "useful for making yourself popular at parties." But Rudolf took refuge in music to comfort himself, not to entertain others, something his practical-minded father could never have understood.

Hamet's return may have changed the focus of family life, but it did little to alter the course Rudolf had already set for himself. He was fast becoming the star of his amateur children's dance group and was proud of their local performances. Still, even at the age of nine, he could see that his father wasn't much interested in his dancing. Fearful of provoking his displeasure, he stopped practicing at home and shared his enthusiasm only with his sister Rosa and Albert. Since his father never assumed for a moment that Rudolf was seriously involved in his dance lessons, he didn't interfere with what he considered a childish whim that was sure to pass.

Rudolf's love of dance drew him closer to Rosa, who was teaching eurythmics and winning prizes for her dancing in local contests. Rosa planned to become a teacher, as her mother once had, and was pleased to share with Rudik whatever she knew about dance, sometimes taking him along to her amateur dance group. Once in a while, she would bring home ballet costumes to show him. "That, to me, was heaven. I would spread them out on the bed and gaze at them—gaze at them so intensively that I could feel myself actually inside them. I would fondle them for hours, smooth them and smell them. . . ."*

The obsession he managed to conceal from his father did not so readily escape notice in the schoolyard, where his ineptitude in sports was mocked. During games of soccer, he would regularly miss the ball because he was busy practicing his pirouettes. In gym class, he fared no better, drawing the ire of both his classmates and his teacher, none of whom imagined that he would ever come to anything. While the other

---

*When Nureyev's own ballet costumes hit the auction block at Christie's New York, others could evidently still feel *him* inside them. The costumes brought more than eight times their highest estimate, some selling for as much as forty-five thousand dollars.

boys executed their exercises exactly the way their instructor demonstrated them, Rudolf preferred to add his own little flourishes. "He was not like the other kids," says classmate Marat Hismatullin, who became a baritone with the Ufa Opera. "He was feeble and did things in his own way. When our teacher Mr. Korasyion asked us to stick our arms out to the side, we stuck them out in a straight line without bending our elbows. When Rudolf held out his arm, he always curved his elbow and his fingers. Of course our teacher got very angry at him because he wouldn't do what he was told. All the boys made fun of him."

Whenever he lost himself in daydreams, his classmates would pick fights with him, elbowing, pinching and shoving him to get a reaction. To Taisiam Khalturina Mikhailovna, his class mistress at School Number Two, their taunts appeared to be driven by envy, though it is difficult to know whether her recollection captures her feelings as she felt them at the time or her later reading of the situation. "At the lesson, Rudik would look at me with his eyes wide open listening, but I could see he was in his own world. He would be fantasizing about something, without noticing it himself. The boys wanted to know what he was thinking about, so they pushed him from all sides until he retaliated. They wouldn't calm down until he fought back."

When Rudik *did* retaliate, the means he used only further alienated them. He had learned early on that the best form of protection was to let no one come too close. But since he lacked the heft of the other boys, he would "fall down and start crying wildly to attract attention that he was hurt," recalls Hismatullin. "Whoever pushed him would stand there saying, 'Look here, I just elbowed him and he fell down and cried like mad.' Since I was stronger than he was, I would try to protect him, not because I liked him, but because I felt sorry for him. He seemed helpless." Rudolf's outbursts ended as quickly as they began. "Of course he would cry when he fought with other boys," says Albert. "But he would calm down quickly and forget about it. He was not a sniveler."

Although he didn't dare practice his folk dances at home, he managed to perform them just about everywhere else — on the street, at school during May Day and other public celebrations and in amateur competitions. "Folk dancing," he would later explain, "is a fiery dance. Temperament is very important . . . so from early years, I know how to be onstage, and how to command and how to shine." His third-form school report praised nine-year-old Rudik as "an active member of the artistic club. Dances very well and very easily." The following year he won his first dance prize, a book of photographs championing the glories of "Old and New Moscow." Inside, the inscription read: "To Nureyev, for the best dancing in the audition of amateur groups of Zhdanov district of Ufa. 1948." It was signed by the head of Ufa's Young Communist League.

Rudolf had by that time joined the Pioneers, the Communist youth group to which every Soviet child belonged. Like the Boy Scouts, the Pioneers were organized around activities meant to foster civic-mindedness and group loyalty, except that in the Pioneers, every song, dance and story was laced with a political message. "A Pioneer is loyal to the Motherland, the Party, Communism . . ." began the Pioneer code, which, in keeping with the Stalinist climate, encouraged children not only to place a high premium on conformity, but to suppress any show of independence. At the time Rudolf joined, the Pioneers' role model was a fourteen-year-old boy named Pavlik Morozov who, during the period of farm collectivization, reported his father to the authorities for hiding grain from the state.*

Rudolf, Albert and the neighborhood boys attended the Palace of Pioneers on nearby Gorga Street, a large wooden house divided into classrooms, each graced with a portrait of Stalin. "About wise and beloved Stalin, the people make wonderful songs," they sang. The Pioneers offered free dance classes and it was here that Rudolf began to broaden his repertoire. Soon he was sampling dances from all the Russian republics, which his teacher simply adapted from Pioneer magazines published in Moscow and Leningrad. Fellow Pioneer and sometime partner Pamira Suleimanova remembers that Rudolf was "like a sponge. He was wonderful to dance with because he was so sure of himself. He took the lead and was so secure that I never worried." Sometimes they performed together at the military officers' club, where there was a real stage. The greater aims of the Pioneers, however, were lost on young Rudolf, who would never embrace the notion that the individual took second place to any collective. For him, national holidays were exciting only because they presented him with opportunities to dance. "Because nothing connected with groups ever appealed to me I wasn't a very eager Pioneer," he recalled, adding for equal measure, "and I can well imagine my group wasn't too fond of me either."

At the same time, he continued to dance in the children's group at School Number Two. One day a ballerina from the Ufa Ballet came to choreograph a dance. When she saw how readily ten-year-old Rudolf and Albert took to her instructions, she urged them to study at the House of Teachers with a former ballerina from Leningrad by the name of Anna Ivanovna Udeltsova. The House of Teachers was on the outskirts of town, about four tram stops from home, and Rudik went on his own to investigate. Anna Udeltsova didn't accept just anyone and insisted that Rudolf audition for her by performing selections from his well-honed folk repertoire, among them a gopak—performed in a circle, the dancer's arms

*In his biography of Stalin, Robert Conquest reports Stalin's private reaction: " 'What a little swine, denouncing his own father,' he said, adding that his example must nevertheless be used politically, as a weapon against the recalcitrant peasantry."

akimbo—and a lezginka, a dance begun on tiptoe with the dancer slowly sinking to his knees. When he finished, she broke her stunned silence. She had spent most of her life teaching children to dance, she told him, and only now, watching him, could she see that with his innate gift, he had "a duty to learn classical dancing" and to study at the Maryinsky school in St. Petersburg, still calling the company and its city by the names they were known by in her youth. She invited him to join her class.

Rudolf was already accustomed to praise, but Udeltsova's words made him blush—and at once fueled his nascent hopes. Ever since he had stepped inside the Ufa Opera House and discovered a new world, his only thought had been to travel there. He had been dreaming "of the savior, who would come, take me by the hand and rescue me from that mediocre life. . . ." Now it was as if a secret passageway had been revealed. Not only did Udeltsova glimpse the potential he felt within himself, she wanted to help him get to Leningrad, the mecca of dance as far as he knew. While he had no clear picture of Leningrad or its ballet school, he had heard its name evoked whenever he danced well. To him, Leningrad was the summit, the highest form of praise. And luckily for him, Udeltsova was not simply steeped in Leningrad's ballet traditions; her daughter lived in Leningrad, and Udeltsova visited every summer to keep abreast of the new faces in the world of dance. Back in Ufa, she would regale her students with descriptions of everything she had seen.

Small, tidy and quietly intelligent, Anna Ivanovna Udeltsova was forever "beaming with kindness," remembers an Ufa neighbor. "There was that typical Slavic quietness about her. She could never stand up for either her pupils or for herself. But she loved her profession, she made that clear." She was also something of a snob who regarded Rudik as "just a little Tatar boy, an urchin, shabby, untamed," a view she did little to conceal from him. Indeed, as she was to recall years later, she asked her husband to "help him with the social graces." Called Anna Ivanovna by her students, Udeltsova looked a decade older than her sixty-one years when Rudolf and Albert came to study with her in 1949. Even then, Rudolf thought of her as "a very old woman," although she would live to the age of one hundred and three. Her deeply lined face and white hair spoke of the difficulties she had endured following the Revolution, when her husband, Sergei, had been sent away to a Siberian labor camp. He had managed to survive, but on his return to Leningrad, he and his wife were exiled to Ufa.*

Anna Udeltsova's aura of sweetness evaporated the moment class

*Rudolf claimed inaccurately in his memoir that Udeltsova was exiled to Ufa *before* the Revolution.

began. "Straighten your back! Look at your legs!" she would admonish in her pinched voice, offering words of kindness only when something was particularly well executed. Her classes drew all levels and ages, and Rudolf and Albert were the least experienced and youngest of her students. "She was tough," says Albert, "but Rudik and I didn't mind because we were learning how to do things in the right way." She taught them the rudiments of ballet: the five positions, the plié, the battement, the arabesque, the tendu.

Rudik's most valuable lessons, however, took place after class whenever Udeltsova invited him to her home for tea. Only then would she speak to him of her prime years in St. Petersburg, when she danced for Diaghilev and rehearsed alongside Pavlova. Her stories of the fabled ballerina, with their emphasis on Pavlova's devotion and divinity, inducted Rudolf into the romance of ballet and opened his eyes to the kind of religious dedication that great artistry demanded. Here before him were others who had realized his dream. For the first time, he began to think about dancing, not simply about steps.*

After eighteen months, Udeltsova concluded that she had taught her "dear boy" all that she could. She had even choreographed a sailor's dance expressly for him. Shortly thereafter she was transferred to the Railway Workers Club (Club Zheleznodorozhnika), so she passed Rudolf on to her close friend Elena Konstantinovna Voitovich, who led an amateur dance group. Once again, Albert followed Rudolf to the class, which was held at the Pioneers Palace on Karl Marx Street, just a few blocks from their homes.

Elena Konstantinovna Voitovich was something of a local celebrity, whose ties to St. Petersburg's storied past were even more pronounced than those of Anna Udeltsova. Born in 1900 to a general in the czar's army and a lady-in-waiting at the czar's court, Voitovich had studied at the Imperial Ballet School, graduating in 1918. Despite the shifting political fortunes of her family—a Soviet encyclopedia of ballet identifies her as "the daughter of petit bourgeois parents"—she was invited to join the corps de ballet of what came to be known as the Kirov Ballet. Although endowed with a pliant jump, Voitovich never advanced beyond the rank of coryphée,[†] one step up from the corps de ballet, and retired from the company in 1935. Two years later, she and her husband were exiled to Kuybyshev, and eventually they made their way to Ufa. Like Anna Udeltsova, who preceded her there, Elena Konstantinovna Voitov-

---

*Later, when looking back with more experienced eyes, he would articulate his fascination with Pavlova's religious dedication to her training. Her technique was impressive in itself, he wrote, and yet "by the very atmosphere she distilled around her, she threw a veil over all outward manifestation of technique, creating an impression of utter spontaneity each time she danced."

†In his autobiography, Nureyev calls Voitovich an ex-Kirov soloist, though in fact she was never promoted beyond the level of coryphée.

ich could never have imagined that she would one day live in any other city but her beloved St. Petersburg. Their derailed destinies proved Rudolf's good fortune.

BY THE TIME Rudolf came to study with her in 1950, Elena Konstantinovna Voitovich was fifty years old and recently widowed. Childless, she lived with her mother near the Ufa Opera House and devoted herself to teaching dance. Aside from running the Pioneers' amateur dance group, she served as ballet mistress of the Ufa Ballet, the only company Rudolf had ever seen. She had even helped stage *The Song of the Cranes* and regularly coached Zaitouna Nazretdinova, the ballerina Rudolf had seen that fateful New Year's Eve. The fact that Voitovich taught the dancers at the Ufa Opera House made an impression on twelve-year-old Rudolf, who naturally longed to take his place alongside them.

Tall, thin and stately, her light brown hair cut short, Elena Voitovich had a decidedly reserved disposition that many mistook for aloofness. But in the classroom, she came alive, her energy and intelligence palpable. Her most unusual asset was her powerful jump, which she could still demonstrate. Insisting on excellence from all her pupils, she wanted them not merely to dance well, but to dance well enough to qualify for the Ufa Ballet. "She was so kind out of class," says a former pupil, who became close to Voitovich in later years. "But in class, we were afraid of her. If she said something and you missed it, you wouldn't dare ask a second time."

Rudolf never had to ask a second time. He followed Voitovich's instructions with such rapt attention that he appeared to "live inside the dance," according to another Pioneer classmate. Whether performing folk dances, character dances or ballet combinations, twelve-year-old Rudolf was the standout, somehow managing to command the kind of authority in the studio that he failed to summon in the schoolyard. "He didn't have close friends in the Pioneers," recalls Irina Klimova, who today teaches dance at a former Pioneers Palace not far from the one where she and Rudolf studied, "but no one teased him and no one disputed that he was the best." Klimova was five years Rudolf's junior and looked up to him as a role model. In the Russian dance they performed together, she remembers how he was admired for his ability to carry her aloft on his shoulder while turning in a circle. Among the younger Pioneers, it was considered an honor to be asked by the class star to help him remove his boots, and even today, nearly a half century later, Klimova still recalls making him a bouquet of paper flowers for a special flower dance.

Rudolf's first leading role in a ballet came in *The Fairy Doll*, which Voitovich had staged especially to showcase his skills as a partner.

Dressed in white pants and a crisp white shirt, Rudolf danced with Sveta Bashiyeva, who performed in pointe shoes. Thrilled to find such a receptive pupil, Voitovich not only catered to him in class, but was soon inviting him home for tea and sharing stories of her career with him, just as Anna Udeltsova had done.

Rudolf also came under the wing of Irina Alexandrovna Voronina, another exile from St. Petersburg, who played the piano for his classes at the Pioneers Palace. A warm, maternal figure who also served as the Ufa Ballet's concertmaster, Irina Voronina made it a point to identify the composer of each piece she played. Rudolf's ear for music caught her attention at once and he, in turn, saw that she had much to teach him, not least the piano lessons his father had forbidden. On the afternoons Rudolf stopped by for tea, Voronina would show him how to play simple tunes on the piano. Both Voronina and Voitovich took special delight in Rudolf's afternoon social calls, somehow evoking the St. Petersburg salons of their youth within their drab Ufa apartments. Spiritual allies, Voronina, Voitovich and Udeltsova — Rudolf's troika of female mentors — shared not simply Rudolf's faith in himself but the determination to bring his talents to blossom. Equally important, they gave him a sense of belonging and a vision of his future. Given his single-minded determination, he doubtless would have prevailed despite every discouragement. But like all fledgling artists, he needed assurances from the more seasoned that his efforts were not in vain.

While his mother continued to favor him and show him more affection than she did her daughters, she never encouraged his early interest in dance, or even discussed it with him, which made the support of his mentors that much more crucial. In the lives of most prodigies, one needn't look far to find a parent behind the scenes stage-managing his or her offspring's career. Mozart had an ambitious father; Nijinsky, Yehudi Menuhin and Vladimir Horowitz all had powerful mothers. What makes Nureyev's case so unusual is that from a very early age, his progress was self-determined and self-propelled. His mother appreciated ballet, but had neither the time, the energy nor the inclination to cultivate her taste or to take a stand against her husband. Despite the attention of his teachers and his sister Rosa, Rudolf had to rely primarily on his own wits and wiles to advance, his methods consciously hidden from his father. Under the pretense of going to the shop to buy bread for supper, Rudolf would spend the day at dance class. When he returned home late with stale bread, his mother and sisters suspected where he had been. By not reporting him to Hamet, they tacitly protected him, in part, says Razida, to maintain family harmony. Though Farida didn't express her approval, she didn't raise her voice — or hand — against him either, which Rudolf took as a vote of support. (He would always describe his mother as his "ally.") But according to Razida, Farida was less enthusiastic than Rudolf ever supposed. Like her husband, she had high hopes for Rudolf and imagined an entirely different career for him, the reward for their years of devotion to the party. The fact that their dreams were entirely at odds with those of their son would create lasting turmoil for all of them.

AS HAMET AND FARIDA saw it, Rudolf would have opportunities no one in their family had ever been lucky enough to consider. For generations, they had been tied to the land and to the traditions of village life. Now their children had promising prospects, both educational and financial. Certainly Rudolf would not become a dancer if Hamet had any say in the matter. What kind of career was that for the son of a party member and decorated war veteran? By 1950 Hamet was working as a security guard at an electrical equipment factory, eventually becoming its head of security. He was also active in local party politics and served on a committee that oversaw the allocation of apartments in Ufa. Though Hamet could have used his position to secure larger quarters for his family, his obstinate pride prevented him from even broaching the subject. It was only when the workers at his factory put in a request on his behalf in 1961 that the Nureyevs received a larger flat.

It would be easy to dismiss Hamet as the villain of his son's story, to reduce him to a two-dimensional authority figure determined to crush his son's artistic aspirations. Certainly there are elements of the truth in this characterization, but like most parents, Hamet fervently believed that he had his son's best interests at heart and an understanding of the world that his son had yet to develop. Hamet had grown up during the waning years of imperial rule, when the seeds of revolution were being sown. He had come of age just as the country was riven by civil war. And he had come to manhood as the Communist Party was beginning to define its responsibilities and goals. He had lived through the purges, endured lengthy separations from his family and fought in a world war in part so that his son would be able to rise in the new Soviet society. Dancing was no career for a man, he admonished Rudolf, and it wouldn't put food on the table. He didn't associate ballet with homosexuality as a Western father might, nor were his objections limited to economics: Anyone could be a dancer, regardless of his party loyalty, record or background, but not everyone was well placed to advance to important positions. Most of Ufa's children could look forward to nothing beyond some kind of vocational trade school education. Hamet simply wanted his son to take advantage of all the things for which he had fought.

But Rudolf's desire to dance far outweighed any other concerns, even his fear of his father. He continued to use his bread run as an alibi and showed no remorse when his father beat him for going to dance class. "He beat me up each time he caught me. But I just went on." Razida and Lilya tried to stay clear of such scenes and usually left the house once they started. Rosa, the only sibling who supported him, was by then at a teachers' college in Leningrad. "There was only one method of punishment in our family," says Razida, who of the four children was Hamet's favorite. "Our father was strict, but he was not the kind of father who was always standing there with a stick in his hands. He would scold us if we deserved it."

Getting to dance class on Sunday, the one day Hamet stayed home, put Rudolf's cunning to the test. He would fashion some elaborate errand, but his escape was never assured. By the time he took his place at the barre, his anxiety was palpable. A fellow Pioneer recalls how Rudolf "would be looking all the time to see if his father was coming to take him home." Whenever Razida asked to come to see him dance, Rudolf would insist he wasn't dancing that week. He was afraid that she would report him to their parents and "he knew the problems that would cause," she acknowledges. And while she finally persuaded him to teach her a sailor's dance, Rudolf quickly lost patience. "There's no hope for you! You'd better quit," he said dismissively and never gave her another lesson.

Armed with a zealot's faith in his own abilities, Rudolf continued to dream of a career on the stage, the only place where he felt free to express himself fully. After hearing for years about the Kirov Ballet's school, the Leningrad Choreographic Institute, he learned one day that a select group of Bashkirian children were to be sent there to audition. Believing fortune had finally smiled on him, he rushed home with the news and begged his father to make inquiries. The school was the finest in the country, he told Hamet, who discouraged his interest. But after seeing how much it meant to Rudolf, he finally agreed to find out the procedure for applying. Days later Rudolf learned that the children had already left for Leningrad, plunging him into a state of "black despair." Only years later did he realize that his father was too proud to admit that he couldn't afford the two-hundred-ruble train fare to Leningrad that the audition required.

5

The Road to Leningrad

THE DISCOVERY that Leningrad was not some distant dream hardened Rudolf's resolve to get there. But the more determined he became, the more Hamet blocked him. It wasn't long before Hamet issued a ban on his dancing altogether. Hamet's disapproval and the ensuing battles would dominate Rudolf's late childhood and permanently color his relationship to authority. Recognizing that he could never become what his father wanted, Rudolf gave up trying to please him in even the smallest ways.

At school, Rudolf remained the outsider. As the years passed, the differences between him and other boys grew more pronounced and they soon took to calling him "Froggy" and "Ballerina" on account of the way he walked with his legs deliberately turned out from the hip. However, Rudolf had also grown more arrogant and was learning to answer their taunts with disdain, not tears. Still, his temper was easily triggered. His report cards tell the story: At the age of eleven, Rudolf was "sometimes rude to his friends because he gets mad easily." By fourteen, he was "very nervous and explosive," in the view of his seventh-grade teacher. "He cries and fights with his classmates."

A frequent eyewitness to these skirmishes, Albert did his best to protect his friend, though even he had to admit that Rudik "was not always right." To begin with, he "exaggerated his physical abilities and insulted his classmates. As a result, he would be beaten."

While an insecure child might have tried to curry favor with his classmates in an effort to feel some sense of belonging, Rudolf seemed to care little whether they liked him or not. "He didn't show much interest in other people except as dance partners," Albert recalls. "He was quite self-focused. His only desire was to study ballet. He had a limited circle of people he socialized with. There were Anna Udeltsova, Elena Konstantinovna, Irina Alexandrovna and me." Constant companions, Rudolf and Albert still walked to school, practiced their dances, and played in the yard together. At the first sign of spring, they would sneak out of class and take the trolley to Levaya Belaya, a stop along the Belaya River where in early spring the water was warm enough to swim in. During the summer, they would pass the day swimming, sunbathing and boating on the Djoma River near the House of Teachers, often staying on until evening. Sometimes they played football and volleyball with Genya Kvashonkin, Stasik Yenutin and Marat Saidashev, their neighborhood gang. "We were always together, but that doesn't mean that we stayed away from other boys," Albert says. "Half of the boys from our yard went with us to the Pioneers Palace. So we often went there in a group." On the rare occasions when their parents gave them money, they headed straight for the Matrosov cinema house, where they saw such classics of Russian film as Eisenstein's *Potemkin* and *Ivan the Terrible* as well as many Western films taken from Germany as war booty, including *The Thief of Bagdad*, *That Hamilton Woman*, *Waterloo Bridge* and, their favorite, the *Tarzan* series. Johnny Weissmuller's yodeling hero was another revelation to Rudolf.

Despite only a passing interest in his schoolwork, Rudolf excelled in geography. He pored over maps and scored high marks in a classroom exercise called "Towns." One student would call out the name of a town, and the next had to come up with a town that began with the last letter of the previous town. A veteran traveler in his imagination, Rudolf had journeyed to many distant places from his perch above Ufa's railway station. Coming up with destinations was the easy part.

English was also taught at School Number Two, though the students all spoke English poorly because their teacher couldn't control their class. A tall, nervous woman in her thirties, Elena Troshina had grown up in Shanghai, had studied at Cambridge, and spoke English fluently, all of which was of little interest to her pupils. "Sometimes we drove her to tears." Mathematics was the only academic subject in which Rudolf actively competed, perhaps because it was taught by the school's strict director. "We always tried to be the first to answer his questions because he gave us marks for it," says Albert, recalling that when Rudolf put his mind to it, he could run circles around his classmates. At School Number Two, grades were based on a numerical system running from 1 to 5, with 5 being the highest grade. In the sixth grade, eleven-year-old Rudolf averaged 3s, though he won top marks in literature, geography and physics. Two years later his marks had slipped so noticeably that his teacher complained: "Surely he can do better than 3s!"

The reason for his poor grades was hardly a mystery to his teachers.

"Sometimes he doesn't have enough time for his homework because he is very involved in dancing," his eighth-grade teacher noted in her report, adding, "He always dances at school assemblies."

As far as his teachers were concerned, Rudolf's curiosity, intelligence and aptitude should have made him a strong pupil, and every so often, one of them would show up at the Nureyevs' home to complain about his lack of effort. But they never interfered with his dancing, not even after Hamet Nureyev himself asked them to discourage Rudolf. "Hamet came to see me at school twice," admitted Taisiam Khalturina. "He asked me to talk to Rudolf and to use all my influence as a teacher. 'This boy is a future father and the head of a family,' he told me in despair." Khalturina took pity on Hamet and promised to do what she could. But she knew there was little to be done: Rudik was possessed. Whenever he had to leave class early for a performance, he had always made sure to ask her permission in advance. He was so courteous to her, so solicitous, and she in turn felt some strange allegiance to him, this poor Tatar boy whom the other boys bullied. "I must say that I feel guilty speaking about the elder Nureyev," she recalled, some forty years after Hamet's appeal, "because I never talked to Rudik about it, not even once. I understood the futility of all my efforts."

During the lesson, Rudolf covered his notebooks with sketches of ballerinas' legs, drifting so deeply into his own world that he often failed to hear his teacher. Despite mediocre grades in drawing, he was a talented draftsman whose sketch of Lomonosov,* the eighteenth-century Russian scientist and poet, appeared in a special issue of the class "wall newspaper." For all his possible potential, Rudolf was more interested in looking at pictures than in composing them, and he began honing his eye at the Nesterov Museum† on Gogol Steet, where he learned to recognize at sight the styles of many Russian painters. In time, Rudolf was to fill his own private picture galleries with Old Master works, but in 1952, at the age of fourteen, he had only change in his pocket. His first acquisitions, discovered in local kiosks, were postcard reproductions of paintings he had seen, notably those by Ilya Repin and Ivan Shishkin, and photographs of famous ballerinas. (His picture of Natalia Dudinskaya, the Kirov's prima ballerina, was a favorite.) If his drive to discover the world was unremitting, it was also desultory. He relied for the most part on the books, paintings and cultural activities Ufa had to offer. He saw every performance of the Sverdlovsk Theater of Musical Comedy and later the Omsk Theater of Music during their respective summer

*Director of the Academy of Sciences, Mikhail Lomonosov was a chemist, physicist, educator, historian and poet who codified the Russian grammar.
†Named for the nineteenth-century painter Mikhail Nesterov, an Ufa native.

tours to Ufa, sometimes sneaking through side doors and service entrances to escape paying for a ticket.

While Rudolf found little to inspire his interest at school, he was fanatically dedicated to his lessons at the Pioneers Palace, where during class, Rudolf insisted that his classmates watch him and give him the most minute corrections. "Even if he did something perfectly, he would still ask for corrections," remembers Irina Klimova. Standing before the mirror, he would scrutinize his reflection with the kind of analytic intensity that few of them understood, refusing to go on to the next exercise until he had mastered the one he was working on. Nevertheless, he was not considered vain; he was still in the process of defining himself and lacked the presence and haughty flamboyance he would one day use to legendary effect. Indeed, by the standards of the time, fourteen-year-old Rudolf wasn't much to look at. When pressed, classmates recall an "ordinary-looking," skinny boy with a small build. Whereas the other boys wore their hair clipped short and brushed neatly in place, Rudolf parted his wavy hair at the side and wore it short in the back, but long and tousled in front, so that it hung just above his ears and framed his eyes. When he danced, it was forever falling into his face. Pictures of him taken in his backyard when he was thirteen or fourteen years of age reveal a boyish figure in a white undershirt, with a hollow chest, long, thin arms, a full mouth and soft, pretty features. His expression is at once tough and innocent. In one photograph, he smiles directly into the camera, holding his arms in front of him in a self-conscious posture. In another, with his arms on his hips, he cocks his head in defiance at the camera and curls his lip. And yet his tank top hangs loosely on his undeveloped frame, undercutting his authority. "He never seemed to care about his looks," says Pamira Suleimanova, voicing a view echoed by others, and he paid no mind to his clothes, even if they smelled of sweat. His wardrobe consisted of a pair of pants, a jacket, several shirts. "We didn't have any nice clothes," says Albert, "and if we had patches on our pants and jackets, we were not ashamed of them. The main thing was to look tidy."

Beyond the Pioneers Palace, Rudolf had ample opportunities to perform. In addition to school assemblies, there were concerts to honor public holidays and occasional excursions to neighboring towns with his folk dance troupe. Since Ufa had a tradition of government holiday performances, the best Pioneer dancers were often invited to dance at the various workers' "clubs" around town, each affiliated with a factory, government organization or trade union. It was on Rudolf's first visit to the military officers' club that his cynicism was born. He had become aware of class differences as early as kindergarten, but this particular visit stirred his sense of injustice. "We were all amazed at the polish on the beautiful furniture and the richness of the buffet tables," remembered a fellow Pioneer. "Some of us understood this as a basic necessity, but Rudik didn't accept the rules of the game. He didn't disguise his anger about such 'royal' chambers. His family was poor just like our families, but for some reason, he had a much stronger reaction than the rest of the kids. . . ."

Moments of joy, however fleeting, occasionally flickered across the screen of Rudolf's childhood memories. He was happiest performing with his roving folk dance troupe, his "improvised traveling theater," as he called it. Piling their supplies and equipment into two small trucks, the troupe would arrive in some neighboring town, line up the trucks side by side, remove their sides, and slide a wooden floor across them to make a stage. A red cotton curtain, hoisted across the middle of the trucks, served as their backdrop. It was in these ad hoc performances, often before untutored, restless audiences, that Rudolf learned how to command attention onstage.

His apprenticeship was not without its share of near disasters. One time, before a rowdy audience of railway workers and their families, Rudolf literally came undone. He was supposed to wear a pair of tight navy blue wool pants for his sailor's dance. But when they weren't ready on time, he had to slip on a pair belonging to a dancer with a much broader build and have them pinned in place. He had no sooner taken a few steps than the pins popped and his pants dropped to his ankles. Mortified, he ran backstage to be refastened, only to have the pins go flying—and his trousers take another plunge—shortly after his next entrance. Most fifteen-year-olds would have retreated into the wings at that point, never to return. Rudolf persuaded the organizers to give him one more chance, as he would do with increasing urgency in the coming years. This time his entrance was preceded by a drumroll and the vaudevillian announcement that "Comrrade RRRudolf Nureyev promises to behave and not to play any more tricks." His pants stayed on his hips, but the ribbons atop his pole had become so weighted down with dirt that they refused to float—and wrapped themselves around Rudolf instead.

THE MONTH Rudolf turned fifteen, Stalin died after suffering a brain hemorrhage. The Soviet leader lay in state in Moscow for four days, on the last of which five hundred people suffocated or were crushed to death in the rush to pay their respects, a fitting, if tragic, finale to a thirty-year reign of terror. For Rudolf, however, the big event of 1953 was the opening of the first ballet studio at the Ufa Opera House. He had gained admission on Voitovich's recommendation. It must have seemed to Rudolf as if he were stepping into the world of his childhood fantasies. Not only did he share a dressing room with the Ufa Ballet dancers and watch them in class, he was soon joining them on the very stage where he had first seen them, the stage that had appeared to him as some distant dream eight years earlier. Hearing that the company needed extras, he offered his services and was soon playing every imaginable walk-on role from page to spear carrier. He was even paid a small fee for this honor. From then on, Rudolf would never earn his living through any other means than dance.*

Rudolf's life now revolved around the theater: Class ran till twelve, followed by afternoon rehearsals and, increasingly, performances. The daily routine of class, rehearsal and performance would remain virtually unchanged for the next thirty-nine years, whether the backdrop happened to be Ufa, Leningrad, London, New York or Paris. To accommodate his crowded schedule—and to satisfy his parents' wish that he finish his studies—he requested permission to transfer to the School of Working Youth, where classes were held on a more flexible basis. The petition letter he wrote to its principal suggests that the author was much more versed in making demands than requests. "Due to the fact that I have a full time job, I am not going to be able to attend Middle School No. 2 any longer," he wrote. The nights he wasn't onstage himself, he sneaked into the theater with Albert to see every ballet and opera in the repertoire.[†] Just as his mother had slipped him past its front doors one New Year's Eve, so Rudolf figured out how to pass undetected through its service entrances. Backstage, he and Albert would swing from the ropes, Tarzan-style.

Albert was the only boy from the Pioneers Palace to follow Rudolf to the new ballet studio. The Pioneers Palace was the neighborhood social club, a village green of sorts, that appealed to the other boys precisely because it lacked the solemn air of purpose Rudolf relished at the studio. The effusive Voronina continued to play the piano for his lessons. Rudolf was not as lucky with Voitovich, who coached the Ufa Ballet artists, not the students. Rudolf's training was thus entrusted to Zaitouna Nureevna Bakhtiyarova, an Ufa Ballet alumna with whom he developed little rapport. Since he couldn't leave home before his father had left for work, he frequently arrived late and disheveled for her 8 A.M. class, his

---

*That year, however, it was Farida Nureyeva, not her son, whose picture ran in the local newspaper after her dairy factory reached its quota four months ahead of schedule. Farida was shown bottling kefir.

†The Ufa Ballet had both range and depth, giving Rudolf a good grounding: In addition to such classsics as *Swan Lake*, *Coppélia*, *Don Quixote* and *Esmeralda*, he saw the Bashkirian ballets *The Song of the Cranes* and *The Mountain Tale*, and such Soviet staples as *The Fountain of Bakhchisarai*, *Laurencia* and *The Red Poppy*. That year, the company's chief choreographer, an energetic and intelligent man named Viktor Gasovich Pyari, was praised widely for his new staging of *Scheherazade*.

clothes smelling of sweat from having run all the way. A tough taskmaster who demanded strict obediance, Bakhtiyarova found his disruptions a great annoyance and often made him take his class in the hallway to punish him. She could see Rudolf was talented, yet she deplored what she considered his lack of discipline and wasted no time in upbraiding him in front of the others. In self-defense, Rudolf talked back to her, something no other student dared to do. "He felt there was no reason for her to yell at him," says his class partner Pamira Suleimanova. "We Tatars have to fight when someone yells at us." Once, however, Bakhtiyarova managed to frighten Rudolf into silence (a rare enough occurrence that it's worth noting). Hearing him mutter something nasty about her, she threatened to send him to a prison for delinquent teenagers. After the class she admitted to him that she was "only tough on those who have a future."

Where the other students took one class per day, Rudolf took three, joining the corps de ballet dancers and then the soloists at the conclusion of his first lesson with Bakhtiyarova. He also managed to teach himself a good deal by studying the Ufa dancers and tracing their movements. His role model was Yasha Lifshitz, a Leningrad-trained soloist, whose elegant line and quicksilver jump Rudolf worked hard to emulate.

Even between classes, Rudolf, Albert and Pamira worked at polishing their turns and jumps, though only Rudolf infused an air of competition into their sessions. He was more interested in what he *couldn't* do well than in what came easily to him, a trait he would never lose, even late in his career, when the effect was less than exhilarating for his audience. While Rudolf had the most finished pirouette, Albert had the bigger jump, although they were both the same height. To Rudolf this meant only one thing: He had the physical capability to jump as high as Albert, he simply hadn't yet mastered the mechanics. Day after day, he worked on his jump with a kind of intensity his classmates remember keenly. "He would never stop trying until he achieved what he wanted," says Albert. "Come here and look at me!" he would call to Pamira whenever he struck a pose he considered especially fine. "He wanted someone to appreciate him, to tell him that he was really worth something," she says. A popular singer with the Ufa Opera recalls arriving at the theater one morning to find Rudolf at the entrance, "dying to get to work. When I got to the theater, he was already in his practice clothes. You could always see him sitting at the entrance waiting for someone. Or maybe he was just observing. When he stood, his feet were always in third position. He walked with a majestic bearing as if he were standing onstage."

Where Rudolf and Albert put all their energies into dancing, the other neighborhood boys turned their attention to girls and all the attendant rites of adolescence: smoking cigarettes on street corners, playing spin the bottle, dating. None of Rudolf's boyhood acquaintances remember him joining in any of these, which isn't to suggest that he wasn't experiencing some kind of sexual awakening, though the truth of his sexual identity was likely unknown to him. Rudolf's homosexuality became known to his childhood friends only in later years. According to Albert, Rudolf never showed the slightest romantic interest in men or women, and, says they never talked about sex. But then, few Russians talked openly about sex at that time. Another neighbor, Aza Kuchumova, recalls that Rudolf "didn't go on a date all the time he was in Ufa because he was interested only in dancing."

While keeping whatever sexual yearnings he had to himself, Rudolf was not so furtive when it came to exploring his own body. Without a bed or room of his own, he had no privacy at home, but in the outhouse at least, he could be assured of a few moments to himself. He would later tell a friend about the time he was masturbating in the outhouse when he heard footsteps outside and peered through a hole to see his father approaching. When his father rattled impatiently on the door, Rudolf made sure to let out a satisfied groan so that his father would know exactly what he was up to. "I didn't care that he heard what I was doing," he recalled.

By the age of sixteen, Rudolf had arrived at an uneasy truce with his father, largely because of his newfound status as a wage earner. The ever-shrewd Rudolf had found a way to get the most mileage out of his still-distant association with the Ufa Ballet. Inflating his rank several degrees to "artist," he went around to various workers' collectives offering to give weekly dance lessons for two hundred rubles a month. He was enterprising enough that he was soon earning close to his father's salary. Hamet was no less disapproving of Rudolf's obsession with dance, but he couldn't argue with the fact that his son was earning his keep. This was, perhaps, the ultimate filial rebuke.

Walk-on roles and pocket money may have emboldened him, but Rudolf was still far from Leningrad. A scholarship to the school was his only ticket. Many years later, when asked to account for his formidable sense of purpose, Nureyev recalled the exasperation of those years: "When I discovered that I was meant to dance, and everybody said to me, 'Oh, how talented you are,' and I said, 'Well, why nothing happens? Why I can't get to that wretched school? Why do I have to wait all that time? . . . And finally something came and clicked in my mind that nobody's going to come and take me by hand and show me anything. I had to do it all myself. So that was what I was doing ever since."

But, in fact, he wasn't doing it all himself. He was lucky to have a resourceful ally in Irina Voronina, who was busy campaigning on his behalf. In due course, she convinced a number of local figures to send letters to the Bashkirian Republic's Ministry of Culture, recommending that Rudolf be considered for a scholarship to the Leningrad school. Among these was Zaitouna Nazretdinova, the prima ballerina whose dancing had fired Rudolf's ambitions. To her seasoned eye, the young Nureyev was a hardworking novice, not a polished professional, though as a graduate of the Leningrad school herself, she knew what such training could do for him. "A man from our Ministry of Culture came to me and said, 'Rudik Nureyev wants to go to Leningrad,' and I told him, 'Let him go. He is a capable boy,'" Nazretdinova recalled thirty-nine years later, her bearing still erect and commanding, her hair still black, and tucked into a paisley print scarf, the once-sharp features now obscured by large glasses. "He was just a beginner, but you could see he was confident, that he had stage presence. I would say he was distinguished by his great desire to dance. He was very diligent and not at all sociable when he worked at the theater. He didn't have time for people."

While preparing for his final high school exams, Rudolf was given his first dancing role on the opera house stage, in a Polish dance* choreographed by Voitovich for Glinka's opera *Ivan Susanin*. Rather than simply blend in with the scenery, he was to dance with the corps de ballet, an incremental promotion that was to Rudolf a waking dream. He forgot about his studies and wasn't surprised when he failed his exams, though he knew better than to tell his parents. That task was made easier when the Ufa Ballet invited him along on its month-long summer tour to Rjazan, a town seven hundred and fifty miles northwest of Ufa. The tour gave sixteen-year-old Rudolf his first taste of independence and there was no going home again after that. Rudolf roomed with Albert, who was also brought along as a walk-on, and with hours of free time at their disposal, they enjoyed lazy afternoons and excursions to local landmarks, their newfound freedom wonder enough. Albert gives this account: "Every morning we had breakfast at a canteen and then took the trolleybus to the Oka River to sunbathe and swim. We always had to be back by evening for our performances. After the performance we would supper on our favorite dish, which was fish paste. It was cheap and delicious. We put it on a piece of bread and that was our supper. We didn't drink any tea, just plain water. That's how we lived. We also made cherry jam to take home to our parents. We bought sugar and cherries and one of the opera singers who lived near Rudik in Ufa helped us make it. In our room, we found a beautiful picture album of the sights of Europe and—let the landlady forgive us—we cut out many of those pictures and took them away with us. We spoiled her beautiful album and she must have been dumbfounded when she discovered it."

---

*Although Nureyev claimed in his autobiography that his first dancing role came in a ballet called *Polish Ball*, the curator of the Nureyev Museum in Ufa insists that he appeared in a Polish dance in the opera.

The images of those European capitals surely beckoned, for no sooner did they have a night off than Rudolf and Albert were on the first bus to Moscow, a four-hour journey. They arrived in the heart of the city, at Belorussia Railway Station, and made their way to the Kremlin and then on to Red Square, which suggested to Rudolf "a vast railway station, all different kinds of people. . . ." The Tretyakov Picture Gallery was the sight the boys most wanted to visit and they lingered there the whole afternoon, forgoing meals to allow them a few more hours to explore its treasures. Next, they hit the metro, taking an extra-long ride "because we wanted to experience it," says Albert, who somehow lost Rudolf as they crisscrossed the city underground. Having agreed to meet near the Gorky monument in Belorussia Station should they get separated, Albert dutifully proceeded there and "waited and waited, but Rudik didn't turn up." Fatigue won out and Albert went in search of the nearest hotel, using his student's card to get a cheap rate. The next morning he found Rudolf at the station. He had tried to come back to the station the night before, he said, but the train had stopped running, so he had walked all night. Despite his sleepless night, he and Albert spent the day exploring the Kremlin grounds and the vast spaces of G.U.M. department store before rushing to the terminal to catch the bus back to Rjazan.*

That fall Rudolf joined the Ufa Ballet as an apprentice and threw himself into his classes "like a madman." He was even bold enough to ask Haliaf Safiullin, the company's leading male dancer and a sometime company choreographer, whether he planned to use him in his new ballet. To which Safiullin gently replied, "My dear, you are still young. You have time on your hands." Though he continued to take classes with Bakhtiyarova, he was now permitted to study directly with Viktor Pyari, the company ballet master, and with his mentor Voitovich, who also rehearsed all company productions. But he continued to work from the outside in: His style didn't emanate from a sure and rigorous technique; it had grown out of an innate feeling for dance coupled with an ability to reproduce movements he'd seen. His elevated status seemed reason enough for Rudolf "to give himself airs," recalls Albert, which became more pronounced after Rudolf received word that the Ministry of Culture had partially approved his scholarship to Leningrad. However, he had one more hurdle to overcome: He still had to audition. What Rudolf didn't know was that his application had initially been rejected. According to Zaitouna Nazretdinova, the authorities felt that he was too old to begin training in Leningrad. The school rarely accepted male students beyond the age of fourteen and Rudolf was then seventeen years old. Only after the Bashkirian Ministry of Culture did some heavy lob-

---

*In his autobiography, Rudolf describes the trip to Moscow, but makes no mention of having traveled with anyone else.

bying in Moscow—and played up its longtime association with the Leningrad school—did Moscow agree to deem Nureyev's application "an exception."

When, several months later, Rudolf was tendered what might have been *the* offer of his career—a contract with the Ufa Ballet—he turned it down. It was an honor to be asked to join the company, he knew, but he was holding out for his scholarship to Leningrad.

Theatrical lore is filled with tales of the Lucky Break, that split-second moment when the unknown gets a shot at the spotlight. For Rudolf, that moment came just after he'd turned down the Ufa Ballet, when the republic was choosing dancers for the Bashkirian Decade of Literature and Art, a ten-day showcase of Bashkirian culture to be held in Moscow that May. On the day the Ministry of Culture's representative arrived at the theater to make his selections, one of the soloists failed to show up, bringing the audition to a standstill. The company was about to perform *The Song of the Cranes* and the soloist was one of the *jigits*, Bashkirian horsemen who danced while balancing a pole.

"Could anyone take his place?" the director asked from the stage.

Having been in the audience whenever he wasn't onstage, Rudolf knew the company's repertoire by heart, each ballet imprinted on his memory, with *Song of the Cranes* heading the list. He raised his hand at once, and, after a quick run-through with Viktor Pyari, the part was his. "Dancing for me in those first days had something of the feelings a tight-rope dancer must know—confident that he will reach the far side, yet invigorated with the possibility of danger." Rudolf saw the Bashkirian Decade as an opportunity to be seen in a soloist role by other teachers and dancers from across the country. In the festival program, his name appeared for the first time on its own line, distinct. But during rehearsals in Moscow, the overzealous tightrope dancer sprained his toes coming down from a pirouette and was forced to sit out the opening performance on May 28, 1955. For a young man primed to move, the notion of pacing himself was utterly foreign and accommodated only by necessity. His foot became so swollen that he couldn't fit into his slippers and he had no choice but to stay away from class while his foot healed.

Rest for Rudolf meant taking in the sights he had missed on his trip to Moscow the summer before. The Ufa dancers were billeted together in the Europa Hotel, not far from the Bolshoi Theater, and were required to travel in groups. Rudolf stayed with the group for just three days, before sneaking off to museums and theaters of his own choosing. The festival participants were given free passes to most of the Moscow theaters and Rudolf, recalls Pamira Suleimanova, was known to take in as many as three performances a day. One night the Ufa dancers attended a concert. Rudolf separated himself from the group the minute they passed through the theater's door and proceeded directly to the orchestra, even though he had a ticket to the balcony only. When his Ufa colleagues peered down from their seats, they saw Rudolf seated near the stage, one leg crossed primly over the other, looking "as if he belonged there." What to a contemporary sensibility seems a small infraction struck the Ufa dancers as remarkably brazen. In fact, they worried on his behalf and feared "he would be chased out of his seat, but the ushers never bothered him." Rudolf's offhand familiarity with Moscow surprised the dancers, many of whom, like Pamira Suleimanova, felt intimidated by its vast, sprawling boulevards. "He took me by the hand into the metro and helped me into the train, to make sure I got to rehearsal."

Rudolf healed sufficiently to make his *dekada* debut as a soloist in *The Song of the Cranes* one week later and performed admirably, according to its star, Zaitouna Nazretdinova, who got the lion's share of kudos. Indeed the company's appearances helped put the Ufa Ballet on the map; following the festival, *Pravda* reported that the Bashkirian ballet could be ranked third in the country after the Moscow and Leningrad troupes. But Rudolf sought more than just a good performance. He knew that scouts from the country's top ballet schools were on the lookout for recruits and he hoped to attract their notice in advance of his official audition for the Leningrad school. To Rudolf's mind, Haliaf Safiullin had got it all wrong when he told him he had time on his hands. At seventeen, he himself knew he was old for the Leningrad school. If he was going to make his break from Ufa, he had only a slim margin of time in which to do it. When the scouts didn't come to him as he had hoped, Rudolf did something no one else in their group thought to do: He went in search of them. His strategy was to introduce himself to those Bashkirian dancers at the festival who were already students at the Kirov school and persuade them to introduce him, in turn, to their teachers. His gambit paid off, recalls Eldus Habirov, an Ufa native who had just graduated from the Leningrad ballet school that year: "He approached me at the *dekada* and asked me to introduce him to some of my teachers who had accompanied our group from Leningrad. It was a very unusual request, but I was moved by his insistence and pleased that someone from Ufa wanted to study at the Leningrad school. Two of my teachers said they would see him. In a hotel room in the Europa Hotel, they watched him perform. 'There is no need for you to audition, you should come to the school in September,' they told him. Rudolf was very pleased and thanked me for my help."

At the same time, Irina Voronina, in Moscow as the Ufa Ballet's accompanist, was working some connections of her own. She convinced the great Bolshoi teacher Asaf Messerer to audition Rudolf for the Bolshoi Ballet School. Messerer, a former Bolshoi dancer, allowed Rudolf to watch him teach morning class, which Galina Ulanova, the most celebrated Russian ballerina of the day, regularly attended.*

Messerer informed Rudolf that he would audition him after the class. Rudolf sat in animated silence, anxiously awaiting the moment when he, too, would get to dance for Messerer. Suddenly, before the class ended, Messerer was abruptly called away. With no clue to when he might return, Rudolf waited the whole day, his mood careening from anxious expectation to despair. The next day he made his way once again to Messerer's classroom, only to discover that another instructor had been assigned to audition him because Messerer had been called away on urgent business. His audition was a success, with Rudolf declared a candidate for entry to the Bolshoi Ballet School at the advanced eighth-year level, which Rudolf readily admitted was a near miracle.

But there was a glitch. Unlike the Leningrad school, the Moscow school had no residence for its students and no scholarships established for students from distant republics, which meant that Rudolf would have to pay his own way. Without another miracle, the Bolshoi school held no real possibilities for him, though the endorsement no doubt prodded him to seize the one option left.

"I'm finished with Ufa. I'm going to study in Leningrad," he announced to Pamira Suleimanova on their return to Ufa. Pamira, who had also been awaiting a scholarship to Leningrad, assumed she had not been chosen and began to cry. She didn't then know that the Ministry of Culture had not yet given Rudolf the final go-ahead. Nevertheless, he was confident that the teachers who had auditioned him would recommend him for admission. In his memoir, Rudolf conflated the events leading him to Leningrad, insisting that he went directly from Moscow to Leningrad and bypassed Ufa altogether. In truth, he not only returned to Ufa that summer, he joined the Ufa Ballet on a tour to Penza, three hundred miles west of Ufa, at the end of July. Hamet and Farida came to see him off at the train station, and according to a former company member, Farida cried as she said farewell to Rudolf.

It was from Penza that Rudolf made his way to Leningrad, changing trains in Moscow for the final leg of his journey. What should have been an eight-hour express trip took Rudolf twice the time when he mistakenly boarded the local train and was forced to stand the whole way because there wasn't an empty seat. Sixteen hours after leaving Moscow, and ten years after his first visit to the Ufa Theater, the city he had surveyed only in his imagination finally inched into view: ". . . There were huge, black clouds, hanging very low in the sky. Quite certain we were running into a terrible storm, I wrapped myself up in my heavy rain-coat . . . under

---

*In his memoir, Rudolf makes no mention of his impressions of Ulanova, which he most certainly would have done had he had the rare opportunity to observe her in class that day.

that heavy coat I remember feeling rather lost and alone and completely unprepared for disembarking into a radiantly sunny city. Those oppressive clouds were merely over the industrial suburbs where they hang all the year round. But it was something that, as a country boy, I had never known. . . ."

His first stop was Rossi Street, home of the Leningrad Choreographic Institute, "a consecrated ground of daily work, a link in the chain of continuity," in the words of Ballets Russes star Tamara Karsavina, who had studied there at the turn of the century.* The school's chain of graduates linked some of the most luminous names in ballet: Pavlova, Nijinsky, Balanchine and, later, Nureyev, Makarova, Baryshnikov. But on Rudolf's first day, there wasn't a dancer in sight, only the workers, cleaners and painters who had come to ready the school for the fall term. He had arrived a week early and the school was closed for repairs.

"I'd like to speak to Comrade Shelkov," he announced to the first boy he saw in the corridor. Valentin Shelkov was the director of the school and Rudolf planned to introduce himself without going through the proper channels, the first of many such dicey strategies.

"I'm Shelkov, what do you want?" answered an older man standing nearby, surprised at the cheek of this rumpled teenager.

"I am Rudolf Nureyev, artist from the Ufa Opera. I would like to study here" came Rudolf's reply, a line he'd been rehearsing for a decade. His urgency cut no ice with Comrade Shelkov, who informed Rudolf that he was simply too early and would have to return for his audition in a week's time. Shelkov was not unfamiliar with Rudolf's name. As promised, Abdurachman Kumisnikov, one of the teachers at the *dekada*, had recommended him and Shelkov himself had sent a formal request to the Bashkirian Minister of Culture on July 2, 1955: "During the time of the Bashkirian Decade in Moscow, a teacher of the Leningrad Choreographic Institute, A. L. Kumisnikov, auditioned a young artist of the Bashkirian Theater of Opera and Ballet named Rudolf Nureyev (age 16), who has shown himself to be professionally suited for study at the Leningrad Choreographic Institute. We request that you make provisions in the Directorate of Educational Institutions of the Ministry of Culture of the USSR to send him to us for study, and to allow him a full government scholarship as well as a place in the dormitory."

Nevertheless, Rudolf still had to go through the final selection process. In the meantime, he went off in search of Leningrad, anxiously awaiting the opening of its fabled school, whose doors had for so long been closed to him.

---

*Karsavina's father had been a pupil of Petipa, the legendary ballet master.

6

A Window on the West

RUDOLF SPENT his first week in Leningrad with Anna Udeltsova, who happened to be in town visiting her daughter. Delighted to share with her "dear boy" the city she had long ago described to him, she gave him a place to stay and a tour of the places housing her memories.

While Rudolf's first view of Leningrad had been obscured by black industrial haze, his succeeding impressions were colored by its ever-changing light: pale and diffused, dazzling and cold, slate gray. As he strolled the length of the Nevsky Prospect, its stone palaces warmed by a pastel palette, he discovered a city as nuanced as his own repertoire of moods. "Old Moscow fades beside her rival," the poet Alexander Pushkin had concluded a century earlier. "A dowager, she is outshone." To Rudolf, who had sampled the stolid immensity of Moscow only the summer before, Leningrad was a revelation, "a city blessed by God." Though the horse-drawn carriages and ermine-draped czarinas of Pushkin's day were long gone from the Nevsky Prospect, to Rudolf's hungry eyes, the city evoked all the romance and splendor of that bygone era. Moscow may have dictated the country's political agenda, but the decisions central to Rudolf, those concerning artistic achievement, were issued from this necklace of islands on the Neva River.

Russia's only European city was an enduring monument to Peter the Great, whose sheer doggedness in transforming mosquito-ridden swamplands Rudolf must have admired.* Holding fast to his ambition to wrench Russia from its backward past, Peter forged his new capital on

---

*Nureyev would keep a life-size portrait of Peter in his London drawing room. At six feet seven, Peter was said to possess a will and temperament that matched his size.

the marshy banks of the Neva, first as a fortress to repel the Swedish Army and then, when Baltic trade routes were assured, as a "window on Europe," a bridge to the West. Having studied shipbuilding in Amsterdam and London, Peter understood the value of cultural exchange, which in time would make the city that bore his name synonymous with classical dance the world over. He imported French, Swiss and Italian architects to design palaces for his court and gave them carte blanche to create a master plan for the city, one that would prove to be as proportioned and elegant as a Fabergé egg.

Under Peter's westward-looking successors, the city became a cultural mecca and one of Europe's grandest capitals, from the baroque splendor of the czar's 1,057-room Winter Palace to the austere neoclassicism of the Hermitage, commissioned by Catherine the Great to house her private art collection.

Ballet was yet another European fashion that took root in Russian soil, its seeds first planted in 1738, exactly two centuries before Nureyev was born. It was then that the empress Anna founded a ballet school at the urging of the French ballet master she had imported to teach social dancing to her court.* Numerous French and Italian ballet masters took up residence in St. Petersburg, among them Charles Didelot, who did much to raise the standards of Russian dancing and whose narrative ballets inspired many writers, particularly Pushkin. Thanks to imperial patronage, the Russian ballet quickly grew in popularity and stature, fueled by the contributions of French choreographer and dancer Marius Petipa and two important teachers, Christian Johansson, a pupil of the celebrated Dane August Bournonville, and Enrico Cecchetti, a virtuoso Italian dancer. The Marseilles-born Petipa was the master of the grand spectacle, creating over sixty ballets for the Imperial Ballet during his fifty-six-year reign, including such masterpieces as *The Sleeping Beauty*, *La Bayadère*, *Don Quixote*, *Raymonda* and, together with Lev Ivanov, *Swan Lake* and *The Nutcracker*, all of them ballets Nureyev would stage in the West.

"We copied, borrowed from and emulated every source that gave us inspiration," Petipa's pupil and successor Nicholas Legat wrote of the European traditions that Nureyev, too, would inherit, "and then working on our acquired knowledge, and lending it the stamp of the Russian national genius, we moulded it into the eclectic art of the Russian ballet." By the late nineteenth century, St. Petersburg had replaced Paris and Italy as the capital of the ballet world and in the coming years would produce some of the finest dancers and choreographers, including Pavlova, Karsavina, Nijinsky and Fokine. Beginning in 1905, the city expe-

*The school's first pupils were the children of palace servants, who were trained to dance in court entertainments.

rienced an extraordinary outburst of artistic energy: Alexander Benois and Léon Bakst were designing exotic costumes and decor for the ballet. Stravinsky had dropped his law studies to begin composing his first symphony. Fokine was injecting dramatic realism into the hidebound traditions of the Imperial Ballet, where Petipa's ballets held pride of place.* Like Fokine, Pavlova sought to convey the human spirit in dance.

It was the impresario and aesthete Serge Diaghilev who raised the curtain on Russian art in the West. Diaghilev had hoped to become a composer, but lost heart after Rimsky-Korsakov himself strongly discouraged him.† He went on to help found the avant-garde magazine *Mir Iskusstva* (The World of Art) and served briefly at the Imperial Theaters before challenging the stagnant Maryinsky with his call to arms for a new aesthetic, one that would embrace innovation in all the arts.‡ In 1906, he presented the first exhibition of Russian paintings in Paris; two years later, at the Paris Opéra, the Western premiere of *Boris Godunov*, starring the famous Russian basso Fedor Chaliapin. The greatest ambassador of Russian culture, "a Napoleon of the arts and a Renaissance man in one," Diaghilev set up a kind of rival court, comprised entirely of Russian artists, dancers and musicians.** In 1909, he brought the magnificent dancers of the Imperial Russian Ballet to Paris, enthralling Western audiences with the designs of Bakst and Benois, the music of Stravinsky and the dancing of Pavlova, Karsavina and Nijinsky in Fokine's ballets. The Ballets Russes, as Diaghilev's hugely influential enterprise became known, soon made its home in the West, where it "transformed ballet into a vital, modern art" and provided the inspiration, model and talent for a myriad of new ballet companies, among them England's Royal Ballet.

At home, however, the future of Russian ballet hung very much in the balance following the Revolution of 1917. "The question of whether the ballet would survive on the state stage or would be wiped out as an amusement and caprice of its elect admirers was in the air of the theater," wrote a Petrograd critic in 1918. The story goes that Anatole Lunacharsky, the commissar charged with deciding its fate, fell under the spell of a

---

*Fokine staged several ballets at the Maryinsky Theater, though three of his most famous works, *Scheherazade*, *The Firebird*, and *Le Spectre de la Rose*, were never performed in Russia until the 1990s. *Petrouchka*, however, was shown in the 1920s in Petrograd and Moscow.

†When Diaghilev asked the composer to comment on a symphony he had composed, Rimsky-Korsakov advised cutting it from beginning to end.

‡Nevertheless, he coveted the post of director of the Imperial Theaters, an ambition he never managed to realize.

**For its first two seasons, the Diaghilev company was composed of artists of the imperial theaters on leave of absence. Beginning in 1911, when Nijinsky, then Diaghilev's lover, resigned from the Maryinsky Theater, Diaghilev established his own company as a permanent organization.

group of Maryinsky dancers, who improvised a special performance for his commission. Though the new regime had no use for fairy tales, princes and other such "bourgeois" baubles, it saw no harm in supporting what was deemed an entertaining, inconsequential art form.

A flurry of experimentation ensued, during which Kasyan Goleizovsky and Fedor Lopukhov emerged as Soviet ballet's most innovative choreographers. Like Fokine, the Moscow-based Goleizovsky felt that classical ballet had become ossified and relied too heavily on academic virtuosity and spectacle. Ever on the lookout for novel forms, he advocated the development of pure dance and formed his own chamber group, stirring controversy with his scantily clad dancers, fluid, erotic movement and sculptural forms. He also one of the first to use classical and contemporary music not originally composed for the ballet. For his part, Lopukhov, as head of the former Maryinsky Ballet, not only preserved and restored the great Petipa ballets, he introduced acrobatic elements into classical dance and created some of its earliest abstract works. Music, not story, was his starting point.

Nureyev would come to admire the achievements of both Goleizovsky and Lopukhov, who more directly inspired a young Imperial Theater School graduate by the name of Georgi Balanchivadze (George Balanchine). By the mid-1930s, Stalinism had crushed the Russian avant-garde. Lopukhov's works were banned from the Kirov repertory* and the Silver Age, that glorious period described by the poet Anna Akhmatova as "the time of Stravinsky and Blok, Anna Pavlova and Scriabin, Rostovtsev and Chaliapin, Meyerhold and Diaghilev," was branded "the most shameful and most mediocre" in the country's cultural history. Suspicious of St. Petersburg innovation, Stalin "hoped to destroy the city's oppositional spirit once and for all." That campaign began on December 1, 1934, with the assassination of Sergei Kirov, a keen follower of the city's cultural life who had frequented the opera and supported Lopukhov's early experiments.

Stalin, it was said, spared the ballet only because he was taken with the dancing of Bolshoi star Marina Semyonova. Nevertheless, he had no interest in culture other than as a means of expanding his control. The arts became chained to a rigid ideology, and cultural exchange, the seedbed of renewal, came to an end. Socialist Realism prevailed, and all Soviet art was forced to express the ideals of Communism.

The Red Poppy, the first "revolutionary" ballet, introduced the heroic theme and style to Soviet dancing. Throughout the Stalinist era, the

*Lopukhov later became the artistic director of the Kirov, 1956–1957. He had many problems with the authorities, but during his tenure invited the young Yuri Grigorovich to choreograph the three-act ballet that became his first hit, *The Stone Flower*.

creative ferment taking place elsewhere in the world of dance was unknown inside the Soviet Union. While Balanchine's streamlined, largely plotless neoclassicism took root in America, ballet in Russia went the way of the *drambalet* (drama ballet), in which dancing served the plot line. Still, the innovators of this style managed to transcend "mandatory nationwide optimism" by choosing from world literature stories with tragic themes, among them *The Fountain of Bakhchisarai* (1934), *Laurencia* (1939), *Romeo and Juliet* (1940) and *The Bronze Horseman* (1949.) These ballets, while limited in choreographic invention, gave the dancers ample opportunity to showcase their dramatic range. Marina Semyonova, Galina Ulanova, Natalia Dudinskaya, Vakhtang Chabukiani and Konstantin Sergeyev all made their their mark in the new repertory.

By 1955, the school that had produced Nijinsky and Pavlova was still "an oasis of Russian culture amidst fragments of former glory . . . [as yet untouched] by the general decay so apparent elsewhere in Leningrad," in the words of graduate Natalia Makarova. All the great Soviet stars, like their Maryinsky forebears, took their first steps here. The school's handsome classical building, its yellow facade accented by white columns, occupied one side of Rossi Street, a perfectly proportioned cul-de-sac named for its architect Carlo Rossi, the son of an Italian ballerina.* Though called simply the Leningrad Choreographic Institute when Nureyev arrived there, it remains best known as the Vaganova Choreographic Institute, the name it assumed in 1957 to honor Agrippina Vaganova,† a former Maryinsky ballerina and venerated teacher, who survived the Revolution to become, as Nureyev described her, "the mother of modern Russian ballet."

As late as the 1930s, ballet in Russia had not been codified. It was Vaganova's achievement to draw together and rework the diverse influences on the Russian school into one cohesive method, published at home and abroad as *Fundamentals of the Classic Dance*, the so-called ballet bible. Her method, based on the study of the body's natural responses, demanded harmony and coordination of the entire body. Vaganova-trained pupils became known for their amplitude of movement, their soaring leaps and, especially, their sturdy backs, which enabled them to control their bodies, even in flight. Not only did Vaganova exert a great influence on the style of male dancing in Soviet ballet, she trained a generation of dancers for the Leningrad stage, among them Marina Semyonova, Galina Ulanova, Natalia Dudinskaya and Alla Osipenko. She had also handpicked the school's faculty, guided by the belief that great ballet teachers, like great dancers, were called, not made.

---

*The street is as wide as the height of its building and ten times as long.

†Vaganova (1879–1951) performed with the Maryinsky Ballet and served for a time as both director of the company and director of the ballet school.

* * *

ON AUGUST 25, 1955, it was Rudolf's turn to stand before the panel of experts who safeguarded the school's two-hundred-year-old legacy. His talent was just one among a host of considerations. Height, proportions, flexibility, suppleness, face, feet: All would be measured, appraised and tallied. The starting age for most students was nine or ten and while some joined at twelve and thirteen, rarely did students begin their training any later. However, because the birth rate had dropped during the war, exceptions were sometimes made, but only for the remarkably gifted. As the day of auditions began, the sole person convinced of Rudolf's prodigious gifts was seventeen-year-old Rudolf himself.

Just as his father had seen membership in the party as his ticket out of a dead-end life in Asanovo, Rudolf now saw acceptance into the school as *his* ticket out of Ufa. Even if his father failed to agree, acceptance into the school conferred privileges and status beyond the reach of most Russians. Equally important for Rudolf, all the costs of his education, his holidays and his ballet training would be paid by the state.

Together with a group of Latvian boys, Rudolf was auditioned by Vera Costravitskaya, Vaganova's appointed watchdog. Tall and long-limbed, with an elegant carriage and airtight coiffure, she was famous for her exacting standards. Praise seldom issued from her lips.

As Costravitskaya called out assorted exercises and combinations, Rudolf demonstrated his musicality, his flexibility, his innate expressiveness. He showed her how high he could jump, how swiftly he could turn, how well he understood the vocabulary of ballet. He could speak the language, that much was clear, and he could speak it in a exuberant voice all his own, but he hadn't a firm grounding in its grammar. His turns weren't well placed, his jumps lacked grace, his line wasn't refined. Since Rudolf had learned to dance from the outside in, by imitation and approximation, his style was "soft and fluid," as he himself would acknowledge, not the natural expression of a solid technique.

At last, Costravitskaya delivered her now-famous verdict. "Young man, you'll either become a brilliant dancer—or a total failure." Here she paused, as if weighing the equation. "Most likely, you'll be a total failure!" Her prediction was not the dire insult it would appear to anyone other than a ballet dancer. Rudolf understood that it was not so much a dismissal as a challenge, an acknowledgment that he had a great career ahead of him only if he was willing to work himself raw. Most likely, Costravitskaya assumed, Rudolf would lose heart. Still, having thrown down the gauntlet, she bet on his talent and accepted him into the school. Since his technique was in need of immediate attention, he was assigned to the sixth grade, the class for fifteen-year-old boys led by Valentin Shelkov. In short order, the Bashkirian Ministry of Culture had endorsed his scholarship and dispatched funds to Leningrad for his room and board. The rest was now up to him.

JUST AS HIS Ufa classmates had laughed at the little boy in the girl's coat on his first day of kindergarten, so Rudolf's Leningrad classmates "ogled this feral looking creature," this strange boy from Ufa whose eyes "glittered defiantly," on his first day at the ballet school. Everything about him marked him as an outsider: his tousled hair hanging limply over his eyes, his shabby clothes, his skimpy rope belt squeezing his unusually small waist, his rough manners, his age. "He was wearing horrible soldier's boots up to his knees and an army-style coat," recalls classmate Menia Martinez. "He had only a small suitcase in his hand." Elena Tchernichova remembers looking up from her textbook, opened to a description of Genghis Khan, just as Rudolf was ushered into their classroom. Here he was, she thought, "Genghis Khan in the flesh."

As a pupil from the Bashkir Autonomous Republic, Rudolf was assigned to the dorm housing "minority" students from the Asian republics and satellite countries. Of the school's six hundred pupils, five hundred were from Leningrad and most of them lived at home. The others lived in the dorms, the older ones in the roomier so-called bachelor quarters on the first floor. Rudolf's dorm, located on the third floor, was a long, narrow room with beds lined up barracks-style and enormous windows facing Rossi Street. Separated from his own age group, Rudolf had to share quarters with nineteen other boys aged nine through fifteen, none of whom possessed his single-minded ferocity. In any case, he "showed no interest in making friends," recalls Sergiu Stefanschi, a Romanian student three years Rudolf's junior, who occupied the cot next to his. Without recourse to locks and keys, Rudolf kept his few valued possessions—his musical scores and art reproductions—beneath his mattress. A lifetime of communal living had taught him the importance of marking his turf. The minute he got back to the room, he would lift his mattress to ensure that everything was just as he had left it. "Whenever you're here, keep an eye on this," he instructed Sergiu Stefanschi. "If somebody touches my music, I'll kill them."

Nobody doubted him. Passing by Rudolf's dorm one afternoon, Elena Tchernichova noticed a group of boys huddled by the closed door "like mice." As she approached them, she heard music coming from the room. Her curiosity piqued, she cracked open the door, only to see a boot come hurtling in her direction. Rudolf was sitting on his bed, listening to Bach on a record player, having decreed that no one was allowed back in until he was done.

Rudolf may have ruled the dorm, but he was not given free rein in the classroom, where he was soon running afoul of another regime, as authoritarian and patriarchal as the one he had endured in his father's house. Indeed here, too, just as it had in the Nurcyev home, the military served as the model: The students led highly regimented lives, governed by a respect for tradition, discipline and hierarchy.* By the time Rudolf arrived at the school, long gone were the days when students were given three different uniforms—a black one for every day, a dark blue for holidays and a gray linen for summer—not to mention two overcoats of military cut studded with silver buttons. Though stripped of luxuries and its portraits of the czar, the Rossi Street school had undergone only minor alterations since the changing of the guard: Portraits of Lenin and Stalin replaced those of the Romanovs, and the Romanov wardrobe had been replaced by stiff gray shirts and itchy gray trousers, one per customer. But otherwise, its iron-clad regimen suited the party's objectives: "We all were subliminally taught that great talent counted for nothing in the Academy—therefore, in the nation—unless brought to heel by the established order," wrote dancer Valery Panov in his memoir of those years. "The 'regimen'—that is, *conformity*—was held up as the highest good of all our work, while artistic brilliance that challenged the 'norms' of deportment was positively persecuted. The more gifted a pupil, the quicker the authorities were to expel him if he was rude, childish, or incompetent in general subjects—most of all, if he violated the regulations."

Rudolf, however, could no sooner fall into line at school than he could at home. While the academy's rules were followed as sacraments, Rudolf began to break them, one by one, starting with the first order of the day: breakfast. Classes didn't begin until 8 A.M., but the students were expected to rise earlier to give them enough time to wait their turn in the lavatory and rush to the canteen for their kasha and tea. Their room had only a single cold faucet and "everyone who was waiting shouted to the one washer to *hurry*—and to the child sitting on the toilet to stop fouling the air." Rudolf hated washing and eating en masse, so when the wake-up call came, he simply pulled the covers over his head and waited for the room to clear. Now, instead of running between home, the opera house and the School for Working Youth, as he had done in Ufa, Rudolf had only to walk from one floor to another, and from mid-block to the

---

*Under the czars, the pupils of the Imperial Theater School and the army and naval academies shared the same rank and wore the same uniforms, the insignia on their collars the only distinguishing feature: Crossed sabres meant the army; anchors, the navy; and Apollo's lyre, framed in palms and topped with a crown, signified the ballet. Lincoln Kirstein, who cofounded the School of American Ballet with Theater School graduate George Balanchine, once described it as "the West Point of Ballet." A ballet school, he once observed, "is the most undemocratic thing there is and there are three things they have to learn about this one. One is that there's no justice. The second is that they must never complain. The third is that they must shut up."

top of Rossi Street, for dorm, canteen, classes and studios were all housed in adjoining buildings.

His eleven-hour days were crammed with a wide range of lessons geared toward a career on the stage. Mornings began with courses in the history of ballet, music or art followed by two hours of ballet instruction, the heart of the curriculum. Afternoons were taken up with academic subjects and classes in character dance. Several days a week, fencing, stage makeup, piano and French lessons rounded out Rudolf's crowded schedule. While his courses in the history of the Soviet Union, math and science bored him, he was interested in literature, art and the history of dance. The last was taught by Nikolai Ivanovsky, the school's elegant artistic director, who wore spats and patent leather shoes and bowed his head in greeting to his pupils. A classmate of George Balanchine's and a man of exceptional cultivation, he taught courtly manners by example. Through him, the Petersburg traditions came alive. "He would reenact phrases from certain ballets and it was as if Nijinsky and Pavlova were in the room," says Sergiu Stefanschi. "We adored him."

Another favorite was Igor Belsky, the Kirov's leading character dancer. Imaginative and expressive, he held his students spellbound as he performed a medley of movements from every known ballet. Character dance was one of the distinguishing features of Russian ballet instruction, its rich repertory inspired by the varied folk dance traditions that Rudolf had studied as a child. Rudolf took naturally to his art history teacher, a curator from the Hermitage who was inclined to use the celebrated galleries, rather than textbooks, to illustrate her lessons. Attracted by the beneficent Madonnas of the Italian masters and the untethered brushstrokes of van Gogh, Rudolf was soon making solo visits to the Hermitage every Sunday, his only free day.

He also came under the spell of Maria-Marietta Frangopulo, a thirty-year veteran of the Kirov and former classmate of Balanchine's. Frangopulo supervised the school's tiny museum, a trove of programs, costumes and albums of old photographs, which provided Rudolf with his first real grounding in ballet history. While Western ballet was given short shrift in the school's curriculum—as a result of its "lifeless forms and empty modernistic productions," as students were regularly reminded—Frangopulo was only too happy to share with her students whatever scraps of information she could glean.

Of all the instructors Rudolf met that first week of school, it was his ballet teacher who proved the biggest disappointment. The chain of benevolent command that had begun with Udeltsova and Voitovich came to an abrupt halt with Valentin Ivanovich Shelkov, the school's squat, surly-lipped director, whom Rudolf had met on his first day in Leningrad. Deriding Rudolf at every turn, without apparent cause, Shelkov seemed hell-bent on sending Rudolf running for the first train back to Ufa. "It's not too much to say that Shelkov simply could not *stand* anything about Rudi," remembered classmate Alexander "Sasha" Minz. "He had such a sharply defined character that he simply didn't fit under the umbrella of Shelkov's policy for the school."

However, since Costravitskaya had foreseen his potential for greatness, Shelkov wanted Rudolf in his sixth-grade class—just in case she turned out to be right. Yet all he could see was an untutored boy from the provinces who hadn't a clue about ballet and whom he himself hadn't a clue how to reach. He placed Rudolf at the back of the class, ignored him, and then reminded him to be grateful for such generosity. "Don't forget that you're here out of the goodness of our hearts and the school's charity," he would sneer with the kind of malevolent glee Oliver Twist might have recognized. At other times, he ridiculed Rudolf in front of the others, addressing him as "country boy." Occasionally, Shelkov managed to provoke Rudolf to tears, but if he hoped to provoke him into surrendering, he couldn't have chosen a more misbegotten strategy. "He ruled by discipline," a former pupil says of Shelkov's ballet class–cum–boot camp. "The only thing that made him happy was seeing students in uniforms." Rudolf realized straightaway that Shelkov had little to teach him. "He's a boss, not a ballet master," he announced to Stefanschi with characteristically sharp-eyed judgment.

Rudolf was not alone in his dislike of Comrade Shelkov. Most of the students lived in fear of him, none more so than Stefanschi, who was hauled into his office on several occasions for an impromptu brush cut and an inspection of his collar. "We'd stand straight like soldiers while he checked to see how white our collars were." He accused Marina Cherednichenko, later a Kirov dancer, of perming her naturally curly hair, and patrolled the building for any sign of litter. Few could pass by him without being ordered down the hall to pick up some offending scrap of paper. At night, the students got their revenge by imitating him in their rooms to screams of laughter.

Rudolf hadn't come all the way to Leningrad to suffer Comrade Shelkov's daily assaults, and it was only a matter of time before the apparatchik and the maverick collided. The moment of reckoning came only two weeks into the school term, after Rudolf sneaked out one night to the Kirov Theater in defiance of the rule forbidding students to leave the dorm without permission. He was already in the habit of attending ballet performances nearly every night in Ufa, and he saw no reason to change his ways, especially in Leningrad, where the Kirov Theater beckoned nightly. The prefect of his dorm thought otherwise. When Rudolf returned to the dorm one evening, his mattress and meal tickets were missing and he was forced to spend the night in the window alcove. The next morning he went straight to his literature lesson, but was so exhausted that he fainted as he stood up to answer a question. When he finally came to, he told his classmates about the previous night, making it clear that he saw nothing wrong in his actions. Instead of apologizing, he joked about his harsh punishment and then announced he was off to get something to eat at a friend's house. The class was confounded.

Rudolf's insolence landed him in Shelkov's office before the day was out. The director was irate. How dare he thumb his nose at the rules! he chastised Rudolf. And just who were his friends in Leningrad? Rudolf gave him the name of Udeltsova's daughter, Marina, but Shelkov wasn't satisfied and promptly snatched Rudolf's address book out of his hand. Rudolf had never felt so violated. Although he had yet to establish a life for himself in Leningrad, Shelkov was already peering into its corners and attempting to pry open locked doors.

Fearing that ongoing clashes with Shelkov would get him thrown out of school, leaving him vulnerable to being called up for military service, Rudolf made an unprecedented request: He asked Ivanovsky, the school's artistic director, to transfer him out of the sixth grade and into Alexander Pushkin's eighth-grade class. He knew of Pushkin's reputation and probably figured he had nothing to lose.* He wasn't going to get to the Kirov with Shelkov as his coach, and at seventeen, he couldn't bide his time any longer. By stressing his desire to finish his schooling, rather than complaining about Sheklov's incompetence, Rudolf persuaded Ivanovsky to bump him up to the eighth grade.

Shelkov was not about to lose any ground to the Tatar upstart and professed to be only too pleased to be rid of him. Shelkov predicted that Pushkin would quickly despair of him. "He won't even bother to glance in your direction," he warned Rudolf. As director, he could have expelled Rudolf, but given that Costravitskaya had glimpsed talent, Shelkov hoped to find another teacher to second *his* view. Hedging his bets, he sent Rudolf on with little to recommend him. He was an "obstinate little idiot, a weak-minded evil boy." Worse, he knew nothing of ballet. If he didn't improve, "we will have no alternative but to throw him out of the school."

*Nazretdinova, the first dancer Rudolf saw in Ufa, had studied with Pushkin when she attended the Leningrad school in the 1930s, though it's not known whether Rudolf knew this when he arrived in Leningrad.

7

Pushkin

IF THE NEW TEACHER had been anyone other than Alexander Push-kin, Rudolf would likely have lived out his dancing days on the stage of the Ufa Opera House. But in the reserved and patient Pushkin, Rudolf found his ideal mentor, one he quickly came to admire, respect and ultimately love. The forty-eight-year-old Pushkin was the benign father Rudolf had always dreamed of having, a role model who understood his ambitions and never tried to change them. Their temperaments could not have been better matched. Where Hamet Nureyev and Valentin Shelkov had tried to mold Rudolf in their self-images, Pushkin encour-aged him to find his own voice. "He had patience, his rapport with the students was very low-key," Mikhail Baryshnikov, another Pushkin pro-tégé, recalls. "He was teaching you how to dance, not making you dance. He was teaching you how to look at the dance from your own perspective and be responsible and in command of your mind and your body." And just as important for a boy prone to fits of frustration, Pushkin was "ex-ceedingly calm and balanced. It was almost impossible to quarrel with him," remembers former Kirov ballerina Alla Sizova, Nureyev's frequent partner in his final year at school.

Pushkin also happened to be the finest teacher of male dancing in the country, an exemplar of the traditions, refinement and classical purity that lay at the heart of the Kirov style. A graduate of the Leningrad school and a former Kirov soloist, Pushkin bridged the imperial and Soviet eras: Born in 1907, he had begun studying dance with Nicholas Legat, who, as Petipa's successor and then Diaghilev's ballet master, counted Nijin-sky, Karsavina and, later, Margot Fonteyn among his pupils. It was Legat who had first spotted Nijinsky's talent at his entrance exam and accepted him into the Imperial Ballet School over the reservations of his colleagues. (" 'That youngster can be made into a fine dancer,' I said, and passed him without further ado.'"*) Like Legat before him, Pushkin descended from a long, unbroken line of ballet teachers, each of whom had received, "like runners their wands, the purest technical principles, the cleanest dancing style." Pushkin had joined the Kirov in 1925 and taken up teaching in 1932, while still a dancer. The special class he led at the Kirov drew most of the company's leading male dancers. Though not blessed with the good looks of the Romantic hero, Pushkin was a distinguished soloist admired for his elegant line and best known for his Bluebird in *The Sleeping Beauty*. He retired in 1953 and, from then on, brought his considerable stage experience to bear on the careers of younger dancers.

With his muscular build and strong face, set off by a long nose and receding hairline, Pushkin was a solid, dignified presence in the classroom. Given to wearing crisp white shirts, dark ties and dark pants, he presided with an air of quiet authority, his gentleness belying the exacting nature of his lessons. So deceptively simple was his method that, according to Baryshnikov, "people in his classes for the first time often wondered, 'What is so special here?' Everything, as it were, would turn out by itself." Tatiana Legat, Nicholas's granddaughter and Rudolf's Kirov colleague, remembers that Pushkin's company class was "horribly difficult to get through. You'd think you were nearing the end because your legs were so worn out and then you'd find out that it was just the warmup." Pushkin gave his students a strong grounding in technique, but he also believed in drawing out the individuality and musicality of each dancer, an approach he had inherited from the distinguished Vladimir Ponomarev, his own teacher at the school.† Unlike Shelkov, Pushkin assumed that his pupils had a natural intelligence. He focused on strengths, spoke little and never raised his voice. "He knew very well you cannot explain. That was his strength," says Baryshnikov. "By doing his work over and over, you began to understand parameters of work, range of movement, tempo and all those things."

---

*Legat had also drawn the affection of his students. His relationship with Nijinsky became strained, however, when Nijinsky began a flirtation with Antonia Tchumakova, a dancer with whom Legat was in love. Legat prevailed and Antonia eventually became his wife. Their daughter was the mother of Tatiana Legat, who became not only a student of Pushkin's while a soloist at the Kirov, but Nureyev's colleague and the wife of Yuri Soloviev, Nureyev's classmate.

†Vladimir Ivanovich Ponomarev joined the Maryinsky Theater after graduating from the Imperial Ballet School in 1910. Known for his fluid, noble line, he later became one of the Imperial Ballet School's most revered teachers of male dancing. Among his students were some of the best-known names of the era: Chaboukiani, Sergeyev, Zakharov, Yacobson, Lavrovsky and Pushkin. At his death, Pushkin took over his men's class and continued his methods.

Rudolf liked Pushkin immediately, but the older man, having been warned about him, took little notice of him. As far as Pushkin knew, he'd just inherited a dancer of doubtful provenance, and since Rudolf wasn't yet on a par with the rest of his eighth-grade class, there was no proof to the contrary. Rudolf was only too aware of the catch-up work ahead of him and saw that Pushkin's approval would not come easily. But he also knew that Pushkin's approval was career-making. For the first time in his life, Rudolf felt secure in the knowledge that his training was in the best possible hands. He abandoned himself to Pushkin's expertise without question.

His classmates, meanwhile, hardly warmed to the idea of making room for a pupil as unpolished and unusual as Rudolf. Competition at the school was naturally fierce, the result of a stringent weeding-out process that began upon entry and continued all the way through to graduation. Only two or three graduates each year landed a job with the Kirov or the Bolshoi; a few others found their way into the Maly or the Stanislavsky and the rest were dispersed among the country's thirty-odd state-supported troupes. Having made it all the way to Pushkin's eighth-grade class, their technique approaching professional standards, the other boys looked askance at Rudolf's efforts to compete with them. They were frankly surprised that Pushkin had accepted him into their class from the sixth grade. "Look at yourself, Nureyev," they chided him one day after class as they brought him before the mirror. "You'll never be able to dance — it just isn't possible. You're simply not built for it. You have nothing — no schooling and no technique."

And yet, in reality, it was Rudolf's way of doing things that bothered them most: He took pains with his deportment, phrasing and stage gestures, things nobody else much worried about. He would stand in front of the mirror for hours practicing the way he would present his hand to the ballerina or he might concentrate on the way he would connect one step to the next, not simply on the steps themselves. "He was not so much interested in the emotional aspect of the performance as he was with perfecting his legs and body, which was not typical of Soviet dancers," recalls his contemporary Nikita Dolgushin. "In his preoccupation with external perfection, one could see a Western inclination."

What's more, he was volatile and thought nothing of venting his frustrations in public. He would burst into tears or explode in anger whenever the image in the mirror didn't match the one in his mind's eye. He would force himself to master the steps he found most difficult, just as he had in Ufa. "Cabrioles,* for instance, I did not find easy, so I

---

*The cabriole is a flying movement in which one leg is thrown into the air while the supporting leg rushes up to meet it and pushes it higher into the air.

did them over and over, jumping straight toward the mirror so that the faults showed. I could have done them sideways and looked good without so much trouble, but then I would not have got it right."

Such was his fanaticism that none of the students at the school knew what to make of him. While no less dedicated, they considered Rudolf in a league by himself. Day after day, he could be glimpsed in an empty studio, practicing alone with a feverish intensity. "Oh, look at him, he never stops," they whispered to one another, the thought of joining him rarely considered and dropped the moment he slammed the door. "We heard he was a wild, rude boy," says classmate Marina Cherednichenko, now a Kirov Ballet administrator, echoing a familiar view. "He reacted sharply to things. I don't think anyone was very attracted to him, because he was so antisocial."

Each evening Rudolf would grill Sergiu Stefanschi about what the younger dancer had learned that day in his sixth-grade class. He wasn't interested in Serge's growing pains, his family back in Romania or his dreams for that matter. He only wanted to talk about steps and combinations, and while the rest of the boys in their dorm napped, or played games, Rudolf insisted on reviewing his own and Serge's lessons. "Stand up. Let's practice," Rudolf would command. "I started late, I need to catch up." Finding Serge lying exhausted on his bed one afternoon, Rudolf ordered him to get up. "Why are you resting?" Rudolf wanted to know. When Serge protested that he was tired, Rudolf tore the blanket from him and yanked Serge to his feet. "Oh, leave me alone, you Bashkirian pig!" Serge cried, hoping to sting Rudolf with the insult. But his plan only backfired. "And you are a Romanian pig!" Rudolf screamed as he wrestled Serge to the floor and pummeled him with his fists.

Had Rudolf deferred to the others or shown any interest in them at all, they might have been easier on him. Instead, he kept to himself and fought for his place. His air of superiority annoyed them, though in large measure, their nastiness drove him to take cover in defiance. The Leningraders snickered at his provincial accent, patched pants, unruly manners. "I suffered a lot because of their taunts," he later told a Leningrad friend. "In class, I hated looking in the mirror. I thought I was ugly."

Lonely for companionship that first autumn, he thought of Albert in Ufa. "To my dear friend Albert," he scribbled on a postcard. "In honor of our friendship." On his own, Rudolf imbibed the city's cultural treasures. He took particular delight in the Kirov Theater, the sea-green–and–gold palace one mile from the school, where ballet performances took place each Wednesday and Sunday. Home to the legendary stars of the Russian ballet, the theater was Rudolf's laboratory, the place for important discoveries. Pupils gained stage experience with walk-on roles in Kirov productions. Even these occasions were closely monitored. The students were transported in a bus, which pulled up to the school promptly at seven. ('Their predecessors had traveled in locked carriages, to prevent them from running away.)

In this way, students gained an intimate knowledge of the repertoire and music. Whether onstage, backstage or in the audience, Rudolf devoured the dancing. He memorized each ballet, step by step, and, in his room, reconstructed them from memory. He first tried committing steps to paper. But when he found the last page of his notes hanging in a bathroom stall, he decided simply to memorize them. ("You can imagine what the rest was used for," he told John Percival, an early biographer. "That cured me.") Where his peers concentrated on the dancers of their gender, Rudolf learned both male and female roles. Stefanschi was regularly pressed into service as his partner. "Lights had to be out by eleven-thirty P.M. But when we got back from the theater, we wanted to dance all the solos. We were so excited because the Kirov had all these glamorous performers. And Rudi would say, 'Stand up, Serge, and you will be the girl and I'll partner you.' We'd take the ballet from the beginning."

Later in the year, with the city illuminated from dusk till dawn during the White Nights, they rehearsed their grand manège of jetés coupés in the vast square outside the Winter Palace. Its grandeur was a fitting backdrop for ballet's princes-in-training.

RUDOLF'S CLASSMATES rarely ventured beyond the school's confines, much less sneaked into the Kirov Theater. But Rudolf could no sooner curb his curiosity than he could follow anyone else's lead. When he wasn't at the Kirov, he could be found at the Hermitage, the Philharmonic or at the Pushkin or Gorky Theater. He would sit through any program, even agitprop fare about collectives, tractors and the happy peasants who worked them. "I don't care what they're saying," he told Stefanschi, who accompanied him one afternoon. "I'm only interested in their technique." He was devoted to all forms of art and considered them as interconnected as the myriad islands that constituted Leningrad. This was especially true of his twin passions, music and dance. Most of the music on the family radio had been "played on the occasion of some eminent Russian's death." But through regular visits to Philharmonic Hall, the former nobles' club where Tchaikovsky and Rimsky-Korsakov had premiered their first works, he discovered "the extent to which music could convey pure joy; a strange, even faintly morbid delight." He also began to define his pronounced musical tastes. He revered Bach and Beethoven, preferred Shostakovich and Prokofiev among Soviet composers and, with the exception of Scriabin and Tchaikovsky (his ballet music only), disliked nearly all Russian composers, especially Rachmaninov.

His music, Rudolf would insist, "smelled of Russian sarafans"* and its strong national flavor repelled him.

The lure of the exotic also drew him to Menia Martinez, his first and only close school friend. Open, spontaneous and naturally exuberant, Martinez was the school's first Cuban student and a novelty in a world where gaiety was suspect. Swinging her curvy hips in ankle-length hoopskirts, her light auburn tresses released from their pins, she played Cuban songs on her guitar and danced barefoot in the dorms, sometimes accompanying herself on tam-tam drums. "She would demonstrate Afro-Cuban dances and all the girls would try to imitate her," says Tatiana Legat. A talented singer with a low contralto voice, Martinez regularly gave school concerts and was soon making appearances at the House of Culture of the First Five-Year Plan, situated opposite the Kirov Theater. "A singing dancer was incredible for those times," explains Nikita Dolgushin, his images of Martinez vivid four decades later. "She wore special makeup which seemed to us to be Western makeup; her eye penciling was nothing like our makeup with iron stripes on the eyelids. And she wore spectacular earrings and a Cuban dress with flounces and a tight-fitting bodice." Her tropical origins intrigued Rudolf: She often wore two skirts at a time and never removed her leg warmers during ballet class—
—a privilege granted to no other student. The fact that she spoke Russian haltingly—and with a Spanish accent—added to her allure. "She was crazy and different. Rudi loved that," recalls Stefanschi, who was also enchanted.

Rudolf met Martinez several months into the school year at the home of Abdurachman Kumisnikov, the teacher who had auditioned him at the Moscow *dekada*. Kumisnikov's wife, Naima Baltacheeva, was Martinez's teacher. "She had told me about this young Tatar boy who was a good dancer, although sloppy and a little crazy," Menia recalls. "She said they need to get him in shape." Martinez had glimpsed Rudolf in the hallways and thought him "homely and badly dressed, with messy hair." The daughter of an English professor at the University of Havana who edited a Communist newspaper, Martinez had grown up in a household where books "were sacred." Having heard all the rumors about Rudolf, she was reluctant to befriend him, but discovered that they had much in common. In fact, once they started talking, they found it hard to stop. "Everyone thought of him as this wild boy, but he had an incredible intelligence. He loved books and reading and classical music and old paintings. I was astonished. Where did he get that culture, that sensibility? How was it possible, this country boy with peasant parents?"

She was also surprised to find him sensitive and vulnerable. "I think he had a different attitude toward me because I was a foreigner. I was

*Traditional peasant dress.

from a world he didn't know. Sometimes I would cry over how cold it was and Rudik would hug me. He was so tender with me. That was what first attracted me to him." Menia and Rudolf (or Meniushka and Rudik, as they called each other) were soon spending their free time together. Beyond shielding him from the disdain and, later, the envy of his classmates, Menia's friendship nourished and broadened him. Sophisticated beyond her years, the sixteen-year-old Menia introduced Rudolf to her "Leningrad parents," family friends Mikhail Volkenstein, a molecular physicist, and his wife, Estella Alenikova, the editor of a literary journal. Polyglots both — between them they spoke English, French, Spanish and German — they inhabited a world of books and learning, a milieu intoxicating to Rudolf's rapacious mind. They invited him to concerts, accompanied him through the Hermitage, and introduced him to the works of Pushkin, Shakespeare, Dostoyevsky and Goethe. On Saturdays, they would drive Rudolf and Menia to their dacha outside Leningrad, where, during the fall months, they would all spend the day picking mushrooms. One of Martinez's favorite photographs from those years shows Rudolf riveted, chin in palm, eyes cast upward, listening to Volkenstein, the first in a long line of older male mentors. "I'm a good listener, but not a very good conversationalist," Nureyev later acknowledged. "I'm still and soak up everything. I never become complacent." As a scientist, Volkenstein enjoyed certain privileges, access to tickets among them. When pianist Glenn Gould became the first Western musician invited to the Soviet Union, Volkenstein arranged for Nureyev to have a ticket. Gould's highly emotive style taught Rudolf the importance of breathing "your own life into a work."*

At the end of each day, Rudolf liked to walk down the Nevsky Prospect, stopping in, just opposite the Cathedral of Kazan, at his favorite music shop. He perused its large selection of musical scores and phonograph records, which he was welcome to play on the store's record player. The shop was managed by Elizaveta Mikhailovna Paji, a small, plump, charming woman in her forties with curly black hair, a warm smile and eyes that sparkled with intelligence. Moved by Rudolf's impassioned curiosity, she began introducing him to the many musicians who dropped by. Sometimes, she would ask them to play for Rudolf on the shop's piano. When there were no customers, she would play for him herself.

Like Udeltsova, Veronina and Voitovich before her, Elizaveta Mikhailovna Paji encouraged his questions and admired his probing intelligence. With no children of her own she began to dote on Rudolf and

---

*The telling observation he made of Gould years afterward might just as easily have been made of Nureyev himself: "You might get a most weird and, to most critics, upsetting version by Glenn Gould, but my God! What a titanic talent!" he told Walter Terry in 1978. "Such a talent and inborn sense of dynamism. . . ."

invite him to her home. There he was certain of stimulating conversation and a good meal, unlike the Spartan diet at the school canteen. Her husband, Veniamin, a physicist, would recite his favorite poems, taking as much care with the rhythm and tone of each word as his wife took with each note of music. The couple regularly welcomed many artists and intellectuals. Rudolf reveled in the kind of Petersburg "salon" that Veronina and Voitovich had so lovingly described to him. Through Elizaveta, Rudolf began taking lessons from Marina Petrovna Savva, a leading pianist at the Maly Opera Theater. Marina Petrovna's husband, Nikolai, was a violinist with the Maly Theater. Also childless, they, too, welcomed Rudolf into their home.

Rudolf practiced feverishly on one of many school pianos. Usually, he played Bach, whose compositional rigor he admired. Dancing, however, came first and each night, when other students rested, Rudolf would find an empty studio. He needed to make up for lost time, he reminded Menia, and one ninety-minute ballet class per day was not enough. He wasn't "privileged," as he put it, like Yuri Soloviev and Natalia Makarova, talented pupils who had begun their training much earlier. "I took things calmly, but not Rudik," says Menia, who grew accustomed to his outbursts. "He had this ambition, he was in such a hurry. Once some senior pupils came into the studio while we were working and Rudik threw a chair at them and yelled, 'This is shit! You can't work here.' No one behaved that way. People now say that it was only after he became a star that he behaved like that. Well, he was always like that back when he was a nobody. . . . Our classmates would warn me that if he didn't watch himself, he was going to get expelled. They didn't like him because he wasn't nice to them. He wouldn't even bother saying hello. . . . He was locked in his own world, his own life."

He also refused to join the Komsomol, the youth wing of the Communist Party. Membership in the Komsomol* was virtually obligatory, an inevitable rite of passage, like the Pioneers. Young people joined, not necessarily powered by any political belief but for protective cover: There was safety in numbers. To stand alone meant to stand against and called attention to one's independence.

By January 1956, Rudolf had been away from home for nearly five months. Living at a safe remove from Hamet's censure had eased tensions, and Rudolf was hoping to return for the winter break. Indeed, far from poisoning relations with his father—as most accounts of Nureyev's life have suggested—Rudolf's "defection" to Leningrad ultimately improved them. While angry that Rudolf had left home without permission, Hamet did not interfere with his plans. He had eventually cooled off,

*Many Komsomol leaders were promoted to positions involving state security, including Alexander Shelepin, the man in charge of the KGB when Rudolf lived in Leningrad.

after Rosa made a case for the school's prestige and legitimacy. Hamet was completely in the dark about the security and glamour the Leningrad Choreographic had long conferred on its graduates. "My mother was very happy about it," says Razida, "but my father never showed his emotions. Whenever we spoke of it, he would say, 'Okay, he went. Let's see what happens.'"

That January, Hamet sent a note to Shelkov, asking permission for Rudolf to spend his vacation "at home with his parents." He also hoped the school's director might extend Rudolf's vacation time. For reasons unknown, Shelkov rejected Hamet's request. "Denied," he wrote in large black letters across Hamet's note, pleased, it appears, at the chance to thwart at least *one* Nureyev. One month later, Rudolf sent his father a birthday card that he had obviously chosen in hopes of pleasing him: The panting black cocker spaniel on the front of the card resembled Hamet's beloved Palma. "Dear Papa," Rudolf wrote on February 19, 1956:

Happy Birthday. I wish you many, many years of life, good health, happiness. I hope you grow the garden you want to grow and have a very good rest and go hunting this summer.

Your son, Rudik.

Hamet was disappointed that Rudolf was not following his Stalinist dream. But he was even more disappointed when the dream itself was called into question by Stalin's successor. On February 20, 1956, the day after Rudolf's letter, Nikita Khrushchev unmasked Stalin in a "secret" speech to the Twentieth Communist Party Congress. Although the proceedings were closed, the speech was read out to every party organization in the country. Khrushchev exposed not only Stalin's brutal and arbitrary violence against the party elite, but his monstrous reign of terror during the very period when Hamet was making enormous sacrifices in Stalin's name.[*] It was now publicly revealed that Stalin had ordered the death and torture of many Red Army officers and that Stalin was partly to blame for the country's vulnerability when Hitler struck. For Hamet, as for most Russians, Stalin was the God of his moral universe. Khrushchev's exposé at once shattered that faith and sowed the first seeds of reform. While it would be another 34 years before perestroika paved the way to freedom of expression, a new liberalizing spirit enveloped the nation.

These affairs of state meant little to Rudolf. But the "thaw" opened the window for Soviet companies to tour abroad and brought the first

---

[*]Not that any of Stalin's crimes came as a surprise to Khrushchev, who was Moscow party boss during the show trials and a mute witness to many of the worst atrocities of collectivization and the purges.

Western artists to Russia since the 1930s. The first American attraction to reach the Soviet stage was a production of the Gershwin opera *Porgy and Bess* in December 1955. Cast members visited the Kirov Ballet's school and there saw Rudolf in a student performance of *The Nutcracker*. *New York Post* columnist Leonard Lyons, along on the tour, reported having seen "a Tatar boy, whose headpiece hampered his vision," hold aloft an "Oriental girl. . . . He could not see that the grip was uncomfortable." This was the first reference to Nureyev in the Western press.*

Rudolf encountered his first Western ballet stars in the pages of *Dance Magazine*. A London friend of Menia's had sent them, and three or four issues slipped by the censors. Studying photographs of Margot Fonteyn and Erik Bruhn, he announced to Menia one day as they pored over an issue, "I'm going to dance in all those theaters, too." Just how he was going to manage that neither of them knew, but as far as Menia could see, there was no harm in dreaming of distant stages.

In the meantime, both had role models closer at hand. Every afternoon the Kirov's artists arrived at the school for class in the fifth-floor studio, where *The Sleeping Beauty* had been created sixty-five years earlier. Rudolf rarely passed up the opportunity to observe them. Their presence charged the atmosphere. "They seemed to us almost like divine beings," wrote Natalia Makarova. Pushkin regularly led the class for the Kirov's male soloists, while Natalia Dudinskaya, the company's legendary prima ballerina, led the class for the company's ballerinas, the *classe de perfection*, as it was known. But now and again the two intermingled. A number of the ballerinas liked to take Pushkin's men's class to improve their jump. Since the students were not permitted to sit in the gallery overlooking the studio, "we would stand on top of each other so we could see into the classroom from the doorway," says Marina Cherednichenko. A chief pleasure was the male dancers' show of one-upmanship at the end of class. "We would just stand there, amazed."

Every spring, Pushkin's students prepared the classical variations they would perform for their final exams. Daily class fine-tuned a student's technical know-how, but variations put that technique to the test and took the measure of a young dancer's artistry. The variations were performed on the Kirov stage as part of a school concert and were considered as much a reflection of the student's potential as they were of a teacher's craft. By spring 1956, Rudolf had spent nearly eight months in Pushkin's class. But Pushkin felt he wasn't ready for the stage. Perhaps not wanting to be represented unfavorably, the teacher informed Rudolf that he wouldn't be dancing in the year-end concert. Rudolf prepared a variation anyway, stealing moments in empty studios without the benefit of seasoned guidance. "Pushkin wanted Rudolf to be more academic," re-

*"A trace of uneasiness shadowed the girl's inscrutable face," he added.

calls Menia. "Rudolf did everything organically. But he learned quickly." He chose the male variation from the "Diana and Actaeon," pas de deux an excerpt from *La Esmeralda*, a 1844 work the Ufa Ballet performed.* A fireworks display of technique, Actaeon's solo was one of the most difficult pieces Rudolf could have chosen. It was then closely associated with the former Kirov star Vakhtang Chaboukiani, who had reworked the choreography to showcase his bravura skills and powerhouse jump.

When Rudolf was satisfied he had mastered the solo's demands, he persuaded a reluctant Pushkin to come take a look. Nureyev, Pushkin decided, was ready after all. Never again would he doubt the pupil who would soon become his most famous protégé — and with whom his own name would forever be aligned.

The young man who rode the train home to Ufa that summer had much more to celebrate than the one who had set off for Leningrad eleven months earlier. His father no longer opposed him and his concert debut had, by his own estimation, "made an impression." Even if no one had showered him with compliments, no one had ridiculed him. To Rudolf that was tantamount to acceptance. After a hopeless start with Shelkov, he had won the approbation of Pushkin, and with it, a sense that he "belonged" in his class. Success was by no means assured, but at least there was no one standing in his way. To eighteen-year-old Rudolf, "it was like being awarded a permit, an official right to dance."

RUDOLF ARRIVED HOME to find Albert had been called up for military service. Albert had hoped he might be able to study at the Moscow Institute of Dramatic Arts but needed permission from the Bashkirian Ministry of Culture and had "no strings I could pull." Despite his self-absorption, Rudolf rarely hesitated to go to bat for others. He now took it upon himself to approach the ministry on Albert's behalf. When his arguments failed to make any impression, he grew indignant. But as Albert recalls, "Who would listen to him then?"

Their brief reunion was filled with talk of the passions they had long shared. Rudolf had grown a head taller than Albert and, at five feet eight, was an inch shy of his full height. His sinewy shoulders tapered to a slim, boyish waist, and his legs were powerful, like his father's. His hair was now sandy blond and his cheekbones had grown more prominent, making him look "handsome," as Albert recalls him. It was not just that he stood taller, but he exuded a newfound maturity and "one could feel

---

*Based on Victor Hugo's *Notre-Dame de Paris*, the nineteenth-century ballet by Jules Perrot had been revived in 1935 by Vaganova. Perrot had created the ballet in London in 1844 and staged it in St. Petersburg five years later. A dancer and choreographer at the Paris Opéra during the Romantic era, he also created *Giselle* with Jean Coralli.

his self-confidence." But he was also sensitive to Albert's predicament and perhaps wary of fueling his envy. "He was very glad he was in Leningrad, but he didn't boast about his achievements. He merely said that he was doing quite well and that he especially liked Pushkin. He also shared his impressions with me about Leningrad. He told me about its museums. I was surprised by how much progress he had made in his piano playing. Before he left, he could play only the most simple tunes. When he came back, we visited Irina Alexandrovna [Voronina] and he surprised us both by the way he played classical pieces quite professionally." Rudolf stayed only a week in Ufa, before going on to the school's summer residence on the Black Sea.

Back in Leningrad that fall, Rudolf was happy to find himself transferred to a room housing just six students on the dormitory's ground floor, near to Menia's. In the evenings, the students congregated by the floor's communal stove, sharing tea and the Cuban rice or black beans that Menia would occasionally prepare. She also taught them to make strong Cuban coffee, adding a piece of chocolate to give it more flavor, and how to be more creative in their style of dress since "you couldn't buy anything in the shops then." Under her supervision, they dyed their white shoes black by applying black shoe polish and sewed metal buttons to the toes "to give them a foreign look." On weekends, she and Rudolf saw the Volkensteins, went to the movies or visited an eccentric old woman they had befriended, a balletomane who made them soup every Sunday in the tiny room she shared with her fourteen cats. Sometimes Rudolf persuaded Menia to sing or teach him Spanish slang, which he didn't hesitate to use and never forgot. Many years afterward, a ballet to her: "It's *porquería.*"*

At eighteen, Rudolf had yet to form any serious romantic attachments or to define his sexual identity. Although he and Menia were often glimpsed hugging and kissing, their relationship was affectionate, not sexual. In fact, Menia remembers how surprised she was when Rudolf referred to her one day as "Gina Lollobrigida," the voluptuous Italian movie star he knew from the cinema. "Why did you call me Gina Lollobrigida?" she asked. "Because you have such fantastic breasts," he replied. Menia's figure had filled out over the summer and all the boys were remarking on her body, something Rudolf had never done. "That was the first time I'd sensed something sexual coming from Rudik," she remembers. "He would kiss me a lot, but I never had that passion for him. We would say, 'I love you,' to each other, but I didn't want a physical relationship and Rudik understood that. He would say to me, 'You're still young. When we finish school, we should get married.' I was in love with him, but for what he had inside."

*Garbage.

Their relationship was so ambiguous, however, that many classmates were never entirely sure of its nature. Nikita Dolgushin once gave them a bed to share when they happened to stay overnight at the apartment of his girlfriend, Sania, a pianist at the school who was eighteen years his senior.* "Rudik and I just laughed about it," recalls Martinez. They shared the bed, "but it was a completely naive relationship. All Rudik wanted to talk about was dance, dance, dance."

His inexperience was hardly unusual among young Russians in the 1950s, especially given the sexual puritanism of Soviet life. Sex was never openly discussed, Freud was banned and sex between men was illegal, a law used to intimidate people and send them to jail. If Rudolf was then aware of any homosexual impulses, they were not expressed, perceived or recollected. Such was the fear and loathing surrounding the subject that few of his classmates would have considered broaching it. Homosexuals lived in a twilight world, reviled by a profoundly homophobic society.† The cruising ground for Leningrad's homosexuals was Ekaterina Square, the public gardens dividing the Pushkin Theater end of Rossi Street from the Nevsky Prospect. Sergiu Stefanschi recalls strolling to the dorm one day when a man in the park suddenly grabbed his crotch. "Who knew about such things?" he recalls. One night he overheard some boys in the dorm boasting about how they were going to Ekaterina Square to "beat up" the *gomiki*, as homosexuals were known.‡ "The way they were described to me I thought they must be monsters!" remembers Elena Tchernichova, who was to become a ballet mistress at American Ballet Theatre.

One of the few students then daring enough to express any homosexual interest was "Sasha" Minz, who, according to Stefanschi, flirted with other boys in the dressing room. "Everyone said that Sasha Minz was homosexual," recalls Menia. "He was extremely effeminate—the way he talked, the way he moved—and the other boys would laugh at him. But I never once heard anyone talk about Rudik being homosexual and he never spoke to me about any boy. I think if he had had doubts, he would have told me."

There were no showers in the dorm, so once a week the boys

*Relationships between students and staff were strictly forbidden, so their relationship was kept under wraps. They later married.

†Under Article 121 of the Soviet penal code, passed in 1934, homosexuals faced up to five years' imprisonment for sexual activity. Applauding the antihomosexual measures, Stalin's attorney general wrote that "after two decades of Communism in the USSR, no one has any reason to be a homosexual, and those who persist in their homosexuality should be regarded as counter-revolutionary elements. . . ." Gorky called the law "a triumph of proletarian humanism." It was not repealed until 1993, the year of Nureyev's death.

‡*Gomik* was the term used at the time. Today *goluboy*, which translates as "the blue one," is more common.

trooped off to the marbled public bath near the Moika Canal. Equal parts boyish playground and domestic ritual, the *banya* was perhaps the only outlet for any homosexual tension. There they would run around naked, wrestle each other to the floor, and hit each other with birch leaves, their horseplay a welcome respite from the decorum of their daily lives.

The school did its best to curb raging hormones and, as it did in all spheres of life, encouraged students to keep tabs on each other. When a young Georgian dancer in their dorm persisted in grabbing Menia and asking her to sleep with him, Rudolf urged her to report him to Shelkov. But when she told him, Shelkov only laughed. "Well, naturally he laughed about it. He's in love with the boy," Rudolf said on reflection. That single reference, recalls Menia, "was the only time I ever heard Rudik talk about someone being homosexual."

In 1956, Rudolf was invited to participate in a student concert at the Palace of Culture, the first important showcase he didn't have to ask for. He was to perform Actaeon's variation from *La Esmeralda*, the solo that he had prepared for Pushkin, and a pas de trois in *The Red Poppy*, a Soviet-styled paean to the revolutionary spirit, set in China in the 1920s. Rudolf was cast as one of the three phoenixes who appear in the heroine's dream. His classmates Nikita Dolgushin and "Sasha" Shavrov, the son of Kirov veteran Boris Shavrov, completed the trio. Marina Cheredni-chenko, who was dancing the role of the heroine, recalls their first re-hearsals: "Rudolf wasn't dancing very well and the instructor got angry with him. Suddenly Rudik said, 'I am not going to dance this,' and left the room. It was very rude. None of us ever behaved this way with our teachers. So he went away and rehearsed with Pushkin. The next time he came back, he was much more prepared."

Occasionally, even Pushkin came in for dismissive treatment. "Leave me alone, I know what I'm doing," Rudolf would snap at the older man, who faced Rudolf down with a kind of equanimity to which he was utterly unaccustomed. Pushkin understood that Rudolf was his own severest critic and that his anger was most often directed toward himself. He knew, too, to let the storm clouds pass before directing the boy to the problem at hand.

Rudolf discovered in Pushkin's classroom the male approval that had always eluded him. For the first time in his long, painful struggle to prove himself, he found an ally who could help him realize his dream. (Indeed it was Pushkin who persuaded the authorities to let him out of his military duties, after he was called up for service.) "His combinations provoked you into dancing," Nureyev said later, recalling the joy he felt in Pushkin's class. "They were kind of irresistible . . . tasty, delicious. . . . He associated music with emotion. Steps, gestures had to be filled with feelings." Convinced of Rudolf's talent, Pushkin set to work improving his technique and artistry. To that end, he kept him in his eighth-grade class for two years* and helped him develop his jump, coordination and stamina. He also put Rudolf through his paces at a slower rate than his other pupils. During an exercise known as grand battement, for example, the students would thrust their working leg up into the air and then bring it down, executing one battement with each count of music. Rudolf, however, would be instructed to take twice as long with each battement to build his control and strength. At other times, Rudolf would stand at the barre, extend his "working" leg out to the side, and hold it there for as long as he could.

Frustrated with his body, he would fight against his late start all his life. At five feet eight inches, he was of medium height for a dancer, with sculpted shoulders, short ligaments and thickly muscled thighs and buttocks. His long, flat torso, "typical of an Eastern Tatar physique," according to Nikita Dolgushin, made his figure look slender and "created a certain elegance." His feet, small and wide, were unusually supple, but his legs, while pliant, were slightly short in proportion to his torso. As he saw it, he had none of the natural ability, coordination and airborne ease of Yuri Soloviev, his only rival at the school. With blond curls, a flat round face, gentle blue eyes and muscular thighs and calves, Soloviev was "the picture of a typical Russian peasant lad," as one classmate describes him. So effortlessly did he defy the laws of gravity that he would come to be known as "Cosmic Yuri," after cosmonaut Yuri Gagarin, the first man in space. Rudolf envied and admired Soloviev's jump, line and virtuosity. Although Soloviev studied under Boris Shavrov, not Pushkin, Rudolf watched him rehearse for school concerts. Soloviev's angelic nature made hating him unthinkable and the two struck up an easy camaraderie. "They got along well, but Rudik was jealous because Yuri was the school favorite," recalls Menia. "The teachers would talk about how clean his dancing was. And Pushkin would say, 'Yes, but the talent and temperament that Nureyev has are extraordinary.' Nureyev was the opposite of Soloviev; he was like a hurricane onstage. He would say to me: 'Why everything for Yuri Soloviev and nothing for me?' And I would try to tell him: 'You've got to dance a lot more calmly.'"

Soviet male dancing was then characterized by a certain solidity and groundedness, by "big, slow pliés with landings," according to former Bolshoi Ballet star Vladimir Vasiliev, a contemporary of Nureyev's who exemplified the style. Rudolf, on the other hand, strove to be light, quick and aboveground. He insisted on standing on high demi-pointe to elon-

*Nureyev claims in his memoirs to have studied with Pushkin for two years in the ninth grade, but the programs of his performances during his second year all list Nureyev as an eighth-grade student. Furthermore, the ninth grade was reserved for graduating students only.

gate his legs and line, something no other male dancer did then in Russia.

And while sky-high extensions were the province of the ballerina, not her cavalier, Rudolf pitted himself against the school's most limber girls. His natural turnout and pliant muscles, rare in a male dancer, were astounding in one who started training so late. "One day it was my turn," classmate Elena Tchernichova recalls. "I was tall and my extension high; if he beat me, he was champ for sure. We competed leaning against an old tin stove in the middle of the studio. Up went our legs in a 180-degree split. Rudi called my name. I turned, my leg came down, and 'Oh, I win! I win!' Rudi crowed."

In pas de deux class or recital rehearsals—the only time the male and female students danced together—Rudolf was as demanding of his ballerina as he was of himself. Anyone who wasn't willing to meet him halfway was bound to lose her footing. Once, while attempting a risky lift from La Bayadère before class, Rudolf dropped a skittish young ballerina as he was hoisting her over his head. Students were not allowed to rehearse lifts without a teacher present, but Rudolf refused to accept blame. "She has to help me and she didn't," he said. "I'm not going to drag her up."

Alla Sizova proved a sturdier ally. Lithe and talented, with delicate good looks that called to mind Ingrid Bergman, Sizova was the star of her class. Her exceptionally light, soaring jump, long legs and spirited dancing would later earn her the nickname the Flying Sizova. For the school's year-end concert in June 1957, Rudolf and Sizova were cast in the "Diana and Actaeon" pas de deux from La Esmeralda. With Rudolf supervising their performance, they began their preparations several months in advance. Sizova lived at the home of her teacher Natalia Kamkova in a self-styled dancers' collective. Each night Rudolf came by to review the music with her on Kamkova's record player. Rudolf didn't particularly like Sizova—he told Menia that he found her cold and dull—and he wasted no time in asserting his authority. "Don't forget," he warned Sizova, "your nation was for two hundred years under the Tatar yoke."

Actaeon's variation was already a staple in Rudolf's repertory, but he had as yet to dance with a Diana.* The pas de deux calls for intricate partnering; in addition to high technical demands, among them diagonal turns landing on one knee, Actaeon has to be mindful of Diana's hunting bow. Despite Rudolf's misgivings, their performance marked the beginning of a promising partnership.

---

*In the Greek myth on which it is based, their "dance" is short-lived: Actaeon spies Diana, goddess of the hunt, bathing naked. Fearing that Actaeon might boast about his discovery, Diana turns him into a stag and his own hounds tear him to pieces.

* * *

DURING HIS THIRD and final year at the school Rudolf learned all the great male variations in the classical canon. The bulk of these were by Petipa, whose ballets were as predominant in the Kirov's repertory as they had been in the Maryinsky's. Graduating students were granted the privilege of rehearsing in the Kirov company's fifth-floor studios, where the floor was raked to exactly the same angle as that of the Kirov stage. Equally important, Rudolf danced before an audience at the Kirov Theater itself, an honor reserved for the top graduates. He began with the role of the Prince in the second act adagio of *Swan Lake*, followed by eight performances of *The Nutcracker*. But the performances that launched him—and that people still talk about—took place not in Leningrad, but in Moscow over two days in April 1958. Every spring, Moscow hosted a showcase of the country's top ballet students. The age-old rivalry between Moscow and Leningrad—and the Bolshoi and the Kirov—played itself out on the stage of Tchaikovsky Concert Hall. Each city had its distinctive style of dancing—and its partisans: Where Moscow prided itself on its athletic flair and bravura, Leningrad saw flamboyance and spectacle; where Leningrad claimed unparalleled lyricism, elegance and refinement, Moscow dismissed its dancers as coldly academic. And as Leningraders were fond of pointing out, some of the Bolshoi's finest artists, among them Galina Ulanova, were first Kirov stars. As the birthplace of the Russian ballet, Leningrad was "still considered the final arbiter of taste," remembered Panov. "But when the capital shifted after the Revolution, Moscow got the ministries, the foreign visitors and the need for display for both. Since ballet was still the showpiece of Russia's rulers, the Kirov could no longer compete in prestige, whatever its excellence. The Bolshoi was where Stalin—and therefore the money—went."

Rudolf was chosen to represent the Leningrad school along with Alla Sizova, Marguerite Alfimova, Yuri Soloviev and a promising eighth-grader named Natalia Makarova, who was teamed with Soloviev in the Bluebird pas de deux from *The Sleeping Beauty*, the role that was to become his signature. Moscow had its own stellar candidates in Vladimir Vasiliev and Ekaterina Maximova, both of whom would go on to dominate the ranks of the Bolshoi for two decades.

Rudolf prepared several pieces for Moscow to demonstrate his range, technique and artistry. His program included a duet from Michel Fokine's *Chopiniana* (known in the West as *Les Sylphides*) with classmate Alfimova and a pas de trois from the Soviet ballet *Gayané* that called for him to dance with a torch in each hand. With Sizova, he planned to dance the "Diana and Actaeon" pas de deux as well as the role of the Slave in *Le Corsaire*,* another showstopping pas de deux whose solo bore the flamboyant stamp of Vakhtang Chaboukiani. By the time Rudolf and Sizova arrived in Moscow, the pas de deux bore Rudolf's stamp as well. Teachers occasionally modified choreography to suit a student's talents, but never did students themselves make their own alterations. However, Rudolf "made changes in our coda so that his legs would look longer," recalls Sizova.

To her dismay, Sizova took ill on April 21, the first day of performances. Rudolf was forced to perform only Actaeon's pas de deux of their pas de deux, the third of four items on the program. His performance "astounded the hall," in the words of one viewer, who had already been treated to Makarova and Soloviev in the Bluebird variation and to Vasiliev in the rousing *Flames of Paris*.† "It was the first one the crowd really liked." But it was his *Corsaire* duet with the recovered Sizova on the second night that prompted cries for an encore from the seasoned crowd. It wasn't simply his kinetic fury, suppleness or space-devouring leaps they applauded, but the sensuality that animated his every step. What he lacked in technical polish, he more than made up for with a thrilling, authoritative performance that shattered the academic mold. Nureyev's edgy, explosive quality announced the arrival of a highly unusual graduate. Soviet audiences, recalled Sasha Minz, were utterly unaccustomed to such overt expressions of sexuality on the stage. "[It] was something you did not write or talk about. Any sign of it was taken as some sort of pathology and denounced as a form of anarchism."

While the competition conferred neither prizes nor rankings, Rudolf emerged as the most popular dancer, edging out hometown favorite Vasiliev. Even Vasiliev conceded that Rudolf's dancing had "dazzled" him, a compliment Rudolf relished for its unlikely endorsement. "Nureyev amazed everyone with his animal magnetism and his emotional involvement in the dance," remembers Vasiliev, who four decades later directs the Bolshoi. "Inside him lived this huge strength and dynamism. You had to see him perform live at the time, because when you watch tapes of that period, they don't give you that emotional intensity that he gave off."

Nureyev's dancing directly influenced Vasiliev, the exemplar of Moscow's bravura style for years to come. "Nureyev was the first male dancer to perform his pirouettes on high demi-pointe. At that time, I was doing many more pirouettes than he was. I thought that the beauty of

---

*Based on a poem by Byron, *Le Corsaire* tells the story of a young girl sold into slavery and saved by a pirate and is full of big, soaring jumps for the male dancer. The ballet's composer was Adolphe Adam, best known as the composer of *Giselle*. Created in France, the ballet was revived in Russia by Petipa and later reworked by Chaboukiani.

†Choreographed in 1932 for Chaboukiani and Ulanova, the ballet is set during the French Revolution.

the pirouette was in the number of turns. When I saw Nureyev and those amazing pirouettes on very high demi-pointe that he did, I wasn't able to do low demi-pointe anymore. I started doing the high pointe and fewer turns, just eight or nine as opposed to the twelve or thirteen I was used to doing, but it was a totally different aesthetic: more beautiful and cleaner. After seeing him, I started paying much more attention to the position of my feet."

As a result of their Moscow success, Nureyev and Sizova were included in a state-sponsored film about the Russian ballet—the only Leningrad students so honored—and both the Bolshoi and the Stanislavsky theaters offered Rudolf soloist contracts, waiving the standard first year in the corps de ballet. With his graduation concert two months away, he expected a third offer to come from the Kirov, but there were no guarantees. The Stanislavsky didn't interest him—too provincial, he thought. But the Bolshoi had Galina Ulanova and Maya Plisetskaya, ballerinas he would be honored to partner. And the Bolshoi had been the first company to travel to the West.

Before catching the train to Leningrad, he rushed over to the Bolshoi Theater to see Plisetskaya in the first act of *Swan Lake*. There, during intermission, he met Silva Lon, a Moscow balletomane ten years his senior, who worked at the state ticketing agency for Moscow's theaters. Lon had seen Rudolf dance the day before, but failed to recognize him when she fell into conversation with a group of Leningrad dancers. "How did you like us yesterday?" one asked. "I liked that tall, dark boy from Leningrad most of all," she replied. Rudolf darkened his hair for performances, so she didn't recognize him. "Suddenly this short, light-haired boy stood up and said, 'Why does everyone think that I am tall and dark?' "

Though Rudolf had discovered how to turn the spotlight on himself, he was still suspicious of scrutiny. But when Lon complimented him on his performance, he dropped his guard and told her about the Bolshoi's offer. He was not impressed with the Moscow ballet, he admitted. He was sorry, he said, but he had to leave early to get to the train station on time. While Rudolf struck Lon as self-reliant, he also had what Margot Fonteyn would come to call a "little boy lost" quality that made her want to help him. "He hadn't eaten anything, so I took him to the buffet, fed him and helped him get his things, so he could stay and see the last act of the ballet." From then on, whenever Rudolf came to Moscow, Lon found him tickets and lodging. Before long, he would acquire such doting women in virtually every city in the world.

WHILE MANY of his peers disliked him, Rudolf never failed to win over those he genuinely liked or felt had something to teach him. Toward the end of term, he met Liuba Romankova and her twin brother, Leonid, physics students at the Leningrad Polytechnical Institute. His music shop friend Elizaveta Mikhailovna had asked their mother to introduce "this very sympathetic boy from the provinces" to her children, and one Sunday afternoon, Rudolf arrived in the thin Chinese raincoat he wore year-round because he couldn't afford an overcoat.

The vibrant atmosphere of the Romankov household, so unlike his own, intrigued Rudolf at once. "He came to our place at three in the afternoon and left at three in the morning," remembers Liuba Romankova.* "Can you imagine? Even for Leningraders who are used to keeping late hours—and this was the time of White Nights—it was quite something. We talked about so many things; it was the time of the thaw and we were suddenly flooded with possibilities." Politics, it was clear, failed to interest him, so they spoke of the Impressionists, who were finally on exhibition after being banned for years, and about Osip Mandelstam, whose poetry was once again available. One by one, the family slipped off to bed, parents, grandparents, sister and brother-in-law, but Rudolf didn't budge. Finally, Liuba was the only one left. "Rudik said, 'Maybe it's time for me to go?' which actually meant, 'May I stay a little longer?' I felt he didn't want to leave, so I kept saying, 'No, no, Rudik, stay.'" Still, his admission, thirty years later, that he had envied her cultivated upbringing came as a surprise.†

Elizaveta had introduced Rudolf to Liuba in the hopes of starting a romance. Liuba, however, was in love with her boyfriend, Igor, and thought that Rudolf was smitten with Menia, whom he often brought along. After supper, Menia might treat the family to an impromptu concert of Spanish songs. "She was an absolutely charming girl with the looks of a Vrubel‡ Madonna," Liuba says of Menia. "She was very temperamental and head over heels in love with Rudik, who was very responsive to her. I think he kept this tender feeling for Menia for many years." Tall and thin, with wide brown eyes and dark, bobbed hair, Liuba had studied ballet as a young girl, grown up in a family of balletomanes, and seen Rudolf dance at school concerts. Yet she had never known any of the students at the Leningrad school, for her interests, like those of her brother's, ran more to sports, science and politics. She played volleyball for the Physics Institute and the army sports club and she and Leonid were accomplished skiers. Rudolf dubbed them the *sportivniks*. Before class one day, Menia was surprised to discover Rudolf with iron weights strapped to his ankles, straining to lift his legs. Athletes used

*Now Liuba Myasnikova.
†Concerned for their safety when his memoir was published, Nureyev refers to them as the Davidenkos, the surname of their maternal grandfather.
‡Mikhail Vrubel, the Russian painter (1856–1910).

weights in those days, never dancers. "The *sportivniks* told me these are great for my jumping," he explained. "It makes them strong and afterward, my legs feel very light." Soon, he took to doing his stretching exercises in the Romankovs' living room whenever he stopped by. At the time, recalls Liuba, Rudolf did not stand out for his beauty offstage. But he had beautiful white teeth and an unusually dignified air about him. "Frankly speaking, he didn't strike me as particularly handsome, although everyone admired his looks. But over time, he began to look more imposing, more significant."

RETURNING TO *Le Corsaire* for his graduation recital that June, Rudolf scored another triumph.* His entrance "was like a bomb exploding," remembered the late Sergei Sorokin, a veteran of countless graduation concerts. "The ovation shook the theater." Afterward, dozens of young female fans waited for him at the stage door. "They wanted his autograph," recalls Menia. "They could see that he was becoming somebody special." The concert was the crowning moment of a student's career, drawing fans, teachers, relatives, even members of the Kirov, all eager for a glimpse of the newest prodigies. "I can say with confidence that the greatest success fell at the feet of Alla Sizova and Rudolf Nureyev," the former Kirov ballerina Tatiana Vecheslova announced in the local paper, *Vecherny Leningrad* (Evening Leningrad), devoting the bulk of her review to Nureyev, whom she found at once compelling and confounding:

They danced their duet from *Le Corsaire* brilliantly. . . . Nureyev's performance brought with it a whole host of arguments, though one cannot deny his outstanding talent. His leaps are so light that he seems to be suspended in the air. His pirouettes seem to require no effort at all. He throws himself into his dancing with unmatched expressiveness. His passion, unrestrained by technique, sometimes interferes with his performance. His dancing appears to break out of proper form and is often untidy . . . True, he has his faults, but one mustn't overlook the great work put in during the past three years by this Ballet School graduate, with help from his tutor. If he can only be demanding of himself and merciless with his deficiencies, then he'll have all the makings of an original. . . .

Rudolf had also danced the male solo from *Laurencia*, a ballet created by Chaboukiani as a showcase for himself and Natalia Dudinskaya,

*Performing on the same bill with Nureyev during those two graduation concerts on June 19, and June 24, 1958, were Natalia Makarova, who still had a year to go before she graduated, Yuri Soloviev, who was taken into the corps de ballet of the Kirov that year, and Oleg Vinogradov, who would eventually become the director of the Kirov Ballet, a post he held until 1997.

the most venerated ballerina in Russia. *Laurencia* tells the story of its indomitable Spanish heroine and her fiancé, Frondoso, who lead a village uprising after the local *commendador* exercises his droit du seigneur on the day she is to be married.

Rudolf's student turn as the renegade Frondoso so impressed Dudinskaya herself that she came backstage to congratulate him following his final concert. The forty-six-year-old Dudinskaya was the Kirov's prima ballerina, a survivor of the old guard along with Ulanova, Chaboukiani and Sergeyev. Her soaring jump, on-the-dime turns and charged stage aura had barely diminshed with age. A dazzling virtuosa and favorite pupil of Vaganova's, she had joined the company in 1931, following the enormous success of her own graduation performance in *Corsaire*, which Vaganova had restaged especially for her and the young Konstantin Sergeyev. Her steely technique only hinted at the power she wielded in the theater: As the wife and dance partner of Sergeyev, the Kirov's longtime male star, chief ballet master and sometime artistic director,* she also enjoyed special privileges due to Sergeyev's high standing with the party brass.

Spying Rudolf sitting on a couch backstage, Dudinskaya approached. He was looking very sad, she thought.

"What's the matter, Rudik?" she asked him.

"I don't know how to decide," he answered. "Both the Kirov and the Bolshoi have invited me to join."

With her own career in eclipse, Dudinskaya shrewdly saw that the young Nureyev's luster would brighten her own.† She also knew that Sergeyev had admired Rudolf's dancing in earlier school recitals.

"Stay here in Leningrad," she advised Rudolf. "Stay here because they like you and they know you and because Konstantin Mikhailovich will help you advance."

It was rare enough that Dudinskaya was seeking out a graduating student and almost unprecedented that she should tender the offer she was about to make. In fact, such an invitation had been proffered only once before. Fifty-one years earlier, Matilda Kschessinskaya, the reigning ballerina of the Imperial Ballet and the czar's former mistress, hand-picked a graduating student named Nijinsky.

"Stay here," she repeated, "and we'll dance *Laurencia* together."

His decision was made.

---

*Sergeyev became a ballet master at the Kirov in 1946 and served as the company's artistic director from 1950 to 1956 and again from 1960 to 1970.

†Dudinskaya retired in 1962 after thirty-one years on the stage.

8

The Kirov

THE KIROV'S NEWEST RECRUIT returned home that summer for what he assumed would be a short stay. His family was still living in the one-room flat on Zentsov Street, now even more cramped with the addition of Lilya's new husband, Fanil, who, like his wife, was deaf. Rosa, twenty-eight, was teaching at the local kindergarten, while Razida, twenty-three, was studying at a vocational school.

Albert was also in town, on leave from the army. He was eager to hear all about Rudolf's latest conquests on the ballet stage. Rudolf had just graduated directly into the Kirov's soloist ranks, the first male dancer since Fokine and Nijinsky to bypass the corps de ballet.* "Remember how you dreamed of jumping like Yasha Lifshitz?" Albert reminded Rudolf of their childhood ballet idol. "Now you're better than he is." *The Song of the Cranes* was being filmed in a field outside Ufa. Rudolf dropped by and, over tea with leading lady Zaitouna Nazretdinova, described his Leningrad success and his debt to her for inspiring it.

He remained in uncharacteristically high spirits during his holiday break until he received a telegram from Moscow's Ministry of Culture. It simply stated that as compensation to the republic for paying his tuition, he was being reassigned to the Ufa Ballet. He was no longer a member of the Kirov. The news sent him into a panic. Anointed by Dudinskaya, only to find himself exiled to the one place he had worked so hard to escape! He believed he was being punished for not joining the Komsomol, although it was hardly out of order for the Bashkirian government to demand his services after bankrolling his education. And

---

*Both Rudolf and Alla Sizova became soloists following their graduation concert.

his services were not to go unrewarded: The republic's Ministry of Culture offered him a three-room flat, for himself alone, in the heart of Ufa — no small enticement.

But Rudolf, not about to give up, rushed off to Moscow to plead his case. There, he begged a ministry official to reinstate him at the Kirov, well aware that transfers, even between companies in the same city, were fraught with bureaucratic obstacles. The official wouldn't budge, except to hint that perhaps the Bolshoi might still be interested in him. Seizing what he thought was his only way out, he rushed to the Bolshoi, worked a few angles, and revived his contract offer.

Still, he returned to Leningrad to collect his belongings, deeply disappointed at leaving. He begged Pushkin to help him.* He was soon summoned to the office of Boris Fenster, the Kirov's new director. "There was never any question of throwing you out of the Kirov," he told the bewildered Rudolf. "Unpack your things and stay here with us. Your salary is waiting to be collected!"† So Rudolf turned down the Bolshoi a second time, doubtless earning a few more enemies. He would later dismiss the entire episode as a scare tactic. However, according to the current director of the Ufa Ballet, the Bashkirian government did indeed arrange for his return to Ufa. It decided not to apply pressure after concluding that Rudolf would bring glory to the republic as a Kirov star.‡

Afraid to leave town for fear of another setback, Rudolf passed up his summer holiday on the Black Sea. When Kirov soloist Tatiana Legat returned early from her vacation that August, she was surprised to find Rudolf in an empty studio at the Ballet School. "He was doing his warm-up without music," says Legat, the granddaughter of Nijinsky's first teacher. "He was obsessed. I asked him if I would be in the way, and he said I could join him. So we did our barre together for several days until the others returned. He had an enormous amount of strength and energy. He kept changing his shirt because he was working so hard."

ON OCTOBER 25, 1958, Rudolf made his Kirov debut. He danced the pas de trois in *Swan Lake* with ballerinas Nina Yastrebova and Galina

---

*Rudolf never mentions Pushkin's help in his memoirs. It's likely that the omission was intended to protect Pushkin, who was living in Leningrad when the book was published in 1962.

†The director alone was not authorized to hire, fire or reinstate any dancer. All decisions had to be approved by the theater's trade union and Artistic Council.

‡Clearly some sort of behind-the-scenes deal was struck, for two other outstanding Ufa natives were not so lucky: Eleonora Kuvatova, Baryshnikov's partner at their graduation concert in 1967, and Guzel Suleimanova were also accepted into the Kirov, their first choice, but ultimately "persuaded" to return to Ufa.

Ivanova. But the debut that placed the other male soloists on notice came one month later: On November 20, he donned a black wig and, as promised, played the fiery Spaniard Frondoso to Dudinskaya's Laurencia. Dudinskaya was forty-six and the twenty-year-old Rudolf, in his first starring role, had the precious security of partnering the Kirov's prima ballerina assoluta.

"He learned the role very quickly," a vibrant Dudinskaya recalled thirty-five years later on a White Night in June during intermission at the Kirov Theater.* Rudolf was to be her last Frondoso. "Because of his temperament, his youth and his technique, I thought he would fit the role. I had already danced *Laurencia* with Chaboukiani, who staged it for me, and with Konstantin Mikhailovich [Sergeyev], who were very, very strong partners. And I worried about how Rudi would handle me in certain lifts since it was his first time in a principal role. But he was very attentive and held me very well. He met my expectations."[†]

Rudolf's debut generated electricity on both sides of the footlights. "It was like an eruption of Vesuvius!" recalled Sasha Minz, resorting to the kind of explosive metaphor that Nureyev's dancing provoked. "Many people who were admirers of Chaboukiani said: Rudolf is the new one. Others said no — he's better." His partnering still lacked polish and confidence. His turns were skewed and at times he looked as if he might fall when landing from his jumps. But he infused his performances with passion, energy and an element of risk that ignited the audience. Even the critic Vera Chistyakova had to allow that "such debuts do not happen often.

A dancer with excellent natural gifts — an enormous jump, a rare suppleness and temperament — arrived on the stage. Nureyev immediately showed his confidence in a complex, acute portrayal, captivating us with the swiftness of his dance tempi, the elements of his flight, and with the accurate and, at times, stunning dynamic of his poses, that thoughts of a great future for this young artist involuntarily occurred to us. Which is why one would like to view his debut as only

---

*Another class of graduating students had run through its pas de deux and variations, and Dudinskaya, the doyenne of the school, was cradling a bouquet of pink roses against her gold lamé jacket. Her figure was now matronly, but her large luminous eyes were still vibrant, her carriage still proud and erect. Chaboukiani, Sergeyev and Nureyev — her three celebrated Frondosos — had all died and Dudinskaya was remembering her signature role, the only one she danced with each of them.

[†]Rudolf never forgot her generosity toward him. In 1989, Dudinskaya and Sergeyev were in Boston staging *Swan Lake* for the Boston Ballet and Nureyev called her at the theater. "I asked him, 'Rudi, do you remember how we danced *Laurencia*?' and he said, 'Yes, I'll always remember and I'll always be grateful to you. It's not so often people are grateful to you for good deeds.'" Sergiu Stefanschi also met Nureyev in the West, at the National Ballet of Canada. Nureyev was staging his *Sleeping Beauty* and wanted Serge to rehearse Karen Kain in the role of Aurora. "Tell her about Dudinskaya," he said.

the first height scaled as well as a first sketch of the proud, freedom-loving character of Frondoso. One would like to believe that Nureyev will increase his capabilities through serious work and only then will the hopes pinned on him turn out not to have been in vain.

Dudinskaya also met Nureyev's expectations. Since *Laurencia* had been made for her, "he got everything from the source," as Tatiana Legat puts it. As well, she gave him to understand "that he had to dance with his mind and his heart, not just with his legs." While not a beauty, Dudinskaya was a vivacious and charming performer, whose musicality, bravura and attack Rudolf greatly admired. Two years after their first *Laurencia*, Rudolf watched in "utter astonishment" as the forty-eight-year-old Dudinskaya became the coquettish Kitri in *Don Quixote*, a showpiece demanding technical fireworks. "How do you like the old lady?" he remarked to a friend afterward. "She showed everyone else how to dance."

WITH EACH PERFORMANCE, Rudolf's circle of admirers expanded. Word of his talents had made the rounds in Leningrad, but only a few insiders had seen him dance at the school. That fall, his music shop friend Elizaveta Paji introduced him to Tamara Zakrzhevskaya, a Russian literature student and ardent ballet fan who, Rudolf recalled, "never missed a single one of my performances." Having seen Rudolf's *Laurencia* debut and heard him compared to Chaboukiani, Tamara imagined him "strong, muscular and irresistible." Instead, one afternoon at intermission she met a "slim, badly dressed young boy." He was, to her mind, "the complete antithesis of a star." The discrepancy between his on- and offstage appearance so startled her that Tamara began giggling uncontrollably as they were introduced. "He seemed clearly embarrassed by it all," she remembers. By chance, she bumped into him a few days later outside the theater's ticket office. "He looked at me closely, smiled and asked, 'Would you tell me why you laughed so much the other night?' " She imagined him "differently," she said. At this, Rudolf smiled. "You probably imagined that I would be tall, dark and handsome." Tamara made sure to compliment him on his dancing, and they parted friends.

DURING THESE first months at the Kirov, Rudolf lived in a theater workers' collective. He shared a room with eight others, sleeping on a bunk bed mounted to the wall. But shortly after his *Laurencia* debut, he and Alla Sizova were assigned to a two-room apartment in the prestigious Petrograd Quarter on Ordinarnaya Street, a forty-minute bus ride from the theater. In a city in which entire families shared a single room, this was a rare perk. Rudolf, however, suspected that the Kirov was hoping to push him into a romance. "They're giving me a flat! With Sizova!" he told the Kirov soloist Ninel* "Nelia" Kurgapkina. "They think that by doing so I'll eventually marry her! Never!!!" Although by all accounts, he "couldn't stand" Sizova, Rudolf still hoped to luxuriate in his new-found privacy. He would decorate his room sparingly, he told his Moscow friend Silva Lon, with only "a bearskin rug and pillows on the floor."

Rudolf and Sizova had only just settled in when his sister Rosa moved in with them. Rosa was now teaching kindergarten in Leningrad and as she and Rudolf shared a family name, she managed to secure a permit for the same apartment. It was far from a cozy arrangement. Rudolf and Rosa had grown apart, and he now found her coarse and difficult. She spoke her mind freely, made demands on his time, and showed little understanding of his need for privacy. He was also embarrassed by her. Rosa was a daily reminder of the world he had fled.

To avoid her, Rudolf began staying at the Pushkins', where he knew his teacher and his wife, Xenia Jurgenson, would look after him. The Pushkins lived at the Ballet School in a two-room flat so crammed with fine mahogany furniture that as one visitor recalled, "you had to push things out of the way to move from one spot to another."

In early 1959, Rudolf tore a ligament in his right leg, just hours before his second performance of *Laurencia*. The despair he felt at being sidelined demanded the kind of care only Pushkin could provide. The prognosis was dim: The doctor told Rudolf that he wouldn't be back onstage for another two years. A hiatus like that could damage his career beyond repair. Knowing Rudolf's temperament and domestic discomfort, the Pushkins invited him to live with them so that they could supervise his recovery. Rudolf decamped at once, leaving Sizova to battle it out with Rosa.

Which she did. "Rosa didn't stand on ceremony," remembers Sizova, who by then had invited her parents and sister to share her single room. "She didn't have any subtlety, but still we were friendly. But she never cleaned the apartment. My mother cleaned it. And she had so many men, it was really frightening. She didn't have any friends besides men. Sometimes she went to the ballet, but we never talked about ballet or about Rudik. He never visited her. She came from Ufa alone and lived in this free room. I think she wanted to escape from her parents."

At the Pushkins', in the "calm of domestic life," as Nikita Dolgushin recalled it, Rudolf found "not only the traditions of St. Petersburg but also a home environment and ballet university all rolled into one." The atmosphere mirrored life at the Volkensteins', the Pajis', the Romankovs', all households Rudolf envied. Together, he and Pushkin listened to mu-

*Ninel is Lenin spelled backward.

sic, and joined in lively discussion with the artists and dancers who regularly stopped by for tea. Mostly they spoke of ballet. "All conversations were about what kind of performance you went to see, who was dancing, what you liked or didn't like, how you think it could have been done better," recalls Baryshnikov, who lived with them on and off beginning in the late 1960s, when he was a pupil at the Vaganova School. "It wasn't about the colors in Rubens's paintings or the subtleties or greatness of Schoenberg. People would gather there in the early evenings and in the mornings. There was always plenty of food on the table, which was always beautifully arranged, with crystal, wine, vodka, candles, delicious food. It was a very warm atmostphere. [Xenia] was a wonderful cook. They rarely went out to eat in restaurants. Everything was fresh from the market."

Childless, the Pushkins embraced Rudolf as a son. "Mahmoudka," they dubbed him, "little Mahmoud," a common Tatar name. The Kirov ballerina Alla Shelest dropped by one afternoon to find Rudolf sitting on the floor with a toy train set laid out before him. "Rudolf is playing," the Pushkins whispered with conspiratorial urgency.

The fifty-one-year-old Pushkin and his forty-three-year-old wife were a study in contrasts: Where Pushkin was quiet, "sphinxlike" and soft in manner, Xenia was effervescent, bold, almost mannish. "She looked more like a boxer than a dancer," recalls Menia, perhaps uncharitably. To Rudolf, however, Xsana, as he nicknamed her, "was a pretty woman with that rare gift of making everyone feel better the moment she entered a room; the sort of person who would take you by the scruff of the neck, shake you a bit and make you laugh—and immediately you would feel lighter and gayer." Xenia had recently retired from the Kirov after a lengthy, if undistinguished, career—"a rather coarse dancer with a good jump," in the view of a colleague. This left her time to devote to Rudolf, whom she protected zealously and jealously from any distractions. She cooked, cleaned and cared for him, and, like his mother, was famous for her pies and cakes. There the similarities ended. "She indulged him," says Silva Lon, "so he always did whatever he wanted. It just complicated his already difficult character. He would just say, 'I want.'" To Liuba Romankova, whose parents were among the Pushkins' closest friends, it was plain that Xenia "loved him as a mother, but was also attracted to him as a woman. Her husband was much older and I believe she was willing to do anything for Rudolf."

Rumors circulated that Xenia had seduced Rudolf, a rumor he confirmed to friends years later. ("She was great in bed," he told a number of them in perhaps an inaccurate display of sexual bravura.) To Menia, he confided only that an older woman had seduced him "because she wanted him to have experience." He wanted Menia to know that he wasn't a virgin. His other Leningrad friends, however, never discussed it with him, though they weren't blind to what Liuba calls Xenia's "despotic" devotion. "She wouldn't take her eagle eyes off him for a second. On top of it, she ran her household according to a strict timetable. There was a time for everything, whether it was eating, sleeping, drinking, studying in the classroom or dancing at the theater. In fact, Xenia would even try to prevent Rudik from going out of the flat on his own. . . . She really twisted him round her little finger, but I must say that he didn't object to it."

Whatever the nature of her relationship with Rudolf, Xenia's affection came at a critical moment in his career. Her mix of tenderness, discipline and loyalty sustained him in his struggle to define himself. "Don't listen to the assholes: Xenia taught him that," noted Baryshnikov. According to Liuba, Xenia convinced him that "a great artist should only dance great roles." She was also economic in her use of words, almost cryptic, a manner Rudolf apparently emulated. "He would say something and you would think, 'Whom does he mean?' But you were afraid to be mistaken, as he would say, 'How come you don't know it?' "

Medical predictions to the contrary, Rudolf recovered his strength, spirits and form in record time. Within one month, he was back in class, ignoring the pain he felt daily. (Though not the slights to his honor: He demanded to know from Sizova just who in the company had sent him wishes for a speedy recovery—and just who hadn't.) However, it wasn't until April 7, 1959, five months after his *Laurencia* debut, that he returned in a leading role. He once again partnered Dudinskaya in *Laurencia*, this time minus the requisite black wig that made him look like a monkey.

By then he had begun to ignore a number of other long-standing Kirov traditions. At the beginning of class, novitiates dampened the studio floor with a watering can. This added resistance to the wooden floor. Nevertheless, Rudolf flat out refused to perform the chore and then stalked out of the room. He felt belittled. "It caused a sensation," remembers Sizova. When Ninel Kurgapkina asked him later why he had refused, Rudolf shot back, "There's no shortage of talentless idiots in there who are only fit to water the floor!"

Rudolf's supreme self-confidence and independence aroused indignation in a company where hierarchy, respect and servility were paramount. Although the front lines in company class were reserved for senior members, Rudolf insisted on standing front and center, even when it meant taking another's place. Given the competition for performances—soloists could expect to dance lead roles once or twice a month—the men were particularly loath to make room for the Tatar upstart. Then soloist Vladilen Semenov recalls arriving for class one morning to find Rudolf standing on top of the dressing room table changing into his practice clothes. "Even here, you think you're above everyone else?"

Semenov asked teasingly. "And why not?" Rudolf answered. The Kirov then boasted an impressive cadre of leading men, from the elegant Konstantin Sergeyev to the dynamic Boris Brcgvadze and the princely Askold Makarov. Yet Rudolf snapped at their offering advice. "Who do you think you are to teach me?" he scoffed at Sergeyev one day after the company's longtime premier danseur and ballet master attempted to give him a correction. "That," he said, pointing to Pushkin, "is my teacher."

If they were insulted by his disrespect, the dancers were even more taken aback by the way Pushkin coddled him. When Rudolf happened to overwork his feet one day, Pushkin brought a tub of water into the studio to make him a footbath. Askold Makarov remembers how they all looked on in disbelief. "It's not difficult for me to do," Pushkin explained to them, "and he needs to save his feet."

Not all the dancers disliked him, though, as Nikita Dolgushin points out, embracing a nonconformist was risky. Of course Nureyev was hardly an easy man to embrace. "He felt his provinciality and tried to get rid of it by putting on a mask of contempt," says Dolgushin. "In fact he only pretended. He didn't think he was superior." His "mask" was convincing enough, however, to prompt a number of his colleagues to devise ways to hurt him. Seeing him warming up before a performance, they would crowd him, so that he didn't have enough room to practice. Not that Rudik left it at that, recalls Dolgushin. "He takes a run, kicks them, knocks them down and there are bursts of indignation from both sides."

The fact that Rudolf didn't fit the Kirov mold only further confounded them. He was the first man to dance on high demi-pointe and the first to extend his leg high in the air. Male dancing at that time was "very rough," he observed years later. "They did not believe in lyrical passages, they did not believe that man could exccute woman's steps, and that's what I was doing. They could not be . . . emotional. . . ." As a result, many of the company's male dancers reproached him for his femininity and lack of classical "purity." At the same time, they observed him closely and felt his influence. "More often than not someone would stand on higher demi-pointe than was required, without being aware of it," concedes Dolgushin. "Fifth positions became more correct."

To those in the audience, he didn't seem feminine at all, just exotic. "He was an odd bird in the flock indeed," observed the critic Gennady Smakov, "not only because he was not a 'neat' dancer (which he was never to become) but also because the viewer was so transfixed by the sweeping scope of his movements, his confidence and feline grace, that even the most vigilant eyes failed to catch his technical imperfections. They were in fact of no importance, given the thrill of his presence."

His late start meant that he would always struggle with his technique. He practiced to exhaustion. "The others wondered, 'Who is this strange person?' " says Tatiana Legat. But where he once kicked doors shut while he worked at school, Rudolf now made sure they stayed open so that the students could study the "country boy" their director had declared unfit for training. Dancing well was indeed the best revenge.

WHILE COMPETITION colored Rudolf's relationships with all the male dancers, his ballerinas grew to like him, but only through dancing with him. In the spring of 1959, he won the role of Armen in *Gayané*, yet another Soviet morality tale.* Like *Laurencia*'s Frondoso, Armen was a feisty worker-hero ready to sacrifice himself for the sake of his beloved. Cast in the title role was Ninel Kurgapkina, a leading ballerina nine years his senior with sturdy legs, a formidable technique and a gruff, outspoken manner. "We were both very independent," says Kurgapkina, now a ballet coach in her sixties. "I had my own opinions and knew my own worth." Yet Kurgapkina was put off by Rudolf until they started rehearsing. Rudolf took just two weeks to master the role's complicated lifts and turns. He liked working with Kurgapkina, "a fanatic like him," she acknowledged, particularly when it came to rehearsing the ballet's tricky lifts, such as the one "when he raises me up over him and carries me across the length of the stage with only one of his hands supporting me." Even when she asked him to rehearse the lift a dozen times, he never complained. "That's how he differed from all those 'geniuses' who came after him. . . ." Kurgapkina also welcomed his less-is-more approach to partnering. "Just help me to hold on," she advised him. "Don't mess." From then on, whether his partners liked it or not, Rudolf followed her advice.

As far as the esteemed critic Vera Chistyakova was concerned, however, the jury was still out on Nureyev's prowess as partner. In her review of his first *Gayané* on May 10, she took stock of his development: "One cannot but recognize in his Armen the stately, self-disciplined, proud shepherd. . . . And when, with a burning torch in each hand, he dances around the Kurds, he himself is like a flame — so fervent; incendiary; burning is the rhythm of his dancing. . . . Nureyev's deserved success does not mean that there are no deficiencies in his performance. This time they were more noticeable than in *Laurencia*. Possessing excellent dancing gifts, Nureyev is sometimes careless in linking episodes and helpless in communicating with his partners. . . ."

Despite his growing responsibilities, Rudolf still found time for Menia, whom he half expected to marry. Whenever he broached the subject, Menia would only laugh and say, "We're too young." Menia

---

*This one concerns an Armenian shepherd who thwarts a spy trying to steal rare mineral samples from his collective. For his graduation concert, Rudolf had already prepared Armen's showpiece variation.

was due to return to Cuba in June 1959, six months after Castro's Revolution; she suspected Rudolf hoped to see the world by marrying her. But unlike him, she was anxious to be reunited with her parents. "Even if I have to miss a performance," he promised, "I'm coming to see you off in Moscow."

On the evening of Menia's departure, Rudolf was called to a rehearsal with Dudinskaya at the Ballet School. When Menia came to say good-bye to him, she was told that he was missing. A distressed Dudinskaya begged Menia to find him and dissuade him from traveling with her to Moscow. "Please see to it that he doesn't leave. He will have enemies in the theater if he does," she said. "But I don't know where he is," Menia insisted, secretly hoping that Rudolf would be waiting for her at the train station after all.

Menia had an entourage at the station all right: Shelkov, Dolgushin and many others came looking for Rudolf. But there was no sign of him. Crushed, Menia took her seat and waved good-bye to her friends.

The *Red Star* was ten minutes out of Leningrad when Rudolf popped into her compartment, grinning. He had been hiding in the bathroom.

"Everyone is looking for you," Menia alerted him. He hardly seemed to care. She knew it was impossible to change his mind. Moscow was eight hours away, and with a compartment to themselves, they hugged and kissed, as they frequently did. Only this time Menia sensed that Rudolf wanted to make love. "I was a virgin then and at one point Rudik said to me, 'No, I'd better not. I respect you a lot. I don't want to hurt you.' That's all he said. I didn't think losing my virginity was a bad thing. But it didn't go any further." They fell asleep in each other's arms.

At the airport, Rudolf threw his arms around her neck, kissed her, and began to sob "like a crazy man." He knew what her departure meant. Visas were seldom granted, visits by foreigners were rare and tours abroad still a dream. "I'll never see you again," he cried. "I'll never see you again."

LIKE EVERY Soviet artist, Rudolf longed to be sent on a tour to the West. While Stalin had opposed any contact with the West, fearing the taint of contamination, Khrushchev had raised the Iron Curtain just enough to allow the first Soviet performers to travel abroad. To Khrushchev, foreign tours were effective public relations tools. The Bolshoi's historic London debut in autumn 1956 had proven this, at once whetting the English appetite for vigorous, virile Soviet male dancing and establishing the preeminence of prima ballerina Galina Ulanova. (A rapt Margot Fonteyn would later write that she was "stunned by the revelation that was Ulanova.") The London tour had also served a less visible purpose: combating negative international press arising from the the Soviet invasion of Hungary that same fall and the suppression of Boris Pasternak's manuscript for *Doctor Zhivago*.*

For the artists themselves, winning a spot on a tour was akin to winning the lottery. Travel promised not just exposure, but a per diem in foreign currency, giving those chosen few the enviable opportunity to purchase goods unavailable at home. "A million items from nylon tights to diaphrams [*sic*], woollen sweaters to ball-point pens would have to be bought on our foreign currency pay," Valery Panov recalled of his first tour to the United States in 1959.† "With this chance of a lifetime, no one was fool enough to waste a penny on food. Besides, every uncle, aunt, cousin and sister-in-law would be crushed if you returned without a shirt or an oilcloth to decorate their lives and tantalize their neighbors. All thoughts about pirouettes and grand jetés were buried under stockpiles of sugar, sausage, canned fish, condensed milk, tea and immersion heaters."

The Kirov did not choose Rudolf, however, as one of its candidates for the 1959 International Youth Festival in Vienna that August. Rudolf suspected that his impromptu trip to Moscow with Menia, coupled with his failure to attend the Kirov's political meetings, had caused its directors to pass him over. Still, as had become his habit, he went to plead his case before Boris Fenster, the Kirov's avuncular artistic director since 1956. An innovative choreographer, Fenster had worked for years at Leningrad's Maly Theater. Where Sergeyev, his predecessor at the Kirov, had largely restaged the classics and restricted new repertory to dance dramas with Soviet themes, Fenster brought with him a forward-thinking spirit in keeping with the tenor of the time. Fenster had been the one to formally offer Rudolf his soloist contract; he now took a chance and added Nureyev's name to the list of Vienna-bound candidates. The blue-chip group included Yuri Soloviev, Tatiana Legat, Ninel Kurgapkina, Alla Sizova, Alla Osipenko and Irina Kolpakova.

Once in Moscow to prepare for the competition, however, Rudolf ran afoul of the authorities. He refused to join in rehearsals at a nearby fencing club and rehearsed on his own instead. His objections were perfectly within reason: He had just overcome a serious injury and didn't want to risk jumping in a room without a proper floor or mirrors by which to correct himself. Likewise, the company refused to take any risks with him: Foreign tour rehearsals were interspersed with political "pep

---

*Freedom of expresssion had a long way to go: In 1958, Pasternak was awarded the Nobel Prize after *Doctor Zhivago* had been rejected by Soviet censors and condemned following its publication in the West. Hounded relentlessly, Pasternak, fearing he would be expelled from his homeland, declined the Nobel Prize. He died in 1960.

†On a separate tour that same year, the Bolshoi made its first visit to America and took New York by storm, confirming to the Soviets the preeminence of its dancers.

talks" to inoculate the dancers against the "treacherous temptation" they would confront in the West. Dancers were warned to be especially vigilant against subterfuge by the enemy, which could come in the guise of gifts or invitations to local homes. "To help us avoid such traps, we were to go outdoors only in happy foursomes in charge of a senior person," Panov recalled being warned before departing for America that year. "Wandering alone in a foreign country was 'exceedingly frivolous' anyway and anyone witnessing such a lapse was to notify his leader immediately. . . . Some emerged from these consultations with chattering teeth. . . ."

To the other dancers, Rudolf's flouting of the rules was inconceivable. Matters reached a head during a company meeting, when Rudolf spoke out against Boris Shavrov, a senior Kirov dancer and teacher. Complaining that "all these Shavrovchiki [little Shavrovs]" were "running around the theater," Rudolf railed against the conformism and conservatism that Shavrov and his *chiki* represented. Rudolf had taken a dislike to Shavrov during his student days, after Shavrov had repeatedly refused to allow him to stand in the wings to watch Kirov performances. Shavrov was often cast as the evil witch Carabosse in *The Sleeping Beauty*, a role, Rudolf was fond of saying, "he was born to play."

His speech met with stony silence. "We were all shocked," says Irina Kolpakova, then a Komsomol member (later a party member) and one of the Kirov's most promising young ballerinas. "He showed absolutely no respect toward a well-known teacher." To their surprise, Rudolf was still allowed to go on to Vienna. The incident, though, would become fodder for the KGB and haunt his travel prospects for many a tour to come.

From Moscow, the group traveled all the way to Vienna by charter bus, supervised by a Komsomol leader who would suddenly command them all to sing. Rudolf and Ninel Kurgapkina, however, would "do the complete opposite of what we were asked to do," Kurgapkina recalled proudly. "When everyone else was singing, we would remain quiet. And when everyone else was quiet, we would sing out loud. At which point this little Komsomol guy would berate us. . . ."

To Rudolf, Vienna's fin-de-siècle grandeur, musical past and material abundance were at once startling and exhilarating. He bought a pair of the finest leather shoes for each of his sisters and boots for his mother. But he spent most of his time roaming the streets, often in the company of Kurgapkina, who wore her favorite taffeta dress the night they went out dancing. Their colleagues noticed "how lively Nella looked" and assumed an affair, which wasn't true—not then, anyhow. Still, subtle shifts in mood and demeanor rarely went unchecked or unreported. For company members were encouraged to inform on one another, the price of a ticket for the next tour.

The dance festival was held at Vienna's seventeen-thousand–seat Stadthalle and drew 406 participants from thirty-two countries. French choreographer Roland Petit was there with his Ballets des Champs-Elysées. Rudolf saw Petit's *Cyrano de Bergerac*, his first glimpse of a contemporary Western ballet, and was struck by what, to his eyes, seemed a radically different approach to classical dance, "so very new and strange to me." Rudolf somehow managed to talk his way backstage for an impromptu meeting, even though Petit told the organizer he wasn't to be disturbed. Rudolf seemed "shy and yet extremely curious" to Petit, who, charmed by him, found someone to translate. "He told me that he liked my work and hoped to dance in the West someday."*

The last person Rudolf expected to find in Vienna was Menia Martinez. But there she was, marching with the Cuban delegation in the festival's youth parade. Menia was just as surprised to see Rudolf. "What is this getup?" he asked her suddenly. "At school," she recalls, "we had to dress correctly, befitting the point of view and spirit of the Russians at that time. But in Vienna, I was wearing very tight, bright-colored pants."†

"But look how you're dressed," he complained. "That's not good. Everyone will look at you." Menia was flattered by his jealousy. Over the next few days, Rudolf rarely left her side. "We could get married here in Vienna," he suggested. And once more, she demurred. Her family needed her in Cuba, she said, and anyhow, they were too young and she wasn't about to elope. It upset him that Menia was distracted by thoughts of home, but not because he was genuinely concerned about her life in Cuba. He needed to be the center of her attentions. Always, when his friends put their own needs first, or showed keen interest in anyone else, he questioned their loyalty. "I'm always with you," he lamented, "but you don't seem to care." And he was right. Menia was upset by all the changes taking place in Cuba; Rudolf was no longer her first priority.

Menia had come to Vienna with a group of singers, dancers and actors headed by choreographer Alberto Alonso, the ballerina Alicia Alonso's brother-in-law. Rudolf asked Menia to introduce him to Alberto in the hope of being invited to perform in Cuba. He also took class with Alonso's company, something the Soviet dancers were forbidden to do. "He is never with our delegation and he takes class with you," Kurgap-

*While in hindsight, it is easy to read a good deal into Rudolf's remark to Petit and see it as some kind of message in a bottle, Rudolf meant exactly what he said: He was interested by Petit's work, which was completely unlike anything he had seen in Russia, and he had the foresight to gauge that one day he would want to test himself in a variety of styles. But for the moment, the Kirov was challenge enough. Still very much on the ascent in a company he considered unrivaled, he had many more roles in which he had yet to prove himself.
†The Soviets considered it unbecoming for a woman to wear pants. Any woman wearing them could be refused entry into a restaurant or any public building.

kina warned Menia, perhaps as much out of jealousy as concern. "He can't do that."

Rudolf's success at the festival made his transgressions easier to ignore. On the night of August 16, he and Sizova performed their signature *Corsaire* pas de deux and drew "tumultuous applause" from the seventeen thousand people jammed into Vienna's Stadthalle, wrote the correspondent for *Izvestiya*, calling them "young ambassadors of Soviet ballet." The pair were the only dancers in their category to receive a score of ten, the maximum number of points. Rudolf was pleased with the result, until he discovered that two other pairs in their contingent — Soloviev and Kolpakova and the Bolshoi's Maximova and Vasiliev — were also to be awarded gold medals, even though their scores were lower. "I don't need this leveling," he barked at Sizova, who went on her own to retrieve their medal.* His arrogance offended Vasiliev, who at their last competition in Moscow had freely offered him his compliments. "He didn't like it when someone complimented me or Soloviev," Vasiliev recalls. "He took praise for granted and it caused people to dislike him. He thought he was better than everyone around him and was very protective of his own fame. In our system, we hated it when someone stood out. We considered this bad taste. We did our work and everyone was the same, equal."

After another tearful parting from Menia, Rudolf left behind the romance of Vienna for Bulgaria, where he bought his mother a fur coat. Word of his Vienna triumph preceded him. (YOUNG NUREYEV IS UNIQUE PHENOMENON IN BALLET, ran a headline in the local paper *Rabotnicheskoye Delo*.) As his train pulled into the station, a group of fans had gathered to greet him. "Nureyev, Nureyev," they chanted, passing crates of peaches to him through the window.

En route back to Leningrad, the dancers had to change trains in Kiev. And once more, Rudolf stepped out of line. With a thirty-minute stopover at hand, Rudolf seized the moment to visit Kiev's Prince Vladimir Cathedral. Caught in traffic on his return, he missed the train. He suspected that much would be read into his absence — and much was. "There were a lot of evil tongues in the troupe and they were saying that he had decided to stay in Kiev," recalls Alla Osipenko, the first Kirov ballerina to have visited the West.† Her colleagues wagered that Rudolf would lose his job — should he return. But Osipenko thought they were being ridiculous. He had just gone to look at a cathedral, after all. When

---

*Earlier in the competition, Rudolf performed Frondoso's solo from *Laurencia*. He and Sizova did not have an opportunity to perform *Valse Volonté*, a romantic pas de deux that choreographer Leonid Yacobson had choreographed especially for them. Set to music by Shostakovich, the waltz was the first ballet created for Nureyev.

†At a competition organized three years earlier by Serge Lifar, Osipenko won top honors and was accorded the Anna Pavlova Prize.

Rudolf turned up a short time later, the dancers rebuked him. "Half an hour, you were told!" The matter was added to the burgeoning list of complaints against him.

The first Moscow International Film Festival opened soon after Rudolf returned home. He was delighted when Silva Lon and her friend Val Golovitser invited him to a screening of Alain Resnais's *Hiroshima Mon Amour*, one of the groundbreaking films of the French New Wave. Golovitser, a festival employee, was friendly with a number of dancers, though he couldn't imagine any of them showing an interest in the films of Resnais. But then Rudolf was unlike any other dancer he had met. Golovitser had called him one day from Moscow to say hello, and asked what he was up to. "Bach," was the reply.

After the screening, Golovitser ushered Rudolf into a press conference for the French actress Marina Vlady, the voluptuous blond star of *The Witch*. Rudolf had never met a movie star and eagerly lined up for her autograph. When his turn came, he asked to have his picture taken with her.

"Oh, how I'd love to go to Leningrad," Vlady replied gamely when they were introduced, "but I won't have enough time."

"No problem," Rudolf said, smiling at her. "We'll meet in Paris."

RUDOLF MADE IT to the screen himself that September, when a news clip of *Laurencia* was shown in a cinema house in Ufa. An ecstatic — and vindicated — Anna Udeltsova wrote to Rosa in Leningrad:

Today I've been told that in our cinema house "Motherland" they showed Rudolf in a documentary. Of course I immediately rushed to the cinema and saw my inimitably delicate dashing Spaniard. I looked at my dear boy as if spellbound and the details of the dance escaped me. I should go and see it again . . . start collecting an album of newspaper articles about Rudolf because for Rudolf himself it will be very difficult to do this rough work. I think he needs a secretary. All the articles and newspaper photographs should be glued to a sheet of paper. Otherwise they will get lost. We should perpetuate this unexpected sparkled glory. . . . The thing is that previously, when I spoke about his talent, people used to mock me and said that I was probably carried away by him. All right, yes, earlier, I was carried away by him and now the whole world can witness what was clear to me then, so let God give him good health and strong nerves. . . .

As Udeltsova hoped, the perpetuation of her dear boy's "sparkled glory" had already begun. By the fall of 1959, it had become clear to the Kirov management that Nureyev was a major drawing card. Every star of the company had his or her own clutch of fans, but Rudolf generated excitement among general audiences and fans alike. Some came all the way from Moscow to see him dance. His performances "were like bull-fights, with Nureyev and the audience as bull and toreador," the critic Gennady Smakov later wrote. "The issue of this combat was unpredictable. His very appearance on the stage seemed to stir up an atmosphere of violence and danger." In time, even his detractors forgave him his "irresistible peculiarities," as his flaws came to be called. "His dancing is not perfection," one of them acknowledged to Smakov. "But what he achieves onstage is more than ballet."

Since he rarely chatted with his fans outside the stage door the way other dancers did, Rudolf maintained "an aura of mystery about him." He also inspired slavish devotion, as he was to do throughout his career. Whenever he went on tour, his fans would come to see him off at the station and then gather at a nearby café to discuss his performances. Each of his debuts was keenly anticipated; each detail digested for weeks. Though it was forbidden to throw flowers onto the Kirov stage, Rudolf grew accustomed to taking his bows amid a sea of bouquets.

Nevertheless, his newfound celebrity also brought new demands. As thanks for their devotion, a number of his female fans expected something more from him. When he failed to respond to their romantic overtures, they turned on him, insulting him in the street and telephoning him at all hours of the night. Their calls awakened both Pushkins as well, for he was still living with them. At one of his performances, a disgruntled fan threw an old broom on the stage, the equivalent of a public slap in the face. If Rudolf was rattled, he never let on: Plucking the broom from the stage, he bowed with it graciously, as if it were a bouquet.

Balletomania has long been something of an art in Leningrad, its rules and standards as codified as the art form it honors. Its colorful history began with the Russian debut of the celebrated Romantic ballerina Marie Taglioni in the 1850s. Taglioni's performances so enthralled local audiences that a special exception was granted in order that bouquets could be presented to her onstage. Taglioni stayed in Russia for several years and when she finally departed for France, her personal effects were sold at auction. Her silken ballet slippers went for two hundred rubles, an astonishingly high price for the time. Ballet lore has it that the purchaser then cooked them them in a special sauce, before consuming them at a banquet held for fellow balletomanes.

Despite scant press coverage, Nureyev stirred interest beyond Leningrad's ballet world. At the Philharmonic, he would be greeted by cries of "Nureyev!" whenever he attended concerts. His friend Tamara Zakrzhevskaya usually accompanied him. "He loved being recognized. He wasn't a poseur, but whenever he felt that strangers were looking at him, he immediately straightened his posture." He was also astute about honing his image. In return for a book on van Gogh that his Moscow acquaintance Silva Lon sent him, Rudolf had intended to send her studio portraits of himself. But the photographer "has turned out to be a swine," he wrote to her in October 1959, "and, despite all the times I have been to him, he keeps deceiving me and I have stopped trusting him. Instead, I'm sending you a newspaper cutting with my photograph."

Eager to analyze just what "people were going crazy about," Rudolf decided to study the film made of his *Corsaire* performance in Moscow. He had never seen himself dance before. "Well, of course, I didn't see any of what I was looking for," he remarked years later. "Instead, I felt very strange seeing myself on film. It was like the first time I had sex or something. . . ."

WITH HIS DEBUTS that fall in *La Bayadère* and *Giselle*, Rudolf began taking every aspect of his performance into his own hands. Along the way, he managed to transform not just each new role he danced, but the public's perception of him. Most balletgoers associated the name Nureyev with the virile, heroic roles made famous by Chaboukiani, those demanding temperament and virtuosity: the Slave in *Corsaire*, the Spanish peasant in *Laurencia*, the Armenian shepherd in *Gayané*. But few could imagine him in such Romantic or lyric roles as the ardent, then repentant Count Albrecht in *Giselle*. Nor had he displayed any bent for lyricism or psychologically complex characters.

Now Rudolf was slated to partner Dudinskaya in just such a role, in his first *La Bayadère*, one of Petipa's last masterpieces and a touchstone of the Maryinsky-Kirov repertory. As varied as a five-course meal, the panoramic four-act ballet is a tale of love and jealousy set in the India of the rajahs. The royal Indian warrior Solor is loved by two women: Nikiya, the *bayadère* or temple dancer, and Gamzatti, the rajah's alluring daughter. In its most famous scene, "The Kingdom of the Shades," Solor dreams that he sees his beloved, the dead Nikiya, in an image multiplied by the corps de ballets. "Death as a setting for abstraction had appeared in *Giselle* and other ballets of the Romantic era," Arlene Croce has written. Petipa, however, "extended the implication: . . . Death's kingdom was the Elysium, the nirvana, of pure dance."

Solor was another role closely associated with Chaboukiani, who had devised most of Solor's dances for the 1941 revival. Like Nureyev, he had starred opposite Dudinskaya's Nikiya. Still, as Rudolf saw it, he and Chaboukiani were very different dancers. Chaboukiani, he later recalled, "did not have a big jump, although he gave the illusion of this by his ballon," his ability to hover in the air. Rudolf did, and wanted to show it off. So he slowed down his final solo and introduced a series of double assemblés, double corkscrew turns in the air—the step that would become his signature. The new step so suited the ballet that it was soon copied widely, first by other dancers at the Kirov and eventually by other dancers around the world.

He also revised the costume to suit his particular attributes, a notion that ran completely counter to the Soviet way of doing things. "We were forbidden to change costumes," says Alla Osipenko. "If Dudinskaya was dancing in a particular costume, we were obliged to dance in exactly the same costume. They were simply sewn for us." To extend the length and line of his body, Rudolf danced his final-act solo in tights, rather than in the traditional wide trousers. Finding the customary jacket too constricting, he suggested something shorter and less cumbersome to Simon Virsaladze, the Kirov's chief designer.

He didn't stop there: To create the impression that his legs and body were more elongated than they were, he walked, danced and turned out grandes pirouettes on high demi-pointe, knees fully stretched. This didn't sit well with the ballet's coach, Askold Makarov, who tried to change his approach during rehearsal. "Why do you walk on demi-pointe like the Prince in *Swan Lake*? You are a warrior who just killed a tiger in a hunt and your walk should reflect that." But Rudolf's Solor possessed a certain refinement, his jumps "laced with a touch of effeminate Oriental mannerism," as Gennady Smakov described them. "And you, Askold Anatolievich," Rudolf replied, cutting him off, "just show me the order of the steps. I can figure out the rest without your help."

Rudolf and Dudinskaya had spent months preparing for Rudolf's first *Bayadère*. But hours before the curtain was to go up, Dudinskaya suddenly bowed out. The reason for Dudinskaya's withdrawal was vague, which only served to fuel backstage intrigue, not to mention Rudolf's predebut jitters. Since Dudinskaya never missed a performance, Olga Moiseyeva, her standby, was at home relaxing when the summons came. "I've never so much as shaken his hand," she protested. "How can I go on with a new partner and dance an entire ballet without even running through it once?"

But dance an entire ballet they did. And despite the lack of preparation, "it went like a dream," recalled Moiseyeva, his Nikiya for all four of his Leningrad performances. "There was something almost demon-like about him, as if he himself had arisen from some mystical spirit kingdom."

Rudolf's own assessment, however, was mixed. "The first act went well," he wrote to Silva Lon a few days later; "the second act was somewhat tense, the variations didn't quite work, nor did the lifts. But I'm very pleased with the third act and feel very self-confident about it. . . . I don't know what the general opinion is, but I don't feel conceit, for there is nothing to be conceited about. . . . The costumes and makeup for *La*

Bayadère are my own. And I'm now thinking about *Giselle* (about the costumes)."

For his *Giselle* costumes, he once again took his own sketches to the Kirov's designer and asked for a new jacket to be sewn for both the first and second acts. The jackets he designed were much shorter than the traditional costume, which covered the groin and buttocks.* They were also more fitted and made of lighter fabric.

The rehearsals for *Giselle* had been entrusted to Yuri Grigorovich, the Kirov's innovative young ballet master. Intent on vitalizing the repertory, he chose to stage the ballet with a new dancer in the title role, Irina Kolpakova, and a new Albrecht. With Nureyev, he would have an entirely original approach to the young nobleman who betrays the peasant girl Giselle after falling in love with her. Giselle is unaware that her beloved is not only from an exalted class, but betrothed to a duke's daughter. When the truth is revealed, she dies of a broken heart. Filled with remorse, Albrecht visits her grave to repent of his deception and there is met by the Wilis, ghostly man-hating women who died before marrying. Albrecht begs Giselle's forgiveness and she, in turn, begs the Wilis to spare Albrecht. The Romantic-era ballet, conceived by Théophile Gautier and Vernoy de Saint-Georges as a vehicle for the Italian ballerina Carlotta Grisi, was not without a substantial role for the male dancer. At the Kirov, the tall, strapping Sergeyev had dominated the role of Albrecht for so long that, as Irina Kolpakova recalls, the Kirov's younger generation had a hard time imagining anyone in his place. Sergeyev was admired for his lyricism and princely refinement. Kolpakova was therefore shocked when Rudolf showed no interest in watching him partner Dudinskaya in *Giselle*. To her suggestion that he might learn from Sergeyev, Rudolf replied: "Go to a restaurant and watch how the waiters run from table to table. There you will see great movement."

Rudolf had no intention of following anyone else's lead, however celebrated. To make Albrecht his own, he looked instead within himself. Albrecht is one of those rich, dramatic roles that take the measure of a dancer's artistry and continue to present new challenges as that artistry gains nuance and depth. Albrecht must be "both prince and peasant, Hamlet to her Ophelia," Richard Buckle has written. "He has to perform in the second act an exhausting series of *entrechats, cabrioles, pirouettes* and *tours en l'air* ending in crashing (but not noisy) falls to the ground, while giving an impression of remorse and heartbreak. This must all be done with period style."

*He modeled his tunic after the one worn by Michel Renault, the star of the Paris Opéra, who had performed *Giselle* in Leningrad in 1958.

Sergeyev's interpretation played up the theme of social conflict. Count Albrecht was a man of the world, a member of the ruling class and a calculating seducer of a poor peasant girl. Rudolf's Albrecht, by contrast, was a feckless, impulsive young man, inexperienced in the ways of love and overwhelmed by his inchoate feelings. The artists of Rudolf's generation, observes the Russian balletomane Nina Alovert, "were much more aware of the world at large than their predecessors had been" and preferred to see the story in terms of its moral rather than its social conflicts. Rudolf's own limited experience with Menia had taught him the power of youthful rapture, an experience that likely informed his portrayal. "I first played Albrecht as being totally in love from the beginning," he recalled of this early draft. "He was in love with love. Euphoria!"

This radical departure began on Saturday, December 12, 1959, with Rudolf's debut in *Giselle*. The excitement on both sides of the curtain was palpable. Although Saturdays were working days, the theater was packed that night. People were standing in the boxes, waiting. Backstage, Irina Kolpakova was startled to find her Albrecht wearing not only a new, abbreviated costume, but his "modesty" shorts beneath his purple tights, not over them as was customary. But by then she had come to admire Nureyev's push for innovation, particularly the changes he had made in the ballet's spectral second act when the remorse-stricken Albrecht is commanded to dance to the death by the Queen of the Wilis. (Giselle finally leads him back to life while herself retreating into the land of ghosts.) For his solo, Rudolf had replaced the standard traveling brisés with a succession of "beaten" steps known as entrechats, performed repeatedly in place.* He hoped this would reveal the frenzied stirrings of Albrecht's heart.

When the curtain fell, the theater shook with applause and stamping feet. Georgi Korkin, the Kirov's administrative director, crowed: "This is the beginning of a new era!" Not everyone embraced that view. "Sergeyev and Dudinskaya were mad at us," Kolpakova recalls. "They said, 'Why are you challenging tradition? We worked so hard on this ballet, trying to preserve it, and here you are changing it.' They didn't feel Rudolf was Prince Albrecht."†

But for those who did, Rudolf's performance was a revelation. "He came . . . and he conquered," cheered Vera Krasovskaya. Nureyev, an-

*More specifically, he replaced the diagonal series of brisés (or traveling leg beats) with a round of sixteen entrechats six, triple changes of feet, that are extremely difficult to perform.
†When Valery Panov assumed the role in 1965, Sergeyev urged him not to make any changes. Panov had enormous admiration for Sergeyev, but decided to offer his own interpretation. Afterward, Sergeyev remarked that "there have been many Albrechts over the years, and all went astray somewhere."

other critic wrote, "doesn't so much depart from Sergeyev's traditions as openly challenge them." Yuri Slonimsky, the prominent Russian dance critic, was also present. In an essay published a few months later in *The Atlantic Monthly*, he declared Nureyev's Albrecht "unlike anyone's we have ever seen. Having made Giselle fall in love with him as a whim, he then loses control over himself. The second act, in his version, unfolds like the effects of the torments of love, and we witness the gradual purification of the hero's feeling and the levitation of his soul. The main themes of the ballet become clear to us in Nureyev's meaningful dancing."

Vera Chistyakova seconded that view in *Smena*. "His style is both natural and spontaneous and reflects Albrecht's obvious ardor and despair. The action (of the first act) irrepressibly draws to its fateful conclusion and our emotions are left on edge as we prepare for the events of the second act, an act in which Nureyev really shone."* To many in the audience that night, Rudolf's triumph was indelible. Liuba Romankova feared he had "gone mad or had a heart attack." Tamara Zakrzhevskaya became so involved herself, she felt as if she, too, had just been dancing. "There was a reason for this: Whenever Rudik was dancing, the spectator always experienced an amazing feeling of participation."

His debut was especially notable for another reason: His mother was there to see him dance for the first time on the Kirov stage. To Silva Lon, sitting next to her in the front row, she seemed "like an old country woman," her scarf wrapped tightly around her head. At intermission, she ran straight to the cloakroom to make sure no one had stolen the fur coat Rudolf had bought her in Bulgaria and which she had only reluctantly checked.

Sentiment was rare in the Nureyev family, but that night, Farida was overcome and cried throughout the performance. She had never expected such success, she later told her granddaughter. After that, she periodically returned to Leningrad, though the city frightened her. Once, when Tamara accompanied her to the theater, Farida clung to her arm the whole time. Since Farida spoke Russian poorly, she conversed with Rudolf only in Tatar. "*Akcha bar*? [Got any money?]" he would ask her every time they met. "*Iok* [No]," she would invariably reply, and he'd fish into his pocket for a fistful of notes.

Rudolf had been sending money to Ufa whenever he could. He was then earning 250 rubles a month. Compared with the average Soviet wage of 70 rubles, this was "big money." The extra wages were needed at home, especially after his mother had to retire because of the painful

*Kolpakova would go on to become the prima ballerina of the Kirov. This *Giselle* was her only performance with Nureyev on the Kirov stage.

bursitis in her legs. Rudolf's concern was deeply appreciated by both his parents. Indeed, far from embarrassing his father, his financial support earned his respect. In the spring of 1960, Hamet at last traveled to Leningrad to see Rudolf dance. In the fourteen years since Hamet had returned home from the war, he had never seen his son on a stage. Finally, after much persuading, Farida had convinced him to join her at a performance of *La Bayadère*. The occasion radically altered Hamet's view of his son.

His first glimpse of a grand theater impressed him, but what struck him most of all were the bravos and cries of "Nureyev!" that greeted Rudolf at the curtain call. Though he had seen Rudolf on television, the live accolades were stunning proof of the size of his achievement. Afterward, Pushkin shook his hand and praised him for raising such a talented boy. "When he and my mother came back from Leningrad, my father felt different about Rudik's dancing," recalls Razida. "He saw that other people approved of his passion, so he felt there must be something in it. It was a turning point for him."

Rudolf never discussed his family with his Leningrad friends, and none of them recalls his ever mentioning that his father came to see him dance. Rudolf always described his father as stern, and subsequent chroniclers of their relationship have given short shrift to Hamet, assuming that once Rudolf left home, he and his father severed their ties. But the father who emerges in one of his few surviving letters, written to Rudolf and Rosa in May 1960, shortly after his visit to Leningrad, is anything but uncaring and remote:

Good afternoon, my dear Rudolf and Rosa!

We have received your letter and we are very happy that you are safe and sound. We are all safe and sound and wish you the same. First of all I must thank you Rudik for suggesting we go to the South this year. I'd like to let you know that Mother can't go anywhere this year. Her doctors recommend her to go to Krasnousolsk or Yangan-Tau. But we can't get a voucher. As soon as we get a voucher we'll send her for treatment. . . .

Rudik! As soon as you get your leave come to Ufa. Rosa will probably come here for holiday in autumn. At the moment our main concern is a flat. I have been offered a two-room flat. You will say it's good. No it is not good. First it is far away. Second it's a small flat. There are five doors in one room. It gives access into the other room. So you can enter the second room only through this room, which is pretty inconvenient for our family. Third there is no running water. We have a very good garden. All has been in blossom. There will be plenty of berries and there must be apples—nearly all the apple trees are in blossom. They've started building a house near the plant. By May 1961 they promise to complete the construction. They promise me a flat there. That's all for the moment.

A big kiss to you.
Your papa and mama

9

Distant Stages

WITH MENIA GONE, Rudolf spent most of his free time with Tamara, who was studying Russian literature at Leningrad University. With thick dark brows that arched stiffly above pensive eyes, her lips fixed in a solemn line, Tamara conveyed a brooding, purposeful air. "What did you learn today?" he would ask her each time they met. Tamara soon arranged for him to attend her lectures and, when she saw what an avid reader he was, introduced him to a number of important Russian writers of the 1920s and 1930s, among them Balmont, Gumilev and Voloshin, whose works were available only through the university library or in *samizdat*, underground publications.*

His most thrilling discovery was Salinger's *The Catcher in the Rye*, which he devoured in one sitting. He had somehow managed to secure a copy of *Inostrannaya Literatura* (Foreign Literature), the international literary journal in which the novel had been printed. "No sleep for you tonight!" he announced to Tamara when he handed her his copy. "You won't be able to put it down!" In Holden Caulfield, he encountered an outsider like himself, a rebel who scorns the phoniness of the adult world.

The few friends Rudolf had he kept in compartments. Since he rarely ventured out in a group or spoke about one to another, they barely knew each other. He continued to see Liuba and Leonid "Lyoka" Romankov, spending weekends with them and their sports-minded friends on the Gulf of Finland, at the dacha of a volleyball teammate of

*The Khrushchev thaw had given rise to an anti-Stalinist literary revolution, spearheaded by such literary journals as *Novy Mir* (New World), which began publishing Solzhenitsyn, among other major writers.

Liuba's. He danced to rock 'n' roll at their parties, but thought it unwise to play rugby with them in the snow, fearing that he would unduly strain his legs. He was both "with us and yet at the same time not with us," Liuba wrote in a memoir, recalling how Rudolf would often wander off by himself to gaze at the sea and sunset. "There were moments when I felt that he was quietly studying us all a bit."

His was not an easy temperament to fathom. He would storm off one minute and reappear the next, grinning happily. He saw no need to censor his thoughts, regardless of hurt feelings or social conventions. Despite his frequent, candid conversations with her, Tamara never considered herself anything more than his friend. Privately, she hoped their relationship might develop into intimacy. But she quickly discovered that the closer she grew to Rudolf, the more Xenia protected him. Her own relationship with Xenia grew increasingly strained once Xenia began to see her as a rival. She and Rudolf regularly attended concerts at the Philharmonic; often, as they came out of the theater, Xenia would be standing by the entrance, waiting to take Rudolf home. Sometimes he would see her ahead of time. "Xsana," Tamara would hear him say under his breath. "Then we would go out another way so she wouldn't see us. He was very good to her, but she pressured him too much and he grew tired of it."

Though much less demonstrative than his wife, Pushkin was equally taken with Rudolf. Given their close quarters, he must have detected his wife's sexual interest in his protégé; certainly everyone else seemed to. If he did, there was no discernible rift between husband and wife. "We all knew about that odd ménage and it was much talked about," recalls Nikita Dolgushin. "But no one snickered behind their backs out of respect for Pushkin. He gave the impression that it was taking place in someone else's family." One day while Rudolf was living there, Ninel Kurgapkina came by to listen to records. Rudolf ushered her into a tiny room taken up by an enormous bed and sofa. "So where do you sleep?" she asked him. "Me? Here," he replied. "And what about Alexander Ivanovich?" she pressed on, the logistics eluding her. "I don't know," Rudolf answered vaguely. "He and his wife sleep somewhere else."

Rudolf later confessed to friends that by the time he left Leningrad, he had slept with Pushkin as well as Xenia. One of his friends, who had known the couple in Leningrad and couldn't imagine how he managed it, was taken aback by this dinner table confidence. "You're so immoral!" she exclaimed. "Not at all," Rudolf answered coolly. "Both of them enjoyed it." A colleague of Pushkin's claims that Pushkin was known to have had a homosexual affair in his youth with the brother of a Kirov ballerina. By the time Rudolf came to live in his home, however, the rumors about that liaison had long lain dormant.

Whether Rudolf went to bed with Pushkin is a question that can never be answered. Rudolf was fond of telling contradictory stories: He told the choreographer Rudi van Dantzig that he had "no idea about homosexuality at that time, it never entered my head," and claimed to have had no sexual experience whatsover during his years in Russia, which wasn't true. But he also told a male lover in London that he had once jumped off a Leningrad bus when he found himself attracted to a male passenger. The story about Pushkin may have been fanciful or it may have been true. The Russians have a saying which serves as a useful guide: *Za nogi nie dershala* (I wasn't there holding their legs).

In any case, Rudolf never broached the subject of homosexuality with his Leningrad friends. Only years later would he recognize that he had harbored a secret crush on Liuba's tall, handsome twin, Leonid. "It was shameful and illegal," says Tamara. "He would have been scared to death to discuss it." Despite very real fears of imprisonment,* homosexuality was of course known in the Leningrad ballet world, though only tacitly acknowledged. It was rumored that both Chaboukiani and Sergeyev were homosexual, though given the rampant homophobia of the time, such rumors were often politically motivated.† A gay underground existed, but Rudolf was not part of it. He knew that if caught, he could be sent to jail or blackmailed into serving the KGB's purposes, risks he was not about to take. Even if they weren't persecuted, dancers known to be homosexual were considered "an embarrassment" and kept from foreign tours.‡

RUDOLF ASSUMED a variety of new roles and partners during the 1960 spring season. He partnered Olga Moiseyeva in *La Bayadère*, Alla Sizova in the Bluebird pas de deux from *The Sleeping Beauty*, Ninel Kurgapkina in *Don Quixote* and Alla Shelest in *Giselle*. Of all of them, he felt the keenest affinity with Shelest, a contemporary of Dudinskaya's with as lofty a reputation inside the Soviet Union. The two ballerinas, however, had

*Tamara was acquainted with a well-known opera tenor in Sverdlovsk who was sentenced to a two-year jail term after he was discovered having sex with another man. "He had enemies and they set him up with some boy," she recalls. The tenor spent six months in prison before a friend, the renowned pianist Sviatoslav Richter, persuaded some high-ranking party members into granting him clemency.

†According to Valery Panov, Sergeyev's enemies at the theater called him a homosexual because of his "excess" refinement.

‡Truman Capote visited Leningrad in December 1956 and provoked great curiosity wherever he went. As his biographer Gerald Clarke recounts, Capote had a grand time toying with the Soviets' sense of decorum. After he made a particularly campy exit from the lobby of the Astoria Hotel, kicking up his heels as he went through the revolving door, the somber man from the Ministry of Culture was heard to say: "Ve have them like that in the Soviet Union, but ve hide them."

little in common. Dudinskaya could always be relied on for technical fireworks and consistency; Shelest brought a sense of the unexpected to each performance, dramatic fervor informed by an intensely personal vision. Nevertheless, lacking Dudinskaya's connections, she would always occupy the number two position in the company.

Despite the nineteen years separating them, Shelest found in Rudolf a sensitive, attentive partner who responded to her "every nuance." In *Giselle*, she would say later, she wanted to rely on him "like a woman, such tenderness breathed from his Albrecht." But she could see that he hadn't yet learned how to pace himself. This was especially evident to her during the ballet's second act when Albrecht is nearly danced to death before Giselle intervenes to save him. Sensing that Rudolf was wearing out before the act was through, Shelest, like the superlative Giselle she was, spurred him on. "Hold on, hold on," she whispered in his ear. "It'll be over soon!"

In the first seven months of 1960, Rudolf made eleven appearances on the Kirov stage in addition to performances at the Promkooperatisya, one of the city's palaces of culture. Still, regardless of the roles and partners that came his way, more than his fair share, Rudolf felt he wasn't onstage enough. Thwarted opportunities seemed the only thing on his mind in a letter he wrote to Silva Lon on March 3. "My *Bayadère* is at the Promkooperatisya. . . . They promise me *Don Quixote* in April. Japan is doubtful: There are only 40 going and my ballets are not included. . . . To judge from the newspapers, your theater [the Bolshoi] is on its last legs. But no invitation is forthcoming. Nor is there any invitation for the competition in Cuba. . . . At the beginning of April, our company is to appear on television—me, too, in *Giselle* (after a row) . . . I'm in a dreadful state because of a recent meeting at which it was decided to give the production a routine flavor."

With a view to meeting Western artists, Rudolf had begun private lessons with the Romankovs' English tutor, Georgi Mikhailovich. English and French were taught in Soviet schools, and while unusual, his determination to study a foreign language on his own wasn't especially daring in itself. Conversing with Westerners was another matter; despite the relaxed policies regarding foreign visitors, Russians were not permitted to mix with them. To do so was to arouse suspicions of espionage and risk being summoned to "The Big House," Leningrad's KGB headquarters. And who knew what might happen to you after that? So pervasive was the climate of fear that even a chance encounter with a Westerner was something to be dreaded. Anyone wishing to speak to a foreigner had to seek permission from the company's Personnel Department. Rarely were such requests sought, much less approved.

Nonetheless, Rudolf continued to wade in these dangerous straits: He made it a point to see every foreign troupe that visited Leningrad—

from Alicia Alonso's Ballet Nacional de Cuba to an American touring show of *My Fair Lady*—and then rushed backstage to meet the artists, even when it meant being shadowed by KGB. The agents' faces grew so familiar, he said, he could have drawn them from memory.

My Fair Lady had been the talk of Moscow and Leningrad for months. Every ticket to the five-week engagement had sold out within hours. To prepare the Soviet people for their first American musical comedy, Moscow Radio broadcast the score before opening night. Many Russians were familiar with Shaw's *Pygmalion*, but most failed to understand the show's dialogue. The response was ecstatic all the same: "Get Me to the Church on Time" proved the showstopper.*

Rudolf not only saw the show twice, he struck up a friendship with Lola Fisher, the American actress playing Eliza Doolittle. A "leggy, beguiling blonde," in the view of the *New York Post*, Fisher had understudied Julie Andrews and other stars in the role on Broadway; the Soviet tour was her first big break. In his autobiography, Rudolf recalled his excitement about meeting the Americans. He failed to mention the unusual circumstances that brought them face-to-face.

During Fisher's visit to Leningrad, a classmate of Liuba Romankova's named Radik Tihomirov had been asked to show her the city. Radik had the movie star good looks of Alain Delon and spoke a little English. It quickly became apparent to him, however, that Fisher was not merely interested in him as a guide. ("I left my heart in Leningrad," she told the *New York Post* on her return.) Worried about being alone with her, Radik invited Liuba Romankova to join them for an evening stroll. Liuba spent so much time talking about her friend Rudik's upcoming debut as the spirited barber Basil in Petipa's *Don Quixote* that Fisher decided to come see it for herself and brought a number of her colleagues along.† The Americans looked "bored stiff" during the ballet's first two acts, recalled Liuba. "But we Russians . . . secretly despised the ignorant Americans for being unfamiliar with one of Petipa's most outstanding ballets." But once Rudolf and Kurgapkina began their dazzling pas de deux in the ballet's final act, the theater erupted with applause and cascading bouquets. The delighted Americans asked to be taken backstage. They arrived at the stage door to find Rudolf surrounded by fans. Spotting them, Rudolf fought his way over, his arms laden with flowers, which he presented to Fisher. (His female fans, meanwhile, were indignant that he should hand over their bouquets to another woman.)

*In Moscow, the cast of seventy was fed hot dogs for breakfast "to make them feel at home."

†In his memoir, Nureyev gives the date of his debut in *Don Quixote* as July 26. However, the official Kirov program for his performance, which he autographed that same day for Lola Fisher, lists the date as May 27, 1960.

In turn, the Americans invited him to dine with them at the Europa Hotel. Though in his memoir he recalls declining their invitation, in truth, he went along the next day. The moment he arrived at the restaurant, the entire company of seventy rose to give him a standing ovation. "He was so proud that he was admired by foreigners," says Tamara. Over the next few days, Rudolf traveled with the cast around Leningrad on their chartered bus, something few Russians would have dared. He also visited with Fisher at her hotel, trying out his first few phrases of English. "I whish [sic] you a very happy trip around our country," he wrote across her *Don Quixote* program. For Rudolf, as for Eliza Doolittle, language was the passport to new worlds.

DESPITE BEING TAILED by KGB, Rudolf had special status as a Kirov star. On the heels of their debut in *Don Quixote*, he and Kurgapkina were invited to perform before Khrushchev at a garden party for high-ranking government officials. The affair was held outside Moscow at the dacha of Nikolai Bulganin, a longtime Khrushchev cohort and the former Soviet premier.* The political heavyweights in attendance were of little interest to Rudolf. Apart from Khrushchev, Khrushchev's wife, Nina Petrovna, and Marshal Kliment Voroshilov, Stalin's former war commissar,† he recognized none of them. Still, he was pleased to be sharing the program with leading Soviet artists, such as the composer Dmitri Shostakovich and Sviatoslav Richter, the pianist Rudolf most admired. "I saw with what hunger he seemed almost to devour the notes when it came to his turn to perform. His was a passionate intensity I felt I could understand." Rudolf and Kurgapkina had planned to dance variations from *Don Quixote* because they knew its splashy virtuosity would appeal to the party brass. But when they saw that the stage in the garden was too small to risk space-devouring jumps, they performed only the adagio.

Khrushchev's wife was the country's most powerful balletomane and it was well known that Khrushchev himself admired dancers. Although there was an air of openness that day, and Rudolf and Kurgapkina could readily have spoken to the Soviet leader, "we didn't have anything to say to him," says Kurgapkina.

Predictably, the program also included speeches about the meaning and purpose of Soviet culture, after which Voroshilov, soon joined by Khrushchev, began to sing his favorite Ukrainian folk songs. Rudolf was

*In 1958, Khrushchev had taken over as prime minister himself and combined the post with the first secretaryship of the party, as Stalin had done in 1941. Unlike Stalin, however, he didn't arrest his deposed colleagues. Instead, he transferred them to less prestigious posts without stripping them of their privileges.

†One of the few among Stalin's henchmen to have survived the purges.

struck by this impromptu songfest, particularly by Voroshilov's "thrilling bass voice." But what shocked him was the grandeur of the all-day affair—from the staged hunts and fishing contests to the buckets of champagne and abundant buffet tables covered in starched linen tablecloths. When he sat down to dinner, he didn't know which forks and knives to use. He seemed to have no idea that the party elite lived like czars. "Now I finally see what Communism is," he told Tamara on his return to Leningrad.

DESPITE HIS SELF-ABSORPTION, Rudolf reveled in the success of the colleagues he admired. When Nikita Dolgushin debuted in *The Nutcracker*, Rudolf not only coached him but photographed the performance. He also coached Kostya Brudnov, a young dancer whose natural ability he rated above his own. He even goaded "rival" Yuri Soloviev into asking for additional performances. "Go and bug them. *I* do and they give it to me." Soloviev demurred. Then again, no two temperaments could have been more dissimilar. Soloviev was quiet, sweet-natured and self-effacing to the point of complacency. Where Rudolf lusted after new ideas and experiences, Soloviev was given to simple tastes. And where Rudolf's dancing was unpredictable and daring, Soloviev was known for his extraordinary technique, soaring jumps and deep pliés. "He was an absolutely faultless dancer," notes Dolgushin, "but he lacked nobility and lyricism." Although he and Rudolf were the stars of their graduating class and taken into the Kirov the same year, Soloviev was assigned to the corps de ballet.

His ongoing run-ins with the administration, however, were costing him partners and tours. At a rehearsal of *Don Quixote*, he fought with Mikhail Mikhailovich Mikhailov, the ballet's coach, over his right to change the pacing of his performance. In his first variation, he had performed a series of soft, drawn-out steps before exiting the stage. A staunch guardian of tradition, Mikhailov insisted that he do it again, without slowing down his exit. Rudolf refused and, in a crude play on the older man's name, stormed out of the room saying, "All these Pihal Pihaloviches are trying to tell me what to do." (*Pihal* is the Russian word for "fuck.")

Perhaps in retaliation for what they saw as his privileged treatment, Rudolf's rivals started a rumor that Dudinskaya no longer wanted to dance with him. The rumor was sparked by Dudinskaya's sudden withdrawal from their first *La Bayadère*. Hoping to force a rift, a number of dancers notified Rudolf that Dudinskaya hadn't really hurt her leg, as he had been told, but was envious of *his* success. While this wasn't true, Rudolf believed what they said and became cold toward her. Unaware of the reason for his change of heart, Dudinskaya presumed that he didn't appreciate her, completing this Shakespearean about-face. The next time she danced *Laurencia*, she requested Boris Bregvadze as her partner.

Several months later, Rudolf learned that he wasn't being sent on a tour to Egypt and fell into a morbid state of mind. "How stupid and simpleminded I was at that time," he wrote across a publicity photo he gave to Tamara that June. The photograph showed him dancing with Dudinskaya in their first *Laurencia*. "And I was living only on hope. Now, alas, I have become sober." But no less daring. Returning to *Don Quixote* that month, he simply eliminated his mime passages in the first act. The mime struck him as dated and false, and he refused to fake his way through an insincere performance. Kurgapkina had to improvise her way through their duet. "I'm a dancer, not a mime," he told the higher-ups at intermission. "The mime's not important anyway. I just don't care about it."

He caused a greater scandal by refusing to wear the puffy breeches that went with his costume for the final act, an echo of the historic scandal of 1911 when Nijinsky's refusal to wear the shorts that went with his *Giselle* costume occasioned his departure from the Maryinsky company.* Rudolf had worn them for the first two acts, but finally dug his heels in. The interval dragged on and on while Rudolf argued his point backstage with Sergeyev and an apoplectic Mikhail Mikhailov. The breeches cut off the line of his leg, he said. He wanted to wear only white tights over his dance belt, something no other dancer had ever done on the Kirov stage. "In the West they've been dancing in tights for years, and so will I. What do I need these lampshades for?"

Since the ballet was heading into its final act, Rudolf's understudy had already gone home, and there was no one to replace him. The interval had stretched to nearly one hour and the audience was growing testy. Though threatened with reprisals, Rudolf got his own way. When the curtain came down, the response was thunderous. Still, the conservatives in the audience were scandalized by his "immodesty." To them it looked as if he had forgotten to wear his pants. Backstage, the theater's functionaries rushed to berate the men's costume mistress. "How dare you let such a thing happen," they began, only to be cut short by Rudolf. "Leave Tatyana Nikolayevna alone," he said. "She knew nothing about it. I am the only one responsible."

"It was a scandal," remembers Alla Osipenko, "but the public and

---

*Nijinsky's refusal to wear the trunks was said to have offended the dowager empress Maria Fedorovna, though it's not known whether Nijinsky resigned or was dismissed. In any case, it is widely presumed that Diaghilev engineered the scandal to ensure that Nijinsky would dance only for his company.

the media accepted it wonderfully. Many in the company asked, 'Why is it allowed for Nureyev but not for us?' Because they didn't think of it, that's why."

Rudolf received an official warning and a few more black marks in his "workbook," the ongoing report card kept on each employee by the KGB's in-house personnel director. He also drew an unfavorable review from Vera Krasovskaya. In her year-end roundup, she took him to task for failing to develop the barber Basil into a fully rounded character and for dancing *Don Quixote* as if it were a mere divertissement. Basil was not a particularly profound character, she acknowledged; nonetheless, other Soviet ballet stars had managed to make him interesting. "So why on earth does Nureyev—sporting his 'trendy' haircut—feel he has to stalk the stage with an air of imperturbable indifference? . . . [H]e should learn not to play so fecklessly with his own talent."

Rudolf opened the way for a new approach to costumes and Alla Osipenko was one of the first to follow his lead. Noticing in a photograph that Western ballerinas favored shorter tutus, she promptly took a pair of scissors to her own. "I, too, had a complex that I had short legs and I thought, 'My God, why do I torture myself in these long tutus?'" The women's costume mistress was aghast. "Alla, what are you doing? I will be fired. It is forbidden to dance in such a short tutu."

And a few more rules were rewritten.

RUDOLF'S INTEREST in the West had not gone unnoticed by the authorities. In late September, shortly after being dropped from the tour to Egypt, he was sent on a forty-six-day bus tour of East Germany—one week before American Ballet Theatre was due to open in Moscow.* The possibility that the timing was coincidental is slight. No American ballet company had ever performed in the Soviet Union and Rudolf had been looking forward to the visit with great interest. He was curious about Erik Bruhn and Maria Tallchief, the tour stars, and badly wanted to see *Theme and Variations*, his first Balanchine ballet. As he knew from reading *Dance Magazine*, Tallchief was the former wife and muse of Balanchine and Bruhn the West's preeminent male dancer.

But by the time Bruhn and Tallchief arrived in Moscow, Rudolf was en route to the Berlin Festival, a second-tier competition for Soviet bloc countries, together with Kurgapkina and a circus troupe. The trip was to take him through a number of East German towns after Berlin. He protested that it was like being sent into exile, so Sergeyev tried to give the assignment a positive spin. Didn't he know? Ulanova was sick

---

*The six-week tour included stops in Moscow, Leningrad, Tiflis and Kiev.

and he was to dance in her place. "Not exile, Rudi, but a very special honor!"

Before leaving, Rudolf asked a Moscow acquaintance, the only person he knew with a movie camera, to film Bruhn's performances in Moscow. New publicity photos showed that Nureyev now wore his hair loosely with a fringe of bangs, highly unusual for the time. Across the head shot he gave to Tamara, he scrawled: "Hope that the tour of American Ballet Theatre in my absence will entertain you or perhaps produce a great impression."

Rudolf's own tour was everything he had dreaded: The weather was icy, the stages were dilapidated, the audiences indifferent. Though he and Kurgapkina had been promised every evening performance, they quickly learned that they were just one of several traveling "sideshows," as Kurgapkina recalled them. They danced in cafés and run-down theaters and once, when their bus broke down, they had to wait for eight hours in the cold while it was repaired. Rudolf would later tell friends that he first considered defecting while in Germany. Still, he took advantage of being paid a per diem in East German marks and bought his first musical instrument, a Rosewood piano, which he shipped to Leningrad. He also bought clothing and a little wagon for the baby his sister Lilya was expecting.

In East Berlin, he discovered other pleasures. "I met a very gentle boy in the school there, good-looking too," he recalled many years later during a weekend visit to West Berlin with choreographer Rudi van Dantzig. "He took me around the city and showed me many interesting things. I was very grateful, and also impressed. For me Germany was already more or less the West, even if it was the East part. At the end, we kissed, but I don't remember who took the initiative." Rudolf paused before throwing van Dantzig one more tantalizing tidbit: "By the way, you know that boy from East Germany very well. He is a teacher in your company now." There were also rumors, fueled by Kurgapkina, that she and Rudolf became lovers during the trip. "He's a real man," she boasted to several Kirov colleagues upon their return.*

Rudolf, meanwhile, returned home to find Erik Bruhn the talk of Leningrad. Not only had he missed seeing Bruhn dance, Bruhn had supplanted him in his absence. Even Tamara, his staunchest fan, couldn't stop talking about him. Bruhn had an "amazing" grande pirouette en l'air,† she told Rudolf, with a sweep and finish she had never

---

*Today Kurgapkina denies that they were ever lovers. "He was just very attentive. We were friends in the full sense of this word."

†The grande pirouette is a turn performed on one leg with the free leg raised at a ninety-degree angle to the floor.

seen. (On one measure of music, he spun out three pirouettes in quick succession, not just one, as Rudolf was accustomed to doing.) "Perhaps you shouldn't go to the theater until Bruhn comes again," Rudolf replied. And yet he paid close attention to everything he heard. In rehearsals over the next few weeks for *Corsaire* and *Raymonda* (as one of the four men in the pas de quatre), he reworked his grande pirouette for hours on end, trying to imitate Bruhn's. "No one else at the Kirov was preoccupied with Bruhn," recalls a Leningrad balletomane. He was hurt by Tamara's comment, yet kept returning to it, hungry for clues to Bruhn's talent. Not long afterward, he saw an amateur film clip of Bruhn in *Theme and Variations* that someone in Leningrad had filmed, without music.* In those few seconds of footage, Rudolf saw the dancer he hoped to become. "It was a sensation for me," he said years later. "He is the only dancer who could impress me out of my wits. When I got back to Moscow, he had been dancing there and one of the young dancers said he was too cool. Cool, yes — so cool that it burns."

Still more vexing news awaited him on his return. At his behest, Tamara had gone to see his sister Rosa about giving up his room on Ordinarnaya Street in exchange for two smaller rooms. As much as he preferred to live with the Pushkins, he found Xenia overbearing and wanted a place of his own. But he and Rosa quarreled frequently; though he felt responsible for his sister and helped her financially, he wanted to have little contact with her. So he sent Tamara to deal with her. Rosa, however, "threw a fit and screamed so loud that Sizova's parents ran into the room because they thought that she was trying to kill me," Tamara recalls. "Rudik only has rights to the room on paper, but I am the actual owner," Rosa told her. "I live here and there will be no exchange, especially since I am expecting a baby in the spring."

Rudolf "flushed crimson" when Tamara broke the news, but didn't say a word. "He never showed his feelings," she says, "but I could see he was shocked." Alla Sizova assumed that the father of Rosa's child was someone she had met during her holiday on the Black Sea, while Inna Guskova, an Ufa neighbor living in Leningrad, thought he was "a painter with a long name" whom Rosa hoped to marry. Rudolf worried about how his parents would greet the shameful news and begged Guskova not to tell anybody in Ufa that she was pregnant. Their reaction can only be guessed at. "It's better not to discuss it," is all his sister Razida would say on the subject.

In January 1961, just three months after his trip to East Germany, Rudolf was dispatched on yet another bone-chilling tour, this one to Ioshkar-Ola, six hundred miles east of Leningrad. When he complained

---

*In some accounts, Nureyev recalled seeing the clip in Leningrad; in others, he recalled seeing it during his visit to Berlin.

about spending a whole day and night on a train, Sergeyev promised to speak to Gosconcert, the state impresario, about transporting him by plane. But when Rudolf arrived in Moscow, no plane had been arranged. He already suspected that Sergeyev resented his youth and success and this latest injustice convinced him that Sergeyev meant to humiliate him. But in fairness to Sergeyev,* it couldn't have been easy retiring from the stage to watch young stars like Nureyev replace him as his wife's partner.

It took just one performance on a rickety stage in Ioshkar-Ola to send Rudolf rushing back to Moscow. The moment he arrived, he was summoned to the Ministry of Culture. For having left the tour early and without permission he was to be punished, an official informed him. He would never be sent on another foreign tour. This was particularly distressing, for a Kirov tour to Paris and London was then in the works, and Rudolf desperately wanted to go. And this time he had no one to whom he could appeal.

But at least he had a new role to distract him: the male lead in *Legend of Love*, a new ballet by Yuri Grigorovich. *The Stone Flower* (1957), Grigorovich's first ballet for the Kirov, had proven an enormous popular success† and was one of Rudolf's favorite ballets, though he had never danced it. Grigorovich would later win international recognition as the chief choreographer and artistic director of the Bolshoi, a post he would hold until 1995.

Legend of Love was equal parts fairy tale and political morality tale: A Persian queen sacrifices her beauty to save the life of her sick sister, only to fall in love with her sister's lover, Ferhad, while the handsome young lover saves a village from drought. As Ferhad, Rudolf was intoxicated to be originating a major role. To have a ballet created around your talents is every dancer's wish, and Rudolf relished the hours spent in creative ferment, incorporating images from Persian miniatures and exploring Grigorovich's complex movement combinations. (And Grigorovich was said to be delighted when Rudolf came up with his own ideas.)

A few weeks before the premiere, however, Rudolf was called to a dress rehearsal on the Kirov stage that overlapped with a *Laurencia* rehearsal with Alla Shelest at the Ballet School. When the dress rehearsal dragged on past its allotted time, Rudolf began packing his bag. His

---

*Sergeyev had assumed the reins at the Kirov following the sudden death of Boris Fenster in December. The forty-six-year-old Fenster had suffered a heart attack at the Kirov Theater during the premiere of his new ballet.

†*The Stone Flower* was created at the Kirov while Fedor Lopukhov, Balanchine's mentor, was artistic director. Lopukhov, one of Grigorovich's role models (the other being Fokine), was widely considered Soviet ballet's most innovative choreographer—until his works were banned from the Kirov repertory in the 1930s.

Laurencia was days away and he figured Grigorovich would have to accommodate this scheduling problem. But Grigorovich was not about to let his leading man leave what he considered an essential rehearsal. "I am going to rehearse the *real thing*, not this shit," Rudolf shot back. Infuriated, Grigorovich issued an ultimatum: "If you walk out the door, don't bother coming back." Rudolf slammed the door behind him by way of an answer, leaving his colleagues, once more, in stunned silence.

Grigorovich made good on his promise and, after that, scheduled no more rehearsals for Rudolf, who privately knew that he'd shot himself in the foot. He hadn't wanted to lose face in front of Grigorovich, and here he had squandered the rare opportunity to perform in the new ballet, his ballet. "Replacing him became an emergency," says Irina Kolpakova, who danced the role of Ferhad's beloved.*

Rudolf assumed that he might be refused other performances as well. But a short time later, Sergeyev suddenly informed him that he was giving him back-to-back major debuts in the Kirov's two signature works: Prince Désiré† in *The Sleeping Beauty* and Prince Siegfried in *Swan Lake*. That night, he was beaming when he slipped into his seat at the Philharmonic as the overture began. "Two to zero in our favor," he whispered to Tamara.

Sergeyev's reward to Rudolf was intended as a reproach to Grigorovich. As a choreographer himself, Sergeyev envied Grigorovich's growing renown. Since he could do little to impede his trajectory, he hoped at the very least to upstage him. Rudolf's dismissal from *Legend of Love* gave him his opportunity. (It's also possible he had meant for Rudolf's rehearsals to overlap.) He wanted to show Grigorovich "that he was an idiot for kicking Rudik out of his ballet," explains Tamara.

Adding to this already complicated drama was the fact that Sergeyev's wife, Natalia Dudinskaya, had had a long-standing rivalry with Grigorovich's ex-wife, Alla Shelest, the ballerina Rudolf was supposed to have partnered in *Laurencia*. Shelest had been helping out with the staging of *Legend* at the same time that she was rehearsing with Rudolf for *Laurencia*. Whether Dudinskaya resented Shelest's appearance with Rudolf in *Laurencia* is not known, though she was not above using her authority to make Shelest's life difficult.

Sergeyev scheduled Rudolf's debut in *The Sleeping Beauty* eleven days before the premiere of *Legend of Love*, which suggests that he hoped to steal some of Grigorovich's thunder. (*Swan Lake* followed the next month.) Despite such impressive assignments, Rudolf was deeply disappointed that he didn't dance *Legend* and claimed to never fully under-

---

*"Grigorovich used another boy who couldn't compare to Rudik, but Grigorovich refused to give in," says Kolpakova.

†Known as Prince Florimund in most Western productions of the ballet.

stand why he was dismissed from the ballet. Curiously, he was unwilling or unable to see that a simple apology might have won him his role back. Instead, he blamed his ouster on others. He later surmised that Grigorovich might have been displeased that he was dancing with his ex-wife, Shelest. "I don't know whether someone planned to put us together a lot with this in mind," he later told critic John Percival, "but somehow if it was a plot it worked."* The backstage intrigue kept Rudolf perpetually off-balance, as it did most of the Kirov dancers.† Everywhere he turned, there was something to feed his ever-growing belief in conspiracies against him.

As a result, when the Kirov's Paris and London tour was announced for the coming spring, Rudolf wasn't surprised when he didn't find his name on the list. But then, even those approved for the trip knew that nothing was certain. Passports could be whisked out of your hand on your way to the plane, and you'd never know the reason.

Tours to the West were as long in the making as new ballets, and as carefully choreographed: There were security checks to be run, personnel records to review, character references to gather. Each application required the signatures of the Kirov's artistic director, personnel director and union chief. Once approved, it was sent to the Leningrad Committee and then on to Moscow to the Central Committee's Commission on Traveling Abroad. During the pretour "political" dress rehearsals, the rules were hammered home: Stay together at all times, never go anywhere with strangers, go out only in pairs, exercise vigilance. Report any incidents at once.

Then, a month before the troupe was to leave, Rudolf learned that his name had been added to the roster. At the last moment, the Kirov's Paris impresario had asked for the newest generation of talent, not senior statesmen like Sergeyev, Dudinskaya and Shelest. Sergeyev and Dudinskaya, who had expected to open the tour, were now to come along only as artistic advisers and Shelest not at all. Sergeyev was to appoint a soloist in his place. He selected the twenty-three-year-old Nureyev. "It couldn't have been an easy choice to have to make," Rudolf later acknowledged.

The fact that the theater approved him for the tour is one of the

---

*Shelest insists that Rudolf was offered a performance of *Legend* following the premiere, but turned it down after his request that she dance the role of the Queen was denied.

†Rudolf's longtime partner Alla Sizova also had troubles during the making of *Legend of Love*. Sizova was in the C cast (third cast) of the ballet, and recalls that Sergeyev arranged her scheduling so that she couldn't get to her *Legend* rehearsals after she'd already rehearsed the first two acts. Her problems stemmed from the fact that she was assigned to replace the aging Dudinskaya in *Sleeping Beauty*. "Sergeyev did everything so I wouldn't rehearse *Sleeping Beauty*," she says. "He put me through such collisions that I danced neither *Sleeping Beauty* nor *Legend*. One day Grigorovich came up to me and asked if I wanted to dance or not. I answered that of course I did. I had dreamt of it."

anomalies in his story. He had already proven himself highly independent and rebellious and the last thing the authorities needed was a troublemaker who might embarrass them abroad. But what they needed most
of all was to demonstrate Soviet supremacy, and who better to cast in
the role of cultural foot soldier than Nureyev, the ascendant star of the
new generation? The Bolshoi had already triumphed in London and
America, and now the Kirov would prove that Russia was ballet's world
capital. In the wake of hostilities in the Bay of Pigs in May, the Soviets
wanted to marshal their strongest forces for the Kirov's debut on the other
side of the Iron Curtain. With KGB deputies assigned to watch Nureyev
day and night, the advantages of sending him, at least as far as the Kirov's
directors were concerned, finally overrode the objections.

Rudolf worked furiously under Pushkin's guidance to ready himself
for Paris, the first stop on the tour. At the same time, he was sensitive to
the pain Alla Shelest felt at being unceremoniously dropped from such
a historic tour at the close of her career. One day while coaching Rudolf
and Alla Sizova for Paris, Shelest broke down and Rudolf comforted her.
With people scheming to secure a seat on the plane, his show of empathy
came as something of a shock. "He understood everything," she said,
"despite the great age difference between us." When he invited her home
with him to the Pushkins' apartment, she protested, but he insisted. "We
hardly talked on the way, but all the time I felt warmly his sympathy for
me. This doesn't happen very often in the theatre and it is remembered
for a long time. . . ."

Rudolf worried "up to the last minute" that he would be dropped
from the tour himself.* But on May 11, 1961, he donned his black beret,
shirt, tie and dark narrow suit and took a taxi to Pulkovo Airport with
the Pushkins. Tamara arrived just as Rudolf was heading toward customs.
Moments later, Rosa suddenly showed up with her month-old infant
daughter, Gouzel. "Why did you come here?" Rudolf barked at his sister,
embarrassed that she should have traveled to the airport with her baby.
"Go home immediately." Rosa left without protest.

Finally, his flight was announced. Pushkin and Xenia embraced
him and wished him luck, while Tamara managed to accompany him
through customs. When she came outside to watch him board the plane,
the Pushkins gestured to her to join them at the fence. The three of
them stood waiting for one last glimpse of Rudolf; Xenia spotted him.
"Rudik!" she called out. Rudolf turned, waved, and disappeared into the
plane.

*Before leaving, he visited his parents in Ufa. By then they had moved into their new flat
and Lilya had recently given birth to a girl she named Alfia. Rudolf gave Alfia the wagon and
clothes he had purchased in Germany. The wagon, Alfia recalled years afterward, was the
wonder of the neighborhood.

10

Coup de Théâtre

GREAT FANFARE greeted the Kirov's debut Paris season, just as it had the year Diaghilev brought the first group of Russian dancers west in 1909. That landmark season had introduced Nijinsky, Pavlova and other Maryinsky stars to Parisian audiences and created the vogue for Russian ballet for many years to come. "For so long, more than a century, France had nourished the ballet in Russia with her choreographers and ballerinas," wrote Nijinsky's sister, Bronislava. "Suddenly now, we the Russians wanted to astonish the public of Paris with the Russian ballet." That they did, and for the next two decades, the Ballets Russes proved a major influence on European culture.*

Now, half a century later, their Soviet successors likewise hoped to "astonish" the Parisian public. While the Bolshoi's London debut in 1956 had been a historic success, the Kirov was widely considered its artistic superior and *le tout* Paris eagerly awaited its first look at this new generation of Soviet dancers. But where the dancers of the Diaghilev seasons had moved freely among the city's social, intellectual and artistic circles, the Soviet dancers were kept at a safe remove. No sooner had they touched down at Le Bourget Airport than they were whisked off by charter bus to the Hôtel Moderne, a charmless hotel in the Place de la

---

*"A Diaghilev premiere in Paris was always an event of electric excitement," Balanchine biographer Bernard Taper has written. "There was in the air the feeling, possibly snobbish but with more justification than most snobberies, that *everybody* who mattered was seated in that audience—the *haut monde*, the artists, the intellectuals. With tense anticipation they awaited the curtain's rise, wondering what new discoveries Diaghilev was going to reveal; what new trends in art and fashions in style were about to be set; what new reputations would be made; what scandals perpetrated."

République, one of the least fashionable quarters in Paris. For the rest of the tour, they would rehearse together, eat together, visit the sights together, as sequestered as a jury.

Only Nureyev would go his own way.

EACH DAY, the Kirov dancers rehearsed at the Palais Garnier, the neo-baroque theater that was home to the Paris Opéra Ballet.* The French dancers occupied neighboring studios. When a reception in the backstage Foyer de la Danse† finally brought them face to face, the Russians stood on one side of the room while the French stayed firmly on the other. The Paris dancers Claire Motte, Claude Bessy and Pierre Lacotte were huddled together talking when they happened to notice "this Russian who was slowly making his way over to us, like a cat."

"I'm not really allowed to talk to you," Rudolf ventured in halting English, "but I think that's crazy. You're dancers and I would like to know what you think about Kirov company."

Delighted by this unexpected conversation, the French dancers invited Rudolf out with them. "I'm not allowed," he said. "You will have to ask Kirov director for permission." Lacotte put the matter before Sergeyev, while Dudinskaya translated. "Well, the dancers are very tired," Dudinskaya answered. "It's not good for them to go out." When Lacotte assured them that they were simply interested in talking about dance, they relented. "But come back early." As a show of good faith, Rudolf brought along Yuri Soloviev, his roommate on the tour.

The dancers took them to Claude Bessy's apartment near the Opéra for dinner. Soloviev looked uneasy and barely said a word all night, but as Lacotte recalls, "Rudolf talked enough for both of them." In fact, they had only walked a block when Rudolf began criticizing the way the French moved about on the street. "They just rush around as if they don't know where they're going, as if they have no purpose," he told Lacotte. "I thought, 'My, this one is strange,' " Lacotte says. "He had just arrived and already he was commenting on everything."

Over dinner, Rudolf grilled the French dancers about technique and repertory, ever eager to fill in the gaps of his knowledge. Motte, twenty, was a young Opéra étoile and Lacotte, twenty-three, a dancer and fledgling choreographer. Rudolf was delighted to learn that Lacotte knew *Le Spectre de la Rose*, Fokine's celebrated one-act ballet for Nijinsky and Karsavina, and made him promise to teach it to him during his stay in Paris.‡ Although Fokine had worked at the Maryinsky Theater,

---

*Built on the orders of Napoleon III, the Palais Garnier was designed by Charles Garnier.
†The historic Foyer de la Danse was the setting for many of Degas's paintings of the ballet.
‡Made in 1911 and set to Weber's *Invitation to the Dance*, *Le Spectre* tells of a young girl

many of his most acclaimed ballets for the Ballets Russes were unknown in his native Russia. The only Fokine ballet Rudolf had danced was *Chopiniana,* which was renamed *Les Sylphides* when it was first presented in Paris in 1909.

Afterward Motte and Lacotte drove Rudolf and Soloviev back to their hotel. Rudolf didn't want to get out of the car. "It's been such a wonderful evening, do you think we could go somewhere else?" he asked them. The dancers didn't think it was a good idea. They had promised Sergeyev that they would get Rudolf back by 9:30 P.M.

"He looked so sad as he got out of the car," says Lacotte. As a memento, they had given him a box of chocolates, which he now handed back to Motte through the car window. "I don't want to take these now," he explained. "I'll just take one chocolate and each time I see you, I'll take another."

Lacotte recalls, "That was his way of saying, 'I want to see you again.' We were very touched by that." The trio made plans to rendez-vous the following night at nine-thirty on a side street outside the hotel. "Do you think we should ask permission?" Lacotte asked Claire Motte as they drove away. "Why should we?" she said. "He's an adult and we're not doing anything wrong."

The next night, when they pulled up in Motte's Renault, Rudolf was waiting for them. "He looked so depressed," says Lacotte. "We could see that he didn't think we were coming."

In the days that followed, they showed Rudolf their city as he had "dreamed of finding it," he would say of those first walks along the Seine and visits to the Louvre and Montparnasse, once home to the Impressionist painters he so admired. To Rudolf, the streets "had the atmosphere of a perpetual party." And yet, still he harbored his suspicions: "While Paris looked gay and the people on the streets looked interesting and so different from our drab Russian crowds, they also had a hint of decadence, a lack of solid purpose."

Just as he had defied the rules by going to dinner with the cast of *My Fair Lady* in Leningrad, Rudolf now set off regularly with his French *copains*—without permission, and without bringing along any Kirov comrades. He was elated to be in Paris and wasn't about to pass up any opportunities to explore it. He not only visited Motte, Bessy and Lacotte in their apartments, he saw *Ben Hur* at the cinema and *West Side Story* onstage at the Théâtre Alhambra. The jazzy rhythms of Leonard Bernstein's score and the street-smart vigor of Jerome Robbins's dances utterly

intoxicated with the romance of her first ball. Plucking a rose from her bodice, she falls asleep in a chair and dreams that she is dancing with the spirit of the rose. As the rose incarnate, Nijinsky was famous for his climactic leap through the window, which came to symbolize the force of his legendary elevation.

transported him. He marveled at the way Robbins expressed character through dancing. Afterward, he "cha-cha-cha'd in the street like the Jets," says Lacotte, who began teaching him Le Spectre de la Rose in Claire Motte's rented studio near the opera house.

Nureyev's obvious enthusiasm for "decadent" Western culture did not go down well with his superiors. During a meeting at the Russian embassy that first week in Paris, the Kirov dancers hardly needed to be reminded that foreign travel was a "magnificent honor" and one that would come again only if they demonstrated that the trust placed in them was entirely justified.

Rudolf's breach of this "trust" so early on in the tour gave an ambitious KGB captain named Vladimir Dmitrievich Strizhevksi the opening he had been waiting for. Strizhevski's official title was deputy director of the Kirov, though his KGB affiliation was well known to the dancers. Sergeyev was responsible for all artistic matters, Georgi Korkin for administrative concerns and Strizhevski for the troupe's political well-being. The tour was official state business and Strizhevski, a large, brawny man with a round face and perpetual glower, was to keep his eye trained on anyone who threatened its equilibrium. Not that he was the sole KGB agent in Paris: The Russian embassy naturally had its own supply and Rudolf grew accustomed to glimpsing agents in the shadows just about everywhere he went. "Of course they're following me," he would tell his friends, with an air of resignation, "but what can they do to us? They won't kill us. I'm not spoiling my visit by staying in my hotel. I want to do what I want."

And yet, despite his bravado, he was worried enough to try to elude his KGB chaperones. Each night he rode the company bus back to the hotel, hurried to his room, and then sneaked out a back door to a nearby side street, where Claire Motte would be waiting for him in her Renault. But whenever he arrived back at the Hôtel Moderne past the midnight curfew, Strizhevski would be waiting to check him in. "How dare you come in at this hour!" he'd jeer, only to find that his tirade rankled, rather than frightened, Rudolf, who would shoot him a look of indignation as he continued on to his room.

As Rudolf's roommate, Yuri Soloviev wasn't nearly so cavalier when it came to the KGB. Their first outing together had unnerved him, and he now rarely accompanied Rudolf anywhere except the Palais Garnier. According to Lacotte, Rudolf was always reassuring Soloviev and telling him not to worry about him. But Soloviev was worried for both of them. After all, he was the only Kirov dancer who was willing to be Rudolf's roommate. "Yura felt they got along well, so why not?" says Soloviev's wife, Tatiana Legat, who was not along on the Paris tour. "No one else wanted to room with Rudik. They were afraid." What scared them was Nureyev's unpredictability. Fearful that association with him might jeopardize their chances for future foreign travel, the dancers preferred to distance themselves from someone they regarded as a troublemaker. In Paris, their comings and goings were duly noted, not only by the "KaGeBeshniks" as Rudolf called them, but by the dancers-turned-informers whom the KGB had enticed with rewards or threatened with blackmail. Strizhevski's henchmen prowled the hallways and listened through closed doors, serving as constant reminders that they weren't so far from home after all.

THE KIROV was set to open at the Palais Garnier on May 16, 1961, with *The Sleeping Beauty*. Rudolf expected to dance opening night, especially after he scored an enormous success in the *répétition générale*, the pre–opening night dress rehearsal regularly attended by journalists and bal-letomanes.* Word spread quickly that a dancer named Nureyev was somebody to watch out for. (Indeed, even Natalia Dudinskaya came to remark, years afterward, that when Nureyev first danced *Sleeping Beauty* in Paris, "he stunned the audience. He was such a colossal success that they were overwhelmed. He was a showstopper.")

But Sergeyev didn't want Nureyev to grab the spotlight before the Kirov had established a foothold in Paris. He was also jealous of Nure-yev's enormous success in the role *he* was supposed to have danced. He therefore decided to give opening night to Irina Kolpakova and her hus-band, Vladilen Semenov. While an elegant dancer with an exemplary technique, Semenov was not about to set the house on fire.[†]

Rudolf, however, assumed the premiere would be his and was "very annoyed when he learned that they weren't going to give it to him," recalls Alla Osipenko. "And rightly so." Forgoing the premiere altogether, Rudolf went to hear Yehudi Menuhin play Bach at the Salle Pleyel, and took comfort, as he always would, in the music of his favorite composer.

Kolpakova and Semenov drew enthusiastic, if subdued, reviews. But it was not until the fourth night of the season, when Nureyev first took center stage in an excerpt from *La Bayadère*,[‡] that the French woke up to the explosive strength of the Kirov's male ranks. *La Bayadère* had never been staged in the West. The haunting beauty of the Kingdom of the Shades scene, compounded by Rudolf's exoticism as the warrior Solor, held the Parisians in thrall. Solor dreams of his dead beloved, the *bay-*

---

*Nureyev's solo in the grand pas de deux in Act 3, reworked for him by Sergeyev and Pushkin for his Kirov debut in the role, became the standard version of the part after Nureyev's Western debut. The night of the *répétition générale*, Nureyev partnered Xenia Ter-Stepanova.

[†]He had "a neutral personality," Andrew Porter wrote of his Prince in the *Financial Times* that June.

[‡]Olga Moiseyeva danced the role of Nikiya and among the three soloists was Natalia Makarova.

adère Nikiya, and the stage fills with ballerinas, one after the other, each performing the same sequence in unison until twenty-four ballerinas in white tutus have proceeded down a ramp in diagonal lines across the stage, "rank after rank of remote but radiant figures weaving and bending like a field of corn in the moonlight." Solor's bravura solo is another highlight. Prior to the Paris tour, Sergeyev informed Rudolf that he could substitute for it one of his own choosing, so for his Parisian debut, Rudolf performed his *Corsaire* solo, the showstopper that had won him acclaim while still a student.

"The name Nureyev was already in our minds after his performance at the dress rehearsal, but this was the first time most of us saw him," remembers Igor Eisner, who was to become the French government's Inspector General of dance and a close associate of Nureyev's in the 1980s. Eisner's companion that night was Michel Guy, a future Minister of Culture; sitting in a government box in the center of the opera house was the current Minister of Culture, the writer André Malraux. Thirty years and countless performances later, Eisner still recalls his first glimpse of Nureyev aloft. "He was spinning in the air with his hands on his shoulders and his legs folded up under him. There was a great silence, not a peep, not even an 'Ah!' Then, suddenly, the silence was broken by thunderous applause. We were stunned." His "mercurial" dancing drew repeated gasps from the audience, the likes of which one viewer had heard only in the bullring.

Not since Nijinsky conquered the French capital fifty-two years earlier had a male dancer stirred such curiosity and madness. It wouldn't be long before Janet Flanner informed her American readers that French balletomanes considered Nureyev "the strangest, and uncontestably the most influential, personality—as well as the greatest technician—since Nijinsky, to whom he is the first ever to be so compared." As Nijinsky had before him, Nureyev not only turned the spotlight on the male dancer, but created for him a whole new image. "Since the Romantic period," Nijinsky biographer Richard Buckle has written, "it had been the woman, the Muse, the diva, the ballerina who had been worshipped: to admire a man for his grace and beauty was unheard-of. . . ." Indeed the terms once reserved for Nijinsky—elusive, pantherine, sexually ambiguous—were now applied to Nureyev himself. More than his exotic beauty and technical prowess, however, it was Nureyev's sexual magnetism and temperament that succeeded in charging the audience, men and women alike. Edgy and unpredictable, he danced with an abandon that imbued his performances with the "chilling excitement of a high-wire act performed without a safety net." And like Nijinsky, he possessed that rare ability to "stir up the subconscious of the audience and feed its hidden hungers." At intermission, recalls Lacotte, "all you heard was 'Nureyev, Nureyev.' "

The next day in *Le Monde*, Olivier Merlin waxed ecstatic over the thrilling turnabout in the Kirov's programming and even ventured that perhaps the Russians had saved the best for the second program. "We will not soon forget his arrival racing from the back of the stage . . . with his large, strange eyes and hollow cheeks beneath the plumed turban . . . this was already the Nijinsky of *L'Oiseau de feu*. . . ."

Equally enchanted, his colleagues rushed their own appraisals into print: In *Le Figaro*, Claude Baignères gave pride of place to "*l'aérien* [the aerialist] Rudolf Noureev," while beneath a photo of the *aérien* in question, *L'Aurore* proclaimed: "*Les Ballets de Leningrad ont leur 'homme de l'espace'* " (The Leningrad Ballet has its own man in space).* Soloviev would also come in for high praise from the French critics, as would Alla Sizova and Natalia Makarova among the younger dancers and Irina Kolpakova, Alla Osipenko and Irina Zubkovskaya among the more seasoned ballerinas. Indeed many agreed that their schooling was equal to, if not better than, that of their predecessors in the Diaghilev troupe. (However, "from the point of view of music, design and chore-ographic invention," as Richard Buckle had noted after the Bolshoi's London visit a few years earlier, "the Russians were back in 1900 — Dia-ghilev might never have lived.") The ranks were rich in talent, full of pristine gems, but Nureyev was the discovery of the season, the Kirov's diamond in the rough, its "jewel in the crown," according to *Le Figaro*. And it was the excitement generated by his performances that made the Kirov the hottest ticket in town.

THE NIGHT OF his debut, Claire Motte introduced him to her good friend Clara Saint. Petite and pretty, with a rounded face and figure, Clara had green, almond-shaped eyes and mahogany hair that fell about her shoulders. The daughter of a wealthy Argentine industrialist and his Chilean wife, she had grown up in Buenos Aires, moved to Paris when she was five, and was then engaged to Vincent Malraux, the son of André Malraux. Worldly at the age of twenty, with a reputation for being "a young, free, rich girl," as Viscountess Jacqueline de Ribes recalls her, Clara counted a number of artists and dancers among her influential coterie of friends.

Watching Rudolf dance that night, she marveled at his "remarkable aura." But on meeting him, she was surprised to discover how shy, in-quisitive and naive he was, though the first things that caught her eye were his blond hair, pale green eyes and the scar over his lip. "A dog bit me when I was a child," he explained when he saw her staring at the

*Among the Kirov dancers themselves, it was "Cosmic Yuri" Soloviev, not Nureyev, who was considered the company cosmonaut.

scar. He was "very beautiful," Clara thought, and in his white shirt, black "French-style" beret and narrow, dark and "strangely cut" Russian suit, he had a style all his own. Pleated trousers were the fashion at the time for men, though Rudolf, she noticed, favored trousers that were especially narrow and tight-fitting.

Rudolf liked Clara at once, falling easily into conversation with her, and the two began spending most of his free time together. In his broken English, he never tired of asking questions, or of answering them when the subject turned to dancing. But about his life, he revealed little. He told Clara only that he was born on a train, and that his family were Muslim Tatars who lived in Ufa. "He was completely obsessed with dance," she recalls. "Nobody knew anything about him, so he was mysterious and intriguing." And despite the sexual charge of his performances, his sexuality remained a mystery. Offstage, remembers Clara, "he didn't have a sexual persona, he was almost sexless." Pierre Lacotte, who was rumored to have had an affair with Nureyev at the time, denies that there is any truth in it. "I had no idea he was homosexual," he says today. "He gave absolutely no indication."

Nureyev would later say that he when he first arrived in the West, he was "amazed by the sexual mores." Like a seasoned courtesan, Paris revealed itself to him slowly and seductively: Each night expanded his sense of the possible. He got his first taste of erotica when Clara and Pierre took him to Crazy Horse, the celebrated nightclub revue on the Champs-Élysées. "He was shocked," recalls Clara. "He couldn't believe all these naked girls. He was laughing so much."

At restaurants, he was startled to discover the range of choices available and how easy it was to order a steak. Even so-called Russian restaurants were a far cry from the ones he knew at home. One night Clara took him to Dominique's, a posh Russian restaurant near Montparnasse popular with the émigré White Russians who had fled to Paris after the Revolution. To Clara's youthful eyes, the clientele seemed "very elegant with white hair." As Clara and Rudolf sat down to dinner at the bar, Clara told Rudolf to go ahead and order in Russian. The waiters were old White Russians, but Rudolf refused to speak to them. Baffled, Clara told him it "didn't make any sense for me to translate from English to French, when you can speak to them directly. Just tell them what you want." Rudolf became furious, but wouldn't explain. Clara assumed he was being willful and only later realized that they didn't speak the same Russian. Pedigreed White Russians could still trigger whatever lingering insecurities Rudolf carried with him from Ufa. "We never discussed it, but I think he understood that though these people were waiters, they were very chic. He was embarrassed because he didn't have the right accent."

Soon after meeting Rudolf, Clara received devastating news: Her fiancé, Vincent, had been killed in a car crash in the south of France. To distract herself from grief, she spent every night at the ballet, finding "consolation" there. At the opera house, she introduced Rudolf to her good friend Raymundo de Larrain, an aristocratic Chilean, who had just taken over the Grand Ballet du Marquis de Cuevas. The Kirov dancers had been to see its new production of *The Sleeping Beauty* and had come away with the impression that Western ballet was inferior to their own in every way. Alla Sizova was not alone in thinking that its dancers "were worse than our amateurs," Serge Golovine, its male star, excepted. To the Kirov dancers, the de Cuevas company was a curiosity, a bonbon. It was privately funded, run according to whim and caprice, dedicated to glamorous novelty and filled with a diversely schooled mix of dancers. In short, it was everything the state-run, tradition-bound, time-honored Kirov was not.

In fact, the de Cuevas troupe owed its existence to the largess of the marquis's wife, Margaret, the favorite granddaughter of oil billionaire John D. Rockefeller, the archetypal Western capitalist. The marquis himself was an inveterate snob who had grown up in Chile dreaming of Proust's Paris. Transplanted to Paris in the 1920s, the penniless George de Cuevas met his future wife while working for Prince Felix Yusupov, the assassin of Rasputin, who was then running a house of couture. Bankrolled by Rockefeller money, de Cuevas lost no time in becoming an impresario on a grand scale: He took over the Nouveau Ballet de Monte Carlo in 1947 and renamed it, having in the meantime acquired a title. He toured with the company in Europe and America and quickly became one of the dance world's most beloved and colorful figures.* His flamboyance was the talk of two continents following the costume ball he gave in Biarritz in 1953 to publicize his ballet troupe, an occasion so extravagant that the Vatican saw fit to criticize it. The ball drew the crème de la crème of international society: Elsa Maxwell came dressed as a man, the Duchess of Argyll came dressed as an angel, Merle Oberon danced in a diamond tiara, and the marquis presided in gold lamé with a headdress of grapes and ostrich plumes.

*Among the Marquis de Cuevas's more colorful escapades was his duel with the dancer and choreographer Serge Lifar in 1958, a bizarre bit of stage business that *The New York Times* reported on its front page. Angry that the de Cuevas company had changed the choreography of one of his ballets, Lifar got into a shouting match with the marquis, who struck him in the face with a handkerchief and then refused to apologize. The irate Lifar challenged de Cuevas to a duel and though neither was an experienced swordsman, de Cuevas accepted. Dueling was outlawed in France, so the location of the duel was to be kept secret. Nevertheless, dozens of reporters and photographers arrived in Cannes at the appointed hour. Each man showed up with his second, and it's worth noting that the marquis's second was Jean-Louis Le Pen. The duel ended when the marquis pinked Lifar's arm. "Blood has flowed! Honor is saved!" Lifar cried, whereupon both men embraced.

The marquis had died shortly before the Kirov arrived in Paris, but had lived long enough to see his company's splashy new production of *The Sleeping Beauty*, its designs modeled on the costume balls of Louis XIV. At his death, his wife, who hated ballet, turned over the reins to Raymundo de Larrain, the company's chief designer, who was also reputed to be the marquis's nephew. The marquis's daughter, however, would emphatically deny that there was ever any blood relation between the two men.*

According to the choreographer John Taras, a former de Cuevas dancer later to become a ballet master at the New York City Ballet, the marquis and de Larrain had once been lovers. "The marquis got taken with him and they became very friendly. So he started making sets and costumes for the company. He was a very talented designer. He slept with a lot of people, a very fashionable crowd."

A tall, wiry man with a sharp, prominent nose, wide, protruding eyes and long, manicured fingers, de Larrain bore a resemblance to Jean Cocteau, whose theatrical élan he also shared. Driven by nervous energy, he had, as his friend Violette Verdy recalls, the odd, distracting habit of darting his head "like a bird" as he spoke. Nevertheless, he was blessed with charm, talent and the knack for enlivening any conversation. He drew people easily into his orbit, among them Viscountess Jacqueline de Ribes, the society beauty who was then his mistress, his booster and, not incidentally, "his stepping-stone into society," according to a friend in her set. "He was very crazy and amusing," says Clara, "and invited by everyone, everywhere."

But since Rudolf was the star of the hour, it was Raymundo who now courted him. His first impression had not been favorable. "He's a mujik," he had told Clara and Pierre after meeting Rudolf. Still, he was curious to know what the exotic young Russian thought of his company and invited him to visit. "You have to behave yourself," Lacotte warned Rudolf beforehand. "Raymundo is a very elegant man." To avoid any embarrassing gaffes, he told Rudolf not to tell Raymundo what he had already told him: that he considered his sets and costumes for the de Cuevas *Sleeping Beauty* garish and overdecorated.

But no sooner had they arrived at de Larrain's apartment at 10 Rue Bonaparte, elegantly appointed with its gray velvet walls, than Rudolf told de Larrain precisely what he thought of his company. De Larrain, in turn, responded with his critique of the Kirov's sets and costumes. Irritated by his remarks, Rudolf grabbed a crystal ornament from a nearby table, stuck it on his head, and announced to the group, "Look! A cos-

---

*Nevertheless, de Larrain continued to describe himself as a de Cuevas nephew, even when he later married his tante Margaret, the marquis's wife, when she was eighty and he was forty-two. But that's another story.

tume by Raymundo de Larrain." This hardly impressed his host, who merely pretended to be amused. "See, I told you," he remarked to Lacotte afterward. "He is not a gentleman."

RUDOLF'S "SECRET" outings had not gone undetected by his fellow dancers. "His fans drove him away in their cars and we had no idea where they were going or what was happening to him," recalls Marina Cherednichenko. "We'd come in at night and our director would say, 'He's not here again.' " Rudolf, however, was not alone in keeping late hours. One night, as Strizhevski was about to berate him for returning at 4 A.M., Dudinskaya and Sergeyev suddenly strolled in after him.

"Why don't you lecture them?" Rudolf demanded. "Why can they come in at four in the morning and I can't?"

Strizhevski eyed him coldly. "It's none of your business."

Unbeknownst to the rest of the company, Strizhevski had already alerted Moscow about Nureyev's misconduct. He had "established close relations with politically suspicious persons," he reported to the KGB, citing in particular "a certain Larrin—theater businessman and ballet master" and "Clara San—a woman of dubious behavior" as well as "other elements from among the artistic bohemia."* Moreover, he had violated the rules, "neglected the interests of the collective, regularly spent time with his French acquaintances and came back to the hotel late at night." He had become, in Strizhevski's opinion, a security risk. While awaiting instructions, he stepped up his vigilance. "Rudik didn't give a damn," recalls the likewise unorthodox Alla Osipenko, a glamorous, plainspoken ballerina whom Rudolf had grown to trust in Paris. "He would show up early in the morning and that was that." Rudolf had never danced with Osipenko in Leningrad, but in Paris, they were paired for several performances of *Swan Lake*. Admired for her long, supple limbs, elegant physique and keen musicality, Osipenko "called to mind an extraordinary tropical flower on a long stem," in the view of one Soviet critic, who admired the sense of mystery her dancing evoked.† Having won the Anna Pavlova Prize on her last trip to Paris in 1956, Osipenko had already established a Western following prior to the Kirov's Paris visit. Along with Irina Kolpakova, she was fast becoming the female star of the current tour.

Osipenko paid little mind to the complaints about Nureyev. She

---

*The fact that Strizhevski got names wrong—Clara Saint as Clara San—was fairly typical of KGB reports from abroad, which were frequently poor and lacking in sophistication.

†A favorite pupil of Agrippina Vaganova's at the Leningrad School, she had joined the Kirov corps de ballet in 1950.

remembered how the others had made so much out of his missing the train in Kiev when he had simply gone off to visit its cathedral. She also knew that while most of the dancers were spending their francs on scarves, perfumes and other trinkets to sell back home, Rudolf was investing in wigs, ballet slippers and costumes: the tools of his trade. After rehearsal one day, Rudolf had asked Simon Virsaladze, the Kirov's chief designer, to accompany him to a fabric store to help select the right shade of Lycra for his costume in *Legend of Love*. He still hoped to perform the role Grigorovich had made on him. Since Lycra wasn't available at home, he wanted Virsaladze to advise him about color.

"He's a very strange man," Virsaladze remarked to Osipenko after the excursion. "He might have a temper and maybe he doesn't know how to behave himself, but he's the first dancer in my experience who ever asked me to go with him to buy fabrics for costumes. Can you believe what he said? 'I dream of dancing *Legend* and I want my costume to be the best.' Everybody says that Rudik is a boor. But look what he is indeed."

With Clara, he also visited Galignani, the bookstore on the Rue de Rivoli that he first assumed was a library when Clara took him there. "You can *buy* the books here?" he asked Clara in disbelief as he leafed through volumes on Goya, Manet, Picasso and, much to her surprise, discussed each painter knowledgeably. He spent his remaining francs — the dancers were paid the equivalent of ten dollars per performance — in Le Nain Bleu (The Blue Dwarf), the chic toy shop on the Rue St.-Honoré. There Rudolf played with the most expensive electric train set in the store before finally buying it. Soloviev was as delighted with the purchase as Rudolf was; the two of them stayed awake most of the night watching the train go up, down and across the toy track they had laid out across the floor of their room.

ON YET ANOTHER evening, shouts were heard coming from their room. In class the next morning, Soloviev and Nureyev were the focus of gossip. One story had it that Soloviev had shoved Rudolf into the hallway after some undisclosed dispute. Someone else insisted that Nureyev and Soloviev had been giving each other massages when Nureyev made a pass at Soloviev, who in a fit of anger threw him out. But just who had actually heard or witnessed the fight, no one was saying. Alla Osipenko recalls that while there had never been any rumors about Nureyev's being homosexual — indeed, those who had given his sex life any thought at all assumed he and Kurgapkina had once been lovers — some of her colleagues now jumped to the conclusion that Rudolf had made overtures to Soloviev. As far as Osipenko could determine, "all anyone had seen was Rudik flying out of the room," and though she didn't make much of the incident and never discussed it with Soloviev, she found it "strange to think about Rudolf being a homosexual, especially after the rumors about him and Nelia [Kurgapkina]. But the theater is the theater. You can give a tiny reason or no reason at all and they will say that you are homosexual."

The fact and fiction of Soloviev's actions in Paris will likely never be disentangled, but one thing is certain: Whatever happened was not significant enough to set Nureyev's recall to Moscow in motion. The former Central Archive of the Communist Party contains many documents about Nureyev's defection and nowhere is any incident with Soloviev mentioned. What these top secret documents do reveal, however, is that early on in the tour and well before the alleged incident with Soloviev took place, the Soviets had already decided to send Nureyev back to Russia. While it has always been presumed that the decision to send Nureyev home came swiftly, and at the end of the Paris tour on June 16, these Soviet files confirm that the Soviets had actually ordered Nureyev home thirteen days before the Kirov was scheduled to leave Paris for London. Had the orders been carried out promptly, Nureyev would have disappeared from Paris quietly and, in all likelihood, never have set foot in the West again. But competing interests among Soviet agencies led the authorities to delay Nureyev's departure from Paris, with lasting consequences. The delay not only allowed Nureyev to strengthen new friendships that would soon prove invaluable, but also changed the course of his life, and with it, the course of dance history and East-West relations.

Nureyev himself would never know how early the plans to send him home had been set in motion. Nor would he know that Sergeyev, who he always assumed was the Rasputin behind the plot, had actually tried to block it for as long as he could.* Sergeyev may have sorely envied Nureyev's Parisian success, but he saw how much he stood to gain by it, however reflected the glory.

IT WAS Strizhevski and the KGB's embassy *rezidents* in Paris who first proposed sending Nureyev home from the tour. On June 1, they sent word to Moscow that Nureyev's behavior had become intolerable and was putting the Kirov's security at risk. In response, the Central Committee of the Communist Party quickly called an emergency meeting of the Commission on Traveling Abroad to which Leningrad's party boss was hastily summoned. On June 3, just two days later, the Central Committee dispatched orders for Nureyev's immediate recall. All precautionary measures were to be observed.

The orders threw Sergeyev, Korkin and the Soviet ambassador into

*"Sergeyev had enough power to pull strings all the way from Moscow, and for what?" Nureyev remarked in a 1981 interview. "Because he was jealous."

a terrible quandary. The Kirov had just transferred from the Palais Garnier into the larger Palais des Sports two days earlier, and Nureyev was the male dancer everybody was coming to see. In fact, they'd given him the opening night performance of Swan Lake at the Palais des Sports, even though he was new to the role of Prince Siegfried, having danced it just twice before.* What's more, that week he had been awarded the prestigious Nijinsky Prize. Nureyev was winning favor for the Soviet regime and making all of them look good in the process. He was the star of the tour. How would they explain his sudden disappearance? As far as they were concerned, the KGB were philistines who understood nothing of cultural exchange. Khrushchev was championing internationalism and here they were demonstrating the supreme accomplishment of Soviet culture.

Sergeyev and Korkin decided to stall for time. Nureyev had been cooperative, they reasoned, and they could probably rein him in on their own. Hadn't he dutifully joined a Kirov contingent for interviews and photos at the offices of L'Humanité, the popular French Communist newspaper? In fact, on that very day, Nureyev's picture was on the front page of L'Humanité. He was shown clustered in a group with Sergeyev, Korkin, Irina Kolpakova, Olga Moiseyeva, Alla Osipenko and the French dancer Michel Renault. Inside was a second photo of Nureyev, Kolpakova, Moiseyeva and Sergeyev, an interview entitled "Variations entre danseurs sur le thème de l'amitié" (Variations Between Dancers on the Theme of Friendship) and on the same page, a rave review of the company's opening night performance of Swan Lake starring Nureyev and Moiseyeva.

Ignoring the communiqué, Korkin instead issued Rudolf a stern warning against spending any more time with Clara, a remarkable decision in light of mounting Cold War tensions: Khrushchev and Kennedy were due to meet in Vienna the next month for the first time since the aborted Bay of Pigs invasion in April.

Rudolf took great umbrage at this attack on Clara and at Korkin's censorial tone, not realizing that Korkin was buying him time in Paris. "They have forbidden me to see you," he told Clara and Lacotte. "Well, I'm not going to pay them any attention. I'm not sitting in my room." The official warnings unnerved Lacotte, who thought Rudolf was "playing with fire." Rudolf, however, was more irritated than frightened by the company's attempt to restrain him, though he never once suggested to his French friends that he wanted to stay in the West. On the contrary, he repeatedly implored them to visit him in Leningrad and exacted promises that they would come soon.

---

*Rudolf made his debut as Prince Siegfried on April 1, 1961, opposite Ninel Kurgapkina. He performed the role again on April 16, 1961, with Irina Zubkovskaya. Swan Lake was the last full-length ballet he danced on the Kirov stage before leaving for Paris.

While it may have appeared to others that he was taking undue artistic license as well, Rudolf was simply continuing to do what he had always done: setting his own personal standards, regardless of the circumstances. During a performance of *La Bayadère*, he slipped at the beginning of his variation and promptly exited stage right, leaving the conductor in mid-note, the dancers in mid-step and his colleagues and the audience baffled. "He was furious that the conductor was playing the wrong tempo," recalls Lacotte, who earlier in the week had reprimanded Rudolf after he had taken off his slippers and made threatening gestures at the conductor with them during a rehearsal. "After a few minutes he came back and nodded to the conductor as if to say, 'Now you may continue.' I was thinking, 'if he doesn't dance well, this is going to be a disaster.'" Afterward Rudolf triumphantly announced to Lacotte: "You say I shouldn't talk to the conductor the way I do, but you see, he had to stop. He had to listen to me. I do what I want."*

He also continued to do as he pleased offstage. He went home with Clara to her mother's house on the Quai d'Orsay and had supper in their kitchen, even though he was strictly forbidden to visit private homes. He made lunchtime visits to the Louvre with Michael Wishart, an English painter with the kind of bohemian past—male and female lovers, friendships with Jean Cocteau and painter Francis Bacon, bouts with opium and alcohol addiction—likely to strike terror in the heart of an apparatchik. Wishart had been eager to meet Rudolf and, after leaving a note for him backstage, was delighted to find him standing at the stage door one afternoon. They were shadowed by agents, but Rudolf didn't seem fazed. "Don't worry," he told Wishart. "I can handle it." Though no stranger to the uniquely talented, Wishart had been so "haunted" by Rudolf's performance in *La Bayadère* that he had promptly sent a note to his friend Colette Clark urging her not to miss Nureyev when he got to London. Clark, the daughter of art historian Kenneth Clark, was a close friend of Margot Fonteyn's.

On June 6, Nureyev was recalled by Moscow a second time. Convinced of Nureyev's value to the tour, Sergeyev and Korkin advised the Soviet embassy that Nureyev's behavior had indeed improved. It was "impossible" to continue the tour without him, Sergeyev warned the ambassador, who was likewise basking in the success of the Kirov's Parisian debut. Taking them at their word, he notified Moscow on June 8 that there was no longer any need to send Nureyev home.

The next day, June 9, Rudolf called Tamara in Leningrad. He was thrilled that he had won the Nijinsky Prize, he told her, though he

---

*In the West, dancers were taught to follow the conductor's baton, while in Russia, dancers were permitted to dictate the tempo they wanted. Even so, they never left the stage mid-act if displeased with the arrangement.

couldn't wait to leave Paris because the audience "was a bunch of idiots." He was looking forward to dancing in London before an audience of "real connoisseurs." Tamara, in turn, told him how much *she* was looking forward to the Royal Ballet's Russian debut the next week at the Kirov Theater. She had a ticket for every performance. Rudolf was sorry to miss seeing Margot Fonteyn and the other English stars he had read about in *Dance Magazine.* Tamara promised to give him a full report on his return.

Despite the calm front they presented to Moscow, Korkin and Sergeyev had begun taking added measures to keep Nureyev in check. Sergeyev now ordered Rudolf to avoid his French friends. It was the strength of the collective that enriched the individual, he reminded Rudolf; the individual on his own would come to nothing. As if to prove his point, a curious note in the Kirov's publicity packet reminded critics that although he was "a great dancer with a brilliant future," Nureyev "still needed discipline." None of them knew just quite what that meant.

On June 14, two days before the Kirov was scheduled to depart for London, Moscow sent its third directive ordering Nureyev home. At the same time that Korkin and Sergeyev had been playing up his success, Strizhevski and the embassy agents had been criticizing his conduct in their daily reports to Moscow.* The two camps were working at cross purposes, each battling to win favor with the party brass back home: Where the Kirov's directors were riding high on the Kirov's success and cared only about the company's artistic profile abroad, Strizhevski and the embassy agents cared only about keeping the Soviet dancers in line. Nureyev the crowd pleaser may have brought glory to the Soviet name and shown Sergeyev and Korkin to great advantage, but Nureyev the brazen young man made the Soviet security force look particularly inept. With little regard for Nureyev's significance to the tour, Strizhevski and the embassy agents sounded the alarm and convinced Moscow that security measures had been compromised.

Confronted with a third directive from Moscow, the Kirov's directors had no choice but to comply. They had stuck their necks out as far as they dared. The Bolshoi had always enjoyed much greater favor with Soviet officials and they were nervous that Nureyev's recall might jeopardize the Kirov's standing in Moscow. However, since Rudolf was scheduled to partner Alla Osipenko in *Swan Lake* on the next and final night of the season, it was decided that he would be sent home on June 16, the day the company was set to fly to London. The plan called for Nureyev to be kept in the dark until the last possible moment prior to

---

*The ambassador reported to the Foreign Ministry, while the KGB residents in Paris sent their reports directly to KGB Central in Moscow. According to Arkady Shevchenko, a former high-ranking Soviet official who defected to the West in the 1980s, when the KGB sent information to Moscow, "it never identifie[d] the name of the person who procured it."

boarding. Strizhevski was personally assigned to escort his quarry back to Moscow.

"Look what a marvelous success we had!" Rudolf boasted to Sergeyev the next evening as he and Osipenko came offstage to the sound of screams and bravos. "There's nothing to be surprised about," Sergeyev replied dismissively, much to Osipenko's chagrin. "The audience is always like that."

But to *Le Monde* critic Olivier Merlin, there was nothing matter-of-fact about their performance. It was "the most marvelous interpretation of *Swan Lake* that I have ever seen," he wrote, noting that the names Osipenko and Nureyev "are already joined with those of Karsavina and Nijinsky in the firmament of the sylphs."

That night, as Nureyev and Osipenko were leaving the Palais des Sports, tailed by Strizhevski, a group of fans stood waiting to invite them out for a farewell supper.

"Absolutely not," Strizhevski snapped when they looked to him for permission. "Tomorrow you're flying to London. No one is allowed to go anywhere tonight."

At this, the fans began chanting, "Let Osipenko and Nureyev go with us! Let them go! Let them go!"

Emboldened by the cries of the fans and her glowing reviews, Osipenko played her trump card. "Vladimir Dmitrievich, it's a scandal, just a scandal," she said.

The fans were gaining momentum and there was no telling what they might do if Nureyev and Osipenko were ordered back to the hotel. Bad press on the eve of the London tour would reflect unfavorably on Strizhevski. Hoping to avert a scandal at all costs, he relented. Nureyev would be his soon enough.

"Okay, you can go," he said, directing his comments to Osipenko. "But just remember, you're responsible if he doesn't return on time."

Intoxicated by the heady turn of events, Alla and Rudolf decided to call Leningrad as soon as they arrived at the café, where they were taken by a contingent that included Clara and Pierre Lacotte. (Claire Motte had left for Spain on tour with the Paris Opéra.) As Alla headed for the phone to call her mother, Rudolf stopped her. "Alla, please pass on a message to Alexander Ivanovich [Pushkin] that our performance went off brilliantly." When Alla cautioned him that perhaps she should tone down the message, Rudolf stood firm. "No, tell him that it was brilliant." He was bursting with pride, she thought. Not only had they been given the closing *Swan Lake* of the Paris season, they were also to dance the first *Swan Lake* in London.

It was nearly 3 A.M. before anyone in their lively party made a move to go home. It was by now Alla's birthday and she realized that Natasha Makarova was probably still waiting up for her, with the bottle of vodka they'd been saving for the occasion. With Strizhevski's warning ringing in her ears, she jokingly asked Rudolf: "Are you going home to bed?" But Rudolf told her he and Clara were planning to take a long walk. They parted in laughter, well aware that neither of them had any intention of turning in early.

Excited though he was about dancing in London, Rudolf had grown melancholy about leaving Paris. He didn't want to go straight back to the hotel, he told Clara, who accompanied him on a long stroll along the quays of the Right Bank. "He kept saying how beautiful Paris was and how sad he was because it was probably the last time he would see it."

By the time they reached the Hôtel Moderne, the familiar blue bus was already parked in front and the nearby cafés were slowly coming to life. Trying to cheer them both before departing, Clara reminded Rudolf that she, Pierre and Claire were coming to London in a few days to see him. "Yes," Rudolf replied, "but it's not going to be the same, because Paris is really magic."

The phone was ringing when Rudolf got back to his room. "Should I come to the airport to see you off?" Pierre Lacotte offered. "If you want," Rudolf answered, "but I don't know if I'll be able to talk to you." He had barely enough time to pack before it was time to board the bus for the thirty-minute ride to Le Bourget, a small airport on the southern outskirts of Paris. En route, Gruzinski, the company manager, began distributing the plane tickets to London, an unusual practice given that the dancers never looked after their own tickets, though Rudolf paid it little mind at that moment. However, when Gruzinski inexplicably asked for the tickets back the moment the dancers had begun passing through customs, Rudolf sensed immediately that this was no mere mix-up, and that somehow he was involved, though in what way, he didn't know. He handed over his ticket reluctantly, highly attuned to the briefest exchange of glances.

But as he surveyed the departure lounge, he couldn't get a reading. Sergeyev and Dudinskaya were having a coffee at the bar. The dancers were milling about, waiting to board the 11:30 A.M. BEA flight to London. Strizhevski, Gruzinski and Korkin stood at the door, handing the dancers their tickets once again, and sending them out to the plane, one by one. Their luggage, his included, was already being loaded onto the plane. As far as Rudolf could determine, nothing was amiss.

A group of fans, Opéra dancers and journalists had gathered at the airport to see the Kirov off. Spying Lacotte and his friend Jean-Pierre Bonnefous among them, Rudolf joined them. He had hoped to bring Clara, Pierre told him, but she said she was too tired to come. Just then, Sergeyev and Dudinskaya approached Lacotte and inquired if he was going to see the company in London. "Of course. I want to see Rudolf in *Giselle*," said Lacotte. "Why don't we have a drink?" they proposed, and the group moved over to the bar.

The moment Lacotte turned to speak to Bonnefous, Sergeyev told Rudolf he needed to speak to him privately. All the while he smiled so as not to arouse the suspicions of Rudolf's well-wishers.

"You won't be coming with us now," he said. At this Rudolf turned ashen. He had just received a wire from Moscow, Sergeyev explained. "Khrushchev wants you to go to Moscow and dance a special gala for him." In addition, they had just learned that Rudolf's mother had taken ill. They would be leaving him now to fly to London, while he was to take the Tupolev to Moscow, leaving in two hours' time.

"I know exactly what kind of concert you mean," Rudolf cried, comprehending at once that his career was finished. "No, no, you'll be rejoining us," Sergeyev insisted. But Rudolf saw through this hollow promise. Not only would he never be allowed out on another foreign tour, he would probably be sent back to Ufa or, worse, to some northern outpost, where he would languish in oblivion. He thought of killing himself. As he looked toward the boarding area, he saw Sergeyev talking to Korkin. He assumed they were to blame for his sudden recall to Moscow.

"They're sending me back to Moscow!" he whispered urgently to Lacotte. "I'm not going to London. That's it. I'm finished. Help me or I will kill myself." The day before, Lacotte had given him a silver letter opener as a parting gift. He saw that Rudolf had it now in his shirt pocket.

Lacotte grabbed an interpreter and rushed over to Sergeyev. "If you are sending Rudolf back because he came out with me and my friends, I want to assure you he never said anything against you or his country. We just talked about dance. I'll sign something if you want. Please don't punish him."

Sergeyev lifted his hand and cut him short. "He's not being punished. This has nothing to do with you. His mother is ill and he has to go back for a few days, but he'll be joining us in London, you'll see."

Lacotte didn't know whom to believe. KGB agents had begun circling and he felt helpless to act. He conveyed Sergeyev's words back to Rudolf, who was pacing and crying. "Don't listen to them. It's finished. You have to help me," he implored.

The other dancers saw that Rudolf was in distress, but only Irina Kolpakova, Irina Zubkovskaya and Alla Osipenko came over to speak to him. "They're sending me back to Moscow!" he told them. The ballerinas began to cry and urged him to cooperate. They promised to lodge a protest with the Russian embassy in London, demanding his return, an absurd, desperate promise. "We were all shocked," says Kolpakova. "We told him, 'Don't worry, it's going to be all right,' but of course we knew it wouldn't be. We all understood that something was terribly wrong."

Osipenko was terrified he was going to hurt himself. "Don't do anything foolish," she pleaded. "Go to Moscow." As their eyes met, he made a sign they all knew. It was the sign for prison and it meant the end of a career.

Strizhevski was now rushing the remaining dancers out the door toward the plane, Sergeyev and Dudinskaya among them. Kolpakova, Zubkovskaya and Osipenko were the last in line. With another agent prodding them out the door and onto the tarmac, Kolpakova and Zubkovskaya had no chance to look back. But Osipenko, hearing Rudolf's cries behind her, turned around. Rudolf was banging his forehead against a wall, a sight that would haunt her for years to come. Someone screamed at her to keep moving and it seemed to her only seconds later that she was inside the plane and the stairs were being rolled away.

Instinctively, she appealed to Korkin for help. He was sitting in the first row. "Georgi Mikhailovich, Rudik is in such a terrible state. Do something! Take me off the plane and tell him that we are flying to a government concert in Moscow together. You know Nureyev. He's unpredictable. He will do something." She wasn't thinking about what she was saying. She felt connected to Rudolf after their success in Paris and was afraid he might hurt himself. She hoped that if she offered to go back with him, he would calm down and return with her to Moscow to perform in the concert. Then they would rejoin the tour in London. And yet at the same time, she knew, as did everyone else on that plane, that this wasn't going to happen. Once Rudolf was sent home, he would never be allowed abroad again. How he could possibly save himself, none of them could imagine. There was no precedent. The only "traitors" they'd ever heard about were politicians.

Korkin listened, stone-faced, as she made her impassioned plea. "I did everything I could," he answered with weary resignation. "I can't do anything more."

No one else said a word on Rudolf's behalf. "It was like a coffin on that plane," Osipenko remembered thirty-four years later, the scene indelibly fixed in her mind. "Nobody talked. Nobody drank. Nobody could do anything. And it was my birthday. I turned twenty-nine that day. Even now I get goose bumps thinking about it."

INSIDE THE TERMINAL, Lacotte was having little success calming Rudolf. "If you want me to help you, I can't stay near you," he reasoned, though Rudolf was having none of it. "If you don't stay here," he cried, "they'll put me in another room and I won't be able to do anything."

With Strizhevski only steps away, and two hours before Rudolf's flight to Moscow, Lacotte was "absolutely despairing." He kept looking at the clock. "Tell Rudolf I can take him away on my motorcycle," the journalist Olivier Merlin murmured to Lacotte. "Are you crazy?" said Lacotte. "Look at all the KGB. They'll grab him without any trouble."

Lacotte could think of only one solution and discreetly slipped Jean-Pierre Bonnefous a note. On it was Clara Saint's telephone number. Clara knew Malraux. Maybe she could do something.

At 9:30 A.M. Clara was awoken by an urgent call from Bonnefous. "You must come right away to Le Bourget," he whispered into the receiver. The presence of Russian agents in the hallway frightened him, as it did the rest of the French contingent, and he wanted to get the call over with quickly. When Clara pressed him for details, she could hear panic in his voice. "Rudi wants you to come. I can't talk right now. I'm in a phone booth."

Twenty-five minutes later Clara pulled up to Le Bourget in a taxi, wearing large sunglasses and a silk scarf thrown over her head. Bonnefous was waiting for her outside. The Kirov dancers had boarded the plane for London, he explained, and Rudi wasn't on it. He was being sent to Moscow in two hours. "That's impossible," Clara replied, exhausted after only three hours of sleep. "Where is he?" Bonnefous led her past the glass doors into the airport and indicated with his eyes that Rudolf was sitting at the bar. Clara looked over and saw Rudolf wedged in between "two large men, two monsters, like in the movies." She knew little of Cold War politics except what she'd gleaned from the movies, but she couldn't stand to see Rudolf "taken by force" and knew he needed help. Nearby she saw Lacotte, Merlin and several of the Paris Opéra dancers. She could see they were discussing the situation and clearly agitated, but no one was taking any action.

"What do you think he wants to do?" she asked Bonnefous. When he replied that Lacotte had indicated that Rudolf wanted to stay in Paris, Clara urged him to go ask Rudolf himself. "Do you think I can?" Bonnefous answered. Clara saw at once that she was going to have to act on her own. The Paris dancers clearly feared for their own careers and "didn't want to interfere. They all hoped to dance in Russia one day. They just stood there panicking, wondering what to do. But me, I had nothing to lose."

As Clara approached Rudolf, Strizhevski stood up. "I just want to say good-bye," she said, testing to see whether Strizhevski and the other agent understood English. When it was clear that they didn't, she leaned forward to kiss Rudolf on each cheek and feigned an emotional parting to allow her a few more necessary kisses. "Do you want to stay?" she asked as she kissed him. Her heart was beating very fast. "Yes, please do something," he answered as she leaned toward the other cheek. "Are you sure?" Another kiss. "Yes, yes, please, I want to stay." Clara smiled at the agents. "They just thought I was this young girl saying good-bye," she remembers. "They were so strong, they didn't care about me."

When Clara returned to the others and told them that Rudolf had asked for her help, they warned her not to get involved. "It's very dangerous," they whispered. "We know it's terrible, but we can't do anything." Clara realized she was wasting precious time and began discreetly surveying the airport for other options. Spying the sign marked AIRPORT POLICE near the staircase, she casually made her way to the second-floor office.

"There's a Russian dancer downstairs at the bar who wants to stay in France," she announced to the two plainclothes policemen at the desk. They asked if she was sure he was "only a dancer." They had never heard of him. Are you sure he's not a scientist?

"Yes, he's a great dancer," she insisted, and explained that she'd seen him dance at the Paris Opéra and the Palais des Sports by way of proof. "They're sending him back because he spent time with French people. He's not like the others, he was more independent. They were probably afraid he'd run to the French embassy if he got wind of their plan, so they waited until they got to the airport. But I know he really wants to stay and they're planning to send him back to Moscow. Can't we do something?"

Clara knew that the French police were virulently anti-Communist and was betting on the chance that they might be eager to help. "Look, we can't go to him, he has to come to us," they explained. "If he comes to us, then we'll take care of everything."

"But how?" Clara asked. "There are two men guarding him."

The policemen promised to accompany Clara downstairs to the bar. She was to go first and order a coffee. They would follow ten minutes later and stand near her. When they had taken up their positions, she was to approach Rudolf again and explain to him that he had to go to them on his own.

Clara's legs were "like rubber" as she went to bid farewell to "poor Rudi" one more time. "It's so sad that he's leaving," she lamented to Strizhevski, hoping to convince him that she was just an overwrought French girl. For added effect, she made a show of great affection to give the impression that she was whispering something tender in Rudolf's ear. "It's so sad you're leaving us," she said for all to hear, and then, sotto voce, added, "See those two men at the bar? They're waiting for you. You must go to them." As they exchanged one last kiss, Rudolf simply said, "Yes," as he kissed her cheek.

Five minutes later Rudolf bolted from his chair to the bar, a distance of just a few yards. "I want to stay in France," he cried in English just as Strizhevski and the other agent lunged and grabbed him. A tug-of-war ensued for a full minute. "That's enough!" the French police shouted at the Russians. "You are in France!" At this, the Russians had no choice but to let go of Rudolf. As the French police ushered him upstairs, the embassy agents rushed to the phones to relay the bad news.

Leaving the bar, Clara was met by a cluster of thirty disapproving bystanders. "All the dancers were saying to me, 'What have you done? It's terrible! Don't you realize it's going to be awful for him? They're going to take him back, they're so powerful. What you did was terrible!' " Georges Soria, the Kirov's Paris impresario, rebuked her for jeopardizing future cultural exchanges with the Soviets. "There'll be no more Bolshoi or Kirov after this," he yelled at her. "Listen," she tried to explain, "I did it because he asked me to."

CLARA MADE HER WAY upstairs and found Rudolf drinking coffee surrounded by assorted gendarmes and inspectors. He didn't look well and at that moment he was convinced that the French were about to turn him over to the Soviets. His distrust of authority was so profound that he thought it was only a matter of time before the Soviet authorities engineered his release. What he didn't know was that Le Bourget's chief of border control, Gregory Alexinsky, had a vested interest in thwarting any such attempt. A specialist in the problems of political refugees, he was White Russian by birth, the son of a former Socialist deputy in the Duma who had been imprisoned for criticizing Lenin. His family had fled Russia in 1919. Fearing that the Soviets would see a conspiracy if they learned that a White Russian had granted Nureyev protection in France, Alexinsky decided not to address Rudolf in his native Russian. He also took care not to put his name on official documents, even though it meant getting others to sign their names to orders he had given.*

As Clara took a seat, Alexinsky and his deputies directed questions at her that Rudolf had trouble answering. Did he really want to stay? Did he have a job? How would he support himself? His luggage had gone to London, Rudolf answered. He had nothing. "I'm sure he won't have any trouble finding work," Clara interjected. The inspectors weren't convinced. Are you sure about that? they repeated. "I'll take care of him until then," Clara answered.

To clear themselves further of any accusations that they had entrapped Rudolf, the French officials wanted Rudolf to spend several quiet minutes in the adjoining room, contemplating his decision, alone. The

*By uncanny coincidence, Alexinsky was a longtime friend of former Paris Opéra Ballet director and dancer Serge Lifar. He recalls that a few days after Nureyev's defection, Lifar also passed through Le Bourget on his way back from Stockholm. "I was in a room downstairs and all of a sudden I saw a stream of passengers and noticed Lifar, who very expansively threw his arms around me saying, 'My dear commissioner, I am so glad to see you! You have witnessed a fantastic event here the other day.' I knew what he was talking about, but I said anyway, 'Which one?' And he said, 'But Nureyev's escape, a few days ago!' I said, 'Of course.' He told me, 'People don't realize that this is a second Nijinsky, a great artist that Russia has just lost.' And he said that if the Opéra de Paris hires him, it would be marvelous."

room had two doors, they told him. One would lead him into the departure lounge for Moscow through a back entrance; the other into one of the inspectors' private offices. But just as he got up to move, Mikhail Klemenov, the Soviet embassy's cultural attaché, rushed into the room, insisting that he speak with Nureyev. Alexinsky put them together.

To his every entreaty and threat, Rudolf answered "Nyet." Finally Klemenov said, "You refuse to return to your great fatherland?" and Rudolf answered, "Yes, I refuse." Klemenov suddenly slapped Rudolf hard across the face, and the French intervened. "We told him there was no need for fisticuffs," recalls Alexinsky.

"What you did was terrible!" Klemenov hissed at Clara on the way out. "This boy is going to be so unhappy here with you."

In the sanctuary of the quiet room, Rudolf thought of home. He thought of Pushkin, "a kind of second father to me"; Tamara, "the girl I liked, perhaps loved"; the Kirov, "to me the first ballet company in the world, all that I held most dear and had made me into what I am." He also thought of his family in Ufa and what might happen to them if he didn't return. Staying in the West meant severing his ties to everyone who mattered to him. Stripped of familiar faces, his new freedom "wore an austere look," he thought.

He had flirted with the idea of defection before but had never had the courage or opportunity to see it through. "What would your reaction be if I decided to stay in the West?" he had asked Liuba's brother, Leonid, the week before he'd left for Paris. "It's your decision," Leonid had replied, believing Rudik would never take such a risk. But then, neither did Rudik himself. Not then, anyhow. One day he would leave, anyone who knew him well was certain of that, but even he hadn't counted on defecting in Paris — or London for that matter. Still, he knew the fate of Valery Panov, the Maly Theater soloist who had been sent home abruptly from San Francisco two years earlier. Panov had shown too much interest in the West and had yet to be sent on another foreign tour.

Before leaving Leningrad, he had given Tamara a photo of himself. "I am sustained only by hope," he had written on it, a play on the Russian saying, "A young man lives on hope alone."

There were no guarantees in the West, but at least his future remained an open question and his to determine. What choice was left to him? If he went back now, he'd be mercilessly interrogated by the KGB. He would lose everything he had struggled for. Frustration would erode into bitterness, a life sentence impossible to endure.

Years later, when asked about his decision, Nureyev acknowledged that he could never have survived under such stifling conditions. He would surely have gone mad, he said, the way Nijinsky did after Diaghilev fired him from the Ballets Russes and "severed his lifeline to the stage."* Nijinsky, he observed, "knew himself only when he was dancing. His mind was blocked, constipated, and so he went mad. Even when they let you dance in Russia, you are terribly compressed. I had the feeling that if I didn't try everything, then my life would be wasted. Still, I would never have had the courage to do it unless they goaded me."

NUREYEV'S LIFE in the West, much like his birth in the East twenty-three years earlier, began precariously, unexpectedly and in transit. Just as his mother had left familiar surroundings to join her husband in a war zone thousands of miles from home, so Rudolf now faced uncertain prospects: He had no passport, no luggage, no money, no home. And there was now a corps of disgraced Russian agents in Paris, with careers on the line, eager for a chance to redeem themselves. "It would be very dangerous to send him to a hotel tonight," the French inspectors advised Clara. "The Russians might try to follow him and take him back." Could she find him a place to stay? Clara was sure she could, but she would have to make some calls. With assurances that he would call her that afternoon, Alexinsky sent Rudolf off to police headquarters under escort, sneaking him out of the airport through a back door. From there, he was taken to the Ministry of the Interior, where, following interviews with officials of the counterespionage branch, he was given a refugee visa.

Clara, meanwhile, headed down the front staircase, only to be overwhelmed by a mob of forty photographers angling for a shot of the Russian dancer's presumed love interest. "Where is he? Where did he go? What happened?" they shouted at her. Two hours earlier, as she had scrambled into a taxicab, she was just another young Frenchwoman on her way to the airport; now she suddenly found herself the focus of media scrutiny, cast as the heroine in a Cold War drama. She tried to answer the questions they fired at her. "I have no idea why he should have asked for asylum here," she answered repeatedly, evading questions about his whereabouts. "I cannot imagine him being involved in politics. His whole life is dancing," she said to one reporter. "No, we are not engaged," to another. "No, he's not married, but there was nothing serious between us."

Not since Captain Charles Lindbergh landed the *Spirit of St. Louis* in 1927 had Le Bourget seen such a tempest.† Then the Parisian news

---

*The event that occasioned Nijinsky's dismissal from the Ballets Russes late in 1913 was his sudden marriage to a young corps dancer named Romola de Pulszky. Upon hearing the news, Diaghilev, the twenty-three-year-old Nijinsky's mentor and lover, was thrown into a black rage: He promptly fired Nijinsky, his most brilliant star, and dropped his ballets from the repertory. It wasn't long before Nijinsky suffered a breakdown from which he never fully recovered. He spent the last thirty-one years of his life in and out of sanitariums.

†On May 21, 1927, Lindbergh concluded his historic flight across the Atlantic Ocean at Le Bourget.

vendors had shouted in the streets, *"Bonnes nouvelles!* The American has arrived," and local patrons poured champagne for American tourists. *"Tu avais dansé toute cette nuit* [You have danced through the night]."

This time it was the flight of a Soviet dancer that sparked headlines and imaginations worldwide. Like Lindbergh before him, Nureyev became an instant cause célèbre, a romantic hero for the age.* Within hours of his defection, his six quick, momentous steps into the arms of the French gendarmes would be recast as "a dance to freedom," a dash "through the barrier," a "leap to freedom," and not least, a *coup de théâtre*, while Rudolf himself, his name still largely unknown in the West, would be identified in headlines as everything from a "Red dancer" to "the new Nijinsky." London's *Daily Express* would have him "leaping like Nijinsky himself down the vaulted hall, shouting in English at the top of his voice: 'I want to stay in France . . . I want to be free.'"

More than a dancer, he was a political symbol: As the first Soviet artist ever to defect, he demonstrated at the height of the Cold War that the Iron Curtain could be pierced. Suddenly ballet was front-page news. "It is good that he lived to see the Soviet Union crumble," American dance critic Arlene Croce would observe after his death, "for he was Mikhail Gorbachev's advance man as well as Mikhail Baryshnikov's."

And yet never was there a more reluctant political symbol than Nureyev. Politics neither interested nor motivated him. His defection was not an act of defiance; it was an act of will propelled by his instinctive need to dance. That reflex had shown itself whenever authority had stood in the way: His father had forbidden him to study and he had flown off to Leningrad; Shelkov had threatened him with expulsion and he'd escaped to Pushkin's class; the Ministry of Culture had ordered him home to the ranks of the Ufa Ballet and he'd pleaded his way back into the Kirov. Since that first childhood visit to the theater, Nureyev had fought for his place on the stage with a sense of destiny, a battle he waged, and would continue to wage, not only with his opponents but within himself. "Rudolf's defection was the most natural thing in the world," Baryshnikov, who followed his lead in 1974, acknowledged years afterward. "For other people, including me, there were years of thoughts and plans and doubts and the long business of working up your courage. But Rudolf didn't need courage. He had so much courage that it wasn't even courage anymore. . . . So for him to bolt at that French airport—it was like a bird in a cage, and suddenly the door is open."

---

*Across the Atlantic, Cecil Beaton spoke for many when he confided in his diary that the young Russian dancer's "sudden decision to give up the life that he had been accustomed to . . . and his desperate effort to start life afresh" had "affected tremendously my imagination."

11

Fallout

Paris, June 16, 1961

Two KGB agents were stationed outside her mother's house when Clara returned from Le Bourget. Ignoring them, she immediately found Rudolf a safe haven for the next few days. Her friend Jean Loup Puznat worked in the film business and was only too glad to offer Rudolf his parents' roomy apartment opposite the Luxembourg Gardens after Clara described her eventful morning. Despite exhaustion, she rushed out to buy Rudolf a few essentials: a toothbrush, pajamas, a few shirts, some pants. By the time she got home, Pierre Lacotte was on the line. He was calling from a phone booth, he said, because there were KGB agents outside his apartment. He was getting a lawyer, just in case. Moments later the French inspectors called from the ministry and Clara gave them Puznat's address. Since he was not connected to the ballet world, no one would think to look for Rudolf there. When she spoke to Rudolf to tell him she would see him that night, he had only one question: "What about my class? Where will I do my class?" Clara took a breath. "Listen, take your class in the apartment for the next few days, because for the moment, you can't go anywhere."

London, June 16, 1961

At London (now Heathrow) Airport a group of reporters converged on the Kirov dancers the moment they arrived from Paris. Did they know that Nureyev had just defected? The news caught them off guard and cast a cloud of confusion over the entire company. Some believed Rudolf was on his way to Moscow to perform for Khrushchev; others believed he was simply on his way to Moscow. Still, others knew at once that it must be true. John Tooley, there to greet them as assistant general administrator of Covent Garden, recalls finding the company "in the depths of depression and dismay." Nevertheless, the Russians did their best to put on a brave face. "There is nothing mysterious," Korkin told reporters, still under the assumption that Nureyev was on his way home. "Nureyev has returned to Leningrad because his mother is dangerously ill. Why all this fuss?" And company manager Valentin Bogdanov, the man in charge of the boarding passes, claimed that all was as it should be. "There is none missing," he said.

Before anyone could piece the story together, the dancers were hustled off to a welcoming luncheon at the Oxford Street Corner House in London's West End. En route, thoughts ran wild before their bus broke down and they were forced to walk the rest of the way. Many were outraged by Nureyev's apparent act of treachery and appalled that he had "left us in the lurch." There were rumors that he'd been drugged by the French. Some said he was in love. Others presumed "it was another of Rudik's tricks." Meanwhile, Alla Osipenko, "the Odette of the Leningrad company," as the Kirov's Swan Queen was described in the London press, was distraught at losing her Siegfried. Her agitation was only made worse by the luncheon, which to her chagrin turned out to be a surprise birthday party in her honor. "Nobody was in the mood for this birthday party," recalls Osipenko, who had to smile for the cameras as she cut her cake. "You should have seen the faces." After lunch they checked into the Strand Palace Hotel in London's West End, where a group of reporters ambushed her. "Miss Osipenko, do you know that your partner Nureyev has defected in Paris?" Osipenko claimed she didn't know anything about it. "I was feeling very upset because I knew that if the reporters were talking about Nureyev, something must have happened to him." In the hotel corridor she ran into Kirov designer Simon Virsaladze. "I just heard on the radio that Nureyev asked for political asylum," he said, rolling his eyes in dismay. That night "nobody slept," she says. "We were all talking and walking from one room to another. Some people couldn't believe that he would have defected."

The next morning the dancers were called to a meeting. "They didn't tell us anything directly," Osipenko remembers. "I was simply told, 'Alla, you will dance with Soloviev in *Swan Lake*.' I had never danced with Soloviev before. He was too short for me." And Soloviev was new to the role of the Prince. But Sergeyev insisted. "It's urgent that you rehearse together and learn to dance it quickly," was all he said. "They didn't explain," she says. "But there was no more talk of Nureyev."

Leningrad, June 16, 1961

Five hours after Rudolf left Le Bourget under police escort, his friend Tamara was making her way to the Kirov Theater to see the Royal Ballet. That night Frederick Ashton's *La Fille Mal Gardée** was to have its Russian premiere, and she was anxious to get to her seat. No sooner had she settled into her plush blue seat than a friend yelled over to her that someone was looking for her in the lobby. There she ran into an old friend of hers, looking somber. "Sit down, I have something to tell you," he told her. "It's about Rudik, isn't it?" she asked anxiously. "I just heard on the BBC that Rudik has asked for political asylum in France." Tamara had never heard the term "political asylum." "It's nonsense, Rudik knows nothing of politics," she said reflexively. The man tried to explain. "It has nothing to do with politics. He asked to stay in France."

Tamara rushed to a pay phone to call the Pushkins but got no answer. Next, she called Elizaveta Mikhailovna Paji, their music shop friend. "She was crying over the phone," recalls Tamara. "She had already heard. 'Is it true?' she asked me. I said I didn't know. She asked me to come over immediately, so I got on the bus and went there. She lived in a communal apartment, so I was surprised when she opened the door in her slip. Elizaveta's husband was sitting there quietly, looking really sad. Both of them really loved Rudik like a son. Elizaveta Mikhailovna was running around the room, crying. Later we tried to call Pushkin, but he still wasn't home. We wanted him to find out from us because he had high blood pressure and we were afraid that someone would tell him suddenly and he would go into shock. He didn't get home until one A.M. When I finally reached him the next morning, he said simply, 'I already know.' His blood pressure had gone up and he was in bed after an acute attack. Xenia was in Pyarnu [in Estonia], so I sent her a telegram: 'Mahmoudka in trouble. Come home.'"

Over the next twenty-four hours Rudolf's Leningrad friends tried to make sense of the rumors and deal with their shock. The official press made no mention of Nureyev or the Kirov. "We heard he was hit by a car," Tamara recalls. "Then we heard that he was taken to Moscow and was in a mental institution. We didn't understand what could have happened." Their profound sense of loss drew them together. As Rudolf was now a traitor, they had no choice but to hide their grieving from others. At the same time, their ties to him were known. They all knew that any day now they could expect the KGB at their doors. As an important

*Tamara recalled that the performance was *Ondine*. However, *Ondine* had premiered the night before. Given the events that night, it's not surprising that the program got confused in her memory.

physicist working on a secret project Elizaveta's husband, Veniamin, was especially worried.

Ufa, June 16, 1961

Rudolf's sister Rosa was also reeling from the news, but telephoning her parents in Ufa was no simple matter. Neither they nor anyone they knew had a private phone, so she had to cable them to call her in Leningrad. That took a few days. Razida was away at the Black Sea on vacation at the time and returned to find her father "in a dark mood." She could see straightaway that he was suffering. "It was painful to look at him. He was a Communist and a commissar, so he took it very hard. He lost weight and aged quickly. My mother reacted differently. The only thing she was concerned about then was whether Rudik would have enough to live on. 'Does he have enough money?' That's what worried her."

Leningrad, June 18, 1961

On June 18, three days after making her Leningrad debut, Margot Fonteyn learned that a Kirov dancer had defected in Paris. Her colleague Georgina Parkinson relayed the news after speaking to her husband in London. "Of course, nothing was said in Leningrad," Fonteyn recalled, though a certain Kirov ballerina who had come "shyly" to her dressing room a few times now "appeared no more." The ballerina, though never named, was Alla Shelest. As Nureyev's frequent leading lady, Shelest was plainly at risk. According to Fonteyn, Nureyev later confirmed that the Kirov ballerina in question "was the one he had admired the most." She was a very sensitive artist, he said, "and he had learned a good deal from watching her." Shelest, in turn, would recall that Nureyev's defection "destroyed any idea of the normal course of things. He was the first. It was impossible to understand how this idea might come to his mind. I was so sorry I had lost him."

Liuba Romankova had been away on a romantic weekend in the country with her new boyfriend, a ski instructor, when the news first broke. She remembers returning home on Sunday, June 18, to a "persistently" ringing phone. Her parents were away on holiday and there was no one in the flat. "I rushed to the phone, hitting against every bit of furniture that was in my way, and heard someone say, 'Rudik defected in the West.' I stood there for a while as if paralyzed. It felt like a death because I thought I would never see him again."

Moscow, June 18, 1961

Within forty-eight hours of Nureyev's defection, KGB boss Alexander Shelepin* had prepared his damage report for the Central Committee of the Communist Party, following an emergency meeting of the Committee of State Security.† The haste with which Shelepin filed his summary suggests the Soviets' profound embarrassment at this sudden blow to Soviet prestige. A simple plan had been badly botched, and he now had a major international scandal on his hands, one that threatened to undermine Western credibility in the Soviet system.

Hereby I report that on June 16 1961 NUREYEV Rudolf Hametovich born 1938, single, Tatar, nonparty member, artist of the Leningrad Kirov Theater who was a member of the touring company in France betrayed his motherland in Paris.

According to the information received from France June 3 this year, NUREYEV Rudolf Hametovich violated the rules of behavior of Soviet citizens abroad, went out to town and came back to the hotel late at night. Besides he established close relations with French artists among whom there were homosexuals. Despite talks of a cautionary character conducted with him, NUREYEV did not change his behavior.

Shelepin went on to summarize the state's thwarted efforts to have Nureyev sent back to the Soviet Union and provided information about Nureyev's family in Ufa. He naturally wanted to make himself look as good as possible, so he distanced himself from blame and pointed the finger at both the KGB workers in France and at the party functionaries in the Kirov who had approved Nureyev for the tour to Paris. From the intelligence he had gathered about Nureyev, Shelepin now wrote that he was convinced that Nureyev should never have been sent abroad in the first place. Since a mind-boggling number of overlapping agencies had been involved in the preparation and supervision of the tour, it wasn't hard to pass the buck. "NUREYEV was characterized as an undisciplined, unrestrained and rude person," Shelepin wrote, after reviewing the character description the Kirov had compiled on Nureyev. "Earlier [he] went abroad more than once."‡

But as for incriminating political evidence prior to the tour, the KGB apparently had "no compromising materials against either him or

---

*A pro-Stalin hardliner, Shelepin was known in some circles as Iron Shurik, a play on "Iron Felix" Dzerzhinsky, the founder of the secret police.
†The initials KGB stand for the Russian words for "Committee of State Security," a name the secret police adopted in 1954.
‡The term "abroad" was applied to any travel outside the Soviet Union. As a member of the Kirov, Nureyev had traveled to Vienna, East Germany and several other Eastern bloc countries.

his relatives." In other words, it had no evidence of dissident activity or suspicious contacts with foreigners. (Curiously, Nureyev's friendly overtures to the American cast of *My Fair Lady* were never mentioned.) Nevertheless, Nureyev's family would soon be enlisted in the campaign to win Nureyev back to the motherland.

With the Kirov slated to begin its first American tour that September, the Soviets were in a hurry to put the Nureyev scandal behind them. To that end, Moscow and Leningrad each appointed a high-level task force to identify those responsible and punish the guilty. The investigations were to begin upon the Kirov's return from London.

Paris, June 16, 1961

The hours following his defection were no less distressing for Rudolf than they were for those who loved him. As he tried to sort through the sensations that now bombarded him, he was overcome at the thought that his decision was irrevocable. He could not go home again, and as much as he might have wished at times to cut his ties, the fact that he might never again see his mother pained him beyond description. He was exhausted and crying when Clara and Pierre arrived at the apartment. "I never thought it would happen this way," he told them. His mind seesawed between matters large and small. "I'll never see my mother again," he cried. "I have nothing. My shoes, my wigs and all my presents are on the way to Moscow." Rudolf, recalls Lacotte, "was in a fog. He was so frightened. He had no strength; he was just lying on the bed."

In an adjoining room, Clara and Pierre listened to the reports of his defection over the radio. As Clara saw it, the only way to revive him was to get him back onstage as quickly as possible. She immediately thought of the only ballet director she knew: Raymundo de Larrain.

The savvy Raymundo saw Nureyev's value at once and promptly offered him a contract. Though the highly eccentric Marquesa de Cuevas was thinking of disbanding the troupe once and for all, Raymundo managed to persuade her to continue as its patron and to underwrite Rudolf's eight-thousand-dollar-a-month salary, which made him one of the best-paid dancers in the world.* Rudolf and Raymundo had arrived at his salary together. In Russia, Rudolf had already learned how to leverage his artistic capital. Once he was in France, it took him a scant few weeks to translate that skill into Western terms. "Here, in the West, I feel I'm going to ask for as much money as I can obtain," he would tell

---

*The only other dancer to rival his salary at that time was Maria Tallchief, who was paid two thousand dollars a week by Sergei Denham's Ballet Russe de Monte Carlo in 1954.

a reporter just two months later, showing the business savvy that would make him the richest dancer in history, "because the amount of money one receives is what decides one's worth."

Hoping to capitalize on his own investment, Raymundo wanted Rudolf to make his de Cuevas company debut in *The Sleeping Beauty* on June 23, the same night and in the same ballet that Rudolf was supposed to have made his London debut in with the Kirov. "It's marvelous, extraordinary," Raymundo told Clara excitedly. "We'll have a special evening for him. Let's tell the press right away." Clara cautioned him that Rudolf was in danger. "Not yet," she said. Lacotte, however, remained cynical of Raymundo's newfound appreciation: "He forgot all about having said that Rudolf was a *mujik* when he saw how wonderful the publicity would be for his season."

Paris, London, June 17, 1961

Twenty-four hours after his defection Nureyev was front-page news around the world. The story was perfect fodder for the burgeoning medium of television news, which had played a decisive role in the 1960 American presidential elections and made a star of President John F. Kennedy. Now, all at once, Nureyev was everywhere, the first dancer caught in what David Halberstam calls "the glare of the new media society," a society that would "culminate almost three decades later when *People* magazine sold more advertising than its older and more traditional sibling, *Time* magazine." His defection had all the elements of a great story, and best of all for a hungry press corps, it had continuity. Coverage begat more coverage and as interest in him grew, the public wanted to know more and more about him.

Passing a newsstand on the Avenue Matignon, Clara was shocked to see herself on the cover of just about every major European daily, her hair wrapped in a scarf, her eyes concealed behind large dark sunglasses. Since Rudolf had been sequestered when the story broke, the newspapers had run photos of her instead. DANCER'S GIRL FRIEND AT AIRPORT QUESTIONING, announced the *Daily Mail*. GIRL SEES RUSSIANS CHASE HER FRIEND, claimed the *Daily Express*, which went on to report that Nureyev had "skipped to freedom to the delight of a red-haired girl," who was "looking very impressive in green sweater and skirt." Despite her repeated protests to reporters, Clara was the coquette of the hour, the Juliet who had captured the heart of the Kirov's Romeo.

The Russians were only too happy to blame it all on love and, in a rare display of journalistic détente, went along with the story: RUSSIANS SAY ROMANCE CAUSED DANCER'S FLIGHT, *The New York Times* announced on Sunday, June 18, having just the day before reported that

Nureyev had apparently come to Paris with the idea of defecting. "It is a very disagreeable subject and we are sad about it," a woman, identified as an interpreter with the Kirov, was quoted as saying. "But he is young and the girl is very beautiful." Eschewing the limelight, Clara recalls her sudden, if fleeting, celebrity as "a nightmare." (It may have proved her baptism by fire, for she went on to become the publicity director of Yves Saint Laurent Rive Gauche.) Indeed, though the press at the time failed to report her behind-the-scenes role in Nureyev's defection, she never bothered to correct the record, nor did she and Nureyev ever revisit that moment together. But then Nureyev never invited any reminiscences. "It's done, we don't have to talk about the past," he told Lacotte shortly afterward.

NUREYEV BEGAN his autobiography with the story of his defection. His account is less interesting for what it is—a straightforward, though incomplete, account—than for what it reveals about how Nureyev wished to be perceived and how little he knew at the time.* Because the records of his defection were state secrets during Nureyev's lifetime and only recently declassified at the request of the author, it has been impossible until now to look beyond the accepted story to give a full account of that historic event. Nureyev drew only on his own memories and given his highly agitated state of mind that day—he himself concedes he was suicidal—he is not the most reliable witness. "Never did Rudolf give the right story about his 'departure,' " contends Lacotte. He was also not privy to the many conversations and events that took place before, during and directly following his defection. It should also be remembered that his memoir was published only one year after his defection, at a time when he was not free to give a full picture even if he had wanted to. Over the years his story evolved, changing in tone, content and focus, his role and motivation going through constant revision. No two versions of his defection are quite the same. The media both followed his lead and added their own flourishes.

Nevertheless, his account remained consistent on several major points, the most curious of which is the date he continued to give for his defection. In his autobiography Nureyev makes much of his preoccupation with dates, omens and horoscopes and then writes that he defected on June 17 rather than June 16, an odd mistake given the amount of press coverage it received and the fact that Nureyev claims to have

*The reason for these omissions or displaced points of view may have something to do with the fact that when he told his story to his French ghostwriters, Nureyev had no desire to probe into his state of mind or reveal himself to his audience.

confirmed the date. "It's very strange, but while I can remember the exact date I entered the Leningrad Ballet School, and while, without a second's hesitation, I can name the hour I first appeared on the Kirov stage, I always have to check which day it was that my life took such a violent new turn at Le Bourget airport. Actually, it was the 17th of June. I'm very superstitious; I wish I had checked on my horoscope that day." Even odder, nearly every book, article and film about Nureyev, including his obituaries, give June 17 as the date of his defection.

There are other inconsistencies in his account, which until now have never been questioned, verified or confirmed by other eye-witnesses. Contemporary evidence casts doubt on the accuracy of Nureyev's recollections: In describing his reaction to the news that he is to be sent home, Nureyev plays down his distress to the point where his responses seem strangely muted. "I felt the blood drain from my face. Dance in the Kremlin indeed. That was a likely story. . . . I knew exactly where I stood and also what this immediate recall to Moscow would entail: no foreign travel ever again and the position of star dancer to which I was entitled in a couple of years would be forever denied me. . . . I felt I would rather kill myself. . . . I said to Sergeyev that in that case I would go and say goodbye to the dancers. I walked over towards them and told them of the decision to pack me off back to Moscow. It was a surprise to everyone but they all understood what it implied. Most of the ballerinas — even those who had always been openly against me — started to cry. I know theatre people are easily moved, but all the same I was surprised that they displayed so much warmth and emotion."

It is the reactions of others, not his own, that he described. (He was careful not to mention the ballerinas by name, for fear that any references to their kindness could have grave consequences for them.) Nowhere does he mention that he was crying, that he hit his head against a wall or that the ballerinas were responding as much to his despondency as to his unlikely news. (When Alla Osipenko and Nureyev met again for the first time in 1989, she was surprised to discover how little he seemed to recall of his desperation that day. "Oh, but you don't remember how you were!" she told him after he denied having hit his head against a wall.)

Furthermore, Nureyev also fails to mention that he begged Lacotte to stay near him so that the KGB wouldn't hustle him off to the waiting plane. Rather, it is "a friend" who does the begging, just as it is another friend who looks pale and worried: "A friend . . . was shaking me by the arm and begging me to stay calm, to go back to Moscow, assuring me that after a little time I would be back at the Kirov as if nothing had happened. I was aware of faces: another friend, looking pale and worried, walking round and round me in agitation. . . . I felt in a daze but I asked someone to ring Clara and say 'goodbye,' feeling I would never have the chance to see her again."

If the recollections of others present are to be believed, Nureyev did not have the presence of mind to hatch a plan; according to Lacotte and Jean-Pierre Bonnefous, it was Lacotte's idea, not Nureyev's, to call Clara. Nureyev goes on to say that he was hiding behind a column when Clara arrived at the airport and that "I cried out to her that I'd taken my decision" when it was Clara who approached him and asked him what he wanted to do. He also claims erroneously that Clara came back into the departure area flanked by the two French inspectors and that he flew to them when in fact he was wedged in between the two KGB policemen at the bar when Clara returned on her own to say good-bye to him "one last time." And as the inspectors were not in uniform, he could not have known their identity. It was only when Clara whispered instructions to him that he knew what he had to do, though Nureyev gives the impression that Clara was following through on *his* plan. Nureyev would complain to friends in later years that the press had romanticized and exaggerated the story of his defection. While he was not wrong, he was also something of an accomplice in his own mythmaking: In the second paragraph of his memoir, he describes his moment of crisis and places himself—for the sake of drama, rather than accuracy—on the tarmac, beneath the wing of the aircraft bound for Moscow: "Its huge wing loomed over me like the hand of the evil magician in *Swan Lake*. Should I surrender and make the best of it? Or should I, like the heroine of the ballet, defy the command and make a dangerous—possibly fatal—bid for freedom?"

A few pages later he writes: "And then I made it—in the longest, most breath-taking leap of my whole career I landed squarely in the arms of the two Inspectors. 'I want to stay,' I gasped. 'I want to stay!' "

Toward the end of that career, in an interview he gave for a British television documentary about his life, Nureyev gave a highly distilled, pared-down version of those events and left Clara and all references to "breath-taking leaps" and "gasping" out of it altogether. "So I'd been told, 'You have to walk very slowly, six steps exactly, and say, "I would like to stay in your country." ' And that is exactly what I have done. I went directly to those two commissars. . . . No jumping, no running, no screaming, no hysteria. Quietly I say, 'I would like to stay in your country.' "

ON MONDAY, JUNE 19, the Kirov made its London debut before a glittering crowd that included Princess Margaret, her husband, Antony Armstrong-Jones, and actress Vivien Leigh. Russia's Minister of Culture, Ekaterina Furtseva, the only woman on the all-powerful party Presidium and a crony of Khrushchev's, was also on hand, having, as *Time* magazine noted that week, "dropped into London for a visit." Alla Osipenko and Yuri Soloviev starred in *The Stone Flower* and no one looking at the company that night would have been able to discern that anything was amiss. As far as *The New York Times* knew, Nureyev "was not scheduled to dance in the premiere of any of the ballets." And in its rush to get out the story, *Time* magazine ran a photo of Yuri Soloviev with the caption "Defector Rudolf Nureev."

Despite the company's attempts to downplay his significance, the press pursued the story with an ever more watchful eye. No article about the Kirov failed to mention the progress of the "runaway Russian." On the eve of the Kirov's debut, the *Observer* reported that his defection was going to "rob" London "of the chance to see one of the three or four best male dancers in the world." British impresario Victor Hochhauser felt his loss keenly enough to threaten a lawsuit should Nureyev dance with the Grand Ballet de Marquis de Cuevas during the Kirov's season. The fact that de Larrain had invited him to appear in Paris on the same night he was due to appear in London — and in the same ballet — was, as he saw it, "unethical and irresponsible."

Behind the scenes Sergeyev and Dudinskaya scrambled to fill the void left by his sudden departure and spent long hours rehearsing other dancers in his roles. Of all those who filled in for Nureyev, it was Soloviev who benefited the most from the unexpected exposure. Thrust into prominence on the London leg of the tour in both *Swan Lake* and *Sleeping Beauty*, Soloviev, as Andrew Porter declared in the *Financial Times* that month, "is conquering London as Nureyev conquered Paris. We have seen no one quite like him."

Alla Osipenko also came in for high praise from the English critics — "She is both as flexible and as taut as steel — a very remarkable dancer," observed one of them — but she never got a chance to reap the rewards of her success. As far as the KGB was concerned, she was aligned with Nureyev. She had been his partner in Paris and had spoken out on his behalf on the plane to London. The first hint of trouble came as she was about to greet fans backstage on opening night. "When they ask for Osipenko," a KGB agent advised her, "tell them she is behind you." Osipenko had danced in a black wig and since the London balletomanes didn't know that she was naturally blond, they rushed to compliment Lolya Petrova, the ballerina they now assumed was Osipenko. Further indignities followed: She was no longer permitted to room with Natasha Makarova. "I was told I was a bad influence." And each night she was locked in her room by someone from KGB. She would not travel to the West again for another six years.

✴   ✴   ✴

IN PARIS the Soviets now launched their counterassault. They wasted no time informing the French government that should Nureyev be hired by the Paris Opéra Ballet, a state-subsidized company, all Soviet-French cultural exchanges would come to a halt. Not wanting to mar relations with the Soviet Union, and wary of provoking the then-powerful French Communist Party, the French capitulated. At the same time, Serge Lifar,* the Paris Opéra's flamboyant former director, took the opportunity to declare that Nureyev was "the unquestionable star of the Leningrad Ballet," and was, along with Frenchman Serge Golovine, one of the two best male dancers in the world.

After four days in hiding, Rudolf finally insisted on sneaking out to class and rehearsals in preparation for his de Cuevas debut. Raymundo de Larrain had begun receiving threatening phone calls, accusing him of harboring a "traitor" in his company. Though not easily intimidated, he was unnerved enough to hire two private detectives for his new star, who now found himself in the curious position of being under constant surveillance by both French bodyguards and Russian agents. His circumscribed life — class, rehearsal and lunch — was even more regimented and controlled than it had been at home. Separated from Pushkin, Xenia, Tamara and the small circle he trusted, he felt even more depressed and uprooted. Already he had begun to receive telegrams from his Kirov colleagues, urging him to return home. "I am well protected, but I ask myself, 'how long must I hide?'" he wondered aloud that week to one of the dozens of journalists Raymundo had ushered backstage to meet him. "I shall never return to my own country," he told another, "but I shall never be happy in yours." He longed for home, Nureyev would say later, but journalists at the time misunderstood him and wrongly assumed that he longed to *return* home.

Parisian audiences didn't have long to wait to see Nureyev back onstage. On June 23, eight days after closing the Kirov's Paris season and seven days after bolting from the KGB, Rudolf made his first appearance with a Western company, dancing the role of Prince Florimund in the de Cuevas Ballet's production of *The Sleeping Beauty*. That same night London cheered its first look at the Kirov's *Sleeping Beauty*. Meanwhile, the photographers, policemen and balletomanes who jammed Paris' two-thousand-seat Théâtre des Champs-Elysées threatened to turn Nureyev's debut into a sideshow. They greeted him with a standing ovation, interrupted his performance four times with applause, and brought him back

*The last premier danseur of Diaghilev's Ballets Russes, Lifar led the Paris Opéra Ballet from 1930 to 1958, drawing renewed attention to French ballet and to male dancing. Accused of collaboration during the Second World War, he left the Opéra in 1945. Cleared of the charges, he returned in 1947, though his performances for a time drew hecklers.

for twenty-eight curtain calls. Rudolf, however, felt "like a Christmas tree" as he took to the stage wearing a blue-and-gold beaded costume and the kind of diamanté tiara he had mocked on his first visit chez Raymundo.*

Ballerina Violette Verdy,† in the audience the night of his debut, recalls her first impression of a dancer who was to become a lifelong friend. "I could not get over his intensity, his focus and, of course, his beauty. He was not so much wild as he was untamed and unpolluted. You could see the purity right away in his dedication and total involvement in the role. . . . He had conceived the part of the prince as a man in search of an ideal, with the wonder of discovering it—and with that extraordinary sense of being mesmerized by what he was looking for, and being mesmerized by what he was finding. I had never seen such a vulnerable, exposed quality. . . . He was invested in the part and the part was speaking for him. That was very tantalizing and made the audience all the more curious about him."

Harold Schonberg of *The New York Times* was also present and judged Nureyev "a brilliant executant of the role," who "fully deserved the ovation he received" in his first appearance with a Western company. He went on to observe that "as a stylist, he may not be the most finished of artists as yet. . . . He is however a dancer well on his way to genuine stardom. And he does have the one thing no premier danseur can be without—a personality that comes right over the footlights. When he is on stage, everybody in the audience knows that somebody with a commanding presence is at work."

One week after his defection Nureyev was on his way to becoming the most scrutinized dancer in history, his offstage life commanding as much attention as his sold-out performances. "I didn't like the way I was dished up as a sensation," he complained to a reporter that month, thinking it was all behind him, "and I resented the public curiosity about everything concerning my person." Unaccustomed to the postwar media circus—and as yet untutored in the ways of manipulating it to his own ends—he also resented the constant intrusions on his preperformance rituals. At the Kirov, he had been in the habit of preparing for the stage by spending the day alone, resting quietly and focusing inward. But in Paris, Raymundo scheduled interviews for him day after day, prompting Rudolf to wonder whether he hadn't "made a hopeless mistake."

*In *The New York Times*, Harold Schonberg concurred that the production "sometimes represents French taste at its worst."

†Verdy was one of the most versatile of ballerinas. She had just joined the New York City Ballet, having already danced with the Ballets de Paris and American Ballet Theatre, as well as starred in the Roland Petit film *The Glass Slipper* and performed with Jean-Louis Barrault's renowned acting troupe.

During the company's month-long run of *Sleeping Beauty*, Rudolf was to appear alternately as the Prince and in the virtuoso Bluebird pas de deux, a role that, by all accounts, he had never danced with much distinction at the Kirov. (He "seemed earthbound," recalled one viewer, noting that its technical demands seemed to tax him to exhaustion.) Nevertheless, as Rudolf saw it, he had always been thwarted in his efforts to stamp the role with his own interpretation, wanting to show not simply a bird in flight, but a bird "tempted by a mysterious enticement to fly elsewhere." Rudolf figured that, at least in the de Cuevas troupe, he could dance the Bluebird the way he hoped to.

As it happened, the obstacles he feared came from unlikely quarters. Hours before his Bluebird debut at the Théâtre des Champs-Elysées, a journalist came backstage "and asked a lot of foolish questions which had nothing to do with ballet. She spoke of 'le beau Rudi' and 'la dolce vita' and all kinds of nonsense." Even more distressing were the letters from the Soviet embassy her photographer now handed him. One was from his mother, another from his father and the third from Pushkin. He knew better than to read them before a performance, but they were his first communication from home and he couldn't wait.

Come home, his mother begged him. Come home. His father's letter was equally to the point. How could a son of his betray the motherland? he asked. There was simply no excuse.

His parents' anguish tore at him, he recalled, even though he understood that "propaganda and their own warm feelings were all mixed up. I felt they wanted me back sincerely yet at the same time they had been indoctrinated and told to get me back. . . . I could feel resentment that no one among the people I hold most dear had ever succeeded in understanding me."

Pushkin's letter pained him most of all: The person he assumed knew him best "didn't seem able to understand me. He wrote that Paris was a city of decadence whose rottenness would only corrupt me; that I would lose not only my dancing technique but all moral integrity if I stayed in Europe." Rudolf seemed curiously unaware that Pushkin had been scripted and would have had little choice about the tone and content of his letter.

Already unsettled, he had barely begun his variation when a group of French Communist agitators began shouting "Traitor!" and "Go back to Moscow!" while pelting the stage with tomatoes, banana skins and paper bombs filled with pepper. The jeers and catcalls were countered with cheers of encouragement from other members of the audience, a cacophony that threatened to drown Tchaikovsky's music altogether. "It was just the kind of scandal that Paris relishes, consumes and renews itself with," recalls Violette Verdy.

The annals of ballet were certainly rich with precedent: The premiere of Nijinsky's *Le Sacre du Printemps* on May 29, 1913—which had taken place in the same theater—is just as famous for the riot it set off as it is for its groundbreaking score and choreography.* And in another celebrated Ballets Russes incident a group of surrealists interrupted the premiere of a new ballet by Nijinsky's sister, Bronislava, in 1925. "Oh, not again," Nijinsky's beleaguered mother had declared, "another scandal to get Diaghilev a front-page review."

The Communists this time around also helped generate a few front-page reviews, even if they failed to sabotage Nureyev's performance: Dancing on through all the noise and tumult, he later claimed to have felt "pleased to be serenely dancing while those fools were making such a vulgar exhibition," though this was no doubt an afterthought. More likely he was shaken by the unforeseen assault, given the letters which preceded it.

The next night his performance was interrupted once again, although only by admirers, who showered the stage with flowers in a show of gratitude and solidarity. "He was in such a state," says Rosella Hightower, the veteran de Cuevas star who worked closely with him in those first days. "Dancing was the only thing he had to hold on to. He was completely alone in a world he didn't know."

As fate would have it, Bronislava Nijinska returned to the Théâtre des Champs-Elysées that month to see Nureyev dance the Bluebird, which her brother had performed to great effect during *his* first Parisian season in 1909. Nijinska had supplied much of the choreography for the de Cuevas production of *The Sleeping Beauty*. Afterward she delivered her verdict: "He is the reincarnation of my brother."

Jerome Robbins, Pierre Bergé and Yves Saint Laurent also turned out for the event of the 1961 season. The trio were in the middle of dinner that month when Robbins happened to mention how much he'd love to see Nureyev dance. "So we said, 'Why not tonight?' " remembers Bergé, Saint Laurent's lover and business partner. The performance was sold out and due to begin in twenty minutes, but Bergé pulled some strings with the director of the theater and got them all seats. Bergé and Saint Laurent had already seen Rudolf dance with the Kirov, and were convinced, as Bergé tells it, that Rudolf was destined to become "a superstar" because "he had the look, the face, the arrogance, the attitude. And he knew very well that he possessed it." But according to Bergé,

---

*The primitive rite represented in Nijinsky's choreography, Stravinsky's groundbreaking score and Nicolas Roerich's sets and costumes was a far cry from the ballets to which Parisian audiences had grown accustomed. Backstage, Nijinsky stood on a chair shouting counts to the dancers, while out front, Diaghilev tried vainly to restore order.

Jerome Robbins was nonplussed. "He was surprised by Nureyev, nothing more. At the time, many dancers and choreographers felt that it was only because Nureyev was a Russian who defected that people were talking about him."

Indeed, the English critic Arnold Haskell, the West's prime champion of Soviet ballet, gave voice to that view in the *Dancing Times*, in a column entitled "A Sorry Affair." Lamenting the way this "crazy mixed up dancer" had "let down his comrades," Haskell claimed that Nureyev could save his career only by turning away from the corrupting process of Westernization. "I fear that he is in for a grave disappointment when he ceases to be a nine days' wonder and when he finds less freedom to express himself as a dancer than in his own country . . . The free-lance dancer, permanently removed from the discipline and background of his school and tradition, rapidly deteriorates. The star needs the company far more than the company needs the star."

On the other side of the Iron Curtain, news of the Bluebird melee reached Leningrad via *L'Humanité*, the French Communist newspaper, which Tamara happened to see at a newsstand on the Nevsky Prospect. There had still been no official word about Nureyev and she was hungry for any information she could find, however distorted. When she called Pushkin to tell him that Rudik had been booed in Paris and that the police had to be called in, Pushkin sounded relieved. "Thank God! He's alive and he's dancing. That's the most important thing."

Rudolf's defection had created problems for all of his Leningrad friends. Both Tamara and the Pushkins had been visited by the KGB and ordered to write letters urging him to return. Don't bother sealing your letters, they were warned. Tamara made sure to write in a style so uncharacteristically ornate that Rudolf would know that her hand had been forced.

But her problems didn't end there. In her distress over Rudolf's defection, she had missed an exam and was soon expelled from Leningrad State University for underachievement. When she appealed to the dean, he sent her on to the school's party secretary, who informed her that her academic record wasn't at issue. "You must understand Comrade Zakrzhevskaya, that above all we are guided here by political factors. We are suppposed to write 'Philologist and Teacher of Russian Language and Literature' on your diploma. And being a teacher implies trust. The state is entrusting you with its most precious possession: its children. How can we possibly entrust their education to such a politically naive person as yourself?" Since Rudolf had accompanied her to lectures, he was well known to her classmates; indeed many of them had begun attending his performances once they learned he was a star of the Kirov. When Tamara protested that it was the Kirov Theater that had approved his going to Paris, the party secretary replied: "Let them answer for their own. The university must only give diplomas to those tried and true." Over the next six months Tamara would run from office to office, pleading her case and missing valuable classes before she was finally reinstated in November. She was given ten days to make up the work she had missed.

As far as the authorities knew, Nureyev had shared his Leningrad flat with Alla Sizova. Days after his defection the KGB went to interrogate her mother while Sizova was still on tour in London. Fearing the worst for her daughter, Sizova's mother had become so unhinged by the experience that she had to spend several weeks in a psychiatric hospital.

Rudolf's English tutor, Georgi Mikhailovich, was also targeted early on by the KGB and summoned to "the Big House," Leningrad's KGB headquarters. "They asked him who Rudik's friends were and he told them about the Romankovs' children," recalls Liuba Romankova, who, like Rudolf, had studied English with Georgi Mikhailovich. "He immediately called me and said, 'Lubochka, I had to reveal it because they know all.'" Liuba was then working at the Ioffe Physics Institute, where she, too, was soon summoned to the "first department," its security section, which, like every other, kept tabs on political reliability and diligence as well as a lifetime dossier on each employee.

Her friend had betrayed his motherland, she was informed. "I wouldn't shake hands with him if I met him," the deputy said in disgust.

"No wonder you wouldn't," Liuba replied, preferring to "play the fool," as she puts it. "You are not acquainted with him."

WORLDS AWAY in Ufa, the news of Nureyev's defection drew the fury of Anna Udeltsova. "For me it was a terrible blow," she later told the British filmmaker Patricia Foy, who traveled to Ufa in 1990 to prepare a documentary on Nureyev. Udeltsova was by then a tiny white-haired lady of one hundred and three and if one didn't know better, it would be easy to come away from the film thinking that this sweet old woman had been devastated by the loss of her beloved pupil. But in 1961 she had a different reaction. According to Inna Guskova, Rudolf's onetime neighbor, Udeltsova "cursed him as much as many others did" when she learned of his defection. "One of her relatives told me that she shouted, 'He is a bastard! How did he dare?' Only when she read in his memoir many years later that Rudik called her his favorite teacher in Ufa did she begin loving him again."

Not everyone in Ufa cursed the Nureyevs' son. Hamet's distress was visible and none of his neighbors was unkind to him, recalls Rudolf's niece Alfia, who was then living with the Nureyevs. Most of them worked with Hamet at the nearby plant and though they all knew his son, "no one called him a traitor. They simply said, 'We are sorry we won't see him again.' " Hamet wasn't expelled from the party, nor was he fired from his job, but he wasn't promoted anymore and neither were his daughters. Farida was a pensioner, so she didn't have much to lose, except the one thing she would come to care most about: seeing her only son. Hamet never spoke to Rudolf again.

Though the family would never be officially informed, the chief of Ufa's visa department had been instructed not to issue foreign passports or exit visas to any of Nureyev's relatives.* Nevertheless, Farida and Rosa went to the Ministry of Culture in Moscow in hopes of meeting with Minister Furtseva and persuading her to let Farida go to Paris to bring Rudolf home. Furtseva, however, refused to see them, the first of many fruitless missions to Moscow for Rosa. The KGB continued to urge the Nureyevs to make contact with their son. "They didn't ask us to tell him that he was a traitor," as Razida remembers it. "On the contrary, they said, 'Write him a letter, telephone him, tell him to come home.' But I didn't know where to call him. And, stupid me, I called KGB in Moscow to find out his telephone number. The man I talked to said he didn't know it, but he would try to find it out. When I called him the next day, I was informed that he had been dismissed."

Finally, in August, a number was relayed to Rosa in Leningrad, who, in turn, cabled home instructions. Farida and Razida called Rudolf in Deauville, the fashionable seaside resort on the Normandy coast, where the de Cuevas troupe was then rehearsing. Famous for its casino and thoroughbred racing scene, a magnet for the smartest society of Europe, Deauville was at the furthest remove from Ufa. "I asked him what was in my heart because I didn't believe he would do better abroad," recalls Razida. "He told me it wasn't his fault. He said Russia was his native country and he wanted to come back, but only after he'd seen the world." Farida was having none of it and pleaded with Rudolf to come home.

"Mama," he finally interrupted her, "you forgot to ask me one question."

---

*In 1993 the director of the Ufa Ballet happened to meet Ufa's former visa chief and the two fell into a conversation about Nureyev's defection, a subject they couldn't have discussed openly until then. "He told me how uneasy he had felt about the orders he was given," remembers Radic Gareev. "But he was a military man and he had no choice. The order was marked 'strictly confidential' and said: 'No contacts with Nureyev. No visas for his relatives.' "

"What is that?" she asked him.

"Are you happy?"

Farida did as he asked.

"Yes," Rudolf answered her, though Farida scarcely believed him.

NUREYEV'S DEFECTION had shaken the Kirov to its roots and sent tremors through every state agency and subcommittee involved in the Paris tour, from the ministries of Foreign Affairs and Culture to the Soviet embassy in France, and from the KGB to the Leningrad party bureau. All of them were implicated in Nureyev's act of treason, though each did its best to place the blame elsewhere. That July the Central Committee launched its investigation. Appointed to head the task force were the chairmen of two Central Committee departments: the Commission on Traveling Abroad, which approved all foreign travel, and the Department of Culture, which oversaw the Ministry of Culture and, in turn, the Kirov.

One by one the Kirov dancers were summoned to the Big House and asked to account for Nureyev's behavior abroad. Who were his friends? Did they think he had planned to defect? With their first American tour only two months away, they naturally had a lot at stake. The United States was the destination they coveted most of all.

"The walls of the KGB were thick, but word leaked out about who said what," remembers Tamara. "Soloviev was the only one who said that Rudik had planned to defect. When I heard about it, I immediately went to see Soloviev to ask him if he had really said that about Rudik. He said, 'Yes, I believe he intended to do it.'" By way of proof, Soloviev told her that Rudolf wasn't buying Western consumer goods the way the others were. He seemed to be saving his money. Why? "Because he was going to defect," he said. But the contents of Rudolf's luggage told another story. His suitcase had been returned to the Pushkins and one glimpse inside told Xenia, Pushkin and Tamara that Soloviev's claim "was utter nonsense." Along with blue fabric for his hoped-for *Legend of Love* costume, Rudolf had purchased several blond wigs for *The Sleeping Beauty*, as well as ballet slippers and a makeup case. It was obvious to all of them that Rudolf was buying the things he needed for his Leningrad performances. The exception was the electric train set, the memento that brought their Mahmoudka home to them most acutely. The Pushkins assembled the train in their apartment and it was still there, years later, when Mikhail Baryshnikov came to live with them. "There was a shrine to his memory," he recalls. "Everything he left behind was sacred, his toy train, his clothes."

Even if we assume that Soloviev didn't know about Rudolf's wigs and costumes, he certainly knew about the train set. He had stayed up half the night playing with it like a schoolboy, he told his wife on his return to Leningrad. So why did he tell the KGB that Rudolf was saving his money or that Rudolf was planning to defect? Fear is the likely answer, a motive that cannot possibly be overstated in light of the Cold War paranoia that drove the investigation. Refusing to cooperate in a matter of state security could only be viewed as a sympathy vote for Nureyev. The KGB leaned hard on Soloviev to supply evidence against Nureyev, with whom he'd shared a room in Paris for nearly five weeks. How was it, they prodded him, that he didn't notice anything suspicious?

"Yura had a lot of trouble in the days after Rudik defected," says Tatiana Legat, recalling the many interrogations her husband endured. "We were terribly afraid. Terribly! Yura was brought to the organs* and I don't know what he said or what he signed, but I know that they wanted to know how it could have happened. He had to say how lucky he was that he hadn't been tainted by Nureyev."

But did he tell the authorities that Nureyev made a pass at him in Paris, as some of his colleagues believe? According to Tamara, Soloviev began spreading that rumor once back in Leningrad. But whether the claim is true and just what, if anything, Soloviev told the KGB during or after the Paris tour continue to be a matter of fervent and contradictory speculation. Tatiana Legat says that Soloviev confided in her that he had been "so startled by Rudik's advance that he had slapped him across the face and avoided him for the rest of his stay in Paris." But she has no idea, she says, whether her husband reported on Nureyev while in Paris. "He only said that he and Rudik had a good laugh about the fact that they had been asked to report on one another."†

Years later, when asked by his former classmate Elena Tchernichova whether he had made a pass at Soloviev, Rudolf replied, "Yes, of course I did. He had such a cute butt." By then Rudolf was not in any danger and may have been merely toying with her. Tchernichova also claims that Soloviev once admitted to her after a few rounds of drinks that he had indeed reported Nureyev's advance to the KGB in Paris. He was afraid of being implicated, she heard him say, and did it to protect his career. Still other close friends of Soloviev's insist that it would have been out of character for Soloviev to have turned informer. "Even if he had

---

*The "organs" referred to the organs of state security.

†Had Soloviev figured decisively in the events leading to Nureyev's defection, as many believe, his claims would likely have been mentioned in one of the many documents about Nureyev's defection in the Central Committee archives. Surely in his first report to the Central Committee, KGB chief Shelepin would have cited the episode, had he known about it, as further proof of Nureyev's "decadent" behavior abroad.

been told, 'You're a very good man, please tell us something,' Yura couldn't do it," says Alla Osipenko. "He was a very honest man. It would have been against his nature to do it. It's true that on that tour we were encouraged to inform on each other. But based on my own experience, I can say that it didn't always happen. When I traveled, I always roomed with Natasha Makarova and I can swear that neither of us informed on each other."*

Soloviev's troubles didn't end there. In the months that followed, "they tried to make him join the party because they wanted him to help them, but he refused," recalls his wife. "They even fired Mironov, the secretary of the theater's party organization, because he failed to get Yura to join, so you can imagine how horrible it was." Nevertheless, the news wasn't all bad. "When Nureyev left, Yura took over his parts." There was the London premiere of *Swan Lake* with Osipenko and later the New York premieres of *The Sleeping Beauty* and *Le Corsaire* with Sizova. "After London, Yura was in demand, so I guess you could say Nureyev gave him a push. Every cloud has a silver lining."†

It wasn't long before the Soviets were erasing Nureyev from the history books. His name disappeared from the list of honor graduates at his alma mater and his *Corsaire* solo was excised from *A Leap by the Soul,* the film about Russian ballet made at the time of his student triumph in Moscow. An article about him was stricken from all future copies of a book about the Kirov Ballet. Any magazine sent from abroad that contained his photograph arrived with the offending image pasted over. Still, at secret gatherings, Nureyev's fans would later screen amateur films of him, taken from the wings or in class. (Baryshnikov first saw Nureyev dance in one of these films.)

Not all news about Nureyev was suppressed: On occasion, items were fed to the Kirov dancers when they served the purposes of propaganda. When Alla Sizova heard that the French unions had thrown tomatoes at her former partner in Paris and booed him off the stage, she assumed, as did many of her fellow dancers, that Soviet artists died a quick death in the West. But when she happened to boast that "Nureyev won't fail in the West with *our* education," the KGB came calling. Mention of Nureyev's name—regardless of the context—provoked suspicion and censure. "Two agents showed up at the theater and started ques-

---

*Nearly ten years after the Paris tour, when Valery Panov submitted an application to emigrate to Israel, a meeting was held at the Kirov to encourage Panov's colleagues to condemn him for betraying the motherland. The company was then preparing for a tour and the dancers knew that if they hoped to be chosen, they would have to comply. According to the photographer Nina Alovert, only a few dancers refused to discredit Panov and among these were Soloviev and Mikhail Baryshnikov.

†Soloviev committed suicide in 1977.

tioning me. 'Do you understand what you have said?' they asked me. So I told them that I meant it must be terrible to work abroad and then they left me alone."

Nureyev had never been particularly popular among his colleagues and while some of them were sorry to lose him, no one considered him indispensable. Nureyev was a young star, not an established one, and in the view of many, he was a fool to abandon the prestige and security he had known at the Kirov. "Well, of course he was a talented man," says Sizova, thirty-odd years later, "but he wasn't the only one. For us, the loss of one dancer was nothing. Our theater could get along very well without him. What shocked us was not that he was gone, but that he could have acted in the way he did. How could someone with our training and our background do such a thing? This was not something we could understand."

THE INVESTIGATION was completed in a matter of weeks and on August 2 the commission delivered its findings to the Central Committee. The three-page report, cosigned by the chiefs of the committee's Cultural Department and Commission on Traveling Abroad, gave a summary of the key events and players and naturally assigned blame. "From the first days of his stay in Paris, Nureyev established close relations with politically suspicious persons: a certain Larrain — theater businessman and ballet master — . . . Clara Saint, a woman of dubious behavior, and other elements from among the artistic bohemia. Nureyev roughly violated the discipline, neglected the interests of the collective, systematically spent time together with his new acquaintances, coming back to the hotel late at night. By the beginning of June, when Nureyev's behavior had become unbearable, the deputy chief of the ballet company, Comrade Strizhevski, and the embassy workers put forward a proposal about sending Nureyev from Paris ahead of time."

The report went on to describe how the order for Nureyev's recall had twice gone unheeded: "Instead of the immediate execution of the received instructions, the directorate of the theater, as well as the embassy workers, considered the dispatch of Nureyev inexpedient, though it was already evident that the further stay in France of this renegade who had lost his honor and conscience was fraught with dangerous consequences."

Faulting the decisions made all along the chain of command, the investigators concluded that Nureyev's dispatch from Paris had been bungled from start to finish.

Nureyev was preparing for the flight to London together with the collective of the ballet company. At the airport before boarding the London plane the director of the theater, Comrade Korkin,* took Nureyev aside from the line for boarding and informed him that it was necessary for him to go to Moscow because of his mother's illness and because of his participation in important concerts in Moscow. Having learned about it, Nureyev declared that he would commit suicide as sending him back from abroad would bring about the gravest consequences for him. Nureyev was left at Paris airport . . . in a state of nervous excitement. . . . At the airport Nureyev informed his French "friends" present there, who later helped him tell the police of his intention to remain in Paris. Comrade Strizhevski, who was at the airport, was not able to prevent the traitor from carrying out his intention, as the police interfered.

With twenty-twenty hindsight, the report now charged that Nureyev's "outrageous behavior from the first days of his work at the Leningrad ballet" should have disqualified him from consideration for the tour. How was it, the writers asked, that someone who had "turned the collective against himself, dared insult his colleagues and was known in the collective as a scoundrel and immorally unstable person" could have been approved to go abroad? In their view, there could be only one explanation: Sergeyev, Korkin and the theater's party boss had approved Nureyev's application without sending it to the party committees of the theater and the ballet company for further scrutiny.

There is good reason to believe their claim: Nureyev was not among the dancers initially approved for the Paris tour and was added only at the last minute, after the organizers informed Sergeyev that Paris wanted to see younger dancers. Sergeyev and Korkin needed Nureyev in Paris and probably suspected—as Rudolf had all along—that he would never make the cut if his file were sent through the proper channels. Given the petty rivalries that colored decision making at these in-house committee meetings—and not least Rudolf's less-than-glowing character profile—he was right to worry that he would be dropped from the lineup.

More significant than the details of the report, however, is the picture it paints of a system at once obsessed with control but unable to maintain it away from home. The Soviets assumed that by their keeping such tight reins on the tour there could be little room for error. Yet paradoxically, they possessed no such omnipotence. The presence of so many agencies and officials, each with different and often conflicting agendas, ultimately left no one in control.

With the Kirov's tour to the United States slated for early Septem-

*According to Nureyev and other eyewitnesses, it was Sergeyev, not Korkin, who told him he wasn't going on to London.

ber, the Central Committee ordered a second investigation, this time into the company's political vigilance both before and during the Paris tour. On August 15, just forty-eight hours after East Germany began erecting the Berlin Wall, Leningrad's district chief of science, schools and culture delivered his findings to the party's local committee. His report was prosaically entitled "On the Mistakes of the Leningrad Kirov Academic Opera and Ballet Theater Leadership in the Preparation of and During the Tour of the Ballet Company Abroad." Excerpts of the meeting were forwarded to the Central Committee and in turn the Ministry of Culture.

In the opinion of the Leningrad committee, Nureyev's "treacherous act" was the direct result of lax political instruction and irresponsible leadership at the Kirov (an ironic allegation given Hamet Nureyev's career as a *politruk*). The report charged that during the tour "no political work was carried out in the collective and the political and Komsomol groups were inactive." And not only did the directors "make up a false character reference praising Nureyev," they twice ignored orders to return Nureyev to the USSR. Indeed, according to the report, "Sergeyev had categorically asserted that it was impossible to continue the tour without Nureyev," prompting the committee to conclude that Nureyev "was under Comrade Korkin's and Sergeyev's protection." Not surprisingly, the report made no reference to Nureyev's drawing power in Paris or to his contributions to the Kirov's success.

In the wake of this latest investigation, Korkin was fired for "political shortsightedness" and expelled from the party. Sergeyev, meanwhile, was summoned to the Ministry of Culture for further questioning. Security measures at the Kirov were to be intensified: All those bound for American were ordered to undergo stringent monitoring and political instruction. Priority was to be given to card-carrying party members. But of course, by tightening the reins even further, the authorities learned "only the wrong lessons," as Valery Panov put it.

The fate of Strizhevski was left to KGB chief Shelepin to decide. A memo to the party's Central Committee, dated August 26, 1961, noted that the KGB boss had issued an official reprimand to Captain Strizhevski "for the unsatisfactory organization of the agitation-operative work among the members of the [Kirov], and for not taking timely measures for dispatching Nureyev to the USSR." The reprimand marked him for life.

By the time the Kirov departed for New York in early September, Korkin had been replaced by Petr Rachinsky, a hard-liner and former fireman. Tatiana Legat had joined the tour, replacing Nureyev as her husband's roommate, while Alla Osipenko had lost her top billing and was left behind in Leningrad. Of the principal players, only Sergeyev managed to come through the political drama unscathed. He would rule the Kirov for the next nine years, until the defection of another star, Natalia Makarova, finally and irrevocably spelled the end of his reign.

New Horizons

AFTER TWO MONTHS in the West, Nureyev was uncertain about where he was heading. He was pleased to be dancing sixteen times each month, rather than the standard three at the Kirov, and he enjoyed partnering Rosella Hightower, the de Cuevas company's enormously popular prima ballerina. But on the whole, he thought the company—and its fashionable audience—lacked the discipline, respect for tradition and seriousness of purpose he had known at the Kirov. "He felt it wasn't his world," says Hightower. "He didn't want to conform to anyone else's ideas. He wanted to make his own ideas."

He was also convinced that de Larrain cared more about decor than dancing. One night he simply refused to go onstage in one of the beaded bolero jackets de Larrain had designed. "He threw it on the floor and told me it was nothing but shit and distracting," de Larrain later complained.

"Raymundo and Rudolf did not have the same point of view on beauty and the theater and they fought," recalled Jacqueline de Ribes, who was ringside for many of their battles. "[Raymundo] was very unrealistic. He didn't know how to talk to people. He was too grand." Yet he guarded Rudolf with a proprietary air, steering him clear of any competitor who might lure him with a better offer. He effectively barred Pierre Lacotte from speaking to Nureyev after he heard that Lacotte had provoked Nureyev's interest in starring in a film about Nijinsky. When Lacotte tried to bring the producer backstage to meet Nureyev one day, de Larrain ordered them both from the theater and admonished Lacotte to stay away. As a result, claims Lacotte, he didn't speak to Nureyev for another two years, though Rudolf was never to know the reason. Even so, Rudolf complained later that Raymundo "never let me meet with anyone." De Larrain had hoped to sign Rudolf to a two-year contract, but Rudolf steadfastly refused to commit himself beyond six months.

Offstage Rudolf worried constantly about being kidnapped by the KGB; he insisted on sitting on the floors of taxicabs, for fear of being followed. Most days he sought refuge in the studio alongside Hightower, who shared his passion for work and was eager to learn from him. She admired his sharply analytic mind and marveled at both his remarkable turnout, unusual in a male dancer at the time, and his exaggerated fifth position, "Pushkin's sign of the cross," in Hightower's words. "To Rudolf it was a sacred position. Pushkin was his world and he would never do anything that went against his training."

"The integrity was such that it was almost overwhelming," concurs Violette Verdy, one of Nureyev's first friends in the West. "He was going to the cathedral, to the pure thing. I met him at a time when he was still testing his ground, when he was less devoured by social life. He wasn't narcissistic then. He was open and curious and interested in anything good."

He watched, listened and avidly took in a staggering range of sensations. When Jean Fayard of *Le Figaro* came to interview "the Soviet dancer who chose freedom" in mid-July, he was struck by the breadth of his interests. That week alone, Nureyev had been to see the Mexican Ballet, the Russian film *The Letter*, a Gustave Moreau exhibition at the Louvre, Ford's *'Tis Pity She's a Whore* at the Théâtre de Paris and a gallery show devoted to the work of Georges Méliès, the renowned silent film–era set designer. His new life was not without its sybaritic moments. During a break in the de Cuevas schedule in July, Clara and Raymundo invited him to the south of France, where they had booked rooms at La Réserve, an Italianate villa-hotel in Beaulieu with its own private beach. In the warm azure waters of the Mediterranean, Rudolf found the perfect balm for his nervous exhaustion. The discovery that he could actually rent his own motorboat deepened his pleasure and he was happy to spend hours at a time tooling around the hotel's private port, swimming and sunning himself. Naturally a number of photographers were on hand to record his latest exploits, though even *they* couldn't disrupt his idyll. "He was in the papers every day and people were crowding around him," Clara recalls. "He was already being treated like a star."

It wasn't long before the American photographer Richard Avedon tracked him down in Paris and invited him to pose for a portrait for *Harper's Bazaar*. A celebrated fashion photographer since the 1940s, Avedon was also known for his bold portraits of celebrities, who appealed to him, he said, because they "have the faces of men and women familiar with extreme situations." The Duke and Duchess of Windsor, Tennessee Williams and Dorothy Parker had all sat for him, and now, two months after his bolt from the KGB, so did Nureyev, for whom extreme situations were a matter of course. Rudolf took at once to Avedon's manic energy, and during the session, which took place in a studio near the Hôtel St. Regis, the photographer kept the champagne flowing. Suddenly, around midnight, Avedon proposed doing some nude photos. "Rudolf was almost drunk by that point and looked pretty hesitant," recalls Clara, who decided not to stick around for the finale.

The following morning Rudolf telephoned Clara. He was stricken with remorse. "He said he was furious, that it was a mistake, that it was stupid of him." Any fears of overexposure were soon allayed by the September issue of *Bazaar*. Avedon's portraits showed two faces of Nureyev: In one he is sweetly grinning, accessible; in the other he is at once insolent and alluring, all pouting lips and tensile strength. Nureyev glossed over the episode in his memoir, noting only that when he saw the photos Avedon had taken, he felt reassured "he had understood me. . . ."

IT WAS WHILE rehearsing in Deauville that August that Rudolf fell into a brief affair with Maria Tallchief, the most famous American ballerina of the day. A star since the 1940s, first with the Ballet Russe de Monte Carlo and later as the prima ballerina of the New York City Ballet, Tallchief had also appeared as a guest with American Ballet Theatre, whose landmark tour to the Soviet Union in 1960 had introduced American ballet to the Russians. Tall and long-legged, with black hair, olive skin and large brown eyes, the exotically beautiful Tallchief had been born in Fairfax, Oklahoma, the daughter of an Osage Indian father and a Scotch-Irish mother. She had grown up in Hollywood, where she had taken ballet lessons with Bronislava Nijinska and seriously studied the piano with an eye toward a concert career.

Tallchief's reputation and Native-American roots naturally intrigued Rudolf, but so did her close ties to the two people he most wanted to meet: Erik Bruhn, the West's preeminent classical dancer, and George Balanchine, its preeminent choreographer. Tallchief had married Balanchine in 1946, the third of his four wives. Though the marriage had lasted just five years, Tallchief had stayed on in the role of muse and prima ballerina, and many of Balanchine's signature works—among them *Symphony in C, Orpheus* and *Firebird*—had been built around her talents.

By the time she met Rudolf that summer, she was separated from her second husband, a Chicago businessman, and had just come out of a stormy relationship with Bruhn, which had unraveled during their tour to Russia. If their artistic liaison was hailed for its harmony, their personal relationship was anything but, and had ended bitterly the month before

Tallchief arrived in Deauville after Bruhn accused her of smothering him. The story goes that her parting shot to Bruhn, with whom she later admitted to being quite smitten, was to promise to find a new partner. "There is a Russian that has just defected. He is in Paris and I'll find him. *He'll* be my new partner!"

When quite by chance, she found her young Russian in Deauville, the thirty-six-year-old Tallchief "fell in love with him in a flash," remembers Rosella Hightower, who also had Native-American roots. "It was a meeting of two flamboyant temperaments—the Tatar and the Indian. They had a lot in common." Tallchief, for her part, couldn't help thinking that Balanchine must have been just like Nureyev as a young man, an observation she later related to the choreographer. Nureyev was so curious, so hungry for knowledge, she thought, and, not incidentally, "so very attractive, so boyish and handsome . . . I couldn't take my eyes off him."

By a curious twist of events, Tallchief was on her way to Copenhagen to dance with Bruhn at the Royal Theater. Bruhn had been asked to invite Tallchief to dance with him for a special gala and, according to his account, had sent her a decidedly formal letter, leaving no doubt about the terms. Rudolf naturally jumped at the chance to meet Bruhn and quickly convinced de Larrain to grant him a brief leave of absence. He was "obsessed with Erik," Tallchief recalled, and spoke of him constantly. He had seen only a film clip of Bruhn dancing, but the clip, and the fevered response to his appearances in his Russia, had been enough to convince him that "whether friend or enemy, I had to find out what makes him tick, and how it makes him tick, and learn the ticking."

One way to learn the ticking was to study with Bruhn's trusted teacher, Vera Volkova, a Russian émigrée who had been working at the Royal Danish Ballet School for nearly a decade. As the foremost authority on the Vaganova method in the West, she was considered one of the most influential teachers in Europe and especially skilled with male dancers, whose ranks included Stanley Williams, with whom Nureyev would later study in New York. Born in prerevolutionary St. Petersburg, she had studied with Vaganova and had later toured the Far East. Eventually she had emigrated to London with her British husband and opened her own school, which after the war attracted most of the leading British dancers, Margot Fonteyn among them, as well as all the top foreign dancers who passed through London. Nureyev knew better than anyone that his technique needed refining, and he hoped that Volkova or Bruhn might nurture his talent the way Pushkin had. That quest for mentors, begun in Ufa, would continue to the end of his life.

En route to Copenhagen, Rudolf and Maria Tallchief stopped off in Frankfurt, where Rudolf was to be filmed for German television, partnering French ballerina Yvette Chauviré in extracts from *Giselle* and *Le*

Spectre de la Rose, the Fokine ballet Pierre Lacotte had begun teaching him in Paris. At Nureyev's insistence, the taping was to be kept quiet until the last day, and nothing whatsoever was to be leaked about Tallchief's presence in Frankfurt. Nevertheless, an American reporter soon found them and even managed to snare an exclusive interview with Nureyev, who, he seemed surprised to discover, was "almost neurotically antagonistic toward the press."

Nureyev had good reason to be out of sorts: Vaslav Orlikovsky, the Basel Ballet's director, who had arranged the program, didn't know the complete *Spectre de la Rose*, leaving Rudolf no choice but to piece together the rest on his own, using vintage photographs of Nijinsky in the role.* And since no live musicians were provided as he had expected, he had found himself in the rather curious position of dancing to phonograph records, hardly circumstances worth having left home for, save for the handsome four–thousand-dollar fee.† The Russian-born Orlikovsky seemed equally exasperated with Nureyev. "He practices more than any other dancer I've ever seen," he complained to the reporter Franz Spelman, voicing a familiar refrain. "Yesterday he asked me three times to delay a final take because he felt that he had still some more training to do. He is the most ambitious man I've ever encountered, the perfect perfectionist. But off the stage, he can be the sloppiest, rudest man. So moody! So hard to get along with! One never knows where one stands with him."

Ignoring the gag order on Tallchief, Orlikovksy let loose with a description of the pair in their offstage hours. "At night he sits silently in his hotel room," he told Spelman, "permitting Maria Tallchief to massage his feet, and no one can utter a word while the phonograph goes full blast: the Mozart *Requiem*, Brahms' *Fourth Symphony*, *Tristan and Isolde* and that endless *Symphony Divine* by Scriabin. . . . he plays that piece sometimes three, five, 10 times in a row. . . . I took him to the Troika Restaurant here—the best Russian place west of Moscow. He hardly touched the food. 'It is all imitation!' was his only comment. . . ."

Equally intriguing was the interview with Nureyev himself, the first extended one he had ever given. Resentful of the questions about his private life—in Russia, he said pointedly, "only the secret police does this"—he simply recast his personal history, something he would do with increasing relish as the years wore on. His most peculiar claims were

---

*In his biography of Nureyev, John Percival suggests that Pierre Lacotte was on hand to show him the ballet, though Lacotte was not in Frankfurt at the time. Lacotte recalls that he had taught Nureyev some of the ballet in Paris, but had never finished because Raymundo de Larrain tried to keep him away from Nureyev.

†In his first Western television appearance, Nureyev danced in Act 2 of *Giselle* with Basel Ballet dancer Irène Skorik and *Le Spectre de la Rose* with the Berlin-based ballerina Gisela Deege.

that his father had taught him folk dancing and that he had been invited to join the Kirov after Sergeyev had seen him perform with a group of Ufa dancers at the Kirov Theater.

But when asked about his future plans, the twenty-three-year-old Nureyev outlined with remarkable prescience and confidence the goals he intended to accomplish — all of which he would. "I'm on my way to see the people of the Danish Ballet. Later on I shall go to London. From there, I hope to go to New York. Of course I would like to work under a man like Balanchine. And I certainly would like to appear at Covent Garden. But I don't want to go on anywhere in the circumstances which existed in Paris. I don't want to be considered as a freak, or as a curiosity. I want to retain my own dancer's identity. But now I'm aiming for it: my own identity — as a dancer, and later on as a choreographer and teacher — even if this would mean forming my own group."

FROM FRANKFURT, Rudolf called Pushkin and was relieved when he finally got through after several failed tries. He asked Pushkin not to worry about him. He was alive and well and dancing, he said, the constant clicking in his ear a reminder that the line was bugged. He also spoke to Xenia, who, though heartbroken over his departure, was "the only person not afraid to continue relations with Rudik," recalls Liuba Romankova. "Alexander Ivanovich was afraid to lose his job, but since Xenia was a pensioner, there wasn't much they could do to her. Rudik would make arrangements with her to call at set times. Sometimes she would call me when she knew he would call and I would go over to their place. It was always a big secret."

The second call he made was to Copenhagen, at Tallchief's suggestion. "There's someone here who wants to meet you," she alerted Bruhn from a pay phone. "His name is Rudolf Nureyev." Bruhn assumed she was joking. "So I passed the phone to Rudolf and that's how they met," recalled Tallchief, who would soon have cause to regret that introduction.

13

Rudik and Erik

NUREYEV'S ARRIVAL in Copenhagen came at a pivotal moment in Erik Bruhn's career: At thirty-two, Bruhn was at the height of his renown, yet saw himself at a dead end. A brooding prince in the tradition of his most famous countryman, he could give the most sublime performance and come offstage feeling despondent. He once confessed that he had achieved artistic harmony onstage perhaps five or six times in his entire career. "For two or three days after, I was almost sick. I was burnt up completely. Then came the thought of recapturing that unbelievable state. You try to achieve the same feeling. You work for that, and you despair." Hobbled by self-doubt, Bruhn was his own worst critic. "He dances to please some abstract ideal of perfection," the critic Clive Barnes observed. "There is no dancer alive with more style, more grandeur, and more passion." Hailed for his unrivaled technical and artistic perfection, his elegant line, his classical finesse, Bruhn was the dancer's dancer, the quintessential danseur noble. He was also to the manner born. Ten years Nureyev's senior, he had begun his training at the age of nine and joined the Royal Danish Ballet ten years later, quickly becoming the company's "idol." Although famous in his native Denmark, he was unknown in America when he joined Ballet Theatre in 1949. By 1955 he had become an international star. Yet despite all the acclaim and accolades, by September 1961 Bruhn felt he had traveled as far as he could go. "There seemed to be no other dancer around. Everybody was looking to me. I felt alone. . . ."

Nureyev's sudden appearance offered Bruhn the competitive stimulus he had despaired of ever finding. However, the stimulus of Nureyev would present Bruhn with considerably more challenges than even *he* might have bargained for.

Among these was Maria Tallchief, with whom Bruhn had abruptly ended his short-lived affair one year earlier. "He was always running away from Maria like mad," recalls his close friend the choreographer Glen Tetley, who had joined them on ABT's 1960 Russian tour. No sooner did Tallchief arrive at Copenhagen's Hotel Angleterre with Rudolf in tow than she rang Bruhn at home and invited him to join them for a drink. Bruhn vividly recalled this meeting: "It was late afternoon and the place was very dark. I greeted Maria and there sat this young dancer casually dressed in a sweater and slacks. I sat down and looked at him more carefully and saw that he was very attractive. He had a certain style about him . . . a kind of class. It was not a natural elegance, but somehow it worked. He did not speak very much, probably because his English was still not very good. It was something of an uncomfortable situation because of my relationship with Maria. She and I covered it up with lots of unnatural laughter. Rudik mentioned much later that he had hated the sound of my laugh. . . . It was all I could do to get through that hour we spent together."

After that, they saw each other only in the studio during class with the Royal Danish dancers and Vera Volkova. Maria and Erik, meanwhile, rehearsed in the afternoons, while Nureyev studied privately with Volkova. But in the evenings Tallchief had Nureyev to herself. Still, she could see that "a great attraction was developing" between them, "even though it was clear that Rudy's adoration was overwhelming. Erik was the type who needed to maintain his independence. Yet Rudy was so appealing that one was drawn to him spontaneously. I felt it myself. . . .'"

As he now took stock of Bruhn, Nureyev saw his ideal: the long-limbed, impeccable figure fixed in his mind's eye whenever he faced the classroom mirror. Rudolf, at five feet nine inches, was neither broad-shouldered nor elegantly long in the leg like Bruhn, and had less than princely proportions with his long, sculpted torso and muscular thighs and calves. He could see that Bruhn was in command of a seamless and flawless technique, while he was still struggling to correct his body, to make "an instrument of it," in Violette Verdy's words, "at the same time as his soul and his talent were revealing themselves. He was the battleground on which all this took place."

Rudolf was also what the Danes called "a dirty dancer," remembers Peter Martins, then a fifteen-year-old apprentice with the Royal Danish Ballet. "Not clean, sort of messy. When it came to dancing, he didn't quite measure up. We Danes were very meticulous. For us, what mattered was not how many turns you could do or how high you could jump, but how you took off and landed. I don't think it ever occurred

NUREYEV: HIS LIFE] *192*

to Rudolf that classical male dancing could be as refined as that. We sort of dismissed him. All of us young ones didn't care that he was a famous defector and we couldn't understand why Erik brought him in. Erik was our idol, not Rudi. But we soon discovered that there were virtues to his dancing. He introduced a Soviet vocabulary of male pyrotechnics that hadn't been seen much before. I got the sense that Erik was equally impressed with him, but Erik was much more discreet about it. All Rudolf did was watch Erik. He was so impressed with Erik's style and cleanliness, but when he tried to copy Erik, he couldn't do it."

That didn't stop him from criticizing his schooling, however. "That's wrong, it's not Russian," he would tell Bruhn, who would patiently explain that the Danish school was equally valid, even if Rudolf was unfamiliar with it.* The creator of that distinctive school was August Bournonville, the influential nineteenth-century dancer, choreographer and director, who developed the fleet and airy technique that became the signature of successive generations of Danish dancers. His ballets formed the basis of the Royal Danish Ballet's repertory of classics, the most famous of which was *La Sylphide*. Bournonville was also responsible for reasserting the importance of the male dancer; by the 1960s the Royal Danish Ballet was famous for training the best male dancers outside Russia.

As the epitome of the Bournonville dancer, Bruhn was Nureyev's polar opposite, the Apollo to his Dionysius, poetic not powerful. Where the Soviet school favored big, soaring, powerful jumps with sustained poses, the Franco-Danish style of Bournonville shunned fire for finesse, calling for crisp, nimble footwork, quick changes in direction, fluttering beats and incremental steps building to a crescendo. Bruhn moved audiences with the effortlessness of his dancing; Nureyev thrilled them with the effortfulness of his. Bruhn's performances were dignified, ethereal, elegant; Nureyev's were defiant, dangerous and unquestionably sexual. The recognition that each possessed qualities the other desired kindled their mutual passion. "Erik had it all from the beginning," Rudolf told Rosella Hightower, a favorite partner of Bruhn's at Ballet Theatre in the 1950s. "I had to break my legs and arms and back and put myself together again." And yet Bruhn was equally inspired by Nureyev. "It was through watching him that I could free myself and try to discover that looseness of his." Indeed, had Rudolf not come along, he would have "quit," Bruhn admitted.

Despite their differences, their greatest affinity lay in their perfec-

*Though Agrippina Vaganova had studied under one of Bournonville's foremost pupils, Christian Johansson, a leading teacher at the Imperial Ballet School until his death in 1903, she did not include Bournonville technique in her own curriculum at the Leningrad Ballet School.

tionism, their insistence on upping the ante with each performance. But where Nureyev was driven to perform whatever the circumstances, Bruhn, like a skittish thoroughbred, was often sidelined by his sensitive constitution. To Nureyev, talent was destiny, demanding of him every sacrifice. To Bruhn, talent was a burden, something to be borne, not celebrated. Even at age fifteen, Bruhn was such a standout pupil at the Royal Danish Ballet School that senior members of the company came to watch him in class. That early recognition only unhinged him. "I became frightened of my capacities. . . . Of course, I continued dancing, but that initial fear never left me." To this day colleagues like former Danish ballet star Flemming Flindt don't recall ever having seen anybody as "amazing" in class as Bruhn. "But he was never very keen on performing. He once said to me, 'One thing I'm very good at is getting offstage fast.' That was a typical Bruhn remark."

Rudolf, by contrast, had fought his way to center stage. At seventeen, he was a long shot beginning his training at the Leningrad school. His personality had been tempered by battle. As far as he was concerned, the fight would never be over. Unfortunately, his firebrand style and unyielding application were just as alienating to the Danes as they had been to the Russians. Bruhn, in fact, was the only Danish dancer who bothered to strike up a friendship with him; the others considered him strange, rude and untutored. How did Nureyev dare to stand front and center of every class, when Bruhn stood at the back and drew little attention to himself? "He was disrespectful to the teachers, just doing what he wanted," recalls Peter Martins. "He would stop a class and say, 'It's too fast.' Erik seemed to be slightly embarrassed about hanging out with this young kid. In the Danish ballet, you can't get away with prima donna scenes."

But Erik also understood that Rudolf was in the throes of culture shock. "Why don't the Danish people respect you more?" Nureyev had asked him one day, unable to fathom why the Danes didn't make more of a fuss over Bruhn the way the Russian balletomanes did over their favorite dancers. "What do you expect them to do—crawl on their hands and knees when I come around?'" Bruhn responded.

Nureyev might well have replied yes, for he was soon besotted with Bruhn, a discovery he tried in vain to conceal. This naturally took a toll on Erik's relations with Tallchief, which grew ever more tenuous as their performances neared. In her Royal Danish debut, Tallchief was to appear in the pas de deux from *Don Quixote*, a bravura technical showpiece, and Birgit Cullberg's darkly dramatic *Miss Julie*, based on the Strindberg play about the psychosexual warfare between a sadistic valet and a young noblewoman. Certainly there was enough offstage tension on which to draw. "Whatever Maria was trying to get herself into or out of was not working *yet*," Bruhn realized later. "I can see that it was not an easy time for her, and it wasn't an easy time for me. It was certainly a confusing time for Rudik." Glen Tetley, who was in town performing with Jerome Robbins's company, recalls "enormous hostility from Rudolf" toward Tallchief. "Maria imagined something was happening between them, but nothing was." It was "a puzzling time," Tallchief acknowledged. "It didn't only have to do with sex, although I suspect that Rudy and Erik began having relations. . . . Being between them, I could never quite tell who was in control."

During a break one day, Nureyev pulled Bruhn aside. He *had to* talk to him, he whispered with conspiratorial urgency. He wanted to have lunch with Bruhn alone—without Maria. Tallchief, however, was not about to be kissed off so lightly. When Nureyev informed her of his lunch plans, she "had a fit," according to Bruhn. In a scene ripe for Strindberg, she rushed from her Royal Theater dressing room, screaming. Nureyev went running after her, and Bruhn trailed after both. At that moment, the entire Danish company streamed out of morning class to witness Nureyev, Bruhn and Tallchief chasing one anther around the opera house. With the gala days away and Tallchief threatening to decamp, Bruhn canceled his lunch à *deux* to appease her. Their performances went ahead as planned and the three of them even had dinner together afterward, but Tallchief soon left Copenhagen, without either partner.

Rudolf fell in love with Erik the dancer first, and the man second, though the two became inextricably linked in his mind ever after. That he was in love with Bruhn was not the anguished discovery it was for many young men attracted to others of their sex, but the natural and perhaps inevitable response to meeting his ideal. With characteristic determination, he simply went after what he wanted, with a freedom that had been off limits to him in Russia. Rampant homophobia—and the fear of reprisals—had taught him to repress any homosexual feeling he may have had, and he now found the West as liberating in sexual matters as it was in those artistic. Bruhn was not the first man he was attracted to, but certainly the first one he felt free to pursue. "I doubt Rudolf ever knew he was homosexual until he met Erik," observes John Taras, a ballet world insider and one of Nureyev's first friends in the West. At twenty-three, Nureyev was still relatively inexperienced sexually. His relationship with Menia Martinez went unconsummated, and his affairs with Tallchief, Xenia Jurgenson and Ninel Kurgapkina had been short-lived. It was, after all, on that trip to East Berlin with Kurgapkina that Nureyev discovered his pleasure in kissing another man. He was more attracted to men than women and "it masturbated my head to have sex with women," he confided to a friend, by which he meant that it "twisted and turned things around."

Whether Bruhn was his first male lover is unknown, but he was unquestionably his first and greatest love and, together with Pushkin, the most influential male figure in his life. Older and wiser in the ways of the world, Bruhn was someone who could point the way and help Nureyev navigate the tricky shoals of the international dance world. He was, in that respect, another father figure. Most important of all, he was someone Rudolf looked up to, "the only dancer who has anything to show me I don't already know."

Theirs was as much a passion of ideals as of physical attraction. Each was entranced by what he lacked himself, Rudolf by Bruhn's refinement and standing; Bruhn, by Rudolf's youth, passion and fearlessness. "Rudolf took Erik completely off guard," recalls Glen Tetley. "Erik was totally smitten from the beginning and I don't recall his ever having that reaction to anybody else. It was the first time in his life that he was totally in love, that kind of hypnotic, physical, deeply erotic love. Erik was always rather veiled and immaculate and here was someone who was anything but. Rudolf could be the devil incarnate, one hundred percent animal, all impulse and just intuitively going after it. Erik was just flipped by the magnetism. And Rudolf saw this immaculate body and these perfect positions, this suave manner. Erik was the ideal, the god."

Tall and blond, Bruhn was strikingly handsome, with the kind of virile good looks that appealed to both sexes. His "Greek-god face," as Tallchief described it, was set off by a square jaw, high forehead and searing blue eyes. Heads turned whenever he entered a room. Though primarily drawn to others of his own sex, Bruhn had had both male and female lovers since his first serious affair with ballerina Sonia Arova at the age of eighteen. The pair had become engaged soon after falling in love in London in 1947, when both were dancing with the Metropolitan Ballet.* Even then, Bruhn was known to be ambivalent about his sexuality. A former colleague remembers a cast party in London during which a fellow dancer impersonated Arova singing, "I wonder who's kissing him now, I wonder who's showing him how." "Well, we all knew what that meant. Oh, yes."

Bruhn and Arova were often apart. In 1949 Bruhn was invited to join Ballet Theatre for its New York season. Bruhn was then unknown in America, but had an enthusiastic supporter in Blevins Davis, Ballet Theatre's president and chief patron, who persuaded company founder Lucia Chase to hire him and then, unbeknownst to Bruhn, guaranteed his salary. He also booked Bruhn a first-class passage on the SS *America* and accompanied him on the journey. It didn't take Bruhn long to recognize Davis's motives. "During the trip I realized that he had certain inclinations. He paid attention to me in certain ways. I was quite innocent about all that and I was still happily engaged to Sonia Arova. . . .

*A short-lived, though admired, British company.

But nothing mattered. I was going to the United States and I was going to dance with an important American ballet company. When we landed, it seemed that a whole new world was waiting for me."

At Ballet Theatre, however, Bruhn was dismayed to discover that nearly everyone assumed he was Blevins Davis's boyfriend. The rumor upset him, not only because of the homosexual stigma but because this implied that he had not been taken into the company on the basis of his talent alone. The rumor had gained ground after Erik went to stay with Davis at his home in Independence, Missouri, for several weeks. He undertook the trip at the urging of Lucia Chase, who saw that Davis was interested in Bruhn and was only too eager to keep her chief patron happy. For his twenty-first birthday, Davis threw him a party to which he invited his close friend Bess Truman. Bruhn, however, was not interested in Davis and spent most of his visit fighting off his advances.*

Bruhn traveled between Denmark and America over the next few years, seeing Arova whenever he could. The pair finally called off their five-year engagement after Arova followed Bruhn to Ballet Theatre in 1954 and there discovered " a different Erik."† Bruhn, she quickly realized, was the company "Golden Boy" and "close" to dancers such as Scott Douglas who were known to be homosexual. She began to suspect that Bruhn might be gay as well. Without discussing the subject directly, she expressed her misgivings about their future to Bruhn. "Erik felt we should stay together. But I wasn't sure that I would be able to cope with that kind of situation. He still felt very close to me, but I felt strange. I was too young to understand anything more. I didn't want him to settle for anything that would be frustrating for him in the end. I didn't see a clean future." Although no longer Bruhn's fiancée, Arova remained one of his most enduring confidants.

Bruhn's offstage life was scrupulously private and even his few close friends knew only scant details. While he had never hidden his homosexual romances, as did most performers of his generation, he avoided any discussion of them. "In those days it was not something that was talked about," says Arova, recalling the Danish dancer she and Bruhn knew who had committed suicide over rumors of his being gay. Bruhn's friend Marit Gentele was not the first to recognize that Erik did not regard himself as exclusively homosexual. Copenhagen may have been more tolerant of homosexuals than other cities in Europe at the time, but as the Swedish-born Gentele saw it, "There was a conservative ethos at the Royal Danish Ballet and homosexuality was frowned upon. There was a tradition of dance families and many in the company were the children of former dancers. There were very few gay dancers."

---

*It was years before he forgave Chase for setting him up.
†It was Davis who eventually brought Arova into the company.

Bruhn's renown in America had grown steadily, but it was not until 1955, with his debut in *Giselle* opposite Alicia Markova, that he established himself as the top male star in American ballet. The great English ballerina was then twenty years his senior.* "It may well be a date to write down in the history books," declared *The New York Times'* John Martin, the country's first major dance critic, "for it's as if the greatest Giselle of today were handing over a sacred trust to what is probably the greatest Albrecht of tomorrow. . . . His dancing was like velvet. . . ."

If Bruhn was the only dancer Nureyev regarded as a peer, he was also the only person whom Nureyev allowed to wield power over him. "Teach it to me," he was always saying to Erik. "If Erik was brilliant in a role, Rudolf would not be satisfied until he had become brilliant in that same role," says Rosella Hightower. "It was a great incentive for him for a very long time." Equally enraptured with Nureyev, Bruhn helped him in every possible way, imparting as much of his learning as he could, even when Nureyev threatened to overshadow him. Their relationship was tempestuous and unremittingly intense from the start. "Pure Strindberg" was the way Bruhn characterized it a few years later. "Rudolf was overwhelmed by his feelings for Erik," says Arova, "and Erik didn't know how to cope with him. Rudolf exhausted him." Violette Verdy recalls that "Rudy was so strong, so new and so hungry after the desert of Russia. He just wanted what he wanted."

Offstage as much as on, the two had vividly contrasting personalities: Easily provoked, Nureyev exploded; quiet and controlled, Bruhn imploded. Hoping to protect them from gossip, and save Rudolf money, of which he had little, Bruhn invited him to live with him in the boyhood home he had recently purchased from—and still shared with—his mother. A charming, two-story brick house in Gentofte, a suburb of Copenhagen, it stood on Violet Road in a quiet, tree-lined middle-class neighborhood. For the sake of appearances, Rudolf and Erik occupied separate bedrooms. The trouble was, Bruhn's mother took an instant dislike to Rudolf, perhaps seeing in him a threat to her son's preeminence and respectability—and competition for her son's affections. She had already read about Rudolf in the papers when her son introduced them, and while she didn't know the nature of their relationship, she suspected it soon enough. She and Rudolf "had what seemed to be a violent reaction to each other," Bruhn recalled. "It was like lightning."

Not that Bruhn and his mother had ever had an easy time of it, either. An imposing, vibrant woman with red hair, Ellen Bruhn had been as formidable a force in Erik's young life as Hamet Nureyev had been in Rudolf's. "I was exposed to a female force I couldn't cope with,"

*Markova had formed a legendary partnership in the thirties with Anton Dolin; together they were considered the period's finest interpreters of *Giselle*.

Bruhn recalled of his childhood. "There was a period of time when I couldn't stand being with women." Like Rudolf, Bruhn had grown up with three older sisters, the only son in a household of women, which also included his beloved aunt Minna, his mother's sister. Highly independent, his mother worked as a hairdresser and ran her own thriving salon. His father, Ernst, a kind, handsome charmer whom Erik grew to resemble, had spent twelve years in Russia as a civil engineer. But after returning to his native Denmark and marrying Erik's mother, he had never been able to make much of himself. He regularly squandered the money his wife gave him on gambling and liquor. The couple quarreled incessantly and finally separated when Erik was five. Still, they never separated completely. Ernst Bruhn paid regular weekly visits to the children, and though nearly every meeting ended in a fight with their mother, she continued to help him out financially. Years later, when he was dying of cancer, she was constantly by his side.

Disappointed in her husband, Ellen Bruhn shifted her attentions and ambitions to their only son, turning him against his father in the process. As his mother's favorite, he incurred not only his father's jealousy, but his sisters'. In retaliation, they beat him up at every opportunity. But when Erik would beg his mother not to spoil him in front of them, she would taunt him, "If you can't take it, you're not strong enough. You're just like your father." His mother, by Bruhn's account, rarely showed her favorite much love or affection. "When she did, it was enough to keep me going for a few years. It was so strong that you never forgot it." Equally memorable was her punishing way of making him feel worthless. When he did what she wanted, he was the most important boy in the world; when he didn't, he was his father's son.

Bruhn was an unusually shy, quiet child who retreated so far into himself that his first teachers supposed he was retarded and prescribed remedial classes. His mother chose dance lessons instead and the boy eventually came into his own, albeit reluctantly. At his first dance recital nine-year-old Erik froze before the audience and fled the stage. Overcome with shame, he steeled himself, asked his teacher if he could try again, and returned to perform his Russian folk dance without a hitch. His mother, however, never stopped criticizing him and never once attended any of his recitals at the Royal Danish Ballet School. "She just assumed I was a big nothing," said Bruhn, who often daydreamed that he was invisible. She even failed to turn up for his professional debut. (When, years later, she finally asked to come see him dance, Bruhn took his revenge by forcing her to stand in line for tickets.)

By the time Rudolf arrived in Denmark, however, Ellen Bruhn had come to admire her son's achievement and had grown much more protective of him. Whether out of gratitude, need, or both, he never abandoned her or his boyhood home. "I don't know how I managed to survive her," Bruhn said in attempting to come to grips with her powerful influence. "On the other hand, without her, I might never have been provoked into proving myself so much. I think every artist needs, not a mother like mine, but an element of opposition to push you into achievement."

Away from the tensions of the Gentofte house, Bruhn and Nureyev pushed each other to achieve in the studio, working side by side in near silence, with Bruhn leading the class, confident in his role as teacher. He had tried taking a class from Nureyev before one of his performances with Tallchief, but had dropped out midway through because he found Nureyev's long, slow barre work too hard on his muscles. Each body warms up differently and Bruhn, with his Bournonville schooling and softer, more pliant muscles, was accustomed to a shorter barre and faster pace. He and Rudolf both spoke the language of classical ballet, but the way they spoke it—their accent, their phrasing, their colloquialisms— differed. At first, they merely took stock of their differences. "At the time his English was very limited and I felt that the more I explained, the less he understood," Bruhn recalled. "But we looked at each other, and we worked together. We could see that whatever we were talking about *worked*." Gradually they began experimenting with each other's styles and inspiring—and challenging—each other more directly, a process that would continue over the next twenty-five years and far outlast their rather more volatile romance.

They also continued to take classes with Vera Volkova, the teacher Bruhn most revered, though Nureyev was disappointed to discover that Volkova was not familiar with the Vaganova method as he knew it. (When she had studied with Vaganova, the famous teacher was still evolving her method.) Nevertheless, Nureyev liked the colorful Volkova herself, especially after he learned that she had danced with Pushkin in her youth, a link as welcome as their common language. Her idiosyncratic command of English, so like his own, also made him feel at home, as did her insistence on driving her pupils beyond their own perceived limits. "Pull God's beard!" she would cry. "Head is like you are smelling violets over right shoulder."

Rudolf was visiting Volkova at her flat one night in October when the phone rang. Volkova ran to answer it and returned a moment later to say that he had a call from London. London? he wondered. He didn't know anyone in London.

"It's Margot Fonteyn here," England's most famous ballerina announced without fanfare. "Would you dance in my gala in London?"

Dame Margot's charity matinee in aid of the Royal Academy of Dancing was to be held one month later. Rudolf had never seen Fonteyn dance, ". . . but, of course, name was magic!" He was honored by her invitation and liked the "cheerful, friendly, generous way she talked." He agreed at once to what would become his London debut.

That's at least the way Nureyev recalled their first conversation in his autobiography.* Fonteyn, however, claimed not to have spoken to Nureyev on the phone at all on that occasion. As she told it, the idea to enlist Nureyev had come from her friend Colette Clark, who together with Mary, the Duchess of Roxburghe, was organizing the RAD gala. The Russian prima ballerina Galina Ulanova had just dropped out of the event (or been pulled — presumably as a result of Nureyev's defection) and Fonteyn, Clark and the duchess were left scrambling for a last-minute replacement. "I hear that Rudolf Nureyev, this dancer who defected from the Kirov, is sensational," Clark ventured. Her friend the painter Michael Wishart had written to her from Paris the night he saw Nureyev first dance with the Kirov, and her sister-in-law Violette Verdy had been raving about him ever since witnessing his de Cuevas debut. Fonteyn had of course been making her own debut in Nureyev's homeland when he defected and hadn't paid much mind to the story at the time. But now she saw he would be a brilliant addition to the roster. It was left to Clark to track him down, which she finally did in Copenhagen, where, Fonteyn was delighted to learn, he was studying with her former teacher Volkova.† Clark and Volkova relayed messages between them.

Nureyev knew just what he wanted to dance — and with whom. Could he partner Fonteyn in *Le Spectre de la Rose?* Volkova asked on his behalf. Fonteyn balked. "I've never set eyes on him," she told Clark, "and anyway, I've asked John Gilpin to dance *Spectre de la Rose* with me.‡ Ask Vera if he is a good dancer." Within a day, Clark returned with an answer: "Vera says he's adamant about dancing with you and that he's marvelous." Fonteyn wasn't convinced. "He sounds rather tiresome to me." But Clark persisted. Word had it that he was extraordinary. "They say that he has such a presence he only has to walk on the stage and lift his arm and you can see the swans by the lake. . . ." Skeptical, Fonteyn held her ground. "The more I hear of him, the worse he sounds. I don't mean as a dancer, but why should he decide to dance with me

---

*Though the mistaking of dates forms something of a pattern in his autobiography, Nureyev quoted Fonteyn as saying that her gala was to be held in October when in fact it was set for November 2. Surely Fonteyn would not have got the date wrong.

†Volkova claimed that Fonteyn called her to ask if she knew of Nureyev's whereabouts, but Colette Clark and Fonteyn remembered that it was Clark who spoke to Volkova on Fonteyn's behalf.

‡Fonteyn was luckier with *Spectre* than Nureyev had been in Frankfurt: While he had pieced it together from his session with Pierre Lacotte and photographs of Nijinsky, she was coached by Tamara Karsavina, Fokine's original young girl.

when he's only twenty-three and I've never even met him?" Clark could only reply, "Well, Vera thinks he's a genius. She says he has 'the nostrils,' you know what I mean? People of genius have 'nostrils.'" And at this, she flared her own to demonstrate.

In the end Nureyev agreed to dance with Rosella Hightower instead. He held out, however, for one last request: Could Sir Frederick Ashton choreograph a solo for him? Ashton, the master craftsman of English ballet, with over fifty-one works to his credit, was taken aback. Dancers rarely, if ever, asked choreographers to fashion dances for them, particularly when they'd never met. Nevertheless, Ashton was intrigued enough to agree and even granted Nureyev one more liberty he had never before extended to any dancer: He let him choose the music. Nureyev picked the brooding *Poème Tragique* by Alexander Scriabin, whom he revered, along with van Gogh and Dostoyevsky, "for the generosity and violence I feel they share."

Fonteyn invited Rudolf to meet with her in London to discuss plans for the gala. Terrified of being kidnapped, Nureyev agreed to the trip only after Fonteyn proposed that it be made in secret, free of persistent reporters, flashbulbs and, Rudolf could only hope, Soviet agents. The resourceful Fonteyn was perhaps the only ballerina schooled in political misadventure. Her husband, Roberto "Tito" de Arias, was the scion of a prominent Panamanian political family and then Panamanian ambassador to Great Britain. Several years earlier Fonteyn had been briefly imprisoned in Panama after her husband was implicated in an attempted coup there. Fonteyn had gone to Panama on a vacation just as her husband and his cronies were hatching plans for a revolution. When the plan was discovered, Fonteyn, acting as a decoy for Tito's escape, set sail in her own boat, which was loaded with guns and ammunition beneath the floorboards. She was caught and jailed for the night before being deported to Miami. By the time she arrived in New York, the press corps was waiting for her, intrigued by her ballerina-behind-bars mystique. Fonteyn skillfully dodged their questions and yet won them over nonetheless.

With that same clear sense of purpose, Fonteyn now hastily arranged a visa for the passportless Rudolf and invited him to stay with her. She also promised to send her car for him at the airport. But on the day he arrived at London Airport, there was no one to meet him. He called Fonteyn at home.

"Here is Nureyev," he announced. "Where are you?"

Fonteyn hadn't expected him for another two hours. Chagrined that the fearful Russian was stranded at an airport of all places, she assured him that her car would be there promptly.

"I will take taxi," Nureyev offered, but Fonteyn wouldn't hear of it.

Forty minutes later, Nureyev was once more on the line.

"Here is Nureyev."

"Didn't the chauffeur find you?" asked the confounded Fonteyn, an immensely poised woman who set great store by her attention to detail. She begged Nureyev to stay put while she got hold of the chauffeur.

"No. I will take taxi," he insisted.

When Nureyev finally stepped out of the cab at Fonteyn's South Kensington home, she noticed the nostrils at once. He was smaller than she expected—she was standing above him on the doorstep at the time—and his "funny, pinched little face," she recalled, had a "curious pallor peculiar to so many dancers from Russia."

Fonteyn's home in Thurloe Place, an elegant square of identical limestone Georgian houses near the Victoria and Albert Museum, was also the Panamanian embassy. As Rudolf stepped inside, his attention was drawn to the oil portrait of Fonteyn in the foyer. Painted by Annigoni, it showed Fonteyn in traditional Panamanian dress. A long stairway led to the airy blue drawing room on the second floor, which was furnished with embassy-style French furniture and floor-length maroon drapes. Rudolf was expecting formality, but there was nothing of the grand ballerina about Fonteyn, whose low-key, gracious manner appealed to him at once. As Nureyev, Fonteyn and Colette Clark sat down to tea—five lumps of sugar for Rudolf, Fonteyn duly noted in her memoir—the two dancers took the measure of each other. "I was bowled over straight away by the warm, simple way she welcomed me, without any fuss." According to Clark, Fonteyn was also "very sweet, chummy and flirtatious with him." Fonteyn, for her part, recalled feeling relieved when Nureyev finally dropped his guard and smiled at something fanciful she said. "I didn't know Russians laughed," she confessed to him, struck by the way his face registered his every emotion. "They were so serious when we were there."

Fonteyn had to dash off to a cocktail party and left Clark to accompany Nureyev to a performance of *Giselle* by the Ballet Rambert. Its director, Marie Rambert, had founded the first permanent English school and company in the 1920s and given Frederick Ashton his start as a choreographer. A pioneer of modern British ballet, she had danced in the corps of the Ballets Russes and assisted Nijinsky during the making of his *Le Sacre du Printemps*, in which she also performed. Nureyev would claim in his memoir that Rambert seemed to him "an amazing vital little person," whose "dark eyes sparkled as she spoke of Nijinsky." In fact the two disliked each other on sight. Clark knew it wasn't going well when Rambert, a good friend of hers, suddenly switched from Russian to English during her backstage meeting with him. "She liked sweet, good, innocent people and cosy Rudolf was not. He had a powerful personality even then. I think he rather frightened her; he certainly frightened me. He wasn't interested in anyone but Margot, strangely enough. He knew that she was the important one."

Fonteyn, however, wasn't entirely won over. "I liked him nine-tenths," she told Clark that night, "but once or twice I saw a steely look in his eye." That look was not one of coldness, as Fonteyn would only later come to realize, but "a manifestation of fear." And like a cat's hiss, it was "ready to show itself at the slightest suspicion of attack."

Over the next two days, Rudolf explored London by foot and double-decker bus, going unrecognized from the Tower of London to the National Gallery. He was expecting "old narrow picturesque twisting streets" and was surprised not to find the city of menace that Dickens had so convincingly evoked for him. "I'm sure London must come as a surprise to you after Russia," Clark said to him, expecting to hear him extol its virtues. "Only thing that surprises me is that houses here are all the same," he replied.

Fonteyn herself was dancing *Giselle* during his visit and had arranged for her good friends Nigel and Maude Gosling to bring Rudolf to the theater for his first look at the Royal Ballet. Nigel was the dance and art critic of the *Observer*; his wife, Maude Lloyd, one of the first ballerinas of the Ballet Rambert. With Maude's insider's know-how allied to Nigel's interpretive skill, they wrote dance criticism under the pseudonym Alexander Bland, a name they adopted from Beatrix Potter's *Pigling Bland* story. Rudolf was to prove their most enduring subject. They, in turn, would become his surrogate parents in the West, offering him the care, support and protection he had known at the Pushkins.

Distinguished rather than handsome, tall, straight-backed and balding, Nigel had a serene air and a calm, authoritative voice. His interest in ballet had been sparked by his meeting the South African–born Maude. On a whim, he had asked to take lessons at the Rambert school and Maude became his teacher. The two were married five years later, in 1939. Lloyd had been a favorite muse of the choreographer Antony Tudor, who created for her the leading role in *Lilac Garden*, the psychosexual drama that became his signature work. It was Richard Buckle who persuaded the Goslings to join forces in writing about dance for his magazine *Ballet*. A warm, gentle presence, Maude was a beloved figure in the English dance world. Her delicate, pretty features, set off by soft white curls, were rarely darkened by a frown. Her ability to get along with anyone was evinced by her long and close friendship with Tudor, who was known for his acerbic tongue and dark moods, which made dancers wary of working with him.*

---

*Acclaimed as "a choreographer of human sorrow" for his psychologically probing ballets, Tudor nonetheless had a knack for reducing dancers to tears.

The Goslings had seen Rudolf dance with the Kirov in Paris and were among his earliest champions. In response to Arnold Haskell's "A Sorry Affair," the Goslings leaped to Nureyev's defense with "A Sorry Affair — Indeed!," Alexander Bland's celebrated rebuttal. Fulminating against Haskell's misreading of the facts, easy assumptions about Soviet freedoms and his spurious conclusion that Nureyev would amount to nothing more than a "nine days' wonder," Bland wrote: "The fact is that Mr. Haskell, like myself, has never met Nureyev; we do not form part of that 'small minority who know the actual facts' (who does?); and therefore are in no position to throw either bouquets or brickbats. In this case a decent silence would have been preferable to a statement repugnant to all those who respect the right of the individual, which might mislead ignorant readers about our attitude to refugees from Communism, which in fact — in Mr. Haskell's own phrase — 'degrades the word freedom.' "

On arriving at Fonteyn's home to meet Rudolf, the Goslings found no one in the drawing room. Twenty minutes later, a tousled-haired Rudolf flew into view, rubbing his eyes, dressed in a dark sports shirt and tight pants. He had fallen asleep, he explained, prompting the couple to wonder how this "gypsy" would ever slip unnoticed past Covent Garden's dressy crowd. Five minutes later Nureyev had not only changed into a dark suit but somehow transformed himself into a totally different person — "slim, smooth and handsome," or so he now appeared to Nigel Gosling. "In those first few minutes I had caught a glimpse of Nureyev's character and perceived his astonishing power to change." Rudolf's omnivorous curiosity also struck him. "Tell me about this man Freud," Rudolf asked him that night, the first of many such conversations between them. "What windows did he open?"

Having already danced in his mind everywhere, Rudolf was amused rather than impressed once inside the Royal Opera House. Its pink-shaded lights reminded him of a café. (From Ufa to Paris, imposing chandeliers hung in every opera house he had known.) He laughed when a safety curtain — an iron curtain, no less — was lowered between the acts. But his first view of Fonteyn's *Giselle* mesmerized him, despite the fact that the Royal's recently revamped version was different from the one he had danced at the Kirov. Still, he admired Fonteyn's lyricism and musicality, and felt the thirty-year-old British company stood up admirably, even in comparison with the two-hundred-year-old Kirov. At that moment his professional future was still very much a question mark. The Grand Ballet de Marquis de Cuevas had fallen short of his expectations and he now saw how the Royal Ballet might fulfill them.

At dinner with the Goslings afterward at a nearby restaurant, Rudolf went to wash his hands and was informed that the bathroom was in the basement. Nigel accompanied him and as they went down a narrow dark corridor, Nigel could sense Rudolf's hair standing on end. He feared he was being led into some kind of trap.

As a favor to Fonteyn, Rudolf had agreed to an interview with Nigel to help publicize his upcoming London debut in her gala. The *Observer* had paid his fare from Denmark in exchange for the exclusive, which Rudolf insisted be published after his "secret" visit. "I forget quickly," was all he would say for the record about his defection five months earlier. Gosling, in turn, made no mention of his scare at the restaurant. "Quiet, elegant, soft-spoken, he walks with the fastidious intentness of a cat—one of the larger, wild cats," he wrote instead, a characterization echoed time and again in descriptions of Nureyev in the West. "His manner is gentle, with a hint of something formidable behind; his style is 'cool'; his physique, slight-seeming from a distance, looks tough as you get close."

It was precisely those feral qualities that endeared him to Ninette de Valois,* the Royal Ballet's tenacious director and one of the few people to take to him straightaway without reservation. "The Irish and the Tartar understood each other at sight," recalled Fonteyn. "Of course, he was just the kind of rebellious talent and engaging *enfant terrible* that she loved." Like Marie Rambert, de Valois had also danced with Diaghilev's Ballets Russes, before moving on to found the Vic-Wells, the company that became the Royal Ballet. During her company's summer tour to Leningrad, word had quickly filtered through to her that "the best young Russian" had defected in Paris, and she had determined to keep track of his progress. However, it was at Rudolf's request that Fonteyn introduced them. "Her wit, shrewdness, humanity and intelligence delighted him," she recalled. A formidable woman of great determination and vision, de Valois had maintained a strict national bias while building her company and had only occasionally invited "foreigners" to appear as guests. Never having seen Nureyev dance, she was not about to tender any invitations, though she awaited his debut with great interest.

Before returning to Denmark, Nureyev accompanied Fonteyn to company class at the Royal Ballet school, but under an assumed name— Zygmunt Jasman, a Polish dancer due to dance in her gala. Nureyev went to change in the dressing room reserved for the Royal's leading men and there ran into David Blair, Fonteyn's new partner. "You're that Russian fellow aren't you?" Blair pressed him. When Nureyev insisted that no, he was "Jasmine," as he pronounced it, Blair took him at his word and sent him off to a less distinguished changing room.

Before long, Rudolf would be the one to send Blair packing.

* * *

*De Valois's real name was Edris Stannus.

BACK IN Copenhagen with Erik, Nureyev quickly grasped that there was little he could do to escape Soviet surveillance. One day Erik received a letter from the Soviet embassy in Copenhagen. His performances in Russia had been such a success that Gosconcert, the state impresario, had invited him to dance with the Bolshoi for a season, the first Western dancer to be so honored. Bruhn now assumed it was news about his engagement. But when he asked Rudolf to translate, he was disappointed to learn that the Bolshoi had decided to "postpone" his appearance, no doubt as a result of his association with a "traitor."

Shortly thereafter, Bruhn received an invitation from the former Ballets Russes star Anton Dolin, asking him to partner Sonia Arova in London during a special two-week engagement. When Bruhn called her in Paris to make arrangements, he asked her to book him a double room. He made no mention of Nureyev, fearing the line might be tapped.

On their way to Paris by train, Rudolf visibly paled each time they crossed a border, terror-stricken that he might be kidnapped and sent back to Russia. Did he have the right papers? he kept asking Bruhn, whose reassurances failed to calm him.

Arova met them at the Gare du Nord. She knew instantly who Erik's companion was, but not the reason for the nasty glance Rudolf shot her as they were introduced. "You remind him of Maria," Erik told her later, and he filled her in on their recent contretemps. In fact, with her large, expressive eyes, generous mouth, auburn hair and "dark, smoldering looks," as Bruhn described them, she did resemble Tallchief.* Nevertheless, in Erik's mind at least, the similarities ended there. "You're dealing with a very different person here," he advised Rudolf. Still, Rudolf let down his guard with Arova only after he was certain that she had no designs on Bruhn. "From what they said, it had ended badly with Maria," Arova remembers. "Rudolf felt that she had misled him about her relationship with Erik. 'It wasn't true what she told me,' he kept saying. Of course, the moment Rudolf met Erik, he had no more time for Maria."

The Bulgarian-born Arova shared with Rudolf not only a bond with Bruhn but Tatar roots, a common language and a dogged self-sufficiency. Her career had been set in motion by the legendary Russian basso Fedor Chaliapin, an old family friend, who, while visiting her parents' home one night, had been prevailed upon to sing. While everyone else listened raptly, six-year-old Sonia had improvised a dance. This had so impressed the singer that he had persuaded Sonia's reluctant parents to let her study ballet. When the war broke out, she was smuggled into Paris, disguised as a boy. Like Nureyev, Arova had fought her way to the front ranks

---

*Such was their resemblence at the time that in Nureyev's autobiography a caption accompanying a photo of Nureyev, Bruhn and Tallchief backstage at the New York City Ballet misidentifies Tallchief as Arova.

through hard work and adaptability. A bold, vivacious performer, she was also one of the most versatile, having danced with many leading companies in Europe and America, among them the Ballet Rambert and the de Cuevas company. Rosella Hightower recalls her as "unusually generous, even when she wasn't given the opportunities she should have been. She was never petty about protecting her reputation."

She took in stride Erik and Rudolf's love affair, which would not have been the case had Bruhn arrived in Paris with a woman. Rudolf was the first male lover that Bruhn openly acknowledged to her. "We had resolved things nicely and cleanly, so I didn't compare myself. I was actually very helpful towards their relationship, which is why Rudolf felt he could trust me. He could see there was no double play. Whereas Maria had been adamant. How come Rudolf could prefer Erik to her? I didn't feel that way."

In Paris, Arova, Nureyev and Bruhn took class and rehearsed together in a rented studio near the Place Clichy. Fearing encounters with the KGB, Rudolf carried a switchblade in his pocket. "We're being followed," he'd suddenly alert Bruhn and Arova, who would struggle to keep pace with him. At night, they dined at Arova's Rue Lécluse apartment, where Rudolf took comfort in her mother's Bulgarian cooking and care. "Mamushka" he called her. His own mother was never far from his thoughts and he often tried to reach her by phone, even after Arova warned him repeatedly that he might put himself and his mother in danger by calling. "Yes, I know," he answered, "but I've got to make her understand it would be death for me to go back there."

In the studio, Bruhn took the lead. As he and Arova rehearsed for their London appearances, Rudolf studied him "like a hawk," memorizing him. The pair was to dance the pas de deux from Bournonville's ebullient *Flower Festival at Genzano*, which was new to Rudolf, and the pas de deux from *Don Quixote*, which he had danced in Leningrad. When Rudolf saw that his approach differed from theirs, he tried to correct them. He took it as a given that the great Maryinsky tradition in which he had been reared was superior. During the coda of his pas de deux, Rudolf's habit was to follow his partner's solo by walking slowly to center stage, getting into position, and then signaling for the music to begin. But in the West, as Arova explained to him, "we didn't break the atmosphere to have a rest. We connected the variations. By the time the ballerina finished her variation, the male was standing there ready to start. We didn't wait for him to walk onstage and take his preparation as if to say, 'Now I'm going to perform a trick.' "

Gradually, they led him to see that the Russian approach was not the only one, "but there were big arguments," says Arova. "We never had a dull rehearsal." While Rudolf struck her as complex and reserved, as "someone who was really searching," he also seemed curiously set in his ways. Still, she and Bruhn wanted to learn what he knew. "We were like sponges around him."

His nerves frayed from all the tensions, Erik had been unable to focus on Rudolf in Copenhagen. But once in Paris, he finally had the presence of mind to take a closer look. "I had been looking but not actually seeing. Suddenly I saw!" What he saw was someone he wasn't entirely equipped to handle. "Erik was this protected Dane who never let any emotion out and he was not prepared for Rudolf's enormous appetites," says Glen Tetley. "Rudolf opened a door into Erik's life that Erik wasn't used to." Another friend contends that Rudolf "kept the child in Erik alive." Bruhn later described himself as "relaxed" in Paris, though Arova paints a different picture, recalling that Bruhn was having trouble dealing with Rudolf. The two fought constantly, she says, and regularly cast her as go-between. "You're going to wither out between those two!" her mother warned. "It was never an easy relationship," says Arova. "Erik was very controlled and Rudolf was the moody one. Erik was trying to make him understand things and when he couldn't, he'd get frustrated and they'd have these rows. Then Erik would go for a walk and Rudi would come running into our apartment looking for him. Rudolf wanted so much out of Erik. He was always demanding of him and Erik would say, 'But I have only so much to give and then I feel I'm being drained.'"

It wasn't long before Bruhn began to believe that Nureyev wanted more from him than he was able to give. While his close friends knew Bruhn to be warm and generous with a lively, dry sense of humor, one of them recalled that he could "turn in a second and become extremely hostile and cold" when he felt that someone came too close to him. It was this dark side that he revealed when he drank, which he did with alarming frequency through the sixties. "Erik's alcoholism was one of his secret torments," remembers Violette Verdy. "He had a streak of cruelty about him and when he drank, he became so sarcastic and hurtful."

Frustrated by persistent rumors that Rudolf was trying to unseat him, Bruhn accused him one day of having come out of Russia just to "kill" him. He knew it was "a vicious thing" to say, but felt somehow compelled to say it. "When he heard that, Rudik got so upset, he cried," Bruhn acknowledged. "He said, 'How can you be so evil?'" If Bruhn could sometimes be cruel, he could also be remarkably generous, and many dancers owed their careers to his guidance, as Rudolf would always claim he did.

Rudolf was due to begin rehearsals with Frederick Ashton. So in mid-October, when Arova and Bruhn traveled to London for their performances with the Dolin troupe, Rudolf went with them. Ninette de Valois came to see them at the Golders Green Hippodrome and was so taken with Bruhn's dancing that she invited him to dance with her company as a guest artist during the following spring season.*

Rudolf, meanwhile, threw himself into his rehearsals with Ashton with such unrelenting exertion that Fonteyn could only wonder, "Surely he ought to save himself somewhere?" She had watched his first rehearsal and later described the experience in telling detail: "He was actually desperately serious; nervous, intense and repeating every step with all his might until he almost knocked himself out with the effort. From time to time he stopped to take off his leg warmers before a very difficult step; after the exertion he stopped again, let out a breath rapidly and forcefully with a sound like a sibilant 'Ho.' On went the woolen tights. After a few more steps he changed his shoes and put the leg warmers back on top of the woolen tights. So it went on for two hours. He was working like a steam engine." Fonteyn was not yet familiar with Nureyev's enormous reserves of strength, or his driving need to test himself.

Rudolf and Ashton were both under pressure: Ashton, to launch the most talked-about dancer of the season; Nureyev, to prove that he was more than just a Russian defector. A fastidious man with quiet manners and a droll charm, the genteel choreographer was celebrated for the wit, lyricism and gentle simplicity of his ballets. Born in Ecuador, the son of a British businessman, he had been obsessed with ballet since boyhood, after seeing Pavlova dance in Peru. His most constant muse, however, was Fonteyn, for whom he had choreographed over twenty-eight ballets. "In her," wrote Arnold Haskell, "Ashton has undoubtedly found someone who can evoke and reveal the deeper sides of his art." Faced with Rudolf, Ashton felt suddenly "like a ringmaster, wondering if this beautiful animal would perform his tricks or whether I would be mauled in the process." It was Nureyev's unleashed power that Ashton meant to convey in this new solo, the idea for which sprang to mind during their first rehearsal.

Nureyev arrived "looking nervous, solemn and unfriendly," remembers veteran Royal Ballet conductor John Lanchbery, who was dumbfounded that "this fabulous-looking boy with the funny mouth" could have picked Scriabin's *Poème Tragique* for his London debut. Lanchbery had orchestrated the score and couldn't imagine a more apt musical choice: "It was exactly the right length, madly danceable, and Russian to the very last note."

Ashton was not one to discuss ideas while choreographing and only after the company pianist had played a few bars did he address Lanchbery. "This is where the curtain will go up." As the pianist repeated the

*Though the company had long objected to guest artists, Fonteyn and her partner David Blair were due to dance in Australia at the time and it was hoped that Bruhn's popularity might compensate for their absence.

introductory bars again and again, Ashton stared hard at Nureyev, listening to see what the music suggested. Suddenly he turned to the dancer Michael Somes and asked him to get the cloak worn to rehearse Albrecht's visit to Giselle's grave in the ballet's haunting second act. The tall, virile, irascible Somes, Fonteyn's longtime partner, had pretty much retired that year from leading roles after de Valois had made it plain that she thought it time he quit. Still, Ashton relied on him in the studio to such an extent that he would soon become the company's répétiteur, teaching roles and maintaining standards of performance.

When Somes returned, Ashton instructed Nureyev to put on the cloak and go to the far end of the studio. "When I say 'Now,' I want you to run to me," he said. Nureyev ran toward Ashton. "No, no, no," Ashton stopped him. "I want you to run as fast as you possibly can, straight to the front of the stage, as if you might fall into the orchestra pit."

This time Nureyev's cloak caught the wind like a sail. Ashton had the entrance he was after.

The Nureyev family in 1937, the year before Rudolf was born: *(from right)* Hamet, Rosa, Farida, Razida (on her mother's lap), Lilya, Hamet's sister-in-law and his brother

(left) Major Hamet Nureyev on the Western front in 1943. *(right)* Five-year-old Rudik in 1943 with a toy pistol. His first sights and sounds were of men preparing for battle.

Farida Nureyeva bottling milk at a kefir factory in Ufa

The Nureyev family circa 1948. Hamet never appeared without his medals in family photographs.

(left) Rudolf, age twelve, at the Palace of Pioneers in his first major role in a ballet. He is shown here with Sveta Bashiyeva in *The Fairy Doll*, which was staged especially to showcase his skills as a partner. *(right)* Rudolf, age thirteen, in the backyard. "He never seemed to care about his looks," said a classmate.

Rudolf at the barre in Ufa

Rudolf as a student at the Kirov School in 1958, with his mentor Alexander Pushkin, his frequent partner, Alla Sizova, and her teacher, Natalia Kamkova

(left) Rudolf with Menia Martinez in Leningrad. "She was very temperamental and head over heels in love with Rudik, who was very responsive to her. I think he kept this tender feeling for Menia for many years." *(right)* Menia in performance. Naturally exuberant, she was the school's first Cuban student and a novelty in a world where gaiety was suspect. "She was crazy and different. Rudi loved that."

Rudolf and Alla Sizova dance *Le Corsaire* at their graduation concert, June 1958. "His entrance was like a bomb exploding. The ovation shook the theater."

(left) Nureyev's first starring role at the Kirov was as the fiery Spaniard, Frondoso, in *Laurencia*. Here he partners Natalia Dudinskaya, the company's prima ballerina, who had demanded to dance with him. Two years later, Nureyev gave this photograph to a Leningrad friend and scrawled across it: "How stupid and simpleminded I was at that time! And I was living only on hope. Now, alas, I have become sober." *(right)* Nureyev in *Laurencia* wearing the black wig that many thought made him look like a monkey.

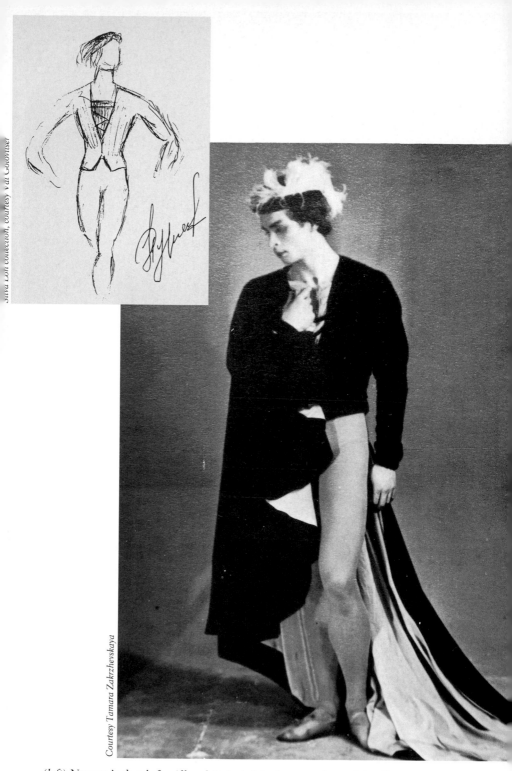

(left) Nureyev's sketch for Albrecht's jacket in the second act of *Giselle*. Nureyev rewrote a number of rules at the Kirov, beginning with his costumes. Designed to make his legs look longer, his jacket was both more fitted and much shorter than the traditional one, which covered the groin and buttocks. *(right)* Nureyev wearing the jacket he designed in his debut in *Giselle*, 1959.

Nureyev in Leningrad

(left) Pushkin's wife, Xenia Jurgenson, one of the many women who doted on Nureyev, with a friend in Leningrad. (right) In Moscow, the twenty-one-year-old Nureyev meets his first movie star, the French actress Marina Vlady. This is one of the rare occasions when Nureyev was not the one signing autographs.

(left) Though few Soviet citizens dared to mix with foreigners, Rudolf pursued every Western artist who passed through Leningrad. Here he appears in front of the Hotel Europa with Lola Fisher, the Eliza Doolittle of an American touring production of *My Fair Lady*, and Leningrader Radik Tihomirov. *(right)* As punishment for mixing with Westerners, Rudolf was sent on a forty-six-day bus tour of East Germany the week before American Ballet Theatre was to make its Leningrad debut. He missed seeing Erik Bruhn, Ballet Theatre's male star, whose performances left Soviet audiences spellbound—and Nureyev with a new rival. On this publicity photo, which he gave to Tamara before he left for East Germany, he wrote, "Hope that the performances of American Ballet Theatre in my absence will entertain you or perhaps produce a great impression."

Rudolf at the Leningrad airport on May 11, 1961, minutes before boarding the plane to Paris, where he would defect the following month

(left) Nureyev's defection grabbed headlines around the world. Meanwhile, Clara Saint suddenly found herself at the center of a Cold War drama. (right) KGB chief Alexander Shelepin's report to the Central Committee of the Communist Party. It begins: "Hereby I report that on June 16 1961 Nureyev Rudolf Hametovich born 1938, single, Tatar, non-Party member, artist of the Leningrad Kirov Theatre who was a member of the touring company in France betrayed his Motherland in Paris."

(left) Nureyev emerges from hiding to meet the press at the Théâtre des Champs-Elysées in Paris six days after his defection. (right) As members of the de Cuevas Ballet look on, Nureyev rehearses the Bluebird pas de deux for the company's production of *The Sleeping Beauty*.

With Erik Bruhn in the studio. Rudolf was obsessed with Erik, whom he studied "like a hawk," as if memorizing him. "Teach it to me," Rudolf was forever saying to him.

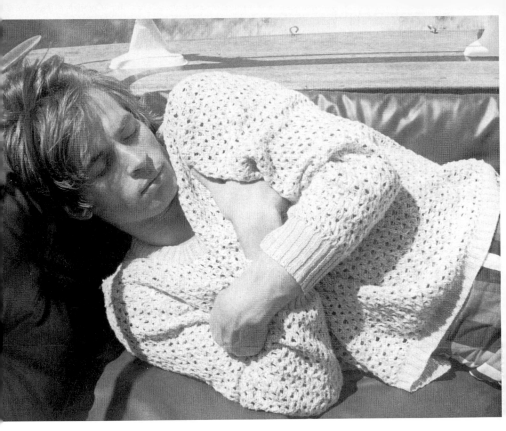

On a break from the Nervi Festival, July 1962

With Erik Bruhn and Sonia Arova's new husband, Thor Sutowski, on the Côte d'Azur

Margot Fonteyn was forty-two when the fiery twenty-three-year-old Nureyev arrived in London and reignited her career. *(top)* The pair dance for the first time in *Giselle*, in February 1962. *(center)* In Nureyev's staging of The Kingdom of the Shades scene from *La Bayadère*, 1963. *(bottom)* Nureyev in *Le Corsaire*, November 1962

Nureyev and Fonteyn in Frederick Ashton's *Marguerite and Armand*, 1963. No other dancers have ever been permitted to dance it.

With Fonteyn in Nice, 1963. "She gives maternal dignity to all the natural functions I am sure," quipped Cecil Beaton. Beneath the polished exterior, however, was a warm-hearted woman with a streak of Brazilian vivacity.

(left) Nigel and Maude Gosling, Nureyev's surrogate parents in the West. (right) Nureyev, Joan Thring, Fonteyn and Keith Money in Bath, England, 1964, moments before Fonteyn learned that her husband had been shot and was hovering near death.

Nureyev and Fonteyn in Kenneth MacMillan's *Romeo and Juliet*

In *Paradise Lost*, choreographed for Nureyev and Fonteyn by Roland Petit in 1967. Mick Jagger and girlfriend, Marianne Faithfull, attended the premiere. She and Jagger were "obsessed" with Nureyev, said Faithfull, and "couldn't help but be influenced by him." "I saw the patriarch of mankind have the first orgasm, standing marvelously on his head," wrote Richard Buckle.

From the dance stage to the dance floor, Nureyev was never far from a photographer's lens.

(*left*) With American and British royalty: On Fifth Avenue with Jacqueline Kennedy, May 1967. (*right*) With Princess Margaret, Lord Snowdon and ballerina Merle Park backstage at the Royal Opera House following the London premiere of Nureyev's production of *The Nutcracker*, February 1968. "He was more beautiful than I can describe," recalled Princess Margaret, "with his flared nostrils, huge eyes and high cheekbones."

14

"Actually, I Am Romantic Kind of Dancer"

ON OCTOBER 26, one week before the gala, Fonteyn held a reception at her home to introduce Nureyev to the British press. So beloved was the Royal Ballet's prima ballerina that she managed to persuade those assembled not to ask any "political" questions, a remarkable feat given the hard-news value of the "Russian defector," as he continued to be known. "He is a guest in my house," said Fonteyn, implying that was reason enough for the embargo, "and I am sure you will treat him kindly and make him welcome to this country." When asked about reports that he was thinking of returning to Russia, Nureyev used his limited vocabulary to dramatic effect. "I'm here," he said, and smiled. The press was charmed and the subject was dropped. "That boy doesn't need any help at all," Fonteyn quickly concluded. "He just knows exactly what he wants to say."

And he rarely wasted many words saying it. A few days later he was invited to dinner at the Covent Garden flat of Richard Buckle, along with Arova, Bruhn and Ashton. Buckle, a prominent figure in the dance world since the 1940s, was then dance critic of the *Sunday Times* (of London). Rudolf refused to go anywhere unless he knew whom he was dealing with and, according to Arova, after hearing that Buckle had long had "a weak spot for Erik," was not favorably disposed to him. Although Arova didn't realize it at the time, Rudolf was also upset that Buckle had apparently hurt her feelings. Six weeks earlier, when she, Erik and Rudolf had been in Paris, she had mentioned to Rudolf that she didn't like the way her face looked because it "wasn't a classical face." When Rudolf disagreed, she told him that the critic Richard Buckle had said so in a review. Rudolf, she quickly learned, logged everything he saw and heard.

After much cajoling, Rudolf had agreed to go along to Buckle's, though he was barely through the door when Buckle sensed "a wall of animosity." No sooner had the group sat down to dinner than Buckle happened to compliment Arova on how wonderful she looked. At this, Rudolf reached toward Arova sitting next to him, cupped her chin in his palm, and turned to their host. "This is a beautiful face. A real Tatar face," he said, and soon left the table. When Buckle went to look in on Rudolf later, he found him sitting on a sofa reading a book.*

There were few debuts more eagerly awaited than Nureyev's on November 2, 1961, at the Theatre Royal, Drury Lane. No other dancer in history had received as much advance publicity and the packed house was primed. Backstage, however, Rudolf was out of sorts. He was uncomfortable with his costume, and try as they might, Bruhn and Arova failed to cheer him as they took him through his warm-up. When the curtain rose, Rudolf stood at the back of the stage swathed in a red cloak. Rushing headlong toward the footlights, he misjudged his own power and came precipitously close to falling into the orchestra pit. The effect was electrifying, though the crowd's collective gasp so unnerved him that he lost his place for a number of bars and improvised, or so it seemed to conductor John Lanchbery, who didn't recognize the steps. Cecil Beaton felt that his "very blood stream was altered . . . a thrill such as I have not had in the theater since as a ten year old boy I saw Pavlova rush on the stage in the *Bacchanale.*" Seated next to him, Lady Diana Cooper whispered, "He's better than Nijinsky!"

Wearing only a red-and-white sash across his bare chest and gray streaked tights, Nureyev appeared at once anguished and defiant as he hurtled across the stage like a force of nature, "a savage young creature, half naked, rushing with wild eyes on an ecstatic, gaunt face, and a long mop of flying, silk hair," as Beaton saw him. To English audiences unaccustomed to such displays of temperament, Nureyev's "savage intensity . . . produced the shock of seeing a wild animal let loose in a drawing room," noted Alexander Bland. To yet another observer, Nureyev seemed to be "dancing for himself while we the audience are peering through a keyhole on some private ritual."

When finally he slid to his knees and raised his arms and palms skyward—whether in despair or prayer, nobody was certain—Nureyev had all of London at his feet. "We all clapped and cheered and wondered what exactly we had just seen," remembered Keith Money. More than

---

*Buckle recalled the evening in an essay written for Christie's Nureyev auction catalog. Buckle recounted that it was seventeen years before Nureyev finally revealed to him why he had been so antagonistic on their first encounter. "Erik Bruhn, to whom he was devoted, had apparently given him an exaggerated account of his relationship with me in previous years."

his pantherine elevation, his space-cleaving leaps or his dancing for that matter, it was Nureyev's feral intensity and stage presence that lingered most vividly. Such were his powers of projection that whether moving or standing still, he compelled attention. "There could be no question," declared critic Mary Clarke, that Nureyev "was an artist of genius, with a rare ability of projecting emotion through the dance."

That dance had lasted all of four minutes, long enough for "one to glean so much of this natural phenomenon," wrote Beaton. "Even those at a distance could tell of his tact and charm, his warring tendernesses and cruelties, his youthful tastes and bafflement, his authority and his pride . . . Freddie's idiom of yearning wanderers, of D'Annunzio's romanticism and 1910 mysticism combined with this Soviet's ruthlessness to bring about a revolutionary masterstroke." Richard Buckle called it "a dance of despair. . . . Tragic clutching arms, falls on the knees, hair all over the face — thrilling!"

Nureyev, however, never felt that the work showed him to best advantage. He was not alone. Ashton agreed that he had put in "too many ingredients," and a number of critics dismissed the choreography as tawdry and overwrought. Still, few could argue with critic Clement Crisp's later assessment that *Poème Tragique* captured "exactly the image that Nureyev had as an unknown Russian dancer who dared to flee the prison of Soviet art." Perhaps nothing better symbolized that act of defiance than Nureyev's long, loose, flying hair, which titillated that pre-Beatles audience and only added to his mystique. At a time when men wore their hair short, and dancers wore theirs lacquered into place, Nureyev's "beatnik," "sheepdog" and "unruly" hair, as it was invariably described in the press, was both an expression of his individuality and a harbinger of the rebel era to come.

Later in the program, Nureyev returned as a prince, partnering Rosella Hightower in the Black Swan pas de deux from *Swan Lake*. Fonteyn had come by his dressing room at intermission and found him frowning at the blond wig in his hand. "They send wrong wig!" he wailed, but there was little to be done. The Royal Ballet's princes did not wear wigs but Nureyev was insistent. The storm of applause that greeted him at the conclusion of his solo prompted Fonteyn to conclude that anyone who could generate such a response while wearing "that wig" was remarkable indeed.* Watching from the wings, Bruhn, too, was shaken: "Seeing Rudik dance on the stage was a shock. He had a tremendous presence and it was inspiring." But it also unsettled him, and Arova, standing alongside him, couldn't help feeling bad for Erik. "Something incredible had just happened and Erik was thinking, 'Where does that leave me?' "

---

*The critics didn't like his wig either, and Nureyev never wore one onstage again.

While the audience screamed itself hoarse, the critical response was more measured. The sticking point was Nureyev's few technical flaws: His jumps, while soft and high, produced the occasional thump when he landed; his rapid turns, never his strong suit, were sometimes askew and his arms possessed more "boyish grace than masculine grandeur," according to Clive Barnes, who nevertheless predicted, as did many critics, that Nureyev was on his way to becoming "the world's most sought-after international star." The comparisons with Nijinsky, Bruhn, Soloviev and every great male dance star were inevitable: Some saw in him glimmers of French star Jean Babilée, one of the most intriguing male dancers of the postwar era. Others saw "Babilée with a Soloviev technique." The consensus was best expressed by the critic Peter Williams, a longtime observer of the scene, when he suggested that greatness in a dancer was as indefinable as beauty. Nureyev, he observed, was "no paragon like Bruhn, and no immediate sensation like Soloviev. He has faults which can hardly pass unnoticed and the very individuality of his manner comes as a surprise — especially when on his British debut we had been primed by the French press to expect a 'Golovine,' a dancer with whom he would appear to have nothing in common whatsoever. Yet make no mistake, he is the sort of dancer on whom legends alight." To Alexander Bland, Nureyev was a breed apart, "a strange, haunted artist whose medium happens to be dancing."

Backstage after the performance, there was an uproar of activity as well-wishers came by to meet the new discovery. Still, no one was quite prepared, Nureyev least of all, for the scene of mass hysteria that exploded at the stage door. As he and Hightower tried to make their way to Fonteyn's car, the rowdy fans surged forward, straining to touch them and screaming as if they were screen idols, presaging the kind of rock star hysteria Nureyev would provoke in the coming years.

To the English, Nureyev was as much an object of curiosity as Eliza Doolittle had been to the Russians. Once, Nureyev had made his way backstage in the hopes of meeting every new artist who came through Leningrad. Now, for the first time in his life, the world was coming to him. At Fonteyn's cast party that night, Cecil Beaton was among the first to greet him. "I kissed him on the cheek and forehead," Beaton confided in his diary that night. "He was very surprised but I felt the consistency of his smooth, poreless, vellum skin, and was pleased that I had made such a public fool of myself. When I talked to Freddie Ashton about the dance I could not keep back the tears in spite of kicking the door hard behind me."

Though Rudolf and Erik were staying together at the Strand Palace Hotel — the very hotel where the Kirov had stayed following Nureyev's defection — few people at the time knew that they were lovers. Fonteyn's husband, Tito Arias, assumed he was making polite conversation when he casually asked Rudolf at the party, "What were you doing in Copenhagen?" Rudolf's reply—concise, wry and to the point—was pure Nureyev. "Is story better not told," he said darkly. Worried about gossip, Erik insisted on discretion, as he did in all spheres of his life. He later confided to a friend that he had been deeply embarrassed the day Rudolf impulsively took his hand as they strolled down a Copenhagen street. Rudolf, on the other hand, never hid the fact that he was with Erik. "He tried to restrain himself in public," says Arova, "but in private, he was openly affectionate."

The day after his debut, Ninette de Valois called Fonteyn. Nureyev's curtain calls had instantly convinced her to engage him for her own company. It was his soft, sweeping bow and presence, more than Ashton's choreography, that spoke to her of his genius. "I saw an arm raised with a noble dignity, a hand expressively extended with that restrained discipline which is the product of a great traditional schooling. Slowly the head turned from one side of the theatre to the other, and the Slav bone-structure of the face, so beautifully modelled, made me feel like an inspired sculptor rather than director of the Royal Ballet. I could seem him suddenly and clearly in one role—Albrecht in *Giselle*. Then and there I decided that when he first danced for us it must be with Fonteyn in that ballet."

Fonteyn, however, demurred when de Valois announced her plan. One never questioned "Madam," as the forbidding de Valois was known to her dancers, but the forty-two-year-old Fonteyn did wonder whether she wouldn't look like "mutton dancing with lamb" next to the twenty-three-year-old wunderkind. "Don't you think I'm too old?"* Fonteyn had often declared that she would retire in her early forties. Her longtime partner Michael Somes had already retired that year from all but non-dancing parts, and *Giselle* had never been one of her finest roles. Then again, with a sensation like Nureyev waiting in the wings, it didn't take her long to realize that even a few performances with him were well worth the risk.

And so it was settled. The two would dance three performances of *Giselle*, beginning February 21, 1962, for which Rudolf would be paid five hundred pounds. Within weeks of the announcement, two thousand fans had signed a petition calling for Nureyev to join the Royal Ballet.

*   *   *

*This was not a question that the forty-six-year-old Dudinskaya had considered when she invited the twenty-year-old Nureyev to partner her.

OVER THE NEXT three months Rudolf danced his final performances with the de Cuevas company. The first of these, in Hamburg, had to be canceled at the last moment. The stage flooded and the safety curtain jammed. A stagehand had pressed the wrong button—whether inadvertently or intentionally it was never clear—and had set off the fire sprinklers. Since the incident involved Nureyev, the press read much into it. To Harold Hobson of the *Christian Science Monitor*, the flooding was the work of "hostile stage hands" intent on blocking Nureyev from dancing. Nureyev, he wrote, "arouses everywhere he goes sympathy and pity. He is the saddest and most romantic figure seen in Europe since the days of Byron . . . a grieved figure who sought freedom and has found no home. . . ."*

In truth, Nureyev was not so aggrieved as Hobson supposed. He hadn't wanted to dance on the cramped stage in the first place and was annoyed that he had been cast only in *The Sleeping Beauty*. He had wanted to go to Munich to see Erik and Sonia Arova dance their first full-length *Swan Lake* together, which is exactly what he did.

To generate more opportunities to perform, Rudolf formed his own concert group with Bruhn, Arova and Hightower, the first of what would be many independent troupes outside regular companies. In addition to dancing extracts from popular ballets, he and Bruhn decided to create their own works, though neither had any experience as a choreographer. In Leningrad, Rudolf had begun to choreograph a piece to Bach's Concerto in D Minor for Two Violins with Nikita Dolgushin, "a pure ballet without any story line," intending to finish it on his return from Paris and London.

The quartet relocated to Cannes, where Hightower had just opened her own dance school in what had once been the kitchen of a hotel-casino built by Russian nobility at the turn of the century, the perfect place to prepare their creative enterprise. Rudolf, Bruhn and Arova took a furnished apartment together overlooking the sea.

After all the commotion of London, the stillness of Cannes in winter came as a relief. The constant scrutiny had left Rudolf agitated, and he was happy to be working quietly with the few people he trusted. The months spent in Cannes were to prove a remarkably productive, if ascetic, period, "full of inspiration, watching and learning." Each morning over the coffee and croissants delivered daily to their apartment, Rudolf, Erik and Sonia Arova reviewed their progress and discussed approaches; from one-thirty to midnight, they took class and rehearsed in the studio. "The boys were so thrilled that they were going to be shown not just as dancers but as choreographers," says Hightower. Their dedication im-

---

*Beneath the headline EX-SOVIET DANCER SEEKS HOME, the *Christian Science Monitor* published a photograph of the dancer it assumed was Nureyev. It wasn't. It was Soloviev.

pressed Marika Besobrasova, a popular local teacher and former dancer, whose White Russian parents had settled on the Côte d'Azur after the Revolution. She and Rudolf were to become lifelong friends, though the first time she addressed him in Russian on the street, he ran from her, thinking that she must be KGB. Erik, she recalls, was the only person who ever matched Rudolf's passion for dancing. "Rudolf had never met anybody as passionate as he was."

Erik contributed two ensemble pieces: a suite of dances to popular Spanish songs and a plotless work to a toccata and fugue by Bach, in which he and Rudolf danced the same steps, but started from opposite sides of the stage. "Sometimes we had our back to each other while we were dancing, but we did it all exactly alike in spite of having very different physique and schooling." Rudolf turned inevitably to the Kirov repertoire for his first foray into producing and choreographing. Having stored a wealth of balletic detail during his years in Leningrad, he contributed a pas de quatre to Glazunov's score for *Raymonda* and two pas de deux, one from *The Nutcracker*, the other from *Don Quixote*. He worked out most of his *Nutcracker* with Hightower while in Israel with the de Cuevas company in December. Despite the perception of him as a nomad, Rudolf found it difficult to adjust to his newfound gypsy life in the West. His washing and meals had always been taken care of by Xenia and he was not in the habit of performing daily, or even twice on the same program. He was also unaccustomed to taking company class on the same day he performed. Since the de Cuevas troupe was regularly on the road, "we were used to living out of trunks," recalls Hightower. "But Rudolf couldn't attach himself. He felt he was in a kind of no-man's-land." Of his last de Cuevas tour, through Turin, Genoa, Bologna and Venice, he remembered only cold and discomfort. Even snow-laced Venice failed to distract him for long. "It was like a dream. But, oh, what an uncomfortable one!"

Back in Cannes, despite a strenuous rehearsal schedule, Rudolf, Erik and Arova took side trips to neighboring Saint-Tropez and Monte Carlo, chiefly so that Rudolf could try out his sporty white Karmann Ghia. A reflection of his new financial clout, the car had been shipped from Munich. However, since neither he nor Erik knew how to drive, Arova, a "lousy driver" by her own estimate, was often pressed into service. No matter how quickly she negotiated the treacherously curvy roads, Rudolf would always cry out for her to go faster. One day she drove him to Monte Carlo to see Fonteyn, who was performing there in a gala. Rudolf hoped to stay with Fonteyn during their upcoming *Giselle* rehearsals, but he did not come straight out and say so. "Tell me," he said instead. "I must be in London long time for rehearsals. I cannot stay so long in hotel. What you think I do?" Fonteyn wasn't sure and called her husband in London to discuss the matter. What if Nureyev had made a deal with the Russians to do some spying in the West? she asked him. Tito Arias thought her imagination was "overworking" and an invitation was tendered.

THE QUARTET gave the first of its performances at the Cannes Casino on January 6, 1962.* A few days later, the group flew to London, where Rudolf and Hightower performed his *Nutcracker* pas de deux for British television, before moving on to Paris for two concerts at the Théâtre des Champs-Elysées, the scene of Rudolf's frenzied de Cuevas debut. Anticipation ran high for the quartet's sold-out Paris performances. Their debut drew eighteen curtain calls from a glittering crowd that included such denizens of the artistic haut monde as Yves Saint Laurent, choreographer Roland Petit, his wife, the ballerina and cabaret star Zizi Jeanmaire, and French ballet great Jean Babilée. The theater "was vibrant with the kind of collective balletomania that used to seize upon the Diaghilev crowds on a great first night here," Janet Flanner, *The New Yorker* magazine's Paris correspondent, told her American readers. A woman of unpredictable enthusiasms, Flanner had been swept away herself and focused on Nureyev to the exclusion of the others. Head, body, technique, style, presence were all analyzed before she hit upon the source of his hypnotic power: Nureyev's dancing was a potent aphrodisiac. "Dancing alone, he gave to the senses the sharp pangs of perfect pleasure."

The extravagant interest in Nureyev prompted Bruhn to worry that he was being overlooked. Having concluded that Hightower was using Rudolf's notoriety to promote them, he was distressed to find Rudolf's name above his own on their company poster. But what he had yet to grasp was that Rudolf's fame had a momentum all its own. Everything he did was news and people who had never been to the ballet knew the name Rudolf Nureyev. "Everyone in Paris was trying to get him to come to dinner," says Zizi Jeanmaire. "He was the new revelation." Erik didn't begrudge Rudolf's acclaim, but its magnitude troubled him. "He asked me if there was anything I could do," recalls Arova. "But everybody was just interested in Nureyev. I thought he needed to talk about it or else he was going to make himself ill."

On their last night in Paris, Erik injured his left foot so badly that he couldn't partner Arova in his own adaptation of Bournonville's *Flower Festival at Genzano*, one of his signature roles. There was no time to cancel the ballet—they returned from the hospital only forty-five minutes before curtain time—so Rudolf had to go on in Erik's place, in addition

*So hungry was Nureyev to sample new choreography that the previous night he had traveled to Marseilles, one hundred miles down the coast, to partner Hightower in a local production of *La Fille Mal Gardée*.

to dancing all of his own roles in an already taxing program. Though he had never once rehearsed the piece, he had watched Erik in the studio and now ran through the role backstage, in the few minutes before the curtain went up. Onstage, Arova helped him out by whispering the steps to him in Russian. While few in the audience noticed anything amiss in Rudolf's quick study of Bournonville, the critics showed little enthusiasm for the "circus" atmosphere pervading the concert, which "may have been of more interest to the sociologist than dance critic," Marie-Françoise Christout noted tartly in *Ballet Today*, casting a jaundiced eye over yet another frenzied Parisian reception. "It resolved itself into something in three more or less equal parts—dancing, hysterical applause from a roaring mob, and intervals. . . . Clearly their material had been assembled without any great discernment. Only the *Don Quixote* pas de deux bore the stamp of choreography, for neither *Toccata and Fugue*, the result of a collaboration between Bruhn and Nureyev, nor the even more mediocre *Fantasie*, could claim this title. No indulgence can be shown toward such poverty of inspiration."

With Bruhn out of commission, a more pressing problem presented itself: Bruhn was due to appear on American television in one week's time, partnering Maria Tallchief in the *Flower Festival* pas de deux. He now suggested that Rudolf replace him on NBC-TV's prestigious *Bell Telephone Hour*, a leading American variety show, thus giving Rudolf his biggest showcase that year. Most ballet dancers at the time considered it demeaning to perform on television, a medium still in its infancy with regard to filming dance.* In those first days, programs were broadcast live, after a full day of working out camera angles, and dancers had to perform on cement floors, which took a terrible toll on their bodies.

It is doubtful that Rudolf was initially aware of television's enormous impact, but by appearing on a "stage" that reached so many people at once, he led the way in popularizing ballet. His American television debut, on Friday, January 19, was seen by millions nationwide and brought him to the attention of "the-man-in-the-living-room," the public that had never set foot inside an opera house. Even without any advance publicity—curiously NBC failed to recognize its windfall—Nureyev created a stir.† At the *Chicago American* that week, dance writer Ann Barzel was "deluged" by inquiries. "The gist was 'who was that extraordinary young man who danced with Tallchief?' " Once more, the last-minute withdrawal of another dancer had propelled Rudolf onto a larger stage,

---

*Balanchine considered television facile and had little faith that ballet could be adapted properly to the medium. He finally revised that view in the 1970s, with the advent of the program *Dance in America*.

†Also appearing on the program that week were classical guitarist Andrés Segovia, "special guest star" Jane Powell, and singers Sally Ann Howes and Earl Wrightson.

an echo of the circumstances that sent him from Ufa to Moscow for the Bashkirian Decade and from Leningrad to Paris for the Kirov tour.

Rudolf had already planned to accompany Erik to New York; now Bruhn offered to coach him in the role and to lend technical—and emotional—support during his rehearsals with Tallchief. Arova was sent ahead to make arrangements, though according to Tallchief, the producers only reluctantly accepted Bruhn's replacement. None of them had seen him dance. Arova safeguarded his two-thousand-dollar cash fee in her purse. As wary of banks as he was of people, Rudolf insisted on hoarding his money and preferred that Arova carry it around for him. This she did for a few more months, until the day she panicked after a man brushed by her on the streets of New York when she was happened to be carrying sixty thousand dollars in her bag. "I must be nuts," she thought, and promptly opened a bank account in Nureyev's name. The next time he asked her for some money, she handed him his bank book. "I thought he was going to kill me. 'What did you put it in a bank for?' He really had a fit. He didn't believe he could get his money out of the bank."

Though Rudolf was to spend much of his life in planes, he had an intense fear of flying, one he would never conquer. He preferred the window seat so he could see "exactly where we are crashing." No one who flew with him ever got over the unlikely sight of him doubled up with fright during takeoff, his coat drawn up over his head, sweat pouring from his face. By the time Rudolf and Erik finally landed in New York on January 15 after a harrowing flight through a storm, Rudolf was badly shaken. Their plane had been rerouted to Chicago and Rudolf was convinced it was going to crash.

His first view of New York soon revived him, its vitality and romantic skyline a far cry from the "nightmare world of immense buildings" he had imagined. Home to Balanchine, Jerome Robbins and Martha Graham, New York had overtaken London as the dance capital of the world by 1962. The effect of seeing the New York City Ballet perform there, wrote Clive Barnes, "is as exhilarating as horses at Epsom or Mozart in Salzburg." The same day he arrived, Rudolf rushed off to see Martha Graham's company at City Center, where, to Arova's surprise, "nobody recognized him."*

Having already met the most exalted names in French, Danish and English ballet in his first six months in the West, Rudolf lost no time in meeting Balanchine, the most influential choreographer in ballet, with a school, company, style and repertory to his credit. The Russian-born Balanchine had studied at the Imperial Ballet School and danced at the

*Though intrigued with Graham's modern dances, he finally succumbed to jet lag and missed seeing Graham herself perform.

Maryinsky, but had left for the West in 1924, when he found little support for his innovative first dances. Diaghilev had immediately hired him as choreographer for the Ballets Russes and after Diaghilev's death, he was lured to America by Lincoln Kirstein, the patron, poet and tastemaker who helped him found the first American ballet school and company. Balanchine soon transformed the traditions of his youth into an authentically American classic style: fresh, streamlined and accelerated. He also composed a glorious series of ballets, many of them pure dance or "plotless" works, using scores by a diverse range of composers from Tchaikovsky and Stravinsky to John Philip Sousa and George Gershwin.

Apart from the homemade film clip of Bruhn dancing *Theme and Variations*, which Rudolf had seen in Leningrad, the only Balanchine work that Rudolf knew was his landmark *Apollo*, made in 1928, which Alicia Alonso's company had unveiled during a tour to Leningrad in early 1961. "How strange, how weird, how wonderful," he had thought at the time, never imagining that he would be in New York one year later having dinner with Erik Bruhn and the manager of Balanchine's company, Betty Cage. After dinner, Rudolf informed Cage that he was off to see the New York City Ballet perform at City Center. Since Erik didn't want to go along, Cage alerted Balanchine's assistant, Barbara Horgan, to watch out for Nureyev at the stage door. Even in New York, Rudolf worried about the KGB. "It was very cloak-and-dagger in those days," says Horgan. "I had to stand outside waiting for him because he was very nervous about walking around by himself. Then I had to bring him in through the back when the houselights went down."

Rudolf was riveted by Balanchine's *Agon*, a stunning blend of classical and invented movement to Stravinsky's music that was then considered avant-garde. He was also intrigued by *Apollo*, which he badly wanted to dance. While the Soviets hadn't cared for *Theme and Variations* because it told no story, Rudolf believed that Balanchine's ballets told "a story of the body." Afterward Balanchine invited Nureyev to the Russian Tea Room, a favorite haunt of émigré artists. "He wanted to see what kind of man I was, I think. He was extremely friendly. We spoke about Pushkin [the writer], Russian literature, and Tchaikovsky. Of the two operas by Tchaikovsky based on Pushkin, I love *Pique Dame*, he preferred *Eugene Onegin*. So we had small differences of opinion."

The one subject on which they would never agree was Nureyev's future in Balanchine's company. "We had all just seen the Kirov and there was such an extraordinary difference between what they did and what we did," recalls Barbara Horgan. "Balanchine knew instantly that this man had defected from a company that was fifty years behind the times." Horgan joined them for a drink one night in the spring of 1962 and was struck by the way Rudolf hung on Balanchine's every word, eager for his benediction. Balanchine certainly felt affection for Nureyev, a fact that tends to be overlooked in light of their divergent paths. He told Betty Cage that Nureyev had reminded him of himself when he first came out of Russia. "Rudolf," she says, "made George nostalgic for his youth." Nevertheless, Balanchine saw little that interested him as a choreographer. He was far more interested in developing the women in his company than the men, and, to his mind, Rudolf represented the nineteenth-century classicism of Petipa, the domain of princes, warriors and spectral sylphs. Balanchine's neoclassicism, by contrast, was "a contemporary classicism — designed to be seen by twentieth-century eyes and make its effects on twentieth-century nerves." Having built his company into a finely wrought ensemble, he was wary of a sensation like Nureyev, whom he was later to call "a one-man show. I, me, a beautiful man, alone." It was Balanchine's ballets, rather than any particular dancer, that were the real stars of the New York City Ballet, the only ballet company not to post cast lists to sell tickets.

"You don't know how to dance the way we dance and it would take you too long to learn," Balanchine famously replied when Rudolf asked to join his company in the spring of 1962. Still, Rudolf persisted. He wanted to know about all kinds of dancing. "My ballets are dry," Balanchine told him. "But I like them dry," Rudolf had answered. "*That* would attract me!" Balanchine wasn't convinced. "No, no, go and dance your princes, get tired of them, and then when you're tired, you come back to me."

According to Barbara Horgan, who was present, Balanchine's admonition has been misunderstood. "He wasn't simply saying, 'You can't dance the prince here,' he wanted Rudolf to understand that he would have to be willing to remake himself." But Rudolf had already remade himself and didn't have the time or inclination to do it again just then.

In any event, the great classical and romantic ballets defined him. "People don't seem to understand that I must first be seen in roles that I know — a prince in *Swan Lake*, a prince in *The Sleeping Beauty*, a nobleman in *Giselle* — so that I can be seen to the best advantage," he told *New York Tribune* critic Walter Terry that month. "Once I have done this, I will not have to play at being a prince and can experiment with my career. Then to Balanchine." Later he would say that he didn't tire of the princes "and the princes didn't tire of me." But what he failed to add was that he never gave up trying to win Balanchine's approval, even from afar. The fact that a Balanchine work was in a company's repertory was often all the enticement he needed. Balanchine never would invite Rudolf to dance with his own troupe. But seventeen years after those first conversations, he would make him a ballet.

Days after meeting Balanchine, Nureyev was back in the role of a nobleman and rehearsing with Fonteyn in London for their first *Giselle*. As an established ballerina, Fonteyn was accustomed to a show of deference from her new partners, especially when her version of a ballet differed from theirs. While her previous partners had been content to show her off like some precious jewel, Rudolf, she quickly learned, was not about to accept second billing. To his mind, a pas de deux meant a dance for two, not a dance for one, with the other biding time. He was determined to make his Albrecht as important as Giselle, which, Fonteyn later admitted, "came as something of a jolt to those of us accustomed to having most of the limelight." Indeed, his idea of compromise was to suggest, "Don't you think this way better?" The Royal Ballet's production of *Giselle* had been recently revised by Frederick Ashton with help from Tamara Karsavina, who had danced it with Nijinsky.* Rudolf, however, felt that the British clung too rigorously to the traditional Maryinsky version and considered its highly mannered mime scenes particularly outmoded. His portrayal of Albrecht had met with instant success at the Kirov, and it was this more impetuous young blueblood that he now intended to introduce to London.

Not that Fonteyn had any trouble holding her own. "She had steel in her back and mind," was the way her friend Maude Gosling described her, qualities which proved essential to working with "somebody as high-strung as [Rudolf] was. . . ." At the first rehearsals, Rudolf treated Fonteyn with respect, "but from time to time," recalls conductor John Lanchbery, "he would be quite rude to her because he wanted the thing to go his way. And she was the model of diplomacy. He would scream, 'Shit, shit, you dance like shit,' and Margot would turn to him and say in the sweetest voice, 'Well, tell me how am I like shit, Rudolf, because then maybe I can change it.' " Indeed it was Fonteyn's ability to meet him head-on that contributed to their mutual empathy from the start. Giselle may have been deceived by Albrecht, but Fonteyn knew exactly whom she was dealing with. "We entered into some negotiations and each altered a few steps here and there," she wrote of the give-and-take that inspired them both. "What mattered to me most was the intensity of his involvement in the role. Two hours went past in no time at all. I was Giselle and he was Albrecht. . . . I forgot my complexes about mutton and lamb."

The disparity in their ages, temperaments, styles and stature was nonetheless considerable. Fonteyn had first stepped into the role of Giselle in 1937, one year before Nureyev was born, and had already experienced fifteen years of theatrical stardom by the time he defected. Talent, timing and savvy had all played a part in her success. The daughter of a British engineer and his Irish-Brazilian wife, she had spent her early years shuttling between London and Shanghai, where her father

---

*With the rise in esteem of the male dancer during the Diaghilev era, the role of Albrecht had been enriched and strengthened.

was transferred when she was eight. It was as fourteen-year-old Peggy Hookham that she had come to the attention of Ninette de Valois, who saw in the talented little girl the makings of a ballerina for her infant company. (The story goes that her dark eyes and pageboy haircut misled de Valois into asking, "Who is that little Chinese girl on the left?") A year later Peggy Hookham had become Margot Fonteyn and was embarking on the first of her major roles at the Vic-Wells (later Royal) Ballet. "Elegance . . . was discernible, even beneath the careless breadth of adolescent movement," de Valois has written. Fonteyn was just seventeen when she succeeded Alicia Markova as the company's prima ballerina and danced her first Giselle, Markova's most celebrated role. A year later she tackled her first *Swan Lake*. Though terror-stricken at the thought of the thirty-two consecutive fouetté turns on one leg that awaited her in the third act, she was more frightened of Ninette de Valois. "Her word . . . was law, so there was no alternative but to get on with it as best I could." Groomed by de Valois and Frederick Ashton, Fonteyn matured along with British ballet to conquer first London and later New York, where, in 1949, during the Royal's historic debut season, her performance as Princess Aurora in *The Sleeping Beauty* propelled her "from national adoration to international adulation."* *The Sleeping Beauty* had never been performed in its entirety in America, and Fonteyn's charm and simplicity held audiences spellbound.

A luminous dancer of natural grace and delicacy, Fonteyn epitomized the tasteful British school, with her innate musicality, exquisite line and reticence. She not only met the challenges of the classics as de Valois added them to the repertory, but fired the imagination of Frederick Ashton, the company's principal choreographer. So completely did she dominate the ranks that even Moira Shearer only briefly threatened to usurp her position. Hearing that she would alternate with Shearer in Ashton's new production of *Cinderella*, Fonteyn "asked indignantly why he had not even told me before it was announced in the press . . . the prospect of losing my favoured position as undisputed head of the company made me ill at ease and defensive. . . ."

By the time Nureyev arrived in London, Fonteyn had already enjoyed celebrated partnerships with Robert Helpmann and Michael Somes. More than a seasoned star, she was "long the reigning ballerina of the Western world," as *Time* magazine declared, and as revered inside Britain as a member of the royal family—in the days when they still served as role models. She was also the company's major drawing card, her status reflected at the box office: There were matinee, evening and Fonteyn prices.

*Since Moira Shearer was better known, following her film debut in *The Red Shoes*, de Valois had instructed impresario Sol Hurok to focus his press campaign on Fonteyn.

David Blair was next in line to dance with her and while she felt no keen rapport with him, she was hardly casting about for new partners. Still, Nureyev's arrival was opportune. As Lincoln Kirstein had presciently prescribed only three years earlier, "What British ballet could do with is some untidiness, intrusions from underprivileged taste, a sense of legitimate outrage and some red-brick energy . . . maybe there is a public in Britain that might welcome an Angry Young Man on his way to rouse the Sleeping Princess right out of Windsor Forest." Where Bruhn saw himself at a dead end, Fonteyn saw herself coming to the end of a long road, and it was the Fiery Young Tatar who would succeed in rousing them both.

Fonteyn took at once to Rudolf's constant questioning, which forced her to look anew at her own working process. "She was deeply impressed by people who had a cool, ordered, logical way of sorting things out," says her friend and sometime Boswell Keith Money. While Rudolf respected all she stood for, Fonteyn marveled at his schooling, his memory for detail and his ability to show her "with infinite exactitude" how she might improve on a step. "What is your mechanic for fouetté?" he asked her one day as he watched her rehearse the famous whipping turns she had come to master. Fonteyn was struck by the question, one she had never thought to consider. "I faltered in my answer and tried the step again. 'Left arm is too back,' he said, and, with that one simple correction, I recovered my old form easily. I learned a great deal simply from watching him in class. Never had I seen each step practiced with such exactitude and thoroughness. It was paradoxical that the young boy everyone thought so wild and spontaneous in his dancing cared desperately about technique, whereas I, the cool English ballerina, was so much more interested in the emotional aspect of the performance."

Away from the studio, Fonteyn helped Rudolf acclimate to English life. Erik had gone on to Florida for a rest and wasn't due to join him in London until early February. Erik was to have been the first foreigner to partner a Royal ballerina at Covent Garden, but after the frenzy of Rudolf's London debut, Erik was now to follow Rudolf by three weeks.

In January, Rudolf gave his first television interview. Carried by the BBC's program *Monitor* on February 25, 1962, it was conducted by a young journalist named Clive Barnes, who later became the senior dance critic of *The New York Times*.* Unaccustomed to the medium, Nureyev faced away from the camera and looked down, uncertain about where to fix his gaze. But his understanding of his unique qualities as a dancer was never in doubt. "Actually, I am romantic kind of dancer," he explained in Russian-coated English, "but I would like to dance modern

---

*Now dance and drama critic of the *New York Post*.

things and to try every different way which exists. I can't change my style. It's me. I dance what I think, and how I feel. Maybe by some influence I do, I just will develop something else but I'm not going to change, nothing."

He took pretty much the same approach to settling in at Margot's. He arrived with a suitcase full of records only to find that Margot and Tito preferred to unwind in silence. "I am like dying," he admitted one day when she asked what was wrong. "Four days I hear no music." A few days later he confessed that he also hated the cold roast beef she often served in her home. He had never eaten meat cold and couldn't get used to it. Sweetly boyish and endearing one minute, he could turn impetuous and prickly the next, his moods as unpredictable as an English summer. Genuine though his behavior may have been, it was often uncensored. As Fonteyn saw it, he had trouble apologizing and rarely bothered with "standard social phrases like 'Thank you for your help.' They apparently struck him as stilted or false." This of course confounded her household staff, who didn't know what to make of the wild Russian boy in their midst. "There seems to be some murmuring belowstairs," an amused Fonteyn confessed to an American friend.

Michael Wishart came to the house one day to sketch Rudolf. Knowing that Wishart wanted to do his portrait, Rudolf had invited the painter to visit when the two bumped into each other outside the Strand Palace Hotel a few nights earlier. "Make sure you don't show my bald spot," he instructed Wishart, brushing his hair forward, and then promptly fell asleep on the sofa, while Wishart sketched.*

With Cecil Beaton, he was not nearly so accommodating. Beaton had gone to photograph him in January at a local television studio and was appalled to find him in "a terrific rage." Nureyev was still leery of the press and the scene Beaton described in his diary would be repeated many times during that period, in different settings: "He could only glower with hatred at everyone who spoke to him. When formally introduced to me, he would not shake hands, but bowed in a stiff offensive way. No words of politeness came from him, as it was explained I was to take a few pictures of him in his dressing room before the press conference. . . . I was lucky that this trapped fox did not bite me but merely glowered into the lens . . . never in my long career have I met someone before who did not respond a little to my personal approval. . . ."

Certainly no two personalities could have been more dissimilar than Nureyev and Beaton, "the arty lensman," as he was sometimes described in the British press. An arbiter of English high style since the thirties,

*For the oil portrait he made from his sketches, Wishart painted Rudolf with his eyes open.

Beaton was not only the favorite photographer of the rich and the royal, but a celebrated theatrical and film designer best known for his work on *My Fair Lady* and *Gigi.* To Princess Grace, he was "the epitome of Edwardian elegance." Refusing to believe that his well-honed charm had failed him, he reminded Nureyev that they had met at Fonteyn's party, but Nureyev merely regarded him "with ever more suspicion if such a thing is possible." Dropping close friend "Freddie" Ashton's name got him nowhere and his compliment on Ashton's solo only backfired. "Everyone said it was a bad dance, the wrong thing to do," Nureyev replied, deeply offending Beaton, whose dandified manner baffled him.* "Someone showed me a very bad critique today. Why they showed it to me I don't know." Nureyev, Beaton concluded, was ungrateful. "Whether his talent is rare enough to overcome all these difficulties and stupidities and temperament is still very much in the balance."

FOR NUREYEV'S Covent Garden debut, tickets were oversubscribed by seventy thousand applications, and selling on the black market for twenty-five pounds, four times their face value. London had seen Nureyev only in a brief solo and a pas de deux, but this was to be his first outing with Fonteyn and the Royal Ballet and there was great curiosity about whether this mixed marriage of Russian and English styles would take.

"It was like we were going to see a marvelous new species of animal," recalls Princess Margaret of the stir he caused. "Here was this creature from the moon. He was more beautiful than I can describe with his flared nostrils, huge eyes and high cheekbones." Such was the competition for the inside story that when her husband, Lord Snowdon, was given special permission to photograph Nureyev and Fonteyn in rehearsal, his Fleet Street rivals complained about his privileges, and a general press call had to be quickly arranged.† TONY GETS PAGE ONE, screamed a headline after the *Sunday Times* featured one of Snowdon's rehearsal photos on its front page, days before Nureyev's debut. Ashton further fanned expectations by announcing, in the article accompanying several more of Snowdon's photographs, that changes had been made to accommodate Nureyev. Members of the Royal Ballet, Fonteyn included, had always been expected to comply to almost every detail of an existing work, and yet here was its associate director acknowledging that "it would have been absurd and lacking in imagination and tact to have attempted to squeeze [him] into a preconceived mold."

*As Noël Coward saw him, Beaton was "flabby, floppy and affected, with an undulating walk, exaggerated clothes and a voice both too high and too precise."
†Photographers were not permitted in the company's rehearsal studios and the board quickly decided that "no special privileges of this kind would be given in future."

Nureyev's debut on February 21, 1962, effectively shattered that mold and stirred ever more controversy and excitement. He conquered Covent Garden, before an audience that included the Queen Mother. From his first steps, the audience could see "something new happening to the old role." Instead of marching toward the footlights, as was customary, Nureyev crept on stealthily, half-obscured by his cloak, only to disappear before the audience had time to register its appreciation. His Albrecht was not the dashing romantic cad favored by most Western interpreters but a thoughtless teenager in the grips of first love who unintentionally deceives a peasant girl. "We have had all sorts of Albrechts—noble ones, ardent ones, manly ones," wrote Alexander Bland in the *Observer*. "Here is one who combines all these elements and adds a vital ingredient of his own. This is a streak of post adolescent instability which arouses feelings of anxiety and protectiveness. It is the James Dean charm of a boy who will always be in trouble and always forgiven. This excessively youthful interpretation makes the story wholly believable."

Nureyev's immersion in the drama and the subtle naturalism of his acting held the audience spellbound. Shocked into love and responsibility by Giselle's madness and death, he seemed genuinely despairing. "We can imagine the agony of grief he goes through before we see him again, a contrite mourner at the grave of his beloved," Mary Clarke observed in the *Sunday Times*. "When Giselle's ghost appears to him he treats her with a new tenderness, as if surrounding her with all the love in the world." This transformation from "mere petulance to heroic grief" was, in the view of another critic, "ballet acting at its finest."

Steeped in the romantic reverie of the ballet's second act, when the spectral Giselle appears to Albrecht, Nureyev was in his element. He proved a lighter, cleaner and stronger dancer than many critics had expected and his movement appeared so supple that when he made "one of his great loping runs round the stage like a cheetah," as Bland put it, he seemed "to be made of more elastic material than normal humanity." His eyes burning with hopeless passion, he "played the whole second act like a man in a trance, watching visions, a man divorced from the material world," Clive Barnes later wrote. "The full force of the conception only made itself felt at the end when the bewildered yet mature Albrecht is left alone in contemplation. A boy has come to tragic maturity."

Nureyev's greatest achievement, however, was to spur Fonteyn into giving what many considered the performance of her lifetime, twenty-five years after her debut in the role. Fonteyn, who had never before excelled as Giselle, responded to him with perfect sympathy and their great partnership was born. "He threw Margot's game off in a way that stimulated her brain," recalls Snowdon. "He came in like a bull in a china shop." Nureyev's carnal ardor was the perfect foil to Fonteyn's eloquent purity, drawing from her untapped reserves of passion and ethereal grace. Dancing together, their energy and musicality seemed to emanate from a single source. When, near the close of the ballet, she cradled Nureyev's head in her arms as Albrecht lay on the point of death, the audience went completely still, reluctant to intrude on a private moment. John Lanchbery, leading the orchestra that night, had never felt such tension in the house. "The emotions of the audience were screwed up to such a pitch that I was thinking, 'Jesus, is someone going to giggle? Because if so, the whole thing will be ruined.' Rudolf had a wonderful sense of how far he could push things and that performance was pushed as far as it could go."

Stepping out to take their bows, Fonteyn and Nureyev were greeted by an ovation that continued through twenty-three curtain calls. As the audience roared its approval, Fonteyn plucked a long-stemmed red rose from her bouquet and presented it to Nureyev, who, apparently overcome by the moment, dropped to his knee, grabbed her hand, and covered it with kisses. Whether this was a spontaneous act or "a well rehearsed piece of corn . . . it was damned good theatre," confirmed *Dance and Dancers*, and further proof that Nureyev had the instincts of a great star, one "capable of changing the public's attitude towards an art," just as Callas had done for the opera. To the magazine's editors, Nureyev's dramatic gesture presaged a new ballet boom for Britain "as surely as the broken champagne bottle thrown by the unknown Duchess sets a new vessel relentlessly on its way down the slipway. . . . Ballet in London has been needing something explosive to start off another boom. It may seem rude to our own fine stars of the dance to say that these things have to come from outside, but the trouble is that we have all been brought up with our own artists. . . . Nureyev has all the qualities that make for explosions. What is more, he is talked about by people across the length and breadth of the land who never think much about ballet, and certainly have never thought of going to it. Now maybe they will. . . ."

Nureyev and Fonteyn would rarely repeat that curtain call, for Fonteyn disliked him kneeling in salute to her, thinking it looked as if he were deferring to her age, so from then on she dropped to her knee instead.

Having predicted that Nureyev's career would founder in the West, Arnold Haskell, the author of "A Sorry Affair," now reversed himself to concede that it was he, and not Nureyev, who had been led astray by all the hype. "There has been so much publicity about [him], so many rumours and so much misinformation, that it has been difficult to see him in proper perspective. The name of Nijinsky was used by many who were not born when he had already been in the twilight for several years. The role of Albrecht was the perfect test piece for Nureyev as dancer and actor. He proved immediately that his achievement is already tremendous and that . . . given the right conditions, no one will be calling him a second anyone."

Not everyone joined in the chorus of praise. A. V. Coton, the *Daily Telegraph*'s seasoned critic, found it a "deeply intriguing but quite unmoving occasion" and felt that Fonteyn and Nureyev "might have been creatures from two different planets," so ill suited were their temperaments. To Andrew Porter of the *Financial Times*, the soft, wide style of Nureyev's dancing created "too unmanly an impression to complement the ballerina," and his second act was "all lilies and languors." Nearly all Nureyev's variations were new to Covent Garden and while some of them were danced in the Kirov production, many others were his own invention, including the series of entrechats six he introduced when commanded to dance himself to death by the Queen of the Wilis. This was the same solo Rudolf had danced in his few performances of *Giselle* at the Kirov. To a number of English critics, however, the idea that a young dancer would tamper with traditional choreography was tantamount to sacrilege and roundly denounced.

THE PUBLIC, meanwhile, oblivious to these fine points, mobbed the stage door after the performance. The stardom, the acclaim of the British, dancing with Fonteyn — these were all things Rudolf had dreamed about. Yet the night was not the total triumph it might have been because Erik couldn't share in his success, despite having coached him. Erik knew only too well what the night meant to Rudolf: Six years earlier in New York, his own debut in *Giselle* had stunned the dance world. And his partner had also been a renowned ballerina twenty years *his* senior: Alicia Markova, the ballerina Fonteyn succeeded at the Sadler's Wells. Overcome by jealousy, Bruhn, the person who mattered most to Rudolf, had fled the theater in despair. "And I was running after him and the fans were running after me," Nureyev remembered long after. "It was a mess."

And destined to grow messier after Ninette de Valois decided to invite Nureyev back for the company's spring season. Now instead of being the sole male guest artist that season, Bruhn would be sharing the spotlight with Nureyev. Bruhn's precise Danish-based dancing was closer to the British style than was Nureyev's Russian flamboyance and a number of de Valois's colleagues worried that Nureyev would prove disruptive. But change was exactly what de Valois was after and in Nureyev she saw a catalyst, not only for Fonteyn, but for her entire corps of male dancers. His celebrity and box-office cachet weren't lost on her either: His three *Giselles* with Fonteyn could have sold out three times over, and at the last of these, on March 6, he was presented to Queen Elizabeth, Princess Margaret and their aunt Princess Marina. De Valois had spent thirty-two years building a house for British ballet. During the war years, when many of her male dancers were called up, she had refused to bolster their depleted ranks by inviting in dancers from abroad. She feared that she would discourage her own dancers and never develop a tradition for British male dancing. By 1962 the time had come to test its foundations. To those who called her decision risky, de Valois had only one answer: "If one person can come in and spoil the Royal Ballet style, we deserve for it to be spoiled."

TWO DAYS AFTER meeting the Queen of England and nine months after defecting, Nureyev flew to New York to make his American stage debut. Arova was dancing as a guest star with Ruth Page's Chicago Opera Ballet and had arranged for him to partner her on March 10 in the *Don Quixote* pas de deux during the troupe's engagement at the Brooklyn Academy of Music. Arova had made sure to explain to him that he wouldn't be appearing at the city's famed Metropolitan Opera House, but across the East River in Brooklyn. "Who cares?" he had replied. "It's New York. I want to get there, I want to show them." The going rate for guest stars was then four hundred dollars for a single performance; Rudolf asked for twenty-five hundred dollars. "Nobody even argued," says Arova, who negotiated his fee. "They were just glad to get him. When I told him that I didn't dare ask for much myself, he said, 'You go back and ask for more or I won't dance.' "

PREOCCUPIED WITH his own Royal Ballet debut, Erik stayed behind in London. Arova was there to meet Rudolf at Idlewild Airport, but so were a throng of reporters, who peppered him with questions about his family before Arova managed to whisk him off to rehearsal. They had agreed beforehand to a compromise — we'll do half your version and half mine — but once in the studio Rudolf insisted on doing it all his way. 'Well, he has more to lose than I do," thought Arova, who relented and then stayed up half the night practicing the new steps in her hotel room. Rudolf, she recalls, "was very sure of his success."

Two nights later a packed house of dance world luminaries crossed the river for Nureyev's American debut. Leonard Bernstein sat in the front row directly behind the conductor, while Balanchine, Alexandra Danilova, Melissa Hayden, Jacques d'Amboise and Edward Villella sat several rows behind Bernstein. Though the general audience was captivated by Nureyev, the dancers in the crowd were naturally skeptical of all the hype surrounding him. He may have "leapt" to freedom, but could he dance? According to Hayden, a veteran New York City Ballet star, "he jumped very high, but when he landed in deep plié he made a noise. I was sitting next to Balanchine and I said, or maybe he did, that Nureyev was very noisy."

Despite the wait-and-see attitude of the dancers in the audience, the public had no such reservations. The applause following their twelve-minute pas de deux "went on and on, a veritable Niagara," and though Arova shared equally in his triumph, Nureyev had to repeat his variation. "If Nureyev's solo was full of magnificent promise, Sonia Arova's was burnished to exquisite perfection," observed *Dancing Times*. Most of the critics of the day were by now so enamored of the Nureyev phenomenon that they were eager to contribute their own superlatives. "It would have been worth the visit merely to observe Nureyev walk around the stage," declared Irving Kolodin in *Saturday Review*. P. W. Manchester of the *Christian Science Monitor* went further, noting that Nureyev had conquered New York "as immediately and decisively as perhaps no other dancer has done since Margot Fonteyn first appeared here in *The Sleeping Beauty* in 1949." Nureyev, she wrote, was not the virtuoso that Soloviev was and lacked Bruhn's pure classic perfection, but he possessed something rarer, "a quality of mystery, that indefinable something which rivets attention on him even when he is doing nothing more than stand. Because of Nureyev, we can begin to understand what it was about Nijinsky that made him a legend though comparatively few ever saw him dance." To Walter Terry of the *New York Herald Tribune*, he was no mere "novelty," but "an artist, already brilliant, who is at the threshold of what could be the most phenomenal dance career of our age."

The lone dissenting voice belonged to the country's senior dance critic, John Martin, who had not liked what he had seen and was nettled that so many others had. Writing in *The New York Times*, Martin declared that Nureyev's only claim to fame was his defection, which, to his mind, hardly warranted the packed house and wild cheering "no matter how strongly one may feel about those wicked Reds." He had seen Nureyev dance with the Kirov in Paris and had concluded that he was "by no means the best of the lot, nor even as good as the best." Indeed, he even went so far as to call Nureyev's escape at Le Bourget "tragic," arguing, among other things, that Nureyev sorely needed the kind discipline and stability that only the Kirov could provide him. Curiously unaware that it was Nureyev who had sought out Bruhn, Martin mistakenly assumed that Bruhn had come to his rescue: "The one bright note in the picture is that Erik Bruhn (who may really be the greatest male dancer in the world, if, indeed, there is any such thing) has befriended him. . . . If young Nureyev can learn to listen . . ."

Young Nureyev still hoped to dance for Balanchine, though the choreographer failed to come backstage the night of his debut. "His ballets are on a much higher level than the ballets to which I have been used thus far," Nureyev told the critic Anatole Chujoy at the postperformance party, no doubt with the intention of wooing Balanchine through the press. "I am a romantic dancer and Mr. Balanchine's ballets are a new field for me, very different from the field where I work now and I should like to know it better." Balanchine, however, had already made up his mind. "First time he danced in America at Brooklyn Academy of Music," he recalled in 1968, "behind me were about twenty-five boys with red lips sitting and screaming, 'God! oh God!' Frankly we don't need this."

15

The Trial

NUREYEV MAY HAVE BEEN the talk of the dance world on two continents, but he was persona non grata in his mother country and soon tried for state treason in absentia. The closed trial, organized by the KGB, took place on April 2, 1962, at the Municipal Courts Building in Leningrad, not far from Mikhailovsky Castle, one of Rudolf's favorite haunts. Treason carried a maximum penalty of death by firing squad, and the Pushkins feared desperately that if sentenced to death, Rudolf would be murdered abroad, like Trotsky. Hoping nothing less than to save him, they hired a lawyer on his behalf, a bold move given the opposition and potential for retribution. The lawyer, a woman in her mid-thirties, cost them five hundred rubles, nearly two months' wages for a well-paid Kirov artist. While most Soviet citizens did not know much about their rights, they were in fact "protected" by a constitution.

The trial lasted just two hours. Among those summoned to testify before the female judge and the two male representatives "of the people" were Korkin, Strizhevski and Alla Osipenko. Pushkin and Xenia, fearing the worst, stayed home. Tamara, the only "defense" witness, stood with Rosa Nureyeva just outside the courtroom, listening through the door. "Alexander Ivanovich [Pushkin] asked the lawyer to call me because I could present some evidence proving that Rudik had not intended to defect." She planned to recount how she had spoken to him on the phone on June 9, when he had told her that he couldn't wait to leave Paris "because the audience was a bunch of idiots, and that he was looking forward to London, where the audience really understood ballet." But the court declined the attorney's motion to allow Tamara's testimony. Several witnesses from the Kirov had already testified against his intention to defect and the judge deemed her evidence unnecessary.

The first witness called was Korkin, who described how hard Rudolf had worked during the tour. Nureyev sometimes danced twice a day and never complained, he said, adding that his only chance to see Paris was late at night. Next up was KGB captain Strizhevski, who testified that Rudolf had "partied with God knows whom. He came in at four A.M. to the hotel. No one knows where he went." He had tried to reason with Nureyev, he explained, but had been told to "shut up." Sergeyev and Soloviev were both expected in court, but when they failed to appear, their written statements were read aloud by the prosecutor. While Sergeyev praised Nureyev's diligence during the tour, Soloviev, according to Tamara's recollection, claimed that Nureyev had intended to defect in Paris. Osipenko was quick to counter Soloviev's claim. While it was true that he was curious about seeing Paris, she told the court, he had no intention of staying. He was too excited about going on to London. Had he been allowed to join them, she added curtly, "none of this would have happened."

Finally, Gruzinski, the man in charge of the airplane tickets, recounted the scene at Le Bourget. He described how Rudolf had broken free of Strizhevski and run to the French police and how he, in turn, had called the embassy. The Soviet ambassador, he insisted, had tried to convince Rudolf to return home.

The outcome of the trial was a foregone conclusion. The day before, a letter assailing Sergeyev and Dudinskaya for their high-handed management of the Kirov had been published in the pages of *Izvestiya*. It was signed by all the leading ballerinas of the Kirov: Osipenko, Irina Kolpakova, Ninel Kurgapkina, Alla Shelest, Olga Moiseyeva and Ninel Petrova. Sergeyev and Dudinskaya, they charged, had "prevented the new generation of artists from coming up to their level." No mention was made of Nureyev, but much play was made of the fact that Kostya Brudnof and Nikita Dolgushin (two of the dancers Nureyev most admired) had been forced to leave the company to go to work in Novosibirsk. For such a letter to have been published in the Soviet government newspaper meant that party officials wanted both to see Sergeyev punished for Nureyev's defection and to make it appear as if the Kirov dancers seconded their assignment of blame.*

The letter caused a sensation and unwittingly became the center-

*As historian Mark von Hagen points out, their actions were not far removed from the Stalin-era show trials, in which it was not enough to pronounce someone a traitor, usually on trumped-up charges. The government also had to orchestrate a public denunciation campaign, with coworkers and friends expressing their own indignation.

piece of Rudolf's defense. Here was further proof, his lawyer argued after reading it aloud to the court, that the atmosphere of the Kirov Theater was rife with intrigue and that its best young talent was being held back. There were so many problems in the theater and so much tension in the ranks that a simple nighttime walk in Paris had been misinterpreted as something much more dramatic than it was. She went on to blame the KGB for setting a trap for him.

The judge barely deliberated before pronouncing Nureyev guilty. But her reasons for meting out the lightest possible sentence — a seven-year jail term — can only be guessed at. A death sentence would certainly have generated negative publicity in the West, while a lighter sentence would have made it possible for him to return. Possibly she meant to implicate the KGB as well.

The sentence would never be revoked during Nureyev's lifetime.*

*Nureyev's relatives did not formally apply to have him "rehabilitated" until 1997.

16

The Beatnik and the Prince

ONE WEEK AFTER making his New York debut, Rudolf was back in London and living with Erik in the furnished flat they had rented at 22 Roland Gardens in South Kensington. For the next three months, they were seldom apart. Each morning they drove to class in Rudolf's Karmann Ghia, though neither of them had a license or really knew how to drive. The Royal Ballet's rehearsal studios in Baron's Court were no more than ten minutes away by car, but with Rudolf at the wheel, Erik became so agitated that he would have to "open the door and throw up. When I was driving, the same thing would happen to him. The car looked like it had been beaten with a hammer. People would scream at us and call us killers." Fonteyn quickly took matters into her own capable hands and set them up with an instructor from the Automobile Association. The instructor insisted on giving them a driving test. To Erik, this was "worse than going on the stage." He insisted that Rudolf go first, reasoning that if he managed to pass, then he would take the exam, too. If he failed, no dice. A short time later Rudolf returned, waving his license, which was something of a miracle, as anyone who drove with Rudolf in subsequent years would attest. Erik also managed to pass the test, though neither of them ever learned how to park. John Tooley, then assistant general administrator of the Royal Opera House, grew to expect Rudolf's near-daily phone call from the street to his office. "I'm here," he would begin, whereupon Tooley's secretary would be dispatched downstairs to park his car.

Rudolf and Erik kept a low profile in those first weeks. Fonteyn was on tour in Australia, and occasionally they dined with Nadia Nerina, Bruhn's only partner that season, and her husband, Charles Gordon.

"Charlik, Erik say you help me," Rudolf informed Gordon within one hour of meeting him. As Gordon was a merchant banker, Rudolf lost no time in taking advantage of his expertise, just as he did with anyone who was knowledgeable in an unfamiliar area. Since Gordon was also a friend of Erik's, Rudolf assumed he could trust him.

"I am poor man—no money. I want to make money. Tax free!" These last two words caught Gordon by surprise. "I perceived that he was watching me closely," he wrote, "to see how I would react to the use of a term with which even literate accountants were not then entirely familiar." Over dinner, Erik and Gordon spoke of earlier times, while Rudolf, according to Gordon, sat there "knitting his eyebrows and throwing out shafts of boredom—this was talk which did not include him. He needed to be in the centre, to be actively bent on some personal pursuit, whether destructive or intellectually arousing, mischief-making or pleasure-seeking. He cut in on Erik and then demonstrated his astonishing intuition, that special gift he had of being able to see through the back of the head of an enemy or indeed of a friend."

"Charlik hates me," Rudolf announced to Nerina. At that moment Gordon realized that Rudolf "was right, I didn't care for him, yet with his psychic gift he knew the truth before anyone else." Nevertheless, despite his reservations, Gordon agreed to help him and introduced him the next day to his wife's agent, Sander Gorlinsky. Born in Kiev in 1908, Gorlinsky had grown up in Berlin, but the rise of Nazism had forced him to flee, first to Paris and later to England, where he had already left his mark by reintroducing Italian opera to the English immediately after the war. A tough negotiator with "a nose for stars and a lot of personal charm," Gorlinsky was known to appreciate good cognac and fine clothes. "If you're going to get big fees," he liked to say, "you have to dress the part." His client list included such music world figures as Arturo Toscanini, Tito Gobbi and, most notably, Maria Callas, whose Covent Garden debut he had arranged. Would he act for Rudi? Charles Gordon now asked him. Feigning indifference, Gorlinsky took a long draw on his cigar, as if weighing the offer, before answering, "Why not?"

As Rudolf had calculated, Gordon played his part. "In those days, for non-residents and offshore investments, Luxembourg was very practical. I advised Sander that unless he had already done so for his other clients . . . he should form a special Luxembourg company, and that this company 'owned by Rudi' was to have the sole right to receive any fees earned by him, that is, paid without any deductions. This essentially tax-free structure would secure Nureyev's cash flow and establish an increasing net worth." His association with Gorlinsky would make Rudolf a rich man.

✻   ✻   ✻

IT WAS UNPRECEDENTED that the Royal Ballet had engaged two great male guest stars for the same season. It was rarer still to find the two stars attending each other's rehearsals and coaching each other on the side, especially when they were dancing the same roles in *Swan Lake*, *Giselle* and *The Sleeping Beauty*. While competition is an inescapable fact of life in any ballet company, Rudolf and Erik refused to see themselves as rivals. On days when the theater was closed, they made straight for Covent Garden to rehearse on the empty stage, alone. Erik was still recovering from his foot injury and was putting in extra hours to regain his strength. Rudolf was happy to join him. They assumed that audiences would savor their differences the way they themselves did.

But given Nureyev's sudden celebrity and Bruhn's reputation among balletomanes, it was inevitable that the press would compare them. And with both dancers hoping to join the Royal on a more permanent basis, it was inevitable that the Royal would eventually have to choose between them. No foreigner had ever been taken on by the company—at the time only British Commonwealth citizens could become regular members—and the chance that both would be invited to join was remote. Still, neither could have anticipated the way they were pitted against each other, or the pressures that would beset them as soon as the season got under way. "The press had a field day," Bruhn recalled long afterward, not without bitterness. "I mean they . . . watched us like hawks, and it was as if they placed bets on which of us was going to survive."

The *Times* set the tone for the season. "If he is not the world's greatest male dancer, who is?" the paper asked in its first-ever feature on Bruhn in March 1962, only to add that the same might be said of several other topflight dancers, though Nureyev was the only one named. In stark contrast to the front-page blitz preceding Nureyev's debut, the coverage of Bruhn's arrival was confined to the arts pages, where much was made of his low profile in England and his aversion to publicity. "He could prove an even bigger sensation than Rudolf Nureyev," trumpeted *Topic*, the London weekly, predicting that "with any luck, Bruhn should no longer be a mystery man with the general public, the great dancer nobody had ever heard about. . . ."

Still, as Nureyev was the great dancer everybody had already heard about, the press continued to cover his every move. Bruhn couldn't help feeling eclipsed: How could he compete with a Russian defector? It was a question he would still be pondering decades later. "I wonder what my career would have been like if I'd defected," a Canadian colleague heard him say on numerous occasions in the 1980s. And yet Bruhn was decidedly ambivalent about publicity. He yearned for recognition, but loathed drawing attention to himself. His performances were restricted to the stage; away from it, he became so convincingly "mortal" that few recognized him. His ambivalence ruled his life. A friend recalls his genuine surprise when he returned one day from a visit to his bank in Copenhagen. "Someone recognized me," he said, with obvious pleasure. Rudolf, on the other hand, often to Erik's great annoyance, continued the performance long after it was over, almost demanding to be acknowledged. As Rudolf saw it, Erik was not getting his due, a situation that genuinely troubled him. "Rudik kept feeling guilty about the press overlooking me and he was very considerate. That was enough for me. The rest I could not control."

In addition to his guest appearances, Erik was to stage variations from *Napoli*, the first Bournonville ballet to enter the Royal Ballet's repertory. He also taught the British dancers Bournonville technique, classes Rudolf joined, all the while "singing Erik's praises," remembers Monica Mason, then a promising young soloist. "He would tell us, 'Erik has *so much* knowledge. You can see how beautifully he shows steps. You must watch how he does that.' " The women in the company were only too pleased to oblige, since most of them, the young ones in particular, had a mad crush on Bruhn. Rudolf, with his limited English, guarded air and explosive temper, remained at a remove, whereas Erik, with his matinee-idol looks and gentle manner, appeared more accessible. "We were in love with Erik to the point where we would all flush red whenever he walked by," confirms Antoinette Sibley, who worked closely with Bruhn on *Napoli*. "I mean he was gorgeous and just so handsome. We were like teenagers around him." If some of them thought Rudolf arrogant, they had only to see him working next to Erik to realize how humble he could be. "You could see he was soaking up everything he could," recalls Anya Sainsbury, the former dancer Anya Linden. "Along with the arrogance and charisma, there was this humility."

Nevertheless, Rudolf's presence in the studio began to rattle Erik. At every chance, he would evaluate Erik's dancing, "telling him what was good and what wasn't," said Nadia Nerina. He was "forcing his personality on Erik and it made Erik nervous. . . . Erik was always very cool and collected, and would come to rehearsals prepared in his mind as to what he was going to do. He was very organized and he would always appear meticulously dressed. . . . On the other hand, Rudy would come in looking like a ragbag and slop about. Their personalities were totally different. . . ." Erik became so unsettled one day that Nerina refused to continue unless Rudolf left the studio. "Well, he left rather sheepishly and when he closed the door behind him, I could still see him with his nose pressed against the door window watching us."

Rudolf, however, attributed Erik's discomfort to another cause. He knew that Erik felt little rapport with Nerina and was unhappy with his own dancing as a result. Although the South African–born Nerina was one of the Royal's major ballerinas, a formidable virtuoso to whom no technical challenge seemed daunting, Bruhn simply could not work up any enthusiasm for her onstage. He felt there was little warmth or chemistry between them. This of course only compounded his discomfort at having to make his Royal Ballet debut just weeks after Rudolf's landmark debut with Fonteyn on the same stage. The critics, however, were unanimous in their praise of the Bruhn-Nerina partnership. Of their first *Giselle* in early April, *Ballet Today* declared: "This is what we had been waiting for." Yet despite such praise, Bruhn found himself in the unfortunate position of having to overcome the long shadow cast by Nureyev, "talk of whose triumphs was still on our lips." The first Nureyev-Fonteyn *Giselle* had created such a furor, acknowledged Peter Williams, that "it seems likely to overshadow most performances in the ballet for some time to come. . . . Bruhn is the kind of artist upon whom any male dancer can safely model himself. To copy Nureyev could easily bring disaster. . . . There was none of the wild rapture of Nureyev, yet [Bruhn] remained completely true to the spirit of romanticism."

Unlike Rudolf, Erik did not create his own solo for Albrecht or make any significant changes to the choreography. To Nerina, this was as it should be. She had disliked Rudolf's "pyrotechnic display" of entrechats six in the ballet's second act, thinking it more exhibitionist than artistic. In what would become ballet legend, she decided to outdo him. During a performance of *Swan Lake* with Bruhn one night, Nerina came onstage to perform Odile's famous thirty-two fouettés in the ballet's third act. (Intent on making the Prince forget his pledge of love to the Swan Queen, the false Black Swan, Odile, tries to dazzle him.) Flashing a mischievous grin, Nerina launched into a series of entrechats six instead, bounding up and down to gasps from the audience. There were not many men who could perform sixteen entrechats six, as Rudolf had done; Nerina performed thirty-two. Rudolf, seated in the audience next to Nerina's husband, sensed at once that "here was a lesson meant for him," or so Nerina's husband later insisted. Outraged, he "glared" at Gordon, got up from his seat and stormed out of the opera house. After that, his relationship with Nerina cooled to below the freezing mark.

On May 3 Rudolf returned to the London stage, performing at a benefit gala in aid of the Royal Ballet. Erik and Nerina also danced that night, while the Queen Mother, Princess Margaret and Lord Snowdon lent the occasion the glamour of royalty. Rudolf appeared in *Les Sylphides*, partnering another guest star, the forty-five-year-old French prima ballerina Yvette Chauviré. His debut was naturally of special interest, not least because Nijinsky had originated the leading male role of the Poet, who, as envisioned by Fokine, wanders among moonlit ruins and dancing sylphs to Chopin's music. Rudolf, more than dance the role, seemed to inhabit it, giving the impression of "complete solitude, of someone searching for inspiration or an ideal," wrote Peter Williams, calling Nureyev's the most fully realized performance he had ever seen, after "many thousand" viewings of the ballet. Lillian Moore of the *Dancing Times* thought him "so abstracted as to be barely conscious of his partner." His dancing had "a strangely disturbing quality, perhaps because it achieves such a powerful effect while breaking so many rules." For his solo, Rudolf danced the version he had learned in Leningrad, not the one familiar to London audiences. Since Fokine had created both solos, there was little argument about its authenticity. The program also showcased the *Napoli* excerpts staged by Bruhn and a new pas de deux by Ashton. But it was *Les Sylphides* that drew the most prolonged and enthusiastic applause of the evening.

The excitement about Nureyev reached an even higher pitch once the *Observer* began publishing excerpts from his forthcoming "autobiography." The opening installment, extravagantly titled "My Leap to Freedom," appeared on May 13, 1962, accompanied by four large photographs. The space devoted to a twenty-four-year-old dancer was considerable, prompting one critic to remark that never in his recollection had the *Observer* "treated a young man in this bold way before." Since Rudolf had yet to lift the curtain on his past, there was an avid and growing public eager to hear the story of this Russian James Dean, as the *Observer* billed him.

His attention firmly in the present, Rudolf had been reluctant to revisit his past. But worried about money, as he would be all of his life, he had been persuaded that in addition to the immediate cash that a memoir would provide him, it might prove a good career move. He had signed the contract with Opera Mundi, a small publisher, in August while on tour with the de Cuevas troupe. Published later that fall, his "autobiography" was ghostwritten by a number of French journalists sent to grab interviews with him on the road, and edited by Rudolf's friend and mentor the *Observer's* Nigel Gosling, thus launching a privileged relationship of benefit to both.

The fact that he was dancing in London while his life story was running in the papers lent an immediacy to his appearances that further fanned interest in him. "He was not only free," recalls Princess Margaret, "but in *our* country and in *our* company." As Bruhn well understood, Rudolf's career would benefit from the curiosity that his exotic background aroused. His memoir, in effect, consolidated his personal myth. Written in the first person, it promised the "heroic" story behind the front-page story and gave the public a sense of intimacy with its subject that few dancers had ever granted. But given the period in which it was published, the memoir conceals as much as it reveals. According to Arova, "he didn't give two hoots about it. He kept asking me to read it and I said, 'I don't know what went on in Russia.' "

Nureyev's growing renown hardly pleased the Soviets, who had every intention of derailing his career in the West. Threatening to end cultural exchanges, the Soviet embassy in London tried repeatedly to dissuade the Royal Ballet from presenting him. When the British resisted, the Soviets promptly canceled the Covent Garden performances of the Bolshoi's Maya Plisetskaya and Nicolai Fadeyechev that spring. They also encouraged Farida Nureyeva to make near-daily calls to Rudolf's dressing room, urging him to return, a ploy which succeeded at least in distressing him. "You have helped a traitor to the Soviet Union," John Tooley was informed by the Soviet attaché when he tried to rush through a visa application for choreographer Robert Helpmann.* "So I'm not helping you." In short order, the Bolshoi's summer visit to London was also dropped, as was Asaf Messerer's guest teaching stint at the Royal. Messerer was the celebrated teacher who had been suddenly called out of town the day Rudolf went to audition for the Bolshoi School. Once again, Rudolf was to miss out on his lessons.

IN HIS FIRST SEASON with the Royal Ballet, Rudolf appeared with Fonteyn only twice, both times in *Giselle*. Curiously, his debuts in the other major classics were with foreign guest ballerinas. He danced *The Sleeping Beauty* with Yvette Chauviré† and *Swan Lake* with Sonia Arova. Erik danced these same ballets with Nerina. The presence of these two great male stars drew the public's attention to the male dancer as never before and benefited the younger generation of British male dancers enormously. These ballet princes even stole the limelight from their ballerinas. So unusual was this turn of events that the *New York Herald Tribune* sent critic Walter Terry overseas to investigate. "A beatnik and a prince have taken London by storm," he reported, noting that both were bringing "a whole new audience" to the ballet.

With his self-effacing refinement, however, Erik exemplified the values of an earlier era. "His grand manner and good manners are so intense that one feels unshaven," Richard Buckle remarked of Bruhn's debut in *The Sleeping Beauty* that April. Rudolf, on the other hand, was of the moment: daring, subversive, young, the poster boy for the coming decade of self-expression and sexual freedom. "Erik Bruhn is certainly a wonderful dancer," Nijinsky's partner Tamara Karsavina told Buckle, "but he lacks Nureyev's nerve." Even Alicia Markova, Bruhn's first Giselle, marveled at how Nureyev had only to walk onstage to command it. To

---

*The Australian-born Helpmann was Fonteyn's first partner and the chief male dancer of the Vic-Wells, later Royal, Ballet. He had collaborated with Nijinska on the de Cuevas production of *The Sleeping Beauty* and was soon to collaborate with Ashton on the Royal Ballet's revised production of *Swan Lake*. Tooley had wanted Helpmann to have a look at the Bolshoi and Kirov productions of the ballet.

†They also danced *Les Sylphides* and, though not a local debut for Nureyev, *Giselle*.

Walter Terry, Nureyev was "a beatnik in ballet tights" with his "shock of unruly hair. . . . But there is nothing crude or gauche about this animal. . . . The discipline of a premier danseur appears to cloak a creature of wild and beautiful movement impulses."

By the early sixties, recalls Arova, "people were ready for a new face. Rudolf walked in at the right time and knew exactly what to do." He also possessed what Snowdon calls "this extraordinary quality of being physically amazing-looking and attractive to both men and women. When you saw him come onstage, you were magnetized by his presence and beauty and the whole thing. Not only just the way he danced and moved. It was very strong and very alive and very masculine dancing. It did change the whole scene."

The year 1962 was to prove as pivotal for the arts as it was for Nureyev. It was the year the Beatles released their first single, "Love Me Do," Bob Dylan his debut album, and the artists Andy Warhol, Roy Lichtenstein and Claes Oldenburg introduced Pop to the New York art world. In Paris, the directors Jean-Luc Godard and François Truffaut were bringing a new focus to film, as was Yves Saint Laurent to couture, while in London, Mary Quant was putting women in miniskirts. The optimistic climate of 1960s London was a restless time, when "centuries of conformity were finally giving way to the Mod revolt." This was the era of the "youthquake," when members of Rudolf's generation set out to forge their own cultural, political and social agendas. Through satire, fashion and even in discotheques, class lines were crossed or obscured altogether. Intent on jolting audiences out of their complacency, the British playwright Joe Orton decided that "the only field still heavily unexplored was the sexual one." By the time of his breakthrough hit *Entertaining Mr. Sloane* in 1963, the Profumo scandal had toppled the Conservative government. From then on little was left unexplored. "The sixties had a term of approbation all ready for the spectacle that was Rudolf Nureyev: far out," Arlene Croce later wrote. "All the 'out' words seemed to fit him. . . . He connected with the rebellious, hyperbolic spirit of the times, and suddenly ballet was in."

As early as May 1962, Richard Buckle was calling Nureyev ballet's first pop star. "Admittedly, ballet had a public before, but it was a public of mad old maids in moth-eaten musquash . . . Now Nureyev is dragging in quite a hep crowd, and as these kids have never seen any ballet before they simply scream their heads off as soon as he leaves the floor.

"Pop dancers, like pop singers, have got to have a gimmick or some special thing about them. . . . Nureyev's thing is that even when he is behaving in a withdrawn and gentlemanly way you feel that he may suddenly snarl and bite you in the neck. . . ."

Where Rudolf seemed to go from strength to strength, emboldened by each performance and partner, Erik grew more and more reluctant.

Hobbled by an injury, he sat out a performance of *Les Sylphides* in April
and postponed his debut in Ashton's *La Fille Mal Gardée* after deciding
he didn't have adequate time to prepare. As the season wore on, Nerina
was dismayed to see Erik losing faith in his dancing. He went as far as
to tell her one day that he was "not a classical dancer." He was the
greatest classical male dancer she had ever seen, she countered, but Erik
would not be consoled. "I did not wish to interfere with his personal life,
but it was obvious that he was extremely upset."

Arova was also making her debut with the company, after Rudolf
asked to dance with her in *Swan Lake* and the pas de deux from *Don
Quixote*. By the time she arrived in June, Erik was at war with himself.
"He didn't feel he was dancing as well he could and he suffered. No
matter what Rudi and I did to make him feel better, we didn't succeed.
That season was very hard on both of them."

Offstage, their relationship deepened, though Bruhn was frightened
by its intensity. Desperately in love, Rudolf could not abide any boundaries between them. "I want so much from Erik," he lamented to Arova
time and again, despairing when Erik couldn't fulfill all of his demands.
It was then, in those moments of thwarted desire, that Rudolf would
explode in frustration, sometimes hurling objects across the room. These
fits of temper baffled Erik much the way they had Rudik's Ufa classmates,
who would never forget how he had flung himself to the ground in tears
at the slightest provocation. The squall would pass quickly enough, but
according to Arova, Erik "didn't know which way to turn. He was worn
out." In all ways. Faced with sexual freedoms for the first time, Rudolf
was determined to experience pleasure. His sexual drive was "abundant,"
whereas Bruhn was, by all accounts, not terribly interested by sex. "Nothing was too much for Rudolf," says Arova. "It must have been hard for
him because Erik wasn't like that." The myth is that theirs was an intensely physical relationship, but the truth is that it quickly became more
emotional and spiritual in nature than sexual, more one of mentor and
adoring pupil than that of two ardent lovers. Years afterward Bruhn likened their meeting to "two comets colliding and exploding." Still, it was
Erik who maintained the upper hand in the relationship.

The nights Erik danced, Rudolf sat with Arova in the orchestra,
studying his performance. He was distressed that Erik wasn't dancing up
to his usual standard and frustrated by what he saw as Erik's inability to
get his mind past his lack of rapport with Nerina. Why couldn't Erik will
himself into surmounting his difficulties as he could? He urged Erik to
request other partners and to make demands—as he had once urged
Soloviev, and continued to do himself—but Erik refused. "It's Erik's
fault," he complained to Arova one night. "He won't put his foot down."

At the Royal Ballet, nobody dared put his foot down—nobody, that
is, except Ninette de Valois, a sharp-eyed dynamo who, in the admiring

view of *New York Times* critic John Martin, combined "the devoutness of a sophisticated Joan of Arc . . . with the procedural methods of the Red Queen." To those "ruled" by her, she loomed as a "totally dominant woman," recalls Christopher Gable, a contemporary of Rudolf's in the company. "What she said went. There was no discussion." As Monica Mason saw her, "Madam kept her distance. One was never conscious of her enjoying a joke or a giggle. But with Rudolf she clearly did. They really laughed together." While the stern matriarch with her own brood, de Valois treated Rudolf like a beloved nephew whose precocity delighted her. "Madam very much loved difficult boys," said Michael Somes. "She didn't love the good boys like me who were always on time." To the astonishment of his colleagues, Rudolf would sit by her legs during rehearsals, and once even put his head on her lap.

In short order, she was granting him diplomatic immunity from the rules. "He would do all of the things that my generation had been trained to believe were beyond the pale," says Gable. "We were all incredibly well behaved and strong and self-effacing. He was wild, undisciplined; he would leave rehearsals; he would break things. He would scream and shout and rave. And he was getting away with it. And getting away with it under Dame Ninette." According to Georgina Parkinson, "he had all of them in the palm of his hand—you name it, Frederick Ashton, Madam. He was seductive, a charmer who knew how to tease and amuse. He was this passionate, fabulous-looking, gorgeous creature. A monster on the one hand, and a pussycat on the other. Madam was like Milquetoast around him."

Enamored of his talent and training, de Valois invited him to her box to watch performances and listened afterward as he critiqued them. Perhaps what most impressed her was that "there was absolutely nothing he wouldn't give his attention to if he thought it was worthwhile. He bothered to listen and he knew how to study. He might gravely shake his head and say, 'No, I don't like it, it's no good,' but that was after having looked at everything from every point of view." Standing in the wings one night as Rudolf came offstage to thunderous applause, she was struck by the standards he set for himself. "All he said to me was, 'Not one clean pirouette, not one good jump. And still they clap!' And then he went on to take another bow." She recognized, as Sergeyev could not, that her dancers had much to learn from him.

The older guard, however, didn't take kindly to seeing Rudolf win privileges that they had been trying for years to secure. Foremost among them was a spotlight on their entrance. "The lights were never on them and Madam didn't want things altered," explains Antoinette Sibley, a fast-rising young soloist who was soon to marry Michael Somes. "But Rudolf just says, 'When I come on, I like light,' and suddenly the light comes on.'" David Blair, for one, never got over the latitude Nureyev was given. "He's allowed to do whatever he wants and we've been here for years and aren't allowed to make changes," he grumbled to Arova. Erik, too, felt stymied, later complaining that just getting a zipper changed on his costume required de Valois's approval. "All my requests were finally agreed to, but it was a hassle."

Rudolf was permitted not only to introduce a new solo into the first act of *Swan Lake*, but to eliminate the second act mime scene altogether. "If you do mime, I will walk offstage!" he warned Arova, who was disconcerted at the idea of having to "improvise" the dramatic action onstage as Rudolf instructed. But to his mind, gesture was preferable to outmoded sign language. The Royal Ballet's production of *Swan Lake* had come directly from the Maryinsky Theater via Nicholas Sergeyev, who had worked under Petipa at the Imperial Ballet. Sergeyev had fled during the Revolution, taking with him the notation notebooks of a number of major Petipa ballets, which he later staged in London. Given de Valois's reverence for the Maryinsky heritage, her dancers knew not to question their inheritance. Rudolf, on the other hand, preferred to look anew at timeworn works, convinced that if these ballets were to resonate with contemporary audiences, he needed to find a dramatic as well as a dancing focus. During the tense dress rehearsal preceding their first performance on June 22, Rudolf insisted on a Soviet-style break in the action following Arova's Black Swan variation, to allow him to come onstage and get into position for his own solo. This, as Arova and Bruhn had tried to explain to him in Paris, was not done in the West. "I hate saying this, Madam," conductor John Lanchbery said over his shoulder to de Valois. "But don't you think it makes it terribly like a circus?" "Oh, Jack," she replied, "it's like a circus anyway. Go on, let him do it."

After Rudolf stopped the orchestra one time too many to ask that the score be played at a slower tempo, Lanchbery finally hit his limit. "Whom do I follow? Him or the score?" he appealed to de Valois.

"You listen to him," came the reply. From that point on, they all knew precisely where they stood.

The critics were not as willing to take their cues from an interloper, no matter how much they championed his talent. To many of them, his small-scaled, naturalistic acting, his way of building character from the inside out à la Stanislavsky, seemed out of sync with the more formal, grandiloquent style then in favor at the Royal Ballet. His new solo provoked the most comment. Intended to convey Prince Siegfried's melancholy and solitude — and to give Rudolf something to dance during a long first act that had him simply walking around onstage — the brief, mournful interlude was set to music Tchaikovsky had composed for the ballet but never used. It fell between the scene in which Siegfried's mother orders him to find a bride and his first meeting with the Swan Queen, Odette. In the version by Petipa and Lev Ivanov, the Prince was given a limited role, in large part because the first Prince Siegfried of that production, Pavel Gerdt, was over fifty when *Swan Lake* was made. Nureyev was hardly the first to revise the ballet. The rise of the male dancer in Russia had prompted both Vaganova and Chaboukiani to give him greater challenges. Though Nureyev's own changes would eventually come to be accepted, few of the critics welcomed them at the time. Among those who did was Richard Buckle, who thought it high time the Royal's fusty production was overhauled. The purists, however, accused Nureyev of aggrandizing his role. (His solo in *The Sleeping Beauty* was also new to the Royal's production, but this one Rudolf had danced at the Kirov, giving it a provenance few thought to question.)

Perhaps more than Siegfried's solo itself, it was the notion that Nureyev was allowed to "chop and change to his heart's content" that most rankled. Clive Barnes, the production's most vociferous critic, did not mince words when he wrote that "the idea of this twenty-four-year-old boy destroying in a few casual rehearsals what it has been the labour of three generations to preserve, is not a pretty one. . . . [Nureyev] has made an unresolved compromise between the Soviet and Western approaches to the role. This was oddly symbolized in the third act, where he wears the black tunic of the Western Siegfried together with an ill-matched pair of white tights such as every Soviet Siegfried keeps in his wardrobe. This black-and-white Prince looked a mess, neither one thing nor another."

Then there was the business of his hair. "It was dressed with a sort of bang over the right eye which belonged to a Teddy Boy rather than to a prince," sniffed *Ballet Today*'s Fernau Hall, who prescribed a wig "or a good deal more spraying."

Still, there was no dismissing his immense presence and personality, or his electrifying hold on his audience. The night of his debut, he and Arova took twenty-one curtain calls amid a hailstorm of roses. Nureyev was "a critic's nightmare," Barnes conceded, a host of contradictions impossible to reconcile. "One says his hair is too long, his jumps are too noisy, his choreography is too untalented, and even his presence occasionally too distrait — and then one ends up lamely by saying: 'But he's still great.' The reason is he has a quality that cannot be assessed, acquired or mistaken. It is the trump card of genius." Whatever it was, it continued to provoke endless debate. "The greatest male dancer since Nijinsky?" Oleg Kerensky asked in the *Daily Mail* on the final day of the season. "Or an over-praised conceited young boy who has hoaxed the ballet world? . . . The argument will not end tonight. . . ."

Nureyev next set his sights beyond the opera house, to the vaster audience promised by television. On a BBC arts program that month, he and Fonteyn performed extracts from the second act of *Giselle*. While Fonteyn was camera-ready, having danced on television numerous times, beginning in the late 1930s, a distracted Rudolf "found it hard to take his eyes off monitor screens." The home audience, however, found it hard to take its eyes off *him*. His striking face, seen often in close-up, projected more forcefully on screen than onstage and an esoteric arts program quickly found itself drawing unprecedented numbers. One week later, Rudolf was back on the screen, dancing the Black Swan pas de deux with Nerina on *Sunday Night at the London Palladium*. That a popular variety show would feature ballet was further evidence of Nureyev's growing fame and drawing power, both of which would go a long way toward transforming the art form from "minority cult to middle-class pastime."

"THE LEGEND of Nijinsky lives again in Nureyev," Tamara Karsavina announced later that month to the students who had come to hear her talk of her career, her partnership with Nijinsky and her schooling in the Maryinsky-Petipa traditions. In the view of Ninette de Valois, Nureyev was the most direct link to that revered tradition, the one from which British ballet had descended. "We were after his past," she said, "and he was after our present." To that end, she moved quickly to accord him the status of permanent guest artist, the Royal Ballet's first after Fonteyn, who was made guest artist in 1959.

Once more, Erik was a casualty of Rudolf's growing fame. The Royal Ballet could not accommodate both of them and Rudolf "was the obvious one to go for," recalls John Tooley, the company liaison with Nureyev, "which is in no way to underestimate Bruhn. But in terms of box-office draw and popular appeal, Bruhn couldn't touch Nureyev.* Rudolf was really what was needed and there was a very rapid awareness of his extraordinary talent on the one hand, and of the kind of lift he could give to the company on the other. Margot needed a new partner and made it quite clear, rather to her surprise, that she was going to find a new life with a younger person. It all fitted, there wasn't much debate, though Erik certainly was not happy about it."

Devastated was more like it. He felt the Royal Ballet was "absolutely right for him," and had no desire to return to Copenhagen on a permanent basis. Blindsided by the company's decision to choose between them, Erik looked "ash-gray" the day he met Clive Barnes for an interview. "I had never seen him look so much like the Prince of Denmark.

---

*At a board meeting on April, 24, 1962, Ninette de Valois announced that she had invited Nureyev to join the company as a guest artist. She also expressed her doubts that Bruhn would be invited back as a guest the following season. In general, "he was not playing to capacity" and there would be more competition for leading roles once all the members of the company had returned from touring.

[He] was very hurt and . . . felt very rejected. He had virtually given up Ballet Theatre for this. . . . He felt his international career was shattered."

Eager to escape from the competitive hothouse of London, Erik left for Florence, where he had agreed to dance *La Sylphide* with the Royal Danish Ballet. But if he hoped to escape Rudolf's constant scrutiny, he did not succeed. Having never seen Erik in Bournonville's masterwork, Rudolf followed him. By July he was back onstage himself, performing alfresco with the Royal Ballet touring company at the Nervi Festival in Italy. "Appearance of RUDOLF NUREYEV who will be partnered by a famous ballerina," the festival's posters announced. "This ballerina may even be Dame Margot Fonteyn herself." It was here, against the backdrop of the Mediterranean, that he and Fonteyn first danced *Swan Lake*. In London the pair had barely got through one complete run-through of the ballet because of constant disagreements over Rudolf's proposed changes. Fonteyn had been pliant in approaching *Giselle*, a ballet in which she had never felt entirely comfortable. But *Swan Lake* was for her as much of a signature piece as *The Sleeping Beauty* and she was loath to tamper with a performance she had spent twenty-five years refining. "Rudolf," she interrupted him at one point, "I have been doing this ballet since 1938."* Rudolf's giggle cued her that she had backed herself into a corner. "I suppose that was before you were born?" To which Rudolf gamely replied, "No, just exact year." That broke them both up, Fonteyn recalled. While as accustomed to getting her way as was Rudolf, Fonteyn, like any seasoned diplomat, knew just how far to push and when to back off from confrontation to try another tack. Had she been any less seasoned, it's unlikely the partnership would have taken. Which isn't to say that she did everything his way. After seeing her dance *Swan Lake* in London earlier in the season, Rudolf had come by her dressing room. He was worried, he admitted, that his different approach to the ballet would "ruin" her performance. "Just you try," she had replied.†

From Nervi, Rudolf boarded a train to Stuttgart, where Erik was to partner Georgina Parkinson in *Daphnis and Chloe*, a new ballet by John Cranko tailored to showcase Bruhn's dramatic gifts. Although the premiere on July 15 proved a great success, Bruhn was "horrified" by his follow-up performance, which, to his mind, fell decidedly short of the mark. His sense of failure, arising partly from the London season, poisoned everything he danced. Rudolf's arrival unhinged him further. "I

*Fonteyn first performed the dual role of Odette-Odile at the end of 1937, though she recalled the year as 1938.

†Nevertheless, by the time she came to dance *Swan Lake* with Rudolf at Covent Garden the following February, she had made enough changes to provoke feelings of betrayal among the conservative ranks.

felt this tension growing, first of all within myself about *Daphnis*, and then the general bad atmosphere that pervaded when Rudik and I were together—taking class together, being seen together. . . . People were provoking us. Jokes were being made, and it just got to me. . . ."

A number of his contemporaries, the Royal Ballet veteran Alexander Grant among them, suspected that "Erik couldn't dance with Rudi watching. There was something that seemed to seize up within him and then he would either injure himself or he just couldn't dance. And Rudi really wanted to see him dance." To Georgina Parkinson, Chloe to Bruhn's Daphnis, Rudolf's arrival plunged Erik into a spiritual crisis. In an instant, Erik "completely withdrew and wasn't available to any of us. He was bad-tempered, irritable, uncomfortable with himself. And then Rudolf offering to appear in the gala was more than Erik could bear."

At Yvette Chauviré's invitation, Rudolf agreed to partner her in a pas de deux.* Erik was also due to dance in the gala evening, but the night before suddenly announced that he was ill and canceled his final appearance in *Daphnis*. When the choreographers John Cranko and Kenneth MacMillan confronted him, he ordered them from his room. The following morning, he was gone. He had driven off in the night, without saying a word to anyone, including Rudolf. Georgina Parkinson was in her hotel room when Rudolf telephoned. "He sounded like butter would melt in his mouth, asking me if Erik was with me. I said, 'No, he certainly isn't,' and asked him why. He said he didn't know where Erik was and that he'd left, taking all his belongings." Among them were Rudolf's travel documents and visas.† With help from Kenneth MacMillan, Parkinson tracked down Fonteyn, who managed to get him the necessary papers, but as she recalls, "Rudolf felt absolutely alone in Stuttgart. Erik had just removed himself because he couldn't deal with one more day. He would claim that he had this back problem or whatever. But it was all Rudolf."

Never one to cancel a performance, Rudolf stayed on for the gala before pursuing Erik all the way to Copenhagen. Within days he had moved into his house in Gentofte, together with Erik, Erik's mother and Sonia Arova, whom Erik was to partner in a centennial gala at the Tivoli Gardens in September. Erik had planned to create a special pas de deux for them, but Arova arrived in Denmark with torn ligaments in her kneecap. Eager to help them out, Rudolf offered to rehearse in her stead. For the next seven days, Erik composed their duet on Rudolf and himself while Arova sat with her leg propped up on a chair, coaching from the sidelines.

---

*Victor Gsovsky's *Grand Pas Classique*, a showpiece made for Chauviré.
†He had traveled first on a French *titre de voyage* and later on a British travel document, provided by the government to foreigners unable to obtain national passports.

The easy esprit of the studio evaporated the moment they got home. Ellen Bruhn had grown no fonder of Rudolf over the year, a feeling she did little to disguise. "You must look after Erik, you must make sure he's okay," she repeatedly reminded Arova. "Erik was the prized possession of that family and his mother sensed that something was wrong," she says. "She just did not like Rudolf and she more or less ignored him. She felt he was stifling Erik." Erik, in turn, worried about his mother, who was having trouble walking and visibly in pain. However, since she shunned doctors, he had no idea what was wrong with her. She suspected she had cancer, she told him, but he didn't take her self-diagnosis seriously. By the time he and his sisters had persuaded her to see a doctor, she was diagnosed with a blood clot in her leg. Still, she refused to enter the hospital and insisted on self-prescribed bedrest. She also made it clear that Rudolf's presence in the house was not helping her get better. "It was a very bad situation," says Arova. "She was getting worse and worse and wanted Rudolf out of the house and Erik couldn't understand why she was so adamant about him. He felt torn. When he asked me what he should do, I told him to make Rudi go to a hotel. And he said, 'I know, but Rudik will not listen.'" But Rudolf did.

The day after the gala, Rudolf and Erik saw Arova off on the night train to Paris. When she arrived, she called them. "Well, Rudik is back in the house," Erik told her. That same day a clot was discovered in his mother's lungs and she was ordered to enter the hospital. Erik and Rudolf, who were due for dinner at Vera Volkova's, offered to accompany her in the ambulance, but Ellen Bruhn wouldn't hear of it. Her daughters would take her, she insisted. Shortly after they arrived at Volkova's, Erik was called to the phone. His mother had fainted getting into the ambulance. By the time he arrived at the hospital, she was dead. An autopsy revealed that she had cancer, and Erik blamed himself for not taking her claim more seriously. He also felt terrible guilt at having invited Rudolf to stay against her wishes and couldn't help wondering whether Rudolf's presence in the house had exacerbated an already explosive situation.

Her death occasioned one of the tenderest moments between him and Rudolf, one Bruhn savored until his own untimely death from lung cancer at the age of fifty-seven. Numb at finding his mother covered by a white sheet, Bruhn, rarely one to reveal profound feeling, had broken down. Rudolf had never seen him cry and instinctively took him in his arms. He sorely missed his own mother and was reluctant to leave Erik alone in a house haunted by illness and memory. So he extended his visit and took care of Erik over the next difficult days of adjustment. His thoughtfulness "bound" them, Bruhn said later. "I mean, he could have just run away. But he didn't."

17

"So You Are Great Ballerina"

BY THE TIME Rudolf arrived in New York in September, to make a return appearance on the *Bell Telephone Hour*, the Bolshoi had taken up residence at the Metropolitan Opera House for a sold-out three-week run. Rudolf settled in at the East Seventy-second Street apartment of Erik's agent, Christopher Allan, and taught the *Corsaire* pas de deux to Lupe Serrano, a leading dancer with American Ballet Theatre. The pair had only one week to prepare for their TV special, hardly enough time to "get a pas de deux in your legs," as Serrano explains. So, at Christopher Allan's suggestion, she took herself off to "some rinky-dink movie theater," where a clip of Alla Sizova dancing her *Corsaire* variation happened to be running. The film had been made following Rudolf and Sizova's performance at the Moscow schools concert, but after his defection, Rudolf had been deleted.*

At his insistence, Serrano joined him at the Bolshoi's performances each evening. He wanted her to study Maya Plisetskaya, the darkly dramatic Bolshoi ballerina, to whom he sent several bouquets during the Bolshoi's engagement. He was unhappy with Serrano's port de bras and hoped that by seeing Plisetskaya perform *The Dying Swan*, she would make more ample use of her arms. He even did his own rendition of Plisetskaya's *Dying Swan* in the studio one day to illustrate his point.

His nightly presence at the Met not only alarmed the Bolshoi's chaperons, it created a dilemma for their American impresario, Sol Hurok. A Russian Jewish émigré who had arrived in New York in 1906 with $1.50, Hurok had become "the Barnum of the Arts." Short, plump

*Serrano does not remember whether Rudolf was featured in the film clip she saw.

and shrewd, Hurok had a knack for divining talent and that ever more elusive quality called star power. As he saw it, the more temperamental the artist, the better, not least because he made good copy. "It's in the nature of a great artist to be [temperamental]," he once said. "There's something in them — some warmth, some fire — that projects into an audience and makes it respond. . . ." His first great success was to introduce Anna Pavlova to the American public and thereafter he toured Fedor Chaliapin and presented Isadora Duncan. For decades the marquee headline "S. Hurok Presents" had promised some of the most renowned names in music, dance and opera: Andrés Segovia, Arthur Rubinstein, Isaac Stern, the Ballet Russe de Monte Carlo, the Royal Ballet, the Bolshoi Ballet, the Kirov Ballet, all of them Hurok clients. Ballet remained an abiding passion and Hurok played a major role in building an audience for ballet in America. An immaculately dressed man, immediately recognizable to theatergoers with his black horn-rimmed glasses and gold-tipped cane, Hurok was also the leading purveyor of Russian culture in the United States and his privileged position with the Soviet government gave him a virtual monopoly on cultural exchanges between the two countries. He was at that moment negotiating to bring the Royal Ballet to New York and, despite pressures from the Soviets, had resisted dropping a moneymaker like Nureyev from the tour. Nureyev's Bolshoi visits naturally complicated an already delicate situation. That the Bolshoi's American tour coincided with the Cuban missile crisis — the nadir of Soviet-American relations — made matters worse still, and Hurok soon flew off to Moscow to plead his case.

All through October, with global nuclear warfare threatened, Nureyev danced with Arova in Chicago, where both were appearing as guest stars of Ruth Page's Chicago Opera Ballet. Rudolf was staying at Page's penthouse apartment on Lakeshore Drive and, after rehearsal one day, persuaded Arova to come home with him for dinner. "So [the three of us] took a taxi to Ruth's house and I said to him in Russian, 'Pay for the taxi.' And he turned around and said, 'Why should I? She benefits from us.' That was his mentality." It was a policy he rarely strayed from ever after.

Page had imported them to appear in the Chicago Lyric Opera's production of *Prince Igor* in her restaging of Fokine's *Polovetsian Dances*. Rudolf appeared as the Tatar chieftain, Arova as his slave girl, and together they stole the opera from the singers.

For a gala program on October 21, the pair teamed up again in three short pieces, among them the *Corsaire* pas de deux. Afterward, as they were dressing for the gala ball, Arova complained of having nothing to wear. Rudolf quickly improvised something out of a piece of shimmering gold fabric. Draping it just so, a skill honed while touring with his Ufa folk troupe, he pinned it into place and Arova had an evening gown.

* * *

NUREYEV RESUMED his partnership with Fonteyn on November 3, in a rousing performance of the *Corsaire* pas de deux at Covent Garden. Staged by Rudolf,* the short ballet was showcased with intervals both before and afterward. Fonteyn had worried that audiences would feel cheated to get so little dancing, but Ashton had reassured her, "Ten minutes of *Corsaire* and twenty minutes of applause. What are you worrying about?"

It was fitting that Nureyev's initial contribution to his new home company should be the ballet that had first brought him acclaim in Russia, a work suffused with the exotic sensuality and savagery that many felt he himself represented. Sheathed only in silvery-blue lamé Turkish trousers with matching headband, his chest bare beneath a gold mesh bolero, his hair flying, Nureyev exploded onto the stage, all Byronic ardor and sinuous grace. The effect came close to caricature. And yet Nureyev, as Mary Clarke observed, "looked not in the least absurd. He wore his costume, as he danced his variation, with such complete conviction of its rightness for him that it became right." Despite its brevity, his *Corsaire* was "worth going a thousand miles to see," declared Alexander Bland, who deemed it "the finest piece of male dancing seen on the Covent Garden stage in this generation."

His soaring jumps, with both feet tucked under him, were wonder enough to those viewing his *Corsaire* for the first time. Equally unexpected was the daring performance he exacted from Fonteyn, whose stock-in-trade was hardly these kinds of virtuoso showpieces. The *Daily Express* marveled at how Dame Margot "shed half her years to match him with contrasting grace and sparkle." The seeds of this renewal had been sown in Nervi when, during a rehearsal of *Swan Lake*, Rudolf discovered that Fonteyn was a much sturdier technician than either of them had supposed. Intrigued, Rudolf bid her to push herself to the limit in the third act's bravura passages. "So you are Great Ballerina. Show me!" And, just as Jean Cocteau had done when Diaghilev commanded him to "astonish me," the forty-three-year-old Fonteyn did the unexpected: She proceeded to extend her technical abilities beyond what they had been at the peak of her career and at an age when ballerinas ease into less taxing roles, if not into the wings. Before Nureyev arrived, it was widely thought that Dame Margot had, in fact, "peaked and was on the way down." Rudolf's "flick of the whip," as Fonteyn's friend Keith Money termed it, "was just what she needed." Seeing the results, Rudolf lost no time in putting those untapped reserves to work.

---

*As John Percival has noted, Rudolf did not receive credit for the choreography in the program.

That Fonteyn, inspired by her young partner, was now giving some of the most daring performances of her career prompted a rush at the box office and near-hysterical press coverage. Celebrities such as Noël Coward, Peter O'Toole and Richard Burton turned out to see what all the fuss was about. Audiences stood vigil outside the stage door angling for autographs and shrieking with delight at the sight of the two dancers, while reporters scrambled to reveal the magic of their rapport. All of London was agog over the chemistry between them. "When I am dancing with him and I look across the stage I see not Nureyev but the character of the ballet," Fonteyn obliged the *Daily Mail* in reply to a question about Nureyev's "greatness." Sounding like Emily Brontë's Cathy describing her Heathcliff, she went on: "I do not see, as I do with others, a man I know and talk to every day. I see the ballet. He is absorbed in the role. He is how I would like to be and he makes it easier for me to dance as I would wish...."

Intent on discovering how much more he could do, Rudolf took risks onstage and inspired Fonteyn to do the same. "God! I've never done half the things I do now," she confessed to John Tooley. Told that her dancing had "suddenly improved" by no less an authority than Dame Marie Rambert, Fonteyn replied, "Yes, now that they look at him instead of me I can relax and really dance for the first time."

Offstage, however, his less than gallant treatment of her startled their colleagues, among them Frederick Ashton, who admitted to being bothered by his "biting remarks" to her. "Saint" is the word most often invoked to describe Fonteyn. "Margot had always been given the kid-glove treatment by her partners," recalls Georgina Parkinson. "But Rudolf insulted the hell out of her. And on top of it all, she took it." Or rather, she took what was useful and disregarded the rest. "People were always terribly respectful of whatever Margot wanted," says Christopher Gable, a frequent partner in the early sixties. "Suddenly Rudolf wasn't! Suddenly, she had a *hugely* demanding, passionate man wanting an equal share in every stage moment. I think it was probably the most stimulating and wonderful thing for her that there was someone arguing with her and shouting at her, and telling her she was rubbish. And she would also argue with him."

Unlike Rudolf, however, who was a law unto himself, Fonteyn had been brought up to please, first her mother, then de Valois, Ashton and Tito Arias. "She is disgustingly loyal..." wrote Richard Buckle. Ashton had initially dismissed her as a headstrong little girl, but she eventually became his muse because of what his biographer calls her "malleability and humility." Ashton illustrated this point in the curious, if well-known, anecdote he chose to relate in a 1989 documentary about Fonteyn. Recalling one of their earliest collaborations in 1935, he described how he had broken her resistance in molding her to his specifications. Frustrated by the lack of attack in her dancing, "[I] bullied and bullied and bullied her and she got more into a state and then finally she burst into tears and rushed up and put her arms around me and said, 'I'm sorry but I'm trying my very best and I can't do any more.' So then I realized she'd really conceded to me and from then on we would be able to work together. . . ."

Over the years Fonteyn had developed a remarkable resiliency that allowed her "never to respond in kind," says Keith Money. "She had this nervous habit of turning things into a joke just to get through the moment. The more difficult and contentious something was, the more she would laugh. It wasn't a real laugh, but it got through the situation, it stopped things from becoming heavy."

She genuinely understood Rudolf, who came to see in her a safe haven at a time when, as Kenneth MacMillan said, "he was desperately in need of mothering." She was always sympathetic about his problems and she understood, above all, that he was tougher on himself than on anyone else. Besides, as Money observes, even if at times she was hurt, "she had been trained all the time, 'Just don't show it.' " Indeed, before going onstage, Fonteyn would have to "work herself up to excitement, she was so calm," said their friend Maude Gosling, whereas Rudolf "was like a racehorse, shaking and sweating. So the two together worked marvelously."

That they found anything in common struck many as peculiar. Were one to judge by appearances, Fonteyn suggested a proper English lady in her impeccable Dior suits (later Saint Laurent), her skirts safely grazing her knee, her blue-black hair pulled high into a French twist, her carriage upright. "She gives maternal dignity to all the natural functions I am sure," quipped Cecil Beaton. But beneath the polished exterior was an exceptionally warmhearted, clear-eyed woman, with a streak of Brazilian vivacity inherited from her mother. Martha Graham recalled seeing Fonteyn break down in tears in the wings one night because she thought she had danced badly. Rudolf quickly whispered something in her ear and Fonteyn began to laugh, "that reluctant laugh that is only Margot's." Rudolf later told Graham that he had whispered "every shocking obscenity he could think of."

Fonteyn, in turn, taught Rudolf how to balance the huge demands of a theatrical career. Interviews, rehearsals, management, costumes, fans, performances, the diplomatic rounds, all of these she managed seamlessly, under great pressure. Rudolf never lost sight of his debt to her. "If I hadn't found Margot, I'd be gone. Big noise, big noise and then gone, burnt out."

In stark contrast with the pyrotechnics of *Le Corsaire*, *Les Sylphides* showed Nureyev and Fonteyn at their most subtle and romantic. Dancing together in Fokine's ballet for the first time on November 6, they seemed "caught up in the music, borne along on the same stream." Fonteyn had rarely danced *Les Sylphides* because she had never had a clear understanding of it; Rudolf's interpretation, she said, brought the ballet into focus for her. If she looked younger next to him, he, in turn, gained in artistry and control next to her. To his fire she added finesse. They quickly became the dream pair, triggering a golden decade for British ballet. As *Dance and Dancers* wrote at the time, "In *Giselle* and *Les Sylphides*, these two, were they to do nothing else, have established themselves among the great partnerships of ballet history."

The nights they danced, their colleagues jammed the wings, craning for a view. But their success was not greeted with cheer in all quarters. David Blair, for one, saw the writing on the wall and took to numbing his pain at the Nag's Head, the pub across the street from the stage door. "I don't know why that bloody Russian bugger's over there partnering her," he was heard to say. "I should be there doing that show tonight." To John Lanchbery, however, as to many others, Blair seemed "too remote and young" for Fonteyn. "Ironically, with Rudolf, who was younger than David, the age gap disappeared completely. Rudolf actually looked more mature onstage in the same way that he looked taller than he really was." Perhaps in hopes of unlocking the secret to Nureyev's and Bruhn's success, Blair had taken himself off to Copenhagen to study with Vera Volkova earlier that fall. Alas, when he arrived in class the first day, it was not Volkova giving the lesson, but Nureyev.

The Royal's ballerinas, meantime, suddenly had to face the fact that the company's star, on the verge of her retirement, wasn't going anywhere anytime soon. Every new generation of dancers feels in some way that the older one is in the way, and with such a brief spell of time in which to make their mark, the clock ticks quickly. Georgina Parkinson was just one of the many young dancers "waiting for Margot to shove off. We'd said good-bye to her so many times and all shed a suitable tear. And here she was, back again in everything. . . . The whole Margot-Rudolf thing was very hard on the dancers who were waiting for their time."

Still, what many now forget is that their partnership was by no means seen as a permanent fixture. Most pundits wagered that it would be a one- or two-year thing at best and then Fonteyn would probably retire. Many of the ballerinas gladly assumed this, figuring their time was soon to come. In the meantime, the enormous interest in the new pair prompted de Valois to ask Ashton to make a ballet for them. She wanted to give Rudolf a proper welcome, to make him feel like a member of the family, and what better way than to offer him his first custom-made role in a major new work?* Ashton had for some time wanted to make a ballet out of the Alexandre Dumas play *La Dame aux camélias*, which

---

*She was not aware that Rudolf had had two ballet roles created around his talents in the Soviet Union. In 1959, Leonid Yakobson had made *Valse Volonté* for him and Sizova to dance in Vienna, while in 1960, Grigorovich had choreographed the role of Ferhad in *Legend of Love* for him. Rudolf, however, never performed either ballet.

was based on the author's love affair with Marie Duplessis, a consumptive French courtesan. One night, as he was sitting in his bath, luxuriating to Liszt's Piano Sonata in B minor, which by some happy accident was playing on the radio, he could envision "the whole thing. . . ." A romantic to the core, he was pleased to discover that Liszt had also had an affair with Dumas's real-life heroine, and wondered whether she might have inspired him to compose "this very piece." A woman of great simple taste, unusual for the time, Duplessis had died at twenty-three, and was soon after immortalized, first by Dumas under the name of Marguerite Gautier and later by Verdi in *La Traviata*. It now struck Ashton that the eloquent Fonteyn was the "epitome" of Dumas's Marguerite, while the charismatic Nureyev was his ideal Armand Duval, the ardent lover she renounces to save his reputation.

Where *Poème Tragique* had been a curtain raiser, a *pièce d'occasion* meant to introduce Rudolf to the British public, *Marguerite and Armand* was to serve as a vehicle for the new partnership, an *évocation poétique*, as Ashton thought of it, that would trade on the stage presence of its two stars. "People now think it's camp," Ashton said later. "How stupid they are. Everyone wants to be stirred—personality is so utterly important."

His aim was to pare down the story of these ill-starred lovers to its essential human drama, "into a kind of tabloid," he told Nigel Gosling, adding, "But I would like it to be strong enough to kill." Rudolf took to his conception at once; the Garbo film *Camille* sprang immediately to mind (indeed, it had influenced Ashton's ballet) and he decided to use Robert Taylor's performance as his model. According to Keith Money, Rudolf's familiarity with the Garbo movie* surprised Ashton and "gave Fred the idea of cinematic cutting, which gave Rudolf . . . a peg to hang his character on, so he felt less nervous and that kept Fred calm."

A few days into rehearsal, however, Rudolf wrenched his left ankle jumping off a bus and the new ballet scheduled for December had to be postponed until the spring. His ill-timed injury, like everything connected with Nureyev, sparked controversy when it emerged that he had agreed to appear with American Ballet Theatre in Chicago over Christmas, the same period he had been scheduled to dance at Covent Garden. "Mystery grows around Nureyev and his foot," declared the *Daily Mail*. *Time* magazine quickly dubbed him the "Troubled Tartar" and cast doubt on his need to recuperate from injury by implying that the injury was his way out of a tricky situation. "I'd rather deal with ten Callases than one Nureyev," a Covent Garden official told *Time*. The double booking, as it turned out, was Covent Garden's oversight, not Nureyev's, though the press department failed to say so.

Rudolf was then staying with Fonteyn's brother, Felix, in his flat on

*He had first seen it in Leningrad.

Thurloe Place, preferring, as he always would, to stay with friends. He felt safe, comfortable and well looked after in the homes of friends and was happy not to pay for his accommodation. Margot and Tito Arias had recently sold their own home on Thurloe Place and had relocated to Panama so the politically ambitious Arias could spend more time there. In London, they stayed with Margot's mother, Hilda Hookham, a disarming, plumpish woman known as B.Q., short for Black Queen, a reference to the ruling Black Queen in the de Valois ballet *Checkmate*. B.Q. had stayed involved in her daughter's career and was "always close enough to know what was happening." In his search for maternal comfort, Rudolf had grown attached to her. Since she lived a few doors down from the Royal Ballet's rehearsal studios, he regularly stopped by for lunch, knowing that she would prepare his steaks "bloody," just the way he liked them. Now she and Fonteyn did their best to cheer him when he checked into a convalescent home for treatment. The uncertainty posed by his dislocated ankle had put him on edge and he was growing increasingly irritable. He had tried dancing through the pain, as dancers are wont to do, but stopped after his doctor warned that he could do further damage to his ankle if he continued. Much greater than his pain was his fear of being sidelined, and any disruption to his dancing was cause for alarm. It didn't help that it was the same ankle he had injured in his first season at the Kirov.*

His separation from Erik only compounded his distress. Erik was then across the world in Sydney with Arova, dancing as a guest of the newly formed Australian Ballet. His absence left Rudolf feeling isolated. He had tried to bridge their distance by telephone. (His daily calls to Sydney had cost him five hundred pounds, he later grumbled to Cecil Beaton.) But Erik regularly refused to speak to him. "Better to have stone in place of heart," Rudolf moaned one day to Fonteyn, who confided to a friend, "Erik is driving Rudolf crazy. He's so cold."

Still mourning his mother's death, Erik needed some distance from Rudolf, with whom he associated those difficult last days of his mother's life. Although he was in love with Rudolf, his feelings were complicated by many forces, not least his acute fear of intimacy, a legacy from childhood, says the Danish actress Susse Wold, one of his closest friends. "Erik couldn't be intimate with anybody. We talked once about that, about his wanting to be close to people, but being afraid to be close. That made Rudolf all the more attracted to him. This was a love that could go on forever, because Rudolf could never really have Erik." Erik's need for what he called "solitary renewal" was something that Rudolf, oddly enough, could not understand. Back in the role of go-between, Arova tried to explain to a disconsolate Rudolf just why Erik was unavailable to him. "He was hurt

---

*That injury had kept him off the stage for several months.

that Erik wouldn't talk to him, so I said, 'Maybe if you call twice a week, that will be enough.' " Erik, meanwhile, was so consumed with guilt over his mother's death that he "hardly slept" while in Sydney. "We would talk all night long," recalls Arova, "trying to get it out of his system."

Desperate to see Erik, Rudolf insisted on flying to Australia. He booked flights on both BOAC and Quantas for November 19, but didn't secure the necessary visas in time, although a horde of balletomanes trooped out to London Airport to see him off. He spent the days getting physiotherapy and teaching Fonteyn the pas de deux from *Gayané*, a Soviet staple that Rudolf was to have danced with her at her charity gala that month for the Royal Academy of Dancing. In his stead, he proposed the Hungarian dancer Viktor Róna, whom he met, cloak-and-dagger-style, in a London parking lot so as not to compromise Róna's standing with the Soviets.

His own standing with the Soviets, though never in doubt, was brought home to him most directly on his flight to Sydney on December 1. As he later recounted it, during a stopover at Cairo Airport, the pilot suddenly asked the passengers to get off the plane because a technical problem needed to be repaired. Rudolf's radar told him that something was up, and as the plane emptied, he stayed cowering in his seat. When the stewardess came to retrieve him, he begged her to help him and insisted he could not leave the plane. She saw he was in a panic and apparently also saw, through the window, two men in raincoats approaching the plane. Quickly, she hid him in the bathroom. "I'll tell them it's broken," she assured Rudolf, who was terrified of being kidnapped. There he sat for several long minutes gazing in the mirror, "seeing myself going grey," he said later, while the KGB men searched the plane and banged on the bathroom door before finally giving up. The plane soon took off, but Rudolf was badly shaken. The fact that his "assumed" name had failed to protect him only heightened the fragility of his new life. Dancing, art, food, sex, every experience had to be crammed in, because at any moment, on any given day, it could all be snatched away. As late as 1990 he had not relaxed his grip. "Things were . . . taken from me, rather than given to me," he said. "So the moment I had a chance on an equal footing, I didn't ever let it go. Not at six or seven or eight or 10 or 12 or 17 or 20 or 35 or 40 or 50, 51, 52, 53 . . . I'll never let it go."

Erik was there to meet him at the airport in Sydney, as were a team of reporters, a now-familiar sight. Why had he used an assumed name? Sydney's *Daily Telegraph* wanted to know. Was he afraid of being kidnapped? "If you don't mind, I'd like to keep it a secret," Rudolf replied. FALSE NAME FOR SCARED DANCER, ran the headline on the paper's story the following day.

Rudolf spent the next two weeks trailing Erik from Sydney to Adelaide. Half a world away, his autobiography hit bookstores in England

and France. Due to dance his first *Theme and Variations* with American Ballet Theatre at the end of the month, he hoped that Erik would teach it to him. *Theme* held special significance for him because it was the work in which he had first glimpsed Erik in Leningrad, albeit on eight-millimeter film and without sound. Their visit grew decidedly "strained," remembers Arova. While they rarely fought openly, "you could feel the tension. Erik was trying to pull away. His feelings hadn't cooled, but he was feeling stifled and I think he began to realize that, as far as his career went, he had to do something drastic." Having reconsidered her position, Ninette de Valois had invited him to make several guest appearances with the Royal Ballet in the spring of 1963. Bruhn, however, now wrote to say that he was thinking of giving up performing for a time and wished to be released from his contract.

Rudolf's holiday in the sun failed to dispel his melancholy. He who dreaded confinement of any kind longed to possess Bruhn absolutely. "I have lost any sense of place, of belonging," he told John Quinn of the *Adelaide News* a few days before his departure. Nureyev, Quinn wrote, "looked a little sad and spoke a little harshly."

The rest cure had at least healed his ankle and by Christmas he was in Chicago, ready to tackle *Theme and Variations, Le Corsaire* and *La Fille Mal Gardée* with ABT. His presence, however, was not enough to sell out the Civic Opera House. Lupe Serrano, his ballerina for the engagement, remembers that Rudolf arrived "in a crabby mood" and had a terrible time with *Theme*, among the most demanding of Balanchine ballets. The male variations are fiendishly difficult and meant to be danced at breakneck speed. Rudolf performed them so slowly and deliberately that "it was not Balanchine as I knew it," Serrano says delicately.

Soon afterward Rudolf went to see Balanchine in New York to thank him for making the ballet.* Balanchine had recently returned from a triumphant debut tour to the Soviet Union, where his sleek classicism had astonished Russian balletomanes. Rudolf, for his part, was "dying of shyness." He had intended to write Balanchine a letter, telling him "how great I thought his ballets were," but "Russian laziness took over." He was therefore dismayed to hear Balanchine remark that *Theme and Variations* was "the worst ballet I've done. . . ." His words fell "like a cold shower."

A second snub followed soon after, this time from the French government, which, in response to threats from the Soviets, canceled Nureyev's appearances with the Paris Opéra in January without informing him directly. Rudolf now had to face the fact that the Royal Ballet was as much a haven as a home.

*Balanchine choreographed the ballet in 1947 for Ballet Theatre, not for his own company.

18

From the Nureyev Front

HERALDED BY "enough publicity to win a general election," *Marguerite and Armand* was the most anticipated event of the 1963 season. Never in the history of the Royal Ballet had a new work received as much advance play. Princess Margaret came to watch it take shape, fifty photographers documented the first dress rehearsal, and both the *Sunday Times* and the *Observer* gave it lavish coverage, with the former offering a sneak preview by Lord Snowdon, and the latter the background scoop by Alexander Bland. Cecil Beaton's designs, Ashton's choreography and the fantasy of a romance between the leads all helped generate excitement.

Work on the ballet had begun in earnest with Rudolf's return to London in January. The experience so intoxicated its principal players that Rudolf had to stop and ask, " 'Does anybody remember what we did?' so nobody remembered and I was getting frustrated and angry and angrier. But I want to know what are we going to do onstage. . . ." Michael Somes, cast as Armand's father, recalled that Rudolf, Margot and Ashton "spent a great deal of time laughing and giggling. They'd be telling a story about something, perhaps not even to do with the ballet." It fell to *him*, insisted Somes, to call them all to order.

Ashton had structured the ballet as a deathbed reverie, with the dying Marguerite reliving her affair with Armand, whom she has reluctantly renounced at his father's urging. In a series of dreamlike flashbacks, she recalls their meeting, their first days of love, her break with him and their last meeting, when Armand, in a fit of anguish over her perceived callousness, insults her by throwing money at her feet. In the ballet's final scene, Armand rushes to Marguerite's bedside, where the lovers are reunited one last time before Marguerite dies in his arms.

The spirit of several fabled figures infused the creative process. In the ballet's prologue, Marguerite sits on a chaise-longue in a scarlet ball gown, surrounded by admirers. The scene was Ashton's reenactment of a reception in Lima, Peru, described to him by his brother, at which Pavlova was surrounded by a group of would-be suitors. A marvelous mimic, Ashton was famous for his impersonations of well-known dancers, Pavlova first among them. "Fred would be running around the room, showing us how Pavlova used to dance," said Somes. He was also fond of quoting to Fonteyn what the real-life Marguerite had said to Liszt as she begged him to take her with him to Italy. "I will be no trouble to you. I sleep all day, go to the theater in the evening and at night you may do what you will with me." Fonteyn preferred to see her, not as desperate, but as emblematic of the kind of vulnerable "feminine woman" she understood Marilyn Monroe to be.

Nureyev also fired Ashton's imagination, prompting "the same revolution in Ashton that he had earlier prompted in Fonteyn," Clive Barnes wrote in his review. "He has challenged both of them to discard their inhibitions. . . ." For Armand's first entrance, Ashton had him strike a pose from Le Corsaire, while the solo he made for him "practically quotes him," in its use of his singular style and steps: turned-out fifth position, high retirés and slow preparations. Apart from this solo, Ashton's ballet was composed entirely of pas de deux, linked in style, though varied in emotional coloring. The coup de foudre of their first meeting is expressed in movement at once "provocative and intense," noted Barnes. "By the next scene, when they are lovers, this intensity is replaced by playfulness, but the second pas de deux of that scene, after Marguerite has resolved to leave Armand, Ashton makes desperate and erotic. For the next scene the mood once again changes, now to fierce anger, and so on to the last pas de deux, which is rarified into the last extremity of Romantic agony."

There was poignancy and perhaps method in Ashton's casting of Michael Somes as Armand's father, a character role, not a dancing one, that required Fonteyn's longtime partner to look disapprovingly upon this rhapsodic union. In describing the scene in which Armand's father orders Marguerite to end the affair, Ashton seemed to suggest that life had intruded on art when he told Alexander Bland, "Michael . . . was standing with Margot, very stern and stiff, and I saw the door open a crack and Rudi looking in very cautiously, in his scarf and everything. I could see him tiptoe round behind me as we went on working and when we began to come to the end of the scene he started stripping off his coat and things, and just at the right moment he flew out from behind me into Margot's arms; it was wonderful."

As Fonteyn experienced it, Rudolf "tore" into their pas de deux "with a passion more real than life itself. . . ."

To Somes, however, Margot and Rudolf were "not partners; they were two star dancers, dancing together brilliantly. They had more or less an equal impact and they fed each other." But then Somes was cast from an entirely different mold from Rudolf, as he himself acknowledged in an unusually frank assessment shortly before his death. "I had done something like twenty of Sir Fred's ballets with Margot and I spent more time making sure that she looked marvelous. Partnering, in my view, is to show your girl when you're dancing with her. The less you are seen, the better she looks. That's why nobody remembers me."

If Ashton had no trouble getting Rudolf to move the way he wanted, he was less certain about how to handle him. After years of working together, he and Fonteyn could sense each other's intentions, but Rudolf insisted on being shown every movement in detail before improvising on his own. Whereas de Valois issued commands from on high, the droll, gentlemanly Ashton preferred to delegate, abhorring confrontation. "He didn't swear or carry on," said Somes, a close friend for forty years. "Fred was brought up in a very public school way and wasn't in the habit of doing things that Rudi was brought up to find completely normal. Fred wouldn't be very pleased with the Siberian behavior sometimes."

When, during one rehearsal, Rudolf demanded that conductor John Lanchbery slow down the tempo, Lanchbery looked to Ashton to guide him, just as he had done with de Valois. "Oh, Jack, you sort it out, dear, sort it out." And with a dramatic sweep of his hand, as if wiping the problem momentarily from his thoughts, Ashton went outside to have a smoke.

Meanwhile, his good friend Cecil Beaton was experiencing problems of his own over the costumes he had designed. He had put red camellias on most of Fonteyn's dresses, but not only was she embarrassed to wear them, her "modesty," as she put it, prevented her from explaining why.* White flowers were insisted upon and white flowers there were. The hat Beaton designed was also discarded. "I could have kicked her," he told his diary. Rudolf proved even testier and at one point refused to wear the jacket Beaton had made, protesting that its long coattails made him look like a waiter and cut off the line of his leg. Taking a pair of scissors to them, he chopped his costume to fit his own ideas and proportions.† It wasn't long before the *Daily Express* got wind of the wardrobe squabbles and blew them into a major story, which only nettled

---

*In the novel, Marguerite wears red camellias on the days she is menstruating.

†The black jacket was even shorter than the one he had designed for his Kirov debut in *Giselle*. Worn with white tights and no "modesty trunks," it would have shocked Soviet audiences.

Rudolf further, resulting in a stormy dress rehearsal. In a letter to Beaton, who was then in Hollywood at work on *My Fair Lady* (for which he would win an Academy Award), the Royal Ballet's publicity director described the scene:

> From the Nureyev Front
> weather: Very Thundery
>
> Dear Cecil,
>
> What a day of . . . storms, rage, hysterics drama and alarms! . . . As it was the photo-call day and we had 50 photographers here I prayed for calm seas. In vain. I went to Rudi's dressing room at 10 A.M. to see how he was. He said, "Do you have anything to do with publicity?" Upon my short "yes" he gave a sort of pantherine snarl, threw a tray of cups of tea across the room, tore off his shirt (yours) and stamped on it. . . . The ballet started at 10:30 and on his first entrance we knew we were in for some-fun. . . . He made no attempt whatsoever to dance, he treated Margot abominably, flung her about, tore his shirt off and flung it into the orchestra, shouted at Lanchberry [sic], fixed us all with the evil eye, flung the riding stock at the stage manager and generally gave such an exhibition of bad manners that we quailled and sank from sight with terror and sheer horror. Fred *must* have been in tears. I didn't dare look at him. Ninette sat clutching my arm in a vice and just moaned. The photographers . . . were struck dumb. . . . Ninette strode up and said "Rudi, I've never told you a lie, the Opera House did *not* give this story to the press." He managed a wan smile, was helped back into his shirt and suddenly the storm was over. We took the pictures . . . Margot ice calm behaved . . . as though nothing had happened. In the second run through, he suddenly danced like a dream . . . the sun had come out!

If Rudolf was particular about the way he presented himself onstage, he was even more fastidious when it came to photographs. A performance, after all, was fleeting—it registered in the present and then evaporated into memory. But the camera recorded those fleeting moments for posterity. This was fine if the photographer happened to catch him in a perfectly rendered pose; there was hell to pay if he didn't. Rudolf liked only full-length pictures of him taken on the stage. Studio portraits, he claimed, distorted the dancer's true line and exaggerated the knee and the foot. Taking his cue from Fonteyn, who loathed the idea of being recorded, Rudolf believed that photographers should "arrive pleading and depart bleeding."

Beaton had also taken photographs of the pair, to be projected onto a scrim as part of his stage design. Suffused with the dreamy languor that was his signature, the photographs were both ethereal and romantic. In the most unusual of these, Rudolf is an apparition in white, dressed in

Armand's billowing blouse, tights and slippers against a white back-ground. Standing on high demi-pointe, he cocks his head in contempla-tion, while his left palm and fingers are turned delicately upward at the end of an outstretched arm.

Thinking Rudolf would be pleased with the photographs, Beaton had invited him to come see them one night shortly before he departed for Hollywood. The pictures were merely "a ruse," Beaton acknowl-edged, "to get him to the house, show him friendliness and perhaps strike up a relationship that might make our working together more agreeable." Spying him at the opera house stalking out of a fitting room, Beaton asked him "in a bandying way" whether he wasn't by chance free that night. "What about now?" Rudolf had replied unexpectedly.

So they had promptly set off in the snow for Pelham Place, where, two months earlier, Beaton had played host to the Queen Mother at luncheon, the social coup of his career, an event also attended by such lesser lights as Dame Edith Sitwell, Truman Capote and Frederick Ash-ton. Rudolf, however, was quite unimpressed by Beaton, who he probably suspected looked down on him, as his Petersburg classmates had. Beaton did, in truth, sneer at him in his diary, describing his "appalling little cracked white leatherette bag," his "dirty winter clothes" and his "shabby imitation fur-lined coat." In any case, Rudolf made no effort to make conversation, polite or otherwise, during the taxi ride across town. "Only occasionally," Beaton wrote, "did I make some parrying joke that caused him, almost in spite of himself, to bear [sic] the long rather yellow teeth." Beaton had spent hours peering through his lens at Nureyev, but seeing him up close in the cab, he observed that "this face, already at 23 so cavernous, becomes no longer young when he laughs. His smile is that of a different person, a rather wordly, urbane, sophisticated man of ma-turity."

Rudolf had come simply to see his pictures and offended Beaton by failing to greet his butler or to admire his sitting room, which, on this cold, wintry day, was perfumed by lilacs and warmed by a roaring fire. When Rudolf complained of exhaustion, Beaton, wanting badly to please him, quickly pulled out a floor mattress. And there Rudolf lay sprawled before the fire, looking for all the world like some pampered rajah, as he sipped alternately from his whiskey and his tea, in between bites of brioche and buttered toast. At the same time, though with considerable difficulty, he picked through Beaton's portraits of him, discarding the ones he deemed unworthy, setting aside the ones he wanted, and jabbing his finger at others, while demanding, "What you do with this one?" At no time did he convey enthusiasm, except by recommending that Beaton take more photographs of him in performance. "These are all portraits," he scoffed. "As a dancer, I only like full-length pictures." He didn't mean that he wanted to see more of his body, as Beaton assumed, but rather

that he saw himself only as a dancer and therefore wanted to be represented in motion on the stage, not in repose. When Beaton answered
him vaguely, Rudolf cast him a suspicious sidelong glance that Beaton
knew only too well. He had seen it in Garbo, at whose mercy he had
suffered during their on-and-off-again affair.* "I do not like it in her,"
Beaton noted in his diary, "but I hate it in him. In many ways [he]
reminded me of Greta. The same wild untamed quality of genius—of
not fitting. But Greta is subtle and sensitive and has a sense of humanity
even if she is utterly self centered. He has no pity, no concern for others.
He is ruthless and says, 'If they were dead I not mind.' I felt very much
as if I had brought an animal from the woods into the room. I felt at
any moment the furniture might be violently kicked, tables and chairs
turned upside down, the whole place reduced to a shambles. It was quite
dangerous."

He was perhaps overstating things, for Rudolf merely "nodded,
clicked his teeth, rolled his eyes and showed that he knew the meaning
of the word 'louche' " when shown Cecil's bedroom, a study in red with
Japanese cushions. He suspected that Beaton fancied him, but did not
respond in kind. "I don't understand about Nureyev. What sort of sex
life *does* he have?" Truman Capote wrote to Beaton a short time later.
"Is he in love with Erik Bruhn? Myself, I think he (N.) is repulsive. But
then we have never agreed on this subject [of what constitutes attrac-
tiveness]."

The only object in Beaton's house to rouse Rudolf's interest was a
book on astrology, his favorite new subject. Flipping to Pisces, he was
delighted to learn that Chopin shared his sign and read aloud their iden-
tifying "traits": "Melancholy, unlucky, difficult to get on with. Your own
worst enemy." He had recently taken to wearing a gold Pisces medal
around his neck.

"Now let's look up October,"† Rudolf said suddenly. His thoughts
had shifted to Erik, though Beaton didn't understand the connection.

The conversation got around to Australia and in a "veiled way" they
spoke of Erik. But when Beaton remarked that Rudolf's trip must have
been "lovely," Rudolf shot back that he hadn't earned any money there
and that procuring a visa had been difficult. "The people at the airport
know me well enough by now, but they make it difficult to get on an
aeroplane." Given his choice, he said, he would live in France maybe,
or Scandinavia.

It was already dark by the time Rudolf slipped on his coat and set

---

*According to Beaton's biographer Hugo Vickers, Beaton was sick with envy over the
marriage of his rival Antony Armstrong-Jones to Princess Margaret and confided to his diary
that only by marrying Garbo could he outdo Jones. Alas, she turned him down.

†Bruhn was born on October 3, 1928.

off on his own back to Thurloe Place, leaving a downcast Beaton feeling utterly defeated. "No connection had been established," he concluded, "no link forged."

THE FORGING of links took place instead on the stage, the night *Marguerite and Armand* was unveiled to a glittering gala audience that included the Queen Mother, Princess Margaret and Princess Marina. An immediate success, the ballet sealed the Nureyev-Fonteyn partnership and provided it with its signature work. Here was a ballet custom-fitted to each dancer's talents, personality and persona. So identified with its two stars would it become that no one else has ever been permitted to dance it. The role of Marguerite unloosed in Fonteyn new dramatic depths and seemed to encapsulate "Fonteyn's entire career," wrote the American critic Dale Harris, seeing in it "an ultimate truth in metaphorical form about Fonteyn as dancer and human being." Still others felt that Nureyev was best served by the ballet. "[His] half-mocking smile, his abrupt authority, his savage despair—all these are Armand," wrote Barnes. "I can imagine the ballet without Fonteyn; but I find it impossible to envisage it without Nureyev."

Director Peter Brook could envisage it only with both, their performances overwhelming Ashton's choreography. "Extraordinary actors," he called them, "who bring to each moment and each movement that quality of depth which makes the most artificial of forms suddenly seem human and simple." Though an enormous success with the public, the ballet divided critics, a number of whom dismissed it as a star vehicle regrettably lacking in choreographic invention. Few, however, failed to be moved by its stars. Mary Clarke doubted "whether Ashton could wring two such performances from two other dancers."

As roses, peonies and daffodils rained down on them, Fonteyn and Nureyev took twenty-one curtain calls, an elegantly choreographed ritual all their own. While Michael Somes had always made it a point to stand a few paces behind Fonteyn, close to the curtain, Nureyev stood alongside her, sharing equally in the moment. Scooping a handful of flowers from the stage, he presented them to Fonteyn, who, in homage to his homage, plucked a lone, choice stem from her bouquet, kissed it, and offered it back to him. At this, Nureyev bowed low and kissed her hand, sending the audience swooning into the night.

HIS FRIENDS had grown grander, his fame wider, the locales more glamorous, and yet Rudolf was as much the loner in London as he had been in Leningrad. Negotiating its maze of streets with an insider's know-how, he explored the city whenever he could, usually alone, seeing every new film, play and exhibition he could squeeze in between classes, re-hearsals and performances. Some nights he stayed home, talking on the phone, reading or listening to records; most nights he stayed up late watching old movies on television. He camped in a succession of rented, furnished flats and, like his Tatar forebears, traveled light: Apart from the leather bag that held his worn ballet shoes, his most prized possessions were his art books, his movie camera, his collection of toy trains, his hundreds of classical LPs and his portable record player. Music was still an abiding passion, and whenever possible, he sat at the piano, playing Bach. On other nights he dined with Fonteyn and Tito, the Goslings or his new friend Lee Radziwill, Jacqueline Kennedy's sister. Another host-ess was Princess Dina of Jordan, King Hussein's first wife, whom he met through Fonteyn.

But what he longed for most was a more permanent arrangement with Erik, the most important person in his life, he insisted. "My Danish friend Erik Bruhn, who is the greatest dancer in the world, has helped me more than I can express," he told *Daily Mail* columnist Anne Scott-James that spring. "He is the person I need the most." It was not the sort of revealing comment Rudolf was in the habit of making, particularly to reporters, but Scott-James happened to catch him in an uncharacteristi-cally expansive mood. She had planned to treat him to a postperformance supper at Mirabelle. However, the elegant Mayfair restaurant had refused to admit Rudolf dressed as he was, in tight-fitting black pants, thigh-high leather boots, white leather coat and apache cap. His attire anticipated the mania for mod that would put London at the center of the decade's fashion explosion. Rudolf proposed an expensive Knightsbridge boîte he knew, where Scott-James pressed him on his thoughts of home. "I rarely think of my family or of the past," he corrected her, as he sipped his Negroni. "I love my mother, I sometimes talk to her on the telephone, and I am sorry that I can no longer give her any money. But the old life means very little to me and I push all such thoughts away.... Russia had grown too small for me. I do not 'belong' anywhere.... If I miss anything, it is the sincerity of the Russian people. They do more for each other than Western people do. I find the West too sophisticated. It is full of charlatans." At this, he shuddered with scorn. "I have not been lonely here," he went on, "because I do not need people. I never needed them. ... Often I hate people, not just some individual, but people as a whole, particularly the audience." He was angry at himself, he explained. He had given a "lousy" performance that night in *Marguerite and Armand.* "Oh I know there were curtain calls and flowers and the audience went mad, but I thought I was awful."

Hungry for challenge, he continued to test himself in a variety of new guises. At the Kirov he was lucky to learn two new roles in one year. That winter alone, between his Royal and American Ballet Theatre appearances, he took on six. These included Etiocles, one of the warring sons of Oedipus and Jocasta in John Cranko's *Antigone*, and the leading male role in *Diversions*, a plotless ballet by Kenneth MacMillan. In neither was he the featured dancer, but merely a member of the ensemble.

Apart from *Theme and Variations*, which was based on Petipa and thus on a familiar tradition, *Diversions* offered Rudolf the challenge of his first "abstract" role, one devoid of story or character and dependent on "a new kind of expressiveness derived in large part from simple dance patterns of a body in space." At the Kirov, Rudolf had learned to express himself onstage through his portrayal of a given character; now he had to learn how to express himself purely through movement.

If he failed to make a lasting impression, he nonetheless acquitted himself admirably and in roles created for bodies and sensibilities different from his own. His debut in *Symphonic Variations* proved the biggest stretch of all. A touchstone of the British style, it was the sine qua non of the Ashton repertory, lyrical, restrained, delicate and deceptively simple. It was yet another ballet that played up the virtues of teamwork. Rudolf assumed the role made for Michael Somes, "a crucifier," in the words of Donald MacLeary, who also danced it. "There are only six people in it. You never leave the stage, which Rudolf wasn't used to doing."

Rather than postpone his debut, he danced in spite of an infected knuckle. Three hours before curtain time, he had unexpectedly appeared at the opera house, ready to go on, though in pain and running a fever. In a performance hailed for its subtlety, Rudolf nearly succeeded in passing himself off as English. But given his intrinsic "otherness" and his skill in commanding attention simply by standing still, it was perhaps too much to expect that he would blend completely into any group work. "He could only be Rudolf doing Rudolf in whatever he danced," said Somes, who, though not wrong, was known to be notoriously hard on his colleagues. Nevertheless, Ashton never again cast Rudolf in his ballet because according to Somes, he was displeased with his performance. In an otherwise favorable review for the *Guardian*, James Monahan argued that neither "those sinuous, *Corsaire* arms of his [nor] his stage personality, at once so feline and so romantic, became subdued to the reticent British dignity of a Michael Somes." Also at issue was Nureyev's emotional approach to the music, which contrasted sharply with the rather more objective, metrical approach favored by the British. Rudolf's musicality lay not in "matching gesture to beat," as John Percival has written, "but in catching the tone and shape of a whole phrase of music."

By the end of the season it was almost impossible to open a newspaper without reading about him. His infected hand, his performance in spite of it, his favorite recipe (meat stew), his astrological sign—all these topics were duly reported. Even the BBC got into the act, reporting how thousands of flowers were tossed onto the stage after he and Fonteyn closed out the Royal Ballet season with *Le Corsaire*.

The ripple effect was considerable and by the time he set off for New York in April, for his first tour with the Royal Ballet, the American public was primed for his arrival. The company opened at the Metropolitan Opera House, the scene of Fonteyn's dazzling American debut in 1949. "Unimaginable success!" she remembered. That same year *Time* and *Newsweek* had run simultaneous cover stories on her, making Fonteyn the first ballet world figure to appear on the cover of either magazine. This time around, all eyes were focused on her young partner, whose autobiography, replete with striking black-and-white photographs by Richard Avedon, was launched in America the same week the company opened. A sky-bound Nureyev in black tights graced the cover; less characteristic was the back cover head shot, which showed a grinning, boyish-looking Rudolf in an open-necked white shirt, all dimples and cheekbones, his eyes squinting beneath thick, woolly eyebrows, his full lips stretched into a smirk. Only the prominent boyhood scar on his upper lip saved his face from perfection.

New York audiences had seen Nureyev but briefly, onstage in Brooklyn and in his appearances on the *Bell Telephone Hour*. Now they would see him with Fonteyn, and in a variety of full-length ballets. The season opened in a blaze of publicity, with *Newsweek* proclaiming them "ballet's most celebrated partnership." Still, it was David Blair, not Nureyev, who was Prince Florimund to Fonteyn's Princess Aurora on opening night. Nureyev appeared in Act 3 as the Bluebird, never his finest role.* Mindful of his status as guest artist, de Valois had been reluctant to immediately cede the spotlight to him. The press, however, had no such qualms. The "attention he received was out of all proportion to his importance to the company," lamented one veteran observer. "It left one with the feeling that a meteor had obliterated moon and planets and rising stars."

The season, in fact, did not catch fire until the second week, when the Fonteyn-Nureyev team finally made its debut and, with it, dance history. Despite her enormous popularity with New York audiences, Fonteyn alone did not sell out the house without Nureyev as her partner. Their first *Giselle* on April 25 prompted two dozen curtain calls and had the capacity audience "fairly shaking the Met with shattering bravos," wrote Walter Terry in the *New York Herald Tribune*. "When they were together on stage and looked at each other or smiled at each other, or cried out or forgave or faced death, everything else paled and there seemed to be only two people in the entire world. Last night's audience . . . stood and screamed—yes screamed—for a half hour. They were in

*"More Firebird than Bluebird," quipped Doris Hering in *Dance Magazine*.

the presence of greatness and they knew it." Four nights later their performance of the Black Swan pas de deux stopped the show for five minutes of wild applause. During the coda, after all the cheering for Nureyev had died down, Fonteyn proceeded to up the ante with an attitude en arabesque that she held for an impossibly long time. He had dared her to push her technique as far as it would go and now she was outperforming even her younger self. Alexander Grant, who led the Neapolitan Dance in the same act, witnessed this transformation from the stage. "Margot's greatest, greatest thing was that the more challenge she had, the better she danced. Rudolf would be annoyed with himself over something and showing it and would almost let Margot hold herself up. And when she realized that Rudi was being difficult or not giving what he wanted from himself, she would be even more wonderful. And Rudi would have to calm down to match her, because otherwise she would be shooting ahead of him."

Their partnership was equal parts inspiration and competition. Neither felt there was ever "an easy moment" onstage, recalls Keith Money. "Margot knew that Rudolf was going to claim his part of the stage and Rudolf felt that if he turned his back for a minute, the performance would get away from him." Both possessed an unerring instinct for how to connect with their audience, though they achieved their ends by different means. Whereas Fonteyn was the demure ballerina, gratefully acknowledging the public's adoration, her sweetness and humility endearing her to them, Rudolf dared the public not to like him. The more they cheered, the more he distanced himself from them. The effects were long calculated. "Like all performers, I am masochist. Audience is sadist and vice versa. The moment they see blood, see weakness, they will tear you to pieces. They want to be intimidated and when I intimidate them they really have a ball. . . ." The night they first danced *Le Corsaire* in New York, the applause lasted twice as long as the work itself and stopped only when the curtain went up for the next ballet. "Nothing less than a miracle could come up to the expectations," the *Chicago American* advised audiences awaiting their visit. "Fortunately Nureyev is a miraculous dancer."

Offstage as on- , the pair became a national phenomenon, "the hottest little team in show biz," drawing noisy, idolatrous crowds. "We weren't used to people screaming," recalls Antoinette Sibley. "It was quite different from Margot, who was after all such a huge star before. There'd be lots of celebrities and flowers, but that would be very quiet, not like this, not wild and mad people and all that."

There were of course dissenting voices. Former *New York Times* critic John Martin didn't wait out the season before excoriating Nureyev in the pages of the *Saturday Review*, a popular arts weekly. The "international glamor boy," charged Martin, would prove the ruin of the Royal

Ballet and of Fonteyn in particular. "Some of us have tried putting a hand over one eye and trying to look only at her, but it is no good . . . she has gone, as it were, to the grand ball with a gigolo. . . ."

The Soviets, meanwhile, had tried to block his going to the ball altogether. A few months earlier Sol Hurok and David Webster, chief administrator of the Royal Opera House, had met with Soviet culture minister Ekaterina Furtseva in Moscow to discuss Nureyev's presence on the tour. To Furtseva's complaints that Nureyev would arouse "an unhealthy interest and commotion in the press," Hurok countered that his exclusion from the lineup would arouse an even greater commotion and generate nothing but anti-Soviet publicity. Worse, he, Hurok, would be tarred as an agent of the Soviets, thus undermining his ability to showcase Russian artists during this time of heightened East-West tensions.

Hurok carried the day, though not before the matter had been taken up by numerous departments of the party's Central Committee. But it did not end there. Unable to impede Nureyev's ascent in the West, the Soviets now vilified him at home. The month of the Royal Ballet's New York season, Nureyev's defection to the West was officially announced in the Soviet press. In an article headlined HE LOVES NO ONE AND BE-TRAYS ALL, *Izvestiya* broke its two-year news blackout to brand him a traitor "to both his country and Soviet art," one who had "deteriorated as a dancer" and reached "the limits of moral debasement." The paper quoted Paris Opéra Ballet director Serge Lifar, who in an earlier interview published in *Paris Jour* had called Nureyev "unstable, hysterical and vain. . . . The discipline is work, not whiskey at 5 o'clock in the morning. . . ."

In New York, his comings and goings continued to be widely chronicled, while the ardor of his fans called to mind the frenzied adoration once bestowed on Rudolph Valentino, Frank Sinatra and James Dean. And one year before the Beatles hit these shores, he inspired several Manhattan hairdressers to produce the "Nureyev Coiffure" for their female clients, a look achieved by combing the hair over the right ear. "It looked like something the lawnmower missed," *Newsweek* reported in a column devoted entirely to the subject of his hair, prompting an understandably flummoxed Nureyev to wonder: "Is it the hair that makes success?"

If he was now cagier about deflecting questions he found silly or intrusive, he was still a straight shooter when it came to questions about his dancing. Was it true that he hated the audience? a journalist from *Newsweek* asked him over dinner at the Russian Tea Room. The interview with Anne Scott-James had been reprinted in a number of U.S. newspapers. "Maybe an artist doesn't belong in any place," he answered in earnest. "An artist dances for himself. He needs the audience to test his strength, his power." He suspected she would jump on this, and she did. "Maybe the public shouldn't know such things," he said quickly, understanding full well that if *he* said it, they would. As he stepped out onto Fifty-seventh Street, a concert was ending at Carnegie Hall next door. Where just one year earlier he had gone unrecognized on the streets of New York, he now caused a stir wherever he went. Seeing him, a crowd gathered, thrusting programs for him to sign. Rudolf, however, walked past them, remarking with more prescience than he supposed, "After fifteen years, they will start running after someone else."

Attracted by his glamour, Greta Garbo, First Lady Jacqueline Kennedy and Princess Grace of Monaco all came to see him, one star recognizing another. Garbo was characteristically nonplussed. "Those poor fellows having to lift all those big girls," she said after a performance at the Met. "It's so silly." Nevertheless, she and Rudolf hit it off, or so Rudolf reported to Beaton. Jacqueline Kennedy was also in the audience for his New York performances, having heard all about Rudolf from her sister, Lee. The tension when he danced with Fonteyn was "extraordinary," she recalled many years later. "You lost yourself in it. I remember there were 40 curtain calls. People's hands were black-and-blue pulp. Seeing [them] has made up for having missed Nijinsky and Chaliapin. It has been one of the strongest artistic experiences of my life. . . ." One night she asked to go backstage to meet Rudolf, but Sol Hurok wouldn't hear of it, reportedly going as far as to lock the door to Nureyev's dressing room. He had already had enough trouble and wasn't about to broker Nureyev's first meeting with the wife of an American president. You might fall and hurt yourself, he cautioned the First Lady, who took his advice and departed, leaving Rudolf fuming at Hurok inside his dressing room.

Hurok's victory was short-lived. Mrs. Kennedy soon sent a private plane to New York to bring Nureyev, Fonteyn and Ashton for tea at the White House. She and Rudolf were charmed by each another, their youth, glamour and aura binding these two sixties icons, he, ballet's most famous prince, and she, the queen of Camelot. It was the beginning of a thirty-year friendship that would see both of them become heroes "for a generation determined not to be boring, dedicated to pursuing excellence." Fonteyn, who had met Jackie earlier, found her "almost fey, with that breathless voice and those wide-set eyes." After tea, she ushered them into the Cabinet Room before offering to go see "if the President is busy." The minute she left, Rudolf made a dash for the President's chair. He wanted to know what power really felt like. That year the United States and Russia would sign the first nuclear testing ban and agree to install the first hot line between the White House and the Kremlin. Within moments, President Kennedy himself was welcoming Rudolf into the Oval Office.

* * *

FOLLOWING A PARTY for the Royal Ballet in Toronto, Rudolf tried pirouetting down the middle of the street back to his hotel at 3 A.M., when a policeman approached him. He was handcuffed and promptly hauled off to the station, from which Royal Ballet manager Michael Wood finally retrieved him after a good deal of appeasing. With Le Bourget a not-so-distant memory, this momentary loss of freedom shook him, as the English dancer Lynn Seymour learned when she put in a call to his hotel room. "I said, 'You poor baby. What happened?' Evidently no one else had called him. He was mortified, unbelievably mortified." He was also back in the headlines.

The tour wound down in July, with sold-out, celebrity-studded performances in Los Angeles. In the audience for a Nureyev-Fonteyn *Giselle*, Cecil Beaton marveled at how popular ballet had become. Young people were as excited as their parents over "this old barnstormer," their interest sparked primarily by Nureyev.* "The 'bigness' of his pride . . . was something we don't see in the theatre nowadays." The night Beaton saw *Marguerite and Armand* onstage for the first time, he had driven directly from the set of *My Fair Lady*, inviting along as his guests Audrey Hepburn, her husband, Mel Ferrer, director George Cukor and Christopher Isherwood. Hepburn was "in a state of elation" during the performance, while the hard-to-please Cukor yelled himself hoarse. "I never remember shouting in a theatre before," Beaton recalled his saying, "and although it is painful for me to gush your work is beautiful!" Beaton's own feelings about the ballet were mixed. He was disturbed to find his costumes changed without his permission and he thought the lighting "very rough." But once the ballet began, "one sits with blood tingling on edge in case one misses a romantic nuance. . . . Margot's performance is her best and she shows herself another Duse . . . the ugly little frog that she is becomes a beauty through the quality of her spirit. Nureyev too is the quintessence of all romantic passion and looked so beautiful smiling in the early scenes and like a tragic clown . . . at the last. . . ."

In Hollywood, as in New York, Nureyev was the most sought-after guest in town. At producer Frank McCarthy's party for him, Bette Davis, Natalie Wood, Hedda Hopper and Beaton mingled among the guests. Rudolf told Davis how much he admired her. He had seen *All About Eve* in Leningrad; ever since, she had remained "the greatest" for him. Finding Rudolf "slightly drunk and very coy," Beaton finally succeeded

---

*In Beaton's unpublished diaries, Fonteyn was given short shrift, which may have had something to do with their run-ins over his *Marguerite* costumes. The line that reads, "Margot was superb," in the published diary disguised a colder assessment: "Margot was an adept little pupil—ugly as a frog and without allure, but honest, hardworking and coldly sober."

in drawing him out. "We hugged and kissed and displayed a great love for one another and I proposed that he should come and live with me," Beaton told his diary. "It was all very agreeable and an amusing comedy. But in between the lines he threw me a few home truths." Heading the list were gripes about the huge taxes he was forced to pay on his American television fees. He then commanded about two thousand dollars for a night's work, nearly double the amount he was paid for his appearances on British television. More poignantly, he complained of feeling isolated within the Royal Ballet. He suspected that he was resented, as indeed he was. Ballet people, he said, were "so silly." They followed orders; they never thought for themselves. "Nobody understands me, perhaps Margot a little from time to time, and Freddy's nice, but he offers me nothing, and they hate me. But I don't care." He was lonely, he said, and missed Erik terribly. Already a month had passed without their meeting and "there's no hope for us. We can't work together. Our friends don't like us to be together. It is *always* travelling for me; always on the road—without a window."

FOR THE SUMMER HOLIDAYS, Rudolf arranged for Erik to join the company of dancers that he and Fonteyn were to lead around the Mediterranean, and then on to Japan and Honolulu.* There had briefly been talk that Bruhn and Carla Fracci might also be showcased during the "Fonteyn Follies," as the Fonteyn Concert Tour was known to its participants. According to Bruhn, they had discussed mixing up the pairings so that Nureyev would occasionally dance with Fracci, and Bruhn with Fonteyn, whom he had never partnered. Rudolf had encouraged him to dance with Fonteyn, but Bruhn was reluctant to encroach on his territory. He also worried that he and Fonteyn were "too much the purists," without enough contrast to create a spark. Perhaps more to the point, Bruhn found her difficult to get to know and "so extremely ladylike in every situation" that he felt uncomfortable. Then again, it's impossible to know in what measure his assessment was colored by her rejection of the Bruhn-Fracci team. As Bruhn later told it, Fonteyn was not keen to include Fracci.†

Nor were the tour organizers keen to include Bruhn, once the trip was under way. "We didn't really have a job for Erik, so I said he couldn't come," recalls Joan Thring, the tour's feisty manager. "Rudolf got really angry with me. In the end, we decided that Erik would be a brilliant

*The tour included stops in Athens, Nice, Tel Aviv, Haifa, Jerusalem, Nagoya, Kyoto, Osaka and Honolulu.
†That year Bruhn and Yuri Soloviev were both awarded the Nijinsky Prize, the same prize Rudolf had won in 1961 the month he defected.

teacher, so we agreed to take him as far as Greece. I asked Rudolf who was going to pay for Erik. Rudolf said, 'I pay,' and gave me all these old airline tickets, with the carbon copy left in, from all his travels around Europe. 'Here,' he said to me, 'you cash this and it will pay for Erik's ticket.' He actually thought they were cashable. I told him they were just rubbish. I got slapped for the first time. He was a great one for flashing out."

On the plane to Athens before takeoff, Rudolf asked Thring whether she had booked him a room with a double bed. At her reply, "not specifically," Rudolf swore at her in Russian and returned to his seat. A few minutes later Thring marched down to where he and Erik were sitting, demanding to know what *pizdyushka* ("cunt") meant. When Erik asked what was wrong, Thring told him about the double bed, embarrassing Rudolf, who did not want Bruhn to know he had involved her in a private matter. "I told them they would have a room each, both with double beds, and they could sleep in whichever one they wanted, but I wouldn't be called names." Later they explained to her that *pizdyushka* meant "everything nasty you could think of." *Pizda* quickly became her pet name for Rudolf.

With the Bolshoi Ballet ensconced at the Royal Opera House for the month of July, the group had assembled in Cannes for rehearsals at Rosella Hightower's studio. Fearing a cancellation by the Bolshoi, John Tooley had urged Rudolf not to come to London while the Russians were in town. "I am sure you realize by now that your own countrymen's feelings about you are, at least on the official level, extremely cold," he wrote. "You must also know what we feel about their attitude and the fights I have had here and in Moscow." The Côte d'Azur was then an outpost of the international set and "a kind of crossroads of celebrities and culture," in the words of the French dancer Hélène Traïline, recalling how Rudolf and Erik stuck out from the rest. "Even people who didn't know who they were would turn to look at them because they were so sublimely handsome. You were struck by their beauty." They spent all their time together, though Erik was "much more reserved," says Thring, unlike Rudolf, "who was always very warm and cuddly, like a little boy, which is what he was."

In Monte Carlo, the little boy shelled out $110,000 for his first home, an isolated mountaintop villa at La Turbie, perched two thousand feet up Mont-Agel with views of the Alps and the coastline. Fittingly, it was called Arcadie. Having grown up in cramped, airless quarters, he craved his own aerie, from where he could see 360 degrees around him and yet remain at a distance. "It's really the house I've always dreamed of: outside, mountains, sky and not a human being in sight; inside big white spaces — I hate small rooms, they make me feel I'm in prison — old beams and best of all, a fireplace." His dining room was illuminated by an enormous chandelier covered with candles, his favorite form of lighting.

Monte Carlo had held a storied place in the ballet world, ever since Diaghilev used its opera house as his creative base from 1911 until his death in 1929. The person Rudolf assigned to find him a villa was his friend the prominent ballet teacher Marika Besobrasova and her husband, Jean, a lawyer, who had met Rudolf in Paris while he was still a member of the Kirov. It was Besobrasova who also found him his caretaker, Serge, and his beloved housekeeper, Claire, a doting white-haired Frenchwoman who Rudolf claimed was the best cook in France.

The purchase of his villa made Rudolf Russia's leading capitalist. "How Much Bullion in the Ballet?" wondered the *Daily Mail*, a question Farida Nureyeva must have been asking after learning of the sale via the KGB. Finally, here was proof that her Rudik wasn't starving in the West. "Now I know he has enough money," she told her daughter Razida.

But in Rudik's mind, he would never have enough of it, no matter how many houses he owned, or millions he amassed and stored away in Liechtenstein bank accounts. If high living was a magnet, earning money was a driving force. The expense of his new villa became an immediate concern. Keith Money, along on the tour as a photographer, recorded a telling episode in his diary, which says much about Fonteyn's deft understanding of Rudolf's financial hunger. Hours before a performance at the Herod Atticus amphitheater in Athens, Rudolf suddenly announced that he was not going to dance that evening. Fonteyn, who was busy stitching her pointe shoes on the stage, kept on with her task, the frown on her brow the only hint of her displeasure. "Well, that's for you to decide," she said finally. "I suppose I can do one or two extra solos."

Rudolf had expected her to protest and wasn't sure what to make of her response. The silence hung between them. "It was like watching two dogs meeting from different ends of town, rather than two people who work together in such close physical harmony," observed Money.

"But I expect they won't be satisfied with *that*," Fonteyn began again. "Perhaps we'd better just give the money back?"

"Huh?"

"Give the money back. If you're not dancing."

"I see," Rudolf said after a long pause, and then wandered off through one of the stone arches, lost in thought. Fonteyn, meanwhile, went on with her sewing, fairly confident, it seems, that he would turn up after all. Which he did, hours later, acting as if he were expected all along.

His appearance at the Athens Festival provoked the usual diplomatic sparring. As a result of his participation, the Soviets canceled the scheduled performances of Sviatoslav Richter, the pianist Rudolf had most admired in Leningrad. The memo to the Central Committee, ordering this last-minute cancellation—"due to the fact that the defector R. Nureyev is participating"—was signed by Leonid Brezhnev, who was soon to become the new Soviet leader.

In the meantime, the defector's merits were endlessly debated. "The Russian jumps about very energetically," Nancy Mitford reported to Beaton from Athens. "Nureyev told a Greek friend* . . . who had him on his yacht that the English only cheer when he leaps and know nothing about ballet. . . . Lifar, whom I saw in Venice, says he's a lazy boy and won't work. . . . I suppose you've seen him in London? Rather handsome . . ."

The "Follies" fare included Nureyev's version of the third act of *Raymonda* as well as an extract from *La Sylphide* that Bruhn reworked especially for Nureyev and Fonteyn. While Fonteyn continued to be stimulated by the new technical challenges Nureyev gave her, Nureyev, in turn, was stimulated by his work with Bruhn, a creative ménage à trois that nourished each of them, although perhaps Bruhn the least. Rudolf had long been eager for Bruhn to coach him in the role of James, the Scotsman hero of Bournonville's *La Sylphide*. In this quintessential Romantic-era ballet, James falls in love with a wood sprite on the eve of his wedding and follows her into the forest. Searching for a way to capture her, he wraps a magical scarf around her, unaware that the evil witch Madge has poisoned it. Her wings destroyed, the sylph dies in the arms of her heartbroken lover.

Bruhn was the definitive James, and in his effort to emulate him, Rudolf naturally wanted to master the demands of the Bournonville style. Bournonville "was like Bach to me, a craftsman, transcending his craft," he recalled in 1978. With its emphasis on buoyancy and precision, on bounding beaten steps and quicksilver shifts of weight, it contrasted sharply with his own pliant, expansive style of dancing.

It was Bruhn's belief that a dancer gave life to a role only by infusing it with his understanding of the character, with whatever was "true" to him at the moment. In his view, James was an idealist and the Sylphide "a poet's dream of something beautiful he wants to make real." The character appealed to Rudolf's romantic nature, while the choreography allowed him to show off his elevation and beats. The pas de deux proved a favorite with audiences on the tour, as it did later that fall with viewers of the popular television variety show *Sunday Night at the London Palladium*. Ballet's new pop stars were in good company: Also featured on the program was a fast-rising new band called the Rolling Stones.

*   *   *

*Presumably Aristotle Onassis.

A CHANGING of the guard took place over the summer and by September 1963 Frederick Ashton had become the new director of the Royal Ballet. One of his first acts was to commission Nureyev to stage the Kingdom of the Shades scene from *La Bayadère*, the ballet in which Rudolf had scored his initial success in Paris two years earlier. This early Petipa classic was not known to Western audiences when the Kirov first toured it in 1961. Rudolf was to have danced it during the Kirov's tour to London and Ashton had apparently fought "against some resistance" to have him mount this now-celebrated extract. "I was adamant that time should be found to put it in."*

Nureyev's youth and explosive nervous energy had prompted skepticism. But with his prodigious memory for steps and talent for teaching, he quickly proved himself an exemplary coach—and, in time, Petipa's staunchest champion in the West. Ever since his student days, he had longed to both dance and choreograph, hoping not only to make his mark on the stage but to leave his imprint on the repertory. While he had produced a number of short pieces for himself and a partner, the Shades scene, a cornerstone of the Russian repertory, was to be his first production for a large cast. The ballet starred Nureyev and Fonteyn (as the Indian warrior Solor and the temple dancer Nikiya) and showcased both the company's corps de ballet and three outstanding soloists who would go on to become leading ballerinas: Lynn Seymour, Merle Park and Monica Mason.

As with all the classic nineteenth-century Russian story ballets he would go on to stage, Nureyev drew on the Kirov version, though he did not reproduce it step for step. Petipa's choreography was, for him, a guide, not a precise blueprint. "When I change, where I change, is for reason, for good reason that we dance these ballets today, not yesterday." Another reason was that Petipa had favored the ballerina. In *his* version of the pivotal scarf duet, in which Solor and Nikiya dance together linked by a long, transparent scarf, Nureyev had Solor mirror her movements, rather than merely observe them, in keeping with his belief that a pas de deux was a conversation. How could there be a conversation, he suggested, "if one partner is dumb?" He also replaced a waltz for the corps de ballet with one from another act, and devised a new configuration for the finale, taken from an earlier act.

More than teach steps, his greatest challenge was to convey the ballet's style: Unity and precision were vital to its success. This was especially true of the hypnotic opening sequence, in which Solor dreams of seeing his dead Nikiya, as row upon row of ghostly white figures cross the stage, repeating the same step. The Royal Ballet had a number of

---

*It is not clear whether Ashton initiated the commission or whether he had inherited a directive set in motion by Ninette de Valois.

Petipa ballets in its repertory, but these, as John Percival observed, had become Anglicized over time. Nureyev now demanded a greater degree of attack in the dancing, and a lusher, more voluptuous movement style, particularly in the port de bras. He also taught the ballerinas to dance more slowly, with greater control, to exploit the tension of a particular phrase or step. Monica Mason recalls how Nureyev slowed down her variation to showcase her elevation. The company's female dancers weren't usually asked to go for height in their jumps, but Nureyev, she says, expected her to jump "the highest I could every single jump! He wanted it done like a man's variation. He made you understand that you should never make anything easy for yourself. He believed it was your duty to show the audience how difficult something was."*

His effort in performance was his signature and the means by which he thrilled his audience. In calling attention to the difficulty of a step, he telegraphed not only his own excitement at carrying it off but the notion that dancing itself was a risky business.

During an orchestra rehearsal of *Bayadère*, he kept struggling with his solo, but refused to stop working on it even after the musicians had gone home. Finally, he ran out of stage time. "Rudi dear," proposed assistant director John Hart, "why don't you make it simpler for yourself? I mean, no one would know." Rudolf was baffled by the suggestion. "How I work if I don't give myself something I can't do?"

From the start, he set exacting standards from which the entire company benefited. With an eye for spotting young talent, he gave opportunities to several promising dancers, believing, as he always would, that talent should take precedence over seniority. Framed by dancers half her age, Fonteyn was forced to assert her technical authority, something she wasn't convinced she could do. His role model was Dudinskaya, with whom he had rehearsed, though never danced, *La Bayadère* at the Kirov.

While ruthless with himself, Nureyev was the model of generosity when it came to coaching other dancers, feeling a kinship with those who had to struggle as he did. Lacking the natural coordination of a Bruhn, he had to work "very, *very* hard to maintain his technique," recalls Georgina Parkinson, one of the soloists he chose for the ballet's second cast. "He didn't turn naturally and really had to work on his pirouettes." Any dancer intent on improving her technique or working out a step had only to ask to win his assistance. "We all put ourselves in his hands," Parkinson says of the golden generation that included Sibley, Park and Seymour, all of them

---

*After seeing Rudolf's Shades scene in the 1970s, following her own defection, Natalia Makarova told Mason that Rudolf had slowed down the solo. "We never did it that slowly at the Kirov," she said.

Nureyev protégées. "De Valois, who had nursed us all, gave us to Rudolf to learn from. He was our example, sweating away, working his guts out, striving, striving, the whole time." Like any good teacher, he knew precisely what he wanted out of a dancer, "and precisely how to help you achieve it," says Monica Mason. He also encouraged them to study with outside teachers, something they had never done, in particular with the four-foot-one-inch Russian dynamo Valentina Pereyaslavec, to whose New York studio the Royal Ballet dancers now flocked whenever they were in town. "It was all Rudolf's doing, with his obsession for improving." Rudolf also arranged for Pereyaslavec to occasionally teach company class in London. In her class, no one could change an exercise or take it easy or choose where they would stand. All this was determined by Madame, who barked her instructions in a booming voice that "you could hear around the block." Nevertheless, she treated Rudolf "royally. She just worshiped the ground he walked on."

As absorbed as he was in his own performance, Nureyev never lost sight of anyone else's. Well after *La Bayadère* was launched, he continued to help the dancers find the most efficient way of performing each step. Standing in the wings, he would analyze the dancing onstage, just as he had as a student. But now when the ballerinas exited into the wings, he would give them notes before going onstage for his own variation. "Cabriole better," he counseled Mason. "Still more *petit battement*. I go. I dance."

It was a sold-out house that greeted *La Bayadère* on opening night, with Nureyev adding some unscheduled drama by disappearing into the wings before completing his first big solo. Having landed badly coming out of a circle of looping turns, he felt himself losing his balance and had dashed into the wings to avoid an onstage spill. There was a tense moment when no one was sure what had happened, or whether he would return, but minutes later he was back for the scarf duet. The scandalmongers insisted on making much out of the mishap, reporting that Nureyev "had flounced off . . . in a fit of temperament . . ." (NUREYEV ON "WHY I RAN OFF STAGE: ALLOW ME MY MISTAKES," ran a headline in the *Daily Express*.) Regardless, his *Bayadère* proved an unqualified success and showed Nureyev to be not only a dancer of rare power but "a major new resource for Western ballet," wrote Clive Barnes. The corps had never looked more uniform, the soloists dazzled, and Fonteyn revealed a "whole technical armoury that one hardly knew she possessed." Nureyev himself earned a few more superlatives for his breathtaking series of double assemblé turns, establishing them as the hallmark of male virtuosity. To audiences at the time, his turnout looked exaggerated, even "absurd," as Arlene Croce was later to observe, noting how "the truly remarkable feature of that signature step — the double assemblé — was the tight fifth he held from takeoff to landing. It was the double revolution in the air that caught the eye, and at first everyone who tried the step stumbled coming down, as Nureyev himself sometimes did. Then his imitators caught on, and the step today is a commonplace, along with full turnout."

With *Bayadère*, Nureyev proved that he was much more than a novelty act: Here was a unique dancer whose talents extended beyond those simply of a performing artist. In just two years in the West, Nureyev had changed the face of British ballet. He had popularized ballet, propelled Fonteyn to fresh heights, set new standards for the male ranks. "Now with *La Bayadère*," wrote *Dance and Dancers*, "he has presented us with a great classic to cherish, and what is equally as important taught us how to dance it. . . ."

He next set to work mounting more staples from the Kirov repertory. He not only supplied three dances for a new production of *Swan Lake*,* directed by Robert Helpmann and choreographed principally by Ashton, he staged the "Diana and Actaeon" pas de deux for himself and Svetlana Beriosova; Vainonen's *The Flames of Paris* for Christopher Gable and Anya Linden; and in early 1964, the *Laurencia* pas de six for a television program transmitted live from Covent Garden, with himself and Nadia Nerina in the leading roles and Antoinette Sibley, Merle Park, Graham Usher and Gable as the soloists. The "traitor" was fast becoming Russian ballet's most active ambassador.

He was already the leading advocate for the male dancer, his influence reflected in Ashton's decision to give, for the first time, equal prominence to both partners in a ballet, *The Dream*. Attracted by Nureyev's example, an increasing number of boys were drawn to a career in ballet. Before 1963, the number of boys enrolled at the Royal Ballet School had never exceeded ten; by 1964, there were seventeen, the largest increase in its history.

Just as he had challenged rigid distinctions between "male" and "female" movements at the Kirov, so Nureyev continued to redefine them at the Royal Ballet. In the process, he changed the image of the male dancer, who, in his view, "had forfeited his right to use the *whole* dance language." While the company's older male guard resented him, feeling understandably displaced, younger, promising dancers like Gable and Anthony Dowell welcomed him as an entirely new kind of role model, as Ashton hoped they might. "There was a tradition in my generation of dancers that you had to be really heterosexual onstage, because you had to prove that you weren't 'one of those,' " recalls Gable, Nure-

*He was due to dance the premiere in mid-December but had to withdraw after he was knocked down by a motorscooter in the King's Road and hurt his ankle.

yev's contemporary. "So the English style was reticent, withdrawn male with a capital *M*, and self-effacing. Rudolf wasn't inhibited by any of that. He moved in a far more lyrical way than any English dancers would have dared at that time. He had very floaty, romantic arms, and he wasn't afraid of very soft movement at a time when the male standard was Eddie Villella* or David Blair and Michael Somes—very manly dancing. He was completely comfortable with his sexuality and his sexual orientation and he had no interest in anything other than expressing the music and the choreography in the way that seemed appropriate to him. People like me suddenly saw that there was no need to prove your maleness by using this sort of wooden and reserved style that said, 'I'm a man.' And so he gave us permission to take away all those barriers."

Apart from their youth, promise and repertory, Gable and Nureyev shared little in common as dancers. Tall, fair and glamorous, with blond curls framing his handsome face, Gable was widely admired for his dramatic talents, seen to best advantage with Lynn Seymour as his partner. However, with Nureyev on the scene, challenging the standards and extending the limits of possibility, Gable saw that he would have to work harder. The British public had come to expect a higher level of technical proficiency and Gable had no choice but to deliver it. "Rudolf had areas of vocabulary that no English dancer was attempting, because we didn't know how to go about it. You'd see boys fighting to figure out what coordination you need to achieve these double-double things he was doing. Suddenly a whole generation were taking on that virtuoso technique. He was totally open and giving of all the information that he had." And duly rewarded. While his contemporaries earned a weekly salary of about forty pounds, Rudolf's contract guaranteed him three hundred pounds *per performance*. (That year he gave eighty-five performances, sixty of them with the Royal Ballet.)

By the fall of 1963 Gable was one of the company's most popular dancers and already being touted as Nureyev's potential rival. Gable's "steadily rising star seems almost bound to collide at some point with the flaming Nureyev meteor," reported *The New York Times*. The two were soon paired in Kenneth MacMillan's *Images of Love*, a pas de trois with Lynn Seymour made for a program commemorating Shakespeare's quatercentenary. (The title was drawn from Shakespeare's Sonnet 144, "Two loves I have, of comfort and despair.") Gable was comfort, Seymour despair, and both, in Seymour's words, "struggled for possession of the 'poetic' Rudi. Our threesome was a lightning flash of arms and legs, reaching ravenously towards some ceaseless pleasure."

"You've got so many things that I need to know," Gable admitted

---

*Edward Villella of the New York City Ballet.

one day to Rudolf, "and I don't feel I have anything to offer back." "That's fine," Rudolf replied with disarming candor, "it doesn't matter because you're no threat to me."

There were still many things Rudolf needed to know and Bruhn was his only model. Intent on improving his Albrecht, he went to Copenhagen in early 1964 to watch Bruhn and Yvette Chauviré rehearse *Giselle*. Bruhn had not danced the ballet for two years, and since this was to be his Paris Opéra debut—and his first appearance with Chauviré, a celebrated Giselle—he was reappraising his own approach. The three of them stayed together in Bruhn's house and worked each day with Vera Volkova.

Although basking in the success of *La Bayadère*, Rudolf was envious that Erik had just spent the season with the New York City Ballet, during which Balanchine himself had coached him in *Apollo*. The experience, alas, had ended unhappily after Balanchine cast Bruhn in a performance of the ballet without first giving him a stage rehearsal with the three ballerinas he was to partner. Bruhn balked at performing without adequate preparation and soon bowed out of the season, without ever dancing *Apollo*. His problems with Balanchine were compounded by an incapacitating stomach ailment that only many years later would be diagnosed as a perforated ulcer. At the time, however, his doctors could find nothing wrong, leaving Bruhn to conclude that emotional stress was to blame. There were days when he could barely get out of bed.

If he hoped for calm in Copenhagen, he failed to find it with Rudolf. By the time Pierre Bergé and Clara Saint came to visit, Erik and Rudolf were "drinking a lot," says Bergé. "Lots of vodka, both of them." Many nights alcohol would poison Erik's tongue and he would lash out cruelly at Rudolf, who quietly endured his taunts.

Bergé had known Nureyev since his first days in Paris and whenever Rudolf returned there, he joined Pierre and Yves Saint Laurent for dinner, often with Claire Motte, Fonteyn and Clara Saint, at whose Rue de Rivoli apartment he sometimes stayed. Though Rudolf and Clara were still friendly, Clara found him increasingly difficult and had begun to pull away. He was not "the same shy person" she had first known. "At a restaurant he would send things back if there was too much salt and he would be very demanding in general. It grew tiresome to be with someone who was so arrogant." Through Rudolf, however, she had met Fonteyn, who in turn had introduced her to Bergé and Saint Laurent. Clara had quickly became a vital member of their circle and would remain so.

Like Nureyev and Bruhn, Saint Laurent and Bergé had markedly contrasting temperaments. Where Saint Laurent was shy, sweet and introverted, Bergé was effusive, playful and a father figure to his younger partner, whose couture house he was instrumental in launching. Bergé, however, was determined "to protect [Yves] and make him happy," which, as Bergé saw it, was clearly not Erik's objective with Rudolf. "Erik was very domineering. He would say to Rudolf, 'What you did tonight was disgusting, just look at yourself, look at your legs, how can you do that?' And Rudolf was absolutely like a pupil before his master."

Though Bruhn's Paris Opéra debut was acclaimed by the French critics, Bruhn was irked to find himself described as Nureyev's teacher in a number of reviews. He assumed the public would think, "What was a teacher doing dancing *Giselle* at the Opéra?"* Once more, Rudolf came from London to see him dance. Rudolf "seemed somewhat down," Bruhn recalled. "He avoided the press and said that he didn't want to see anyone except me. When we were together he seemed more relaxed and we had a good time." One night they went to Maxim's, where "of course, the minute we entered, everybody knew who he was and nobody knew who I was." They ordered caviar and promptly devoured the enormous bowl they were given, thinking the restaurant unusually generous in its portions. The bill suggested otherwise and they could barely scrape together the cash to pay for it. All through supper, Rudolf remained curiously silent about Bruhn's performance. Finally, he said that he and Fonteyn were due to dance *Giselle* in Australia in April. But now he wasn't sure that he could. "After seeing you do it here in Paris, I don't think I can dance *Giselle* anymore."

Rudolf was keenly jealous, and while he would always insist that there was no greater Albrecht than Bruhn, his jealousy never abated. The Italian critic Vittoria Ottolenghi recalls introducing Bruhn to a Rome audience in the early 1980s, prior to a performance of *Giselle* starring Nureyev. Bruhn, then in his fifties, had long since retired. "We have perhaps one of the greatest Albrechts of our time with us tonight," she told the crowd as Bruhn stood to acknowledge their applause. Hearing this, Rudolf was furious. "I thought *I* was the star of the show," was his acid response. Afterward, on their way to dinner in a taxi, he asked Ottolenghi for her opinion of his pirouettes in the second act. "The audience was in ecstasy," she replied, though she herself had seen them performed more affectingly by Vasiliev, by Bruhn and by Nureyev himself. At that, Rudolf turned on Bruhn and said, "Certainly! That's because you never wanted to teach it to me. I've asked you but you've never shown me the real technique behind that pirouette."

Erik was bewildered. "What are you saying? I always taught you everything you asked."

---

*According to Chauviré, it was she who had convinced the Paris Opéra Ballet to invite Bruhn to make his debut with the company. She had insisted that he was not only a great dancer but Nureyev's most important influence.

19

A God, a Man, a Bird,

Himself

BY 1964 THE PATTERN of his life was set. Dancing as often as he could, wherever he could, Rudolf not only appeared regularly with the Royal Ballet but would go just about anywhere there was a good role or interesting program. Performances dictated each day's events, which typically began at 9 A.M. with a scalding bath, tea with five lumps of sugar and toast. By 10 he was at the barre for morning class, swaddled in layers of woolen leg warmers, sweaters and one of his endless supply of caps. Rehearsals followed until 1:30 and then he broke for lunch. More rehearsals, more tea, more costume fittings and meetings filled out the afternoon. Before performances or evenings out, he liked to nap for a few hours. By 6:45 P.M. he was at the theater, warming up on the stage, wrestling with preperformance nerves.

His work consumed him and he did not waste what little spare time he had. Running from theater to theater, he would catch the first act of one play, the second act of another, the final act of an opera and then a late-night film, often in a single evening. He rarely missed a new production at the Aldwych, the Old Vic or the Royal Court or an exhibition at the Tate. When he socialized, he gravitated toward the Sombrero Club, a restaurant in High Street, Kensington, the Caprice in Mayfair, or the Arethusa, a restaurant-club in Chelsea popular with show business insiders. He also liked Danny La Rue's, the fashionable nightclub run by a well-known female impersonator. Other nights he hit the Ad Lib, the smart Leicester Square discotheque and central hub of "Swinging London," whose denizens included the Beatles and the Rolling Stones. A tiny elevator conveyed visitors to the club and in those days, recalls Mick Jagger's then girlfriend, the singer Marianne Faithfull, "being on top of the city and looking down on it like that was very modern and very cool."

The day-to-day needs of Rudolf's life now fell to Joan Thring, the tour manager responsible for the "Fonteyn Follies." Despite their initial clash, Rudolf had come to admire her pluck. "You crack very good whip," Rudolf had told her. "I like you look after me." As his secretary and manager, Thring invited guests to dine, arranged for housekeepers and masseurs, vetted the seating plans for dinner parties, and made sure that his life ran as smoothly as he wanted it to. While Gorlinsky negotiated his fees and invested his money, Thring paid his bills, signed checks, and organized his travel. When he worked with outside companies, Thring was included in his contract, which also guaranteed him twenty-eight hundred dollars per performance, first-class travel and all of his expenses.

A former model turned publicist, Thring was a tall, willful woman with a raucous laugh, striking hazel eyes and straight dark brown hair that fell to her waist. She had worked briefly as a court reporter in Australia before marrying Frank Thring, a celebrated Australian actor, with whom she moved to England. By the time Rudolf met her, Joan was divorced and working as a press representative in the theater. Formidable in her own right, she took a firm line with Rudolf, seeing her role as equal parts nanny, den mother and lion tamer. "There were a few moments when I first worked with him that I thought, 'My God, what am I getting into?'" But, like everyone else, she was readily charmed by him. "On the whole, he was terribly cuddly, jolly, like a real teddy bear, and you couldn't help but love him. I defy anybody who was close to him not to be a little in love with him." She recalls his "enormous charm and enormous excitement. He was like a naughty child. He liked lavatory jokes, silly jokes and you'd do anything to see that face light up."

His celebrity allowed him to get away with behavior that could only be described as outside any normal bounds of propriety. Yet Thring never appeared fazed by it. And Rudolf trusted her because she was "absolutely gung ho" and nothing he asked seemed to daunt her. She rented a furnished ground-floor flat for him in tony Eaton Place, which Rudolf nearly burned to the ground one night playing with the paraffin-fueled train set she had bought him. With his Karmann Ghia with Erik in Denmark, she ordered him a beige Mercedes 320SL sports car, which cost $10,500 and which Rudolf drove as if it were a bumper car, earning him countless fines and prompting his friend Peter O'Toole to quip that "it's like the way I used to drive. I've given up driving." As always, Rudolf took little notice of red lights and stop signs.

* * *

HE ALSO CONTINUED to see the Goslings, eager to imbibe Nigel's expertise in art and to fill in the gaps of his knowledge. Nigel's "generosity of mind . . . seemed to belong to an earlier age," observed a friend, "yet he was fully in touch with the culture of his day." Nigel was the father Hamet had never been, soft-spoken and scholarly, with a whimsical, witty sense of humor that never called attention to itself. Quietly self-assured, he was a man of firm convictions who, during the war, had bypassed military service as a conscientious objector and had served instead in the British Red Cross. Unlike Hamet Nureyev, he had had options: Born into a family of country gentry, he was schooled at Eton and Cambridge and had worked first for the Diplomatic Service in Berlin before turning to painting and writing fiction. But it was as a critic of art and dance that he made his name, a métier to which he brought an open mind and diplomatic finesse.

Though Rudolf seldom read Nigel's dance criticism, he would "never miss reading [him] on art," said Maude, who recalled how "astonished" Nigel was by Rudolf's "quick mind" and "instinctive knowledge" of painting, art and music. He was equally struck by Rudolf's metamorphic temperament, by turns "shrewd, tough, easily hurt and cynical. The acute sensibilities of a forest pygmy seem preserved in a member of the jet set." The forest pygmy in Rudolf made sustained concentration difficult. His method of thinking was, as Gosling described it, "lateral and spasmodic . . . a series of blinding flashes rather than a steady gleam."

In awe of Rudolf's talent, Gosling was, by all accounts, in love with him, too. "He knew that in his middle age he had suddenly come upon a young man that was the biggest talent he'd ever met in his life," explains Jane Hermann, a New York friend and the former director of presentations at the Metropolitan Opera House, who often stayed with them in London. "He adored Rudolf. He wasn't so much critical as amused by his naughty-boy quality. It was the antithesis of the wellborn Englishman. Here was this raw, brilliant talent who was basically self-educated and a peasant, who felt that he had the right to behave in almost any way he wished. Nigel found great humor in that." The Dutch choreographer Rudi van Dantzig, another houseguest, had a similar impression. "They were both at his feet from the first days. Rudolf was Nigel and Maude's spoiled child. Like a mother, Maude could sometimes see his bad sides, but Nigel was always boiling over with admiration and love."

With the Goslings Rudolf behaved as any coddled son might. He used their home as a base and regularly rang them in the middle of the night whenever he needed to talk. The Gosling household's casual, familial atmosphere provided him with the kind of balance he had known at the Pushkins' and earlier, at the Volkensteins'. "Nigel and Maude were like my family, a foundation stone in my life, a base which I could pull towards or push away from."

If Nigel suggested the gentle Pushkin, Maude was no Xenia. She never criticized Rudolf, nor did she ever try to guide or advise him, even though Rudolf regularly asked her for her opinion of his performances. "Although we came to love him like a son, I never tried to be his mother. That would have been an insult to his own mother, whom he adored." Rather, she saw to it that Rudolf had "a quiet, peaceful place so he could come in, pick up any books he likes, plop himself down on the sofa and not talk if he doesn't want to, which is very often, and be left alone." They were there for him "when he wanted to talk to us. If he didn't want to, he wouldn't." Everything was geared to his needs.

That was how he remembered his early childhood, and in Maude, Rudolf saw the mother he knew before Hamet returned from the war. In later years, he liked to recall a dream he had as a child. "My mother was so very happy and she told me again on the phone about it, that when . . . as a child, I was very cheerful. Cheerful. And very happy. And one night I was laughing a lot. Just laughing, laughing, laughing. So happy. Golden Age!"

While Rudolf's presence "filled the house," Maude never considered him demanding or arrogant. "No, in fact he was rather tentative. He had a very light, soft voice. He spoke very little. If one word would do, he never used three. He understood the English language but he didn't like to speak it because he was afraid of making a grammatical error and he never wrote it because he thought he might spell it wrongly. He hated to make a mistake." Rudolf never kept diaries and, once in the West, rarely jotted so much as a note. In all the years of their friendship, the Goslings received only two postcards from him, while bags of fan mail multiplied, unopened, in their home.

On a moment's notice, the Goslings would drop everything to accommodate him, prompting many of their friends to wonder whether they didn't pay him more attention than they did their own son, Nicholas, who was four years Rudolf's junior. Rudolf sometimes wondered this himself. Maude made him chicken broth to take to rehearsals and had a steak waiting when he got home. Her close friend Muriel Monkhouse—Tiny, as she was called—lived with the Goslings and helped cook the meals. On performance days, they didn't sit down to eat until after midnight. After dinner, Nicholas would often set up the projector so that Rudolf could watch the films his parents had rented for him. Their "Roxy nights," as Rudolf called them, went on for years, until he had seen all the great classic films he'd missed in his youth, those by Eisenstein and Chaplin and the Marx Brothers. Occasionally Nigel would bring home "blue" movies for him, recalls Joan Thring. "Nigel would ask me to ask Rudolf if he had any favorites. He was so fond of Rudolf and he loved to see him laugh. We'd set up a screen and sit on the sofa. None of us were embarrassed; it was quite extraordinary, really."

His close friendship with Rudolf placed Nigel in a curious position: He was mentor, adviser and father figure to a dancer he regularly reviewed. While he wrote about Rudolf with marked insight and feeling, he could not look at him dispassionately as other critics could. Rudolf knew that he could depend on the Goslings, and knew, too, that he could trust them never to be indiscreet. Even when they came to write his books about Rudolf, first *The Nureyev Valentino* and *The Nureyev Image* and later *Fonteyn and Nureyev*, they offered nary a glimpse into his emotional and sexual lives. They also chose not to reveal their own enduring friendship with him. So gentle is their approach and so strong their sense of decorum that nowhere in their ruminations on Nureyev's major roles, works and career highlights is Rudolf shown in anything but a flattering, golden light. The closest they come to criticism is to refer to Rudolf's "Protean complication of character." The more turbulent forces that drove him remain hidden from public view. As the guardian of the Nureyev legend, Gosling was no more inclined to speak ill of him than to fight in a war.

Another trusted friend of those years was the dancer Lynn Seymour, with whom Rudolf had first become friendly on the 1963 American tour. Insomniacs both, they liked to chat on the phone after performances and frequently bumped into each other at galleries, clubs and movies. The Kabuki flavor of *Images of Love*, made a short time later, prompted Rudolf to dub her Kabuki Lil, a nickname he soon shortened to Lil. Waifish, flamboyant and, like Rudolf, an outsider, the Canadian-born Seymour was to become the great dance actress of her generation, at once headstrong and expressive both on and off the stage. The "flower child" of the Royal Ballet, as Richard Buckle called her, Seymour was more rounded of figure and bolder than her British colleagues, qualities Kenneth MacMillan would later put to good use in the many roles he made for her. Like Rudolf, she had struggled against an imperfect body. "We both felt we had to work extra hard to get anywhere near where our peers were. That's where our affection for one another grew." A bent for lusty language also bound them, as did a shared sense of the absurd, which frequently saw them convulsed with giggles in the studio.

WITH BEATLEMANIA in full swing, twenty-six-year-old Rudolf, like all of Britain, longed to meet the Fab Four. Thring knew their publicist, Wendy Hanson, who arranged to take him backstage after one of their concerts in Hammersmith. But the Beatles were watching TV, one set per Beatle, and merely mumbled, "Oh, hi," in Rudolf's direction. More typical was the response of Marlene Dietrich, who stopped by his dressing room one night just as Rudolf was on his way to dinner with Sean Connery, then the star of the James Bond films, whose wife, Diane Cilento, was a friend of Thring's. Rudolf had met Dietrich only briefly backstage in New York and now promptly invited her to join them at the Caprice, together with Thring and the Connerys. But when Thring arrived at the restaurant, ahead of Rudolf, Dietrich was seated at a table for two. "I have a tête-à-tête with Rudolf," the actress, then in her sixties, informed Thring. "Well, I'm afraid you don't," Thring corrected her, somehow managing to usher the "peeved" Dietrich to the larger table. "She was mad about him." At dinner, she insisted on talking about how much she loved potatoes and peasants. Finally, Connery had had enough. "Fuck off, Marlene," he said. "You've never loved a peasant in your life!"

From the Caprice, they went on to a party in Chelsea, where the first person to greet them was April Ashley, "a famous sex change," says Thring. "She used to be George the sailor." Rudolf was riveted by her. Ashley, however, was riveted by Dietrich, and started gushing about how she had been a fan since the age of eight. Clearly irritated at this unwitting reference to her age, Dietrich demanded that Rudolf take her home. Fearing that Dietrich might "chain him to the bed," Rudolf begged Thring to take her off his hands, but she refused. "I'll drive her home," he said, "if you promise you'll wait here for me. If I'm not back in twenty minutes, you come get me.'"

He returned safely in one piece, though Dietrich did not give up. Having made a tracing of him from a newspaper photograph, she slipped it under his door one night when he wasn't home. "With love from Marlene," she wrote. Still, in her memoir, published in 1989, his slights to her vanity did not go unpunished. "I've never known a vainer man," she wrote, recalling how he constantly complained of having legs that were too short. "My job was to assure him that this was not the case, that he was perfect on stage." Seeing Baryshnikov, she added in a final coup de grace, always made her think "of Nureyev and his fixation." To her mind, Baryshnikov had not only ideal proportions but greater confidence, a sense of balance she attributed "to the fact that he loves women. He's not a loner. . . . He's healthy, thank God!"

While Rudolf enjoyed a special rapport with women, his interest in them was primarily social or aesthetic, not sexual. He admired beauty wherever he found it, but while he occasionally had liaisons with women, he rarely made much effort to bed the opposite sex. Not that much effort had ever been required, as his experiences with Xenia, Ninel Kurgapkina and Maria Tallchief had shown him. "He had female lovers, whom he'd get fascinated with for a while," says Lynn Seymour. Indeed, despite his appeal to both genders, the majority of his fans were female and there was never any shortage of women wanting to sleep with him. "Some socialite beauty would throw herself at him and he couldn't resist." Lee Radziwill was apparently one of the few to succeed. A number of their friends have remarked on how persistent she was. "Lee kept pushing and Rudolf finally just gave in," says one of them. "It wasn't a real affair, just one or two nights. She thought so much of herself that probably when she got him into bed, she thought that was it, there would be no more of anything else. She got very possessive with him." Radziwill, her husband and their two young children lived in a three-story Georgian town house near Buckingham Palace, staffed by a cook, a butler, two maids and a nanny. By all accounts, her marriage to "Stas" Radziwill was not a happy one. Though Rudolf was often cavalier to her, "she didn't seem to care," recalls a mutual friend, who hosted them both at her home on numerous occasions. "She had these romantic ideas about him." Her third husband, the director Herbert Ross, speculates that "women were simply attracted by that sort of raw animal quality he had. There was always a slight element of danger with him." For her part, Lee couldn't see what Rudolf saw in Erik. "He was cold," she recalled years later, "but he must have had something because Rudolf was crazy about him."

Even when he didn't want to sleep with women, Rudolf courted their adoration. "Part of his charm was to get women to fawn all over him," says Jane Hermann, who knew him for sixteen years. "Gay or straight, he flirted like crazy." And young or old as well. Edward Albee would occasionally invite his mother to join them for lunch at New York's "21" Club and recalls how "fascinating" it was to watch the interplay between them. "Here was this sixty-year-old woman deeply enamored of Rudolf and he was absolutely *charming*, laying it on with a trowel."

For a long time, Rudolf didn't define himself as being homosexual. "He saw himself as a sexual being," says Querube Arias, Fonteyn's stepdaughter. "There was a sexual element to all his relationships." Eventually he would turn exclusively to men for sexual fulfillment. "With women, you have to work so hard and it's not very satisfying for me," he told Violette Verdy years later. "With men, it's very quick. Big pleasure."

But since men in the sixties weren't as free to throw themselves at him as were women, Rudolf "had to go looking for them," recalls Thring. His separations from Erik made monogamy increasingly difficult, and Rudolf's love for him did not preclude frequent brief encounters. Keyed up after performances, he found it hard to relax and rarely managed more than five hours' sleep. Often he went walking late at night, frequently on the hunt for sexual adventure. His sexual charisma, a wellspring of his power onstage, was no less potent once the curtain came down. After giving entirely of himself in performance and spending the better of the day preparing for it, he would indulge his body afterward. Sex, like a good meal, momentarily replenished him. His supreme self-confidence derived in part from the pride he took in being "prodigiously endowed," as one of his lovers described him. The filmmaker Derek Jarman remembered seeing Nureyev on the King's Road late at night. "Rudi used to go [there] because a lot of people just walked up and down it." According to Michael Wishart, another fixture of the London scene, Rudolf went in for "rough-trade pickups, sailors, lorry drivers and the like. He was not attracted to conspicuously effeminate men."

His favorite haunts were small, furtive bars like The Arts and Battledress. La Douce was where the mods went; open until dawn, it had a coffee bar upstairs and a small dance floor downstairs. These places attracted a predominantly homosexual clientele, though Rudolf was "nervous to be alone in them. He felt it was bad for his image," recalls Thring, who regularly accompanied him. With his profound distrust of strangers, he worried about being watched and arrested. Spotting someone he liked, he would send Thring over "to be nice to him." Afterward she would drop both of them at Rudolf's flat and then go home. His visitors rarely stayed on past morning. Sometimes Thring set him up with men she knew, like the blond Australian model he went home with one night who afterward complained that he had to do all the work.

These dalliances were, by their very nature, transitory. Sex was one thing, intimacy another, and for Rudolf the two were not the same. For Erik, they were. The danger in one-night stands and anonymous sex held little appeal for him, and he could not accept Rudolf's promiscuity, which he viewed as a betrayal. He was "horrified by Rudi's enormous appetite for people, as a lover, physically," recalls Glen Tetley. "Erik was a very fastidious person, he was basically very chaste, and he could not condone Rudolf's appetite."

To Rudolf's friend Antoinette Sibley, his rapacious sexual drive was simply part and parcel of his approach to life. "He certainly loved sex, but whatever he did, he did to the nth degree. I don't think sex was any different from anything else." Occasionally, Rudolf and Thring gatecrashed late-night parties. The host of one of these, Ned Sherrin, the producer of the satirical television revue *That Was the Week That Was,* recalled how Rudolf "would enter confidently, sure that a host was delighted to see him, patrol the room in a businesslike fashion, and leave quite soon, with whoever he had decided would be his companion for the night." The West was understandably a libidinal paradise to a man banned from expressing his desire during all his years in Russia. For the first time in his life, he had the license to do as he chose and the opportunities to choose whom he wanted. Not that homosexuality was condoned by the English courts. In the early sixties, homosexual acts were criminally punishable, with the maximum penalty of life imprisonment. Though the landmark Wolfenden Report of 1956 had called for the legalizing of homosexual acts between consenting adults in private, it would not become law until 1967; in the interim, the subject was "frequently discussed both inside and outside Parliament."

At a time when well-known figures went to great lengths to mask their homosexual liaisons, Rudolf was relatively open about his sexuality. "He never denied it among friends who were gay," recalls Edward Albee. "But who knows how far the openness went?" John Lanchbery, who led the orchestra for most of Nureyev's appearances with the Royal Ballet, insists that "the gay world knew he was gay all right. He would go to a bar and choose a young man and negotiate a price, or whatever. He was quite blatant." As Christopher Gable and many others describe him, Rudolf was "constantly surrounded by adulation and sexual approval."

To the gay men of the era, Nureyev became a kind of icon. In a letter to the reclusive aesthete Stephen Tennant, Michael Wishart described a week of Nureyev performances in decidedly nondance terms. "A Royal Gala in which he danced beautifully the pas de deux from . . . La Sylphide in a fetching (Danish) kilt and pretty tartan socks. Also an unworthy jaunty number in an angora polo necked pullover and charming girlish white tights. . . . Then he was Actaeon in gold-lamé. . . . Last night as Solor . . . he was a god, a man, a bird, himself. A lovely white feather bolt upright from his turban and a sequin décolleté."

Although his relationship with Bruhn was an open secret in the ballet world, Nureyev never discussed it publicly, and rarely privately, even with his closest friends. For all his flamboyance and adventuring, Nureyev was an exceptionally concealed man, with an intense inner life he largely kept to himself. "He never talked about his relationships," says Lynn Seymour. "Occasionally this little thing would drop, but it was never very specific. I think Rudolf liked companionship but also treasured his solitude and was always afraid of anyone getting too close somehow."

The press, in any case, consigned their relationship to the closet and, in the parlance of the times, referred to Bruhn as Nureyev's "great friend." The press was more complicit in those days and wouldn't have considered Nureyev's exploits with men news that was fit to print. But since sex lay at the heart of Nureyev's allure and image, it was natural enough that the media should play up his magnetic presence onstage and his large female following offstage. "When he leaves the theater," reported Time, "hordes of glaze-eyed females of all ages have been known to surround his car and fall on their knees chanting 'Thank you, thank you.' "

Still, Nureyev knew to fear the censure of a gossip-hungry press and shrewdly protected his public persona. His frequent social appearances with Fonteyn and other high-profile women proved a useful decoy. Yet unlike many other closeted gay celebrities, Nureyev never cultivated a belief that he was heterosexual. For years he gamely fielded questions from journalists about whom he was going to marry. He never spoke the whole truth, but he never lied. Was he thinking of ever getting married? "No, no, I never want to be locked in cage," he told Don Short of the *Daily Mirror* (London) in late 1963. "To me ballet is too important. Everything else must be sacrificed for it. There must be no obstacles." To a reporter from *Time* magazine, he declared in 1965 that "women are silly, every one of them, but stronger than sailors. They just want to drink you dry and leave you to die of weakness." He could not accept love unless it was mutual, he told Leon Harris in a 1968 interview for *Esquire*. "It is a big prison when you are in love or are loved. Jesus! Love is what you look for all your life, every second, every day. But when it is somebody there with the love pouring out of them, it kills you when it's unwanted, it kills you. Why ruin my life, some girl's life? I don't want to marry."

Over the years his answers grew increasingly coy, though he continued to dodge the subject of his homosexuality. And how's your sex life? asked the intrepid Sally Quinn of *The Washington Post* in 1974. "Sporadic," Rudolf replied. "Oh but the ladies will be so disappointed with that tiny morsel," she persisted. "The ladies," he replied, "will just have to remain tense."

"To know what it is to make love as a man and woman is special knowledge," he told Elizabeth Kaye in a 1990 interview for *Esquire*, just the sort of quotable, cryptic comment he was fond of making.

To audiences of the 1960s, however, Nureyev was heterosexual and probably Fonteyn's lover as well. MARGOT, MY PERFECT PARTNER—BY NUREYEV was a typical headline. The success of *Marguerite and Armand* was due in no small measure to the public's belief that there really was a correlation between the on- and offstage passions of its stars. "It was as though the audience was watching through the keyhole," recalled Violette Verdy, a popular guest at the Royal Ballet in the 1960s. "And you also thought that maybe, maybe, hopefully, the whole thing really was a bedroom. . . ." The heat they gave off onstage, and the fact that they were often seen together, fed rumors of an affair which persist to this day. Even among their closest friends and colleagues, the nature of their relationship continues to be a subject of debate. Everyone has an opinion, but few have any facts.

Were they lovers? That depends on who is telling the story.

Fonteyn evaded the question in her autobiography. "As I was obviously very fond of Rudolf and spent so much time with him, it was food for scandal to those who liked it that way. I decided there was little I could do but wait for it to pass. The truth will out eventually, I thought." But how truthful is Fonteyn's autobiography? Keith Money calls it "Margot's best-case scenario," as good a description as any of most personal memoirs. "She has perfected the art of answering questions at length and saying absolutely nothing," Buckle once wrote of her. "She would never, even under torture, admit that pink was her favourite colour for fear of offending orange and mauve." Certainly her life with Tito Arias improves in the telling; the portrait she paints of wedded bliss was not one her intimates recognized. At the very least, her memoir obscures some plainer truths.

The pair had met in 1937, when Fonteyn was just eighteen and on tour with the Sadler's Wells Ballet in Cambridge, where Tito was a student. At a party one night, she saw him dance the rumba and fell instantly in love. His feelings for her, however, remained a mystery, as did Tito himself, who "never stayed long" and "vanished again as mysteriously as he had come." His father had been briefly president of Panama and Tito himself had his sights set on a political career. Soon he sailed for Panama, leaving Fonteyn heartbroken. When they took up again the following May, her feelings had barely diminished, "but were now fenced in for self-protection." They saw each other only briefly after that, once for lunch and once for supper, and then not a word passed between them for another twelve years.

Fonteyn had long imagined herself married by the age of thirty-five, at which point she assumed she would retire. But at the age of thirty-four, she felt lonely and incomplete. There had been an affair with the urbane and hard-drinking Constant Lambert, the company's brilliant longtime musical director, and another, "recklessly passionate" one with French choreographer Roland Petit. Both affairs, however, went unmentioned in Fonteyn's autobiography.

The day Tito Arias reentered her life, Fonteyn was preparing to dance *The Sleeping Beauty* at the old Met in New York. Suddenly a stage doorman brought a visiting card to her dressing room. "Roberto E. Arias, Delegate of Panama to the United Nations," it said. The gentleman, she was told, would return at the end of the ballet. But at intermission, there he stood at her dressing room door, looking very fat, she thought, with chubby cheeks, a far cry from the slender dark-haired boy she had loved. The next morning, he woke her and insisted on coming up for breakfast, whereupon he asked her to marry him. Fonteyn assumed he was joking, a strange joke to be sure, given that he was married with three children. Fonteyn barely took him seriously. They were practically strangers by then. This time around, however, he persisted, showering her with roses, diamond Cartier bracelets and compliments. For the party he threw in her honor, he sent thirty-word telegrams to each guest. In Los Angeles, he was determined to impress her with his famous friends Merle Oberon, Danny Kaye and John Wayne, who loaned them his boat for a day trip to Catalina Island. By Christmas, she had agreed to marry him, won over by his charm and keen mind. Many of her friends looked askance at this unlikely union and wondered whether she hadn't talked herself into loving him. Though Ashton gave her his blessing, he distrusted Arias and his "gold bracelets, pomaded hair and glib Latin charm." Fonteyn was admittedly vulnerable to the headstrong Tito, but her eyes were open: Life with Tito, she assured herself, would never be boring.

The next few years were proof of that. Their wedding in February 1955 was a media circus.There were so many photographers jammed into the tiny Panamanian consulate in Paris that she could barely hear the ceremony above the explosion of shutters. Two years later came Tito's farcical coup attempt in Panama. Politics consumed him and he was forever flying off to Panama to plot revolution or run for office when he wasn't serving as ambassador. His business affairs were also filled with intrigue.

Fonteyn reveled in the heady mix of power, art and glamour that life with Tito brought her. She met Castro and Churchill and Jordan's King Hussein. She went for cruises on the *Christina* with Tito's longtime crony Aristotle Onassis and his lover, Maria Callas. Juggling two careers, Fonteyn dutifully fulfilled her obligations as an ambassador's wife. Hardly anyone would have suspected that she approached much of it with great trepidation. People only noticed that she did it all so efficiently and so well. "We were all so jealous of Margot," concedes Princesss Margaret. "She was so endowed with talent. . . . She'd get up to say a few words on the spot and they'd be beautifully expressed." According to his daughter Querube, Tito saw himself as Margot's protector, a role Fonteyn both encouraged and accepted. Querube, who regularly stayed with them on school vacations and later joined Fonteyn on tours, recalls that they liked to spend many hours "talking away" about politics and ballet gossip. Her father, she says, thought of Margot "like those figures in the ballets, like a Giselle that needed taking care of. She wouldn't take any steps without him." As late as 1990 Fonteyn said in a television documentary: "Until I married Tito I had absolutely no idea who I was offstage. And then I married him and I knew: I was Mrs. Tito de Arias."

Yet tales of his philandering are legion. Her mother had warned her before their marriage that she wouldn't be the only woman in his life. Being half Brazilian, "she knew what it was all about," explains Theodora Christon, Fonteyn's longtime private secretary in New York. "I don't think B.Q. quite approved of him." Neither did many of Fonteyn's friends after Tito made passes at other women in Fonteyn's presence. Even their closest Panamanian friend, Louis Martinz, recalled how Tito had "this girlfriend whom he would have to the house who was a society woman, not just some hooker."

Fonteyn was hardly blind to his womanizing—"oh, that's one of Tito's ladies," she once surprised Theodora Christon by saying—but she endured it nonetheless. "We all knew what was going on, but nobody talked about it. She just took it as part of what he was and accepted it." Keith Money, who disliked Tito intensely and eventually fell out with her over him, chalked up her equanimity to her coping mechanism. "Margot's way of getting through life was to have sort of steel bulkheads like in a ship, and if she couldn't cope with something, whatever, a relationship, a problem, whatever, if she couldn't solve it by dusk, it went into a box, the box went into the cupboard, the cupboard was locked and the key was thrown away." Still, there were times when his philandering, and her inability to track him down, made her anxious and unhappy. Once, when Tito's secretary was spending too much time in their company, Fonteyn confessed that she "didn't know how much more she could take."

Rudolf "hated" the way Tito treated her. "He was quite nice to him for her sake," says Thring, "but he didn't approve of him." No doubt he was also put off by Tito's high-handedness and lack of interest in ballet. Not only did Tito refer to Rudolf as "that crazy Russian," but much as he admired his wife's talent, he seldom attended an entire performance. "He only went to the act he liked," says his daughter Querube. "Margot wanted him to be there, so he'd say, 'Okay, Swan Lake, I'll see Act Three.' So she would tell him the exact hour to be there."

There is no question that Nureyev and Fonteyn loved each other deeply; one only had to see how she lit up in his presence or the way they laughed conspiratorially to feel the bond between them. "There was a real connection between them, in many ways more than with Tito," says Joy Williams Brown, a close friend for thirty years. "She never pretended not to love him." Louis Martinz, who was briefly a lover of Nureyev's, described Fonteyn as "a lady with two great loves: her husband and Rudolf." She was in any case fiercely loyal to both: She would turn down opportunities to dance major ballets with other partners if they happened to be ballets in Rudolf's repertory and she never approved photographs of them that didn't make Rudolf look good as well. But according to Maude Gosling, she was careful not to overstep the bounds of propriety and was therefore "less generous in her praise of Rudolf than she would like to have been because she didn't want to upset Tito."

In the minds of those who tended to them daily, Rudolf's preference for men, Fonteyn's allegiance to Tito and common sense ruled out an affair between them. Bruhn once described his partnership with Carla Fracci as "a love affair without scars," one "consummated on the stage," and this was how most of Fonteyn's intimates saw her passion for Rudolf. To Joan Thring the idea that they had anything more than a close friendship is "completely out of the question. A love affair between them, as well as dancing together, would have destroyed some part of it sooner or later. Margot wasn't that silly. She wouldn't have jeopardized it. I was with them so much, I would have seen something, and there was never any sign of anything like that." There are those who think that Rudolf would never have put a partnership so central to his career at risk. Theodora Christon, who had regular access to Fonteyn during her tours to America, is equally dismissive. "Number one, he liked boys. So the idea that he was hopping into her bed was kind of ridiculous to those of us who knew the whole thing." "Go next door and find out what the boy is doing," she would instruct Christon. "And be careful to knock." "They didn't have the same circle of friends," insists Christon, "and the Dame was very much in love with her husband."

Many of Rudolf's closest friends also doubt they were ever lovers. "Although there was all the gossip, I was around at the time, and I didn't get any sense," says Seymour. "With Margot it's so unlikely. She worshiped her husband. I don't think it would have occurred to her. Rudolf adored and respected her, but I think it was a very deep friendship."

Still others find it credible. "We all suspected it," says Georgina Parkinson. "Knowing the people involved, it's not unlikely," concurs Jane Hermann, who met them both in the mid-1970s. "Rudolf was an extremely sexual animal. Anybody who knew them would say without question that they deeply loved each other. Whether or not that love was consummated, neither ever told me." Another well-placed source claims that they were lovers for years and that Fonteyn was exceedingly jealous of Rudolf's female friends.

The few direct comments attributed to Rudolf are characteristically inconsistent. His friend Genya Polyakov recalled Rudolf's confiding that they had indeed been lovers. Having shared many such confidences with Nureyev during the last years of his life in Paris, Polyakov saw no reason to doubt him. "He said that Margot liked the physical side of their relationship, but he said it a lot more crudely." Of all the women in his life, Maude included, Margot was the one with whom he felt the keenest rapport, even if he sometimes spoke of her disparagingly. "I've got to push that old woman around," Michael Wishart recalled him saying. Still, he trusted her completely and late in his life he told several friends that he should have married her. However, by then Fonteyn was dying and the remark seems to have been filtered through regret.

From time to time Nureyev would hint to various lovers that several women had become pregnant by him, without naming names. According to one biographer's undocumented and highly speculative account, the forty-five-year-old Fonteyn was one of them. Medical evidence, however, appears to discount that possibility. Theodora Christon, a registered nurse when she worked for Fonteyn, insists that Fonteyn experienced numerous gynecological problems throughout her career and stopped menstruating prematurely, a fairly common occurrence among professional dancers and athletes. When Fonteyn became ill with ovarian cancer in the late 1980s, her doctors needed to know whether she had ever been pregnant. Fonteyn said that she had not, recalls her stepdaughter Querube, who oversaw her care until her death. If that claim is true, it seems unlikely that Fonteyn would have lied at that stage of life, particularly when her health was at issue.

IN APRIL 1964, with Erik's Albrecht vivid in his mind,* Rudolf set out for Australia, where he and Fonteyn were to dance *Giselle* and *Swan Lake* with the Australian Ballet. This was the same fledgling company that Bruhn and Arova had danced with in late 1962, when Rudolf had flown from London to Sydney to see their performances. Nureyev and Fonteyn were to dance four times a week during the monthlong tour, which included stops in Sydney and Melbourne. Before the trip to Australia, Fonteyn had flown to Panama, to spend several days with Tito on the campaign trail. It was on this trip that, according to several sources, she came face-to-face with the fact that Tito was having an affair with the wife of a political crony.

Whatever her state of mind, she arrived in Sydney to find that she had to work much harder to keep pace with her younger partner. She recalled how when they had first danced *Giselle* together, Rudolf was relatively inexperienced and had performed with "something of an amateur's enthusiasm." But as the newness had worn off, he had begun whipping himself into a rage almost nightly, to generate the necessary excitement. Fonteyn was only too aware of his "looking around for an excuse, no matter how flimsy, to shout one or two profanities before an important evening." His method worked well, even if a few hapless souls "had to be sacrificed in a good cause," she wrote, characteristically putting a positive spin on a dicey situation.

In Melbourne, the lure of Nureyev and Fonteyn drew record numbers to the ballet, despite unheard-of ticket prices and long queues. The daily press was full of complaints about the prices, but that didn't deter thirty-five hundred people from packing the Palais Theatre nightly from

*In the two years since his London debut in the role, Rudolf had revised his interpretation. In the fall of 1964, critic Fernau Hall assessed the changes in *Ballet Today*: "In his desire to show Albrecht as tortured by guilt, he previously made him too soft and so spineless . . . but this time he achieved a proper balance between the vacillations and weakness caused by guilt and the proper manly pride of a man in love; between the assumed simple manner of a villager and the noble presence of an aristocrat. . . . In Act II his performance was one of the finest I have ever seen. . . . His fusion of acting and dancing was specially strong in his performance of the *double tours en l'air*: to do this step at all, a dancer must use considerable strength, elevation and speed, yet Nureyev somehow managed to make the turns slow and elegiac, canted slightly forward and expressing growing exhaustion as well as his tender feelings for Giselle. Only a dancer with complete command of the technique of the step could so alter its style and impact, in harmony with the dramatic situation."

May 5 to May 16. Having read about twenty-minute ovations in London and New York, the crowd did their best "to beat the record for clapping." The "point of interest," noted one critic, "was that the curtain was not bounced up and down to drag out the applause. It was down for 10 seconds at a time, before rising again." Their fourth act pas de deux from *Swan Lake*, wrote another critic in a typically breathless assessment, was "one of the loveliest love duets ever seen in Melbourne."

As the exotic novelty on the tour, Rudolf was happier than Fonteyn had ever seen him. He was delighted to be onstage nearly every night, and had grown more accustomed to life on the road. Still, by the end of the tour, they were both anxious to get home, Rudolf to Copenhagen to see Bruhn dance with the Danes, and Fonteyn to Miami for a rendezvous with Tito on her birthday. Stopping off at London Airport on his way to Denmark, Rudolf was met by the now-familiar gaggle of reporters. The *Evening News* recorded that "a girl met and kissed Rudolf Nureyev on arrival at London Airport today, sat with him for two hours in a lounge and then kissed him goodbye when he flew off on holiday." The girl was Joan Thring.

The same day, Fonteyn arrived in Miami to discover that Tito was still in Panama, where he was preoccupied with his candidacy for the National Assembly. He couldn't get away, he said when she telephoned. The election votes were still being counted. Anxious to see him, and presumably to make her presence felt, she flew to Panama. But Tito was too embroiled in the election to pay her much notice. Feeling lost in the shuffle, she soon left for Stuttgart, for yet another round of performances with Rudolf.

20

Nureyev and Fonteyn

RUDOLF HAD SENSED that something was wrong even before the photographers pounced. It was June 8 and he and Margot were in the English spa town of Bath for the opening of Yehudi Menuhin's annual music festival, during which they were due to perform. They were returning from dinner with Joan Thring and Keith Money when Menuhin's wife, the former ballerina Diana Gould, intercepted them and, pulling Fonteyn aside, whispered to her urgently, "Tito has been shot. He's alive and in the hospital." Fonteyn had long feared that Tito might be gunned down and now "the dreaded thing had happened." The photographers, meanwhile, were jostling one another, vying to snap photographs of Rudolf and Margot together. "They were trying to make a big affair out of them," remembers Thring. Although neither Thring nor Rudolf was sure of what Gould had said, Thring saw that she had to get Rudolf away from the press. "I told him to find out where his room was and to go and stay there until I came for him. He didn't question it at all, he just went."

Thring immediately called Panama, no easy feat, while Fonteyn sat in her hotel room with Kenneth MacMillan and Money, drinking brandy to still her nerves. Finally, Thring managed to piece together enough details to give Fonteyn some news. But the moment she began to speak, Fonteyn screamed and ran down the hallway to a vacant ballroom, unable to listen. There, Rudolf and Thring found her crumpled in an armchair, crying. Rudolf took her in his arms and tried to calm her down. It was another four hours before she allowed Thring to tell her any more. "I told Margot who shot him. She said I had it wrong. Then I made her talk to her brother-in-law, and I didn't have it wrong. I told her if she wanted to see Tito alive, she had to go now." Fonteyn spoke to Tito's brother, but the connection was poor. Should she come straightaway? she asked him. She had a premiere the next night. Was it all right if she came after that? "Out of danger," she heard him say. So she decided to stay.

The next day's rehearsal was palpably tense. During a run-through of *Divertimento*, a new pas de deux created for them by MacMillan before the Australian tour, Fonteyn understandably lost her way, at a moment when she was to have been mirroring Rudolf's quirky, sinuous movements. The duet showed them as "mythical creatures performing some insect-like ritual," said Keith Money, who photographed it. With help from Rudolf and MacMillan, Fonteyn recovered her composure— so much so, in fact, that by the evening's performance, she was able to dance the work twice: the second time, after an encore was demanded.*

The next day she flew to Panama. The uncertainty of her situation only underscored for Rudolf the enormous load he was then shouldering himself: He had been commissioned by the Spoleto-based Festival of Two Worlds to stage the entire three acts of *Raymonda* for the Royal Ballet touring section, its junior company. He and Fonteyn were to star in the ballet's premiere one month later and were to dance every performance. This was to be Rudolf's first evening-length production, and while he knew the ballet well, he had never danced its leading male role.† Naturally Fonteyn's departure prompted anxious moments.

Raymonda was Petipa's last success, made in 1898, and though popular in Russia (the daunting title role was among Dudinskaya's greatest), it was virtually unknown in the West. One reason was its complicated plot. A chivalric tale of manly virtue, *Raymonda* told the story of Jean de Brienne, who, returning from the Crusades to marry his betrothed, is forced to fight a rival to win her hand. While Rudolf had stuck pretty closely to the Kirov production in reconstructing *La Bayadère*, he was more ambitious in his staging of *Raymonda* and stripped the ballet to its bare essentials, the better to showcase its lively dancing. He now kept as much of the choreography as he could remember and added to it some connecting passages and dances of his own. He dispensed with the long passages of mime, convinced that audiences were intelligent enough not to need "all those traffic directions." Crammed with steps, his dances

---

*They also performed the pas de deux from *La Sylphide*.
†At the Kirov, he had performed only in the male pas de quatre, one of the chief variations of the last act.

were filled with the kinds of technical challenges in which he reveled. Fonteyn had always hoped the whole three-act ballet would be done for her; she liked movement she could "attack," and the ballet's panache and color greatly appealed to her.

With the timing of Fonteyn's return uncertain, Rudolf partnered the two ballerinas who stepped in for her: Lynn Seymour in *La Sylphide* at the Bath Festival, and Annette Page in *The Sleeping Beauty* in London. "We were all so worried for Margot," says Seymour. "The news got horribler and horribler and things became more unsure." In Panama, Fonteyn struggled with grim realities. She was shocked to find Tito strapped to a narrow table, unable to move even his head. A tube protruded from a hole in his neck and drugs were fed to him intravenously. Two bullets had lodged in his chest; another had punctured his lung; a fourth had struck him in the back of his neck, near his spine. He was paralyzed, permanently, as it would turn out, though Fonteyn admittedly "refused to conceive the possibility of permanent, serious injury" for a long time to come. The forty-seven-year-old Tito had been shot by Alfredo Jimenez, a disgruntled associate, who had intercepted his car at an intersection and shot him at point-blank range. One story had it that he was angry that Tito was sleeping with his wife. Tito's version was that he had refused to fudge election results to make Jimenez his substitute deputy, as Jimenez had requested. Jimenez would never be brought to trial, leading Tito's detractors to conclude that it was a crime of passion. The press, however, reported it as a political crime.

Over the next few days, Tito regained his ability to speak. Together with his doctor, Fonteyn decided to have Tito transferred to England's Stoke Mandeville Hospital, a renowned spinal injuries center. Would it be safe for her to leave? she had asked his doctor. She had performances in London and would fly back immediately if Tito was in danger. There was only one kind of danger they need worry about, the doctor replied, and in that case, "you would be too late."

Two weeks after the shooting, Fonteyn was back onstage in London. In quick succession, she managed *La Bayadère*, *Giselle*, and *Marguerite and Armand*, six performances in total over ten days, while rehearsing Rudolf's *Raymonda* at the same time. Struck by her resilience, Rudolf prescribed his favorite curative, giving her an unwieldy solo that would have taxed any ballerina under the best of circumstances. But Fonteyn never complained, even though Rudolf would have accommodated her if she had. When Keith Money proposed that he might want to trim a bit here and there to make it easier on her, Rudolf surprised him by saying, "Oh! They not do that in Russia! I just gave it to her, to see how she do it!"

Fonteyn left for Spoleto the day after Tito arrived in England for

treatment at Stoke Mandeville.* The strain began to show. Fonteyn injured a calf muscle and Rudolf was "almost dangerously on the boil with
suppressed nerves," Money recorded in his diary. During a rehearsal
break in Spoleto, he whipped a ballet shoe at Thring's head. It smacked
into the scenery, his aim just wide. "Joan just blinked and scarcely broke
stride and said, 'Stop it!' as if she were admonishing a slightly fractious
child." Thring, like Fonteyn, never took his outbursts personally; she
knew that he was angry with himself most of all. On this day he was
unhappy about the sets and costumes, which Beni Montresor, the designer chosen by the festival, had fashioned according to his own ideas
of how best to show off the ballet's two stars. He had done away with
the rich brocades and period details Rudolf had requested and given the
ballet a decidedly modernist look, with colored gauze screens and plain
velvet costumes. The sets were thought to be ill suited to a nineteenth-
century ballet and roundly criticized.† Nureyev's *Raymonda*, as Ashton
described it, was "Petipa seen through the mind and body of Nureyev."
With colleagues, he went further, charging that in cutting out the Russian mime, Nureyev "had left no dramatic element in the ballet." This
approach, as well as the sets and costumes, would need to be rethought,
he advised, before he would consider commissioning it for the main
company.

Raymonda was due to open on July 10 for a nine-day run. The day
before the premiere, Fonteyn was making up her face for the final dress
rehearsal when Thring came backstage with more bad news. Rudolf followed. Tito had suffered a serious relapse, she said. If Fonteyn wanted
to see him alive, she had better get to London at once. There was a
flight at two-thirty leaving from Rome. She was booked on it. Fonteyn
hesitated. She knew how much Rudolf had riding on this *Raymonda* and
there was no one standing by to replace her. But Rudolf insisted that she
go and "was unusually gentle and seemed dreadfully upset for me."
Though he was now without his Raymonda for opening night, he told
her not to think about the ballet. "You must pack and leave right away,"
he said softly, and then escorted her to the hotel to make sure she did.
"He understood she had to go and was not resentful," says Thring. "Peo-

---

*Where he was to remain for the next two years.
†The only person in Spoleto who did appreciate the sets was the American modern dance
pioneer Paul Taylor, the festival's other dance attraction. "His rehearsal had just ended and
mine was about to begin. And he was standing there arguing with the designer, so I butt in
and said, 'Well, I'll take the set if you don't want it.' " Taylor knew who Rudolf was and thought
him "a nice spunky little guy." The two became fast friends, though it would take some convincing on Rudolf's part before Taylor would eventually agree to work with him. During a
performance of his *Aureole* in Spoleto, Taylor caught sight of Rudolf in the wings, trying to
mimic the steps.

ple assume he was always so self-centered, but he was very kind and sweet about it."

He was not as gentle with Fonteyn's stand-in, Doreen Wells, whom he "threw" about the stage "like she was a bag of potatoes" during their quick run-through of the entire ballet. "He'd explain things to her," says Thring, "but she never came out the right way. I thought he was going to kill everybody in sight." At a party that evening at the home of composer Gian-Carlo Menotti, the festival's director, the guests were informed that everyone was to serve himself. "Nureyev never serves himself," he cried, and then threw a plate of spaghetti against a wall. The outburst, like so many others, quickly acquired the status of legend and, with it, an alternate version that it was a glass of wine that was thrown. But related out of context, it encourages a view of Nureyev as Diva, when in fact, he clearly had cause to be distressed. He had just lost his primary partner and had no idea when, or if, she would return to dance with him.*

The premiere did not please him. Wells was intrepid, though uninspired, and the company wasn't entirely up to the challenges he had set for them. But his own dancing won unanimous praise, as did his choreography, even if, as Alexander Bland wrote, "it showed more promise than achievement." The ballet had been announced for the company's fall tour, but its bare-bones setting proved so unpopular that after a visit to Lebanon's Baalbek Festival, it was dropped from the repertory. Undaunted, Nureyev would return to *Raymonda* many times throughout his career.

Despite a harrowing bedside vigil, Fonteyn made it back for the final performance in Spoleto. Tito's heart had stopped beating, his temperature had shot up to 108 degrees, and he had lapsed into a coma. Although he came through the crisis, he permanently lost his speech.† Nevertheless, no one seeing Fonteyn in *Raymonda* would have discerned her distress. Noël Coward, who hadn't much cared for the ballet the first time around, found it "magical" after staying on to see her dance with Nureyev, a performance that brought them thirty-two curtain calls. "She was exquisite," he wrote in his diary, "and her presence lighted up the whole thing . . . the two of them together will go down in my memory as one of the *great* moments of my life in the theater. . . ."

For the first time in weeks, Rudolf showed signs of enjoying himself. He was "just so amused by Noël," with whom he and Thring spent the

---

*To Paul Taylor, who observed the scene firsthand, it was simply another performance. "He knows that Spoletini adore temperament, always expect it from artists, and would feel gypped not to witness any . . . so he generously gives everybody an extra performance by smashing several wine glasses against the wall—stylishly Russian and the only courteous thing to do."

†He would partially regain it, though only those closest to him could make out his rasping sounds.

weekend in Rome, tooling around and visiting the Sistine Chapel. The West End's consummate bon vivant, Coward thought Nureyev "a curious wild animal, very beguiling and fairly unpredictable." Rudolf reveled in the role and actually bit Coward at dinner, "but it was only on the finger and didn't draw blood," wrote Coward, clearly pleased to have been targeted. From there, Rudolf traveled on to Baalbek, Lebanon. In nearby Beirut he insisted on walking around on his own late at night despite the presence of Soviet ships in the harbor. Thring was so worried about his being kidnapped she tried locking him in his room. "Margot and I were like his jailers; we took turns locking him in and he'd be absolutely livid. I'd tell him, 'You only need one Arab to pick you up and sell you to the Russians.' And he'd say, 'Oh, they won't do it, they won't do it,' but he was always slightly edgy about it."

Fonteyn would later say that financial straits had convinced her to rejoin the tour in Baalbek. Tito's campaign had depleted their savings and she was faced with his uncertain prognosis and mounting hospital bills. Her partnership with Nureyev had led to the highest performance fees of her career and she felt she had to keep performing. While this was true, it's more likely that at that moment she needed to get back to the stage, the only place she felt completely at home. "Real life often seemed so much more unreal than the stage, or maybe I should say my identity was clear to me only when I assumed some make-believe character." The role of Mrs. Tito de Arias would test her for the next twenty-five years, which she would spend caring for Tito, who was confined to a wheelchair, paralyzed from the neck down. For the two years Tito was to remain hospitalized, she would travel three hours by train every night to visit him, getting up at dawn to feed him before heading back to London in time for class and rehearsal. She even took driving lessons so she could drive herself to and from the station. After performing, she would rush off, sandwich in hand, to see Tito, then sleep at a nearby hotel. Her devotion was all-encompassing, and Rudolf, like the rest of her friends, could only wonder at it.

The shooting shifted the balance of power between husband and wife. Not only had Fonteyn become his protector, Tito was entirely dependent on her. In time, she took him with her on tour, to dinners and parties and on friends' yachts, determined that his life should be as full as her own. By 1965, she was signing her letters to friends Margotito. "She never allowed him to become the body in the wheelchair that nobody paid attention to," says Theodora Christon, who helped look after him. "He was still a force." It was her will that made him so. That spirit took nourishment from her magical union with Nureyev, one to which she now applied herself with added urgency.

✻   ✻   ✻

THREE MONTHS after staging his first full-length ballet, Rudolf was at work on his second, a new version of *Swan Lake* for the Vienna State Opera, with himself and Fonteyn in the leading roles. Five years earlier, twenty-one-year-old Rudolf had pleaded his way onto the Kirov's tour to Vienna and traveled there, closely chaperoned, on a company bus. This time he was received as a star and granted the freedom to choose casting, designer and working conditions. "There was enormous anticipation about his coming here," recalls Michael Birkmeyer, then a young dancer in the company and now director of its school. "It was like when the Beatles arrived. People were lining up around the opera house trying to get in."

To produce and direct ballets had always been Rudolf's ambition, one he now felt he could satisfy only by looking outside the Royal Ballet. He was hungry for new experiences, and apart from *Marguerite and Armand*, Ashton had created no new roles for him. Much as the company welcomed his contributions, it had other dancers and other choreographers to keep happy. Anxious as ever to extend his reach—to create an entire work, not just a part in it—Rudolf decided to make his own opportunities.

The most ambitious of dancers, Nureyev chose the most beloved of Tchaikovsky's ballets, though still a novice choreographer and while still defining himself as a dancer. That year there had already been two revivals of *Swan Lake*, one by Robert Helpmann in London, the other by John Cranko in Stuttgart, and Rudolf had danced in both of them. Though Rudolf had devised dances for both of these, he felt that, overall, the Prince's role was too limited, particularly in the Royal Ballet's version. "He sits on his ass for 35 minutes and then suddenly has to walk. Impossible." Now, in the fall of 1964, Nureyev hoped to give the Prince his due, and himself a showcase in the process.

As might be expected in Nureyev's *Swan Lake*, the Prince is the central figure, while everyone else is "a projection of his own mind." His inner longings are embodied by Odette-Odile, the White Swan and the Black Swan, dual characters who represent his spiritual and carnal desires. "It's a story very particular to the Romantic period, and it's a dream of ideal woman, escape from reality," he explained. As this was Vienna, the home of Freud, he conceived of an introspective Prince Siegfried, a manic depressive at odds with his environment. In discussing his conception, he could easily have been talking about himself when he described the Prince as "an unusual man ready for unusual things to happen to him." Tradition had to be respected, he added, "but surely not past the point where it obscures dramatic meaning—the valid modern kind that fires the imagination."

As the critic René Sirvin has observed, the themes Nureyev expressed in his highly personal staging of *Swan Lake* would recur in a number of his productions. "Water, for example, in diverse forms: lake, island, underwater scenes, waves, storms. . . . The separation from the beloved one you try to rejoin, the pursuit of an ideal one will only reach once one has triumphed over physical and moral trials. . . . The heroes must confront an enemy or rival before reaching their goal, or they must conquer liberty. . . . Another constant in his choreography: the dream. The flight to wondrous, fantastic kingdoms at the borders of the real and the imaginary in order to escape from a closed and smothering world."

Music, however, was his starting point and in Tchaikovsky's score, Nureyev discerned a darker mood than had been reflected in other versions. Thinking the traditional Soviet happy ending inappropriate, he could envisage only a tragic end for his brooding hero and had him drown in a flood that engulfs the stage in the last act, an idea borrowed from Soviet choreographer Vladimir Bourmeister's version for Moscow's Stanislavsky Theater. Though he followed the traditional choreography by Ivanov for the celebrated second act lakeside scene, he reset the other three acts, choreographing a elegiac final pas de deux for the Prince and Odette, and gave himself a role that employed his full range.

At his invitation, Erik joined him in Vienna. Rudolf had hoped that they might collaborate on the ballet, but they couldn't come to any agreement on interpretation. At the time, Bruhn questioned Rudolf's addition of the first act solo for the Prince, which Rudolf had choreographed for the Royal Ballet to establish the Prince's unique character. Erik also thought Rudolf's choreography was cluttered with too many steps, a view many critics would come to share. According to Birkmeyer, they fought constantly. Although Erik left Vienna before the ballet's premiere, there was no rupture between them.

Three years later, Bruhn would do his own version of the ballet for the National Ballet of Canada. He drew upon Rudolf's production; as Rudolf saw it, Erik stole many of his ideas. Not only did Bruhn add his own solo to the first act as Rudolf had done, he adopted many of the revisions to the score that Nureyev had chosen. But there was one significant difference: Bruhn had transformed the evil magician Von Rothbart, a role traditionally played by a man, into a woman he called the Black Queen. He wanted to equate the Prince's relationship to this menacing figure with that of his relationship to his mother, the Queen. "Well, everybody, including Rudik, got very upset over this major alteration because the whole ballet was now seen on Freudian terms," Bruhn said later. Rudolf was not alone in believing that this change had sprung from Bruhn's own complex psychology, "from something deep inside him that I think probably Freud couldn't analyse," observed Celia Franca, who originated the role. When eventually Rudolf danced in Bruhn's production in 1972, he incorporated aspects of his own production, with Bruhn's permission. Referring to the last act of this hybrid *Swan Lake*, he told the *Los Angeles Times*, "I use my own choreography. Erik had modeled his on mine anyway, so I said, 'Why not go the whole hog?'"

Rehearsals for Rudolf's *Swan Lake* did not go smoothly. The Vienna State Opera Ballet was the stepchild of the opera house and not only inexperienced in the classical style but encumbered by strict union rules that annoyed Rudolf no end. Intent on clearing out the deadwood, he cast according to talent, not rank, and soon had a scandal on his hands. But scandals, as Rudolf knew, were good for business. "If I'm just a good dancer, I would be on the culture page," he told Michael Birkmeyer. "Now I'm on the front page because I did something stupid." Though Birkmeyer was only a corps member, Rudolf groomed him for the role of the Prince in an alternate cast. "Rudolf didn't care about the scandals," he says. "He told the dancers off. If he thought they were fat, he said so. He worked like hell with us for about six weeks. He said, 'Either they do it the way I want or I go.' That was it. The company was never so good as when he worked with us." Eager to avail himself of his vast storehouse of knowledge, Rudolf would spend long hours driving home some technical fine point or coaching the other dancers. While ardently pursuing his own challenges, Rudolf was to prove a stimulus to any company he danced with, not only because he attracted new audiences and enormous publicity but because he set a standard of commitment that no other dancer could match. If the dancers worked hard, he worked harder. Whether they liked him or not, few of them failed to be invigorated by him.

Chief among them was Birkmeyer, who was on the verge of quitting dance when they met, but stayed on because of Nureyev and became the company's leading male dancer. While eager to learn from him, Birkmeyer had a tough time rebuffing Rudolf's advances. "For him sex was a game. When he saw something he liked, he had to have it." With thick brown curls framing a handsome face, Birkmeyer had the kind of rugged good looks Rudolf desired. His heterosexuality was no deterrent; in fact, the more Birkmeyer resisted, the more relentless Rudolf became. Obstacles had always been a spur for him. "He would say, 'Mikey, how do you know? You never tried.' I just couldn't, not even as a boy. Till my late forties, he never stopped trying."

As expectations for his ballet mounted, Rudolf grew increasingly irritable. He demanded that the Vienna Philharmonic slow the tempo of Tchaikovsky's score, and was promptly advised that no one, most certainly not a dancer, told the renowned orchestra how to play. "Stick to your profession, this is ours," violist Wilhelm Hübner, the orchestra's president, remembered colleagues advising the dancer. Another day he threw Fonteyn out of a rehearsal after telling her to "fuck off," and Joan Thring was summoned to Vienna to deal with him. "The company couldn't believe he could speak to Dame Margot like that. I thought, 'They hadn't heard anything!' " She knew it would be all right, that they would have supper together and then it would be as if nothing had happened, but she was told that "nobody could control him."

By the time she arrived, Rudolf had calmed down, though his tension was hardly eased by the army of photographers who had descended on the opera house for the ballet's open dress rehearsal. Spotting a dancer wearing a costume he didn't like, he ripped it onstage, and immediately "there was a noise of Hasselblads going off like World War III," recalls Lord Snowdon, who was among them. "The Viennese photographers were trying to get a picture of him in a mood, or doing something from a news point of view." Distracted by the noise, Rudolf turned on them. "Out!" he ordered. "Everybody out! Even *you!*" he said, pointing his finger at Snowdon, who, though taken aback, promptly packed up his bags and went down to the theater's canteen. A few minutes later Rudolf found him there. "I'm sorry about that," he said, giving Snowdon a big hug.

A playful man with an irreverent sense of humor, Snowdon had been fascinated by dancers ever since boyhood, when he was first introduced to ballet by his uncle the celebrated theatrical designer Oliver Messel. Princess Margaret shared her husband's passion for ballet and loved sitting in on rehearsals, especially when Nureyev and Fonteyn were dancing. Reflecting on Nureyev's ardor in rehearsal photographs, she later remarked, "He always gave everything he had whenever there was a lens pointed at him." Both she and Snowdon were "fond" of Rudolf, whom they occasionally had to lunch at Kensington Palace, prompting one rumor that the Russian was giving her ballet lessons. "We died with laughter over *that*," she recalls.

Snowdon was in Vienna to photograph Nureyev's *Swan Lake* for *Life* magazine. Though he took pictures of rehearsals and performances, Vienna made him think of *The Third Man*, which sparked his idea to photograph Nureyev and Fonteyn at the city's famous Prater fairground, on the giant Ferris wheel that figured prominently in the Orson Welles film. But when neither responded favorably, he snapped them riding bumper cars and playing football instead. Removing them from their rarefied realm, Snowdon showed them clowning in a carefree moment, a side of them the public had never seen. "We had great fun together going off to the fun fair. I loved Rudolf though he used to tear up photographs of mine. I'd say, 'Rudolf, don't do that; they're very expensive. We may be getting a cover on *Life* magazine.' And he'd say, 'All right, you get one cover, I no tear up photos.' It was all a childlike acting performance, which was very endearing." Although the Vietnam War claimed the cover on November 27, 1964, Snowdon's photos were given eleven pages, unusual at a time when, as he recalls, even the magazine's editors considered ballet "an elitist kind of art form that didn't relate to its readers."

Nureyev's *Swan Lake* opened on October 15 at the Vienna State Opera House and was a dazzling popular success. At their last performance, Nureyev and Fonteyn were given an astonishing eighty-nine curtain calls over four acts, the most ever taken, according to *The Guinness Book of Records*. By then he had won over the Vienna Philharmonic. "Everyone was a Rudolf fan," recalled Wilhelm Hübner. Although the critics agreed that Nureyev had created a poetic showcase for himself, a number of them thought that he had yet to fully prove himself as a "creative talent." His *Swan Lake*, wrote one critic, "provides intriguing glimpses of Nureyev's choreographic powers. His full range cannot be judged, for he has thus far tried his hand only at known works. . . . However, here in Central Europe where the classics are often petrified mummies, Nureyev's attempt to bring a classic up to date was blessed. Blessed, too, is the disturbance and controversy he brings to our stages. . . ." The ballet proved a box office hit, even with other dancers in the role of the Prince, and a shot in the arm to the Vienna State Opera Ballet, which took Nureyev's production into its regular repertory. As a result, company director Aurel von Milloss invited Nureyev to return whenever he wished.

Back in London, Rudolf and Fonteyn danced *Giselle* and *Swan Lake* at Covent Garden, while Rudolf revived the Grand Pas from Petipa's *Paquita* for Fonteyn's annual RAD Gala on November 17. He and Fonteyn danced the leading roles, though Rudolf once again boosted the careers of several promising Royal ballerinas by casting and coaching them in the ballet's solos. His own dancing was soon put on hold, however, when Rudolf followed Ringo Starr into the London Clinic to have his tonsils removed. Incapable of inactivity, he hopped across the Atlantic at Christmas to see Erik's new production of *La Sylphide* for the National Ballet of Canada.

At Rudolf's suggestion, Erik had invited Lynn Seymour to dance with him at Toronto's O'Keefe Centre. Rudolf surprised them one afternoon, bursting into rehearsal "in sleek boots and a black fur speckled with snow," Seymour recalled. He took them out to his favorite steakhouse that night, but when the maître d' refused to admit him without a tie, Rudolf thrust his fur coat into the man's face, demanding, "If this isn't worthy of your restaurant, then nothing is," and then stalked outside to pelt the windows with snowballs. Erik was appalled by his behavior; the two argued and marched off in separate directions. Minutes later, Rudolf came trudging back through snowdrifts to rejoin Seymour, his mood utterly transformed. "Do you know how to make snow angels?" he asked suddenly, and with childish delight, fell backward to demonstrate, fanning his arms. For the next several hours, they played in the snow, "singing, laughing, and throwing snowballs into the sky." Rudolf, she quickly realized, wasn't one to dwell on unhappy moments. "He didn't have that gloomy Russian thing of moodiness and beating the breast. None of that. Not like Erik, the Danish brooder."

Erik was both staging and starring in *La Sylphide*, his first major production. Rudolf tried not to draw attention away from him, but couldn't help himself. His mere presence provoked such interest that he agreed to a press conference on December 31, the day of the ballet's premiere. He was in Toronto solely as a spectator, he insisted.

That would have been the case had Erik not strained his knee the following night. Once more Erik propelled Rudolf to center stage by proposing that he dance in his place for one performance. On January 5, 1965, Rudolf made his debut as James, the bewitched young Scotsman who spurns mortal happiness for the idealized love of the sylph. Rudolf had danced only the "scarf" pas de deux that Erik had fashioned for him and Fonteyn the summer before; now, on three days' notice, he learned the entire ballet, even though he was injured himself, having badly wrenched his ankle slipping on the ice. "I don't care if it's broken," he told Seymour as he bound it. "I've wanted to do this ballet for a long time." Moments before the curtain went up, the pair were convulsed by giggles after hearing the announcement that "Rudolf Nureyev will replace Erik Burke at this performance."

Bruhn was not amused. Sitting next to him that night was Betty Oliphant, the company's ballet mistress, who was to become a close friend. "I had the strong feeling that Erik regretted very much his decision because the next day his knee was fine and he was going to perform. Rudi was superb, but he really wasn't James. We were determined that Erik was going to get the same kind of ovation that Rudi did, but it was more difficult because the mass hysteria for Nureyev was going full steam. Erik danced as he had never before or since."

With Seymour as their Sylph, Erik received twenty-five curtain calls to Rudolf's nineteen, each spurring the other. "It was the most beautiful James I have ever seen him do," Bruhn would say years later. During rehearsals, Rudolf had proposed making amendments here and there. "I do that this way," he would say. But Erik kept the reins tight. "It's Bournonville. You don't change." In his own account of his debut, Rudolf recalled being pleased with his performance, given his injuries. "Very foolishly, I took one of the bandages away, so I let the blood spread even further inside of my ankle. However, I rebandaged again and waited for the second act. I danced. I did all the steps. I didn't change or cut anything. Everything was as was rehearsed. The next day of course my legs were both very enormous, and Erik miraculously suddenly recovered and he danced to glorious acclaim."

Nureyev's unscheduled debut brought an unprecedented level of publicity to the ballet's opening week. Nevertheless, the critics reserved their highest praise for Bruhn, calling him the master of the Bournonville style. But as Ralph Hicklin pointed out in the *Globe and Mail*, comparisons between the two dancers meant little. "One does not compare Gielgud's Lear with Olivier's and decide which is the better. . . . Nureyev wears the face of a haunted boy—one whom we can easily believe entangled in the supernatural love affair with a sylph. . . ." Bruhn's interpretation was cooler, he wrote, "an approach that allows the dance to speak for itself."

Rudolf returned briefly to London on January 7, only to turn around ten days later to fly to Washington with Fonteyn for Lyndon Johnson's inauguration. They arrived in the midst of a blizzard. Preoccupied with crashing, Rudolf kept his nerves doused with whiskey in the first-class cabin. Inaugural galas were typically star-spangled affairs, but such was the popularity of the Tatar Prince and his English Dame that Nureyev and Fonteyn had been added to the celebrity lineup. Performing before the President and the ten thousand others who jammed the vast National Armory on January 18, 1965, were some of the biggest names in the entertainment world: Barbra Streisand, Harry Belafonte, Carol Burnett, Johnny Carson and Julie Andrews. Still, it was Nureyev and Fonteyn, performing the pas de deux from *Le Corsaire*, who won the most thunderous ovation of the evening. Many in the audience had never been to the ballet. "Excellent, wonderful," Vice President Hubert Humphrey said afterward, "and I don't usually cotton to that kind of dancing." His ankle still bandaged, Rudolf supplied "the most breathtaking moments of the show," reported *The New York Times* in a front-page story. Afterward, as he always did, Rudolf stepped out for a solo curtain call. Everywhere he looked, as far as his eye could see, there were people clapping and cheering and calling for more.

21

Rudimania

HE DID NOT STAY to savor his conquest. Two days later, he was back in London, immersed in rehearsals for *Romeo and Juliet*, Kenneth Mac-Millan's first full-length ballet. With Nureyev and Fonteyn cast as the lovers, more than one thousand fans camped outside the box office at Covent Garden waiting for tickets to go on sale. What the public didn't know was that the behind-the-scenes drama was as charged as the ballet itself. Indeed, its enduring success as a Nureyev-Fonteyn vehicle belied its battle-scarred path to the stage.

MacMillan had in fact created the ballet for his muse, Lynn Seymour, and her partner, Christopher Gable, whose bodies, temperaments and sensibilities had given life to the central roles. The ballet was to be MacMillan's statement about the pair, just as *Marguerite and Armand* had been Ashton's about Fonteyn and Nureyev, and he fully intended that *Romeo and Juliet* should launch them as international stars. Seymour and Gable had been active participants in MacMillan's artistic process. The three of them, in fact, collaborated so closely on the making of *Romeo and Juliet* that they took to referring to it as "our ballet."

But others saw it differently. To Sol Hurok, again producing the Royal Ballet's spring tour to America, it was inconceivable that the ballet should open in New York without Nureyev and Fonteyn. Either they danced the premiere, he warned the company's leadership, or the tour was off. As their popularity ensured the tour's success, Ashton, in consultation with the board, not only agreed but advised MacMillan to give the London premiere to them as well. "I told him that if he wants a local success he should use Seymour and Gable, but for an international success he must have Margot and Rudolf." That season the ticket prices, which had for some time been higher when Fonteyn danced, went up for Nureyev's performances.

Devastated by the sudden loss of control over his own ballet, Mac-Millan briefly considered withdrawing it, but he could scarcely afford to scotch his first major showcase. The rancor left him so depressed, however, that he felt powerless to do much of anything. Seymour, meanwhile, was beside herself. Shortly before rehearsals had begun, she had discovered she was pregnant. She knew that a ballerina could hope for fifteen prime dancing years at most, twenty if you were Margot Fonteyn, and she hadn't wanted to leave the stage just as she was about to have her moment. So she had opted for an abortion.* Three days later, she had returned to the studio. Her Juliet was as much Seymour as Capulet, "the culmination of all my fantasy roles as a dancer."

Making matters more joyless still, Seymour and Gable now had to teach their roles to Fonteyn and Nureyev. At age forty-six, Fonteyn was tackling the teenage Juliet. Seymour and Gable would perform the ballet during the season, but it was the first cast that was awarded the spotlight, the press attention and the glamour of an opening night. "It was awkward for them and a slap in the face for me," says Seymour, "but at that time you didn't question things, you just got on with it."

Several choreographers had staged *Romeo and Juliet*, among them Ashton and John Cranko, but it was Leonid Lavrovsky's groundbreaking production for the Bolshoi that was the most widely admired. MacMillan, however, was most influenced by Franco Zeffirelli's 1963 stage production for the Old Vic and was intent on conveying that same realism and accent on youth. MacMillan was known for vivid drama ballets built around strong characters, and his choreography stood out for its poetic line and intense imagery. To give the story a modern reading, he focused on the family drama and made Juliet its catalyst. Juliet, as MacMillan saw her, was passionate and willful, a free spirit much like Seymour herself, while the virile Romeo was a youthful dreamer. "Romeo is a nice, normal fellow," MacMillan told her, "but it is Juliet's decisive personality and rebellious temperament that provokes the affair." He saw them not as "ethereal lovers, miming impassioned vows," but as two randy teenagers caught up in the tumult of first passion.

The pas de deux he devised for the famous balcony scene was meant to have an off-kilter, dizzy quality to convey that feeling. Mac-Millan's Romeo, whether made for Rudolf or not, was the first new role to present him, as Clive Barnes observed, "neither as an abstract hero nor as one of the puppet princes, but quite simply as a human being."

*She waited until her husband left for Leningrad with Nigel Gosling. Her husband did not know that she was pregnant, and in the end, her decision cost her her marriage. Several years later, however, she would give birth to twins.

According to Gable, however, Rudolf had little respect for MacMillan's intentions and had no qualms about amending the choreography to showcase his strengths. To his mind, the thirty-five-year-old MacMillan was young and inexperienced, while he knew best what suited him. "He felt that the pas de deux didn't focus enough on Romeo," says Gable. "So he decided to do a series of double something or others all the way around the stage, which got a round from the audience, and then he picked up the pas de deux at a later point. If he felt that the audience wanted to see an explosion of his skill at a certain point, he'd put something in. And if he felt that a lift was going to make him tired for his solo, he'd cut it out."

That he cut out one of the most beautiful lifts in the pas de deux — when Juliet drapes herself across Romeo's shoulders in a half-moon shape — was something MacMillan could barely tolerate. To him, the steps and their movement quality were paramount. He felt little rapport with Nureyev and now sank into "a seminervous breakdown of misery and wasn't helping much." Still, to his close friend Georgina Parkinson, cast as Romeo's first love, Rosaline, he confided that he was "furious" that Nureyev and Fonteyn were changing his choreography. "Kenneth hated Margot in it, but he let them do what they liked and thought of Lynn and Christopher as his first cast." Poles apart physically, the four performers naturally offered different readings. Whereas Nureyev's Romeo was a mischievous Renaissance playboy sparked into deeper feeling only after his meeting with Juliet, Gable chose to play him as an full-blooded, earthy young man from the start. Seymour's Juliet was headstrong and impetuous, while Fonteyn's was more romantic and demure.

With three weeks to go before the February 9 premiere, Rudolf and Margot had yet to learn the entire ballet. Still nursing a bad ankle, Rudolf further aggravated tensions when he refused to risk doing any section "full out." Three days before the premiere, Gable and his wife were dining at Seymour's flat and into their second bottle of claret when Gable got an urgent call summoning him to the opera house. The curtain was about to go up on the Shades scene from *Bayadère* and Rudolf wasn't sure he could dance. Gable raced across London to find Rudolf standing backstage in costume. "Sorry, honey," he told Gable, "I can't go on." Gable had fifteen minutes to slap pancake makeup on his face, affix a turban, and tug on tights that hadn't had time to dry. Did he want to run through anything with her? Fonteyn asked. She and Rudolf had by that point changed portions of their pas de deux, and Gable had to wing the performance. He was hardly pleased when Rudolf came backstage afterward to give him corrections. However, since Rudolf never missed a performance unless he was seriously injured, Gable began to hope that he might replace him on the opening night of *Romeo* after all. He quickly realized that Rudolf was saving himself for his debut. Disillusioned by the experience, and frustrated by the lack of support for them, MacMillan, Seymour and Gable would all leave the company within the year.*

On February 9, 1965, a gala audience, including a fleet of royals, packed the opera house. The ballet's premiere concluded with forty-three curtain calls lasting over forty minutes. Fonteyn made her first and last curtsies to Tito, who was in a first-tier box in a wheelchair. She had arranged for him to be brought in by ambulance from Stoke Mandeville; even the stagehands wept.

Seldom had the London critics been so unanimous in their praise as they were for MacMillan's achievement and Nicholas Georgiadis's sumptuous set and costumes. Not everyone was as enthusiastic about Nureyev's Romeo. Andrew Porter in the *Financial Times* considered the ballet as a whole a "triumphant success," but wasn't entirely swayed by either of the leads. "The Fonteyn/Nureyev *Romeo* was not a drama of character development but a touching lyrical suite of contrasted scenes. . . ." The *Guardian*, which carried a front-page photograph of Nureyev on the day of the premiere, gave opening night nearly half a page with two large photographs. Richard Buckle, in the *Sunday Times*, was one of the few to praise Nureyev's vivid characterization. "[He] specializes in a kind of mocking approach. This Romeo's courting of Rosaline is catlike, satirical. But love pricks him into spurts of ecstasy, expressed by wheeling suddenly round the stage. . . . Nureyev's was a portrait in depth." The popular view was perhaps best expressed in the *Times*, which concluded that he danced "better on half a foot than most men do on two."

It didn't matter that the cognoscenti preferred the Gable-Seymour *Romeo*; in the public mind the ballet belonged to Nureyev and Fonteyn, an identification sealed after they were filmed in the ballet that summer.† Their partnership was what sold the ballet, and this MacMillan resented above all. "He wanted it to be his ballet," says Parkinson, "and they made it theirs right from the word 'go.'" Their success was repeated in New York, where *Romeo and Juliet* premiered on April 21, 1965. Many in the gala audience, among them Mrs. John D. Rockefeller III, three Kennedy sisters, UN Ambassador Adlai Stevenson and ballet's newest convert, Hubert Humphrey, had come only to see Nureyev and Fonteyn. After thirty-three curtain calls, the audience finally let them go. Banking on the pair as box office gold, Hurok refused to announce more than one

---

*Though one of the Royal Ballet's most talented choreographers, MacMillan was not encouraged to stay, and perhaps because Seymour and Gable were MacMillan's muses, Ashton showed more enthusiasm for Sibley and Dowell. MacMillan and Seymour left for the Berlin Ballet, while Gable gave up ballet altogether to pursue an acting career. He would star in Ken Russell's film *The Boy Friend* opposite Twiggy.

†The film opened in the fall of 1965.

week ahead which nights they would perform, thus ensuring that those eager to see them would hedge their bets by purchasing tickets for as many performances as possible. His gambit paid off: The entire three-month tour was nearly sold out before it even began and scalpers were commanding up to $420 for $14 tickets. In Washington, seven thousand people crowded into the Coliseum to see their opening night appearance in *Giselle*.

The curiosity and excitement peculiar to the 1965 tour centered primarily on Nureyev, whose fame was exploding. *Time* and *Newsweek* featured him on their covers the same week and fans crowded the stage door, chanting, "We want Rudi, Rudi in the nudie." Rudimania was in full force and Rudi was rarely far removed from a photographer's lens or a journalist's query. He was "the Man of the Hour" (*Time*); "the Russian Revolution" (*Newsweek*); "the New Boy in Town" (*The New York Times*).

While the critical response to him was for the most part adoring, a backlash was also building that would continue throughout his career. To his detractors, Nureyev was a celebrity first, a dancer second. Modern dance pioneer Ted Shawn, while acknowledging his talent, labeled him a publicity-mad "money grabber who is pushing back the cause that I've been working on for years—to get proper recognition for the male dancer in America. Nureyev is a very bad influence on the dance, with his long hair and his misbehaving. Young men with ambitions to dance will look at him and say 'That's what it takes to be a great dancer.'" Voicing a view shared by many colleagues, *New York Times* critic Allen Hughes worried that the press was turning the tour into the "Nureyev Show" at the expense of so many other equally talented dancers. But just two days later, his own paper ran "Nureyev in New York: Tiger in Need of a Haircut," reporter Gay Talese's account of the day he spent trailing the dancer around town. "Everywhere [he] walked yesterday—across Madison Avenue, down Park, into the Russian Tea Room for lunch—people turned to stare at him. . . . Why this sudden electricity in New York?"

Vogue editor in chief Diana Vreeland, a keen observer of the scene, saw that public tastes were changing. Society was passé, she had announced to Cecil Beaton some months earlier, noting that "today only personality counts, with very few exceptions unless it is a 'new beauty.' . . . Youth is the best thing we can get." Had she added "anything British," the list would have been complete. By 1965 the British invasion was sweeping America, propelled by the Beatles and the Rolling Stones, Vidal Sassoon and Mary Quant, Twiggy and Jean Shrimpton. *Time* declared London "the city of the decade." *Darling*, the John Schlesinger film starring Julie Christie and Laurence Harvey, depicted its sexually liberated scene.

Personality, Beauty, Youth, Freedom: Nureyev personified the decade's obsessions. The London fashion world claimed him as a trendsetter. The *Sun* singled him out as the year's "champion Mod dresser," outclassing runner-up Lord Snowdon. The *Daily Express*, meanwhile, insisted that "No Adam, no Eve, can ignore the influence of the looks of Nureyev. When a young man races for a bus, with his leather jacket hanging from his finger, he's holding it Nureyev style. When Russian student caps take the suburbs as well as the King's Road by storm, you know who launched that craze. . . . Among girls who like to be first with the newest, there is a natty 'Nuri' way to wear trouser suits—buttoned tight at the midriff, collar flipped up, hands in pockets . . ."

He was "the catch of the season," declared *Newsweek*. "The cry is not Baby Jane! Caterine! Isabel! Amanda! but Rudi!" Andy Warhol, enjoying his own breakthrough moment as "the Pope of Pop Art," oversaw a party for him that season at the Factory, his silver-painted studio on East Forty-seventh Street. The idea for the "Fifty Most Beautiful People" party had come from Tennessee Williams and his friend Lester Persky,* who had called to invite Warhol to their own soirée. Williams had recently met Nureyev in London and had hinted to Persky that he and Nureyev had had a sexual encounter in London.† Warhol offered to let Persky and Williams host their party at the Factory, and his anointed Superstars, "spaced-out heiresses, hustlers and drag queens," mixed easily with Nureyev, Williams, Judy Garland and Montgomery Clift, while Edie Sedgwick chatted up Brian Jones and later stood high up on a rafter, doing the twist. "Rudi!" screamed Judy Garland as she flung her arms about his neck. "You filthy Communist! Do you know that Tennessee Williams thinks I can't act? Let's go find out if he thinks *you* can dance. . . ."

That May, Rudolf was frugging at the opening of Arthur, the chic Manhattan discotheque run by Richard Burton's ex, Sybil. Built on the site of the old El Morocco, it had black walls and banquettes, white tables and colored lights over the dance floor. The opening drew Sybil's film and theater friends, many of them investors, including Mike Nichols, Warren Beatty, Danny Kaye, Harold Prince and Edward Villella. Sonny and Cher played a set, as did The Four Seasons, and model Tiger Morse showed up in an outlandish silver dress illuminated by tiny Christmas lights. "You name them, they all wanted to meet Rudolf. He was like a Beatle," recalls Burton,‡ who modeled her club closely on London's Ad Lib. "After that, people would come to the club wanting to know if Nureyev was there."

Together with Fonteyn, Rudolf embarked on a public social life

*Persky, then an advertising executive, was soon to produce a number of Williams's plays as well as such films as *Shampoo* and *Hair*.
†"I hope for Tennessee's sake it was true," Persky said later.
‡Now Sybil Christopher.

across America. In New York, they dined at Orsini's with Jackie Kennedy, his "favorite American woman," he told reporters. In Washington, they were feted by the British ambassador; afterward, Rudolf hit Whiskey a Go Go with still more Kennedys: Bobby, Ted, Joan and the Stephen Smiths. Yet amid all the clamor and adulation, the frenzied fans and fawning hostesses, Rudolf remained ineffably the outsider. "I'm tired of American parties," he confessed to *Newsweek*'s Ainslie Dinwiddie, who caught up with him mid-tour. "They're like an enormous performance with a bad director. If I give a party, it is not to bring people together at the right time and place and bring gossip columnists to mention them in the newspapers." He was perhaps a little disingenuous. In public, he just about demanded attention. And while he may have felt discomfited by all the attendant fuss, he was, as Edward Albee points out, "enormously self-aware of the image he was projecting at all times. I'm sure we relaxed and talked, but I can't remember him ever being 'offstage,' so to speak."

Someone who craved public devotion couldn't have wished for a bigger stage than *The Ed Sullivan Show*, on which Nureyev and Fonteyn first appeared on May 16, 1965. As host of the country's top-rated variety program, Sullivan was to television what Hurok was to the stage, an impresario who greatly influenced the nation's cultural tastes. Nureyev and Fonteyn had already drawn scores of newcomers to the ballet, but with fifty-two million viewers, the *Sullivan Show* was the largest single audience they would ever attract. Equally important, the show conferred celebrity and stature in the minds of the masses. Many had seen Nureyev on magazine covers; relatively few had seen him in motion. Those who might never have considered watching a ballet, let alone a male ballet dancer, did so because Ed Sullivan headlined them.

The pair danced extracts from *Swan Lake*. As had become his standard practice, Rudolf arrived for rehearsal with the camera sequences already mapped out in his head. He had no more confidence in television crews than he did in photographers and spent the day directing the cameramen on how best to shoot them. Seeing that one of the cameras was placed too low, at an angle that he felt would distort his line, he put his foot over the lens and refused to continue until it was raised. Afterward, at lunch with Fonteyn at the Russian Tea Room, he was equally insistent about how he wanted his steak cooked. Theodora Christon, who joined them, remembers that "he picked the thing up, looked at it, put it down and began speaking Russian to the waiter. He couldn't get him to understand what he wanted. So he went into the kitchen to show them. Rudolf had taken his shoes off under the table and the Dame just looked at me, sighed, and said, 'Is he wearing shoes, dear?' "

The following week, Sullivan "rushed them back to our stage," as he told his viewers. "In the seventeen-year history of our show no stars ever have won the excited acclaim that greeted last Sunday's appearance of ballerina Margot Fonteyn and the magnificent Rudolf Nureyev. . . . I'm going to ask you through the country and Canada and Australia: get on the phone right now, call your friends and tell them that Margot Fonteyn and Nureyev have been added to tonight's program — so get right on the phone!" Later that fall, on October 30, 1965, Nureyev appeared on ABC's Jimmy Durante special, partnering Lynn Seymour in excerpts from La Sylphide. No introduction to the ballet was given, leaving viewers apparently baffled at seeing Nureyev in a kilt and overdone makeup. Then again, as one critic noted, the lack of information may have been a ploy to make the viewers more receptive to Durante's later send-up of the ballet, with the jaunty comedian trading his dark suit and trademark rumpled hat for kilt and slippers, while Rudolf looked on, smiling.

His popular appeal was further enhanced with the release that same month of An Evening with the Royal Ballet, a filmed ballet performance in which Nureyev partnered Fonteyn in Le Corsaire and Les Sylphides. Though other dancers were featured, it was these two that made the film a box-office success. Grosses topped one million dollars, a record for an all-ballet film. Over two nights during the week of December 6, 1965, the film was shown in more than fifty theaters in New York and New Jersey alone.

While the Royal Ballet company benefited from the intense public scrutiny, the other dancers couldn't help but feel eclipsed. Press coverage dwelt almost exclusively on Nureyev and Fonteyn. Because they were allotted virtually all opening nights, their pride of place in reviews was inevitable. As a result, the public felt cheated when they didn't dance. In Chicago during the 1965 tour, Seymour and Gable replaced Nureyev and Fonteyn in a performance of Romeo and Juliet and went on to the most hostile crowd either had ever encountered. Gable saw ticket holders "crying in the lobby because they'd got these terrible understudies. We worked our asses off and by the end of the show we got the audience. But the next day, the gist of the reviews was 'If the understudies were this good, can you imagine what the real thing would have been like?' "

That bias was not confined to America. On the company's fall tour to Italy, with no Hurok to bolster public interest, there were many empty seats whenever Nureyev and Fonteyn were not promised. The press was similarly blasé. By the following year, company morale was beginning to sag under the weight of their fame. Disheartened by what they saw as the unfair treatment of Seymour and Gable, many of their colleagues began to wonder, as John Tooley recalls, "How much longer are we going to have to endure this?" In Monaco in the summer of 1966, it was Rudolf and Margot who danced Romeo and Juliet at the Royal Palace and who dined afterward with Prince Rainier and Princess Grace. When the company next moved on to Athens, Annette Page, another budding

Juliet, complained to Ashton about their dominating the casting. She was not the first, nor would she be the last. "We were all chomping on the bit," concedes Antoinette Sibley, then twenty-seven, whose partnership with Anthony Dowell was gaining ground with Ashton's encouragement. "Because of their presence, we weren't getting out there enough." Ashton felt hamstrung, trying though he was not to run a national company "for the benefit of two people."

"I admire your spirit in coming to me," he told Page, "but you've got to realize that the only reason we've got this tour booked at all is because of Fonteyn and Nureyev. They're not interested in us, they're only interested in THEM!"

RUDOLF MAY HAVE BEEN busier than any other dancer at the Royal Ballet, but as far as he was concerned, he wasn't nearly busy enough. He wanted to be onstage every night as well as to coach, choreograph, produce and teach, and no single company could satisfy all of his appetites. "He has a great deal of knowledge, ability and imagination," Fonteyn noted, "and if you have these things you can't sit still." Where most ballet stars built their careers inside their home companies and took on guest engagements from time to time, Rudolf considered himself stateless both onstage and off. With a keen understanding of his marquee value, he now sought to establish footholds in other parts of the world. "For me," he said, "a country is just a place to dance. Your roots are your work. Work is sacred."

In the summer of 1965, immediately following his and Fonteyn's conquest of America with the Royal Ballet, Rudolf joined the Australian Ballet for several performances at the Nice Opera House. The Australian troupe was on its way to London and was quickly offered a full European tour on condition that Nureyev and Fonteyn appeared as guest stars. Rudolf struck a deal with codirectors Peggy van Praagh and Robert Helpmann typical of the arrangement he would make with many young companies: Their dancers would be seen by audiences they couldn't hope to attract without him; he would get as many performances as he wanted; their company would acquire a nineteenth-century ballet, taught by Nureyev himself; he would have at his disposal dancers on whom to test his choreographic ideas.

Rudolf had already taught *Don Quixote* to the Australian dancers when he decided that his *Raymonda* would offer Fonteyn a better role. The ballet had been seen only in Spoleto and Lebanon, and he was anxious that it should have a wider viewing with a new set. In November, he and Fonteyn joined the Australians for an eight-week sweep through Birmingham, London, Paris, Copenhagen, Los Angeles and Honolulu. In London one night during the tour, Rudolf met the actor Keith Baxter at La Poppote, a restaurant behind Harrods popular with actors and journalists. Rudolf invited him out for a drink and they soon fell into a casual affair.

Tall, robust and masculine, with coal-black hair and "Celtic good looks," Baxter cut a glamorous figure in English theatrical circles. The son of a Welsh docker and a graduate of RADA (the Royal Academy of Dramatic Art), he had once shared a flat with fellow actors Albert Finney and Alan Bates. He would later star in the West End and Broadway productions of *Sleuth*, and had just completed shooting the Orson Welles film *Chimes at Midnight*, an amalgam of Shakespeare's Henry IV plays. Baxter starred as Hal to Welles's Falstaff.

Rudolf knew little about Baxter when they met, although a couple of years earlier Orson Welles had hoped to pair them in the segment he had been asked to direct in *The Bible*, a Dino de Laurentiis epic that was eventually canceled. He had cast Baxter as Jacob and wanted "somebody very beautiful" to play the Angel. So he asked Rudolf. The day Rudolf went to meet Welles at the Ritz, Welles's wife, Paula, "was in such a twitter" about Nureyev that Welles asked Baxter to usher her from the room, "so she didn't fuck the whole thing up," as Welles put it. Seeing Rudolf approach, however, in a white leather coat, the pair hid behind a pillar. Welles described how he wanted Rudolf's Angel to wrestle with Jacob. "But what are my lines?" Rudolf pressed him. "There aren't any lines," Welles replied. "You mean," Rudolf said suddenly, "I just make with muscles?"

At a time in his life when Rudolf had few friends his own age, he and Baxter developed an easy camaraderie, "friendship overlaid with eroticism," in Baxter's words. Rudolf, six years his junior, struck the actor as "terribly lonely" and "relatively unspoiled. He was a terrific giggler." Friendships were difficult, for Rudolf's English was not much more than rudimentary, so "the easiness of chitchat was denied him."

Rudolf was eager for Baxter to see him dance and invited him to Paris, where Baxter was already going to dub scenes in *Chimes at Midnight* with Jeanne Moreau. The two spent most evenings with Fonteyn and with Rudolf's Parisian circle: Clara Saint, Yves Saint Laurent, Pierre Bergé, Roland Petit, Zizi Jeanmaire and Claire Motte. Seeing Rudolf arrogantly "flick" his hands at waiters, Baxter dubbed him Modestovich. One night they were dining with Fonteyn at Maxim's when Aristotle Onassis sent a note over to their table, inviting them to join him and Maria Callas. "It was extraordinary watching Onassis's face looking round the table," recalls Baxter. "It was like seeing a great collector admiring his treasures."

Over the next several months, Rudolf and Baxter saw each other whenever they could. Fascinated by the theater, Rudolf loved listening

to Baxter talk about it. He even choreographed a dance for him to perform during his West End run in *The Rivals* opposite Sir Ralph Richardson. "When I took it into rehearsals, Sir Ralph looked at me in utter
amazement because two days before, I couldn't put one foot in front of
the other. 'Oh, that's a wonderful dance,' he said and then I told him
who taught it to me."

In public settings, Rudolf still walked warily, fearing that at any
moment a car might come along and snatch him. Once, when he and
Baxter were rowboating on the Serpentine, "happily splashing the oars
into the water and laughing," another, larger boat filled with four men
suddenly crashed into them "and fear suffused his face immediately."
Only when they were alone in Baxter's flat, reading and listening to
music, sitting on the windowsill staring across the Thames, did "his face
lose its fear." Since both were lousy cooks, they regularly ate at restaurants. Once in a while they warmed up canned tomato soup and drank
Stolichnaya, "two bottles one night," and then they "danced on the roof
and I pointed out the MI6 building where our spies were programmed.
That sobered him."

Neither was in love with the other; however, Rudolf, says Baxter,
sometimes pretended to be, "though it was only a pretense and he knew
it too — the deep love of his life was Erik." The shadow of Erik was ever-
present. "Aaah. It's such a pity," Rudolf said with a great sigh one night.
"What's a pity?" Baxter asked him. "Because I'm so in love with Erik."

IN THE SPRING OF 1966, Rudolf joined Erik in Rome, where Erik had
invited him to partner Carla Fracci at the Teatro dell'Opera. Bruhn was
then at another crossroads. He felt isolated at the Royal Danish Ballet,
which had just passed him over as its new director, and he had no major
guest engagements booked. He told a reporter, "I thrive on differences,
on complication."

He found plenty of both at the Rome Opera, where he spent three
months staging new works, dancing and teaching its fledgling ballet
troupe. The experience drained him and brought a recurrence of his
stomach pains. Though Bruhn also danced with Fracci, he gave Rudolf
all six performances of *La Sylphide*, a remarkably generous showcase
given the disparity in their situations. During rehearsals, Fracci kept calling Rudolf Erik and was surprised when Rudolf looked pleased. "I don't
mind," he said, "I love Erik." And Rudolf, she recalls, sometimes called
Erik Daddy. Never during their five years together had their trajectories
been so sharply contrasted: While Erik was approaching the end of his
career, Rudolf, at twenty-eight, was rapidly expanding his range. In 1966
alone, in addition to his appearances with the Royal Ballet, he was to

mount three new productions and dance the leading roles in all of them. Though typical for an Olivier or a Gielgud, this was unheard of in the ballet world.

His next challenge was to choreograph an original ballet from scratch. Emboldened by his success with *Raymonda* and *Swan Lake*, he tested his creative powers further with *Tancredi*, made for the Vienna State Opera Ballet in May 1966. The ballet gave him the chance "to show what I learned about the West, and what I can do with it choreographically," though without the benefit of obscurity to cloak his missteps. The score, by German composer Hans Werner Henze, had been adapted from an earlier ballet and given a new scenario. Rudolf further amended it to fit his own conception of the story. His work continued to express the idea of otherness and isolation. There were clearly aspects of Nureyev in the troubled hero, Tancredi, who, after emerging from a mother figure, steps out on his own, only to be rejected by his companions. His major crisis comes in the form of two female figures, one chaste, the other carnal, the spirit and the flesh, both of whom attract him. Forced to choose between them, he suffers a series of hallucinations before splitting in two. After a final struggle, he dies and returns to the womb.

Despite its pop psychology appeal and Nureyev's fluid movement style, his fantasy proved heavy going, and it was judged by the critics to be as schizophrenic as Tancredi himself. While baffled by its meaning— "one of the wildest, strangest ballets of our time," reported *The New York Times* on its front page—they saw in it evidence of a promising, original choreographer. Only Alexander Bland deemed it a success by suggesting that the ballet was "deliberately designed" to be "slightly mystifying," and that it proved that "we have a real choreographer on our hands with ideas that go far beyond mere classical dance-steps. It is rather sad that this continuously intriguing and often beautiful demonstration had to happen so far away [in Vienna]." Nureyev's dancing in the title role was also admired, as was Barry Kay's set, a labryinth suggesting the shadowy corridors of the mind. The ballet, however, was given just four performances, two of them starring Nureyev,* and then dropped from the repertory. Still, Rudolf did not consider it a failure, but rather a productive experiment, a kind of apprenticeship that had allowed him to express his own distinctive dance ideas.

RUDOLF SPENT his summer holiday with Erik at his new villa in Monte Carlo. A number of friends had converged there, among them Sonia Arova and her new husband, Thor Sutowski. A tall, blond American-

---

*Michael Birkmeyer and Karl Musil alternated.

born dancer eighteen years Arova's junior, he bore a striking resemblance to Erik. During a tour of the villa, Erik urged Rudolf to show them "what you've got." At this, Rudolf walked over to his enormous fireplace, pulled out a brick, slid another one over, "and pulled out this Russian double-headed solid gold eagle studded with diamonds and rubies." Lee Radziwill had given it to him as a gift, but he wasn't sure if he liked it. "I think it's a little too ostentatious," he said, before stuffing it back in its hiding place. Rudolf had decorated the house like a church where he indulged "my obsession for religious props . . . I have stained glass and iron doors and crosses. It is a joke or a kind of absolution I seek there for my sins. . . ."

EVEN AS HE WAS creating *Tancredi*, Rudolf was already thinking about *The Sleeping Beauty*, which he was to stage for Milan's La Scala in September 1966, with Fracci and himself in the leading roles. At La Scala, as in Vienna, the ballet company stood in the shadows of the opera; Rudolf's goal was to infuse life into its languid dancers. As the new star of Italian ballet, the thirty-year-old Fracci was unaccustomed to competing with her partners, but Rudolf liked to push his ballerinas to their limit, to show them their own strength. "He didn't partner his ballerina," she says; "he danced with her." A delicate, darkly pretty dancer with finely etched features, parchment-white skin and a hairline accented by a widow's peak, Fracci would go on to dance with Rudolf in nearly all of his productions. Early on, however, Rudolf thought her "lazy" and worried that she lacked stamina. But as Fracci recalls, "he saw that I didn't have the body to do things in the Russian style, so he helped me a lot technically. You had to be strong and show you could do it. If you didn't, he would think, 'She's nothing.' "

The most daunting tests he still reserved for himself. In *The Sleeping Beauty*, his first work for La Scala, he faced his greatest challenge to date. Petipa's supreme achievement and his finest collaboration with Tchaikovsky,* the ballet was the hallmark of the Maryinsky and Kirov style, Nureyev's touchstone. As he admired Bach's music for its structural logic, so he admired Petipa's ballets for their masterly construction. Drawing on both Petipa's ballet and the Versailles court satire Perrault intended in his 1697 tale, Rudolf spent months reading the memoirs of Saint-Simon in order to understand better the rituals of the Sun King's court. One of his ideas was to re-create a *ballet de cour*, those formal spectacles in which Louis XIV himself took part. Rudolf offered a solemn tableau of pomp and ceremony. Dispensing with the spun-sugar delicacy

---

*Its initial success in 1890 was due chiefly to Tchaikovsky's music, which the composer considered his finest ballet score.

and decorative entertainments predominant in other productions, he set it amid the court at Versailles, dressed by Nicholas Georgiadis in muted browns, blacks and golds.

While he drew heavily on Petipa, Nureyev did not touch such signature elements as the famous Rose Adagio. But Nureyev never believed in the sanctity of the classics. He amended several sections and added others both to increase the male role and to provide the ballet with a more coherent dramatic motivation. In Petipa's version, made for the aging Pavel Gerdt, Florimund scarcely dances; in Nureyev's grand staging, he scarcely stops, dominating the second act with several solos.

Nureyev also gave the Prince a more sharply delineated character: His Florimund was a conceited young fop, at once insolent, flirtatious and charming. He gradually awakens to his responsibilities after seeing his beloved Aurora in a vision. In this way, both the Prince and the Princess experience an awakening. To better convey his state of mind, Rudolf introduced a long solo full of the twists and turns that come of such a conversion. The witch Carabosse and the Lilac Fairy became more equally matched adversaries, the better to heighten the theme of struggle between death and rebirth, decay and renewal.

The Sleeping Beauty opened at La Scala on September 22, 1966, to enormous popular acclaim. Critics applauded Nureyev's exultant dancing and the grandeur of his vision. They were at odds, however, with the larger role assigned the Prince and Nureyev's fussy new choreography. Clive Barnes later wrote that it conveyed "an apparent desire to match every musical note with a step and to chase every musical phrase into the ground."

Almost immediately, Rudolf plunged into a revival of Petipa's Don Quixote for the Vienna State Opera Ballet. In this "pseudo-Spanish Russian ballet," set to Ludwig Minkus's flashy score and only loosely based on the Cervantes novel, Nureyev revealed his flair for comedy. The ballet tells the tale of Kitri, the coquettish daughter of an innkeeper who is in love with the local barber, Basil. Her father, however, hopes to marry her off to a rich older suitor named Gamache. In Nureyev's streamlined version of the Kirov's production, the real hero and heroine are the runaway lovers, while the Spanish nobleman of the title is a minor character who totters through the ballet in search of his Dulcinea. "I wanted the story not to be about Don Quixote but about how people react to him, how they take advantage of him and devise ways to mock and laugh at him. Yet they go crazy doing this, they are as fanatic as the knight is."

Predictably, the biggest changes Nureyev made affected his own role as Basil. This time, his dropping the mime and wearing white tights without breeches did not scandalize the Viennese as it had the Russians. Crammed with difficult dancing, here fiendishly fast, there fiendishly slow, Nureyev's Don Quixote proved as exhilarating to the Vienna dancers as it was to its first-night audience. The critics, however, were more measured in their appraisals. While staunch champions like Alexander Bland praised the ballet's wit, panache and rich opportunities for dancing, the *Sunday Telegraph* considered the staging "inept," and wondered how it would fare without Nureyev in the leading role. This was to become a common complaint about many of his productions: Their chief attraction lay in Nureyev's riveting performance and virtuosic new solos, not in his choreographic invention. Still, audiences reveled in seeing Nureyev "clowning like a tipsy monkey," Richard Buckle later wrote. A decade and countless revisions after the ballet's premiere, John Percival concluded that in the case of Nureyev's Basil, "nobody else brings quite the same sparkling audacity to it. . . . It is remarkable, in fact, to what an extent his acting is done through his dancing. . . . It is almost tempting to look for an autobiographical element in his portrait of the young man who, with nothing but native wit to help him manages to end up a winner while others who started with every advantage come a cropper."

RUDOLF NOW HAD the far-flung career he'd coveted. Yet he longed for the kind of muse relationship that Fonteyn had known with Ashton. He wished that Ashton and Balanchine, the world's two finest living choreographers, would mine his talent by developing new works for him. Neither was keen. They considered him overextended and unmalleable. Balanchine also preferred to discover his own dancers, and looked disdainfully on Rudolf's fame. "You cannot fly around all over the place and maintain a focus," he once said of him.

In his first days in the West, Rudolf had eyes only for Balanchine. To his lasting regret, he had rebuffed Ashton's early efforts to rehearse him in the nineteenth-century classics. "You don't put yourself in my hands," Ashton had complained. Nureyev had wanted to protect his schooling and his style, and Ashton, he felt, had "no formal knowledge." He came to revise that view. "I thought he doesn't understand classical dance. 'Not this year, next year,' I said, and again, 'Not this year, next year.' . . . I was willing in my head but my heart just wouldn't do it. And that took a long time and finally he lost interest and got cool hands."

The situation was more complicated than Nureyev assumed. As director, Ashton had an entire company to consider. And in Antoinette Sibley and Anthony Dowell, he had dancers willing to surrender themselves to his artistic goals. "Rudolf I think questioned this," says Dowell, later to become director of the Royal Ballet. "He was too strong a force. If Fred knew you weren't going to give yourself totally, he wasn't interested." To his nephew Anthony Russell-Roberts, Ashton confided that he found it "utterly exhausting to be in Rudolf's presence." That feeling colored his choice of cast. While "fond" of Rudolf and admiring of his gifts, Ashton could never be "demanded upon," insists Alexander Grant, his close friend and former lover, at whose Battersea home Ashton lunched each Sunday. "Asking Freddie to make a ballet for you was fatal. It would put him off." In any case, Ashton seldom made ballets expressly for men, and according to Somes, whose loyalty to Ashton was equaled only by his jealousy of Nureyev, Ashton had said all that he had to say about Rudolf in *Marguerite and Armand.* "So what more was there to say but say it again in some other ballet?"

In January 1967, when Maude Gosling's oldest friend, Antony Tudor, returned to London to make *Shadowplay* for the Royal Ballet, he chose Dowell for the leading role. The night of its premiere, the Goslings threw Tudor an impromptu supper party and Rudolf spent half the night by Tudor's side, asking for his own ballet. Drawn to Tudor's acuity, Rudolf felt himself "being totally perceived" by the choreographer "in a single, stunning glance." Perhaps he was; however, this and subsequent queries came to nothing.

In the meantime, the Royal Ballet needed some dazzle for a Covent Garden gala—and a new Nureyev-Fonteyn vehicle for its upcoming American tour. So Ashton invited Roland Petit to make a ballet for them. The great hope of French ballet since his emergence in the 1940s, Petit had stunned Paris and London with a succession of popular ballets notable for their Gallic sensuality and bold sense of theater. It was as a cat in his *Les Demoiselles de la Nuit,* made for her in 1949, that Fonteyn had danced her first major role outside her home company.

Rudolf and Petit had first collaborated several months earlier in Paris on the filmed version of Petit's *Le Jeune Homme et la Mort,* based on a scenario by Cocteau. With Petit's wife, Zizi Jeanmaire, one of the most popular entertainers in France, Rudolf had starred in the role made famous by Jean Babilée, as the poet who kills himself for love, only to discover that his temptress is Death.

Le Jeune Homme et la Mort was one of the first dance films staged for the camera and not simply a filmed stage performance. Petit directed it after working on a number of movies in Hollywood. Thinking that Rudolf had "the face of a movie star," Petit edited the film to make ample use of close-ups. "I would tell him how photogenic he was and remind him to put on some lipstick before we shot, telling him he was like Marilyn Monroe, because he would take the light like her. And he was so happy. He'd say, 'I'm photogenic?' and I'd say, 'Yes, yes, like Marilyn Monroe." The medium of film and Petit's close-ups allowed the viewer not only to observe for the first time "incremental changes in [Nureyev's] expression as they [occurred]" but to "get the perfume of him."

In London, Rudolf played host to Petit. Hearing him complain one day of exhaustion, Rudolf arrived at his door the next morning in his

Mercedes and drove him to and from rehearsals for the remainder of his stay. He also delighted in testing Petit's boundaries. "He knew me to be a man of the world and he loved trying to shock me." He took him to seedy bars "where men were dressed as women; not beautiful boys but ugly men dressed as women. He wanted to show me that he was a man of the world too."

With *Paradise Lost*, Petit hoped to show ballet's most romantic twosome in a radically new light. For him this meant dispensing with tutus and tiaras and emphasizing Rudolf's sexual vigor for all it was worth. In Petit's Garden of Eden, Adam and Eve were chic, sexy and thoroughly modern. Petit had drawn his inspiration from a poem by novelist Jean Cau; the company, however, was expecting Milton. At the first orchestra rehearsal, the composer-conductor Marius Constant began by telling the musicians, "Gentleman, I expect you have all heard of Milton's *Paradise Lost?*" When they all murmured, "Yes," he warned them that "this ballet has nothing whatever to do with [it!]"

Amid flashing neon lights and Martial Raysse's Pop Art decor,* Nureyev and Fonteyn crawled, twisted and somersaulted to Marius Constant's cacophonous score, he in white tights and suspenders, she in the briefest white plastic minidress this side of the King's Road. Moving as if they were a single organism, they composed a series of abstract forms, as intricately poised as a Calder mobile. A bold vehicle for its stars, Petit's ballet amplified the daring, synergy and split-second timing that defined their partnership. In the most memorable sequence, Rudolf circled the stage with a loping run before diving headfirst through the huge scarlet lips of a large female face, "the kind of thing," wrote Fonteyn, "that really only happens in French ballets."

But as this was London, the ballet titillated its first-night crowd. "I saw the patriarch of mankind have the first orgasm, standing marvellously on his head," wrote Buckle, describing one of its many indelible images. Rudolf's stage aura, it was agreed, had never been used to more thrilling effect.†

Among its biggest fans were Mick Jagger and his girlfriend, the pop singer Marianne Faithfull, who were photographed arriving for the premiere. Faithfull vividly recalls the excitement of seeing Nureyev dive through those scarlet lips. "That may have been the moment that I felt he was most connected to what we were doing. The erotic element was always there in his dancing, but here it was much more overt." Afterward she and Jagger went backstage. "Mick knew him slightly by then. I thought they were quite similar as performers, in their intensity and erotic

---

*Henry Moore had been invited to do the decor, but had refused.
†While the ballet was well received, it was given only seven performances in London and several more in America before it was dropped from the repertoire.

thrill." She and Jagger were "obsessed" with Nureyev and went to all his first nights, apparently to study him at close range. "Mick and I and everybody we knew couldn't help but be influenced by Nureyev, by his individuality and concentration. He had that quality of being lost in his own thing. He was staggeringly beautiful and somewhat removed. There's something about artists like him that you can't catch and never will."

Certainly Jagger's naughty schoolboy image, all pouting lips, waifish charm and sexual authority, owed something to Nureyev's example. What they shared was an electric physical presence that charged both men and women, gay and straight. But did they charge each other? Joan Thring once joined them for lunch and recalls them behaving "like two delinquents." Their interest in each other was obvious. "They were both icons of the age, and young, and you never knew which way they were going to go. I don't know whether they ever got together. They probably did because they were certainly well on the way. They were very flirtatious."

If the blurring of sexual lines was part of the creative mix of the era, so was the new drug culture. Twelve days before the opening of *Paradise Lost*, Jagger and Faithfull had been busted for acid at Keith Richards's country house. Jagger was briefly jailed and the papers couldn't get enough of the story.

Rudolf steered clear of the drug scene, not only for fear of being deported but because he dreaded losing control over his body. Houseguests were admonished: "And whatever you do, no drugs in my house!" The director Tony Richardson invited him to a party one night at his Chelsea flat, but when Rudolf arrived to find the other guests "absolutely out of their brains," he left immediately, fearing that he might end up in the papers or in jail, as Jagger had.

It was, therefore, all the more ironic that he should become a folk hero for being busted himself in July 1967, in the heart of hippiedom during the Summer of Love. On tour with the Royal Ballet in San Francisco, Rudolf and Margot had just danced *Paradise Lost* before a sellout crowd when a fan approached Fonteyn at the stage door and invited her to a "freak-out" in the Haight-Ashbury section. She and Rudolf were on their way to supper at Trader Vic's with friends, but she was curious enough to take the address. On the way home, she persuaded Rudolf to check out the party. Only reluctantly did he agree to go along to the six-room apartment near Golden Gate Park. The first hint that this wasn't a run-of-the-mill soiree came when they couldn't find anything to drink. They were just about to leave when someone shouted, "Fuzz!" and in the commotion that followed, they were swept up to the roof, where Fonteyn kept warm by throwing her white mink over her knees. Rudolf jumped to an adjoining rooftop, hoping to flee via the fire escape, but he, Fonteyn and sixteen others were arrested in a raid and whisked to the city jail in a paddy wagon. There they were fingerprinted, questioned and booked on charges of "visiting a place where marijuana is kept."

Awakened at five o'clock in the morning by a call from Fonteyn, a surprised Vernon Clark, the Royal Ballet's manager, bailed them out for $330 apiece. By then a mob of reporters was on hand to record their release. Though the charges were swiftly dropped, the story made headlines around the world. When an intrusive TV camera was shoved too close to his face, Rudolf exhaled heavily onto the lens to fog the picture. "What children you are!" he scoffed from the taxi window as they rode away. The unwanted publicity hardly hurt him and delighted Hurok: Not only did it bolster sales at the Hollywood Bowl, the next stop on the tour, it gave Rudolf and Margot newfound cachet with the under-thirty generation, who now embraced them as renegades. Coming on the heels of their sold-out performances in *Romeo and Juliet* and *Paradise Lost*, their detour to Haight-Ashbury boosted their youthful luster. Suddenly Nureyev and Fonteyn were symbols of the counterculture.

The tour had begun in New York, where the Royal Ballet was seen for the first time at the "new" Metropolitan Opera House at Lincoln Center. Across the plaza, or "the ballet battlefield," as one critic termed it, Bruhn and Fracci were dancing with the American Ballet Theatre at the same time, making it one of the most exciting dance seasons the city had ever known. Over three weeks in May 1967, audiences saw both Erik and Rudolf in the roles of Albrecht and Romeo.* On the same evening, in fact, Bruhn partnered Fracci in *Giselle* at one theater, while Nureyev danced it with Fonteyn at the other. Once more, the press pitted them against each other. "Bruhn's dancing," reported *The New Yorker* of his Romeo, "was elegant in the extreme. . . . It did not, though, have quite the uninhibited boyishness of Mr. Nureyev's." *Time* magazine introduced Bruhn to its readers as "the man whom Nureyev considers the finest male dancer in the world" and quoted Rudolf as saying, "His technique is too good to be believed."†

Rudolf and Erik, if not exactly impervious to the comparisons, were better able to handle them now that they were starring with different companies. And the fact that Bruhn finally had a sublime partnership all his own, one that critics were calling the highlight of the ABT season,

*Bruhn and Fracci danced only the balcony scene, choreographed by Bruhn and set to the Prokofiev score.

†That summer Vera Volkova, the Copenhagen-based teacher of both Bruhn and Nureyev, visited Leningrad for the first time since she had left in the early 1920s. Everywhere she went, she reported, and by every dancer she met, she was asked about Bruhn, who had made such a lasting impression during his visit there with ABT in 1960. She also met with Pushkin, her old partner in Shanghai, and one can safely assume that Rudolf was the focus of that conversation.

helped to soothe lingering resentments. Bruhn had agreed to return to ABT on condition that Fracci be invited to dance with him in her New York debut. The enormous success of their partnership rekindled Bruhn's faith in his dancing, and it was a much more contented Erik who greeted Rudolf in New York. To the bafflement of a press corps eager to play up their rivalry, the two dancers took class together with Valentina Pereyaslavic, caught each other's performances and went out to dinner.

In many ways, little had changed between them. Still, their relationship was not what it had been in those first years, when they had spent all their time together, working in the studio. Rudolf's fame and rapacity had disrupted that pattern, and gradually both had come to see that a domestic relationship was untenable. Rudolf worried that Erik was turning him into an alcoholic and smarted at his sarcasm. Erik envied Rudolf's huge fees, youth and inexhaustible strength, but not his talent and not his life. They had different desires, different appetites, he said. His close friend Marit Gentele* recalled how he would "mock Rudolf for caring about this countess and that one. Erik disliked all that brouhaha."

Already troubled by Rudolf's promiscuity, Bruhn had no more energy for their battles. "I can't be around him. It's impossible. We'll destroy each other," he told Gentele. "He lost control around Rudolf and he didn't want to live like that," she adds. "Rudolf was everything he wouldn't dare to do."

Though sex was all but over between them, their spiritual ties, having transcended dalliances, conflict and distance, would prove life-long. Rudolf later told a number of friends that he would have bound himself to Erik forever if Erik had only let him. But Erik knew that he couldn't, as he acknowledged in an interview with John Gruen. "Rudik has always claimed that I was an example of freedom and independence — that I would always do exactly what I wanted without regard to others — and it may be so. Well, in those early years that's what happened between Rudik and me — a collision and explosion which could not last. If Rudik had wanted it otherwise, I'm sorry."

Onstage, Nureyev's partnership with Fonteyn flourished. During the Royal Ballet's 1967 New York season, Antoinette Sibley, Anthony Dowell, Merle Park and Svetlana Beriosova all attracted notice. But *Paradise Lost* was the ballet that had sold out first, and months in advance, because it was the only work in which the public felt it was guaranteed to see Nureyev and Fonteyn. Crawling across the stage of the Met one night in Petit's ballet, Fonteyn suddenly thought, 'This is a hell of a way to spend your forty-eighth birthday!' She figured this might amuse Rudolf, but instead of laughing, as he usually did over shared absurdities, he

*Now Marit Gryson.

answered dolefully, "I wish I could think I am dancing still on forty-eighth birthday."

While Fonteyn had no intention of retiring just then, on the closing night of the Met season, when she and Rudolf were due to dance *Swan Lake*, a rumor circulated that this was to be her final New York performance. Few could imagine that they might look forward to seeing a fifty-year-old Swan Queen. (And many of her colleagues hoped they were right.) At the curtain, she and Rudolf were given a forty-two-and-a-half-minute ovation and showered with flowers, streamers and even a laurel wreath, which Rudolf gallantly retrieved from the footlights. The crowd refused to let them go. At first, they had taken their bows in that grandly choreographed way of theirs: I curtsy, you bow, I present you with a rose, you press your lips to my hand. But the ardor of the applause so overwhelmed them that after thirty minutes, they simply stood there, center stage, and smiled.

By night Rudolf played the celebrity-about-town. At the party film producer Sam Spiegel threw for him and Fonteyn at the Plaza Hotel, he chatted up Lauren Bacall. He stayed at Lee Radziwill's eleven-room duplex on Fifth Avenue while Lee was out of town, and there dined with her older sister, Jackie.* On his arrival Lee had made sure that the fridge was stocked with champagne. According to Joan Thring, who accompanied him, Jackie upstaged her. "Jackie then went and bought these huge cheesecakes from Lindy's because she knew Rudolf loved them. Lee was very upset about it." At a dinner party Rudolf hosted one night, the choreographer John Taras informed him that Bronislava Nijinska was in serious financial straits. Since apart from Margot, the only other guests were Jackie Kennedy, Ari Onassis and Stas Radziwill, Rudolf suggested he tell them about her predicament. "I was trying to raise money for her and here were these lovely rich people," although Rudolf did not count himself among them. The next day Taras received an envelope containing five one-hundred-dollar bills. It was from Margot, the only one of them to respond.

Rudolf was by now a regular at Arthur, joining habitués such as Balanchine, Tennessee Williams and the entire Warhol crowd. A "peacock," as the club's proprietress recalls him, Rudolf was "seductive with both men and women." Among the latter was the buxom actress and cabaret singer Monique van Vooren, a jet-set party girl and "the kind of character that exists only in Fellini movies: hyper-sophisticated, hyper-dramatic, hyper-hysterical." The Belgian-born van Vooren had got her start with a bit part in *Gigi* and would later star as a nymphomaniac in

---

*In what would prove a short-lived career, Radziwill was then starring in a critically assailed production of *The Philadelphia Story* in Chicago, which Rudolf went to see later in the tour.

Andy Warhol's 3-D cult film *Frankenstein*. If Jackie Kennedy was one of the few women he stood up to greet in his dressing room, van Vooren was the sort of woman he relied on to fix his tea, run his errands, and be available on a moment's notice. "If Rudolf was a religion, I'd join it," she was fond of telling reporters. Like many of the women in his life, she was thrilled to find herself admitted to his entourage and would do whatever he asked to remain there.

One night van Vooren brought her boyfriend Hiram Keller backstage. Keller, a struggling actor from Georgia, was then waiting tables at Arthur, though his striking beauty, dark looks and blue eyes would soon land him in the chorus of *Hair*, the landmark sixties musical, and a starring role in *Fellini's Satyricon*. (Later he would have a brief affair with Talitha Getty, wife of the American oil heir J. Paul Getty Jr.) Rudolf took one look at Keller, who many thought resembled him, and invited himself on their date to the Copacabana to hear Diana Ross. The next day he asked Keller out for lunch and insisted he accompany him on the rest of the tour, without van Vooren. "He expected me to be his boyfriend and I thought, 'Why not?' If you were twenty-one years old and not doing anything in particular and the greatest dancer of the time asked you to come on tour, hey!" He lasted as far as Boston, the next stop. He was bored, "just sitting around backstage," and resentful of his supporting role. "Rudi had a hard time being with people who were as attractive as he was. He always had to be the one."

His place was quickly filled by others, though rarely for long. At a party at the Ritz one night while still in Boston, he fell into conversation with Philip Core and Jeremiah Tower, two Harvard undergraduates dressed fancifully in frock coats. Core, a painter, and Tower, an architecture major (later to become a leading American chef), both were "just flabbergasted by how well informed and interested he was in talking about painting and music." From what they'd read about him, they were expecting "a frou-frou dancer who talked only about himself." But Rudolf "was like a vampire," recalls Tower. "He wanted to know everything I knew. Then he turned to Philip and wanted to know everything he knew." When Rudolf invited them up to his suite at the Ritz on his next trip to town, they arrived with another friend, whom Rudolf "grabbed after drinking a bottle of Stolichnaya." It was Core and Tower, not Rudolf, who felt obliged to repair to the next room, where, soon, their all-night party resumed.

22

"Nothing Tomorrow, Now, at Once!"

EAGER TO PROVE TO Balanchine that he could dance his ballets, Rudolf made his debut in *Apollo* in the fall of 1967, albeit in Vienna, not New York, and without the benefit of Balanchine's coaching. John Taras rehearsed him, although Rudolf also drew on Erik's recollections of working with Balanchine on the ballet. "He told me what Balanchine said to him about the . . . meaning of every movement." Not only did Rudolf remember each step Taras taught him, he did not make any amendments. "He was very strict about that. At one point I showed him a change Balanchine had made, but Rudolf wanted to do exactly what I had first taught him because it was the original version."

The foundation stone of Balanchine's neoclassical style, *Apollo*, set to Stravinsky's striking score, describes the birth of the god Apollo and his education by the Muses. When it was first announced that Rudolf was to dance the role, a number of critics fussed that Rudolf was too flamboyant, too much a Dionysus to play an Apollo, and that only Balanchine-trained dancers could master its pure-dance poetry and rhythmic nuances. His interpretation, though slower and more solemn than most, convinced many of them otherwise. His Apollo, wrote one critic, "was less of a game, more of a ritual: the Balanchine choreography almost has a Martha Graham effect." To the German critic Horst Koegler, what made Nureyev's approach unusual was his "individual way of placing the accents, his individual way of phrasing. It is still Balanchine, but it is Balanchine spoken with a foreign accent." But as Taras points out, Balanchine's choreography stresses the awkwardness of the boy, the "primitiveness" of Apollo, and this was the quality Rudolf exploited. "Balanchine's Apollo does not become a classical beauty until the very end.

He's a young man being taught to be a god." Certainly one can find traces of Rudolf's own struggle to define himself in his reading of Apollo's ascent to Olympus. As Koegler observed, Rudolf was not so much a false Apollo as "a frustrated Dionysus. All his elementary powers and instincts steer him towards a free life, free from moral considerations, free from social obligations. But the gods have chosen him to belong to their family, and he has no choice but to accept their call. . . ."

Rudolf naturally hoped that Balanchine would ask about his performance. Taras doesn't recall that he ever did. "The only time I saw Balanchine show interest in the ballet was when Misha [Baryshnikov] danced it." The first time Rudolf danced the role in England, in 1969 with the Dutch National Ballet, Richard Buckle wrote that of all the great Apollos he had seen, "Nureyev beats the lot. Nobody has ever put so much into the role." The next year the Royal Ballet finally let him dance it. To Balanchine champion Arlene Croce, Rudolf's "overriding sin" lay in "slowing down the tempi to the point of extinguishing all life from the ballet. . . . Apollo to him is obviously a great and exalted ritual whose mysteries must be unfolded at maximum leisure," while to Ashton biographer David Vaughan, his performance was proof that "there is more than one way to perform a masterpiece."

Rudolf would continue to rethink that performance until the last years of his career, all the while hoping he might dance Apollo with the New York City Ballet. He never would. When Balanchine's successor, Peter Martins, came to see him dance the ballet in New York in the 1980s, Rudolf asked him afterward what he thought of his performance. "It was very interesting," replied Martins, who had danced the role for years, "but it had nothing to do with Apollo." Rankled by his disapproval, with its echoes of the snobbism of his Vaganova days, Rudolf answered bitterly, "It wasn't perfect enough? Wasn't pure enough?"

STATELESS he may have been, but by the fall of 1967 Rudolf had acquired his first home in London. At a cost of forty-five thousand pounds, Number 6 Fife Road was a six-bedroom Victorian house on the edge of Richmond Park. Its thirty-foot drawing room and four large reception rooms seemed outsize even after Rudolf had furnished them with massive oak tables, a Jacobean dining set, dark-colored sofas, imposing candelabra, tapestries, carpets and a life-size portrait of Peter the Great. The two beanbag chairs he brought home from Italy that year provided the only trendy touch. Sunlight rarely leaked through the thick curtains, and in the evening the dining room was illuminated by candlelight.

His homes, like his ballets, reflected Nureyev's taste for opulence and Oriental richness amid a theatrical setting. To Martin Kamer, the assistant to Nureyev's regular designers, Barry Kay and Nicholas Georgiadis, Nureyev's sensibility was "very Novosibirsk, very heavy. We used to joke about it among ourselves. He wouldn't ask what you recommended. He was very much his own man and let his own taste decide. I bumped into him in a London nightclub one night and he said, 'I have corps de ballet and I want you to organize it.' Rudolf got angry if you said you didn't understand, so I knew if he kept talking, I'd find my way. I finally realized that he had said, 'I have Córdoba leather.' He wanted me to figure out how to put it on his walls. It was a very rich, textured wall covering made of antique leather, which you see a lot in Dutch interiors. That's what he was drawn to, very somber baroque things."

Rudolf liked best that the house had its own garden and trees and was at a remove from the center of town. It thrilled him that he could watch deer feeding in his backyard. Walking through Richmond Park, he felt as if he were in the English countryside, which gave him a sense of calm. He had approved the house from photographs Thring had taken and by the time he discovered that it was difficult to reach without a car, he had fallen in love with it. To get himself to Covent Garden, he had to cross the Hammersmith or Putney Bridge, which, given his schedule, made for a high-stress thirty-minute commute. Thring often stayed over to get him up in time for rehearsal and occasionally had him stay at her house in Earl's Court because it was close to the company's studios at the Royal Ballet School. "It was a nightmare for me because he'd get into a frenzy that he was going to be late." Stalled in traffic on their way to a dress rehearsal one day, Rudolf suddenly jumped out of the car at the Sloane Square tube station. But he boarded a train heading in the wrong direction and Thring arrived well ahead of him. "He was beside himself. When he saw me at the stage door, he said, 'Bitch! Bitch!' He just had to attack somebody."

The penury of childhood never left him. It fell to Gorlinsky to assure him that he could afford the things he wanted. Under the new deal Gorlinsky negotiated with the Royal Ballet that fall, Rudolf's fee was increased from one thousand to twelve hundred and fifty pounds per performance. Concerned about being overcharged, Rudolf preferred that Thring and Gorlinsky pay his bills. Seeing a four-poster Tudor bed he liked in a Jermyn Street shopwindow one night, Rudolf told John Tooley, "I want that, I must go and ring Sander," who promptly bought it on his behalf. And Thring would regularly get calls from cabdrivers wanting to collect their fares. And yet, despite a reputation for stinginess, Rudolf was the most generous of hosts. Any colleague passing through London usually wound up at his dinner table, as did friends like Fonteyn and the Goslings. His hospitality, recalled the critic Richard Buckle, was "medieval, baronial: a blazing log fire, immense brass candelabra with wax candles, Spanish leather . . . twelve courses served on silver plate, whisky in pint goblets . . . it was seldom before half-past three in the morning that I left the castle of the unsleeping prince."

Minding that castle was Rudolf's new housekeeper, Alice, a short, plumpish African woman who addressed him only as "sir." Highly eccentric, she liked to go dancing at the Hammersmith Palais and frequently brought her partners home with her. This gave Rudolf "the heebie-jeebies," Thring recalls. "I mean, some stranger with a key." Still, her quirkiness amused him and whenever he was in particularly good humor, she impersonated him. She appeared at one dinner party in a long dressing gown and turban fashioned from a towel, and proceeded to stride imperiously around the table as she served the meal. "She knew how to handle him," says Thring. "Rudolf had no experience in dealing with help." When she came into his room one morning to wake him, Rudolf was so startled by the sight of her that he immediately rang Thring. "Maid has not her teeth." "Well," she replied, "tell her to put them in." But Rudolf insisted, "No, no. You do it."

DESPITE HIS GRAND new home, Rudolf was on the move throughout the fall of 1967: Vienna, Paris, London, then back again to Paris, London, on to Stockholm, Monte Carlo and Copenhagen, before returning again to London, then Vienna and one last stop, in Milan. During these four months in what had become his typical itinerary, he gave thirty-seven performances, appeared in ten different ballets, and partnered nine different ballerinas, among them Fonteyn, Fracci, Chauviré, Merle Park and Marcia Haydée. No opportunity to dance was overlooked. On October 13, in between the dress rehearsal and the premicre of *Paradise Lost* at the Paris Opéra, he flew to London to fill in for an injured Donald MacLeary on the opening night of the Royal Ballet's fall season. He partnered Svetlana Beriosova for the first time in *Swan Lake*, and then, the very next night, made his Paris Opéra debut, four years later than originally planned.

To mark the occasion, Yves Saint Laurent and Pierre Bergé threw a dinner party for him and Fonteyn in their Place Vauban apartment on the Left Bank. Among their attractive male guests was a nineteen-year-old decorative arts student, whom Rudolf wooed to London for weekend visits, instructing Thring to pay his airfare. Rudolf called this latest object of desire "the child." Once when "the child's" plane arrived late, Rudolf met him at the door with a pair of slippers, because he feared that he might be cold and tired. "He was very warm, very affectionate," recalls the student, now a prominent figure in French couture. "He didn't like to talk so much, but the little he said was enough to make you understand what he wanted." Like many of Rudolf's young boyfriends, he had to integrate himself into a life in which he was but a supporting player. He slept in Rudolf's four-poster Tudor bed, accompanied him to class, went antiques shopping with him on his free afternoons, watched silently in his dressing room while Rudolf made up his face for the stage, and ran around London with him in the evenings, to the theater, the opera and the movies. But theirs was a transitory affair, for Rudolf "was very free in his behavior. He liked beautiful boys. If he liked somebody, he took them as if he were choosing a piece of cake. 'Come here, you. Talk to me. Can you join me later?' "

At Erik's invitation, Rudolf staged *The Nutcracker* for the Royal Swedish Ballet in November 1967. Erik had been named the company's new director, and knowing that Rudolf was supposed to mount the ballet at Covent Garden in December, he invited him to work out the kinks first in Stockholm. Rudolf quickly became enmeshed in conflicts. The dancers refused to rehearse past six o'clock and Rudolf provoked them by complaining to the press that lifelong contracts had made them "half-hearted" and interested only in washing machines and improvements to their suburban homes. He expected them to work until midnight while he drove them through what they considered impossible choreography. But their rehearsals had to be fit around his peripatetic schedule, making them feel that they were simply tools for his artistic advancement.

As opening night drew near, tempers flared. Erik, who had been dancing in Oslo, returned to an explosive situation. One of the dancers had accused Rudolf of trying to strangle her and "they had even called in the police! Well, I think that was probably exaggerated, but it is true that Rudik was very rough on the dancers and sometimes unnecessarily so." Nevertheless, his exacting demands galvanized them. "One could almost sense Nureyev's whiplash over their heads," wrote a local critic after repeated viewings of his *Nutcracker*, "for never has such precision and technical verve been shown in this company."

Though a beloved holiday classic, *The Nutcracker* had long been regarded by ballet lovers as something of a Christmas confection, held together by Tchaikovsky's irresistible score. Rudolf hoped to remedy that view by producing a ballet as much for adults as for children. To that end, he attempted nothing less than a wholesale revision of the ballet, first mounted in St. Petersburg in 1892, with a scenario by Petipa and choreography by Ivanov.* His starting point was Vassily Vainonen's 1934 version for the Kirov, in which he had danced many times. But his was to be no innocent frolic through the Kingdom of Sweets, for in both Tchaikovsky's score and E. T. A. Hoffmann's story, he discerned a strong undercurrent of menace. "If you listen to the music, it has enormous depth, enormous feel-

---

*Most of which has not survived.

ing and much more. It's not just a pretty ballet." Neither was Hoffmann's tale simply child's play. Beneath its humor, as the St. Petersburg painter and ballet designer Alexander Benois had observed, "there is a feeling of tension, a kind of delicious languor, as though the heroine, Clara, was both overjoyed and tormented by all that happens to her."

Rudolf made certain that plenty did, thus giving the ballerina a much bigger role. In his version, Clara falls asleep at the Christmas party and dreams of a fairy princess, who is Clara herself, all grown up and dressed in a tutu. But quickly her anxieties take center stage. The world, as she imagines it, is a frightening place, peopled by armies of nasty rats and bats who turn out to be her relatives. Like his production of *Swan Lake*, Nureyev's *Nutcracker* is conceived as a projection of the protagonist's mind.

Rudolf's most drastic alteration was to have the magical Dr. Drosselmeyer, the mysterious white-haired guest who gives Clara the nutcracker doll, reappear as the handsome Prince of Clara's dreams.* This transformation not only added an unusual psychological dimension to the story, but gave Nureyev an intriguing dual role.

During rehearsals in Stockholm, Rudolf dined regularly at the home of Goeran Gentele, the engaging director of the Royal Swedish Opera House, and his wife, Marit, both close friends of Erik's. One night Rudolf telephoned to ask Marit to invite "boys" for him to meet. Minutes later, he called back to say, "Oh, don't bother, I'll bring my own salt and pepper." Lee Radziwill arrived on the scene, clearly still infatuated with Rudolf, and didn't appear to mind when he treated her disdainfully. "Take care of the princess," he would say to Gentele, putting extra emphasis on her title. Still, he loved to be admired by rich, beautiful women, princesses in particular, and welcomed the attention Lee lavished on him. In March 1966, she had thrown him a twenty-eighth-birthday party at her London home, and he was a frequent visitor to Turville Grange, the Radziwills' country estate near Henley-on-Thames.

The Nutcracker opened on November 17, 1967, at the Royal Swedish Opera House to popular acclaim and generally favorable notices. The final preparations had been so frantic that Gerd Andersson, the company's prima ballerina, had sprained her calf muscle and was unable to dance the premiere. Rudolf was understandably distressed. "I come here to dance with you and you get sick!" Having danced despite bandaged ankles, fevers and infections, he could not abide any infirmity of will in others.

When he danced the ballet's premiere at Covent Garden three

*In most productions of the ballet, the magician Drosselmeyer and the Prince are danced by two different dancers. The former is generally performed by an older dancer specializing in character roles.

months later,* he found an indomitable partner in Merle Park. He and Fonteyn had by then begun to dance regularly with others, prompting false rumors that their partnership was ending. But the fact was, neither wanted an exclusive partnership and Rudolf had the greater need to experiment with a diverse range of movement styles. He also recognized that because of their age gap, their alliance could not go on forever and that he had better start developing other partnerships. He had designed the demanding ballerina role in *The Nutcracker* with Park in mind and stuffed it with what he called "knitting," intricate combinations of steps, one following the other. Park had gone to Stockholm to rehearse with him and recalls that he "never liked you to feel comfortable. He liked things to be just a little awkward so that you had to attack it." That she did in a bravura opening night performance that quickly established her as one of the Royal Ballet's most sparkling technicians.

A hit with audiences, Nureyev's first evening-length production for the Royal Ballet would prove one of the company's most popular works. Among its champions was Ninette de Valois, who particularly admired the final pas de deux, in which the Prince and his ballerina performed the same sweeping steps in tandem. As de Valois would later observe, Nureyev was not a choreographer "in the real sense of the word." Rather, he had a talent for reproducing the classics. "He put in a few changes, which he may have lifted from somewhere else, for all we know. And all he had to say was I nicked them there or there or I don't like that, I'll try and improve them, and very often he did and sometimes he didn't. Production is quite a different thing from choreography." The critics were mostly cool to Nureyev's choreography for *The Nutcracker* and to a story line many of them thought unduly complicated. Fernau Hall, writing in the *Daily Telegraph*, saw it as proof that "splendid dancing can disguise but never justify shapeless choreography," while the *Sunday Telegraph*, in a disdainful review entitled "Nutcracker—or Sledgehammer?" dismissed it as "run of the mill stuff that might well be just the thing for Omsk, or even Tomsk perhaps, but has none of the creative invention and imagery we have learned to expect from an Ashton, a MacMillan or a Cranko."

In New York, where the ballet was first shown in the spring of 1968, Clive Barnes spoke for the critical consensus when he wrote in *The New York Times* that the choreography was "never less than efficient but rarely inspired." Nureyev would continue to revise his production, not only at the Royal Ballet, but in the versions he came to mount at La Scala, at

---

*The ballet was first performed at the Royal Opera House on February 29, 1968. For the London production, Georgiadis's opulent sets and costumes replaced Renzo Mongiardino's decor for Stockholm.

the Teatro Colón in Buenos Aires and at the Berlin Ballet. As Peter Williams would later admiringly remark, "More than anything, I find that [his] conception enriches what is one of Tchaikovsky's most hauntingly beautiful scores and gives maturity to something too often associated with nursery gramophones." Writing in the 1980s, Barnes reversed himself and extolled Nureyev's achievement. "No version of *The Nutcracker* that we have ever seen has been more potently dramatic; few have displayed so sharp an imprint of personal style."

RUDOLF HAD NOT HAD a new role from Ashton in five years, but finally, in early 1968, in the brief interval between the Stockholm and London premieres of his *Nutcracker*, Ashton paired him with Antoinette Sibley in a segment of *Jazz Calendar*, a suite of seven trendy variations "full of in-jokes and parodies of contemporary choreography, including his own." With a nod to the swinging sixties, he set his new ballet to Richard Rodney Bennett's jazz score, based on the children's nursery rhyme that begins "Monday's child is fair of face," and commissioned the twenty-six-year-old artist Derek Jarman to design the decor and costumes. "Friday's Child" for Nureyev and Sibley was an overtly erotic, blues-inspired duet strongly influenced by the "classical-erotic-acrobatic idiom" of Petit's *Paradise Lost*. Their rehearsals were "absolute bliss," recalls Sibley — and fortuitously impromptu. "Fred came in the first day and said, 'Oh, I've forgotten the music at home, so we'll just get on and work anyway.' Well, we all just started singing the blues and made it work." Friday's children are meant to be loving and giving; however, "Fred wanted it very sexy, more lust than loving. And Rudolf just started doing these extraordinary things. He was thrilled to be doing it. The hard thing was when the music arrived, after all the work we'd done." Though running a temperature, Rudolf crawled from his sickbed to dance the premiere on January 9, 1968. The ballet was a huge hit with audiences, but not with the critics, who were unsparing in their disapproval. ASHTON OUT OF DATE ran the headline on Mary Clarke's review.

Two months later, Ashton cast Rudolf in the revival of *Birthday Offering*, which he had made to showcase the individuality of seven company ballerinas. This time around, however, Ashton added a tricky new solo for Nureyev, packed with difficult steps. Soon after, Kenneth Tynan, the most influential drama critic of the day, wrote that ballet was a dying art. Queried for his response, Ashton replied, "Yes and it's having a very grand funeral." Certainly the clamor for Fonteyn and Nureyev was as keen as ever, leading Richard Buckle to wonder, apropos of Tynan, whether "an art can be dying and excessively popular. . . . I can only say that if all the applause in all the London theatres where drama is being performed was played end to end it would not add up to half of what greets Fonteyn and Nureyev after one of their evenings at the Garden."

Rudolf found his collaboration with Ashton deeply rewarding, yet Ashton would not create another role for him. "I can't control him in any way," he had told designer Jarman during the making of *Jazz Calendar*. "If you have any problems with the dancers, just let me know and I'll sort it out. Rudi, I'm afraid you'll have to sort out yourself." Jarman had quickly discovered that Rudolf was the despair of the wardrobe department. As the only male dancer to have specific requirements, he wanted his jackets cut short, above the hip, so as to accentuate the line of his leg, and snug-fitting but with enough room around the armholes to allow him to move freely. His neckline was to remain unobscured, which meant absolutely no ruffles or collars, and his costumes had to fasten in the front. This last demand was an enormous hassle because nearly all costumes were made to fasten in the back, but Rudolf was terrified of catching fire from the stage lights. "What if there's a fire and I cannot get out?" he would ask whenever his dresser, Michael Brown, tried to convince him to change his mind. Since he rarely allowed enough time for a fitting, it often took six or more performances before his costume was properly adjusted.

Rudolf had already worn out a number of dressers by the time Brown assumed the job in 1967. His ability to deal with Nureyev's irascible behavior made Brown an indispensable member of his team, though his first experience of those darker moods clearly gave him pause. "Once he knew that someone was scared of him, he'd wipe the floor with them. You had to stand up to him. It took me a couple of years with him, really." Brown, a former professional skater, organized Rudolf's preperformance rituals and readied him for the stage. Most nights Brown would have to dress Rudolf in the wings because he was still doing his warm-up at curtain time. Not that the curtain often rose on time. "Until he was ready, he wouldn't start. He'd say, 'I'm not ready. You wait.' Simple as that. So you waited." Part of his warm-up of course involved working himself into a rage. That's where the opera house staff unwittingly played its part. By urging him to get on with it, the stage managers helped stoke his adrenaline.

Brown not only tended Rudolf's costumes and makeup box but personally prepared his ballet shoes, something he did for no other dancer. While most male dancers wore the one pair of slippers that went with their costume until they gave out and then threw them away, Rudolf mixed different pairs, changed his shoes in between acts, and even scenes, and refused to throw away any of the ones he liked. This meant that Brown was forever patching, sewing and dyeing leather shoes that had grown tough and brittle from years of sweat. His fingers would be "raw, stitching through the leather." And since Rudolf disliked new ballet slippers, Brown would break them in for him by wearing them around his flat. Rudolf kept his shoes, makeup and tights in one big bag, which

NUREYEV: HIS LIFE] 348

he toted around with him wherever he went. In airports, he pulled it behind him on wheels, prompting Merle Park to dub it "his doggy." Rudolf sometimes called it jokingly "Sir Fred." His bag, Brown says, was his life. For regardless of all the trappings—the houses, the hostesses, the Huroks—it all came down to the contents of that bag.

RUDOLF GREW to rely on Brown to such an extent that he insisted on working with him even when he performed in London with foreign companies, each of which had its own wardrobe people on the payroll. "They found it easier if I was there, because then there would be no problems." Brown was also Rudolf's traveling companion on the Royal's tours abroad. Long after the events at Le Bourget, Rudolf feared that the KGB might try to hijack his plane, so he often flew ahead with Brown rather than travel on the company charter. Whether the KGB actually had designs on him is not known, but in the era of Philby, Burgess and James Bond, Nureyev's paranoia was understandable. So much so that Fonteyn, Keith Money and Joan Thring met in secret with a man who called Thring at home one evening in March 1968.

Rudolf's solicitor had told him to call her, he said. "A serious situation" had arisen. It was imperative that they meet at once. Thring was so unnerved that she flew out of her house at Westgate Terrace in Earl's Court and hurried over to 149 Telegraph Road, a few blocks away, where Fonteyn was staying with her mother. Fonteyn, in turn, called Money. "Can you come straight over here? We need a man. Joan is here with some rather mysterious and alarming problem, and we must be back at her house by eight o'clock." The caller, John Merry, soon arrived, accompanied by a female companion he identified only as "Special Branch." It had come to his attention, he now informed them gravely, that Rudolf's phone lines were tapped and that his house was under constant surveillance by Russian agents. They might try to kidnap him, he warned. Already the postman had been stopped and questioned. Didn't they agree that a guard should be placed at his door immediately? At first Thring was inclined to take him seriously because Rudolf had been bothered by incessant nuisance calls in recent weeks. Once in a while there was a clicking noise on the line. He had asked her to speak to his solicitor and she assumed that Merry was part of the investigation. But Merry went on, and the more involved his story got, the less they believed it. "If they really wanted to snatch Rudolf," Fonteyn said, half-mockingly, "there's not a great deal anyone could do." When Merry asked for a high fee to act as Rudolf's bodyguard, they quickly sent him on his way. But they kept the news of his visit from Rudolf, knowing it would only alarm him.

A few weeks earlier, Rudolf's sister Rosa had cabled him from Leningrad. Hamet had died of lung cancer on February 25. Rudolf went white when he read her telegram. Father and son had not spoken for seven years. Rudolf had always maintained a reticence about his family and his father in particular, but he once told Merle Park, his most constant partner after Fonteyn, that he wished that he'd known him better. In an *Esquire* magazine interview before he learned the news, Rudolf made several oblique but telling references to their conflicts. Amused by journalist Leon Harris's bad haircut, Rudolf launched into his theory as to why American fathers objected to their sons growing their hair long. "Boy wants to be beautiful. Father is jealous. He wants to be beautiful too, but either he is afraid of his feeling or he has no hair. Boy should have beautiful hair. All father has to do is give son education, give him all the knowledge the poor bastard can get and then kick him out of house. If boy has to survive, he will survive."

It was inevitable that Nureyev would be claimed as a political renegade in a year of riots and social upheaval, a year that saw demonstrations against the war in Vietnam and the assassinations of both Martin Luther King Jr. and Robert Kennedy. But Rudolf, who had never voiced a political opinion in his life, saw little in common between his own rebellion and that of his Western peers. His had come of necessity; theirs, in his view, was driven by fashion. "So-called worldwide revolt of young people is no revolt," he told Harris. "They're just conforming. They manage to get some cash and have somehow liberated themselves from their parents and that's why they swing. The more they swing, the more in place they are. Their demonstrations are conformity for today's times, not really revolt. Revolt is when you take power in your hands and remake the world your way. . . ." Both Hamet and his son had remade the world they had inherited.

BACK IN NEW YORK in the spring of 1968, Nureyev and Fonteyn opened the Royal Ballet's four-week season in *Romeo and Juliet*. Having pretty much bid adieu to Fonteyn in *Swan Lake* the year before, the critics now marveled at the youthful radiance of her Juliet. Rudolf's dancing, on the other hand, drew praise for its newfound maturity, depth and control. "I learn from you," he told Fonteyn; "keep pot burnished and boiling." Where earlier he had relied on "the almost stylized Romantic image of a lover," wrote Clive Barnes in *The New York Times*, "he now acts with more force, variety and weight of detail, while not sacrificing his former emblematic strength." To another observer, he seemed more at home with the Royal Ballet, and less the "exotic intruder." By night, however, he reveled in playing that role and was invariably the focus of attention, no matter how fabled his companions. "Jackie, Ari, Rudi, and Margot popped in P. J. Clarke's," noted *The New York Times*, "and guess who monopolized the stares? Rudi with tight pants, boots, cap, and short fur jacket."

In the meantime, the stage-door cries for "We want Rudi, in the nudie," had grown more exuberant, following Rudolf's appearance, in the nude, in a Richard Avedon photo for *Vogue*, published in December 1967.* Rudolf was seen from the side, his arms, head and torso thrust backward, his left foot raised to his right knee, accentuating his sinewy buttocks and thighs. It was unusual at the time for a celebrity to appear nude and the photo went a long way toward promoting Nureyev's sexual self-confidence and status as one of the world's most desirable men. In an equally revealing, if less trumpeted, photograph, Diane Arbus caught the guarded intimacy between Rudolf and Erik. Where most photographs of Nureyev played up some aspect of his stage persona, his glamour, romanticism, athleticism, sex appeal, Arbus's photograph gained its power from its grainy restraint. Her photograph conveys the feeling of an interrupted conversation. The pair is shown seated on the floor of a Manhattan dance studio. Their heads and torsos tilt toward each other, barely touching, but their legs are pointing in opposite directions.

Rudolf still continued to pursue Erik. In Copenhagen in October 1968 to dance *Giselle* with the Royal Danish Ballet, he bumped into Glen Tetley backstage at the Royal Theater. Tetley, as it happened, was on his way to a dinner party at Bruhn's home. "Don't tell Rudi," Erik had forewarned him. So when Rudolf invited Tetley to dinner, the choreographer replied that he had other plans. Rudolf had been "drinking quite a bit" and invited himself along. "You can't," Tetley emphasized, but Rudolf persevered, and got into the car that Bruhn had sent for Tetley. A smiling Erik came out to greet the car as it pulled up to his house in Gentofte. But the minute he spied Rudolf, Erik ran back in the house and disappeared up the stairs. He did not reappear for the rest of the evening and the party carried on without him. "I'm sure that Rudolf was upset," recalls Tetley, "but he never let on that he was."

BY THE FALL OF 1968 Rudolf was convinced that the Royal Ballet didn't really want him, except as a partner for Fonteyn. Having spent the better part of the last two years producing and starring in his own versions of the classics, Rudolf now decided to venture not only outside his home

---

*Ironically, the photograph had been taken during Nureyev's first photo session with Avedon in Paris in 1961. At the time Nureyev had been chagrined at his decision to pose naked and had told Clara Saint that he had regretted doing so. By 1967, however, his sense of decorum was no longer an issue.

company but into unfamiliar territory. His first bold move in that direction came with his debut in Rudi van Dantzig's *Monument for a Dead Boy* on Christmas Day, 1968, as a guest with the Dutch National Ballet in The Hague. "It's a kind of new language for me," Rudolf said of van Dantzig's choreographic style, a blend of classical and modern ballet. "In classical dance, we have to be very vertical. Here we use the horizontal as well as most of the muscles in the whole body."

Inspired by the death of a young poet, *Monument for a Dead Boy* had won some notoriety for its frank homosexual theme. Having heard good things about the Harkness Ballet's performances of it, Rudolf asked to perform the work with van Dantzig's company. Van Dantzig scarcely believed he was serious, but a few weeks later, Rudolf called from Milan to find out when they were to begin. Most dancers planned far in advance for a new work and put themselves at the choreographer's disposal; Rudolf told van Dantzig he had a gap to fill in his schedule in two months' time and, over the choreographer's protests, offered him only four days' rehearsal. To Rudolf "a gap" meant a day or two without a performance. He was convinced, as few dancers are, that the more he danced, the better his chances for giving a great performance. He said he danced best when tired. "I know what I am doing, and my muscles just work my way," he told John Percival. At the same time, he fed on the energy he drew from the audience. No matter how much he worked in the studio, he felt that he became fully himself only onstage. There the stakes were higher, the recognition greater. "You can do all those things quite easily without public — it's nothing exceptionally difficult," he explained. "But the moment you have public, there it all takes a very dramatic edge. That may be what makes it all exciting. You transform in front of those lights and in front of the glare of all those eyes." Not all great dancers needed the stage the way Nureyev did. Baryshnikov, too, would come West to avail himself of its choreographic riches, but what he wanted most was to "work on new pieces with new choreographers. For me, the joy was rehearsal — learning a style, putting the dance together. When it came time to perform, I would start to get bored. I wanted to go on to something else. For [Rudolf], it was just the opposite. The rehearsal, the learning, was always too slow. He wanted to get it over with fast, fast. In two, three days, sometimes, he learned a piece that he had never seen before, and then he was onstage. . . ."

He was now onstage three to four times a week, compared with three times a month at the Kirov and his colleagues' twice-a-week performances, and his partners constituted a veritable who's who of balletdom. That fall alone, he appeared in nine European capitals, with nine major European companies, including the Royal Danish Ballet, and performed another new role, Roland Petit's short-lived *L'Estasi* (Ecstasy), at both La Scala and the Paris Opéra.

But as he would with many small troupes, he agreed to appear with van Dantzig's company for considerably less than his now-customary three-thousand-dollar guest fee. When it came to expanding his repertoire, money was never a concern. "What do you mean: rehearse tomorrow?" Rudolf asked when he arrived in Amsterdam ahead of schedule. "Nothing tomorrow, now, at once!" Rudolf tore into the role of the boy who, in a series of flashbacks, recalls an anguished life: his innocent attachment to a young girl, the nastiness of his schoolmates, his unsuccessful sexual affair with a woman, his discovery of true passion with a male friend. The ballet can be read as an allegory of a gay man's awakening. Attracted by the audacity of both its theme and its movement style, Rudolf pressed van Dantzig for details.

"Tell me, what is the ballet about. He loves boys, no?"

"No," came the reply, "it's a boy who isn't sure yet whether he's attracted to boys or girls. He's caught in a series of nightmarish impressions and experiences." Van Dantzig assumed that the theme would resonate with Rudolf's own experience. But he quickly saw that Rudolf had no interest in revisiting past conflicts.

"A stupid boy, then," Rudolf said.

Though a popular success, Rudolf's performance was at odds with van Dantzig's conception. His work was about a boy "who is very shy and insecure in life. An antihero. And that was something Rudolf did not want to be and didn't even try to be. He was brought up to be a hero. The Soviet ballet was built around extraordinary individuals." Ever mindful of his audience, Rudolf insisted on dancing The Nutcracker pas de deux in the same program so that his public could see him in a familiar classical role. "I have to think about my reputation."

Another new work that season was Roland Petit's Pelléas et Mélisande, which was far from the sensation that Paradise Lost had been. Created as a vehicle for the Nureyev-Fonteyn partnership, the ballet, set to music by Schoenberg, was introduced in March 1969 at a gala marking Fonteyn's thirty-five years on the stage, a remarkable milestone for a ballerina. Fonteyn was approaching fifty. The Queen was in the audience for the ballet's premiere, as was Cecil Beaton, who spoke for the majority when he dismissed it as "pretentious and tiresome . . . ugly acrobatics — pullings across floor on bottoms." To Beaton, as to many, "the real vitality came at the end with the curtain calls." Fonteyn and Nureyev's curtain calls were by now as practiced as their pliés, as Beaton discovered a few nights later, when Lord Drogheda, the chairman of Covent Garden, took him into the wings following a Nureyev-Fonteyn Romeo and Juliet. "It was quite a shock to realise how casual M. & R. are about this part of their career — the homage taken for granted," he confessed to his diary. "The flowers held in a rough offhand way, Margot bowing deep to the floor comes from the brilliant lights into the darkness of the wings & while the applause continues asks Garrett [Lord Drogheda] 'How was New York?' R. says to me 'long time no see.' 'Where shall we have supper? At Sheen near Richmond. Ring Joan.' 'Margot your call.' She goes back. The audience continuing in their adulation, Then R . . . 'Oh we go to America — only three months this time.' There — everywhere the cheers — the slow clapping, the flowers. Both dancers now flat-footed human beings but because of the evenings' 'work out' elated and a little excited so that they enjoyed talking to friends with no ear for the hullaballoo the other side of the curtain."

The hullabaloo continued across North America. Writing of their opening New York performance in *Swan Lake*, which Fonteyn, at fifty, had danced more than any other ballerina ever had, Clive Barnes described their particular alchemy as "the odd, essentially unbelievable magic of a legend made fact. . . . There are times when even the most devoted ballet fan wonders just what ballet can convey without the poetically vague, yet always imaginative specifics of words. And then you see a ballet by Balanchine or Ashton, a performance by Fonteyn and Nureyev, and you realize the challenging eloquence of silence."

It was during that fourteen-week tour that Rudolf met Wallace Potts, an aspiring filmmaker, who was to become his steady boyfriend for the next several years. The two were introduced indirectly by Hiram Keller, who was still seeing Monique van Vooren when Rudolf arrived in New York to stay at her East Side apartment. Monique moved into the guest room so that Rudolf could have her bedroom, with its mirrored ceiling. Knowing that Rudolf preferred private homes to hotels, Keller told van Vooren to call a friend of his in Atlanta, who had a guest house he might want to loan to Rudolf when the Royal Ballet performed there in June. By coincidence the friend, a wealthy real estate investor named Ed Barnum, was coming to New York with his young boyfriend, Wallace, and the four of them met. "Ed always hung out with younger people," Keller recalls today. "He took tenements in midtown Atlanta, bought them for nothing, rented them out to college students, and repaired them. He was scary, too, because he had one arm and there was this hook in it. But I was crazy about him." According to van Vooren, Barnum called to ask whether he and Potts could give Rudolf a party in Atlanta. She, in turn, asked Rudolf. "How is boy? Good-looking?" When van Vooren seemed indifferent, Rudolf suggested they come to his dressing room "and if I like him, they can give me a party."

A physics major at Georgia Tech, the twenty-one-year-old Potts was tall and handsome, with an open face, firm jaw, dark brown hair, an athletic build and a casual, easygoing manner. His generous smile revealed crooked lower teeth and his drawl was unmistakably southern. Masculine in a way that appealed to Rudolf, he was not in the least effeminate or flamboyant. Rudolf was the first dancer he'd met and he was instantly won over, as Rudolf was by him. "He was mad for Wallace and Wallace was mad for him," recalls John Lanchbery. "It was awe at first sight," Potts acknowledged, twenty-four years later. When after just three days in Atlanta, Rudolf invited him to join him on tour with the Royal, as he had Keller, Potts promptly accepted.

In Hollywood, they were sunning themselves poolside at the Roosevelt Hotel when Ashton noticed how unhappy they looked. "Rudolf was in a touchy mood and wasn't treating Wallace very well," recalls a colleague, "and Fred pulled Rudolf aside and said, 'Look, Rudolf, boys as pretty as that don't come along very often and one day even you are going to be old and ugly. So why don't you go make it up with him?' "

They went together to Nervi, the seaside resort near Genoa, where Rudolf was due to dance with the Dutch National Ballet in July.* Rudi van Dantzig's first impression was of "a big, friendly, shy boy" when Rudolf introduced Wallace by saying, "He's going to make a film about my work." In the next breath, Rudolf casually informed van Dantzig that he would be dancing in a new work at the Royal Ballet—and that van Dantzig was to choreograph it. This was news to van Dantzig, whom Rudolf had not consulted before making the arrangements. "Rudolf thought [van Dantzig] was so talented," recalls Lynn Seymour, his partner at the Nervi Festival. "He was very Dutch with all those weird qualities the Dutch have—sort of square and yet quite way out. That strange dichotomy." No dancer at the Royal Ballet had ever demanded that a guest choreographer be invited in to create a ballet expressly for him. Rudolf, however, wanted to be seen in a strikingly modern work in London and Ashton had agreed. Rudolf wanted to "shake up" the Royal Ballet, he told van Dantzig, and suggested that the choreographer use electronic music, which had never been heard at Covent Garden. Since this was to be van Dantzig's first major commission, Rudolf assumed he would jump at the chance. But van Dantzig wasn't sure. "That upset him a lot, the fact that I hesitated, that I didn't jump. That was typical Rudolf."

Potts, meanwhile, had decided to return to Atlanta. He had yet to graduate and planned to enroll in a master's film program at the University of Southern California. The demands of Rudolf's itinerary struck him as inconceivable. "He wants me to travel with him everywhere he goes, but I have to finish my studies and he doesn't seem to understand," he lamented. But leave he did, which, to van Dantzig, was "quite an accomplishment given Rudolf's strength of will."

Potts, of course, would be back, and van Dantzig soon flew to London to make Rudolf his ballet.

*At the Nervi Festival, he danced Monument for a Dead Boy and partnered Lynn Seymour in Giselle and a pas de deux from Romeo and Juliet.

23

I Want, You Must

ALL DANCERS WAGE a losing battle against time, gravity and younger rivals, although Nureyev may have been the first to believe otherwise. In *The Ropes of Time*, the first full-scale work created especially for and about him, Rudi van Dantzig explored that theme. Rudolf was the Traveller through life, attended by Death, and at his request, he was onstage for the ballet's entire thirty-five minutes. Having noticed that thirty-one-year-old Rudolf had started to lose suppleness in his jumps and landings, van Dantzig wanted to investigate the struggle to maintain ascendancy. He was also intrigued by the notion of how a great dancer deals with the inevitability of successors. He illustrated this in movement toward the middle of the ballet, when the Traveller, dancing a solo, is joined by a male dancer, then another and another, until the stage is filled with dancers, all performing the same steps as the Traveller. Rudolf, recalls van Dantzig, had trouble accepting even the notion of his own decline. He would "go on and on," Rudolf told him. "He actually said, 'I have fought to get here and I will not allow other people to become better than me.'"

Life intruded on art during rehearsals. Rudolf had specifically asked van Dantzig not to use a stand-in. Yet he continued to take on foreign guest engagements, sometimes disappearing for days at a time. The choreographer decided he couldn't make any progress without one. He appealed to Ashton, who proposed Anthony Dowell. On his return, Rudolf was hardly pleased to find the younger dancer in his place. He took it as a sign that van Dantzig had lost confidence in him. Dowell looked to Rudolf as a mentor, but he had also gained a sizable following of his own as a result of his partnership with Sibley, then considered second only to that of Nureyev and Fonteyn. To demonstrate his displeasure, Rudolf rehearsed "in the most awful way," so the choreographer couldn't see what his steps looked like. Quickly, van Dantzig called for a run-through of the entire ballet and, in front of the other dancers, asked Dowell to take over. But it was Rudolf who stepped forward.

"Is your name Anthony?" the choreographer asked. The company gasped, and Rudolf stormed out. Ashton, however, reportedly giggled when told about it. "He enjoyed the intrigue," recalls van Dantzig.

Maude Gosling facilitated their rapprochement. Van Dantzig was staying at her house, in the downstairs "guest" flat that Rudolf often occupied. That same night she invited him to dinner without saying that Rudolf was also invited. All through their awkward supper, Rudolf looked hurt and wounded, while Maude "moved lightly but somewhat hesitantly as if she was continually wondering whether she was disturbing others. . . ." Van Dantzig retired early, but Rudolf was soon at his door, proposing a walk in nearby Hyde Park. He, too, was under great pressure, Rudolf explained, in a rare admission of insecurity. "They seem to see me as a strange, barbaric interloper. They think of me as a threat to their manly solo dancers and the critics tear me down as soon as they can."

From then on, rehearsals went smoothly. Rudolf worked "like a slave" to master the demands of a sculptural movement style that made full use of his plasticity and powers of projection. And yet whenever van Dantzig wanted him to stand still and draw attention to himself quietly, Rudolf insisted he be given steps in order to maintain his momentum. "If I don't have steps, here, I will collapse and I will not be able to recover my full strength at the end of the ballet." *The Ropes of Time* premiered on March 2, 1970, to generally poor reviews, though on the strength of Rudolf's performance alone, it proved a success with many in the audience. More important perhaps, the work's electronic score, futuristic sets by Toer van Schayk and blend of ballet and modern dance succeeded in "shaking up" Covent Garden,* just as Rudolf had intended. The very fact that audiences were so divided, wrote critic Peter Williams, "is what makes ballet a lively art rather than a comatose one . . . it is exciting that a break-through has been made at last, a break-through that might make the artists and the audience extend their vision."

Rudolf would collaborate with van Dantzig on three more ballets, tour with his company regularly during the next decade, and spend countless hours in the studio, at dinner or trading confidences with him and his longtime lover, Toer van Schayk. But van Dantzig understood, as anyone close to Rudolf did in those years, that despite his loyalty

*The electronic music rattled Antoinette Sibley's nerves to such a degree that she soon bowed out of the ballet and was replaced by Diana Vere as the Life figure. (Monica Mason appeared as Death.) "It sounded like glass on a mirror."

and faithfulness, their friendship revolved around Rudolf. So vivid was his presence, so palpable his will that his friends invariably found themselves caught up in his force field. His needs came first and however inconvenient the circumstances, he had no compunction about satisfying them. "He never wanted to be bored. As far as his sexual appetites went, well, as with many homosexuals, there had to be so much change all the time. But Rudolf felt that way about many things he did. He wanted constant excitement. . . . There was this frenzy. Visiting him, I always had the feeling that he was never at peace. . . . He was always saying, 'Let's go to an opera,' 'Let's see a movie,' 'Let's go to a museum.' It was constant running. I don't know where he got the energy from because I was tired from rehearsing him, but he went on and on without ever showing tiredness and on top of that, he couldn't sleep at night. He was always sweating and waking up."

At a dinner party at Rudolf's London home that winter, his housekeeper, Alice, suddenly announced that two young men were at the door. Rudolf had made the appointment some days earlier and apparently forgotten about it. He was in high spirits, however, and cursing under his breath, he jumped up and disappeared. Thring followed, returning moments later to say that he would be back shortly. As Rudolf and his visitors went up the stairs, his dinner guests continued eating "a little uncomfortably," recalled van Dantzig, who was seated at the table along with Fonteyn, Tito, Thring, the Goslings, Toer van Schayk, Sander Gorlinsky and Gorlinsky's wife, Edith, whom Rudolf privately called *la croqueuse de diamants* because "everytime I make a tour she has a new diamond." After a pause, Thring exclaimed with a laugh, "That's just the way he is," adding, "He cooks them like pancakes." Soon the front door slammed and Rudolf returned to the table "flushed," with a mischievous, contented look in his eye. "That tastes really excellent," he said ambiguously, whereupon his French cook, Claire, served him the plate she had kept warm for him, though her icy glance conveyed the full measure of her disapproval.

Rudolf disliked being alone, yet craved solitude, one of the many paradoxes of his character. When company was present, he was apt to go off by himself to read, play the piano, or listen to records, consoled, perhaps, by the murmur of voices in a neighboring room. On the road, he brought with him his traveling library of records and books. He read in fits and starts, usually pocket editions he could easily squeeze into his suitcase; held business meetings in between acts or at dinner parties; and chose his words sparingly. You either caught his meaning or you didn't; he never repeated himself. Neither did he ever account for the time spent away from friends. "He never tells one about what's happened," Maude Gosling acknowledged. "He goes away. I may not see him for months. When he comes back he doesn't say, 'Well, of course I got the

Pineapple Award here, and the something else award there, and I've danced there.' Nothing. It's what's going to happen tomorrow and what are you doing today. What shall we see tonight? . . ."

Risk fed his art as it did his life. With Rudolf flying back and forth among America, Europe and Australia, rushing from one time zone to another, one company to another, one ballet to another, new partners had to grab rehearsals with him on the run. He expected anyone he danced with to be as resilient as Fonteyn, who, like him, could do her daily barre under any circumstances. (En route from Australia to Los Angeles, Rudolf once squeezed in a class during a four-hour stopover.) Antoinette Sibley made her debut as Nikiya in his *Bayadère* having had only one three-hour rehearsal with him, and that in a room with two large pillars smack in the middle of it. "This was a huge break to do it with him. And he made me do *not* the version Margot did, but the version I think Dudinskaya did. He put all the tricks of the trade in for me to do. . . ." Monica Mason's break came when he asked her to be his partner in the *Laurencia* pas de six, most of which she learned in the corridor of a speeding train. His intended partner was injured and he didn't want to change the next day's program. The setting was "ideal," Mason wryly recalls, because "the variation goes sideways across the stage and keeps coming back sideways," though the idea of dancing with him for the first time on such short notice left her terrified.

Fearing boredom more than the occasional bad landing or mishap onstage, Rudolf continued to make his performances risky for both himself and his ballerina. To Lynn Seymour, he was "a completely 'honest' dancer" because he refused "to cheat or take a cheap way out. . . . Making your body do what it naturally won't [was] part of Rudy's definition of technique." His friend Claire Motte, a star of the Paris Opéra Ballet, considered him "the most exacting" dancer she had ever known. In October 1969, the two were rehearsing for a series of *Swan Lakes* at Paris's Palais des Sports, when Motte declared she couldn't continue. Three months earlier she had given birth to her first child. "I want, you must," Rudolf instructed her, and Motte obeyed. A few days later, when Rudolf complained of fatigue, Motte repeated his command. Smiling his "wickedly intelligent smile," he, too, obeyed.

Monica Mason remembers how he would "push you to the edge of the cliff and dare you not to fall off." She was not speaking metaphorically. Tilted forward in an arabesque penché, one leg raised high, she would often feel herself close to crashing to the floor before Rudolf would somehow "make it by the skin of his teeth, and catch [her] by the netting of [her] tutu or even [her] knickers" and pull her up high onto her toes in a relevé. There were other nights when he landed so close to the footlights that she felt sure he was going to end up in the orchestra.

Even between acts, he would "conspire to have things happen."

Waiting in the wings to perform the Black Swan pas de deux with Mason in London one night, Rudolf began rummaging through his shoes. Hearing the approach of their musical cue, Mason looked over to see Rudolf sitting shoeless in the wings. "I remember thinking, 'If this were happening to Margot, she'd be quite calm and she'd giggle and that's exactly what I must do until he's ready. It's a pas de deux, so there's no way I can go onstage by myself.' We missed at least the first step, but he loved that, you see. That was a challenge to you, not to fall apart."

Occasionally, when a performance did not meet his expectations, particularly a performance of a Nureyev production, Rudolf took his frustrations out onstage. The most famous incident occurred during the Royal Ballet's New York season in May 1970, when Rudolf was partnering Merle Park in the opening performance of his *Nutcracker*. He was unhappy with the brisk tempo set by John Lanchbery and, wanting to start over, signaled for a halt to the music. When Lanchbery ignored him, thinking the problem lay in Rudolf's "awkward choreography," not in his tempo, Rudolf kicked Park and strode offstage, glowering. As murmurs of disbelief rippled through some sections of the audience, Park gamely went it alone. "I ran to one corner and shouted, 'Rudolf,' and then did a jeté and ran to the other side and did the same thing. In the meantime, he was breaking some sort of Ming vase on the side. Well, at the end of the pas de deux he came back and I said, 'Thank you very much, nice to see you.' And we finished the ballet." Afterward, in front of several backstage visitors, a contrite Rudolf apologized to Park. She had done such a good job disguising his absence that many in the audience didn't realize that anything was amiss. Not, that is, until two days later. PIQUED NUREYEV STALKS OFF STAGE, ran the headline on Anna Kisselgoff's review in *The New York Times*.

His occasional pique aside, the 1970 New York season was a high point in Nureyev's career. His elevation was easier, his dancing more polished and assured. Clive Barnes thought him "in perfect form" on opening night, dancing *The Sleeping Beauty* with Fonteyn. "His manner was courtly and yet also radiant, princely and yet exultant. He partnered Dame Margot with a deferential brilliance and danced almost more excitingly than I have ever seen him." Arlene Croce detected "a new grandeur. In *La Bayadère*, his physical force makes everyone around him seem even more wraithlike."

He was no longer obssessed with "the technical side," Rudolf explained to a *Newsweek* reporter. "It blocks performance. I think I'm getting rid of the blocks. . . ." To another reporter, he ascribed his improvement to his nonstop performing. Of the forty-eight performances given during the Royal Ballet's six-week season, Nureyev danced twenty-three of them, nineteen with Fonteyn. "Because I feel so alien on the stage, I have a need to be on it more, and more, and more. I find it

NUREYEV: HIS LIFE] 360

difficult to get used to, each time. For some dancers, being on stage doesn't matter so much. Their heart-beat doesn't change—nothing really changes them. But for me, just standing in the wings, before going on, I am already exhausted. . . . Already my knees are shaking. . . ."

The closing performance at the Metropolitan Opera House, a gala in honor of Frederick Ashton, marked the end of an era. After seven years at the helm of the Royal Ballet (and several decades as the chief architect of its style) Ashton was stepping down. Ashton had selected the gala program himself and the only non-Ashton work he featured was the Shades scene from *La Bayadère*, staged by Nureyev and danced by Nureyev and Fonteyn. Ashton had chosen the ballet because it showcased the splendor of his corps de ballet; in so doing, he paid tribute to Rudolf's contribution to the company as well.

Ashton had been forced into a premature retirement by a board wanting change. He was to be replaced by John Field and Kenneth MacMillan, who, in an ironic turn of ballet politics, had reluctantly left the company five years earlier after Ashton hadn't encouraged him to stay. While pleased that MacMillan was bringing Lynn Seymour with him, Rudolf was upset about the way Ashton had been pushed out by David Webster, general administrator of the Royal Opera House. (Ashton had broken down in his dressing room one night and confided the news.) Several years later Rudolf would acknowledge to Princess Margaret, "I can never thank Fred and Margot enough. I'm so grateful for all they've taught me. I thought I knew the whole thing when I came here." In London in July, during the Ashton "farewell" tribute, a retrospective of the choreographer's works, Rudolf saw a number of Ashton ballets for the first time. It was hoped that he would perform *Poème Tragique*, the fiery solo that had introduced him to London, but surprisingly, he said he could not remember it. Still, among the evening's high points was his exuberant portrayal of the leading man in *Les Rendezvous*, a role made famous in 1933 by the Polish virtuoso Stanislas Idzikowsky, who had danced for Pavlova and Diaghilev.

Offstage there were also changes. Apart from Erik, Rudolf had formed no lasting romantic attachments. But that summer, he returned to London with Wallace Potts, who had put his film studies aside to join him. Wallace had called Rudolf in New York after receiving a message from him, though Rudolf told him he hadn't left one. "He said he was dancing at the Met with the Royal Ballet again. He said, 'Do you want to come and see me dance?' And then he asked me, 'What are you doing for summer vacation? Do you want to tour Europe with me?' And being an innocent, never-traveled American, I said yes."

Potts would live with Rudolf on and off for the next seven years, sometimes at his house in London, often on the road, and entirely in his shadow. The "never-traveled" Potts would grow so weary of traveling at times that he would complain to friends that he often didn't know where he was. But in those first years, each was enamored of the other, Wallace with Rudolf's intelligence and fame, Rudolf with Wallace's openness, curiosity and southern charm. Unlike Erik, Wallace had an ease and sweetness that Rudolf appreciated. "There was no side to him," recalls Lynn Seymour. "He was a totally sweet guy." Wallace was accepted easily by Rudolf's friends, who welcomed the stability and companionship he brought to Rudolf's life. "They were very happy together in the beginning," says Princess Firyal of Jordan, who had become firm friends with Rudolf after meeting him through her sister-in-law Princess Dina. "It was very comfortable between them. Of course Wallace also made himself useful to Rudolf." Another friend remembers how they "could be silly together and you didn't see that side of Rudolf very often." Wallace "loved to have fun," recalls Querube Arias. "Nothing shocked him. Rudolf liked to gossip about sex. Wallace could do it and still be kind of dignified."

From the start theirs was an open relationship, which probably contributed to its longevity. "Rudolf must have thought at first it was a one-night stand," says John Lanchbery. "Well, the next thing we knew, Wallace was on tour with us, and I only found out later that Wallace had just thrown his career away to be with Rudolf. Wallace was very handsome, I mean an absolute dish, and he was *mad* about Rudolf, and Rudolf, in a way, was mad about him, except that when he realized that he was being trammeled by Wallace, then he could be bad-tempered and Wallace suffered. . . ." At the same time, Wallace offered Rudolf the calm, comfort and constancy that he longed for and that Erik, as a star in his own right, had been unable to provide. "Wallace was totally devoted to Rudi and not in competition with him," acknowledges Bruhn's close friend Glen Tetley, recalling Potts's "calming influence" on Rudolf. "He would have done anything for him." A good thing, too, for "Rudolf's willpower ran through everything he did, down to what movie you saw or where you ate dinner," explains Jane Hermann. "There was not a question of consensus on anything. You either became subject to his will or you didn't hang around."

As a would-be filmmaker, Potts was willing not only to accompany Rudolf on his travels but to pick up his education on the road, by making film records of Rudolf's rehearsals and performances. His ambition to work in the movies was part of his appeal and Rudolf made an effort to help him get started. He asked Roland Petit to lend Wallace money and, at a party at Maria Tallchief's home in Chicago in 1970, introduced him to the director Herbert Ross, then married to the dancer Nora Kaye. "He was very proud of him," recalls Ross, "and anxious to help him."

One reason he wanted to help was that "he never wanted to keep anybody," recalls John Taras. "Rudolf was very concerned that Wallace have a career. He would do as much as he could to get his boyfriends work because he didn't want to support them." Neither did he want them to work for him, though invariably they did in one capacity or another. Rudolf's overriding demands inevitably shaped his relationships. "His boyfriends became sort of servants to him at times," says van Dantzig. "He didn't see them that way, but at some point he treated them like one. If Wallace was in the room and Rudolf had to catch a plane, he would tell him to take his bag, run to a cab, and hold it."

Potts would say in hindsight that Rudolf "was the only person I've ever been in love with in my life." But he acknowledged that Bruhn was "the great love" of Rudolf's life. "I met Erik, who people said was difficult to get along with. But we hit it off. We got along fantastically. I liked his sarcastic sense of humor. It was like a New York sense of humor—always making wisecracks. I found out later that they had broken up just a year, or even six months, before I met Erik. But he couldn't have been nicer to me."

RUDOLF HAD LONG HAD film ambitions of his own. In the summer of 1970, in what promised to be a fascinating study, Rudolf was cast as Nijinsky in a film about the dancer written by Edward Albee. Tony Richardson was to direct. The chance to embody the dancer with whom he was often compared proved irresistible, for Rudolf had "always felt compassion for [him]. Very early on, I wanted to absorb all his work. I wanted to penetrate the reason he was so extraordinary." On tour with van Dantzig's company in late 1969, Rudolf had danced Nijinsky's celebrated role of Petrouchka, the puppet with a human heart and soul.* During preparations for the movie, Rudolf proposed a daring idea. He wanted van Dantzig to stage Nijinsky's *Jeux* along the lines that Diaghilev had originally envisioned it: as history's first ballet overtly about homosexuality. *Jeux*, made in 1913, showed a man and two women flirting during a game of tennis, but as Nijinsky revealed in his diary, "the story of this ballet is about three young men making love to each other. . . . *Jeux* is the life of which Diaghilev dreamed. He wanted to have two boys as lovers. He often told me so, but I refused. Diaghilev wanted to make love to two boys at the same time, and wanted these boys to make love

---

*Nureyev first danced the role at the Royal Ballet in 1963 after being coached by Serge Grigoriev, the former regisseur of the Diaghilev company, who had been present at the creation of Fokine's celebrated ballet. The ballet, however, was so closely built around Nijinsky's fragile character and small and stocky physique that no performer could expect to impersonate him. Rudolf's first attempt at the role was not successful, for he failed to adequately convey the pathos of the forlorn figure. He would return to the role again and again with increasing success and later credited van Dantzig and Toer van Schayk with helping him to bring his interpretation into sharper focus.

to him. In the ballet, the two girls represent the two boys and the young man is Diaghilev. I changed the characters, as love between three men could not be represented on the stage. . . ." Nor could it be represented in a commercial film in 1970, only one year after New York's Stonewall riots spawned the gay liberation movement. According to van Dantzig, the producers were "worried about showing a ballet about three men" and promptly vetoed Rudolf's idea. Filming was slated to have begun in August, shortly after the Ashton gala, but in June, its producer, Harry Saltzman, pulled out and according to Albee, "there was no more money for our film."

Back in London in August, Rudolf ran into Natalia Makarova one day near the Strand Palace Hotel, where the Kirov was staying during its visit. Makarova was a star of the 1970 tour, along with Soloviev, Sizova and the fast-rising young sensation Mikhail Baryshnikov. Knowing that the KGB were not far behind, they parted after a brief conversation. Although Makarova had been taking a number of liberties during the tour, she enjoyed a favored position in the company and was not terribly worried about reprisals.

On September 4, Rudolf was in Milan to dance his *Sleeping Beauty* when Makarova made her own break with the Kirov. Her defection shocked the company, embarrassed the Soviets all over again, and forced Sergeyev, who knew what this second scandal would cost him, to stay behind in London and beg her to return. But Makarova felt stultified and longed, as had Rudolf, for greater freedom and more choice. Unlike his decision, however, hers had come to her calmly and clearly over dinner with English friends. She had simply asked them to call Scotland Yard and then been escorted to a police station by two young officers.

The Soviets were not alone in assuming that Rudolf was somehow behind Makarova's defection. But in truth, he was deeply upset by it. He hoped to bring his mother and sisters to the West and just when he assumed he was getting somewhere, Makarova set back his cause. Despite his differences with Rosa, he called her regularly in Leningrad. "He was furious," recalls the Australian ballerina Lucette Aldous, who was in London two months later to rehearse with him, "because after that there was no possibility of his family coming out." Nevertheless, he agreed to partner Makarova in November, in a televised performance of the Black Swan pas de deux. The sensationalism surrounding "the pas de defectors" irked him, as did their first rehearsal. The two had never danced together and when at one point Rudolf advised her that "we don't do that here," Makarova replied, "You dance like them." "No," he corrected her, "I dance like me." Still, he showed her every kindness when he saw how disoriented she was. "I have not my Russian shoes," she kept saying.

In Leningrad, meanwhile, Pushkin's wife, Xenia Jurgenson, continued to advise Rudolf from afar. "Tell Rudolf not to dance with Makarova as everyone will think he had something to do with her leaving," she told Monique van Vooren, who visited the city in March 1971 at Rudolf's request. By coincidence Rudi van Dantzig was also going to Leningrad to find a teacher for his company, and Rudolf asked them to join forces. He wanted them to look in on his family and on Xenia, who was now alone following the death of his beloved Pushkin one year earlier. (Pushkin had suffered a heart attack after class one afternoon and collapsed in a park near the school.*) Rudolf and Pushkin had stayed in touch over the years by phone, though Pushkin had been nervous about talking to him. Rudolf had sent him the film version of MacMillan's *Romeo and Juliet*, which friends had smuggled into Leningrad. Pushkin had written to say that Rudolf had done well in the West after all. He was thrilled that Rudolf was dancing with Fonteyn and relieved to see that the rumors of his being "a drunkard" weren't true. "He never fully understood why Rudolf left, but he was so proud of him," recalls Baryshnikov. "Of course the Pushkins were worried about him, knowing his character and how he could be really aggressive with people. They feared people wouldn't understand him and would hurt him."

In the Rossi Street room she had shared with both of them, Xenia Jurgenson spoke little of either Rudolf or Pushkin, though every so often, remembered van Dantzig, "there was the obligatory and very Russian sigh." Instead, she showed them countless photographs of Pushkin's last great protégé, kissing some of them as she did, "like a young girl carrying on about her lover." Her "Mishenka," as she called him in broken English and French, had taken Rudolf's place in their household. She patted the sofa. "Rudik used to sleep here, and now, Mishenka." He was away at rehearsal and she urged them to wait for him. Monique excused herself, but van Dantzig's attempts to leave met with vigorous protest. Finally, long after the conversation had waned, the small, athletic figure of Mikhail Baryshnikov appeared in the doorway. Baryshnikov had never met Rudolf, who had defected three years before Baryshnikov arrived in Leningrad. But he already knew a good deal about him. He had lived with the Pushkins from time to time, while both a student and a member of the Kirov, and had heard Pushkin speak of him. On their wall the Pushkins kept a large photo of Rudolf in *La Bayadère*. (Whenever visitors stopped by, they hastily removed it, leaving a telltale empty patch.) Baryshnikov had seen the smuggled films, and Rudolf had also sent several costumes as gifts, which Baryshnikov wore "with his blessing."

Van Dantzig and van Vooren were eager to see Baryshnikov dance in *Les Sylphides*. They were joined at the Kirov Theater by Rosa, her ten-year-old daughter, Gouzel, and Farida Nureyeva, who had come from Ufa to meet Rudolf's friends. The Nureyevs, like most of Leningrad,

*Baryshnikov taught his class for the remainder of the year.

had never seen anyone quite like Monique van Vooren, for whom the phrase "va-va-voom" must surely have been coined. Her blond tresses piled high, her eyelids thickly lashed and shadowed, she was dressed for the occasion in the skimpiest leather hot pants, breast-clinching suspenders and a long green sable coat, which, to van Dantzig's chagrin, she was forced to check at the door. All eyes were on her as they made their way to their seats. Van Dantzig decided that the Russians would never give him a teacher once they saw them together, and that Rudolf's family would "feel bad when they saw such outrageous clothes." But ten-year-old Gouzel was completely spellbound by her uncle Rudolf's glamorous "girlfriend," which is how Rudolf had asked van Vooren to introduce herself to his relatives. "She was really something," recalls Gouzel, smiling at the memory. "When we walked on the street, the men would jump on her and my mother had to fight with them." By then the family was accustomed to being watched. "We were already on a blacklist, so nothing worse could happen to us," says Gouzel. Her mother, however, always lived in fear that something would. Rosa continued to teach kindergarten, having been deemed unfit to teach older children, and one of her charges was the son of Alla Osipenko, the last Kirov ballerina Rudolf had partnered in Paris. Knowing her line at home was tapped, Rosa would say in code, "I have some sausages for you," whenever she called Osipenko with news of Rudolf.

Van Dantzig hoped to film Rudolf's relatives. When he and van Vooren visited them at Rudolf's old flat on Ordinarnaya Street, however, the light was so poor that he asked them to step outside into the building's courtyard. As they did, their neighbors all opened their windows to peer down at them, making them extremely ill at ease. And when van Dantzig showed Farida the photographs of Rudolf he had brought her, "it was as if she didn't recognize him anymore. She was sort of bewildered in front of all these pictures, some showing him in everyday life with all these hats and coats he had. She looked at them with interest, but as if they had nothing to do with her."

Her son was similarily discomfited at seeing her on film. The day van Dantzig screened his Russian travelogue for Rudolf, the film stock tore just at the moment when Farida was to appear. "See, it's bad luck," Rudolf said. "I don't want to see it."

One year later Rudolf's first Russian-speaking emissary, the Monte Carlo teacher Marika Besobrasova, met Farida in Leningrad. "Tell her how I am, what I represent," Rudolf had said. He wanted her to understand what it was he had achieved. It pained him that he couldn't show her himself. So Besobrasova told her all about the ovations, the premieres here and there and about how the public loved him. Farida began to cry. "And I am the only one who doesn't see that." She pressed Besobrasova for details. How did he live? How did he look? In her bags,

Besobrasova had gifts from Rudolf: packets of dollar bills, pounds of cookies, fur-lined coats, shoes, boots, even evening gowns for his sisters. Evening gowns? she had asked him. Yes, he insisted. He wanted people to know they were *his* sisters. "I bought long dresses that I thought were suitable. Then when I saw his sisters, I thought nothing was suitable."

She considered Rosa particularly "strange" when they met in Moscow. Rosa, who had come to her hotel to pick up the gifts, left her passport in Besobrasova's room. The hotel "spies" discovered it immediately. "Nothing happened to her, but she was called to go pick it up. . . . I didn't realize how dangerous it was for us." Rudolf did, however, and had warned Besobrasova before she left, "the only thing they are afraid of is scandals, so if anything happens to you, make a scandal as big as you can."

NUREYEV'S ENTIRE CAREER in the West was about extending his limits as a dancer, and he never lost hope that a great choreographer would tap his talent in new ways. "I believe there is something in me that is still waiting to be found," he said repeatedly through the years. His questing drive would lead him to nearly every major dance figure during the 1970s, beginning in the fall of 1970 with Jerome Robbins and leading, in the spring of 1979, to Balanchine. No other dancer in the history of the art form had worked with as many major choreographers.

In October 1970, Kenneth MacMillan invited Robbins to London to stage his masterwork *Dances at a Gathering*, a series of inventive solos, pas de deux and ensemble pieces, first performed by the New York City Ballet in 1969. A celebration of pure dance, set to Chopin piano music, Robbins's ballet, though plotless, conveyed the full palette of human emotion. "There's no story," Robbins instructed Rudolf, Sibley, Seymour, Dowell and the other six dancers in the first English cast. "You're just dancing in that space. Dancing, dancing, that's all you have to think about." And that was pretty much all Rudolf could think about during rehearsals because Robbins refused to assign specific roles until two days before the premiere, insisting that the male dancers learn *all* the male roles and the women all the female roles. This highly unusual approach pushed them all "into mental outrage and physical anguish," Seymour recalled in her memoir. A bullet of energy and a "terrifying perfectionist," Robbins was at once "moody, demanding, hurting," in the view of Leonard Bernstein, a frequent collaborator. "But vastly talented." A dancer, director and choreographer for both Broadway and ballet, Robbins enjoyed one of the most diverse and successful theatrical careers; his hits included *West Side Story* and *On the Town*. He had also created a steady stream of masterpieces for the New York City Ballet.

With his eye always on that company, Rudolf hoped to prove to

Robbins that he could meet any challenge. Sibley recalls that he was "desperate to be in every number." He would grab her, saying, "Come on, let's show that we like this, too." Rudolf was chosen by Robbins to open and close the ballet and paired with Dowell in a kind of "anything you can do I can do better" number. Dowell followed Robbins's instructions closely, but Rudolf "would fight him and try to take liberties," says Monica Mason. His amendments, however, met with stern resistance. "Jerry never missed a trick. He would say to Rudolf, 'Now this time I want you at this angle and I want your foot at that height and I don't want it any other way.' And Rudolf would listen. He respected strong men as much as he respected strong women."

The staging of *Dances at a Gathering* was one of the happiest collaborations of Rudolf's career, for it offered him a chance to be seen as a part of an ensemble, not as an outsider.* So fixed was he in the public mind as a visiting superstar, one associated with flashes of temperament and technical brilliance, that choreographers never considered him for group pieces. His success in *Dances*, however, owed everything to his ability to blend into the work's overall conception, without forsaking his individuality. "Nureyev conforms," wrote Mary Clarke, though the phrase seemed an oxymoron, "but he is also the catalyst that brings an extra ounce of performance out of his colleagues."

MacMillan and John Field had indeed set a new direction for the Royal Ballet. For the first six months of 1971, the company was not to perform a single nineteenth-century ballet. Anxious to maintain a steady diet of the classics, Rudolf went on tour with the Australian Ballet. The company had agreed to let him dance every single performance of his *Don Quixote* as thanks for his making possible their North American debut—and no doubt to sell tickets. Rudolf had by then signed on as a Hurok client. With years of experience importing every major European ballet company from the Kirov to the Royal—and with the guarantee that Nureyev would dance six nights a week, plus Saturday matinees— Hurok had no trouble selling out the eleven-week, eighteen-city tour, which began in December 1970. Nobody seemed to mind that they'd never heard of his partner, Lucette Aldous. Nureyev and Fonteyn were still the hottest ticket in the dance world, but even without Fonteyn, Nureyev was a promoter's dream. And since Fonteyn and Nureyev both commanded the same fee, it was cheaper for the Australians to make do with just one of them.

"A few years ago, I could still manage to find time to walk in the streets, to do other things, to see people," he told a reporter who caught up with him at New York's City Center in January 1971. "Now I seem

---

*He also agreed to a lower fee than usual for his appearances in the ballet. Since he was not the featured star, the company could not charge higher ticket prices for his performances.

to spend my time either here or in the apartment. And so, the slow-down begins." He smiled and continued, "You have to give up so much, friendships are difficult for friends are like houses, they eat up your time. But then, there are never going to be a great many people who really share your life. When you come right down to it, who would want to change his life, to give up all this?"

Managing "all this" would never have been possible had Rudolf not had at his service a doting woman in nearly every major world capital. Some he loved, some he used, and all made sure, as Xenia had, that he was never hampered by the more mundane aspects of life. He could call them at a moment's notice, knowing they would drop everything to accommodate him. They picked him up at airports, washed his clothes, prepared his steaks, fixed his tea, made his bed, packed his bags, traveled with him, often paying their own way. "I've never cooked a meal in my life," he'd say laughingly to friends. Apart from Maude in London and Marika in Monte Carlo, there was Lydia Hübner in Vienna, van Vooren and Natasha Harley in New York and Armen Bali in San Francisco, to name just a few. To each, he was a member of the family. Harley, the daughter-in-law of White Russians, regularly hosted dinner parties for him. "He'd call and say, 'Could I come for dinner?'" A few hours later, he would add another name, and then another, until Harley had sixteen at the table.

With Armen Bali he also spoke Russian, though the night they met backstage in 1967, she made sure to tell him that she was Armenian. Short, garrulous and full-figured, Bali was among San Francisco's most colorful characters, with a warmth that put even strangers at ease. Pink lipstick offset a broad smile, her face was framed by dark curls and large-tinted glasses. A survivor like Rudolf, she had grown up in Manchuria, the daughter of Armenian parents who had fled Russia, and had endured both a Japanese prison camp in North China and a displaced persons camp in the Philippines before settling in San Francisco in 1949. In time she came to own Bali's, the restaurant she ran as if it were her own home, opening her arms to anyone in need of one, mostly exiled Russians. The city's legendary columnist Herb Caen once called her "the queen of the ballet groupies," but Rudolf called her his *druk*, a Russian word that means "a friend you can trust." She, in turn, saw herself as his protector. She made him omelets with caviar and sour cream for breakfast, and her special rack of lamb for dinner. She bought him the bed he slept in whenever he was in town, scrubbed his back in the bath, and sat with him until he fell asleep "because it was very hard for him to fall asleep after a performance. A lot of emotions he gave onstage." She threw lavish opening night parties for him at Bali's, which he helped to make famous and where portraits of him dominated the main room. At gala suppers, he had her sit next to him, knowing she would massage his feet under the table. A Gypsy had once predicted that she would see the world with a famous son. Rudolf, she concluded, was that son. Though proud of her own children, Jeannette and Arthur, "they have never given me so much this satisfaction of their talents."

HIS PROTESTS to the contrary, Rudolf found time for both friends and parties—but always at the end of the day, after the business of dancing was done. Despite his frequent travel, he managed to keep track of the few friends he cared about deeply, even if it meant calling them in the middle of the night. Typically, he began mid-topic and picked up from where they had last left off, although months had often passed between calls. On tour with the Australians in Los Angeles, he spent Christmas at the Malibu home of close friends Maggy and Jean Louis. A balleto-mane and former model, Maggy was a glamorous, vivacious woman, whose husband, Jean, was a celebrated Hollywood costume designer. (His most notorious concoction was the form-hugging dress Marilyn Monroe wore the night she sang "Happy Birthday" to JFK in 1962.) Maggy "loved" having Rudolf as a houseguest, recalls her best friend, the film star Loretta Young, "because he just moved in as if it was his house." At the party the Louises threw for him one night in Malibu, with Cary Grant and Bob Hope among the guests, Young made a show-stopping arrival dressed in a sleek black satin jumpsuit, tight-fitting leather boots and a full-length black leather coat, all designed for her by Jean Louis. "When I came in, Dolores Hope said, 'Loretta!' when she saw what I was wearing. The outfit was so unlike me." Rudolf was just coming down the stairs when she arrived and, after giving her the once-over, smiled, turned around, and went back up the stairs. "A few minutes later he came strutting downstairs, wearing *his* all-black leather outfit to outdo me."

Wherever he went he was an object of curiosity and was fast becoming a fixture of the social pages. Monique van Vooren's at-home soiree for him in December 1970 drew both Enid Nemy of *The New York Times* and Eugenia Sheppard of the *New York Post*, along with Bruhn, Makarova and the couturier Valentino. NUREYEV'S BACK IN TOWN—SOCIALLY, announced Nemy's headline. His return with the Australians soon after brought out "all the Beautiful people . . . in the freezing New York cold," noted Aileen Mehle in her "Suzy Says" column in the *New York Daily News*. The occasion was a party for Nureyev given by his former employers, Raymundo de Larrain and the Marquesa de Cuevas, in the marquesa's mansion on East Sixty-eighth Street. Jackie Onassis, "all beautiful smiles in black ruffled organza and a diamond the size of the Christina," chatted with tobacco heiress Doris Duke and socialite C. Z. Guest, while Ari Onassis smoked cigars and sipped champagne. Truman Capote wore a fox jacket and straw hat and mingled with Pat Kennedy Lawford, Prince Egon von Fürstenberg and his wife, Diane. At last, Nureyev arrived "looking excruciatingly sexy (how about that cuckoo scar on his lip—yes, how about it?) while eating a very thick, very rare steak to replace the energy expended in all the leaping and bounding he had just been through. . . ."

With Nureyev as its attraction, the Australian Ballet naturally generated the widespread exposure it had never known. He drew complaints in San Francisco for wearing "transparent tights." The truth was less dramatic. To make his legs look slimmer onstage, he had taken to wearing sheer black nylons over flesh-colored tights, a curious, if eye-catching, choice. The challenge for any troupe that piggybacked on his reputation was to avoid becoming dependent on his drawing power. "The most famous male dancer in the world" was how the unknown Niagara Frontier Ballet* had advertised his presence on its 1971 European summer tour. Rudolf had joined in lieu of a holiday because he wanted to be seen more widely in La Sylphide. But just before a gala performance in Madrid, he pulled a muscle in his left leg. He was in agony and had every reason not to perform. Nevertheless, he decided to make a surprise appearance in the last work on the program. No sooner was it announced that another dancer would replace him in the opening pas de deux than the crowd erupted in boos that did not subside, even after the curtain rose. The dancers were unable to continue and the curtain was lowered. Now it was announced that Nureyev was injured but had agreed to perform later on in an excerpt from The Sleeping Beauty. The jeering continued as before. Finally Rudolf decided that he would have to dance, and went onstage in the opening work,† his leg wrapped in a bandage. Thus reproved, the crowd fell silent, only to cheer him madly at the end.

"Never again," he said afterward. But of course he would, again and again.

"I AM ROMANTIC kind of dancer," Rudolf had said in his first television interview in 1961, "but I would like to dance modern things and to try every different way which exists." By March 1971 there seemed to be no medium or movement style he was unwilling to try. That month he had appeared on a Burt Bacharach television special in a modern dance work by Paul Taylor, set to Bacharach's score from the film Butch Cassidy and the Sundance Kid. He also joined Maurice Béjart's Ballet of the 20th Century for a week of performances in Brussels, with all fifty-eight hundred seats in the domed arena of the Forest National sold out every night.

---

*Renamed the American Classical Ballet for the engagement.
†It was Flower Festival at Genzano, one of the first works Erik had taught him.

Rudolf danced *Songs of a Wayfarer*, a new duet created especially for him and Béjart's leading man, Paolo Bortoluzzi. Set to Mahler's *Lieder eines fahrenden Gesellen*, it showed a man traveling through life, shadowed by his inner self as he seeks his destiny (a theme Rudolf had already explored in a number of ballets). Considered one of Béjart's subtler works, the ballet would become a staple of Nureyev's repertory.

Rudolf had assumed that his work with van Dantzig was all the preparation he needed for future work with any other modern ballet choreographer. But while working with Glen Tetley in London in the fall of 1971, he came to understand that each choreographer had his own style and own singular approach to movement. The American-born Tetley was versed equally in modern dance and ballet, having studied with Hanya Holm and Antony Tudor and performed with both the Martha Graham Company and American Ballet Theatre. Rudolf so wanted to learn Tetley's erotic *Field Figures* that he "begged" Tetley to teach it to him and then rearranged his schedule to make the time.* Flattered by Nureyev's commitment, Tetley cast Rudolf in his next new work for the Royal Ballet, *Laborintus*, premiered on July 26, 1972, at the Royal Opera House. Danced to music and a sung text by Luciano Berio, *Laborintus* pictured modern life as a descent into the inferno. The challenge for Rudolf was to perform in an "unclassical" style, one that included falls, rolls and an anguished duet with Lynn Seymour that required him to contort her limbs into twisted sculptural poses.

During rehearsals, Rudolf invited Tetley home to Richmond Park for lunch and there "opened himself up. . . . He talked about his life and how he had stripped all his roots away and how many times he had felt that he wanted to kill himself." He could not see "the meaning of it all," Tetley recalls him saying. "As beautiful as the house was, it was desolate. . . . There wasn't any homelife there." Rudolf and Joan Thring had by this time parted company. He told friends that he had fired her, citing her possessiveness as the cause. But according to Thring, she quit after he ridiculed her in front of two young men he was trying to impress backstage. She had grown tired of his demands. Overhearing them arguing in Rudolf's dressing room one night, Fonteyn remarked to a friend, "One is as difficult as the other."

While his appearances with the Royal Ballet had tapered off considerably, from eighty-two in 1969 to twenty-five in 1971, he and Fonteyn had dominated the Royal's 1972 tour to New York earlier that spring. Although Rudolf had also partnered Seymour, Mason and Park, his partnership with Fonteyn went unchallenged at the box office. Andy Warhol,

---

*He even forced Hurok to include the ballet on the Royal's 1972 tour to America because he wanted to be seen in the work in New York. When Hurok balked, Rudolf refused to sign his contract until Hurok relented.

however, was interested only in Rudolf, whom he hoped to feature in *Andy Warhol's Interview*, the first magazine devoted entirely to the cult of celebrity. While no one "believed in the fame game more than Andy Warhol" and no one "played it better," Warhol was then a novice interviewer and nervous about handling Nureyev, whom he "adored." Rudolf was in rehearsal at the Metropolitan Opera House the day Warhol showed up, accompanied by staff writer Bob Colaciello* and photographer Robert Mapplethorpe, a promising young artist whose sexually explicit photographs would later bring him notoriety.

The enterprise, though prearranged, was probably doomed from the start, given that Rudolf thought Warhol "ugly" and that Warhol disliked Mapplethorpe, who had been invited along at Rudolf's request. Then again, it was hard to tell just who was performing for whom.

"What color are your eyes?" Warhol opened.

"The interview is canceled," Rudolf replied, switching off Warhol's mini tape recorder to ensure that it was. He had agreed to photographs only, he said, so Warhol and Mapplethorpe went to work with their Polaroid cameras instead. Warhol slipped the photos into his jacket pocket, but Rudolf insisted on reviewing the results. He liked the close-up of his high-boned face. But then Warhol zoomed in on "dancedom's most famous crotch," reported Colaciello in *Interview*. Rudolf would have none of that, at least not while a reporter was present. As soon as he saw the snapshot, he flung it to the floor and then planted his foot firmly on top of it. Mapplethorpe moved in quickly to snap dancedom's most famous foot pressing on Warhol's photo. This only infuriated Warhol, who shot Mapplethorpe "a nuclear look." Rudolf, meanwhile, grabbed Mapplethorpe's camera, tore out the undeveloped film, and crumpled it into a ball.

"Don't you like your foot?" Mapplethorpe asked him.

"My foot, yes," Rudolf answered, cracking his first smile as he teasingly tapped the tip of Mapplethorpe's nose. They could photograph him, he said, provided that he approved the ones they took away with them.

Nearly all their Polaroids became strips of torn paper.

Soon Rudolf resumed rehearsing, propelling himself through leap after vaulting leap. "He's so great," exclaimed Warhol for the record, clutching his torn film as mementos. "I didn't know a person could be that great. He should be in the movies."

With the release of *I Am a Dancer* three months later, Rudolf made the first of several bids at movie stardom. The quasi-documentary had begun as a sixteen-millimeter film for French television. It was then partially reshot at EMI's film studio outside London and expanded to thirty-five-millimeter to take advantage of Nureyev's big-screen potential.

---

*Who was later to drop the *i* and become *Interview*'s editor.

Linked by offstage glimpses of Nureyev at the barre, in rehearsal and surrounded by fans at the stage door, the film showed him primarily in performance. He danced Tetley's *Field Figures*, the only modern work, with Deanne Bergsma; *La Sylphide* with Carla Fracci; *Marguerite and Armand* with Fonteyn; and the grand pas de deux from his *Sleeping Beauty* with Seymour. His loyalty to Seymour was nowhere more evident than in this invitation to dance with him. Seymour had recently separated from the father of her twin boys, and MacMillan had replaced her in Balanchine's *Serenade* because of her weight. Depressed, she was at home in bed the day Rudolf telephoned. He needed her for the film, he explained.

"You'd best ask someone else," Seymour replied. "You'll get a hernia trying to lift me."

"You'll do it, Lil," he insisted, and then told her he had to hang up or else they'd be late for class. In this way he coaxed Seymour back into the studio and into shape for their pas de deux. "He believed in you despite vicissitudes. He wasn't a fair-weather friend, that's for sure." Seymour's intensity drew from Nureyev some of his most fully realized performances, most notably in *Romeo and Juliet*. And yet, though he loved dancing with her, the ups and downs of her emotional life precluded a steady partnership.

I Am a Dancer disappointed him. "I screamed, I yelled, and did everything possible to cancel it," he told the *Guardian* before the film's premiere. "I wanted to buy it, burn it, destroy it." To that end, he claimed to have offered the producer thirty thousand pounds. He also refused to promote the film, or to allow his name to be used in the title, reportedly out of deference to Fonteyn, who was also featured. *I Am a Dancer* did a brisk business at the select theaters in which it was shown, first in London and then in New York. Audiences were intrigued to see him close up in class and to hear him speak about his work. Nevertheless the portrait was more *cinéma* than *verité*. It revealed nothing of Nureyev's personal life and failed to convey "the animal quality held in check by superb discipline that [made] his performances so exciting." "As 'biography,' " observed *Variety* in a typical assessment, "the pic is timid to a fault."

The same could hardly be said of its star. In July, the month of the film's release, Nureyev officially crossed the frontier from classical to modern dance by joining the Paul Taylor Dance Company on a tour to Mexico City. At the time, ballet and modern dancers regarded each other warily across a great divide. Rudolf "took the plunge, he took the largest gamble, he had the most to lose." It was unusual enough for a ballet star to perform with a modern dance troupe, especially so for one as aligned with the nineteenth-century ballet classics as was Nureyev. But then Nureyev was, as Arlene Croce later wrote, "the kind of dancer who causes

categories to have a nervous breakdown. . . . He seems able to go anywhere and do anything, and even those who have never seen him on
the stage have an impression of him as an extraordinary unconfined
being. . . ."*

A protégé of Martha Graham's, Taylor was a tall, bulky man known
for his sly humor. Rudolf had wanted to work with him ever since their
meeting in Spoleto eight years earlier. But Taylor had never been much
interested in ballet dancers and had agreed to the experiment mainly out
of affection for Rudolf and after weighing the financial advantages.
Rudolf's reasons for choosing Taylor were as strategic as they were opportunistic: He had yet to perform in Mexico and he wanted to try a
completely foreign technique. This was no easy task: It required him to
dance barefoot, contract his back, and to find a lower center of gravity,
all things that were contrary to his Vaganova training. Where classical
ballet reveres a turned-out position, an unbroken flow of movement and
the ideal of transcending gravity, modern dance celebrates groundedness;
its dancers drive their weight into the floor, emphasizing their connection
to the earth, not their affinity for the sky. Additionally, Taylor's style
forces dancers to split their bodies in half; "from the waist down you are
animal, weighted. From the waist up, everything is ethereal, uplifted,
open. You have to be into the floor and up in the air at the same time."
Rudolf was not only audacious enough to take over two of Taylor's own
roles, in the lyrical *Aureole* and the satirical *Book of Beasts*, but humble
enough to acknowledge "how far Paul and I are apart, how much I have
to learn, the work I must put in to achieve his demands. . . ." Rudolf did
not ask for a fee.

Initially, Taylor's dancers were sworn to secrecy. "One of the first
things Paul told us was, 'I like him very much; I'm not in love with
him,' " recalls the former Taylor dancer Senta Driver. "I think he knew
there would be speculation. He was trying to establish his attitude toward
Rudolf and prepare us to accept him." What struck Driver on meeting
Rudolf was the "fluorescent, almost unearthly" glow his face emitted. "[It
was] what made people turn around and look at him. There was a brilliance, even when he was earnestly working. It wasn't something that
you turned on and off." Rudolf, who had never danced barefoot, was
fascinated by the business of how modern dancers tape their feet to
protect them. In the Taylor company, this ritual involved heating adhe-
sive bandage with a match and applying it between all four small toes
and then around the foot until it "looked like a sandal." Rudolf, however,
relied on Taylor to tape his feet for him, which sometimes took an hour

*The fact that Mikhail Baryshnikov would come to head a modern dance troupe in the
1990s and that ballet companies now regularly commission modern choreographers to make
new works owes much to Nureyev's pioneering efforts.

to do. "So there was Paul kneeling at Rudolf's feet every day," says Driver. "It was the only service I have ever seen Paul do for anybody. Ever. In the beginning it made sense, but it's not hard to learn. Rudolf never did it himself."

Rudolf recalled Taylor as being "extraordinarily calm, but of course rather tense, too. I imagine he thought, here comes a ballet dancer, star, he will be content with a few rehearsals. But I was pulling everything out of him. He said it was great for his dancers to see how I work—like a dog. And that's the way I work—like a dog." Through no fault of Rudolf's, Hurok all but ignored Taylor in selling the Mexican engagement. Rudolf had asked to include a few performances of Balanchine's *Apollo,** inviting several members of the Boston Ballet along on the tour. As a result, the audience was filled with what one critic called "ballet freaks and the curiosity-seeking chic, as rude and regressive a group as could have possibly been found." Taylor still remembers being awakened in the middle of the night by a call to his hotel room from the distraught local presenter. "He said everyone expected all the dancers to be on pointe and couldn't we please change our program and do The Dying Swan or something?" He was sorry, Taylor replied, "but this is all we have." The closest Rudolf came to a feathered creature was in the role of the Squonk in *Book of Beasts*, "a big shaggy thing," in Taylor's words, that was actually meant to be a send-up of both the Dying Swan and Nijinsky's Faun.

Despite Rudolf's best intentions and incessant hard work, "he never really realized that he couldn't just throw on the modern technique like a cloak," says Taylor, who always felt that Rudolf was miscast in the Handel-inspired *Aureole*, a work Rudolf continued to dance throughout his career. "He wanted to do it and I didn't care. But you need long arms and legs [for a piece like that]. He did have the presence, though, which carried it, and the audience loved him." In those first performances, he had trouble with the final explosion of split leaps across the stage. Already his jump had lost buoyancy and elasticity, as Rudolf acknowledged to the Taylor dancers. His major problem, however, was that he didn't pace himself properly in rehearsal. According to Driver, he would start with the first section each day and run through it five times "full out" before going on to the next one. As a result, he never reached the last section, "which is where all the jumping is. If the lead person does not jump out in these leaps, people behind him have to hover like helicopters. We'd be praying for him to get it."

In Taylor's view, a well-crafted dance could withstand innumerable interpretations. And yet to his eyes, Rudolf "looked like a ballet dancer

---

*Since the Boston Ballet had *Apollo* in its repertory, Rudolf managed to secure the rights to perform it by inviting along several of its ballerinas.

doing a takeoff of a modern dancer." He admired him enormously, but "more for his valor than for his dancing." Over the years, Rudolf would press Taylor to make a new piece for him, but Taylor never would. Like most choreographers, he looked askance at using guest stars not fluent in his language. And Rudolf never had the time to immerse himself fully.

Still, he had succeeded in breaking down barriers and throughout the 1970s would go to great lengths to make sure he was seen in Taylor's work both in London and in New York. In October 1974, he flew from Paris to New York for one day only, just to appear in a Taylor season on Broadway. His guest stints not only brought new audiences to modern dance but generated much-needed income for Taylor's company. In fact Taylor was desperately in want of money at the time Nureyev approached him. By performing Taylor's dances, Rudolf made it possible for Taylor to keep making them.

24

No Nureyev, No Job

"IF COVENT GARDEN can't provide you with work and incentive, you go and get it somewhere else," Nureyev once remarked. "Get off your ass; go, telephone, organize, provoke, make performances somewhere else." Convinced that the Royal Ballet did not value him, as he would come to feel about any company when his demands could not be met, Rudolf directed Hurok to find him a company that would give him carte blanche. He had decided early on never to wait for opportunities, and three weeks after the tour to Mexico, he was in Toronto to set his production of *The Sleeping Beauty* on the National Ballet of Canada. For a long time he had wanted to tour North America in this production, the one with which he was most satisfied. And in many ways, the twenty-one-year-old National Ballet of Canada was an inevitable choice. Founded by British-born Celia Franca, a protégée of Ninette de Valois's and a former Sadler's Wells dancer, the company was modeled on the Royal Ballet and its repertory emphasized the classics. The only major Petipa work missing from its lineup was *The Sleeping Beauty*. Equally significant, the company's development had been nurtured by Erik Bruhn, who, since 1963, had worked with it as choreographer, coach and teacher.

Bruhn in fact was to have starred with the company on its first European tour earlier that summer. But in December 1971, while still in peak form, he had suddenly announced his retirement from dancing. The agonizing pains from his as yet undiagnosed ulcer had made performing unbearable. On December 29, 1971, after a final performance as James in *La Sylphide* with Carla Fracci and American Ballet Theatre, the forty-three-year-old Bruhn decided he had endured enough. He assumed, as did his closest friends, that his illness was psychosomatic and

would subside once he removed himself from the pressures of his perfectionism.* Instead, it steadily worsened. His retirement shocked the
dance world, no one more than Rudolf, who could not fathom how any
dancer could give up the stage. To him, it was akin to suicide and a
kind of betrayal. Bruhn was his model and his spur, and he needed him
as a reminder of all he had yet to master.

The National Ballet of Canada hoped to find another role for Bruhn
and, while in London to make its debut that summer, had briefly considered him for the post of director. After meeting with him at Rudolf's
home, however, director Celia Franca concluded that he had too nervous
a disposition for the job. One month later, Rudolf picked up where Erik
had left off, turning what was then a provincial company into an international contender. Just as his staging of La Bayadère had galvanized the
Royal Ballet, so his staging of The Sleeping Beauty vitalized the Canadian
company. It also awakened the potential of the young ballerina Karen
Kain, as it had the Italian ballerina Carla Fracci in 1966. But the scale
of his imagination and ambition was much grander than the company
had bargained for.

Rudolf was both to stage the ballet for its North American premiere
and to dance in virtually every performance save Sunday matinees. A
coast-to-coast tour culminating in the company's Metropolitan Opera
House debut in April 1973 was predicated on Nureyev's drawing power and
Hurok's clout. Hurok had two conditions: that Rudolf be given complete
artistic control and that the company assume the costs of mounting its
most lavish and costly production ever. For the National Ballet it was a calculated risk, one that Celia Franca weighed in private notes: " 1) No Nureyev, no job. 2) No new productions for Nureyev, no job. 3) Nureyev has
final artistic say because our contract with Hurok dictates that if Nureyev
doesn't dance the N.B. doesn't get paid."

The enormous exposure, the chance to work with Nureyev and the
promise of a Met debut clinched the deal. But no sooner had the contract been signed than the $250,000† production budget ballooned to
$412,565 after designer Nicholas Georgiadis insisted on using the most
expensive silks, brocades and satins to build the dazzling seventeenth-
century court. Several members of the board mortgaged their houses to

---

*Bruhn had instructed his agent, Christopher Allan, to send a formal letter announcing
his retirement. In the letter sent to The New York Times, Allen added a personal note: "As you
know, Erik has three or four times after severe illness brought himself back into peak form.
God knows the kind of dedication and determination this must take! His last three performances
in Washington even astounded the whole company of American Ballet Theatre and made the
return of his illness all the more perplexing. It is probably due to the fact that he demands so
much of himself and will never settle for any performance in which he has not tried to better
all previous ones. . . ."
†In Canadian dollars.

make up the difference. "Rudi kept saying that if Georgiadis didn't get his way, he was leaving," recalls then associate director Betty Oliphant. "There was no compromise." The Canadians saw him as extravagant and unyielding, but Nureyev considered himself remarkably accommodating. After all, visions of grandeur did not come cheap. Accustomed to the more ample resources of La Scala, where his *Sleeping Beauty* had been first produced, Rudolf was nevertheless a practical man. Recognizing that he had to take his extravaganza on the road, he agreed to make some concessions, featuring onstage just one coach, for example, instead of the fleet Georgiadis had originally envisioned. From his "enormous, mammoth production of La Scala," as he described it, he had to "draw out of Georgiadis a production which would be able to tour, that stagehands could move, and still the story had to be told and the production had to look awesome. . . ."

Beneath the Dionysian passion of his persona lay a reverence for structure and precision. He wanted the entire company of sixty-five dancers in the rehearsal studio all the time, whether or not they were required in a specific scene. The dancers had other ballets to prepare, but Rudolf believed that each had to be immersed in his *Beauty* to acquire the rigor and stamina needed to perform it. He wanted the authentic Petipa style "as he had got it into his head and into his muscles and into his bones." A "stickler for academic accuracy," he insisted on precise, articulated steps and a decisive, unmannered style of dancing.

Nureyev had sent ahead a ballet mistress from La Scala* to set his *Beauty*. Then, when he arrived two weeks later (dressed for the August heat in layers of woolens, a knit cap and wooden clogs), he made enormous changes. His restless mind was forever revising. Since it was not his habit to offer detailed explanations, "we had to listen carefully and sort of decode his instructions," recalls ballet master David Scott. "People would say he was abrupt, but I think he was trying to save energy wherever he could."

Miraculously, the ballet was staged in under one month, during which the dancers, not just the budget, were pushed to the breaking point. They had never worked with a star of Rudolf's magnitude or temperament; the experience was at once thrilling and terrifying. On bad days they referred to him as Genghis Khan. He not only had them run through the entire three act, seven-scene ballet twice a day, he bullied them into pushing beyond their Canadian reserve. In the process, he gave them what company prima ballerina Veronica Tennant calls "great lessons in theatricality. After working with him, we realized that this was very much a reciprocal occasion with the audience."

Their British-schooled director, Franca, had always eschewed show-

*Gilda Majocchi.

iness; this suited the Canadians. But Rudolf wanted his ballerinas "to sparkle" and insisted on their wearing rhinestone jewelry onstage. Franca may have modeled herself on Ninette de Valois, but she did not share Madam's enthusiasm for Rudolf or his bold, assertive Russian style.* Neither did her autocratic methods meld easily with his. After sparring with him on virtually every aspect of his production, she removed herself to the sidelines and gave Rudolf the run of her company. "She kept away," he recalled, "and didn't get into my soup." But she also stopped turning up for rehearsals, even though Rudolf had cast her as the wicked fairy, Carabosse. Victoria Bertram, the second-cast Carabosse, rehearsed in her place, and then took notes to her afterward.

The company's three senior ballerinas were to alternate in the role of Aurora, but on the first day of rehearsal Nureyev singled out Karen Kain, a tall, elegant, dark-haired beauty and the youngest principal dancer. "Why is *she* not doing Aurora?" he demanded of Franca in front of the entire company. Kain, though cast to dance the Principal Fairy and Florine in the Bluebird pas de deux, was scheduled to dance with Nureyev only in Bruhn's *Swan Lake*.† Rudolf insisted on her as one of his Auroras and coached her, painstakingly, over the next few months on everything from the height of her port de bras to the best way to camouflage her imperfections. "Your arms *not* too short," he corrected her. "No. Is your body too long for arms. You must always stretch arms straight—no round arms, no bent wrist. . . ." Another day he fussed with her hair, pointing out that her face was too long and narrow: "Do like Margot—puff up hair!" Watching her demonstrate Aurora's bounding entrance for the first time, he said approvingly, "She looks like little rabbit jumping over fence."

He insisted that in performance she meet his gaze straight on, "the hardest thing he could ask: intensely shy as I was, having to look into those piercing green eyes was just too much." When finally she could, he would test her concentration. Glancing toward the wings, he would ask, "Cute boy. Who is that boy?" just as she was in the middle of a promenade trying desperately to balance on one leg. "He had an uncanny ability to see everything that was going on onstage at once." Kain, like Fonteyn, rose three inches above him when standing on her toes. Most male dancers disliked taller partners, but Rudolf admitted it made him "fight for his position," and use more expansive movements.

---

*Franca retained fond memories of the Sadler's Wells production in which she had danced the Bluebird variation. Rudolf's Kirov-inspired production, however, "owed little to the English tradition," writes James Neufeld in his history of the company, "or to [Franca's] personal storehouse of knowledge."

†That ballet was also to be performed during the tour.

Kain would go on to become Canada's first homegrown international ballet star. She readily acknowledges that without his goading, she would never have realized her potential. "I wasn't a particularly ambitious or confident person, but with his kind of focus on me I really lit up. . . . The more he asked, the more I gave, and the more I gave, the more I discovered I had. I really went a long way on his steam. . . ."

Rudolf's role models for Princess Aurora were Dudinskaya and Fonteyn. He would describe how Dudinskaya could "spin like a top on her double turns" and insist that the Canadian dancers strive for Fonteyn's line, musicality and delicacy of phrasing. Most of all, they had to prove themselves in the Rose Adagio, one of the most technically testing pieces in the ballerina's canon, full of daunting balances and pirouettes.* "I called Margot last night for advice for you," he told Veronica Tennant after watching her struggle. "She suggested you try for strength of equilibrium in the shoulders rather than thinking about balancing from the toes." This was the clue she needed and Rudolf was pleased at having solved the puzzle. More typically, he delighted in shocking the decorous Canadians. To indicate to Kain the distance he wanted her to cover on pointe during their grand pas de deux, "he didn't say 'penis' but he used sign language to suggest the amount of a good-sized one. Hardly the sort of imagery I'd want to have in my mind at that moment. We'd be onstage and get to that spot and he would have that glint in his eye as if to say, 'You know what I told you.' I knew exactly what was going on in his head."

For all his "verbal vulgarity," as one friend puts it, Rudolf maintained an acute sense of propriety about his private life. He was rarely publicly demonstrative with Wallace Potts but let his affection show in his voice when he spoke of him. In Toronto, he and Wallace stayed at the King Edward Hotel, near the company's downtown studios. Wallace was busily filming Rudolf's rehearsals and was there when he needed him. Finding Toronto's conservatism oppressive, Rudolf occasionally unwound by visiting its few porn theaters. Sometimes he invited Betty Oliphant to join him. The fifty-four-year-old Oliphant, a friend of Bruhn's, was the founder of the company's esteemed ballet school. "He saw me as a kind of mother figure and it really pleased his sense of humor to get this straight Betty to look at porn movies."

The Sleeping Beauty opened at Ottawa's National Arts Centre on September 1, before a capacity audience that included Prime Minister

*Standing on pointe on one leg, her other leg raised in an attitude, she must maintain the pose while four suitors, in succession, turn her full circle. After each revolution, they release her right hand and she must raise her arms to form a frame around her face before placing her hand in the palm of the next suitor.

Pierre Trudeau and his wife, Margaret. Canadian ballet's most opulent production "wears its $350,000* price tag like a sable among muskrat," wrote William Littler in the *Toronto Star*, adding that "it took a long time for the eye to realize that more than a pageant was in progress . . ." Circling the stage with his great manège of leaps in the last act, Nureyev brought the house down. Production problems, alas, threatened to bring the cumbersome set down along with him, convincing Rudolf the stagehands were conspiring to harm him. They played thirteen cities in eight weeks during the first half of the tour. There were more technical snafus because neither the set nor the lighting had been designed to work in these smaller theaters. Some nights Rudolf had to untangle his coach from the forest he was meant to be passing through. At one performance his spotlight went dark just as he was to awaken Aurora[†] from her hundred-year slumber. Venting his anger en route to her bed, he banged together the heads of her sleeping courtiers and then pressed his lips to hers in what was surely the longest, hardest and wettest kiss in the kingdom's history. "That was quite a kiss you gave her," a stagehand remarked. "If I hadn't kissed her," Rudolf replied, "I would have killed her."

Arriving at each new theater, Rudolf would immediately familiarize himself with the stage and its sight lines, taking into account not just the space he needed for his own variations but whether the scenery was properly placed, how many lights were up and the number of crew members required. At the same time, he was performing in three other works. In addition to Erik's *La Sylphide*, there was *The Moor's Pavane*, José Limón's modern dance version of *Othello*, which Limón taught to Rudolf shortly before his death. Where Limon's anguished Moor imploded from pent-up jealousy, Nureyev's "raging" Moor, much like Nureyev himself, "let his feelings come seething to the surface," wrote Ann Barzel, "and showed in his fierce movements." The other work new to him was Bruhn's unorthodox *Swan Lake*. Although Erik was briefly on hand to supervise rehearsals, Rudolf kept changing the choreography. To the dancers' great surprise, Erik did not protest. (The suicide of his friend and agent Chris Allan one month earlier and the decline of his own health must have left him understandably distracted.) Erik's *Swan Lake* was the closest the two ever came to a collaboration. This meant the ballerinas suddenly had to relearn major portions of *Swan Lake* while coming to grips with *The Sleeping Beauty*.

Whenever they felt exhausted, they had only to watch Rudolf drive himself through seven performances a week, with energy left over to coach anyone who asked, to understand a whole new concept of com-

---

*The figure given at the time.
†Vanessa Harwood.

mitment. As the week wore on, he'd insert extra pirouettes into his coda just to prove to himself he could handle them. As Celia Franca admiringly recalled, "He prided himself on that solo at the end, in the wedding scene of *Sleeping Beauty* . . . he'd grit his teeth, and there was no way he wasn't going to finish that whole solo, spinning away and getting as dizzy as hell and then standing up in a clean fifth position, saying 'I did it.' " Karen Kain was literally "hallucinating" from exhaustion after she danced five performances of *Swan Lake* with him in a single weekend. She and Vanessa Harwood were to have split the performances, but Harwood fell ill. "I knew you could do it," Rudolf told her proudly, as if he hadn't done the same. "You and Margot have guts. I was born with only two balls, but you two, you were born with three."

A debatable point, one might argue. No sooner had his *Sleeping Beauty* opened in Toronto and been taped for Canadian television than Rudolf, joined by Wallace, was on a plane to Australia. There he staged, directed and starred in a filmed version of his *Don Quixote*. He was determined to take matters more firmly in hand after his disappointment in his previous film efforts. These included his *Sleeping Beauty* for Canadian television, which won director Norman Campbell an Emmy award. Campbell had deleted all the fairy variations in the Prologue without Nureyev's permission. For Nureyev, this meant the ballet "was castrated, the company was castrated. Instead of the fairy variations, you know what we see? We see the audience clapping. . . ."

Nureyev's Don Quixote, as it was billed, was made for six hundred thousand dollars and shot in a remarkably brief four weeks in an unused airport hangar outside Melbourne, following a week of stage performances in Sydney with its original Australian cast. Nureyev had impressive collaborators in Geoffrey Unsworth, the cinematographer best known for his work on *Cabaret* and *2001: A Space Odyssey*, and codirector Sir Robert Helpmann, who also danced the title role. Helpmann, Fonteyn's first partner at the Sadler's Wells Ballet, had by then appeared in ten films, among them *The Red Shoes* (1948), whose enduring appeal had convinced him that film could "reach towns all over the the world to which a company cannot go." Movies also had staying power. Helpmann liked to recall how he had walked onto a stage in Buenos Aires and been startled to discover that the stagehands recognized him. " 'Ah Red Shoes!' they said — and that was released twenty years ago." Helpmann's malleable face, dominated by large, protruding eyes, was not easy to forget. Nor were his biting wit, charged theatrical presence and wicked sense of humor. His friends grew accustomed to his outrageous pranks, such as the time he arrived at a party in drag, impersonating "a minor European princess, in a hat made out of silk stockings." Rudolf had met Helpmann soon after joining the Royal Ballet, and their friendship deepened during his 1970 tour of America with the Australians in this production of *Don*

Quixote. Helpmann had suggested that the two join forces to make a film that would break new ground. According to Lucette Aldous, Rudolf's leading lady, "Bobby was passionate about doing a ballet film that could be as real as possible. He didn't just want to film it straight from the stage." Rudolf shared his missionary zeal. "The majority of the masses have not been touched by ballet," he told *The New York Times* while rehearsing with the cast. "The movie . . . with a catchy story and lively production, will bring more of the public to ballet."

To that end, he dispensed with the stage altogether. In place of streetscapes painted on backdrops, they constructed sets for each of the ballet's three acts, including a Spanish town square. They also employed cinematic techniques to make the story more naturalistic and easier to follow. Superimposed on a scene of dancing girls, for example, was the face of the dreaming don. For Kitri's costume, Rudolf drew on the Astaire and Rogers films he loved. He had been struck by how, the moment Rogers stood still, her dress seemed to "finish the phrase," as he thought of it. "That's what he told us he wanted," recalls Martin Kamer, the assistant designer. "The costume should finish her arabesque softly and nicely. We looked at all different organzas and washed them until we got the fabric right. To Rudolf the costume was part of the dance."

The director Richard Attenborough, in Australia to promote his film *Young Churchill,* spent a day on the set and admitted to being "amazed" that Nureyev, with no previous experience, had such an instinctive knowledge of moviemaking and camera angles. "I set all the camera shots," Rudolf later told the maverick director Lindsay Anderson. "Every frame, every second on the film is my responsibility, whether you like it or hate it. It's me." He would not relax his grip: He flew the film's editor to London and installed him in his home while he honored engagements in Paris and London.* He juggled performances with Fonteyn at Covent Garden and rehearsals for Balanchine's *Prodigal Son* with editing sessions at home. The reviews were unanimously favorable. He had "done so well" with his screen adaptation, enthused Anna Kisselgoff in *The New York Times,* that he "has actually made it more fun than the stage production . . . probably no dancer onstage today has done more to bring the great 19th-century ballet classics alive and make them relevant to a modern audience." Rudolf, however, was never entirely satisfied with the finished product. The color and sound were adjusted after he flew to Vancouver to rejoin the Canadians on tour. "So now I know. Next time I not only have to lay all the eggs. I have to hatch them too."

From January 29 to April 24, he led the Canadians on their mara-

---

*These included a special two-week Diaghilev tribute at the Paris Opéra in December, in which he danced *Les Sylphides, Apollo,* and *Petrushka,* all on one program, on successive evenings.

thon twenty-one-city march toward the Metropolitan Opera House. Whenever he could, he avoided flying and was driven at night in his chauffeured limousine to the next destination. He was now regularly accompanied by Luigi Pignotti, his full-time masseur and man Friday. A burly Milanese with enormous hands and an easy disposition, Pignotti had been recommended to Rudolf by conductor Zubin Mehta and hired by the Hurok organization with the caveat, "You don't see anything; you don't hear anything; you don't talk." The tour brought the usual rounds of late suppers and parties. In Los Angeles, Nureyev's presence drew Julie Andrews, Yul Brynner, Richard Chamberlain, Paul Newman and Joanne Woodward to the Shrine Auditorium. In Houston, Kain made her debut as his Aurora; afterward, a proud Rudolf threw her an impromptu champagne supper. "You have everything!" he toasted her. "Nobody since Margot has been like this." His delight, she wrote, was as much for her performance as for "his triumph" over Celia Franca. With Fonteyn dancing less and less, he was excited by Kain's possibilities and promoted her at every turn. "The way she does Aurora," he told *Time* in 1974, "there is no one like that anywhere. I don't think they have anyone in Russia like that." Over the course of touring, an affectionate bond sprang up between the dancers and Rudolf; Genghis Khan had become their "papa." For his thirty-fifth birthday, which they celebrated at a pool party in St. Louis, the dancers gave him a present he relished: a jewel-encrusted, fur-lined dance belt* custom-made by the wardrobe master.†

With the success of the tour resting on him, Rudolf grew increasingly irascible the closer they got to New York. At the Chicago Opera House on April 7, when the start of the performance was delayed, the audience began clapping impatiently. Suddenly the curtain parted and there stood Rudolf in his bare chest, his legs wrapped in leg warmers. "You shit-fuckers, shut up!" he screamed, and then retreated behind the curtain. It was one of the few times in his career when he let fly at the audience.

Nureyev's *Sleeping Beauty* premiered in New York on April 23 to a sold-out house, admiring reviews and the usual bombardment of bouquets. Ill prepared for the "the roar of the audience" that greeted them at the curtain calls, Veronica Tennant was equally surprised that their success "meant so much to Rudolf." It was his dancing, his staging and his influence which drew the greatest comment. "So what is a nice company like this doing at the Metropolitan Opera House when its previous New York engagement was a one-night stand in Brooklyn?" Clive Barnes asked in *The New York Times*. "The answer can be given in two words: Rudolf Nureyev." If the National Ballet had yet to prove itself a

---

*A dancer's jockstrap.
†Hy Meadows.

first-rank troupe, wrote Barnes, the Canadians could claim to being "the best decorated company in North America. . . . This is one of the best productions of *The Sleeping Beauty* around. I thought so when I first saw it—with Fonteyn and Nureyev—at La Scala, and I think so now. But the Canadians dance it better."

Several critics found Nureyev's staging too fussy; others yet again questioned his right to "mess with the classics." Still, most agreed that in the additional solos he had given himself, Nureyev had not simply accorded the male dancer his due but championed his possibilities. His solos "are not feats of elevation but slow meditations that show off the body's contours, strength in repose and flexibility," wrote Nancy Goldner in the *Nation*. "They allow the viewer to dwell on the male dancer's stretched muscles and pointed feet and clarity of line and to enjoy the contrast between muscular bulk and small, delicate movement. . . ."

Whatever the critics might write—and they would always have their doubts about his choreography—audience enthusiasm was unrestrained. His local debuts in *La Sylphide* and *The Moor's Pavane* also drew top marks, as did, more indirectly, his coaching of Kain. "If all the [company's] Auroras are as successful as the young Karen Kain," wrote Anna Kisselgoff in *The New York Times*, "the Toronto company has an outstanding reserve of talent for the future. . . ." One year later Barnes would be calling Kain "one of the most talented ballerinas in the western world," and Nureyev's impact on the company "sensational." He had raised its standards, its status, its artistry; before long, the company would recoup its investment. Nureyev was to strengthen his ties to the company through the annual Hurok-sponsored tours that continued until 1977.*

Nureyev's presence cast a long shadow over the company's male ranks, but it boosted the career of twenty-year-old Frank Augustyn, a tall, handsome principal dancer whose high-flying leaps and skimming brisés volés as the Bluebird were widely praised. Augustyn benefited from Nureyev's coaching, and his performances with Kain in the Bluebird pas de deux launched their partnership, the most famous in Canadian ballet. Immediately following their New York debut, Augustyn and Kain flew to Moscow to compete in the Second International Ballet Competition, a kind of ballet Olympics, held that year on the stage of the Bolshoi Theater. For five months their company had shared equal billing with Nureyev. Here on a stage where his name was forbidden, Kain and Augustyn danced the Bluebird pas de deux from his *Sleeping Beauty*, dressed in Georgiadis's sumptuous costumes, which drew "a gasp of appreciation" before they had even danced a step. Seated among the eminent panel of jurors were Nureyev's former partners Dudinskaya and Kolpakova,

---

*At the end of this first New York run, however, he pulled a ligament in his calf. Hurok canceled the Washington stopover.

Bolshoi prima Maya Plisetskaya, Alicia Alonso, Jerome Robbins and Arnold Haskell, the British critic who had derided Nureyev's defection twelve years earlier. Kain remembers how "they loved the way we did Bluebird . . . the port de bras and the style were directly from [Rudolf]. They didn't know that, but they were very impressed. . . ." Perhaps in his protégés, his former colleagues had caught a glimmer of themselves.

The Russian audience, meanwhile, paid them—and Nureyev—the supreme compliment of clapping rhythmically after each of their variations. Nominated by Kolpakova, their performance won first prize for best pas de deux in the competition; Kain, on her own, won the silver medal, having earned a few more gasps when she began her variation in the Black Swan pas de deux with double turns *en attitude* instead of the traditional single turn—yet another Nureyev amendment. There was further evidence of his ballet imperialism in the medal-winning performances of Australian Ballet dancers Marilyn Rowe (who shared the silver with Kain) and Kelvin Coe, a silver winner in the men's division. Nureyev had coached both in his *Don Quixote.*

The night before Kain left for Moscow, Rudolf had called from London. Would she mind buying a fur coat to take to his sister Rosa? She and Augustyn were also due to dance at Leningrad's Maly Theater, and in addition to the hastily purchased coat, Kain stuffed several books about Nureyev into her suitcase. When they met at her hotel, Rosa gave Kain a "vat" of caviar for Rudolf as thanks for the gifts. On her way home, Kain stopped in Paris to see Rudolf, who, while delighted to have the caviar, was dismayed at her taste in fur. "You gave her muskrat?"

RUDOLF WAS in Paris to give a series of sold-out performances of *Swan Lake* with the Paris Opéra Ballet, on an open-air stage erected in one of the courtyards of the Louvre.* Three ballerinas alternated as his Odette-Odile: Noëlla Pontois, Ghislaine Thesmar and guest Natalia Makarova. One month earlier, he and Makarova had made their stage debut, dancing *The Sleeping Beauty* and *Romeo and Juliet* at Covent Garden. Many assumed that these Kirov-trained "defectors" would be natural partners, although they had never been paired at the Kirov. Their musicality and performing styles, however, were enough at odds that neither was entirely pleased with these first performances. Indeed, unlike the musically precise Fonteyn, Makarova had not been trained to time her positions exactly to the music, leading one critic to wonder, "[I]s she stone deaf? Or what?" Having made his own way in the West, Rudolf expected Makarova to do the same. As a result, she prepared for their first *Romeo and Juliet* without her Romeo. They didn't meet onstage until the dress re-

*The first, on Bastille Day, was free and two were rained out.

hearsal, when she appeared "with an intricate Renaissance hairdo that did not go well with my small figure. I sensed that Rudi was startled at the sight and the whole rehearsal turned into one continuous misunderstanding: I mixed up my entrances, all the scenery was unsteady, the balcony almost broke under my feet."

By then Rudolf had been dancing *Romeo and Juliet* for eight years and had "very little patience for Natasha," recalls Georgina Parkinson, who taught Makarova "every little demi-semi-quaver of music so as to make those rehearsals a bit more harmonious." In those first days, she says, Makarova was "very slow to learn. She felt very vulnerable and insecure and needed some TLC, which she certainly didn't get from him. It was not a happy experience." In Paris, the unseasonably icy weather did not augur well for their first performances of *Swan Lake*. Nureyev kept warm on the throne by wrapping a cloak around his legs, while the corps of swans wore leg warmers beneath their tutus. Despite his dread of cold, Nureyev pushed ahead with their performances as planned, though Makarova, in two performances, decided to drop both her solo and the coda of the Black Swan pas de deux.

What doomed their partnership, however, was a mishap that soon assumed the proportions of yet another Parisian *scandale*. During a dress rehearsal of the Black Swan pas de deux, Makarova was completing a series of pirouettes when Rudolf stepped forward to partner her. He assumed she was stopping at seven; she was going for eight. They collided and Makarova landed flat on her back. "She was so angry that she straightened out like a board and just lay there. Rudolf looked shocked but was trying to stay in character." As the taped score went on playing, Rudolf finally raised her to her feet. After some adjustments to her tiara, the performance resumed. There were titters in the French press that Nureyev had pushed her, but the incident would have faded from memory had Makarova not quit Paris soon after, claiming ill health, and then declared, via the American press, that she would never dance with "that man" again. "Never. I am used to ballet that is refined, and a partner must be refined, flexible, sensitive," she said, adding, "Things are difficult for a man who is 35." Her remarks were widely reported and once more carried Nureyev's name beyond the stage. Nureyev, to his credit, did not respond in kind. "Paris was a try-out and it didn't come off . . . just because you can dance together doesn't mean that you are good as partners." (Privately, he dubbed her "Natashtray Macabrava" and vowed that he wouldn't dance with her either.) His fans, meanwhile, freely voiced their disapproval when Makarova returned to *Swan Lake* in the fall, this time with Ivan Nagy in New York. As she made her entrance in the second act, "they started booing so loudly that I couldn't hear any music. I was lost for a few seconds. Then I thought, 'To hell with it,' and I pulled my nerves together. . . ."

* * *

AT LA TURBIE that summer, Rudolf and Wallace set out for a picnic one day with Antoinette Sibley and her second husband, Panton Corbett, who were holidaying in nearby Monaco. A paparazzi photographer snapped Nureyev and Sibley on a dock in their bathing suits, and soon *Newsweek* was reporting rumors of an affair. Such publicity was not unwelcome to Rudolf, for it diverted attention from his actual lover, who had been approaching in the launch with Sibley's husband.

Most of the media attention, however, was directed to Nureyev's unslakable appetite for the stage. One week he was in New York, the next London, the next Milan, rehearsing, coaching, staging, dancing. The finest male dancers reached their peak at age thirty; by forty, most were moving into less taxing roles or off the stage altogether. Every reporter now wanted to know why and for how long was he going to dance. Later they would ask why he refused to stop. The answer was always the same: He couldn't. "I once asked him, 'Why do you fly here, there and everywhere? Why do you work so hard? You'll kill yourself,' " recounts the ballerina Merle Park. "And he said, 'Girl, what better way to die?' I had no answer for that."

Beginning with that first visit to the Ufa Opera House, dancing had promised him an escape, a chance to hold the world at bay for a few magical hours. He had harnessed all of his energy, and all of his fury, to claim his place on the stage. The struggle had marked him. "Don't forget that I am one of those dancers that had to go out and steal his life," he reminded a reporter. "Nobody has ever handed me anything. Nobody. Even as a young boy in Russia, I had to grab life by the throat. I remember . . . entering the Kirov Ballet and being told, 'But who are you? You are just a nobody from the provinces!' " He was forever proving himself to himself, forever pitting himself against adversity, new challenges and unseen barriers, drunk on applause, but never misled by it. "He gave himself no quarter," observes Lynn Seymour.

His two most profound friendships—with Bruhn and with Fonteyn—were rooted in this consuming commitment. Each represented his defining ideals: perfectionism and perseverance. "All my days are about conserving my physical and emotional energies so that I can tap them at any moment on stage," was his reply to one reporter's probing questions about his personal life. "My whole life is about being on the stage, and so I stay very low—I simmer—and I keep to myself." Dancing absorbed him as it did few other dancers and he knew of no other way to define himself. The message was repeated to everyone he knew. Armen Bali, having suggested that he needed to rest, learned not to broach the subject again. "What, do you want me to die? That's my life, my wife, my home, my love. That's it."

"When I stop for a few days, it is terrible," he told the *Los Angeles Times.* "I begin to worry. Is everything all right? Can I still do it? Then, when I begin dancing again and see that everything is in order, I relax. I function. The train runs only when it is on the tracks." To another paper, he explained that a dancer's life was all too short and he was happiest dancing. "So I want to be onstage as much as possible until my body gives out."

In the thirteen years since his defection, he had grown more relaxed. People meeting him for the first time expected to find the temperamental artist of legend and were usually surprised to find instead a thoughtful, intelligent man of the world. Onstage, at the age of thirty-six, he was no longer "the savage young creature" he had been at his London debut. No longer did he hurtle about the stage "with wild eyes on an ecstatic, gaunt face," nor did he hover in the air. But whatever he had lost in elevation and tensile strength, he had gained in depth, nuance and eloquence. The impetuosity of youth had given way to a certain grandeur of bearing and to a more thoughtful, tempered and dramatically integrated performance. Few dancers could animate a role the way he could or draw the public so completely into his domain. And to each familiar role, whether the conceited Prince Florimund, the bereaved Solor, the moody Prince Siegfried or the self-indulgent, then anguished Albrecht, he now brought a deeper musical sensitivity and a greater clarity, while still retaining his wild charisma and sheer technical aplomb. Nureyev's technique had never been his calling card: It was the way he moved, not the precision of his movements, that most compelled attention.

Audiences drawn to the ballet by Nureyev accounted in large part for the ballet boom in America in 1974. In 1961, the year he defected to the West, the country boasted 24 ballet companies; by 1974, there were 216 and the audience for dance had jumped from less than one million to more than ten million. To be sure, there were other stars, among them Makarova, Peter Martins, Edward Villella, Suzanne Farrell and Jacques d'Amboise. But Nureyev was the most visible, accessible and widely traveled. "It's hard to believe," declared *Newsweek* in May 1974, "but today he is more electrifying than ever."

Proof of his dominance came that spring when he appeared at the Metropolitan Opera House in back-to-back seasons with the National Ballet of Canada and the Royal Ballet. For both, he served as guest, catalyst, media magnet and box-office guarantee. Nureyev went straight from one company to the other; he didn't even have to bother changing dressing rooms. "I'm staying put—they're coming to me," he joked before the Royal Ballet arrived in New York.

His debuts that season showed off his impressively diverse range, from the preening, jaded hero of John Neumeier's *Don Juan* to the quietly impassioned lover des Grieux in MacMillan's *Manon* to the spirited country bumpkin Colas in Ashton's *La Fille Mal Gardée*.* This bucolic comedy classic tells of the romance between Colas and his spunky sweetheart, Lise, whose ambitious mother hopes to marry her off to the son of a rich farmer. Unaccustomed to seeing Nureyev in comic roles, much less cavorting around a maypole, audiences were struck by the sheer visceral joy of his Colas. "Never have I seen him look so happy and relaxed on stage," wrote John Percival of his first London Colas two months later, "allowing his innate sense of fun to bubble through into all the situations."

For the first time since its historic New York debut in 1949, the Royal Ballet appeared in New York without Fonteyn. Increasingly, Nureyev danced with Merle Park and Monica Mason. Though Nureyev was in top form, several other male stars gave him a run for his money, among them David Wall and Dowell, two dancers who had benefited from his example. Sibley and Dowell emerged as the company's new golden pair during a season of outstanding performances. Nureyev alternated in various roles with Dowell, among them des Grieux in *Manon*. The role had been created to showcase Dowell's silken technique, but Nureyev brought the character more vividly to life. Both were formidable actors, but as Clive Barnes pointed out, Dowell lacked Nureyev's maturity, just as Nureyev had lacked Bruhn's the season they had both danced with the Royal Ballet in 1962. "In those days [Bruhn's] greater experience always made him more dramatically interesting than the vivid Mr. Nureyev. Mr. Nureyev quickly learned Mr. Bruhn's lesson, which is one of the reasons why today he is Rudolf Nureyev."

His supremacy, however, was no more invulnerable than Bruhn's had been. And it was challenged just as unexpectedly, when Mikhail Baryshnikov defected in Toronto on June 29. The event made headlines around the world and was universally applauded for delivering to the West another Soviet sensation. In contrast to Rudolf's decision, Baryshnikov's was premeditated and carefully planned. And Baryshnikov had the benefit of seeing Nureyev's success.

Baryshnikov and fellow Kirov star Irina Kolpakova had been touring with a contingent of Bolshoi dancers.† At the end of a week of performances in Toronto, Baryshnikov rushed into a waiting car instead of the company bus. He was spirited away by friends to a country estate, where he hid from the press and weighed his next move in seclusion. He was quickly granted asylum, and among the friends who offered counsel were

---

*Refashioned by Ashton in 1960, the original *Fille* had been choreographed in 1789 on the eve of the French Revolution and had since been staged numerous times as a vehicle for many of the greatest dancers of the day.

†Fearing that he might someday defect, the Kirov had kept him tightly reined, and it was only after Kolpakova, a party member, vouched for his return that he was permitted to go on the tour.

Rudolf's former Leningrad classmates Sergiu Stefanschi, then a leading dancer with the National Ballet of Canada; Sasha Minz, who had settled in New York after emigrating to Israel; and Makarova, Baryshnikov's former lover.

Rudolf, who was in London at the time, had met Baryshnikov three years earlier when Baryshnikov was in London with the Kirov. Rudolf had sent a message through a friend,* asking "if I wanted to come have lunch at his house. Of course I did." So early one morning Baryshnikov sneaked out to his house. There they spent the day together talking about the Pushkins and Dudinskaya and Shelest, but mostly about what Rudolf had learned in the West about dancing itself, "about teachers and technique and how the Russians do class and how the French do it, and the English, and how long they warm up and how they do barre and on and on." Baryshnikov was struck by Rudolf's warmth. "I was kind of flattered that he took some interest in me. He liked my dancing. It was nice to see this man extravagantly dressed in this beautiful house. He asked a lot of questions. I thought, 'The guy's okay.' I had heard about how he could be very abusive and unpleasant. Despite all this talk, he was normal. He lived very quietly in a way."

Later, Rudolf showed him his closetful of costumes, taking them out, one by one, as he explained how they were custom-made and tight in the torso, but loose enough beneath the armpits to allow him to move his arms freely. Baryshnikov was a little bored, for he didn't then regard costumes as integral to the art—"now I do. But to him, everything about how the body would look onstage was a matter of passionate interest." The subject of defection was never broached. "It wasn't even in my mind then," Baryshnikov insists. At the end of their visit, Rudolf gave him a book of Michelangelo drawings and a scarf to take away with him.

THREE WEEKS after Baryshnikov's defection, they met again. Both happened to be performing in New York at the same time on neighboring stages. Baryshnikov had been invited to make his New York debut with American Ballet Theatre, partnering Makarova in *Giselle* and other works at the New York State Theater, while a last-minute cancellation by the Bolshoi had brought Nureyev back to the Met for a third time that summer, once again with the Canadians. Over dinner, Rudolf was quick to offer Baryshnikov some hard-won advice. One of the biggest mistakes he made, he said, was to write his autobiography at age twenty-four. "Don't let them do that to *you*." He also urged the younger dancer not to "jump around. Stay with one company." Baryshnikov, however, was hungry to sample new choreography, to work with Ashton and Béjart and Petit. "I

*Chinko Rafique, a former dancer with the Royal Ballet and the Zurich Ballet.

told him I wasn't interested in staying with one company because I wasn't interested in classical dance. I said I'd do the classics, of course, because they would pay me money to do *Giselle* and *Swan Lake* and all those things, but I wasn't interested, from the beginning." While Rudolf had jumped around himself, he felt that his ties to the Royal Ballet had given him a much-needed home base. "Maybe what he was saying to me was, 'It may look like what I'm doing is very exciting, but it's not that easy.'" Another night he took him to the Russian Tea Room, where Nureyev provoked stares and Baryshnikov went unrecognized. When asked for his autograph, Rudolf signed his name, and then passed the paper to Baryshnikov.

He also went to see Baryshnikov dance and was there for his debut as Solor in Makarova's new staging of The Shades scene from *La Bayadère*. And on the nights he was not performing himself, Baryshnikov was at the Met observing Nureyev. Their presence both onstage and in the audience made for an especially exciting season, as balletomanes rushed across the plaza from one theater to the other.

In a poignant turn of events, Baryshnikov's first performances in New York also coincided with Bruhn's return to the stage. The Canadians were performing Bruhn's *La Sylphide* at the Met, and the great danseur noble had agreed to come out of retirement to play Madge the witch, a character role at the furthest remove from his princely domain. The idea was for Bruhn to make his debut as a character artist in New York, with Nureyev in the leading role of James. On August 9, the two friends, their careers inextricably linked, appeared onstage together for the first time since their early concert performances in 1962.

The night was highly charged for them both. The theater was packed with people wanting to see them share the stage. "Rudolf was so excited and proud, he couldn't wait to get out there," recalls Linda Maybarduk, who danced the role of Effie, James's jilted fiancée. Bruhn's own entrance was greeted by bravos and applause. Afterward, as Rudolf took his bow, Erik stood in the wings, trembling. Joanne Nisbet, the company's ballet mistress, had to hold him up and when she asked, "Are you all right?" he answered her in Danish. "He'd forgotten how to speak English, he was so overcome. I gave him a push and then Rudolf just grabbed him and yanked him out onstage." The moment the curtain came down, they embraced.

Bruhn had, in effect, surrendered the classical roles of his prime to Nureyev and moved into a repertoire in which he felt more at ease. With his handsome face and frame transformed, Bruhn's incarnation as Madge proved riveting, if startling. "People were used to seeing me as the noble Prince, and here I was ... a toothless hag, dressed in rags and oozing evil. Well, it was a perfect way to release everything that was evil inside of me."

Rudolf had no doubt of that. When Bruhn (as Madge) threatened to strike him with a stick, he was convinced that he was going to kill him. Erik's approval was still all-important to Rudolf, who was never as nervous as he was the nights Erik was in the audience watching him dance a Bournonville ballet. He would be "sick with nerves," recalls Linda Maybarduk, and Erik would "torture" him by coming backstage and saying nothing. He would just sit there in silence, "which he knew was so much worse for Rudolf than telling him what he had done wrong."

Five days after Rudolf's and Erik's triumph in New York, the National Ballet opened in the same ballet in Toronto. Only this time Baryshnikov danced the role of James. Though Bruhn did not appear as Madge, he coached Baryshnikov for his debut, as he had Rudolf. Following the performance, Bruhn went backstage and told Baryshnikov, "If I had continued dancing the role, I would have liked to have danced it just like that." It was the kind of praise Rudolf had longed to hear.

According to Baryshnikov, Rudolf was jealous of his growing friendship with Bruhn, "of Erik's attention to me. . . . Rudolf didn't have that many friends, especially male friends . . . and obviously Erik was a big problem all his life. He would say to me, 'So you're with Erik again! Maybe you two will get married.' And I'd say, 'Maybe we will.' " Erik was then living with Constantin Patsalas, a handsome Greek-born dancer and choreographer with the National Ballet of Canada. On occasion, the three of them would go out with Rudolf and Wallace Potts. Baryshnikov describes the relationship between Rudolf and Erik at that time as "a battle of egos—each step one of them made was judged by the other," whereas Wallace was more "like a family . . . more down-to-earth." Wallace, he says, "never had any great big ambitious plans. He never challenged Rudolf in anything. From the outside it looked like a lovely relationship."

That summer Baryshnikov was Rudolf's houseguest in London, where he dined with Princess Margaret, Ashton, Fonteyn and Robert Helpmann. Rudolf also "liked to be seen by people and to be recognized. He would make little scenes that everybody would notice, like he's saying, 'Look at me good. What? You don't know who I am?' " He also "dragged" Baryshnikov to "weird cabaret shows," featuring transvestites, English vaudevillians and impersonators. "Sometimes they would imitate him if they knew he was in the audience."

Since both Baryshnikov and Nureyev were Russian defectors, the public assumed they had much in common and regarded each other as competitors. The press was only too happy to play up their rivalry, just as it had done twelve years earlier with Rudolf and Erik. However, apart from the fact that both were Pushkin products and Kirov stars, their styles, temperaments and creative goals were entirely different. "I just happened to have better schooling," acknowledges Baryshnikov. "I studied longer. He knew perfectly well his faults as a dancer. And he knew instinctively that I was not very keen about his dancing per se. I liked his performing, but not always his dancing. It was not a very natural way of moving. There was no internal logic in his phrasing. Everything is about show-manship: 'Look at me, how I do this.' There was no natural flow from the beginning to the end. . . ." Baryshnikov, too, was driven to dance. However, he didn't demand validation from the audience. As Arlene Croce observed the month he defected, "When he walks out onto the stage, he doesn't radiate—doesn't put the audience on notice that he's a star. . . . He attends carefully to his ballerina and appears utterly unpre-possessing. . . . It's obvious that Pushkin has turned out not the last of a line but a new and unique classical virtuoso."

Baryshnikov would insist later that they were never rivals and that Rudolf understood that he wasn't "competing for his spot." In truth, Rudolf wasn't always sure of that. Luigi Pignotti recalls that Rudolf kept an eye on his younger rival and was known to make disparaging remarks about him whenever he felt insecure or threatened. Princess Firyal re-members the call she received from Rudolf after Baryshnikov's Parisian debut. "How was he?" he wanted to know. "Did he give you goose bumps?"

25

Tyger! Tyger!

"ALWAYS I INTRUDE and always I am made to feel this," Nureyev repeatedly told reporters. With the launch of his pickup troupe, Nureyev and Friends, in June 1974, Rudolf formalized what, in the minds of many, had already become the reality: He became the company, making everyone else his guest. His plan was to assemble a group of dancers for one special season, during which he would dance not only every night but in every work on the program, one designed to showcase both his own range and the diversity of dance itself. The venture was to prove easily portable and highly lucrative, and would keep Nureyev onstage to the end of his life.

The first Friends season in Paris, at the massive five-thousand-seat Palais des Sports, featured Merle Park and members of the Paris Opéra Ballet in four short contrasting works, ranging from Bournonville's buoyant *Flower Festival* pas de deux to the neoclassicism of Balanchine's *Apollo* to the drama of José Limón's *Moor's Pavane* and the modern lyricism of Taylor's *Aureole*. This last piece brought to prominence Charles Jude, a young French-Vietnamese dancer, whose Asian languor, suppleness and high cheekbones for many called to mind the young Nureyev. Jude, however, was undecided about his career. "Why are you here?" Rudolf asked him one day. "Because my parents and my teacher want me to be," Jude replied. "But you have the right body, you *must* do this," Rudolf insisted. Nureyev couldn't bear to see indifference in a dancer blessed with Jude's natural ability. It was his goading, courage and example, acknowledges Jude, that changed his mind.

Rudolf had first met Jude on the beach in Èze, near La Turbie, in 1969. Hearing that Jude was the only male dancer in his class at the Nice

Conservatoire, Rudolf sought him out, ever eager to track emerging talent. "I was lying on the beach and someone came to tell me that Nureyev was looking for me. We talked for about ten minutes. He invited me to join him for lunch, but I wanted to be with my friends." Four years later, arriving in Paris for his Louvre performances with Makarova, Rudolf immediately recognized Jude among the corps dancers. He invited him to Maxim's, where he playfully fed him beef stroganoff, ignoring his other guests.

Rudolf's interest was sparked by personal infatuation as well as by regard for talent, the one feeding the other. That he should physically desire his young protégés was hardly unusual. Though the twenty-one-year-old Jude was decidedly heterosexual, it was precisely his inaccessibility that made him all the more appealing. Withdrawn, quiet-spoken and in awe of Rudolf, Jude was flattered by the attention but uncomfortable when it became pronounced. Rudolf's respect for Jude made him in turn cautious and even shy, leading him to enlist Elizabeth Cooper as his go-between. A flame-haired, vivacious pianist, Cooper, played for class at the Paris Opéra. Drawn to her vitality, Rudolf often invited her out with him at night, largely so that she could approach men he liked on his behalf. "He was mostly attracted to straight men, not to homosexuals, and he figured that he stood a better chance if I explained to them who Rudolf Nureyev was." She recalls how dejected Rudolf became one night when Jude didn't come over to their table at Club Sept, a new club popular with the fashion and art crowd.* "He asked me to please go speak to Charles and invite him to come for a drink at the Ritz. Rudolf had a suite there. Charles knew that Rudolf was very attracted to him, and he was afraid. But he said he would come." But Jude never showed. "Rudolf started screaming at me, 'You are a bitch! I want Charles! I want Charles!' " He was so upset, she recalls, that he locked her in a room with his masseur Luigi Pignotti "for the whole night."

Gradually, as Rudolf accepted that there was no chance of an affair, the two became close friends. They traveled, worked and dined together regularly on Rudolf's myriad Friends tours. Fifteen years older than Jude, Rudolf became his mentor, the role Nigel Gosling still played in his own life. He kept in touch with Jude by phone and encouraged him to see films, visit art galleries and plays, and read as widely as possible. "He was very protective and always worrying about my future." He was also charting it, training him and casting Jude in many of his own productions. "After you," he once told Fonteyn, "he's my favorite partner."

---

*Among its regulars were Yves Saint Laurent, Pierre Bergé, Clara Saint, Andy Warhol and a bevy of American models, including Jerry Hall and Pat Cleveland, who was famous for dancing naked on its tabletops.

* * *

THE DAY AFTER Christmas, 1974, Nureyev opened on Broadway* with a new group of Friends, a mix of classical and modern dancers. The 1,903-seat Uris Theater was sold out for five weeks, making it the longest and most successful concert dance engagement in Broadway history.† Although Rudolf had hoped Erik would play Iago to his Othello in *The Moor's Pavane*, Erik turned him down. "We didn't have an argument but I said to him, 'Rudik, I cannot be one of your "friends" on that program, because there isn't one person on it who is a real friend. . . .' It wasn't that I didn't want to dance with Rudik on the same stage, just didn't like that billing." (In all likelihood, it was the thought of "second billing" that irked him most.)

Balanchine, too, had resisted any association, and had agreed to give Rudolf permission to perform *Apollo* only after he realized that his weekly take of the box-office gross would raise a badly needed twenty thousand dollars for his School of American Ballet. "I asked him how much he wanted, and he said, 'Five percent, like I used to get when I was on Broadway,' " recalls his assistant Barbara Horgan. "There was this irritation about Rudolf. Balanchine could be very annoyed at the public about their adulation for a star."

Despite Balanchine's famous dictum "Ballet is woman," the top box-office draws in New York that month were Nureyev and Baryshnikov.‡ But where Baryshnikov danced the classics with Ballet Theatre, Nureyev showed himself in an ambitious mix of styles, dancing four different roles a night, eight times a week, while fans and newcomers alike poured through the doors of the Uris Theater as they might to a hit Broadway musical. "Generally I'm not fond of ballet at all," a garment manufacturer from Queens told *The New York Times*. "You may not like baseball, but when you know Babe Ruth is playing, you go."** Some

---

*Nureyev had made his Broadway debut two months earlier, when he flew from Paris to New York for one day to appear with the Taylor company at the Alvin Theater. He rehearsed the moment he got off the plane, gave matinee and evening performances the following day, and flew back to Paris that same evening. The next day, he performed with the Paris Opéra Ballet.

†The group included Merle Park, American dancer-choreographer Louis Falco and members of the Paul Taylor Dance Company.

‡At a party that month, former Kirov stars Nureyev, Baryshnikov, Makarova, Sasha Minz and Valery and Galina Panov were all reunited for the first time. After two years of anguish that nearly ended their careers, the Panovs had been granted permission to emigrate to Israel as a result of international pressure.

**By the 1980s Nureyev himself had become the standard of measure. Just how far-reaching his legend extended became clear when in describing hockey great Wayne Gretzky, the game's reigning player, his team's owner called him "the Nureyev of sport, the superstar's superstar."

came to see him in the flesh, others to see whether he would "kill himself with a surfeit of dancing," as one critic wrote. "Nureyev was half-dancer, half-gladiator."

To Martha Graham, she of the grand pronouncements and primordial passions, he was Lucifer, half man, half god, "the Promethean figure who brought light, fire." His first forays into American modern dance had led Rudolf to its high priestess, and it was at his behest that the eighty-one-year-old Graham created *Lucifer* for him and Fonteyn in 1975. Given that Graham's fifty-year career was seen as a rebellion against ballet, this historic alliance drew considerable attention. "Not since the lion and the lamb did their fabled bedtime act has there been such an unlikely but happy merging of differences," quipped Clive Barnes in *The New York Times*.

A pioneer of American dance, Graham was descended from pioneering Americans: Her mother was a tenth-generation descendant of *Mayflower* colonist Miles Standish; her father, the grandson of an Irish immigrant. Graham's father, a doctor of nervous disorders, once caught her in a lie. When she asked him how he knew, he replied, "No matter what words may say, movement never lies." Thus were sown the seeds of her artistic credo, which took root after she saw a performance by the American dancer and choreographer Ruth St. Denis. Graham was led to the Denishawn company, the first American modern dance troupe, and in 1926 she founded her own company and movement language.

That language sought to express the human psyche and soul as manifest through myths, archetypes and raw emotion. Rejecting the ballerina's pointed foot as artificial, she flexed her own, forsaking the air for the ground and fairy tales for frankness. Sex was a defining element of her work, and the pelvis the propulsive engine of her technique. Her dancers called her studio "the temple of pelvic truths." "All my life I have been a devotee of sex, in the right sense of the word," she wrote. "Fulfillment, as opposed to procreation, or I would have had children." Nureyev, with his sexual vitality, naturally attracted her.

Graham had continued performing until the age of seventy-six, postponing retirement as long as she could, which inevitably meant ignoring whispers that she could no longer dance. When, in 1970, her own company finally demanded that she retire after forty-nine years on the stage, she plunged into a depression, having "lost my will to live." She stayed home, drank too much, and slipped into a coma. Her "rebirth," as she called it, came in 1973, with a revamped company and approach to life. For the first time, she felt "a sense of urgency that my work should go on even if I was not able to dance myself."

Nevertheless, the transition from making dances for her own body to creating them for others affected her output: In the six years since her retirement she had made only four short pieces. Her company was strapped for cash, and as the choreographer Agnes de Mille cannily observed, "she needed stars to replace herself."

Nureyev reinvigorated her, as he once had Bruhn and Fonteyn, and in his voracious ambition, she recognized herself. "This is the only time that I've ever lived through another person in movement," she said while at work on *Lucifer*. "Rudolf is not a substitute for myself, but working with him gives me a very definite identification." As the Graham dancer Peter Sparling saw it, Rudolf was "someone she could instill with her own persona, someone she could trust to carry center stage much the way she had."

It was in the role of Jocasta, in *Night Journey*, her retelling of the Oedipus tale, that Rudolf had first seen her dance in London many years earlier. "I had never seen anything so magnetic, intense and completing." Afterward he had visited her backstage. Uncertain about what he wanted to say, he had stared at her and said little. By the time they began to work together, their admiration was mutual. In 1974, Graham was glimpsed backstage at the ballet, kissing Nureyev's hands after a performance of *Le Corsaire*. People passing by "stopped in amazement," wrote de Mille, at this startling act of homage.

They charmed each other easily, these two outsize creatures from different worlds and generations. The childless older woman and the unruly child: This was a now-familiar scenario in Rudolf's life. Graham, like de Valois and many others, was not immune to his knack for taming formidable women. She flirted with him openly and eagerly, won over by his impishness and teasing. A "pre-eminent coquette," as her friend Agnes de Mille described her, Graham, at eighty-one, resembled "a miniature Japanese doll." Though racked with arthritis, she kept her gnarled hands sheathed in gloves and her tiny frame draped in caftans designed for her by Halston. Her hair was dyed black, and her face, "frequently lifted and smooth," was now "more gaunt than ever, masklike, colorless, matte, her high cheekbones outlining the skull, her immortality."

To Ronald Protas, Graham's custodian and successor, Rudolf "was just like Martha. She could be a terror, but she was basically one of the softest touches for a sad story you have ever met. They loved each other. She always used to say, 'I wish I could have danced with him.' She never said that about anyone else." (In her autobiography, published in 1991, she added Baryshnikov's name to the list.)

Still, she felt no compunction about putting Rudolf in his place. Annoyed that he never arrived on time to rehearsal, she finally "let him have it" the day he showed up thirty minutes late. "I told him he was a great artist but a spoiled, willful child. And that was just for starters. He only stammered and apologized. It must have done some good. He was never late again."

Having regularly refused to work with ballet dancers, Graham pointedly told the *Times*, "I didn't approach Rudolf, but I felt that as long as he wanted to do something, it should be centered around him rather than for someone else. He was at the moment in his life when he needed to be centered. I'm not saying I was altruistic. He came and worked on the technique and then he went away. It was stop and go. Then I thought of the thing he is, and I started with the idea 'Tyger! Tyger! burning bright/In the forests of the night.' " Rudolf hoped that the new work would reveal an undiscovered side of himself; however, save for a new way of moving, Graham cast him in a familiar role. Her Lucifer was not Satan, but "the bringer of light," the god who falls to earth only to suffer the first stirrings of human fear and passion. Fonteyn was Night, his temptress.

While Graham choreographed directly on Nureyev, scheduling conflicts led her to create the role of Night on Janet Eilber. She then restaged it for Fonteyn, whom she accommodated by making the movement more "balletic." Rudolf had persuaded Fonteyn to appear with him, and though she acquitted herself admirably, she was not interested in learning a new technique. All Rudolf cared to know was, "Is it really Graham? You're not giving it to me differently?" Rudolf was eager to "feed on" new movement. To that end, he trained anew, starting literally from the ground up, learning the contractions, knee crawls, falls and phrasing basic to the Graham technique. Peter Sparling recalls his fascination in watching Nureyev "try to reshape himself."

However, fearing that his audience would think he was, as he put it, "retiring to modern dance," he set a nearly impossible pace for himself. He staged and rehearsed his *Raymonda* for American Ballet Theatre during the same period, and then fitted in a tour to Australia to dance his *Sleeping Beauty* with London Festival Ballet. "If I hadn't done *Raymonda* . . . people would have said 'Aha! He's stepping down. He can't do the classics anymore.' So these things are carefully calculated." But just three days before the premiere of *Lucifer*, he twisted his ankle disembarking from a plane in New York. As a result, he and Halston nearly came to blows at the dress rehearsal. Halston had designed a gold-mesh jockstrap, covered with tiny jewels, which to Rudolf's annoyance "Halston wanted to stitch . . . on my crotch himself. After I had rehearsed all day long, he wanted me to stand for him while he sewed up my crotch. I said, 'Here is my dance belt, sew it on. Let me have one hour.' My foot was enormous. . . ." After Rudolf had stormed off, Fonteyn went quietly to her dressing room without even mentioning the scene to the close friend who accompanied her. Halston, however, wasn't as sanguine. "I will never work with him again," he declared. "That monster!"

Rudolf made his hugely publicized Graham debut on June 19, 1975, with an Ace bandage wrapped around his injured foot. It was the first time his masseur, Luigi Pignotti, recalled seeing him in tears from the pain. His appearance in *Lucifer* that night, at a star-studded benefit, helped to raise two hundred thousand dollars for the Graham company, leaving it debt-free and with money to spare, an unheard-of situation for an American dance company. But this was not your typical dance crowd. First Lady Betty Ford, the benefit's honorary chairwoman and a former Graham pupil, was escorted by Woody Allen, while the audience, having paid up to ten thousand dollars a ticket, included Diane Keaton, Steve McQueen and Paul Newman. Many sported "Martha, Margot and Rudi" buttons. To Rudolf, it was all "like an MGM promotion." Equally strange for some was seeing Nureyev and Fonteyn dance the White Swan pas de deux from *Swan Lake*, the first and last time a nineteenth-century ballet appeared on a Graham bill.* The critics were, in the main, admiring. Nureyev, wrote Arlene Croce, "was not ridiculous. The element of camp in his personality frees him for incongruous undertakings such as this; he gives to the bizarre a touch of authority. . . . It wasn't good Graham dancing but it was good Nureyev. . . ."

"I always thought that whatever Rudolf danced, whether it was Graham or Taylor, or anybody, Rudolf was a great faker," observes Mikhail Baryshnikov. "He never had the chance or the time to truly absorb the choreographer's style and be totally comfortable. But he added so much because he had so much charisma in him, it didn't matter how he did their work. He had respect for the choreographer, but he was never committed one hundred percent to having total respect for the choreography. . . . Maybe he wanted to, but it was like he felt that life was too short to spend six or seven weeks on a twenty-minute piece."

MARTHA, MARGOT AND RUDI were also teamed that month in advertisements for Blackglama furs, the three of them cocooned in mink and clutching hands beneath the tag line "What Becomes a Legend Most?" Each played to his or her persona: Graham the goddess, Fonteyn the glamour queen, Nureyev the imperious Tatar. His shirt unzipped to his solar plexus, he wore a mink Davy Crockett–style cap, the tails arrayed like plumes so that it looked as if a giant bird had perched on his right shoulder. As payment, they each received floor-length coats and Graham, additionally, a donation for her school.

A former Kirov star was never going to be a Graham dancer, and yet Rudolf was not afraid to be seen trying. In December, he performed (without a fee) in Graham's fiftieth anniversary season on Broadway, dancing a variety of new roles: the adulterer Reverend Dimmesdale in

---

*With the exception of a film clip of the pair in *Le Corsaire* shown at a 1994 gala for the company in memory of Nureyev.

her retelling of Hawthorne's *The Scarlet Letter*, Oedipus in *Night Journey* (1947) and the raging brimstone Revivalist in her landmark *Appalachian Spring*, to Aaron Copland's famous score. In explaining the role of the preacher,* Graham had once decreed that he should be "ninety-nine percent sex and one percent religion," a man who knows his power over women and how to use it. In this Rudolf succeeded: His "personal incantational forces vulcanized the less than perfect segments of his performance," wrote Walter Terry. However, Graham devotees roundly booed his debut in *Night Journey* on December 17 after Rudolf fumbled badly with Oedipus' yards-long cape, with which he was meant to conjure some extraordinary images. Hearing the jeers, Rudolf "looked dazed and mortified," recalled one observer, "as if he wanted the floor to swallow him up." He was due to dance the work again that evening. As he and Graham were leaving the theater, Graham was overheard telling him, "Don't worry, doll, it'll be better tonight." For the next decade, Graham listed him as a full member of her company. "You men have to learn to move like Rudolf," Graham would exhort her dancers in teaching them to take command of a moment. "When he faces a wall, he *becomes* the wall!"

"I don't claim to be an expert in modern dance," Rudolf told a reporter in December 1975. "But I improve with each performance. . . . And I take back into classical dance a new awareness of myself." To some the interchange was heresy. To Rudolf, it was essential, and the mixed repertories of today's ballet companies bear him out. "Now we're seeing a fantastic exchange of vocabulary between classical ballet and modern dance. It will become a mutual language. You have musicians playing Mozart, Schoenberg, Ravel, so why not dancers—if they train well, if they become aware of their body as an instrument."

BY 1975, Nureyev's partnership with Fonteyn had lost much of its momentum but none of its allure. Having revived Fonteyn's career in 1962, Rudolf continued to propel it through the 1970s, by giving her the kinds of ballet showcases she was no longer being offered at the Royal Ballet. In sold-out evenings at Washington's Kennedy Center, on Broadway and at London's Coliseum, they continued to trade on the cachet of their union. At age fifty-six, Fonteyn even braved a few performances of *Le Corsaire*, unwisely, given her fading technique. Unlike Bruhn, who refused to compete with his former self, Fonteyn made adjustments in technique. Her artistry and stature were compensation enough for her audiences. Financial pressures drove her on, forcing her to annul the deal she had made with Ashton years earlier that he should tell her when

*The dancer and choreographer Merce Cunningham originated the role in 1944.

she should stop dancing. "But of course when the time came, she made it impossible for me to say anything." She and Rudolf were never entirely sure when their partnership would end. On January 10, 1976, at the Royal Opera House, they gave what turned out to be their last performances together in a full-length ballet. They danced *Romeo and Juliet*, the ballet that had sealed their partnership in the popular imagination.

With Fonteyn edging inevitably toward retirement, Rudolf hoped to forge another brilliant partnership. At an all-star Ballet Theatre gala on July 28, 1975, he "transformed steps into fire," dancing *Corsaire* opposite twenty-two-year-old Gelsey Kirkland, one of the most gifted, if troubled, ballerinas of her generation.* Though Kirkland had invited him to partner her and was "in awe of him," she was then enmeshed in a partnership and love affair with Baryshnikov.† She was also "a rehearsal queen," as one insider puts it, and with Nureyev jetting hither and yon with increasing frequency, his schedule and temperament would never have withstood Kirkland's painstaking and probing preparation. "Rudi seemed to be genuinely proud of me as a dancer," she wrote. "I had heard how difficult he could be with his ballerinas, but on that night he . . . showed me off during curtain calls as if I were an equal sharing in the art. . . . I wished that he were ten years younger." To Arlene Croce, however, he was still "the world's greatest *Corsaire* hero. . . . He may lurch a bit going into a turning jump, but the role draws from him the animal intensity that his own sappy choreography in *Raymonda* and *The Sleeping Beauty* obscures."

He continued to appear with Lynn Seymour and Eva Evdokimova, though neither pairing caught fire with the public. Another favorite was Cynthia Gregory, who stood five feet eleven inches on pointe and, though physically and temperamentally unsuited to him, "by sheer good will and desire . . . made it work," Nureyev acknowledged. "She has such total self-annihilation, she's capable of . . . being so vulnerable that it becomes terrific. . . . The best are like that—giving a kind of love that's totally selfless." Continuing to see great promise in twenty-two-year-old Karen Kain, the thirty-seven-year-old Nureyev enlisted Fonteyn to coach her in *The Sleeping Beauty* and *Swan Lake*, hoping, no doubt, that Kain might do for him what he had done for Fonteyn. Kain joined them in Washington for a "Nureyev, Fonteyn and Friends" season and was to dance with Rudolf directly afterward in New York during his annual engagement with the Canadians. Since Rudolf constantly referred new partners to Fonteyn's working methods, Kain assumed that after thirteen

---

*Nureyev and Bruhn and Cynthia Gregory also appeared together in the pas de trois from the little-known Bournonville ballet *La Ventana*.

†Their destructive love affair, along with Kirkland's battles with drugs, anorexia, bulimia and Balanchine, is chronicled in Kirkland's 1986 memoir, *Dancing on My Grave*.

years as partners, there was by now little disagreement between them. She was wrong.

Swan Lake was Fonteyn's "greatest" role, Rudolf declared when the three of them began working on the Swan's first entrance. "No," Fonteyn corrected him, *Sleeping Beauty* and *Ondine* were far better expressions of her personality. Rudolf instructed that the swan was "a large, regal bird, proud, strong, not sparrow," and that her line must be clear, her arabesque turned out and sustained. Fonteyn parried that he had it all wrong, that Kain should focus on "the feeling of the moment, not the step." Her own motivation came from the story, she explained, not from the technique. "Imagine yourself alone in your bedroom at night," she told Kain. "You're brushing her hair, or grooming your feathers as the Swan would do, when all of a sudden you sense an intruder. Imagine how frozen you feel when your heart starts to pound and you don't know whether you're in danger or not."

Where Fonteyn focused on why she was doing a step, Rudolf was concerned with the form of the step itself. Both achieved their ends by different means, but who could argue with the result? Their approach to Kain's first act solo in *The Sleeping Beauty* was no less at odds. Rudolf insisted she perform it with the power "of a little soldier," very perky and correct, "the way *you* did it," he reminded Fonteyn. No, she insisted, that wasn't the way she had done it at all. "He got a little pouty about it and she just laughed. Then we all realized it was better if only one of them coached me at a time."

While in Washington, Rudolf suddenly announced to Kain that they would dance *Corsaire* together that same evening. She had never danced it before, but Rudolf was too exhausted to rehearse more than the basics. To save time, he asked her to his room at the Watergate Hotel. While Luigi pummeled his muscles, Kain scribbled his instructions in a notebook. But that evening, when the music began for her solo, she realized that she had no idea when to make her entrance. All at once Fonteyn was behind her. "Any second now, okay, go!" she signaled, pushing Kain gently onto the stage.

Kain, however, would not assume Fonteyn's place following the older ballerina's retirement. Rudolf continued to create opportunities for Kain, but to his irritation, she increasingly turned them down out of loyalty to her home company. Much more galling to him, however, was the article by Canadian critic John Fraser that ran in *The New York Times* on July 27, 1975, with the headline NUREYEV, LEAVE CANADIAN BALLET ALONE. While acknowledging Nureyev's catalytic impact, Fraser attacked him for using the company to his own ends, for overshadowing its male dancers, for unbecoming conduct and, most incendiary of all, for his diminishing technique. The time had come, he urged, for him to "pack up and move somewhere else." That he might have done had the company's dancers not applauded him at the curtain calls for the remainder of the season in a show of support and signed a letter to the *Times*, refuting Fraser's claims.* Martha Graham also sent a letter in his defense, the first time in her career she had publicly denounced a critic. Still, sensitive to personal criticism and seeing himself very much as the dancers' champion and "papa," Rudolf was offended by Fraser's nationalist sentiments. The *Times* piece appeared just as the company had engaged both him and Bruhn in discussions about a new artistic leader. Talk of his becoming director was very much "in the air," Rudolf recalled. "But it was never offered."

HIS COSTUME was soaked through with sweat, he was coughing in the middle of his solos, and he had trouble catching his breath. Rudolf was in Paris with London Festival Ballet, dancing *The Sleeping Beauty* at the Palais des Sports with a case of pneumonia and a temperature of 103. At intermission, his dresser, Michael Brown, found him wrapped in blankets, shivering. "You're absolutely mad," Brown told him. "You're going to drop dead on the stage one of these days." But Rudolf refused to rest, dancing through fever in a rain of sweat. Watching him "schlep across the stage" before their performance, "barely able to make it across," his ballerina, Eva Evdokimova, couldn't imagine how he was going to perform at all. And yet somehow, his dancing "got better and better" as the ballet wore on. "Everyone who cares about him begs him to rest," acknowledged the choreographer Murray Louis. "But he won't because he fears that stopping to rest will mean stopping forever."

From Paris, he flew to Los Angeles, a twelve-hour flight, then proceeded directly from the airport to rehearsal. But the following night, February 20, 1976, he was visibly "hanging on for dear life" at the Dorothy Chandler Pavilion as he partnered Gelsey Kirkland in his *Raymonda* with American Ballet Theatre. He could barely breathe and nearly fainted in the first act. A doctor was standing by in the wings. "It was an outrageous performance, a debacle," recalls Herbert Ross, then in preproduction for *The Turning Point*, his popular movie about the ballet world, starring Baryshnikov, Shirley MacLaine and Anne Bancroft.† "Gelsey was drunk or stoned, and Rudolf had pneumonia. Impossible odds. And he had this theory about wearing all these clothes and sweating it all out."

Unbelievably, he insisted on going to the cast party. But when he couldn't breathe, he was rushed to the emergency room against his will.

---

*Veronica Tennant, who wrote the letter, recalls that even the men in the company signed it.

†Baryshnikov was nominated for an Academy Award for his performance as a ballet world Lothario. Kirkland was fired from the film and replaced by Leslie Browne.

Not only did he dread hospitals, he distrusted doctors and feared injections of any kind. He spent the night in an oxygen tent and for the next six days, with no control over his body and not an ounce of energy to force it to work, he sank into a depression. He begged to be allowed to return home to London, but his doctors prescribed rest and sun. His friends Jean and Maggy Louis came to his rescue. Although they had sold their Malibu home and moved to Santa Barbara, they kept a tiny one-bedroom apartment in Santa Monica. "Poor Rudolf, he's so sick, we just had to bring him home," Maggy told Loretta Young, who wondered where they had room. "We slept in the living room and put Rudolf in our bedroom," she was informed.

Rudolf stayed off the stage for an entire month, the longest period he had gone without dancing since his earliest Kirov days. In his weakened state, he longed especially for his mother, who he knew would rub goose fat on his chest to keep the chill away. He hadn't seen her in fifteen years, and though they spoke nearly every week, she never stopped worrying about him. He had offered to buy her a color TV set, but she wouldn't hear of it. "Why not?" her grandaughter Alfia had pleaded. "What if it's the only money he has?" she fretted.

Farida was alarmed to learn that he had been hospitalized; Rosa heard the news on a Voice of America broadcast. For the Nureyev family, the timing couldn't have been any worse. Months earlier, Rudolf's sister Lilya had been struck down by a truck while returning home late at night from her job at an Ufa garment factory, the victim of a hit-and-run. Her husband, also deaf and mute, awoke at sunrise and discovered that she hadn't come home. Since Farida was in Leningrad visiting Rosa, he sent their fifteen-year-old daughter, Alfia, to find her. "I went to my mother's factory to inquire. I was told at the entrance checkpoint that she had been run down at the crosswalk. Her skullbones were fractured and she had a concussion of the brain, which was then practically a fatal diagnosis. My grandmother was urgently called from Leningrad. She wouldn't allow the doctor to operate because they said she might become blind." Lilya spent six months in the hospital, Farida almost always at her bedside. Razida and Alfia brought food to the hospital. Having failed to save Lilya's hearing when she was an infant, Farida couldn't bear to see her daughter suffer again. Lilya would recover and even return to work. But five years later, she would begin losing her memory and, soon, her way home. Whenever she was missing, her family knew they could find her at the club where she had first met her husband in 1957. It was one of the few places she still remembered.

For several years Rudolf had been campaigning secretly to persuade the authorities to allow his mother, his sister Rosa and her teenage daughter, Gouzel, to visit him in Europe. (Despite his prickly relationship with Rosa, his mother refused to come West alone, and Razida and Lilya wanted to remain in Ufa with their families.) "My mother would like to see me; she is over 70 now, but we would be different people to each other — no? we would have to re-learn everything." In the fifteen years since his defection, Rudolf believed that he had created only goodwill for his native country. The Soviets, however, still regarded him as a traitor. He continued to send his family gifts and money, and spoke to his mother when he could. With no phone at home, she continued to go to the local post office to await his calls. This, compounded by Lilya's accident, made him feel keenly the distance separating them. In March 1976, he pressed the British government for help. He asked for a temporary exit visa for his mother, sister and niece, and Prime Minister Harold Wilson promised to use his influence with Soviet officials. He also called on powerful friends like Princess Margaret and Jacqueline Onassis. But each of Rosa's applications was turned down, one because it was allegedly out-of-date, another because it was delivered outside the official postal system. His mother was told that she was too old to travel and pressed to sign documents refuting her desire to leave the country. She refused.

By 1977, Rudolf had grown so "desperate" that he appeared in Washington, D.C., before a federal commission charged with monitoring the Helsinki Conference Accords. He found it galling to air his family problems in public and did so in nervous, barely audible tones. Forty-two U.S. senators joined in an appeal to Soviet Premier Alexei Kosygin on his behalf. In total, the petition had 107,000 signatures, from eighty countries, mostly dancers and musicians from two hundred companies and orchestras worldwide. The senators presented the petition to the Russian embassy in Washington, while Fonteyn presented it to the embassy in London. When no answer came, Rudolf continued to press for their release. Two years later, a number of celebrities lent their names to his cause. Among those whose signatures graced a letter to Soviet Premier Brezhnev were Tennessee Williams, Zubin Mehta, Yehudi Menuhin and John Gielgud. Like so many appeals before and after, it was never officially rejected, but neither did anything come of it.

Recovered from his bout with pneumonia, Rudolf now pushed himself with accelerated frenzy. He feared he had lost his stamina. "I had some very rough moments," he recalled of those first performances in March 1976. "It was frightening." Before long, the thirty-eight-year-old Nureyev was dancing better than he had in years. "Suddenly, even violently, the old Nureyev magic has returned," Anna Kisselgoff wrote in *The New York Times* during the Royal Ballet's 1976 spring season at the Met, "and with all the torrential force that made it famous in the first place." In June, *People* magazine put him on its cover. That same month he launched the Nureyev Festival at the London Coliseum — a seven-week marathon that kept him onstage for forty-six performances, with three different companies,* an unprecedented tour de force. Even those who called it "an orgy of exhibitionism" were impressed by his energy and range. His repertory included *Apollo, Le Corsaire, Songs of a Way-farer, The Sleeping Beauty, Aureole* and a new work, *The Lesson,* by the Danish dancer-choreographer Flemming Flindt. A dark tale of misogyny and masochism, based on the Ionesco play, *The Lesson* is about a sadistic dance master who strangles his pupil. Barely recognizable beneath ashen makeup and a white wig, Nureyev played a depraved old man for the first time. An even greater challenge lay ahead of him in southern Spain, where, in August 1976, Rudolf Nureyev began to transform himself into legendary silent screen idol Rudolph Valentino.

THE FILMING OF *Valentino* began on August 16, 1976, in Almería, Spain. During the next twenty-one weeks, the crew moved on to Barcelona; Blackpool, England; and the EMI-Elstree Studios outside London. Rudolf felt out of his element. He had just regained his momentum and regretted the time away from dancing, though he did his barre daily on the set, to the crew's astonishment.

What he couldn't do was cede control over his creative process to anyone else. He asked to see each take on Ken Russell's playback machine, eager to judge his performance. He amended Russell's original conception of his character because he found it impossibly passive. He could not accept that Valentino allowed himself to be pushed around without fighting back. "However dumb one is," he told Nigel Gosling, "sooner or later one's self-preservation machine begins to work."

Rudolf had first met Ken Russell in 1970, when the director was briefly considered for the ill-fated Nijinsky film. Although Rudolf admired Russell for the boldness of his films, in particular *Women in Love,* adapted from the D. H. Lawrence novel, and *The Music Lovers,* his unorthodox portrait of Tchaikovsky, the two did not hit it off. Five years later, however, Rudolf agreed to a cameo portrayal of Nijinsky in *Valentino.* On reflection, Russell realized that Nureyev himself had the requisite sexual glamour and mystery essential to the starring role. Having cast Twiggy in *The Boy Friend* five years earlier, he no doubt also foresaw the publicity value of Nureyev's film-acting debut. Nureyev was booked through the year, so Russell agreed to wait for him.

Rudolf was reluctant to take such a long sabbatical. "I thought, 'Three months without dancing!' I began to argue about the amount of days it would take." But he felt the need to "expand my territory," as he put it, and hankered after the longevity that a film career could provide.

*Festival Ballet, Nureyev and Friends and the Scottish Ballet.

And what better showcase than *Valentino*, which offered the chance not only to become a movie star but to play one? His approach to the role owed as much to his own experience as a supernova as it did to research. "You can't pretend that you are going to be Valentino or convince anyone that you are him," he said at the time. "You think, 'What would I do *if* I were Valentino?' " He looked nothing like the screen's famed "Latin lover" and star of *The Sheik* and *The Four Horsemen of the Apocalypse*. Yet Rudolf shared with him an erotic charisma and legions of adoring female fans. "Me and my women," Nureyev would sigh with a note of derision, "but where are the men?"

His rapacious nature, however, was far from Valentino's gentle character. Valentino was dominated by women all his life and, Rudolf surmised, "probably not very active sexually." He twice married lesbians and by most accounts was never the great lover in real life that he portrayed onscreen. "But as an artist he never deceived the public," Rudolf emphasized to Nigel Gosling. After all, he "gave them fantasies to take home with them. I suppose I give fantasies to people when I dance — and it's not just restricted to women."

Studying the old Valentino films closely, Nureyev naturally sought his first link with the screen idol through his gestures, his phrasing, his stance. He admired the way Valentino moved, "very slowly and with great elegance." On the occasion of Rudolf's thirty-eighth birthday earlier that March, Wallace Potts had gathered rare footage of Valentino dancing. He meant to surprise Rudolf with it during a party at his London home, with guests including Lee Radziwill, the Goslings, Glen Tetley and critic Peter Williams. After dinner, they all went up to Rudolf's bedroom to watch the film, but the projector's sprockets kept jamming. Furious, Rudolf kicked over the projector and screamed at Wallace, "Fuck you, you can't do anything right!" Wallace ran from the room, leaving the others in shocked silence. "It was so embarrassing," recalls Tetley. "I felt so sorry for Wallace. Here he had found this wonderful treasure to show him."

Since childhood, Rudolf had dreamed of being in the movies. But the long rehearsals and longer days of shooting were not the adventure he had imagined. The first day he was ordered to have his hair cut short at the sides and back. Russell wanted a close 1920s cut. Nureyev dreaded the change but in the end emerged from the frazzled hairdresser with a new look. Loretta Young had attempted to dissuade him from taking the part. "I told him, 'You're an original. Don't try to step into someone else's shoes.' " More complicated was the business of adapting his Russian-inflected English to an Italian-American accent, which he did, more or less, with the aid of a dialogue coach. As a performer accustomed to expressing himself silently, the prospect of speaking lines filled him with apprehension. His friend and costar Leslie Caron, to whom he grew close during the filming, helped calm him by reminding him that she had felt the same way *her* first time out in the 1951 classic *An American in Paris.** "In my case I had to yell at Gene Kelly across the whole set, 'Gerry, I love you!' It was horrendous—worse than performing some sex act in front of a crowd."

Unfortunately Rudolf felt no rapport with leading lady Michelle Phillips, with whom he performed a widely publicized nude love scene. Best known as a member of the sixties group the Mamas and the Papas, Phillips played Natacha Rambova, Valentino's second wife. From the start, she recalled, Nureyev made it plain to her that he had "no interest in women." Whether she was insulted that he didn't desire her, who can say, but in any case she felt that "he hated the fact that he had to kiss me. Anything we did together in the film in that regard, he was forced to do." She later described their collaboration as "the most miserable experience" of her life.

The film's London and New York premieres were gala affairs, the first attended by Princess Margaret; the second, a caviar fete at the Iranian embassy, by Andy Warhol, Martha Graham, Diana Vreeland, Halston, François Truffaut, Maria Tallchief and Erik Bruhn. The film itself, alas, was panned by the critics and sank at the box office.† Still, it was Ken Russell, not Nureyev, who was blamed for its failure: VITAL NUREYEV UPSTAGES "VALENTINO," ran the headline on *The New York Times* review. No one claimed that Nureyev evoked Valentino. But *The New Yorker's* Pauline Kael, the most respected film critic in America, thought he had the makings of a "supremely entertaining" movie actor. "Seen up close, Nureyev has a camp devil loose in him; he has the seductive, moody insolence of an older, more cosmopolitan James Dean, without the self-consciousness. His eagerness to please would be just right for frivolous, lyrical comedy, and he could play cruel charmers—he has the kinky-angel grin. . . . He's a showman through and through."

The night before the London premiere, Rudolf coaxed Ashton to "show us the way Pavlova danced" during a dinner party at his home. Pavlova impressions were an Ashton specialty, honed over the years, and at once Ashton drew on his cigarette, walked to the middle of the room, and began to move with little flitting steps, his hands fluttering with great flourish. Rudolf watched hungrily as Ashton described her effects, all the while running around the room. "She was a genius at keeping your attention, even if she didn't do anything. She was always moving, fingers, head, eyes. She undulated," Ashton said, now pursing his lips and then opening and closing his mouth. "Her face continually changed expres-

*A former ballerina, the French-born Caron had gone on to star in more than twenty films, *Gigi* and *Lili* among them.
†*Valentino* ranked ninety-eighth in *Variety's* top grossing films of 1977.

sions and she moved her mouth as if she was whispering secrets." The moment he turned and fell to one knee, Rudolf jumped from his chair and responded with a Pavlova parody all his own.

Rudolf could also parody himself, as he showed most nimbly in his appearance on *The Muppet Show*, which aired shortly after the release of *Valentino*. His heave-ho *plus de deux* with Miss Piggy in *Swine Lake* must rank as one of the funniest comic moments on television. This Prince Siegfried hears his beloved well before he sees her and the boom-boom-boom of her approaching step fills him with dread, not love. Equally camp is their scene together in a steam room, when Miss Piggy, seeing Nureyev stripped down to a towel, yelps, "Holy maracas!" and, in her best Mae West mode, murmurs, "Don't you, uh, talk to strangers?"

"It depends on how strange the stranger is," he answers, sending the swine into a swoon. Complimenting him on his wit and humor, she eyeballs his famous body before adding, "And the other parts aren't bad either!" As the heat rises, the two launch into "Baby, It's Cold Outside," while Miss Piggy, the show's inimitable femme fatale, does her best to remove his towel with her snout. ("Ahem, well, if you're warm, maybe you're overdressed.") The towel remained in place and, helped by Miss Piggy's amorous endorsement, so did Nureyev's status as a sex symbol.

HIS RELATIONSHIP with Wallace, however, slowly unraveled, and within the year, Wallace would leave him. During their seven years together he had "just wanted to make Rudi happy," as Glen Tetley recalls, but making Rudi happy involved no small sacrifice. It demanded total devotion, with the knowledge that what he gave to Rudolf he could not expect in return. "My heart always went out to Wallace because I thought he was a wonderful, caring man," says Tetley. "Rudi was outrageous in his selfishness. He had the most blazing ego I've ever known in my life. Usually a sense of humor went with it, but he could be brutal." Wedded to his career, Rudolf could not be a true companion to any lover and he willingly admitted as much. "I need them to be there for me," he told a friend, "but I can't be there for them." Erik had been the only lover he had been willing to give himself to fully. Once rejected, he had never been able to offer himself again. Dancing came first, second and third. Increasingly, he chose lovers who made no demands, who were happy to help him serve his needs, not their own.

Like many of their friends, Rudi van Dantzig was saddened, though not surprised, when Rudolf's relationship with Wallace ended. Wallace had once called him, begging to stay at his home in Amsterdam. He needed to hide from Rudolf, Wallace explained on arrival. "I can't keep that life up," he said. "Sometimes I don't even know where we are and

I wonder, 'What are you doing? Who are you?' And Rudolf demands that I still love him." Rudolf called him every day at van Dantzig's, impatient for his return. And return he did, for a while longer.

After their breakup, Wallace directed *Le Beau Mec*, a gay porn film shot in Paris, and struggled through various odd jobs before raising money for another film, a short-lived thriller called *Psychocop*, which he wrote and directed. He never would build a successful film career for himself, but through it all, he and Rudolf remained friends. "Probably became better friends," Wallace later reflected. "You don't have the same passions, but you don't have the same anger or jealousy either."

WHILE STILL AT WORK on *Valentino*, Rudolf also began to rehearse a major new ballet, Glen Tetley's *Pierrot Lunaire*. He had initially seen Tetley's ballet nine years earlier* and had been after the choreographer ever since to allow him to dance it. But Tetley had resisted. As much as he admired Rudolf's dancing, "there was something compellingly earthy, physical and direct about him and the character of Pierrot is innocent, vulnerable and easily manipulated. Rudi could be shockingly earthy."

Rudolf's pursuit of the role had only confirmed Tetley's concerns. In 1968, over dinner at a Copenhagen restaurant with Merle Park and nine other friends, Rudolf had begged Tetley to let him dance *Pierrot*, among the choreographer's most successful works, set to a Schoenberg song cycle. "I hate to repeat this," concedes Tetley, "but he said, 'I'll do *anything* you want me to do. I will shove my hand up my ass and pull my shit out and rub it in my hair.'"

This time around, however, Rudolf simply asked, "Would you let me dance Pierrot?" and Tetley agreed. But, he warned, "I don't want you if you're going to be Rudolf Nureyev doing Pierrot Lunaire. You have to be Pierrot." Despite a hellish schedule that had him up at 4 A.M. for a day of filming, in the evenings Nureyev drove straight to the ballet studio, often putting in two hours at the barre before working with Tetley until midnight. To Tetley's delight, Rudolf proved "touching and vulnerable" in the role of the defeated, moonstruck clown who at the start of the ballet is seen hanging by his limbs from a steel scaffolding. Though a commedia dell'arte figure in common with Petrouchka, Pierrot called for a more internalized performance. Where Petrouchka is overtly physical, in response to Stravinsky's percussive score, Pierrot reflects what Tetley calls the "introspective, gossamer quality" of the Schoenberg score. "He dies many times within the ballet. Eventually he sheds all of his skins and becomes us—a human being."

*In a performance by the Ballet Rambert, with Christopher Bruce in the leading role.

Rudolf first performed *Pierrot Lunaire* in Copenhagen in December 1976; his success in the role made it a personal favorite. He included the ballet on the Friends program he brought to Broadway in March 1977, a season Jamie Wyeth spent painting him from the wings. A portrait painter in the tradition of his famous father, Andrew Wyeth, and grandfather N. C. Wyeth, the thirty-one-year-old Jamie was even granted permission to observe Rudolf onstage as he prepared for the night's performance. His preperformance immersion fascinated the artist, who was bidden to make himself invisible. "He was doing *Pierrot Lunaire* and had his white makeup on. He started to go through his movements, and he'd throw off clothing as he got warmer and warmer. He would get into this frenzy. There were times when he looked at me, but he wasn't even seeing. It would build into this pitch. . . . The curtain was down and I'd start to hear the house filling, the muted voices through the curtain and the orchestra turning up. And here was this silent figure in his white makeup with his hair flying. He was completely in his own world."

Wyeth and Nureyev had first met three years earlier, at a party given by the actor Patrick O'Neal and his wife, Cynthia. When Wyeth asked to paint him, Rudolf turned him down. Determined to change his mind, Wyeth appealed to Lincoln Kirstein, a close family friend and co-chief with Balanchine of the New York City Ballet. Kirstein, however, "loathed" Rudolf, recalls Wyeth, and "sabotaged" his plan. "He just said, 'Nureyev has nothing to do with ballet and you're not interested in ballet anyway.' " By chance, Wyeth bumped into Rudolf some three years later and Rudolf suddenly invited him to paint him. Wyeth was then at work on his portrait of a charismatic young bodybuilder named Arnold Schwarzenegger, the star of the recent documentary *Pumping Iron*. Having dissected cadavers during his studies with a Russian anatomist, Wyeth was intrigued by their striking physical differences: Rudolf, with his sinewy "swimmer's physique," and Schwarzenegger with his "goulash of a body." Schwarzenegger was also intrigued. Anxious to meet Rudolf, he pressed Wyeth to introduce them. "Arnold could barely speak English," recalls Wyeth, "but he was very career-oriented and figured that meeting Nureyev might help him." On March 7, the three of them dined at Elaine's, a popular celebrity watering hole on Manhattan's East Side. They were joined there by Andy Warhol, a good friend of Wyeth's, who later wrote in his diary: "Jamie was having a meeting of their minds."

That meeting had begun badly. "It's a great pleasure to meet you," the "terribly nervous" Austrian said to Rudolf. "And how often do you return to Russia?"

"Every day," Rudolf replied curtly, and then promptly turned his back.

"Well," thought Wyeth, "that's the end of *that!*" But as the night wore on, Rudolf grew ever more salacious and teasing, at one point asking Schwarzenegger, "How do you taste?" When Schwarzenegger held out his arm, Rudolf bit down on it.

That same evening, Rudolf met Wyeth's wife, Phyllis, a Du Pont heiress whose ability to get around though partially paralyzed fascinated him. She had broken her neck in a car accident, she explained, when he asked about her crutches. "Never mind, you have spirit and enthusiasm," he replied. "And don't forget. You must have discipline and routine in your life." The two formed a close bond and Rudolf became a regular guest at Chadds Ford, the Wyeth family compound in Pennsylvania. He once asked Phyllis to cut the crusts off his toast and she set him straight. "In this house, you cut your own crusts. Here's the kettle. You can make your own tea." After that, "he was great, he'd flop around in his clogs, in his old housecoat." He wanted to own a farm just like theirs, with a river running through it, he told them repeatedly, until it struck them that he wanted *their* farm. And he envied Jamie's close ties to his father, intrigued by this dynastic continuity based on art. Father and son loved dressing up in the costumes and uniforms that N. C. Wyeth had used in his illustrations for *Treasure Island* and other books. The day Jamie took Rudolf to his father's studio, Andrew opened the door dressed as a World War I infantryman. Rudolf "got totally into it," dressing up not only in a German uniform and helmet but in the heavy red coat Andrew owned that he claimed had belonged to Ludwig of Bavaria. Rudolf so coveted "Ludwig's coat" that he asked to wear it each time he visited. "They'd laugh at each other as they got dressed up in Andy's studio," recalls Phyllis Wyeth, "and then they'd play the part." Rudolf also took boyish delight in crossing the Brandywine River in Phyllis's horse-drawn carriage. Sometimes its wheels stuck in the muddy crossing, triggering Rudolf's memories of the road he once traveled en route to his weekly bath in Ufa.

RUDOLF HAD NOT ATTEMPTED an original ballet since his psychodrama *Tancredi*, a decade earlier. Now in 1976, while learning *Pierrot Lunaire*, he began to choreograph his own version of *Romeo and Juliet* for the London Festival Ballet. He desired a new romantic vehicle and decided "there's nothing to do but do one myself." Though he was closely linked to MacMillan's version of the ballet, he intended to use the same story and music in entirely new ways. The result, wrote Anna Kisselgoff of its American premiere in 1978, was "highly theatrical, somewhat controversial, sometimes tasteless, often beautiful and pure Rudolf Nureyev."

Nureyev's *Romeo and Juliet* was set apart from the many other ballet versions by its shift in focus to a tough, gritty tragedy of sex and violence in a doomed city. Most treatments of the ballet were based on the libretto fashioned by its composer, Sergei Prokofiev, and on the version choreographed by Leonid Lavrovsky. Rudolf went back to Shakespeare's play, even to the stories on which it was based, and made a close study of both the text and Renaissance life. Nigel Gosling spent hours in the Round Reading Room at the British Library doing research on his behalf. Rudolf stripped "all traces of Victorian sentiment" from Shakespeare's tragedy; he saw the lovers "racing not only toward each other, across the barriers of hatred that separated them, but also toward death." More than any other of his productions, this one expressed his preoccupation with the tenuousness of life. His turbulent Verona teemed with bawdy, full-blooded characters, ruled by fate. "His concentration was on the violence of the time and how ephemeral life was," recalls Patricia Ruanne, his ballet's original Juliet. "Their passion had to move fast because there wasn't any time. His thinking was, what you wanted out of life you had to get straightaway, because if you thought about it too long, you might be dead."

The ballet's prologue was representative of his approach. A group of macabre, hooded figures playing dice was followed by a cortege straight out of Goya, complete with a cart full of plague victims, surrounded by mourners. As he had once studied paintings in the Hermitage, determining how they achieved their effects and why his eye was drawn to one painting over another, so he now saw each dancer as a painting in his ballet and determined the effects he meant for each to have on the public. Drawing on Zeffirelli's filmed version of *Romeo and Juliet* and Robbins's choreography for *West Side Story*, he had Romeo, Benvolio and Mercutio cavort playfully but competitively, like strutting teenagers. The dueling Capulet and Montague entourages suggested rival gangs, their rowdy dances embellished with rude Italian hand gestures and hair pulling. Never had he used his dramatic flair to such vivid effect.

Rudolf surprised many by not enlarging his own role as Romeo. He did, however, give extra prominence to Romeo's best friend, Mercutio, a role he also planned to dance. Yet it was Juliet who appeared to be a projection of Nureyev himself. Willful, insouciant, sure of where she is going, his Juliet was a tomboy and he briefly considered casting a boy in the role (as was the custom in Shakespeare's day). His Romeo, by contrast, was weak, in love with love, eager to follow her lead. Their lustiness showed itself in their bedroom pas de deux. Far from a lyrical expression of young love, it was frankly sensual. It is hardly surprising that Nureyev's lusty, highly sexed manner should be reflected in his dance language. The choreography was also rigorously athletic, and Rudolf such a risk taker that Patricia Ruanne would cry during rehearsals at being pushed "way beyond" her limit. "He had such strength in his hands; and if all else failed, he'd just grab a lump of flesh and hang on to that. I'd come offstage with all these little blue half-moons everywhere. . . ."

His choreography was a hodgepodge of influences: If its weaving patterns for the corps suggested Balanchine, its falls, contractions and spiraling pirouettes pointed to Martha Graham. And yet the ballet also bore all the hallmarks of the Nureyev style: quick changes in direction, big jumping steps and tricky, complicated enchaînements designed to impress the audience with their difficulty. As John Taras saw it, Nureyev choreographed for his own body, not for the dancer in front of him. This was certainly the case with Juliet's first solo, whose series of jumps and whipping turns has proven nearly impossible for anyone who has ever tackled it. "It requires too much stamina," insists Ruanne, who later taught it to Eva Evdokimova, neither of them short on technique. "You get halfway through it and you feel as if you're going blind and deaf because all your oxygen is going to keep your heart ticking."

The key reason for its difficulty was Rudolf's foul mood the day he devised it. Though it was Easter morning, he had come into the studio expecting to work on the bedroom pas de deux. He was greeted instead by a note from his stand-in, Jonas Kåge, showing a smiling bunny with an erection. "Sorry, the Easter bunny got me," he had written. Rudolf hadn't counted on making a solo, so he "threw together" a variation for Ruanne "that *he* would have done very well, but it fell on my shoulders to cope with it." When she protested that she couldn't get through it, Rudolf put her on notice, as he had done so many times with Fonteyn. "You will."

Completed following his return to London in the spring of 1977, *Romeo and Juliet* opened on June 2 at the London Coliseum and was later seen in Australia, Paris and New York. A hit with audiences because of its star, the ballet divided the English critics. Some, disconcerted by its lack of tenderness, compared it unfavorably with MacMillan's version for the Royal Ballet. Others admired its theatricality and Ezio Frigerio's elegant sets but judged the choreography uninspired. One of the few to endorse it unequivocally was Nigel Gosling, whose review neglected to mention his own contribution. The ballet met with greater success in New York a year later, although critical opinion once more favored Nureyev's dramatic sensibility and high-voltage performance over his choreography.

The first weeks of performances "nearly killed" the Festival Ballet principals, as Ruanne vividly recalls. Rudolf permitted no alternating casts, forcing the lead dancers to struggle through the same grueling ballet eight times a week, as he himself had learned to do. "He told us, 'You cannot think or breathe or eat or sleep anything but the production until it's over. You don't cook, you certainly don't drag yourself around a supermarket with a trolley. You eat out and have half a bottle of wine to make sure you sleep. If you really can't face the day, don't do class, but do a good barre yourself before the performance. You have to streamline your life around that only thing that counts, which is that performance every night.' " What he failed to add was that he had others to do his bidding—and more. Peter Martins recalls his astonishment the day he was rushing to change for Stanley Williams's class at the School of American Ballet and discovered Rudolf in the dressing room. "Luigi took everything off him, his shoes, socks, pants. Put his dance belt on, his sweater, his shoes. I said, 'Rudolf, please, I know you have a lot of money, but can't you even dress and undress yourself?' And he said, 'Do you understand how much energy it takes to do all this? So I pay Luigi.'"

BY 1977, the four-year cold war between Nureyev and Makarova had come to an end. Their mutual friend Armen Bali had been working behind the scenes to heal their rift. In early 1976, she had hoped to smuggle Rudolf into Makarova's wedding, but pneumonia had laid him low. Later that fall, they were reconciled onstage when Nureyev stepped in for an injured Anthony Dowell in *Dances at a Gathering* at Covent Garden. Afterward they dined together at Mr. Chow, along with Ken Russell and Fonteyn. In short order, they agreed to return to Paris, scene of their celebrated falling-out, to dance *La Sylphide* with the Scottish Ballet. Such was their success that Makarova consented to appear under the Nureyev banner in June, during the 1977 Nureyev Festival at the London Coliseum. With Makarova, Seymour and Fonteyn all performing with him on the same stage and, in the case of *Les Sylphides*, in the same ballet, the season proved a high-water mark in Nureyev's career. It also proved something of a endurance test: He danced every night of the six-week season, having just come off the opening run of his *Romeo and Juliet*, during which he gave twenty-five performances in a three-week period. Still, his festival appearances "very seldom suggested any lack of zest or any of that leadenness of limb which is a dancer's minimal penalty for over-work," marveled the critic James Monahan. "Maybe at 39 he did not dance quite as he used to at 29 but he always gave full measure." Makarova, he noted, "seemed to be a tonic to him."

Two years later, Makarova was in San Francisco with American Ballet Theatre when she suddenly found herself without a partner in *Swan Lake*. Dowell had taken ill, and on a day's notice, Rudolf flew from New York to replace him, having been summoned by Armen Bali. At first, he didn't believe Bali was serious. "Does she really want to dance with me?" The morning paper announced the switch and the opera house was filled to standing-room capacity—for a Thursday matinee. Despite occasional disagreements, and the disparaging remarks Rudolf sometimes made about her intelligence, he felt a bond with Makarova. At the party Armen Bali threw for them at her restaurant, "you couldn't pull them apart," Bali remembers. "They were talking and holding hands and nobody could interfere. I told him, 'Rudi, your soup is getting cold,' and I got kicked out because he was talking to Makarova about the dance."

26

Nomad de Luxe

BY THE LATE 1970S Fonteyn had pretty much retired to her farm in Panama, though she occasionally joined Rudolf for special or lucrative engagements. Among these was a gala in Manila on August 26, 1977, hosted by her friends President Ferdinand Marcos and his wife, Imelda. It was here, in Manila of all places, that Nureyev and Fonteyn danced *Marguerite and Armand* for the last time.

The hours before a performance were for Rudolf hallowed time, but he and Fonteyn had grown accustomed to putting on their makeup together in the same dressing room, something Rudolf did with no other partner. Accompanied by Tito, Tito's manservant, Buenaventura Medina, and Luigi Pignotti, the pair were guests of honor at the presidential palace. Rudolf had only to remark that he wished to go sailing, and Marcos immediately offered to put a sailboat at his disposal. The next morning, he and Luigi arrived at the dock to find the presidential yacht, with the President, his son, his daughter, various and sundry ministers and an orchestra aboard. An elaborate luncheon ensued. "In the middle of lunch, Rudolf said, 'But, Mr. President, I didn't ask for this city. I asked for a sailboat,'" remembers Luigi. "So the president snapped his fingers, and in five minutes, they got a sailboat ready. I spent the day on the yacht and Rudolf was behind us in the sailboat. He was very happy, very satisfied."

After dancing, he was happiest anywhere there was sun and water. His dream, he told his friend Princess Firyal, was to wake up each morning with *"mes pieds dans l'eau."* Later he would purchase his own island, but for the moment, there was no shortage of offers to holiday on the islands and yachts of grander friends. Rudolf was at heart a simple man who abhorred pretension, but he was also socially ambitious and in awe of the rich. Not the newly rich or the hidebound rich, but the fashionable rich, people of taste and achievement who hankered, as he did, to remake the world around them. Despite the high fees he commanded, at the time about five thousand dollars per performance, Rudolf never considered himself rich or ever lost the fear that he would die in poverty. He hungered not so much for money itself as for the freedom, power and security it conferred. "He was in awe of the purchase power of money, with the idea that you can have what you want," says Princess Firyal.

Beginning in the late 1970s, this child of Communists spent nearly every Christmas with Baron and Baroness Guy de Rothschild at Ferrières, their sprawling belle epoque castle north of Paris. He was also a frequent guest on the *Atlantis II*, the yacht of Greek tycoon Stavros Niarchos, who gave him use of his private island Spetsopoula as well. Niarchos later named a racehorse for him and gave him one share as a gift. The colt, sired by the celebrated Northern Dancer, was undefeated* but had to be retired after one year because of a leg injury. Put to stud, Nureyev became one of the highest-priced stallions of the time, a status in which Nureyev the man no doubt took pride.

Nureyev had been introduced to Niarchos by the tycoon's great love, Princess Firyal. The two were instantly impressed by each other, Nureyev by Niarchos's great wealth and power, the self-made Niarchos by Nureyev's intelligence and rise from humble origins, "coming out of Russia, from a town like that!" Still, the Greek's longtime friend and neighbor Rosemarie Kanzler casts a more cynical eye. "Stavros was always competing with Ari [Onassis] for publicity, and since Ari had Callas, Stavros decided he'd have Nureyev."

The first time Niarchos invited Rudolf on a cruise, this one to Turkey, he worried that Rudolf would "act like a prima donna" and show up late for meals. Lunch was to be served promptly at one o'clock, dinner at nine-thirty. Would Rudolf adhere to this? he asked Firyal. "Well, every day at one o'clock, Rudolf was the first one at the table. He followed the rules more than any of us." At night Rudolf went off on his own to Turkish villages, making sure to set out after all the guests had gone to bed and to return before they awoke. "He didn't want us to know he went cruising at night, but I'd find out because the next day he'd tell me how nice the village was. I would tell him to be careful. This concern was shared by a lot of our mutual friends. First of all, there could be violence, someone could stab him. It was dangerous for him to wander around by himself. But he did, a lot."

Firyal and Niarchos belonged to what Lynn Seymour dubbed "Rudolf's Rich Groupie Set." In New York, there was Jacqueline Onassis,

*Although the horse won all its races, it was disqualified on one occasion.

in Rudolf's eyes elegance itself, and unsurpassable. "He much preferred Jackie to Lee," says Phyllis Wyeth. There were also Judy and Sam Peabody, whose Fifth Avenue home was yet another oasis. In Paris, Marie-Hélène de Rothschild welcomed him into her gilded circle. At the Hôtel Lambert, her magnificent quarters on the Île St.-Louis, she presided over gracious luncheons and dinners, mingling politicians, aristocrats, authors, artists and film stars. As one might expect of "the undisputed queen of Paris society," as W *Magazine* once crowned her, *La Baronne* entertained in grand style, often in the Hôtel Lambert's Galerie d'Hercule, one of the most ornate rooms in Paris. Here Rudolf would dine beneath a baroque ceiling painted by Charles Le Brun, who had also created Versailles's Hall of Mirrors. For all his world-weariness, Rudolf was not entirely at ease in such formal social settings. The childhood taunts of "dirty Tatar" were not easily forgotten. Leslie Caron recalled how he "felt nervous about manners in society—things like the proper use of knives, forks and napkins. When I was filming with him, if he was invited to go to an embassy or chateau where there would be 'grandees,' he would always ask me to go with him." And yet, as much as he was "extremely sensitive to 'good society' and how one ought to behave," he took great pleasure in what Caron calls "the provocation of being himself—wearing clogs instead of shoes, and hats inside a château, for example."

Despite their wildly disparate backgrounds, Nureyev and Marie-Hélène de Rothschild were in many ways kindred spirits. Both were enormously charismatic, vehement in their likes and dislikes, loyal, domineering, inquisitive and flamboyantly theatrical. Rudolf was drawn to her elegance, taste and vivacity. She, in turn, admired his wit, acuity and passion for culture. "He was very clever and cunning and could see pretty well through people," she recalled years later. "He either liked you or disliked you. He was rarely indifferent." "She loved Rudolf," said their mutual friend Douce François, "and he absolutely adored her." Rudolf, whom she nicknamed NuNu, also shared her affinity for the opulent: richly textured fabrics, sumptuous decors and jewels of vibrant hues. Yves Saint Laurent was for both the couturier of choice, though only Rudolf got most of his clothes for free. "He always noticed what I was wearing, my jewelry especially. Sometimes he'd take it off me and put it on himself." In later years, whenever he was working on a new production, he eagerly showed her the sketches for the sets and fabrics for the costumes.

Seeing herself as a patroness to writers and artists, Marie-Hélène was not a snob in the usual sense. According to Jacqueline de Ribes, a friend since childhood, "she didn't like the obvious social climber. She had a great sense of quality." Where Rudolf summoned fantasies on the stage, *La Baronne* had the means to create them in "real" life. ("The Rothschild style revolves around me," she once told a *Vogue* editor.) She was best known for the spectacular parties she gave at Ferrières. For her Proust Ball in 1971, described as "the Ball of the Century," Yves Saint Laurent designed a satin gown to match the ropes of pearls she planned to wear. Footmen lined the corridors holding candelabra, while her guests, among them Elizabeth Taylor, Princess Grace of Monaco and the Duchess of Windsor, came arrayed in plumes, jewels and couturier-designed costumes of their own. Their escort, Richard Burton, meanwhile, chatted with JFK's former press secretary, Pierre Salinger, about "Rudi Nureyev and his wickedness." At her Surrealist Ball the following year, attended by Salvador Dali, the guests ate off fur-lined plates, a reference to sculptor Meret Oppenheim's famous furry teacup.

The most coveted invitation was to the Rothschilds' annual Christmas fête for twenty close friends, which Rudolf attended whenever he could. Staying at Ferrières, recalled one guest, "was so luxurious—my God, the bathrooms, the lace sheets, the maids—so beautifully run." Every guest was required to bring presents, and, according to the designer Oscar de la Renta, "if Marie-Hélène didn't like your wrapping paper" because it clashed with her decor, she would have the gifts rewrapped. After dinner, everyone would gather in the salon around an enormous tree for the opening of the Christmas gifts, which was something of a ceremony and lasted hours, because Marie-Hélène insisted that they be opened one by one. "Rudolf loved it that I gave myself presents 'from me to me,'" she recalled. "He started doing that, too."

And not just at Christmas. In Turkey he would buy "piles" of kilims, in Japan "hundreds" of obis, hoarding possessions as he did money. "You're the only Russian Bedouin I know," Princess Firyal of Jordan once told him. He was certainly a curious mixture: On the one hand, he was still the cautious, self-made man who rarely picked up a check and forever grumbled about the high cost of help; on the other, he was happy to spend money, sometimes big money, on silks, furniture, tapestries, rare maps. "It's another facet of his sensuality," was the way Lynn Seymour explained it. "He liked to feast the eyes."

After performances late at night, he continued to go window-shopping for antiques; his new friend Tessa Kennedy, a fashionable London decorator, often accompanied him. "I took him up to this carpet warehouse where all the carpets in the world are bonded and they were usually in lots of about fifty. So we'd get about twenty-five each. He's got millions and millions of carpets rolled up underneath every bed that he owns." Lively and adventurous with bright blue eyes, blond hair framing her round face, Kennedy had led a gilded life from her earliest days. An heiress to a Yugoslavian shipping fortune, she and her twin sister had made news at the age of two when they became the first twins to cross the Atlantic in an airplane. But it was as "the Runaway Heiress" that she grabbed international headlines in 1958, when, at the age of eighteen, she eloped with the "penniless" society painter Dominic Elwes, a nephew of Nancy Mitford's, to Cuba. There they met Ernest Hemingway and were befriended by the legendary mafioso Meyer Lansky. Since Tessa was below the then age of consent, her father made her a ward of the court, while a warrant was issued for Elwes's arrest. He was jailed for one month. Elwes committed suicide in 1975; by then Kennedy was married to the American film producer Elliot Kastner, the father of two of her five children. By the time she met Rudolf, she had built a clientele that included King Hussein, Richard Burton and Stavros Niarchos, for whom she had designed the interior of his new yacht. Her sense of fun and adventure appealed to Rudolf, who felt relaxed in her company. Kennedy, in turn, looked on him as "a brother—very, very understanding, loyal and wise."

With the exception of Erik and Nigel Gosling, Rudolf's most enduring relationships were with women. Jane Hermann admits that their relationship was entirely symbiotic and rooted in their value to each other. With the demise of the Hurok organization following Hurok's death in 1974, the Metropolitan Opera House had hired her as its own in-house impresario. Nureyev's *Romeo and Juliet* was Hermann's first project. "I was in a position where he could use me very well, and in the first ten years of our relationship, it was mutual. I had him on that stage and was selling tickets through the roof. But you lived your life in accordance with his constant requirements. He'd call the Met and say, 'Why don't I have any toilet paper in the house?' or 'Get me a cleaning lady.' As much as I adored him, I'd think, 'Thank God this is only a three-week run.' Once Rudolf appeared, he almost expected that you were available for dinners, shopping, movies. If you couldn't do for him what he wanted done at a given moment, he moved on to the next person. Then you made the decision: Either you acquiesced in order to maintain the relationship, which I did at times, or you backed off and let it cool until there was the next time he wanted something."

Despite the loyalty he demanded and received, Rudolf feared being smothered, which is one reason why he preferred the company of rich, older women. Not only could they pay their own way, they weren't after him for sex, or so he assumed. This didn't stop him from flirting with them, though whenever they reciprocated too keenly, he would worry that they had misread his intentions. "He was deathly afraid that some of us would embarrass him in that way," says Hermann. "He just felt that any woman who gave him great affection automatically was dying to bed him."

One friend who did harbor such hopes was Douce François, a pretty, dark-haired Chilean heiress who was reportedly so crazy about Rudolf that she had her hair cut short to enhance her boyish appearance. Stylish and outgoing, with a generous smile, Douce was the stepniece of the late Arturo Lopez-Willshaw, a fabulously wealthy Chilean homosexual. Lopez had married his cousin, Patricia Lopez de Huici, Douce's aunt, and lived with her in "his small Versailles" in Neuilly, installing his boyfriend, Alexis de Redé, in an apartment in the Hôtel Lambert. A great tastemaker of the day, de Redé was Marie-Hélène de Rothschild's closest friend, and even after the Rothschilds purchased the Hôtel Lambert, de Redé was permitted to stay on. Arturo Lopez had also been a great admirer of Raymundo de Larrain, Douce's longtime boyfriend. Following the demise of the de Cuevas Ballet, de Larrain formed his own company, under the sponsorship of Jacqueline de Ribes. When after two years the Viscountess could no longer afford to underwrite a ballet troupe, Raymundo began photographing celebrities for *Vogue* and other magazines. It was Raymundo who had introduced Douce to Rudolf. Douce loved the ballet and longed to be part of Raymundo's glamorous world. "She was madly in love with him and at one point, he wanted to marry her," says Jacqueline de Ribes, Raymundo's longtime confidante. "He thought she had money." After he and Douce broke up in the 1970s, the forty-two-year-old Raymundo shocked all their friends by marrying his former "Tante Margaret," the Marquesa de Cuevas, then eighty and wildly eccentric.

As many of their friends saw it, Douce's friendship with Rudolf allowed her to continue the life she had known with Raymundo. "Rudolf brought excitement, took her places, introduced her to people," says Firyal. And she rewarded him by devoting herself entirely to his needs, doing every possible errand to make his life easier and hers more meaningful. "There wasn't any question that she was in love him," says Jane Hermann, an assessment echoed by nearly every one of their friends. "She wanted to live with him and knew it was possible for him to be attracted to a woman." Like many women in love with homosexual men, she fooled herself into believing that she could trigger his attraction. But the more she tried and the more possessive she became, the more she repelled him. "Douce, she eats my air," he told Jamie Wyeth. Luigi Pignotti recalls that she practically followed him to the bathroom. "She never understood Rudolf. She put too much pressure on him." Even her friend Alexis de Redé concedes that "Douce could be too much of a nanny sometimes."

In retaliation, he would chastise her in front of friends or cut her off and refuse to speak to her for several months. "Douce finished," he would say, and Marie-Hélène de Rothschild would try to broker peace between them. "She would tell him, 'You have to be kind to this woman who is devoting so much of herself to you,' " says Jacqueline de Ribes, adding, "Douce was a *masochiste*." She was once driving Rudolf to a rehearsal at the Palais Garnier when he grew impatient with her and jumped out of the car at a red light. Douce, however, proceeded to drive alongside him as he walked, all the while begging him to get back in the car. That incident was in many ways a metaphor for their relationship: Rudolf striding away on his own, Douce, following, imploring him to rely on her. "From the word 'go' he treated her like a badly paid, overworked secretary," contends conductor John Lanchbery. "And I mean she *loved* it. She was wonderful about being treated like that, putting up with all sorts of insults."

His willingness to allow Douce and others to serve him prompted friends to chide him for exploiting them. "He knew the difference between his equals and his slaves and would only step out of line when he could," says Princess Firyal. "He figured if they want to, why not let them? I'd call to invite him to dinner and I'd ask, 'How many of your slaves are you bringing?' He once said to me, 'You're very unkind about my slaves. They're not doing anything they don't want to do. There's something in it for them. I go as far as they let me.'"

Any friendship with him had to be predicated on the understanding that Rudolf prized his freedom. "He didn't want to belong to anybody," says Luigi Pignotti. Yet because he had a knack for making each of his friends feel that he or she was the most important person in his life, they naturally resented sharing him. After all, it was flattering to be needed by a hugely famous man, particularly one as exciting and intelligent as Nureyev, but as Tessa Kennedy observed, "a lot of women are terribly possessive of him for stupid reasons and also very jealous of each other—which he *hates*." This wasn't strictly true. Despite his extraordinary ability to compartmentalize his life, he delighted in arousing jealousy among his most devoted friends and repeatedly seized opportunities where he could stage-manage the life around him. He liked to pit them against one another from time to time, to test loyalties and add a little drama to an otherwise quiet outing. "If he knew that Douce wanted to go to La Turbie, he would invite someone else who didn't care, just so that Douce would be jealous of the one who went," says a longtime friend. And knowing that Lillian Libman and Jane Hermann each wanted exclusive rights to him, he would sometimes invite them both out to dinner with him in New York. Libman, formerly Stravinsky's secretary and a Hurok publicist, worked for the Nederlander organization, which produced Nureyev's Friends seasons on Broadway. According to Hermann, "he loved setting up this battle of these two broads who would vie for his attention."

Throughout his life Rudolf maintained an enormous regard for learned and powerful men. Another new friend was Jacob Rothschild, who, as a trustee of the London's National Gallery, once had the galleries opened for him at midnight. The two shared wide-ranging interests in collecting, and Rudolf regularly sought his advice on paintings he wanted to buy. An avid patron of the arts, Rothschild was a "tall, imposing man, deceptively shy, with a subtle warmth under a cool, judicious manner," in the view of Lynn Seymour, who knew him well. In the spring of 1978, Rudolf and Seymour joined Rothschild at his villa in Corfu, after their performance at Venice's La Fenice was unexpectedly canceled. It rained and rained, prompting Rudolf to stay in bed, buried beneath layers of sweaters, listening to Tchaikovsky. When finally the sun did emerge, they swam, sailed and gave themselves class in a makeshift studio. Pressed into performing by the other guests, Seymour agreed to reprise one of the dances Ashton had made for her as part of an homage to Isadora Duncan. Rudolf took charge of the event and set up lights on a terrace overlooking the sea. "You must dance in the moonlight, Lil," he advised. But no sooner had Seymour floated onto the terrace, poppy petals in her hands, than her frightened young son ran toward her and clung to her leg. Rudolf realized at once they'd been upstaged. "Performance canceled," he announced.

IN THE FALL OF 1977, Rudolf had partnered Seymour in three performances of The Sleeping Beauty at Covent Garden. He couldn't have foreseen that these were to be his last performances with the Royal Ballet for four years. He had always regarded the company as his home, even as his allotted performances had dwindled throughout the 1970s. In 1977 they totaled just thirteen, down from forty the year before and eighty-two in 1969. Wanting to encourage younger dancers, director Kenneth Mac-Millan had felt it necessary to phase out Nureyev and Fonteyn. His successor, Norman Morrice, took things further and, on assuming the reins in 1977, promptly announced a ban on all guest artists, an elite group that included Nureyev, Makarova and Baryshnikov. Morrice, like MacMillan, hoped to give the Royal's own dancers more opportunities to perform.

Rudolf was stunned to find himself branded an outsider and lumped together with dancers who, for all their contributions as performers, had not transformed the face of British ballet. What made Morrice's ban particularly galling was that he himself had been tapped for the job of director. However, in discussions with John Tooley, the general administrator of Covent Garden, he had expressed his misgivings about sacrificing performances in order to lead the company. "If I interrupt my dancing career to become a director, make a hash of it, which I might, then I can't continue my dancing, because then I've lost it." He would dance a while longer, he said, and then see about becoming director. "The constant cry of Nureyev throughout all the years I knew him was 'I have to perform as often as I can,' " recalls Tooley. "And the truth was, the Royal Ballet could not contain that demand."

Morrice's ban effectively severed Rudolf's fifteen-year partnership with the company. Feeling unprized and betrayed, Nureyev aired his grievances in the press. Tooley dispatched a private memo to Morrice, asking him to find a way to "mend fences" with the dancer. Nureyev's complaints, he feared, were harming the company's image. He proposed tempting him with a new ballet, a work by Antony Tudor, perhaps, or Ashton's *A Month in the Country*, which Rudolf longed to do. "Could Fred be persuaded?" he wrote. "Again, I am thinking only of *occasional* appearances. I believe it to be important for R.B. to find a way of meeting Nureyev in some of his wishes."

Rudolf, for his part, instructed his agent, Sander Gorlinsky, that priority was to be given to any offers from the Royal Ballet. When, after seven months, none had been tendered, Rudolf pulled the company's rights to perform his stagings of the Shades scene from *La Bayadère* and the third act of *Raymonda*. Three years passed before the company invited him to dance at Covent Garden. Then his acceptance came only minutes before the season's casting was to be announced at a press conference. So the company rescinded its offer, saying it feared that the sudden change in casting would create too many problems with the other dancers. Tooley wrote to him to apologize. "The last thing we want is a further deterioration of your relationship with the Royal Ballet." In spite of bruised feelings, Rudolf still longed to dance with the company. Hearing that David Wall had injured himself before the performance in which Rudolf had hoped to dance, Rudolf told Nigel Gosling that he'd be willing to "help out." Eager to make him happy, Gosling dispatched a note to Tooley, conveying Rudolf's sentiments with all the delicacy of a seasoned mediator. "If you didn't want to talk to Rudi direct—always the best way, as you know, I would gladly take the temperature of the water tactfully and tentatively and let you know. (Of course he doesn't know I am writing this.) . . . Naturally nothing would make me happier than to see R and the RB together again."

The estrangement made him bitter. "The moment [Margot] ceased to dance . . . there was incredible urge to demote me, to turn me from identity into nonentity," he said in a Thames Television interview. "Only thing I was serving was to fill the house, to be tea cozy to keep teapot warm, and then get rid of as fast as possible. Clear the deck. Bring public in and then clear the deck. Go to America; fill those theaters; kick in the ass. Out." It was to be yet another year before the two were reconciled.

AT THE AGE OF FORTY, the world's most famous dancer was hardly lacking for work, nor had his hold on his public slackened. In his numerous liaisons with other companies, Nureyev was never to experience the kind of sustained creative dynamism he had known at the Royal Ballet. Still, his appetite for new movement remained undiminished and there was no shortage of choreographers willing to build works around him. Rudi van Dantzig created three for him, Murray Louis two, though none proved enduring vehicles. Nureyev pushed himself nightly, his performances as much public demonstrations as private endurance tests. That same drive permeated his personal life. He regularly sought out casual sex, and while he never stopped looking for the ideal companion, his nature and the pace he had set for himself inevitably limited him to passing encounters.

Robert La Fosse was among his conquests. Rudolf "cruised" the talented nineteen-year-old dancer with American Ballet Theatre during a rehearsal of *Swan Lake* on the stage of the Metropolitan Opera House. "He stared at me for five minutes while he was sitting on the throne as the Prince." La Fosse, his boyishly handsome face set off by blue eyes and a blond pageboy, had grown up in Beaumont, Texas, and was admittedly "freaked" when Nureyev invited him to his dressing room after the rehearsal. "He was sitting there naked when I walked in. He wanted to show himself off to me. He was very well endowed, abnormally so, and very proud of it." La Fosse already knew of Nureyev's reputation: His brother Edmund had had an encounter with him in a bathhouse a few years earlier, and it was no secret that Nureyev was "well known in the bathhouses." In fact, at a time when gay men were openly celebrating their sexuality as never before, a time which saw the proliferation of gay bathhouses and sex clubs, Nureyev's promiscuity was hardly uncommon. The freedom to act on one's sexual desires where, when and how one chose was central to the gay liberation movement of the 1970s, as it had been to the sexual revolution that began in the 1960s. The bathhouses were for many gay men "virtual convenience stores" for immediate, available, anonymous sex.

La Fosse, who quickly became a star of Ballet Theatre and, later, the New York City Ballet, was "in awe" of Nureyev. Not long before, he had chased after Rudolf's limousine one night as it pulled away from the stage door of the Met. "I was at an age when my libido was on high drive, and the idea that it was Rudolf Nureyev was extraordinary. This was not someone you said 'no thanks' to." A few months after meeting, the two ran into each other at Studio 54, the era's temple of hedonism, a former-opera-house–turned–television-studio–turned–discotheque, where the crowds waiting outside would yell, "Take me with you!" to those allowed past its velvet ropes. Inside, the handsome young waiters wore nothing but silk shorts, and sex and drugs were celebrated with equal verve. Among its regulars were Bianca Jagger, Halston and Liza Minnelli. Truman Capote had declared it the best nightclub he'd ever seen. "It's very democratic," he said. "Boys with boys, girls with girls,

girls with boys, blacks and whites, capitalists and Marxists, Chinese and everything else—all one big mix!"

Spying La Fosse on the dance floor, Rudolf promptly invited him to Washington, where he was on his way to dance *Romeo and Juliet* with the London Festival Ballet. "I have to go get my things," La Fosse replied. "No, no," Rudolf insisted, "we go in car *now*." They left immediately in Rudolf's limousine and for the next week La Fosse wore Rudolf's leather pants to the ballet each night. The affair was over quickly when La Fosse saw that there was no chance of a romance, which he naively hoped might develop. "It was a total fantasy for a while, but he had no interest in me except as this cute little thing. He was extremely sexual and not at all affectionate. I felt like a trick."

He was soon replaced by Frank Duvall, a nineteen-year-old French student who joined Rudolf on the Dutch National Ballet's first tour to America. Tall and attractive, with sandy brown hair and green eyes, Frank was eager to explore each new city. Since Rudolf felt tired and ill for much of the tour, Duvall regularly went out with the other dancers. His fluency in Russian made Rudolf suspicious. "Don't you think Frank is a spy?" he asked Rudi van Dantzig repeatedly. "I'm sure KGB put him on to me." Van Dantzig saw Rudolf's constant need for companionship as his safeguard against loneliness. In Vienna in early 1979 to work on *Ulysses*, a new ballet for Nureyev and the Vienna State Opera Ballet, he and Rudolf wandered the city each night in the bitter January cold. "It was as if he was afraid to go back to his hotel," Van Dantzig recalled. At one point Rudolf confided, "I don't know what it is, I sometimes feel desperate. You know, I just want to jump out of the window, to get it all over with." As Glen Tetley had been years earlier, van Dantzig was "flabbergasted" at how alienated Rudolf appeared. He suspected, though, that Rudolf would have objected to that characterization. "In a way he was lonely, but in another way, he enjoyed having friends and sharing things with them, not with the idea of getting something out of it, but for the sheer joy of it. There were periods when I thought our friendship was over and he was always the one to phone and say, 'When do we see each other?' If I had suggested to him that he was lonely, he would have gotten very angry. Once I asked him if he missed Russia and he accused me of putting thoughts in his mind that weren't there, just to make him what I wanted him to be. And he would deny that he was lonely and unhappy. But I definitely got the feeling that he was."

Nureyev was sustained through these low moments by his belief that through sheer force of will, he could have whatever he wanted. Yet even he was surprised when the one choreographer he had most wanted to win over finally reached out to him.

He had been waiting seventeen years.

27

Balanchine

"I WAS THINKING, What about Nureyev for *Bourgeois?*" George Balanchine suddenly asked his assistant, Barbara Horgan, one morning in 1978. The New York City Opera had asked him to create a new version of *Le Bourgeois Gentilhomme*, based on the Molière play, to music by Richard Strauss.

Horgan wasn't sure that she had heard him correctly. "Whatever made you think of him?"

"Well," Balanchine answered matter-of-factly, "he's got good character for it."

The role Balanchine had in mind was Cléonte, the prankster who assumes various disguises—tailor, dancing master, fencing teacher, Turk— to win his beloved from her pretentious father, Monsieur Jourdain, the bourgeois who would be a gentleman. Patricia McBride was cast as Cléonte's lover, Lucile, Jean-Pierre Bonnefous as M. Jourdain and students of the School of American Ballet as the corps.

"For ages I've wanted to have a comic ballet," Nureyev told *The New York Times*. "And it took Mr. Balanchine to make one for me." It also took Mr. Balanchine to downplay his choice of Nureyev for the starring role. Given their history, Balanchine's "no star" policy and the fact that they were two of the greatest names in twentieth-century dance, their alliance occasioned surprise and interest. "He is just like anyone else," Balanchine was quick to point out. "We are all from the same mother. We were brought up in the Maryinsky Theater." Rudolf, however, regarded the ballet "as a gift from God," recalls former New York City Ballet principal dancer Patricia Neary, then director of the Zurich Ballet.

Rehearsals began in February 1979, with the premiere slated for

April 8. Whatever steps Balanchine gave him, Rudolf made sure to add something more difficult, like double assemblé turns, just to prove that he could do them. But his powers were on the wane: his elevation had gone, his spine had lost its suppleness, his pliés much of their pliancy, although he could still turn well. "It should be simple," Balanchine corrected him at one point, "just a little joke. . . ." Rudolf especially wanted to impress him because Baryshnikov, in a bold move, had joined his New York City Ballet the previous summer. "I would love to be the instrument in his wonderful hands," Baryshnikov had said at the time.

Ironically, it was Nureyev and not Baryshnikov for whom Balanchine created a new work. Still, Rudolf envied their relationship and made snide comments about it to Peter Martins. "He was always making remarks about Balanchine not taking him under his wing. I used to say to him, 'Would you come and dance for seven hundred dollars a week? That's what I get.'" (Baryshnikov, too, had agreed to work for the NYCB rate.) Not only did Balanchine coach Baryshnikov extensively in a number of major roles, *Apollo* among them, he took a paternal interest in him outside the theater and regularly invited him home for dinner. The two would spend long hours talking about food and women and reminiscing about Russia. Balanchine "was like a father to me," said Baryshnikov.*

Rudolf naturally assumed that if *Le Bourgeois* proved a success at the New York City Opera, Balanchine would invite him to dance it, and perhaps other works, with his own company. "Balanchine knew he was very serious," recalls Martins, "but it wasn't his dancing he talked about, it was Rudolf as *a thing*." Balanchine's disregard for Nureyev was implicit in his response to Martins's request for a raise. Martins wanted to buy a new co-op, he told Balanchine. "You don't need it," came the reply. But when Martins insisted that he really did want to live there, the choreographer sneered: "You want to be rich like Nureyev? He has a villa in Monte Carlo, a house in London. Nothing but problems. Everywhere someone to take care of things. You should have a studio apartment. No problems, so you can dance. You don't want to be like Nureyev."

Knowing that Balanchine was in poor health, having suffered a heart attack the year before, Rudolf was especially solicitous of him in the studio. He encouraged him to take rests, which Balanchine refused to do, and had Luigi bring him borscht or chicken soup each day from the Russian Tea Room. "Are you going to go home and lie down or something, have lunch?" Rudolf asked him one day after a long rehearsal and

*When Lucia Chase retired from the artistic directorship of American Ballet Theatre, Baryshnikov was invited to take her place. Balanchine advised him that he could return to the New York City Ballet, "your home," as he put it, if the new job didn't work out. Baryshnikov became director of ABT in the fall of 1980.

costume fitting. "No, no no. Home? I don't go home," Balanchine replied. "I just go and snatch a little bit of vodka and that's it." Sometimes,
in order to make him sit awhile, Rudolf pretended to need extra time.
"Mr. Balanchine," he would say, "I have to stand and figure out the
counts." (Balanchine apparently believed him. "He learns so slowly," he
complained to Barbara Horgan.)

The two men spoke in Russian, although Rudolf found it difficult
"because I'm so used to thinking in English. My English is not that great
and my Russian is bad. But we got on very well." The relationship wasn't
that simple, according to Susan Hendl, who, in her first assignment as
ballet mistress, assisted Balanchine with the staging. Not only did Balanchine repeatedly ask her for her opinion of Nureyev, but Nureyev kept
wanting to know what Balanchine thought of him.

As both of them had grown up ardently interested in music, Rudolf
was curious to see firsthand how Balanchine approached music as a
dance maker. He recalled being fascinated by the way Balanchine broke
down the counts for the ballet's pas de deux. First, he would ask the
pianist to play the last bars of the section. "Then he would figure out
some pose or other combination for how the pas de deux should finish,
but that was just tentative because next he asked, 'Play now the climax
before that.' He was working backward, analytically, finding where the
dance with the music had to climb. After hearing that earlier climax,
from which the music would ascend, he said, 'Now let's choreograph.' "

But as his angina attacks increased, Balanchine soon felt unable to
choreograph. To Rudolf's grave disappointment, Balanchine bowed out
of the ballet. In his stead, he asked Jerome Robbins and Peter Martins
to choreograph some of the dances. Robbins wasn't interested, remembers Hendl, and the rehearsals were distinctly "edgy." Martins, who had
produced only one ballet at that point, was hardly keen either. "Rudolf
expects you," he told Balanchine, "and *I'm* going to walk in there. It's
not going to happen."

"It'll happen. You do it, dear."

"And I walked in there and I remember Rudolf wanted to kill me,
but he behaved. He did what I wanted, but he would always make a
point of suggesting something else. 'You want this way? It could be this
way, too.' But it was all done in humor because we knew we had to
finish the ballet." Before the premiere, Balanchine returned to polish
the choreography.

For all the verve and high spirits Rudolf brought to his comic role,
the ballet was not a success with either the critics or audiences. In *The
New Yorker*, Arlene Croce dismissed it as "a pretentious bore," and saw
in it scant evidence of a true collaboration between Nureyev and Balanchine. Nureyev's numerous costume changes, she suggested, were an

apt metaphor for "the quick-change artist that Nureyev has become, hopping from company to company, from role to role."

Balanchine himself was pleased with Rudolf's performance when he saw it several weeks after the premiere ("Yes, good. It'll get better"), but was never to work with him again. The ballet fared much better with the French critics when Nureyev starred in it again later that year at the Paris Opéra. (In the early 1980s, when, at Rudolf's invitation, Susan Hendl arrived at the Paris Opéra to stage a revival of the ballet, she was shocked to discover "that Rudolf had changed it so much. It was like a different production." But since Balanchine had never particularly cared about the ballet, Barbara Horgan, the director of the Balanchine Trust, simply advised Hendl, "Let him do what he wants.")

As with Balanchine, City Ballet cofounder Lincoln Kirstein also appeared to have had a change of heart about Nureyev. After ardently dissuading Jamie Wyeth from painting him, Lincoln "suddenly thought Rudolf was an interesting figure." He even bought one of Wyeth's portraits of the dancer. "This was typical perverse Kirstein," Wyeth notes. While Nureyev was at work on *Le Bourgeois Gentilhomme*, Kirstein invited him to dine several times at his Gramercy Park town house, where the two engaged in long conversations about dance history. One night the doorbell rang after midnight and in walked Margot Fonteyn. Rudolf had wanted to give Kirstein a special surprise. "Lincoln was just astounded," recalls Wyeth.

During the making of *Le Bourgeois Gentilhomme* Rudolf became infatuated with a young dancer, albeit briefly. His new lover's name was Robert Tracy, a twenty-three-year-old student at Balanchine's School of American Ballet. Tracy had the good fortune not only to be one of twelve students picked by Balanchine to dance in his new ballet but to attract the eye of the ballet's star. At five feet ten inches, Tracy had a slight build, questioning brown eyes and thick, curly brown hair that fell over his forehead. Boyishly appealing, he was not especially handsome, nor was he among the school's most gifted students. Despite a strong jump and long legs, he was never going to advance beyond the corps de ballet. "He worked very hard," recalls a former classmate, "but no one considered him particularly talented." Soft-spoken with a studious air, Tracy had grown up in Milton, Massachusetts, where his father taught high school English. He had studied Greek and Latin at Skidmore College, where Melissa Hayden encouraged him to begin his dance training. Hayden, a former leading dancer of the New York City Ballet, remembered him as a "bright young man" and one of the few students in her ballet class intent on dancing for a major company. Upon graduation, he danced for one year in the corps of Maria Tallchief's Chicago Lyric Opera Ballet and lived with the actor Hinton Battle, a star of the hit

Broadway musical *The Wiz*. With Hayden's and Tallchief's help, he then won a scholarship to the School of American Ballet.

Tracy met Nureyev in February 1979 as both were heading to Stanley Williams's men's class at the School of American Ballet. Tracy had heard that Rudolf had been in Greece and, wanting to strike up a conversation, inquired about his trip. After rehearsal, Rudolf asked Tracy where he might buy batteries for his boom box and Tracy offered to find them for him. Rudolf invited him back to his suite "for tea" at the old Navarro Hotel on Central Park South. "That's when everything started," Tracy recalled; "he seduced me that afternoon."

Rudolf had a date that evening with his friend the socialite Judy Peabody to see Twyla Tharp's company. When Peabody arrived in her limousine to pick him up, Rudolf asked Tracy to call him the next day and hopped in. Tracy assumed he was joking. "I thought he had thousands of boys. Later, of course, I realized he did." When the two ran into each other in class a few days later, Nureyev wanted to know why he hadn't called. Tracy was flattered. He had been intrigued with Rudolf ever since first glimpsing him in *I Am a Dancer* six years earlier. "You really wanted me to call you? Me?"

Rudolf took Tracy out that evening to Arthur Kopit's new play, then to a Visconti film and, around midnight, to Elaine's. The next day, Tracy moved into Rudolf's suite at the Navarro, where he stayed for three months. He had begun work on an oral history of Balanchine's female muses and delighted Rudolf by reading aloud his interviews. In the weeks that followed, Rudolf introduced Tracy to friends such as Jacqueline Onassis, Sam and Judy Peabody, Phyllis and Jamie Wyeth, Freddy and Isabel Eberstadt. Record industry mogul Ahmet Ertegün and his wife, Mica, gave a party for Rudolf at Le Chantilly one night and included Mick Jagger and his new girlfriend, Jerry Hall, among their guests.

"This is my friend Robert Tracy," Rudolf would tell friends, proudly showing off his young lover. Tracy's youth attracted him, especially since his own was fading, but so did his inquisitiveness and desire for knowledge. Though dance was their mutual passion, they also frequented movies and plays. Phyllis Wyeth recalls Tracy as a welcome departure from some of the less seemly boyfriends Rudolf had brought to Chadds Ford. "There were one or two other little boys that you really didn't want to have at the dining room table, but Robert was an educated, polite young man, with good manners." As Violette Verdy saw him, Robert had "a childlike quality in spite of his intelligence and social know-how. It was charming."

Theirs was a relationship founded on complementary needs: Where Nureyev relished Tracy's youthful enthusiasm, Tracy saw in Nureyev someone to admire, a father figure and role model. Tracy's father had died when he was just nine and in Rudolf he found "a rich replacement

Rehearsing the National Ballet of Canada in his production of *The Sleeping Beauty*. The ballet was staged in under one month, during which both the dancers and the budget were pushed to the breaking point.

With Wallace Potts outside the Uris Theater in New York during a Nureyev and Friends season, 1974

With Karen Kain in his production of *The Sleeping Beauty* at the Metropolitan Opera House in New York

Nureyev as James and Erik Bruhn as the witch Madge in Bruhn's staging of *La Sylphide* for the National Ballet of Canada, August 1974. Bruhn came out of retirement to play a role at the furthest remove from his princely domain. The two shared the stage for the first time since their early concert performances in 1962. Erik's approval still meant everything to Rudolf. When Bruhn (as Madge) threatened to strike him with a stick, Rudolf was convinced that Bruhn was going to kill him.

With Mikhail Baryshnikov in London in 1974 shortly after Baryshnikov's defection

With his masseur, man Friday and friend, Luigi Pignotti, in New York

In *Songs of a Wayfarer*, choreographed for Nureyev and Paolo Bortoluzzi *(left)* by Maurice Bejart in 1971

In *Lucifer* choreographed for Nureyev by Martha Graham in 1975. "This is the only time that I've ever lived through another person in movement," Graham said at the time.

Martha, Rudi and Margot play to their personas in Blackglama's celebrated "What Becomes a Legend Most?" ad campaign.

With costars Kermit and Miss Piggy in 1977 during the taping of *The Muppets Show*. Nureyev was happy to parody himself as he showed most keenly in his heave-ho *plus de deux* with Miss Piggy in *Swine Lake*.

Nureyev and his longtime agent, Sander Gorlinsky, leaving the Metropolitan Opera House stage door, with Nureyev's ever-present fans trailing

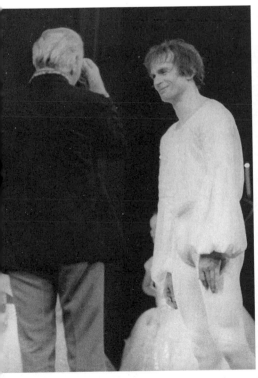

(*left*) Nureyev never stopped hoping that George Balanchine would make a ballet for him. When finally he did, in 1979, Balanchine fell ill and was unable to finish it. Here Balanchine rehearses Nureyev in *Le Bourgeois Gentilhomme*, April 1979. (*right*) As the repentant Albrecht visiting Giselle's grave. "Go and dance your princes," Balanchine had admonished him, "get tired of them, and then when you're tired, you come back to me." Nureyev never did tire of the princes "and the princes didn't tire of me."

In two of the roles made famous by Nijinsky: As the Faun in Nijinsky's *L'Après-midi d'un Faune* with the Joffrey Ballet in New York, March 1979. In the final moment that scandalized the ballet's first audience in 1912, the Faun masturbates with a scarf left behind by a nymph.

In Fokine's *Le Spectre de la Rose*, Joffrey Ballet, New York, March 1979

(left) With his new boyfriend, Robert Tracy, on Santorini, 1979 *(right)* On Ahmet and Mica Ertegün's boat off Bodrum on the Southern Turkish coast, 1979

With Andrew Wyeth in Chadds Ford. The two loved dressing up in the uniforms that N. C. Wyeth had used in his illustrations. "They'd laugh at each other as they got dressed up in Andy's studio and then they'd play the part."

In the title role of Nureyev's original ballet, *Manfred*, for the Paris Opéra Ballet, December 1979

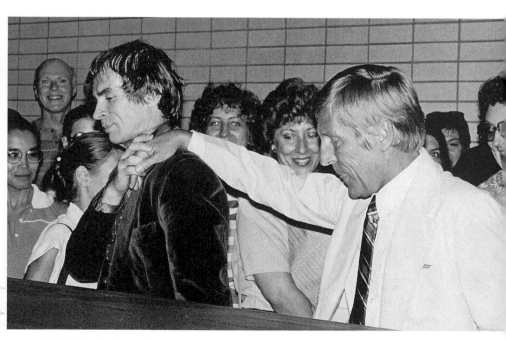

With Erik Bruhn at the stage door of the Metropolitan Opera House, 1983. Their love for each other, having transcended dalliances, conflict and distance, proved lifelong.

Sharing the stage with Mikhail Baryshnikov in Martha Graham's *Appalachian Spring* for a benefit gala at City Center in New York, October 1987. Nureyev had hoped that Graham would give him the ballet for the Paris Opéra Ballet, but after his angry outburst at the post-performance supper, the two never spoke again.

(left) With protégée Sylvie Guillem in the Seychelles, 1986. Guillem shows off her sky-high arabesque standing atop a tortoise. *(right)* The fifty-year-old Nureyev taking a curtain call with protégé and close friend Charles Jude following a performance of *Songs of a Wayfarer* at the Metropolitan Opera House in New York, 1988.

Returning home to Ufa for the first time since his defection twenty-six years earlier. Here Nureyev greets his sister Razida at the airport.

(left) Nureyev, celebrating his fiftieth birthday at the home of director Herbert Ross in Los. Angeles, 1988, with John Taras, Herbert Ross, Jeannette Etheredge and Lee Radziwill. *(right)* At his fiftieth birthday party with Douce François.

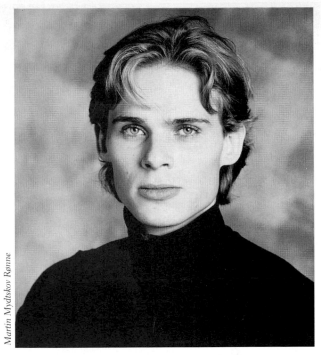

Martin Mydtskov Rønne

The Danish dancer Kenneth Greve, Nureyev's last protégé, whose Apollonian good looks suggested the young Erik Bruhn

Nureyev on a visit to his alma mater, the Vaganova Choreographic Institute, during his return to Leningrad in November 1989

Acknowledging the applause of the Leningrad audience on his return to the Kirov stage for the first time in twenty-eight years. Nureyev appeared as James in *La Sylphide*, dancing on a bad foot and a torn calf muscle. He probably shouldn't have danced, he acknowledged afterward, "but I'm of the school of Margot Fonteyn . . . if you could stand, you could dance."

Though seriously ill, Nureyev insisted on attending the premiere of his production of *La Bayadère* for the Paris Opéra Ballet on October 8, 1992. Flanking him are French Minister of Culture Jack Lang and Paris Opéra president Pierre Bergé moments before Lang decorated him with the insignia of the Commander of Arts and Letters

At the gala supper for his *La Bayadère* with his friend Marie-Hélène de Rothschild

Reluctantly, Nureyev returns to Paris from his house on St.-Bart's with Charles Jude, October 1992

Nureyev's ornate tombstone at the Sainte-Geneviève-des-Bois cemetery outside Paris. Designed by Ezio Frigerio, it is a traveling trunk covered by an Oriental carpet fashioned from Murano glass mosaic.

for the male figure I didn't have," he confided to a friend. "I was scattered when I met him and struck by his strength of purpose. It was a case of hero worship." Beyond the thrill of meeting celebrities, Tracy was pleased when Rudolf sought his opinion of his performances.

From their first meeting, Tracy felt that Rudolf was testing him, "seeing if I would make him tea, bring him a Coke. . . . He wanted friends to be servants, because he was too cheap to pay real ones." After their affair was over, Tracy chose to remain in Rudolf's circle. An older, rather more embittered Tracy would later say that at the time they met, he was playing a lackey in *Bourgeois Gentilhomme* and "remained a lackey for the next thirteen years." However, it was a role that was largely self-assigned. Even as a college student, he knew how to make himself indispensable to those he admired. Melissa Hayden remembers how he was "always doing things" for her. "I would say, 'I have to drive to Manhattan,' and he would insist on taking me. He was that sort of person."

From the start, Tracy was given to understand that he was not the sole man in Rudolf's life. In addition to the hustlers he sometimes hired, Rudolf was still involved with Frank Duvall. One day he casually asked Tracy, "What are you going to do when my boyfriend arrives from Paris?" "Disappear," Tracy replied. But when Duvall arrived with a case of syphilis, Rudolf enlisted Lillian Libman to have him treated—and assigned Tracy to look after him when he was performing. Robert quickly learned to make way for others. "Rudi was never going to commit himself exclusively to one person," says Violette Verdy. "He said to me once, 'I don't have time. I am running always. If they can't follow me, I'm gone.' "

IN MARCH 1979, the month before he opened in his first Balanchine ballet, Nureyev starred on Broadway in a tribute to Serge Diaghilev. The great Russian impresario had brought to prominence a host of major talents, George Balanchine among them. It was his tenure with Diaghilev's Ballets Russes, Balanchine later said, that shaped and refined his artistic sensibilities.

The Joffrey Ballet's "Homage to Diaghilev," commemorating the fiftieth anniversary of his death, had been Nureyev's idea. He wanted to dance in a single evening three of the roles made famous by Nijinsky, Diaghilev's most celebrated protégé: the title role in *Petrouchka*, the Specter in *Le Spectre de la Rose* and the Faun in *L'Après-midi d'un Faune*. Like Balanchine, Robert Joffrey had always resisted guest stars. His company was then seriously strapped for cash, however, and Nureyev, he knew, was box-office gold. So when producer James Nederlander offered to underwrite the revival of *L'Après-midi d'un Faune* if Nureyev starred in three of the four ballets on the program, Joffrey agreed not only to the flat fee Nederlander offered him but to contribute his productions of *Petrouchka* and *Parade*. He also agreed to Nureyev's demand that no other dancer substitute for him. While Joffrey was hardly keen to see his dancers play backup to the superstar, he was an ardent student of dance history who shared with Nureyev both a missionary zeal and a commitment to ballets of historic and artistic significance. Joffrey saw himself in the role of dance curator. In addition to popularizing dance in America through a wide-ranging, accessible repertory (his rock ballet *Astarte* was the first ballet to appear on the cover of *Time*, in 1968), he had made his company a showcase for distinguished revivals of modern classics. In his youth, Joffrey had hoped to someday dance Nijinsky's ballets. But "as the next best thing, he lived vicariously through Nureyev."

L'Après-midi d'un Faune was the first and only surviving ballet of the four Nijinsky himself choreographed and the only Nijinsky role that was new to Nureyev. Its premiere on May 29, 1912, had scandalized Parisians, with its strange, stilted movements and erotic depiction of desire's awakening. The Faun fondles a scarf left behind by a nymph in a scene culminating with a final ecstatic moment. The first-night audience was so outraged that Diaghilev, remarkable showman that he was, ordered the dancers to repeat the entire performance immediately. Set to Debussy's lush score, the ballet drew on sixth-century B.C. Greek friezes and Egyptian reliefs and featured the designs of Léon Bakst.* Nijinksy portrayed the Faun, "a strange being, half human, half animal," whose "frank animality" prompts a group of nymphs to flee from him. As Lydia Sokolova, one of the original nymphs, recalled of Nijinsky, ". . . the manner in which he caressed and carried the nymphs' veil was so animal that one expected to see him run up the side of the hill with it in his mouth. . . ."†

The making of *Faune* had proven something of an ordeal for Nijinsky. He had such trouble expressing himself verbally that he required 120 rehearsals‡ to communicate his complex ideas to the Ballets Russes dancers. Nureyev learned the role from William Chappell, a former Diaghilev dancer and close friend of Ashton's, who taught him the intricacies of the ballet's turned-in angular movements and exotic stances, with the body twisted to look flat. Nureyev admired the way Nijinsky had broken new ground and "completely annihilated himself as a dancer" by ignoring "his most spectacular, appealing qualities."

In *Le Spectre de la Rose*, Nureyev was the spirit of the rose that

---

*These were re-created for the Joffrey by Rouben Ter-Arutunian.
†She continued: "There was an unforgettable movement just before his final amorous descent upon the scarf when he knelt on one knee on top of the hill, with his other leg stretched out behind him. Suddenly he threw back his head, opened his mouth and silently laughed. . . ."
‡By some accounts, 200.

haunts a young girl after her first ball. Nijinsky's famous leap through the window had made a fantastic impact at the ballet's debut in 1911 and came to symbolize Nijinsky's legendary elevation. Nureyev had studied the ballet from a number of sources, including the notes Margot Fonteyn had taken from Tamara Karsavina, who originated the role of the young girl. Pierre Lacotte had taught him some of the ballet in 1961. Baryshnikov had shown him the version he had learned, Fokine ballet master Nicholas Beriozoff yet another, and he had also studied photographs of Nijinsky in the role, all of which convinced him that since everybody [was] defending the "authentic" version, he had best select "what would be the most natural thing, what would be the best by my standard, to my mind, and I put it together."

He had already danced *Petrouchka* as early as 1963 with the Royal Ballet.* However, he had never been satisfied with his interpretation, thinking he had copied Nijinsky too faithfully rather than made *Petrouchka* his own. He now believed that to make an old work breathe, "you have to try to say it with your own tools." To Nureyev that meant playing him less as a passive waif than as a trapped puppet buoyed by a defiant spirit. He also dispensed with the makeup Nijinsky had worn because it didn't suit his face, the exaggerated red lips, putty cheeks and red wig making Nureyev look more wicked than despairing. As envisioned by the ballet's librettist and designer, Alexander Benois, Petrouchka was "the personification of the spiritual and suffering side of humanity." The ballet is set during a street fair in St. Petersburg, where a magician is presenting a puppet show. After he drops the curtain, his puppets — Petrouchka, the ballerina and the Moor — come to life. Petrouchka loves the Ballerina, but enrages the jealous Moor. The character's triumphant quality drew Nureyev to him. In the ballet's final image, after the Moor has killed him, Petrouchka's ghost mysteriously appears on the roof of the puppet booth. "Petrouchka must live — that is the mystery of him!" Diaghilev reportedly remarked of the ending he invented.

Intrigued as he was by the Nijinsky legend, Nureyev had dissuaded critics from comparing them since his first days in the West. The two dancers had studied at the same school and were both sculptural, as opposed to linear, dancers. Yet where Nureyev was narrow-waisted with broad shoulders, a long neck and muscular legs, Nijinsky had a wide waist, sloping shoulders, a thick neck and stocky legs. They also shared an exotic stage presence and animal magnetism, enough at any rate to have prompted Nijinsky's sister, Bronislava, to call Nureyev "the reincarnation of my brother." Their personalities, however, could not have been more different. Emotionally fragile, Nijinsky was entirely depend-

*The ballet, first performed in 1911, featured choreography by Michel Fokine, music by Stravinsky and decor by Alexander Benois.

ent on his mentor and lover Diaghilev. Nijinsky's emotional and sexual capitulation to Diaghilev intrigued Nureyev. When asked about their relationship, he made a pointed distinction between the Nijinsky-Diaghilev liaison and Nijinsky's marriage to a young dancer: "What is interesting to me was their sort of abnormal relationship, which produced very interesting things. The result was very beautiful and everlasting. Then there is the normal relationship, which produced zero. So, what is normalcy?" Nijinsky's career had lasted only a decade, from 1907 to 1917. Nureyev, after twenty-one years on the stage, showed no sign of slowing down.

Still, his decision, at age forty, to invite comparisons to Nijinsky, who was twenty years younger when *he* danced the same roles, fueled critical controversy. Bruhn had urged him years earlier not to dance any of Nijinsky's ballets. At the time Rudolf agreed with him. "Now, however, I can afford to be foolish," he said in 1979. "But is it foolish? It is not easy, though it is possible, to be 19 or 20 at 40. Look at Margot Fonteyn. . . . With Nijinsky, I feel . . . a genuine compassion. . . . Some of the critics say I do not do something 'authentic' or that I take liberties with the classics. Do they know Nijinsky better than I? Have they studied him? They *look* at the poses in his photographs. I look too — but I can *feel* the movements that led into those poses and flow out of them. . . ."

He had seen those poses come briefly to life the night Kyra Nijinsky, the dancer's sixty-four-year-old daughter, gave an impromptu demonstration of her father dancing. On meeting her at Armen Bali's restaurant in the fall of 1978, Rudolf grilled her about her father. Suddenly, she cast off her big gold shoes, climbed up on a table, and, according to Rudi van Dantzig's firsthand account, "threw a little laugh in Rudolf's direction that hovered between madness and ecstasy and waved her round, heavy arms. . . . She adopted poses that were known from her father's photographs, acted the coquette and flirted and moved on stocking feet from table to table." A former dancer herself, Kyra was a "hypernervous" woman, who wore a "pathetic little hat with glitter," her teeth stained by red lipstick. Rudolf couldn't take his eyes off her. "Look at her hands," he urged van Dantzig. "Look at how she curves her arms around her head. I'm sure that's what Nijinsky did in *Le Spectre de la Rose*. And those shoulders, so soft and seductive when she turns them."

His own evocations met with mixed reviews from critics who, like Nureyev, had never seen Nijinsky dance. Anna Kisselgoff of the *Times* was not alone in dismissing his *Spectre* as "wrongheaded." Many critics expressed disappointment at Nureyev's labored jumps, insularity and failure to communicate the Specter's unearthly qualities. Only Clive Barnes deemed it "an exquisitely judged performance." Barnes, however, did not care for Nureyev's Petrouchka, which he felt lacked "that bleakness of the soul that the choreographer seemed to suggest in his marionette movements of despair." Arlene Croce of *The New Yorker* was less forgiving, calling him a "truly terrible Petrushka—waggling, flapping, hunching like a small boy in need of a bathroom and turning up a piteous little face. It takes something for Rudolf Nureyev to become as a little child, and his effortful bad acting is inflamed by pathos—he's a sob-sister Petrushka."

L'Après-midi d'un Faune was the only ballet that came in for generally high praise. But since it contained not a single classical ballet step, Nureyev was insulted by the insinuation that he could no longer dance. "Nureyev in the title role . . . gives us a very good idea of what this historic ballet was meant to be," wrote Kisselgoff. Barnes, writing in the *Post*, declared unequivocally that Nureyev "marvelously caught all those hard-edged poses and postures imprinted on our minds from a dozen or so Nijinsky photographs. . . ." In contrast, Croce wrote that he failed to "luxuriate in the movement. . . . When he lies on the rock or tenses his prone body in the air, he doesn't give us a feeling of blood-heat steeping his vitals."

Still, as hoped, the four-week Diaghilev season rescued the Joffrey Ballet from financial ruin. It also set an all-time box-office record at the Mark Hellinger Theater, prompting Nederlander to repeat the program later in the summer at Lincoln Center's New York State Theater. In June, Nureyev reprised his Nijinsky roles in London with the Festival Ballet to largely tepid reviews and sold-out houses. Only the Goslings, writing as Alexander Bland, were uniformly admiring. It is worth noting that Nureyev was staying in the Goslings' downstairs flat at the time and spending most mornings in conversation with Nigel while Luigi pummeled his muscles. As Bland they were then completing *Fonteyn and Nureyev*, their fourth Nureyev monograph,* and Bland's review of Nureyev's *Spectre* fairly pulses with the "blood-heat" Croce found missing from Nureyev's *Faune*.

The intangible bond between Nureyev and his great forebear . . . emerged strikingly . . . This is the most elusive of all the Nijinsky roles and for years I have believed that the little ballet was dead . . . Suddenly it came alive again . . . How was the miracle achieved? . . . Nureyev has grasped that the essence of the role is not so much in graceful airborne lightness as in a quality which Nijinsky must have had in abundance, what wine experts call "body." . . . The mysterious night-bloom which he conjures up is no faint poetic fantasy but one of those darkly crimson roses, "blood drops from the burning heart of June," which evoke passion rather than sentiment. Suddenly it became believable that those who saw Nijinsky in this slight and usually trivial ballet remembered it for ever. . . .

---

*It was preceded by Nureyev's autobiography, which Nigel Gosling had edited, as well as *The Nureyev Valentino* and *The Nureyev Image*, a study of Nureyev's career.

What made this June 23 performance especially memorable was Fonteyn's appearance—at age sixty—in the role of the young girl. Nureyev had also persuaded her to dance the chief nymph in *Faune*, surprising many who assumed that she had given her farewell performance one month earlier, in the gentle solo Ashton had choreographed for her sixtieth birthday gala at Covent Garden.* Nureyev and Fonteyn had not danced together since their final performance in a full-length ballet two years earlier; Fonteyn's unexpected appearance marked the last time Nureyev would partner her. Fittingly, *Spectre* was the ballet in which Nureyev had first hoped to partner Fonteyn at his London debut in 1961. He was then twenty-three, Fonteyn forty-two. But Fonteyn had already engaged another partner and was, in any case, wary of dancing with a young man she'd never met. Now when she went up on pointe, the strain showed, but her presence inspired him all the same.

AS HE HAD DONE with Wallace Potts and other boyfriends, Rudolf flew Robert Tracy to London to see him dance. Tracy was only too happy to go; he had never been to Europe. Since Rudolf had rented his home in Richmond Park, they stayed in his flat at the Goslings' and dined some nights with Princess Firyal, who recalls that Rudolf "seemed really happy and proud to introduce Robert to his friends. Robert was very lucid and full of energy. He was watching and learning and quickly carving a niche for himself in Rudolf's life."

At the beginning of July, they returned briefly to New York so that Rudolf could dance with the National Ballet of Canada in what would turn out to be his last New York season with the company. Although he had appeared annually with the Canadians since staging his *Sleeping Beauty* for them in 1972, he was unhappy that director Alexander Grant had refused to give him as many performances as he wanted. A former muse of Frederick Ashton's, the short, stocky Grant was a thirty-year veteran of the Royal Ballet and one of the most celebrated dramatic dancers of his day. Intent on bolstering the Canadian ballet's male ranks, he saw no choice but to allot Nureyev fewer performances. Nonetheless, during the company's 1979 New York season, Nureyev danced twelve performances out of fourteen, appearing in *The Sleeping Beauty, Coppélia* and *Giselle*. His impact on the company was "enormous," allows Grant, its director from 1976 to 1982. "His *Sleeping Beauty* was a great milestone in the company's history. The dancers all adored him and never stopped talking about him all the time I was there."

On July 6, he gave them a new reason to talk about him after he

*The four-inch headline on the next day's *Evening Standard* read, DAME MARGOT GIVES HER LAST LONDON PERFORMANCE—FONTEYN'S FAREWELL.

refused to awaken his Princess Aurora during a performance of *The Sleeping Beauty*. Late in the second act, moments before the Prince spies his Princess, a spotlight was supposed to follow him up on the staircase as he made his way among the slumbering courtiers. But on this occasion, his spotlight failed to come on. Rudolf grew increasingly agitated as he stood in the dark, snapping his fingers to cue the lighting man. Feigning sleep on a nearby bed was his Aurora, Karen Kain, who heard him stomp off the stage and kick the lighting boom as he cursed loudly. "He's gone offstage!" her ladies-in-waiting whispered. Kain wasn't sure what to do. If she woke up sans Prince Charming, then what? "I'm lying there and my mind is racing. Nobody's waking up and I'll have to do something." There was more commotion in the wings after Rudolf tried to slap the stage manager and then attempted to rip the notice board off the corridor wall. Suddenly, he emerged onstage from a totally unexpected direction and made straight for Kain, whom he awakened with a smacking sound that passed for a kiss. The problem was, he was far too early. One look at Rudolf told her that he "was so angry he was past being angry." So to fill the bars of music until her cue, Kain smiled, yawned, and lolled about on her bed as if slow to wake up. Rudolf looked anything but the happy Prince as the curtain fell at the end of the act. "I no do Act Three," he announced. "Find Frank!" Frank Augustyn, however, had long since gone off to the movies. The intermission extended to forty-five minutes as Nureyev debated whether he'd go on.

Finally he returned for the wedding scene but was hardly in a festive mood. "He didn't give the audience a thing and didn't dance well as a result." Kain recalls feeling jilted. "When he was angry, instead of giving me a hand for a promenade, he'd give me a finger. So I would have to stand there on pointe holding on to his finger, trying not to look tense." Instead of the twenty minutes of wild applause she and Nureyev customarily received in New York, there was only polite clapping.

THE FOLLOWING MONTH, Rudolf took his first extended vacation in years, bringing Robert Tracy with him. They toured the Greek islands and southern Turkey aboard the *Aspasia*, the yacht of Greek shipping magnate Perry Embiricos. Joining them on the two-week cruise were Embiricos and his boyfriend; Rudi van Dantzig and his new boyfriend; designer Toer van Schayk; Douce François and a crew of eight. Douce was clearly happy to be the only woman on board, and was forever "trying to be 'on' for Rudolf," Tracy later told friends. The group converged in Piraeus and spent their days exploring the islands, swimming and sunning themselves on sandy beaches. At night, a bell would summon them to dinner, the exquisite fare more reminiscent of Paris than Greece. On hilly Santorini, they trekked from one coast to the other. Even in the smallest villages, there was someone who recognized Rudolf and wanted proof of his appearance there. Mothers sent their daughters scurrying for autographs; tourists snapped photos.

In Turkey, Rudolf scoured bazaars for more kilims, jewels and burnooses, in which he would array himself at night. Dragging his companions through the back streets of small harbor towns, he would suddenly stop and inhale with great pleasure. "This smells like home," he would say, recalling the Muslim foods and aromas of his youth. "My roots are here. I smell it in the air, in the dirt."

After two weeks, Rudolf and Robert joined Jane Hermann in Bodrum, on the southern Turkish coast, at the home of Ahmet and Mica Ertegün, whose vacationing houseguests included the decorator Chessy Rayner, Princess Ira Fürstenberg and the publisher George Weidenfeld. Weidenfeld, an imposing man of wide tastes, conversed with Rudolf about Pushkin's *Eugene Onegin* and the novels of Nabokov and came away with the impression that he was "a very intuitive man of the senses, who was nevertheless intellectually curious." Mica Ertegün knew that Robert and Rudolf were a couple, though she "didn't get the impression it was much of a relationship. Rudolf didn't seem particularly affectionate or interested." He passed the days swimming, sailing and visiting with such fashionables who passed through as the *parfumeuse* Hélène Rochas; her handsome boyfriend, Kim d'Estainville; and Oscar de la Renta. Even when he was in repose, Rudolf's theatricality asserted itself. Seeing the way he draped himself in a Turkish robe after a swim, his head wrapped imperiously in a turban, Mica Ertegün couldn't help feeling that "he made the rest of us look like peasants." Still, as Jane Hermann remembers, he was rarely in repose for long. "I climbed over more stuff, more places because he had to see everything. I wouldn't have bothered going around to every bazaar in Istanbul and every rug seller. But he made you see things and, because of who he was, people opened themselves to him."

Their summer holiday took them on to Rudolf's villa at La Turbie, by which time Hermann and Tracy had begun to get on each other's nerves. Tracy, like a number of Rudolf's friends, found Hermann crude and possessive of Rudolf. She, in turn, resented Tracy's assumption of privileges as Rudolf's boyfriend, particularly his inclusion in business meetings concerning the Metropolitan Opera House. The tensions exploded one day after she made some offhand "crack about Rudolf," and Tracy repeated it to him. "Robert felt that I disliked him because I wanted a very clear separation of church and state. Rudolf never made that separation. His idea of a business meeting was whoever was sitting at the dinner table. I was afraid Robert was privy to too much. But my feeling was it wasn't only Robert, it was a lot of his entourage, Douce, Jeannette [Etheredge]* and others. When it came to the business affairs of the Met, I did not feel that these people should be privy to those discussions or have access to backstage whenever they wanted it. You don't take a major institution's affairs and discuss it with a lot of balletomanes who are going to use it for dinner table conversation. . . . Douce also took great umbrage at me one day when I told her it was none of her business. It is a huge, difficult job to put a season together. You don't need the intercession of amateurs."

HIS SUMMER TOUR of the Greek islands only fueled Nureyev's latest preoccupation: Lord Byron. The turbulent poet was to be the subject of his first original ballet for the Paris Opéra, now under the direction of his old friend Violette Verdy. Nureyev set his *Manfred*, based on Byron's dramatic poem as well as on the poet's life, to Tchaikovsky's *Manfred* Symphony, inspired by the same poem. Just as a friend of Tchaikovsky's had urged the composer to write a symphony based on Byron's *Manfred*, so Nureyev's friend the cellist Mstislav Rostropovich had piqued Nureyev's interest in 1977 with an idea for "a wonderful new role" for him. Rostropovich waited an entire week and then disclosed it, "like manna from heaven," Nureyev recalled.

Byron haunted his imagination and he read all he could about him before embarking on his ballet. And yet, as much as he loved the music, he was uncertain about how to dramatize such a metaphysical tale as *Manfred*. Byron's poem had been inspired by both the savage beauty of the Alpine landscape and a friend's reciting of Goethe's *Faust*. In the end, as John Percival has written, Rudolf's subject was not really the poem or Byron's life as much as it was "about what has been dubbed 'the romantic agony'—the sense of doomed longing, the fervour and despair that fill so much of the art of the period."

The central role he conceived as a vehicle for himself, and it is not hard to see why Manfred/Byron appealed to him. Manfred is another solitary traveler through life "whose gift to humanity has been an unconquerable individual will." In common with the heroes of many of Nureyev's ballets, Manfred, much like Byron himself, is a tormented character, riven by opposing desires and haunted by guilt. "The thing about Byron is the duality," Rudolf told Flora Lewis of *The New York Times*. "He says if you wake up and feel famous one day, you must expect to feel infamous another day. There is love and hate, all contradictions. He took his own money to help the Greeks, there were shabby and pathetic episodes, and he died an unheroic death, of a chill. But then

*Armen Bali's daughter.

he became the symbol of Greek unification, so in his downfall he was up again."

The ballet was yet another work that reflected Nureyev's enduring interest in the pull between innocence and experience, sacred and profane love. His stream-of-consciousness narrative is replete with allusions to incest and homosexuality and a profusion of characters from monks to mountain spirits. The Poet revisits events in his life, all the while pursuing Astarte, his spiritual twin and muse, a character based on Byron's sister. The Poet, in turn, is pursued by the ghosts of loved ones and by a growing band of black-clad figures, symbols of the guilt that haunts him. Nureyev's Poet, noted one critic, "is forever divided between debauchery and the ideal, between black masses and poetry; he is constantly in flight, from England to Switzerland, to Italy, to Greece, where he at last finds the liberation of death, leaving the spectator himself breathless."

The sheer physicality of the role left Nureyev breathless as well. At a time when critics had begun to speak of his decline, Nureyev responded by giving himself the most taxing role of his career, one that kept him onstage for the ballet's entirety and had him partnering eleven different characters. For more than sixty-five minutes, he drove himself through leaps, pirouettes, tours en l'air, quick changes in direction, all without pause and at a breakneck pace. His choreography incorporated nearly everything he had learned up to that point—from the formal structures of Petipa to the contractions and rolls to the floor of Martha Graham.

Nureyev choreographed the part of Manfred on his alternate in the leading role, the Paris Opéra star Jean Guizerix. Tall and muscular, with a brooding Basque face, Guizerix had the requisite magnetism and technique. For the role of Astarte, Rudolf chose Florence Clerc, who shared the role with the willowy Wilfride Piollet. There was a dual structure behind Nureyev's casting: Florence Clerc was newly married to Charles Jude, whom Nureyev cast as the poet Shelley, Byron's close friend, while Piollet was married to Guizerix. Nureyev choreographed several male duets intended to represent Byron and Shelley's friendship. "Does it shock you?" he challenged Flora Lewis of *The New York Times*. "Men speak together. Why shouldn't they dance together?"

Rudolf grew close to both couples during the making of *Manfred*, though as Clerc recalls, given Rudolf's affection for Jude, he "warmed up to me slowly." From then on, they appeared regularly on his Friends tours. As Guizerix saw him, Rudolf was "torn and scorched inside," much like Byron's hero. "It was difficult to find calm in him. He was a very profound man, with a desire for things to happen the way he wanted them to. He was always digging deep in the earth to advance, as if he was continuously plowing the soil."

Indeed, despite his air of self-sufficiency, he needed constant assurances that he was loved. "It was a paradox," says Piollet, "because even though he needed a lot of tenderness, he didn't allow people to be so tender with him."

THE PREMIERE OF *Manfred* took place on November 20, 1979, at the Palais des Sports—but without Nureyev in the leading role.* Two weeks earlier, he had broken a metatarsal in his right foot while dancing *The Nutcracker* in Berlin. With his foot encased in plaster—the first broken bone of his career—he was incapacitated for four weeks. Guizerix took his place, but without its promised star, ticket sales sagged. Sales were little helped by the poster for the ballet, which showed a heavily made-up, effeminate face that scarcely resembled Nureyev's. "A monstrosity," Nureyev said of it, "a horror."

Though he was able to perform the last two weeks of the run, the five-thousand-seat Palais des Sports remained half-empty. The New Year's Eve performance was canceled. Even more disappointing were the reviews, with or without its star in the leading role. While everyone agreed it was an ambitious, if relentless, showcase for Nureyev, Irène Lidova spoke for the critical consensus when she called it "confused, disorderly and disconnected." Among its staunch defenders were Alexander Bland and John Percival, who had flown over from London for the first performances. The ballet's theme and music, wrote Percival, had "inspired Nureyev to his best choreography yet."

While in Paris, Rudolf stayed with Douce François, at her Rue Murillo apartment near the Parc Monceau. Douce moved into a smaller bedroom so that Rudolf could have use of her master suite, with bathtub. Susan Hendl, then in Paris to stage *Le Bourgeois Gentilhomme* at the Opéra, remembers how Douce "was always there for him and so loving." If Rudolf often treated her as a servant, he sometimes showed her kindness. In October 1979, a month before *Manfred* premiered, Rudolf was in Zurich to stage his production of *Don Quixote* for the Zurich Ballet. One night, he asked director Patricia Neary to arrange a birthday party for Douce. "We'll start out with caviar and champagne and then we'll have bratwurst," he informed Neary. "I'll pay for it, you just get the food."

He never did reimburse her, however, so Neary took the money out of his paycheck. "Anyone who was willing to love and give to him, he took from them," she says. "Often he would turn to me and say, 'Go get me tea,' and I'd say, 'I'm sorry, I'm not the waitress here. I'm the director. I brought you here. Someone else will get your tea.' If he didn't have

*An injury had also kept Jude from performing.

this enormous respect for your money or for what you were producing, you could be stepped on. Obviously Douce enjoyed being a gofer."

In Paris, Douce kept his thermos filled with sweet tea, washed his tights, chauffeured him wherever he needed to go. "Douce wanted to keep Rudolf for herself," observes Charles Jude. "He would ask Douce to call me to join him for dinner or to see a movie. And she would tell him he should stay home, that she would cook for him. It was the people who wanted to go out with him—without her—that she objected to." Robert Tracy, on the other hand, had grown accustomed to Douce's possessive presence, and that December, after Rudolf sent him a ticket, he joined them in Paris, staying on for the Rothschilds' Christmas fête at Ferrières.

NUREYEV'S MARATHON SCHEDULE of performances was no less peripatetic in 1979 than it had been a decade earlier. With his ties to the Royal Ballet considerably frayed, he had stopped viewing London as his home base. His house in Richmond was now regularly let to friends; during his annual Nureyev Festival in London, he stayed in the Goslings' basement flat. That year he bought two apartments, one in Paris, the other in New York, which would serve as his principal residences for the rest of his life. Douce found him his twelve-room pied-à-terre at 23 Quai Voltaire* in the Seventh Arrondissement. Looking over the Seine and beyond it to the Louvre, the apartment took up an entire floor. The large drawing room's expansive windows fronted the quai. With his penchant for the sumptuous and the sensual, Rudolf hired the decorator Emilio Carcano, a protégé of Renzo Mongiardino, the celebrated Italian designer whose assignments had included Marie-Hélène de Rothschild's Paris town house and Princess Firyal's London home. Although Douce supervised the renovation, Marie-Hélène de Rothschild "went over now and then to give Rudolf advice." His instructions to Carcano were to "build" the apartment around his collection of antique furniture, which ran the gamut from seventeenth-century-style Venetian chairs and early-nineteenth-century Russian Karelian birch chairs to an Empire daybed and Dutch rococo chamber organ. Such eclecticism made Carcano initially dubious, but he was soon won over by his client's "instinctive taste" and brilliant eye. He quickly learned what Nureyev's colleagues had long known, that Rudolf "knew exactly what he wanted and was oblivious to the dictates of fashion."

The effects Carcano created were decidedly theatrical, plush and old-world, suggesting a stage set of a doge's palace. Silk waistcoats and

*Earlier residents of the Quai Voltaire included Diaghilev's patron and friend Misia Sert and the Marquis de Cuevas.

velvet jackets—costumes from Nureyev's productions—hung on a coat-rack in the entrance hall. The hall had faux *bois* walls, while its floor was patterned with black-and-white tiles from a château. The main salon was a symphony of texture and color: Japanese obis of rich-hued silks; Kashmir shawls; heavy patchwork curtains culled from the myriad eighteenth and nineteenth-century fabrics in Nureyev's collection; a mirror-and-giltwood cornice; sofas covered in golden-tinged Genoese velvet; walls covered in Spanish seventeenth-century leather wall panels embossed and painted with birds, squirrels and flowers. Even the two en suite bathrooms were dressed and adorned, one in imitation of marble inlay, the other green with gold stenciling and outfitted with a copper bathtub and elaborate brass taps.

To Pierre Bergé the apartment suggested "Rudolf's fantasy of things he never had or knew in Russia." It was here that Nureyev's far-reaching interests were best expressed, whether in the antique maps and fifty-six-inch-high Victorian globe, the architectural stage designs and Kabuki woodcuts, the pianofortes, organ and hammered dulcimer, or in the hundreds of paintings and studies of nude men. To many of his visitors, the apartment's most memorable feature was these pictures of the male form, even hung "one on top of the other," according to Leslie Caron. "There was not enough room for them all on the walls, so they would be stacked behind couches, under beds." The paintings were an expression not merely of Nureyev's sexuality but of his dancer's pursuit of the ideal form. Still, visitors like Antoinette Sibley found it slightly disconcerting to sit in his dining room "and everywhere you look there's a load of flesh. What's strange is his bedroom didn't have all these pictures."

Nureyev's New York apartment was located on the fifth floor of the Dakota, the imposing Victorian building inhabited by many celebrities of the performing world. Purchased for $350,000, the four-room apartment was on Central Park West at Seventy-second Street, within easy walking distance of the Metropolitan Opera House. At Rudolf's suggestion, Tracy moved out of the third-floor walk-up he shared with a photographer and into the Dakota, where his neighbors included Leonard Bernstein, Lauren Bacall, John Lennon and Yoko Ono. Fearing that he might lose his scholarship should his teachers get wind of his "improved" situation, Tracy kept quiet about his glamorous setup around his peers at the School of American Ballet. "We were never quite sure what his relationship with Nureyev was," says one of them. (Two years later, in 1981, they would move into a grander seven-room apartment on the second floor that Rudolf purchased for $1.8 million.)

Tracy was able to get by on the $200-a-month stipend he received from the School of American Ballet. He not only lived rent-free, he never paid for a meal or plane ticket as long as he was with Rudolf. If they were alone, Rudolf picked up the check; if they weren't, Rudolf made sure someone else did. There were dinners with Balanchine, Baryshnikov and Jacqueline Onassis; summer cruises on the Mediterranean; and New Year's parties in the early 1980s at the St. Moritz "chalets" of Christina Onassis and of Stavros Niarchos. Tracy was naturally excited by the worlds opening before him and intelligent enough to put his connections to good use. Even before graduating, he appeared on Broadway with Nureyev and the Boston Ballet, first in *La Sylphide* in 1980 and later in Nureyev's *Don Quixote*. He also benefited enormously from Nureyev's coaching. In return, he took care of Rudolf's apartment and organized his New York social life. Rudolf's friends grew accustomed to Robert's call, alerting them to Rudolf's impending arrival and inviting them to see him dance. This suited Rudolf, who "didn't want to spend money on little things, like cleaning ladies and housekeepers," says Natasha Harley, who often played hostess for him at the Dakota, sending over her own cleaning woman before Nureyev arrived in town, and catering the dinner parties he gave after performances.

EVEN WITH ALL THE CARE he received, Nureyev's own mother still remained beyond reach. Despite appeals by British Prime Minister Harold Wilson and U.S. President Jimmy Carter, the Soviets were unmoved by criticism that they had breached the Helsinki agreement on human rights, which stressed the importance of reuniting separated families. At seventy-four, his mother was suffering serious eye trouble and appeared "resigned," Nureyev said, "to never seeing me again. In fact, she actually said goodbye to me."

Nearly twenty years after the events at Le Bourget, the taint of "defector" continued to shadow him. In March 1980, the Rome Opera suddenly canceled his scheduled performances in *Swan Lake* because guest choreographer Yuri Grigorovich, on leave from the Bolshoi, had been forbidden by Moscow to work with him.* Still, Nureyev remained convinced that President Carter lacked the will, not the means, to bring his relatives to the West. "All I wanted was for them to visit me for a few weeks," he lamented to a reporter in April 1980. "But humanitarian problems never seem to penetrate the skin, meaning brains, of any politician, including Mr. Carter."

Three months later, he received a call that surprised him. His niece Gouzel, Rosa's daughter, was in Mexico City and on her way to visit him. Rudolf had last seen her the day he had left Leningrad, nineteen years earlier, when Rosa had rushed to the airport, with the one-month-old in her arms. "He was shocked to hear from me," recalls Gouzel,

---

*Grigorovich was the choreographer who had created the leading role in *Legend of Love* for Nureyev at the Kirov.

who had married an Ecuadorian student to get out of the Soviet Union. Rudolf quickly called Natasha Harley. "I have a big favor to ask," he said, as he had many times before. His niece was about to arrive in New York and he had given her Harley's number. She didn't speak any English. Would she mind looking after her?

Rudolf was then performing at the Met with the Berlin Ballet. He was starring in *The Idiot*, based on the Dostoyevsky novel and choreographed by fellow Kirov refugee Valery Panov. Nureyev performed the wise fool Prince Myshkin with striking results: In the ballet's most memorable image, he swung high above the stage, virtually nude, suspended from a giant bell. The plight of Panov and his wife, Galina, had drawn world attention. With Nureyev and Panov reunited onstage for the ballet's New York premiere, *The Idiot* received a twenty-minute ovation, which became thunderous when the two former Kirov stars embraced at the curtain call.

The day after his niece arrived, Rudolf went to meet her at Harley's apartment on East Sixty-eighth Street. At nineteen, Gouzel bore a striking resemblance to her uncle Rudolf with her high, pronounced cheekbones, gray-green almond-shaped eyes and full mouth. "They kissed each other and he asked her how she was," recalls Harley. "He had a very happy look in his eyes, but she was very much afraid of him and answered in a timid way. He wanted in the worst way for her to do something." Gouzel stayed with Harley for over one month, a trying time for both. Harley found underwear strewn in her living room and heard constant complaints about life in America. "She didn't like anyone or anything. She kept saying everything was better in Russia." Her adjustment was equally trying for Armen Bali, who looked after Gouzel during an extended stay in San Francisco. "She didn't know how to clean her body or her hair when she came." Eventually, Rudolf bought a flat for Gouzel upstairs from his own at the Quai Voltaire and encouraged her to attend the Sorbonne. He even sent her to Monte Carlo to study ballet with Marika Besobrasova, to whom Princess Grace had entrusted the training of her daughters. "I tried, but it was useless. Gouzel would stand with her back to the barre. I told him that she didn't want to learn," Besobrasova recalls. Her lack of direction frustrated Rudolf enormously. "Explain to her that she has to study or find work," he pressed Harley, hoping she might be more influential with Gouzel. "I'll pay for it but she has to *do* something." Having forged his own way in the West, he couldn't fathom her lack of ambition. "Gouzela gave him nothing but headaches," says Armen Bali.

Sadly, so did his sister Rosa after she followed her daughter to the West two years later. Relations between Rudolf and Rosa, always strained in Leningrad, were hardly improved by the greater gulf that now separated them. On one of Rosa's first evenings in London, she insisted on making Rudolf the dishes their mother used to prepare. Ballerina Eva Evdokimova, his most frequent partner after Fonteyn and Merle Park and a guest that night, was struck by Rudolf's discomfort at his sister's cooking and her need to "mother him." As Charles Jude recalls, he was "very emotional about seeing his family again, but disappointed in their behavior." Rosa had been granted an exit visa to visit her daughter and soon "married" the brother of Douce François to obtain her citizenship.* Rudolf's success in the West had so preoccupied Rosa in Leningrad that she assumed that *she* would look after him once they were reunited. According to Jude, "there was a big scandal when she came to Paris. She had a memory of Rudolf as a little boy and she was shocked to see how he spoke, how he ate. He wasn't the same Rudolf. She didn't recognize her brother. When she said all these things to him, he told her to leave, that he couldn't see her anymore. So he put her up in his house at La Turbie, where she lived alone. My family lived nearby in Èze, so I would see her when I went to the market. She and Rudolf hardly talked to each other." While Rosa was at La Turbie, Rudolf asked Marika Besobrasova to take care of her bills and look in on her from time to time. But Rosa had become so paranoid that she trusted few of Rudolf's friends. She took to calling Besobrasova in the middle of the night with strange complaints, such as the time she accused the caretaker of trying to poison her. Once, after Rudolf had invited friends to stay at La Turbie in his absence, Rosa refused to let them in. He was "shocked," recalls Armen Bali. "He said to me, 'What have we done? Send them back!' " In 1982, in Cannes with the Ballet Théâtre de Nancy, Rudolf invited Rosa to see him dance. At the supper afterward at the Cinema Palace, Luigi Pignotti heard Rudolf speaking heatedly in Russian to his sister. Suddenly, Rudolf turned to him. "If *she* stays here, *I'm* going back to Russia."

IN HIS EARLY FORTIES, an age when most male dancers are well past their prime, Rudolf continued to seek new challenges. Many of these fell short of his ambitions. He still hoped that a choreographer might unlock some undiscovered part of himself, but new ballets now rarely came his way. Choreographers reveled in the possibilities of the young or, in the case of Ashton and Fonteyn, in the deepening artistry of a constant muse. Forced to create his own showcases, Rudolf staged his productions for companies the world over and forged alliances during the 1980s with such lesser-known troupes as the Zurich Ballet, the Boston

*When Douce's brother asked Rosa for a divorce in order to marry a woman he loved, Rosa refused. It took years before she finally relented.

Ballet, the Ballet Théâtre de Nancy and Japan's Matsuyama Ballet. On each he left his imprint, elevating standards, profiles and income. But as in the past, every company he appeared with—from the venerable Paris Opéra Ballet to the London Festival Ballet—grew wary of playing a supporting role to a superstar. Although their dancers were stimulated by his presence, the prospect of perennial second billing inevitably sparked resentment. Nevertheless, the response to his name still led impresarios to insist that he be the featured star with any troupe that wasn't a household name. "There was a time when it was easier to ... dance with good companies," he acknowledged in 1981. "Now it's more closed, nationalistic almost. . . ."

In the spring of 1980, he had suddenly found himself at the center of an international incident. The Metropolitan Opera House canceled a visit by the Paris Opéra Ballet when its dancers objected to Nureyev's inclusion and threatened to strike.* Since this was to have been the Paris Opéra's first U.S. visit in thirty-two years, the scramble for exposure was intense. Many of its male stars refused to appear as "window-dressing for the over-the-hill Nureyev," as one of them rather uncharitably put it. "We have our own great dancers who deserve a chance to be seen." Be that as it may, Jane Hermann insisted on Nureyev and the box-office insurance he guaranteed. New York audiences, she argued, were unfamiliar with the Paris Opéra Ballet. Its director, Violette Verdy, supported the decision, pointing out that Nureyev had already brought considerable attention to the company, the world's oldest ballet troupe. "Now the boys feel really threatened by Rudi," she said. Rudolf felt betrayed that Charles Jude was among the most vocal of the group threatening to strike, though there was nothing personal in Jude's position. Still, Rudolf refused to speak to him for several months.

"All this may sound terribly French," wrote Anna Kisselgoff in *The New York Times*, "but the issues go beyond the question of whether the Paris Opéra Ballet . . . was destined—in the words of *Le Figaro*—to remain 'the Tomb of the Unknown Dancer.' . . . Will box office considerations . . . now always predominate over artistic considerations? Is the American public obliged now to see the same guest stars with every foreign company, whether they fit into the specific esthetic of that company or not?"

Nureyev was scheduled to dance *Manfred* during the tour and so wanted his ballet to be seen in New York that he agreed to curtail his performances. But there was only one concession the dancers would accept: no Nureyev. As a result, the tour was canceled. In the end, the

*The dancers' resentment was further inflamed when the Danish dancer Peter Schaufuss was also engaged as a guest star.

Paris Opéra's loss was his gain: The Martha Graham Dance Company appeared at the Met in its stead, with Nureyev as its guest star.*

Calling him "a fiend for working," Graham shrugged off criticisms of her association with a ballet star. She cast him in *Clytemnestra*, one of her major works, first performed in 1958 with Graham and Paul Taylor in the roles of the unfaithful queen of Agamemnon and her lover, Aegisthus. Nureyev was compelling as the wild-eyed Aegisthus, who, aroused at his lover's impending murder of her husband, draws her scarf through his legs in a masturbatory gesture recalling Nijinsky's *L'Après-midi d'un Faune*. "A dancer must learn not to destroy the beautiful, tragic animal that is part of him," Graham told her opening night audience, clearly seeing in Nureyev a dancer who felt fully the primal impulse behind her movement. Andy Warhol, however, thought him "terrible, he just doesn't know how to be a modern dancer."

Graham also understood Nureyev's need to keep dancing. She, too, had defied age, the critics and physical pain in order to continue performing. A calcium spur on Nureyev's right heel now cut regularly into his flesh, requiring him to wear a complicated bandage he called a "sandwich." (To best kill pain, he advised a reporter, "you must think of something else.") There were times when he could barely stand or walk, and yet somehow he danced: In 1980 alone, he gave 249 performances. Just how well he danced was a subject of some debate. For many, his abiding charisma could not make up for the strain and decline in his dancing. "Where once he dazzled by the ease of his virtuosity," wrote the British critic David Dougill in the *Sunday Times*, "what is now most apparent in his dancing is sheer persistence and daredevilry." Having championed him from the first, the critic Mary Clarke wrote in 1980: "He looks wonderfully slim and boyish, but one must confess that the elasticity and elevation, and therefore the excitement, have gone from his dancing. . . ." The harshest assessment came from Arlene Croce, who wrote that "for some time, his appearances have belonged to the history of his career rather than the history of his art."

To his fans, Nureyev remained an electric presence whose artistry continued to gain in nuance and depth. If he wasn't on the mark every night, he could still regularly summon the old art and magic. For many, this was more than enough. His solos "had enough excitement to last any evening," Anna Kisselgoff wrote after seeing him dance *La Sylphide* with the Boston Ballet in November 1980.

The chorus of approval was led by Nigel Gosling, who, when it came to criticizing Nureyev, remained a conscientious objector. "There are a few friendlies, but on the whole the smarty-pants critics knocked him from the moment he appeared in the West," he told *The New York*

*Liza Minnelli also appeared as the narrator in one work.

Times in 1981, twenty years after Nureyev's defection. "At first, it was because he was so much himself he didn't fit into any slot and so couldn't be 'compared' to anyone else. . . . Then it was his 'wild' life style and pop-star following—he was 'vulgarizing' ballet. Now it's his age—they want him to quit 'for his own good,' before he 'disgraces' himself. . . ."

To many observers he did just that in the summer of 1981, when he appeared at the Met with Milan's La Scala Ballet in his own *Romeo and Juliet*. Carla Fracci was his Juliet and Margot Fonteyn her mother, Lady Capulet. The illustrious names sold tickets, but prompted one critic to complain, "Why were Rudolf Nureyev, 43, Carla Fracci, 45, and Margot Fonteyn, 62, playing . . . characters whose ages Shakespeare put at late adolescent, 13 and late 20s at most?" Another dismissed Nureyev himself: "When he dances Romeo's opening solo, he looks as if he's wrenching himself into a new step or direction before he's had time to breathe life into the old one."

As much as the criticism stung, Nureyev harbored few illusions about his waning powers. "I stopped expecting perfection a long time ago," he said at the time. "But I still ask the maximum of myself and those I work with, because it gets results." One year later, on tour in Athens with the Zurich Ballet, he was asked at a press conference how many performances he had given that year. "Probably I've danced every single day but ten," he replied. (In fact he gave 189 performances that year.) And how many of those would he call very good or exceptional? "Maybe three," Rudolf answered. Patricia Neary, who was beside him, assumed he had misspoken. "Did you say *three?*" she whispered. "Yes," he replied. A few days later, she asked him whether he was usually disappointed in his performance. "Most of the time, yes," he said. "I always feel I could be better."

Increasingly, he struggled to do things that had once come easily, but he refused to cut corners or simplify complicated movements. If anything, he drove himself harder. In *The Sleeping Beauty*, for example, having already added five solos for the Prince, he now endeavored to make each solo more difficult. Eva Evdokimova, his steady partner in those years, recalls how effortful his dancing had become. "Where other dancers would adapt to make themselves still elegant, Rudolf would push harder and harder. He needn't have." When Maude Gosling would suggest gently that he could "do it much easier," Rudolf disagreed. Once he relaxed his struggle, he feared he would lose his strength. "If I start doing it easier," he told her, "then the next time I'll do it more easily."

In the fall of 1982, after a five-year absence, Rudolf was invited back to the Royal Ballet to dance a number of ballets, including *La Bayadère*, *Giselle*, his own third act of *Raymonda*, *Apollo* and *The Prodigal Son*. He also staged *The Tempest*, his first original new work for the company. One day he ran into Monica Mason, who had recently stopped dancing.

"You mean, you don't *want* to dance anymore," Nureyev pressed her. No, she corrected him, she *couldn't* dance anymore. She was in too much pain most of the time. "If you wanted to dance," he dissented, "you wouldn't mind the pain."

Still, he had already begun preparing for his postperforming career. After years of scouting, he had recently purchased a farm in Virginia that he planned to one day run as a dance academy. Its faculty, he hoped, would include Fonteyn and Bruhn. It promised to be an ideal retreat for his later years, a place to cultivate a new generation and hand down hard-won traditions. Occasionally, he would say that he ought to retire sometime soon. But as his friends knew all too well, he expected them to object. Michael Birkmeyer, a Nureyev protégé and star of the Vienna Opera Ballet in the early 1980s, made the mistake of agreeing with him one night as he ferried Rudolf from the Vienna airport to the Hotel Imperial. "Yes, stop while you are still at the top," he concurred. "Go away as the king of ballet." The next morning in class, Birkmeyer asked if he'd given the subject any further thought. Rudolf turned on him. "Stop dancing? Are you crazy? You're an asshole! It was your idea, not mine."

And so he went on, night after night, year after year, country after country. "It's my life," he told a reporter. "There are so many bright, well-educated, cultured people who go around wanting to know who they are. They can't find themselves. My life is focused." His friends understood this and defended his decision to continue. Jacqueline Onassis even overlooked her aversion to the press and visited him at the Dakota the day he was to be interviewed by a reporter for *The New York Times Magazine*. She was as "awestruck by him" as he was by her. "I think he's heroic," she made a point of saying; "he's dancing against the clock. Here is a man who will dance as long as he can, to the end, to the last drop of blood."

In the meantime, he looked for other ways to express himself. He tried musical comedy, appearing as a song-and-dance man in a Julie Andrews television special, and he made another stab at movie stardom in James Toback's critically assailed spy thriller *Exposed*. Rudolf played a renowned violinist who seduces a high-fashion model, only to use her in his campaign against a master terrorist. This time out, however, Nureyev received second billing to Nastassja Kinski, the sensuously beautiful star of Roman Polanski's *Tess*, whom Richard Avedon had famously photographed with a python coiled around her naked body. It was Kinski, in fact, who pushed for Rudolf as her leading man, after spying a head shot of the young Nureyev in a movie poster store in Hollywood. Toback quickly endorsed her choice, noting that Nureyev and Kinski "could have been twins." Toback flew to London, where he read Rudolf his script at 3 A.M. at an all-night restaurant. By dawn Rudolf had agreed to do it.

The director had neglected to stress that *Exposed* was "Nastassja's movie," and Rudolf was "a bit chagrined after he saw that was the case."

He would have been even more distressed had he known that the film's producers were dead set against him from the start. *Valentino* had flopped, they argued, and, as Toback recalls, "David Begelman said, 'Can't we find an American heterosexual to play this part?' They felt the public viewed Nureyev as a homosexual. They sent me thirty other names, which meant 'Please use anyone other than Nureyev.'" Toback had final choice, however. He based his decision not on *Valentino* but on Nureyev's television interviews, in which he glimpsed "a strange, perverse, deranged quality. He didn't convert to the screen in the traditional romantic lead way that he might have thought. There was a quirky madness to him that he couldn't hide."[*]

Although Nureyev had agreed to an all-cash fee of $200,000 for twenty-three days of work, one week before shooting began he suddenly raised his price another $150,000. Toback, who had struggled to finance his film, had no choice but to pay him out of his own earnings. The filming itself went smoothly, and Toback and Nureyev often dined together on location in Paris and New York. A Harvard graduate and former English professor, Toback remembers "lengthy discussions" about Dostoyevsky, Mahler and philosophy. "Whatever I was reading, he would be curious about or he already knew it. Rarely would anything new go unattended with him." Rudolf was drawn to the subject of sex as much as the act. He "grilled" Toback about his sexual history. "He was interested in sex in whatever manifestation it was in. He would interrupt his lunch hour to go cruising and would always come back with a smile on his face." He had recently discovered Flaubert's letters from Egypt. "Sex was very liberating for Flaubert," he told a journalist at the time. "Well, for me, too, it's liberation . . . liberation."

Knowing that Nastassja Kinski had "real romantic notions" about Nureyev, Toback hoped they might transmit to the screen. Rudolf liked Kinski and thought her alluring, but when Toback tried encouraging his interest in her, Nureyev answered, half in jest, "Tell her to sew on a prick and cut off her tits and I'll think about it." As a result, Toback reworked their only love scene and had Rudolf play her body with his violinist's bow. Rudolf complained of fatigue all through their midwinter shoot and worried about growing older. Toback and Kinski were startled to hear him say, "I'm not as beautiful as I used to be," and rushed to reassure him that indeed he was.

Pleased with his performance, Nureyev promoted the film widely

---

[*]Toback, later to write the screenplay for *Bugsy*, wrote *The Gambler* and wrote and directed *Fingers*, a box-office dud which nevertheless had its admirers in François Truffaut and Norman Mailer.

on talk shows and invited Jacqueline Onassis to an early screening in Manhattan. But when Rudolf's character was shot in the film's final shoot-out, she let out "this yell," according to Toback, covered her face, and didn't remove her hands until the lights came up. "I apologize," she whispered to Rudolf. "I just couldn't look at that." The critical response pretty much echoed that view, and audiences stayed away. Thus, with the release of *Exposed* in April 1983, did Nureyev's film career effectively come to an end.

BY THE TIME SHOOTING had begun in late 1981, Rudolf's on-again, off-again relationship with Robert Tracy had nearly run its course. It had never been monogamous. The two regularly accompanied each other to the St. Marks Baths in New York and Rudolf continued to keep up his active sexual pursuits. But in the summer of 1981, while the pair were on tour in Caracas, Rudolf accused Tracy of stealing a beautiful Venezuelan boy he liked. The young man, however, had merely given Tracy a lift back to his hotel after a party. Rudolf refused to believe him, and when Tracy returned to their suite, he punched him in the eye. Frightened, Tracy spent the night in an adjoining room. The two soon reconciled, and a mood of elation took over; that quickly evaporated one week later in Verona, after Rudolf blamed Tracy for making him late for class. Their arguments were largely about power: Rudolf had it, Tracy didn't and resented being seen, as he told a friend, "as the young boy who serviced Rudolf." He was also jealous of Rudolf's newfound attraction to an Italian dancer. Tracy left, though he didn't go far: He had already begun an affair with Contessa Giovanna Augusta, a wealthy Italian admirer of Rudolf's, whom he joined in Rome. Rudolf thought him ungrateful. He had been teaching Tracy the role of the Bluebird in his production of *The Sleeping Beauty*, which Tracy was to have danced for the first time the following week with the Vienna State Opera Ballet. In leaving, Tracy forfeited that rare opportunity.

Eight months passed before the two spoke again. Then, at the suggestion of their mutual friend Violette Verdy, Robert contacted Rudolf on tour with the Boston Ballet in Tennessee. Rudolf now invited Tracy to dance in his *Manfred* later that summer with the Zurich Ballet. Robert agreed and, soon after, joined Rudolf in London. They stayed at his flat at the Goslings'—but in separate bedrooms. Without discussion, they both understood that their sexual relationship was over. When they went on to Greece to holiday on the Niarchos yacht, they occupied separate suites. Nureyev trusted Tracy enough to allow him to move back into the Dakota. He would live there for the next ten years, fulfilling his role as Rudolf's caretaker and social secretary. "They had this mercurial relationship," says Jamie Wyeth. "One day Rudolf would be terrific with him and the next he would be screaming at him. But Robert was very helpful to him; he organized things and got things done."

ON MAY 21, 1982, Nigel Gosling died of cancer in a London hospital. Rudolf, in Chicago with the Boston Ballet, flew immediately to London to comfort Maude. He even attended Nigel's funeral, the only one that he ever did. "When someone close to him was dying, he had to go away," says Charles Jude. "He was afraid to be near death." The seventy-two-year-old Gosling had been ill for some time, but Rudolf had grown to depend on Nigel's counsel and friendship and deeply grieved his loss. "It's like losing my father; more than that," he told Rudi van Dantzig. "As long as Maude survives, she means home to me."

Less than one year later, Balanchine lay dying in a New York hospital of a malady only later diagnosed as the rare Creutzfeldt-Jakob disease, which has recently been associated with mad cow's disease. At the time, however, his friends understood only that Balanchine's mind was deteriorating rapidly. Despite his dread of hospitals, Rudolf hastened to Balanchine's bedside in January 1983, bearing caviar and a bottle of Château d'Yquem. Their mutual friend the designer Rouben Ter-Arutunian accompanied him. Though gravely ill, Balanchine was so pleased with his gifts that he stretched out his arms to embrace him. He had forgotten how to speak English and was most comfortable in his native tongue. Rudolf hoped that Balanchine might want to give some of his ballets to the Kirov, but his suggestion met with utter indifference. "When I die," Balanchine replied, "everything should vanish. . . ." Another day Balanchine's doctor entered his room to find Rudolf kneeling by the choreographer's bed, tears streaking his face. He had desperately wanted Balanchine as a father figure, but Balanchine had always refused the mantle. To the end, Balanchine never stopped disappointing him.

Two years earlier, for the New York City Ballet's Tchaikovsky Festival, Rudolf had offered his revised *Manfred*. A number of choreographers had been invited to contribute works, and Rudolf was anxious to know what Balanchine and Kirstein thought of it. "Has Lincoln seen *Manfred*? What did he say?" he repeatedly asked Jamie Wyeth. After viewing it on video, however, Balanchine promptly turned him down. Rudolf cried when he learned of the decision.

But by then he had already persuaded the Zurich Ballet to stage *Manfred*. Under Patricia Neary, the Zurich Ballet had become a satellite Balanchine company, and it was Rudolf's hope that Balanchine might see *Manfred* again and change his mind. In December 1981, six months after the New York City Ballet's Tchaikovsky Festival, Balanchine arrived in Zurich. He was not pleased to learn that "his company," as he thought of it, was dancing *Manfred*. "I really don't want to see that," he told

Neary. "No choreography, right?" The dancers were challenged by it, she said brightly. "And they would love it if you came to see it. After all, you are our artistic adviser." "I didn't advise you to take this ballet," Balanchine remonstrated. In the end, he was "surprised at how much dancing there was in it and by how hard everyone had to work," recalls Neary. "He said, 'Not bad, but too many steps.' "

Balanchine was not nearly so compliant the following October, when Neary informed him that "their" company was to make its American debut in Nureyev's *Manfred* and Nureyev's *Don Quixote*, with Nureyev promised at every performance. "That's like prostitution," he said.

Balanchine died six months later, on Saturday, April 30, 1983. On the day of his funeral, the Zurich Ballet opened in Washington, D.C., in Nureyev's *Manfred*. In an advance press release announcing the company's U.S. debut, the Zurich Ballet was called "Nureyev and George Balanchine's European Company." By the time of the tour, the company's publicity posters had amended that claim to simply say, "George Balanchine's European Company."

28

"Ritorna Vincitor!"

IN SEPTEMBER 1983, Nureyev became the artistic director of the Paris Opéra Ballet, his first permanent post since arriving in the West twenty-two years earlier. Then the Paris Opéra had refused him work, fearing reprisals from the Soviets. And just three years earlier, its dancers had refused to appear with him in New York, causing the cancellation of its first U.S. tour in thirty-two years. By 1981, however, the Opéra was in need of dynamic leadership, having gone through eight different directors since Serge Lifar's departure in 1958. While Lifar had ruled the Opéra for thirty years, his successors had been little more than caretakers of a moribund organization. Rudolf's friends had been among them: John Taras, Violette Verdy and Rosella Hightower, from whom he inherited the job after nearly two years of negotiations.

His career in the West had been spent galvanizing established troupes and boosting fledgling ones. Now Nureyev faced perhaps his most challenging assignment yet: limbering up an ossified company. Founded by Louis XIV in 1661, the Paris Opéra Ballet was the oldest ballet company in the world and, until the nineteenth century, the foremost. Petipa had begun his career there before decamping for St. Petersburg, which, under his leadership, became ballet's new world capital.

Riven by intrigue, subject to political vicissitudes and known for its insurmountable bureaucracy and rigid hierarchy, the Paris Opéra Ballet was "the only place in the world where dust transforms itself into cement," Jean Cocteau wryly observed. That description might have just as easily fitted the Kirov Ballet when Rudolf arrived to challenge most of its hidebound traditions. Having stood up to the Soviets, Rudolf possessed the requisite arrogance and authority to take on the French. Even a ruthless negotiator like Jane Hermann — "Hermann the Sherman tank" Rudolf dubbed her — conceded that she would have been "reduced to a mass of jelly by the machinations of the French, but Rudolf's innate cynicism, his basic assumption that people are not wholly loyal, makes it possible for him to function in a society where it is de rigueur to lie."

Rudolf had declined the post when it was first proposed in 1973, preferring to focus on his dancing. But in 1981, after Jack Lang became Minister of Culture under François Mitterrand, a search for a dance director was again under way. Lang and his lieutenant, André Larquié, turned to Igor Eisner, the Ministry of Culture's widely admired Inspector general of dance, who, without hesitation, proposed Nureyev. A former journalist and a highly cultivated man whose companion, Michel Guy, was a former Minister of Culture, Eisner had been in the audience for Nureyev's Paris debut with the Kirov. Twenty years later, Eisner flew to Verona to discuss his taking over the Paris Opéra Ballet.

Nureyev had been a regular guest of the company throughout his career. In recent years, he had staged the Shades scene from *Bayadère*, *Manfred* and the enormously successful *Don Quixote*. "He had been courting the company and he badly wanted the job, even knowing the inconveniences." During a late-night dinner at the Trattoria Sergio, Nureyev laid out his conditions. He would remain in Paris only six months out of the year, not necessarily consecutively, so as to avoid paying French taxes. He would perform forty times a year at the Opéra and would be free to pursue other engagements. He was also to be guaranteed the right to mount one production of his own each year, and the administration was to build three large studios inside the Palais Garnier to accommodate all the new activity he planned. (The largest of these he would call Petipa; the two others, Balanchine and Lifar.) As they parted, Rudolf bade Eisner, "*Ritorna vincitor!* [Return when you have won!]," quoting the famous line from Verdi's *Aida*, said to a departing commander on his way to war.

The Soviet embassy objected vociferously to the appointment. Jack Lang, by then set on Nureyev, faced the Soviets down with the backing of President Mitterrand himself. Some of the Paris dancers also expressed misgivings. They considered his celebrity an asset but worried that he would be tough on them and dance too much. As a concession, Nureyev agreed not to dance the first nights of any full-length ballets with the Paris company.

The Paris post marked a new era in Nureyev's life. "Maybe it's finally time to bring all the eggs together in one basket and hatch them together," he said, mangling his metaphor to striking effect. Still, he was in no hurry to slow down, despite chronic aches and pains and the sudden onset of recurrent and unexplained night sweats. Before taking on Paris, he appeared with the Boston Ballet on Broadway, dancing every performance of his *Don Quixote*, matinees included; with Japan's Matsuyama Ballet, returning to Japan for the first time in twenty years; and with the Zurich Ballet, with which he toured to Washington and Chicago. The 1983 Nureyev Festival in London—twenty-four days of nonstop dancing with three different companies in seven different ballets that June—was followed by his first New York appearances with Natalia Makarova in July. At Jane Hermann's suggestion, Roland Petit had agreed to cast them in his *Notre-Dame de Paris* for his troupe's summer stint at the Met.* Their performances sold out immediately. "Rudolf and Natasha hadn't had a good relationship in a number of years," recalls Hermann, "and every balletomane in New York was waiting to see which one was going to walk out first or who would hit whom."

As it turned out, Nureyev and Makarova got along fine; it was Nureyev and Petit who nearly came to blows. Nureyev failed to rehearse the ballet properly, shortened his costume, improvised his own choreography, and made it plain that he was not interested in portraying a hunchback, even a famous one. At one performance, when he was meant to be expressing Quasimodo's angst in the solo Petit had devised for him, he substituted the Prince's variation from his own *Sleeping Beauty*. He performed his signature manège of coupé-jetés around the stage, a set piece of classical virtuosity out of keeping with the role. "I don't know if the public had any idea where the choreography came from," recalls Hermann. "But as far as they were concerned, Rudolf and Natasha could do no wrong." Petit, however, was beside himself. His fury was made all the more acute after he overheard Nureyev inviting Makarova to dance the ballet with him at the Paris Opéra, one of two Petit ballets scheduled for Nureyev's first Paris season.

The party afterward at Jane Hermann's East Thirtieth Street home was a raucous, drunken affair for which Rudolf uncharacteristically supplied a case of Dom Pérignon. Petit kept his distance from Rudolf, who was nestled next to Martha Graham on a sofa. When Rudolf demanded that Petit come over and greet Graham, as Makarova had done with a great sweeping bow, Petit pretended that he hadn't heard him. There are various versions of what followed, but the next thing Zizi Jeanmaire knew, Rudolf let loose with a volley of expletives at her husband. "I'm going to bash his head in," Petit told her. She feared they were going to punch each other and jumped between them, yelling for them to stop.

---

*Petit's company, the Ballet National de Marseille, was one of twelve major dance companies in France.

Jeanmaire finally dragged Petit home, but not before he vowed never to give Nureyev his ballets. "I don't want your fucking ballets," Rudolf replied. When, after several months, he refused to apologize, Petit withdrew them from the Paris season. It was several years before they spoke to each other again, and then it was as if nothing had come between them.

RUDOLF'S FIRST ORDER of business in Paris was the Opéra's 161 dancers. He determined to do for the company what he had done for himself. He began to both extend and polish the company's classic heritage, while opening it up to the diversity of dance styles that he had already embraced. He strengthened its ties to Petipa, introduced classes in Bournonville and Balanchine technique, and prescribed a steady diet of both the classics and modern ballets. "My body has Petipa, my head has Bournonville, and my heart has Balanchine," he liked to say.

He lost no time in enriching the repertory to showcase its rich but largely untested talent. His first season included his own stagings of Petipa's *Raymonda* and *Don Quixote*, as well as Balanchine's *Le Bourgeois Gentilhomme* and Pierre Lacotte's revival of *Coppélia*, the French classic created at the Paris Opéra more than a century earlier. To honor his English ties, he planned evenings devoted to Ashton and Tudor, and to broaden French tastes, he intended to import not only modern masters, such as Martha Graham, Paul Taylor and Merce Cunningham, but such contemporary mavericks as William Forsythe, Karole Armitage and Michael Clark. Remarkably, it wasn't until Nureyev invited the Graham troupe to Paris in January 1984 that an American modern dance company had performed at the opera house. On the opening night of Graham's *Phaedra's Dream*, in which Nureyev danced a leading role, the ninety-year-old choreographer was finally recognized by the French.* As she clutched Nureyev's hand onstage, Culture Minister Jack Lang placed the Légion d'Honneur around her neck, announcing modestly, "The entire world of dance is honored by this nomination."

The Opéra dancers were among the world's most glamorous and technically accomplished—clean beats, high extensions, beautiful feet. Nureyev, however, saw the need to make them more engaged, versatile and refined. To be sure, not all of them welcomed the Nureyev work ethic. As civil servants who could not be fired, they had strong unions, steady paychecks and the security of a pension after twenty years of service. Rudolf circumvented Opéra protocol by pairing dancers of differing rank, something that had never been done, and by assigning unseasoned

*The engagement was a personal triumph for Graham, who had been lambasted by the French press on her first visit to Paris thirty years earlier.

dancers major roles, thereby serving notice that all roles were up for grabs, regardless of position or age. As ever, he hated to see fledgling talent go unattended. He handed the leading male role in *Coppélia* to a nineteen-year-old corps dancer named Laurent Hilaire and cast twenty-year-old Isabelle Guérin as Kitri in *Don Quixote*, her first starring role. He also awarded Hilaire and fellow corps dancer Manuel Legris a show-stopping duo in *Raymonda*, which brought them both to immediate prominence. However, his pairing of Legris with the étoile Claude de Vulpian, an established ballerina, did not go unchallenged. She marched into Rudolf's office and announced that she couldn't dance with a boy from the corps de ballet. To no avail. "Before Rudolf I would never have had that chance, it was not the French mentality," says Legris. "He changed all that."

"He wanted to have enormous power and he got it," concurs Monique Loudières, another étoile whose career he boosted. "He would ask for more and more, people would say he was crazy, but they agreed to his demands because he was Nureyev." Despite considerable administrative interference, he stuck by his policies, prompting one French daily to declare, four months into his campaign, NUREYEV LAUNCHES STAR WARS. Yet within three years, the strength of the Paris Opéra Ballet would lie in its outstanding young stars, among them Laurent Hilaire, Manuel Legris, Isabelle Guérin and Sylvie Guillem, all of whom were under twenty-five when Nureyev elevated them to the top rank. (Under the French system, once admitted to the corps, the dancers advanced incrementally, but only after a twelve-member jury approved their promotion. The highest rank of étoile, or star, was bestowed at the discretion of the artistic director.) Sylvie Guillem, stimulated by the opportunities Nureyev provided her, was soon being touted as the most exciting ballerina of her generation. Tall and slender, with long limbs, hyperextended developpés and a striking range, Guillem possessed a prodigious technique and, in time, a temperament to rival Nureyev's own. She also had confidence to spare. A talented gymnast as a child, she began her ballet training late, at age twelve, but quickly became a standout at the Paris Opéra Ballet School.

For all his focus on youth, Nureyev did not discount the company's older guard, as he felt Baryshnikov was doing at American Ballet Theatre.* To Nureyev, they were the company's living legacy and he made sure to find a place for those he most admired. He hired Claire Motte as company ballet mistress and brought Yvette Chauviré out of retirement to play a character role in *Raymonda* and to assist him with the ballet. Motte had befriended him during his first days in Paris with the Kirov, while Chauviré, the greatest French ballerina of the century, had danced

*Baryshnikov served as director of ABT from 1980 to 1989.

with him in his first seasons with both the Royal Ballet and the Paris Opéra Ballet. To her mind, he arrived "at just the right moment, at a time when the Opéra was exhausted. He restored Petipa to France, and though he had an absolute respect for the rigor of everything classical, he wasn't stuck in the classics. We were dancing well, but thanks to his demand for perfection, things became a little cleaner, a little more perfect. So it all flowered anew."

One of his first acts as director was to remake the company's technique, replacing the "frou-frou and decoration," as he thought of it, with the Vaganova principles that had been bred in his bones. He insisted on the purity of each position, and like his role model, Bruhn, he abhorred any distortion or showiness for the sake of effect. "It's too French," he would say, and they all knew what he meant. "Each gesture and expression had to say something. There could be nothing gratuitous," explains Isabelle Guérin.

The fact that he took daily class with his dancers, offering corrections as he went, made a deep impression on those who had never seen him dance in his prime. Laurent Hilaire recalls being struck to find the forty-five-year-old Nureyev in the class for the men's junior dancers. The class was taught by Alexandre Kalioujny, whom Rudolf considered the Opéra's finest male dance coach. "It was a shock to see him working as a real student, as if he were fifteen years old, so concentrated at every moment. He would never quit for anything." Daily class allowed Nureyev to both maintain his dancer's physique and keep watch over the ensemble. "He really managed to change the look of the company by being in class all the time," says Patrice Bart, the veteran Paris étoile who became company ballet master in 1986 with Nureyev's encouragement. "Before he arrived, there were a lot of teachers who had their own ideas. . . . If Rudolf disagreed with the way a step was being taught, he'd stop the class and explain how he wanted to see it done. He cleaned up the style and managed to get the whole company working the same way."

To help them gain stamina and experience, he dispatched a number of dancers to other companies, usually to perform in his productions. He also forced them them to learn new ballets quickly, without the endless preparation to which they were accustomed. Manuel Legris had just one week to master Nureyev's role in Don Quixote before his debut at La Scala. "I said, 'My God, I can't. I've never done Don Q.' And he said, 'Try and do. You have two rehearsals with me and you go.' " He taught by example, not with words. Sometimes just one word would do, "but with that one word you could understand the entire ballet," insists Legris. "Sometimes you just watched his eyes. You had to pick up the clues very fast." For those who did, the rewards were invaluable. His coaching of Charles Jude for his Royal Ballet debut in the Shades scene of Bayadère had the London critics comparing Jude with the young Nureyev, "who first astounded us in this production."

Nureyev's premiere season as director was applauded by critics on both sides of the Atlantic. The company was dancing better than it had in years, many said, with a renewed vigor that was all to Nureyev's credit. Change had not come without a price, however. Many dancers disliked their new *patron*, who did not mince words. Nor did he express himself fully—or in French if he could avoid it. He spoke French only when he had the time, English when he was in a hurry and Russian when he swore at them, "which was often," recalls one. "It was difficult for him to explain precisely, so when people didn't understand him, he got frustrated," explained his close friend Genya Polyakov, the Russian-born ballet master he brought to the Opéra from Florence. "He was not easy to follow." There are repeated tales of tea-filled thermoses sent crashing to the floor and ashtrays thrown at studio mirrors. His "acts of provocation," as André Larquié called them, were his way of asserting his will and testing the strength of his opponents. Once, after he had smashed yet another thermos, Monique Loudières rebuked him in front of her colleagues. Seeing how angry she was, he quietly retrieved a broom and swept all the broken pieces from the floor. "He just stayed in a corner, sort of shrinking, like a child who just threw a tantrum. He actually preferred people who stood up to him. He hated weak people."

His demanding temperament, however, made him appear intimidating and unapproachable. "He was always right, even when he was wrong," says Isabelle Guérin, whose irreverent sense of humor and knack for impersonation made her one of his favorites. "He wouldn't yield, he had to prove he was right. People didn't understand him very well because he had a very strong disposition and, at the same time, was very, very shy. He had trouble reaching out to people."

Still they were quick to forgive him his excesses when they saw how much he had to teach and how eager he was to pass on his knowledge. Sylvie Guillem's appearances with him throughout the mid-1980s taught her "a lot about the way to be onstage." He brought with him not only a great of sense of occasion, but "all this presence and artistry," she recalled. "You can create something with him. . . . He has something to say onstage, not with his body anymore, but there is something else he gives." His authority had intensified with age, as had his ability to animate a role with his powers of projection. Manuel Legris observed how he "took the light" and never rushed his performance but slowly assumed command.

While the Opéra was the center of his life in Paris, he regularly hosted dinner parties at his Quai Voltaire apartment. Meals were prepared by Manuel, the Chilean cook Douce had hired. Lit by candlelight, the apartment was designed for nighttime living and kept at stifling temperatures because Rudolf was forever cold, no matter how many layers of Missoni sweaters and Kenzo scarves he wrapped himself in. After dinner, he delighted in introducing his young protégés to the musical comedies he loved, forcing them to stay up late into the night to watch the movies of Astaire and Kelly. Hundreds of videocassettes lined an antique walnut cabinet in his dining room. A large-screen television, curiously out of place amid the baroque splendor of his drawing room, was almost always on. "Look, there's the world," he would say, pointing to his television set. He had every channel available, yet never watched a complete program because he was afraid he might be missing something on another channel. An inveterate insomniac, he read into the early hours, tackled Bach on his harpsichord, or phoned his family of friends without regard for what time it was in Paris — or anywhere else. But he was always at the Opéra first thing in the morning, driving himself there in his Mercedes, and he rarely arrived home until the evening's curtain came down.

There were complaints that he was crowding the repertory with his own productions. Yet Nureyev actively pursued outside choreographers. He had hoped to entice Ashton to Paris to stage his *Month in the Country* and *La Fille Mal Gardée*, but he seriously compromised their already tenuous relationship by announcing his intentions before securing Ashton's approval. "Freddie went crazy," confirms Alexander Grant. "He said, 'I haven't given him permission to do it and I don't like the Paris Opéra because they're impossible to work with and you can't use who you want and every choreographer who goes there ends up in tears. I'm not going to be bothered with it." Ashton and Nureyev had "a big row," says Grant, after Ashton refused to give him the ballet. According to Ashton's nephew Anthony Russell-Roberts, the more "aggressive" Rudolf became, the more Ashton dug in. Paradoxically, as much as he loved French style, music and food, Ashton "deeply distrusted" the French and feared they would mock his lyrical English style. "They'll call it English goo," he complained to Grant.

Nureyev's plans to stage *Pierrot Lunaire* also came to naught after Glen Tetley refused him the ballet on the grounds that his technique was disintegrating. Nureyev, he decided, could no longer sustain Pierrot's "airborne quality." Nureyev surprised him, however, by putting the company's needs ahead of his own. In his place, he offered the popular Patrick Dupond, even though he cared for neither the dancer nor his rock star persona. Tetley thought him "very generous" but had absolutely no desire to work at the Paris Opéra. "I did that once and it was the number one worst experience in my life. Sure they're wonderful dancers, but heavens, the attitude!"

Indeed, when Nureyev was not present to keep them in line, the dancers fell back into their old ways. The English choreographer David Bintley pulled up stakes soon after arriving, appalled at the lingering resistance to new teaching, not to mention the absenteeism at rehearsals. Rudi van Dantzig had showcased Dupond and Guillem in his first Nureyev commission for the company, but he found matters "so desperate" that, inspired by Bintley's example, he went home to Amsterdam before starting work on his second. "I was getting one hour's rehearsal time a day and none of the dancers I wanted." Rudolf called him daily, begging him to come back. "It's impossible for me to have two works cancelled in one season, first Bintley, now you. They'll throw me out, my career with the Opéra will be finished. . . . My professional life is on the line with this piece.'" Van Dantzig held his ground for a while, then caved in. "I didn't even ring him, just turned up at his apartment. And he opened his arms to me. He never, ever bore grudges."

The problems Nureyev faced at the Paris Opéra were partly of his own making. There were complaints that he spent too much time away from Paris and that he danced much too often when in town, depriving younger dancers of important roles. In the summer of 1984, shortly after the French press reported that the wardrobe department was refusing to dress him because he'd thrown a bottle at one of them, Nureyev hit the esteemed teacher Michel Renault following an argument over Renault's methods. The incident provoked the dancers' union to call for Rudolf's resignation and made all the local papers. IMPOSSIBLE NOUREEV! screamed one French daily, while another, milking the incident for scandal, likened it to the infamous duel between Serge Lifar and the Marquis de Cuevas. Nureyev was fined six thousand francs.

His need to dance, and to dance first nights when he had agreed not to, fueled dissent among the ranks. It also gave voice to the claque that regularly booed him on opening nights. For the Paris premiere of his *Romeo and Juliet* in October 1984, Nureyev appeared only at the curtain call in his role as choreographer. Greeted by catcalls and whistles, he smilingly responded with a gesture unfamiliar to the ballet stage but perfectly in keeping with the hot-blooded vigor of the evening's bawdy fare. His *bras d'honneur** stunned the demonstrators into silence and provoked laughter from the rest of the house.

Two months later, the dancers briefly went on strike to protest his new production of *Swan Lake*. When he arrived at rehearsal and asked who wanted to do his ballet, only Charles Jude stood up. The famous Soviet version of *Swan Lake* by Vladimir Bourmeister had long been a crowd-pleasing Opéra staple and the dancers were reluctant to replace it, particularly with Nureyev's taxing and psychologically dense version. Many complained that there was too much dancing in his productions,

_____
*An "up yours" sign.

while others simply rejected the amendments he had introduced. "In the beginning, they didn't like his ballets and he was very sad about it," remembered Genya Polyakov. Nureyev, however, loathed the Bourmeister, with its happy Soviet-style ending, which saw Odette and Siegfried reunited in death. In his version, following Tchaikovsky's original scenario, Siegfried drowned in a storm.

The standoff with the dancers forced him into a compromise. Their "gentleman's agreement," as he termed it, alternated performances of his own and the Bourmeister productions. But he did not let the matter end there. When Sylvie Guillem made her much-anticipated debut in his ballet, he turned the occasion into a show of strength. On December 29, to cries and gasps from the audience, Nureyev appeared on the stage to name the nineteen-year-old Guillem *étoile*, the youngest in the company's history. She had jumped three ranks in just eight days.

In time, the dancers decided they liked his version better after all, despite its demands. "You do all the other *Swan Lakes*, it's like nothing," observes Manuel Legris. "The man has only the adagio in the second act and the Black Swan pas de deux. In Nureyev's production, the man has many more solos, with very difficult combinations. After dancing one of his ballets, everything else seems easy."

The conflicts at the Opéra had left even Nureyev battle-weary. It was in this frame of mind that he went to see his doctor, Michel Canesi, in the fall of 1984. The two had met the previous year through their mutual friend the arts patron Charles Murdland, a trustee of the London Festival Ballet. Boyish, outgoing and fresh out of medical school, the thirty-year-old Canesi was a dermatologist with a specialty in venereal diseases. Though he was friendly with a number of dancers at the Paris Opéra, he was struck immediately by the intensity of Rudolf's gaze, by the way he appeared to take his full measure. During Rudolf's first visit Canesi simply examined him "for some very straightforward things" and gave him a blood test. There was nothing "significant," and a year elapsed before he saw him again.

This time Rudolf complained of not feeling quite right. A recent bout of pneumonia had him worried about his lungs, particularly since his father had died of lung cancer. He was having trouble maintaining his weight and was still plagued by the night sweats that left him "drenched in the morning." But also preoccupying him were the rumors that Rock Hudson had AIDS, a devastating new disease that scientists were only beginning to comprehend. Though the news of Rock Hudson's illness would not be made public until 1985, Hudson had in fact learned of his AIDS diagnosis in June 1984 and was at that moment in Paris for treatment. Could he too have the disease? Rudolf asked Canesi.

The first reports of a "gay cancer" had begun appearing in the mainstream press in 1981, fueling panic among homosexuals, who initially and inexplicably appeared to be its main targets. For some then unknown reason, the immune systems of the afflicted gay men shut down, leaving them defenseless against even mild infections. The two most common symptoms of the new disease were a rare and strange form of pneumonia, called *Pneumocystis carinii*, and a disfiguring form of cancer known as Kaposi's sarcoma, previously seen only in older men of Mediterranean or Jewish descent. Neglect and ignorance characterized the media's AIDS coverage from the start. Stigmatization and isolation of those who had it quickly followed, a list that soon included Haitians, hemophiliacs and IV drug users. As Randy Shilts observed in his landmark history of the epidemic, *And the Band Played On*, only when it started killing heterosexuals did AIDS become newsworthy.

By the spring of 1983, Rudolf couldn't help being concerned about the mysterious disease: With cases increasing at a staggering rate, the mainstream press had finally broken its silence. An avalanche of coverage incited a wave of AIDS hysteria from San Francisco to Stockholm. "EPIDEMIC: The Mysterious and Deadly Disease Called AIDS May Be the Public-Health Threat of the Century. How Did It Start? Can It Be Stopped?" blazed the cover of *Newsweek* in April. The same month in New York, following one of the first conferences on AIDS, the organizers and speakers gathered for a cocktail reception at the Dakota apartment of Rudolf's neighbor Leonard Bernstein. At that time, scientists were still struggling to understand the disease and its means of transmission and had yet to identify the virus that caused it. By the time Nureyev took over at the Paris Opéra, the number of known AIDS cases in the United States had passed the five thousand mark, while France was reporting the largest AIDS caseload in Europe, with ninety-four diagnosed patients.

Given his specialty in sexually transmitted diseases, Michel Canesi had first heard about the disease while still a medical student and had kept abreast of new developments through his friendships with Luc Montagnier, the French doctor credited with discovering what became known as the HIV virus, and Willy Rozenbaum, a pioneering AIDS researcher. In November 1984, nearly a year before AIDS testing became publicly available, Canesi sent Rudolf to see Rozenbaum at Pitié-Salpêtrière Hospital, the only medical center in Paris where the testing was being done. Rudolf was instantly recognized, and it was soon the talk of Paris that Nureyev had AIDS.

The sad fact was that his tests did indeed reveal that he was HIV-positive and had been so, according to his doctor's estimate, for at least four years. What this meant, however, wasn't entirely clear, and Rudolf didn't appear unduly distressed when Canesi broke the news. Like many other doctors in France at the time, Canesi believed that only about 10 percent of those who tested positive would develop full-blown AIDS. Canesi made sure to advise Rudolf about precautions, but researchers faced many unanswered questions and no cure was forthcoming. The lack of information intimidated Canesi, who was nervous about taking on such a famous patient. "I thought, 'What if I make a mistake? I'll have the whole world coming down on me.' It wasn't easy."

Rudolf confided in only those few close friends he felt could handle the news; the rest were kept in the dark, many until the last year of his life. "I will be dead very soon," he told Genya Polyakov without a trace of melodrama, though according to Polyakov, Rudolf was initially "frightened" by his diagnosis. He asked Opéra president André Larquié to call Canesi "about my condition," knowing that he would someday need his support. He also advised Robert Tracy to see Canesi about treatments, without once using the word "AIDS." Tracy would later discover that he, too, had the virus.

Contrary to accounts that Nureyev ignored realities, he grilled Canesi about the disease and made him promise that he would let him know when "the time had come." He left it up to his doctor to worry about his health and trusted that he would tell him whatever he needed to know. Canesi had many patients who couldn't get their minds off their HIV status. What separated Rudolf from the rest was that "he took the problem and handed it to me. *I* was to deal with it."

At a time in his career when he was still in demand, he feared that some countries, mainly the United States, would refuse him entry if he were known to be HIV-positive. Equally significant, he dreaded being labeled "the dancer with AIDS," suspecting that the public would come to define him by his disease, not his artistry. To his mind, an acknowledgment of his HIV status was tantamount to coming out publicly as a homosexual. If he had any doubts about this, he had only to see the press crush that greeted the news that Rock Hudson had AIDS in July 1985. Papers around the world were rushing into print reports of Hudson's homosexuality, a secret the actor had kept hidden from the public during his long years as Hollywood's matinee idol. To prominent figures like Nureyev, disclosure meant a loss of privacy and a curtailing of freedoms which Nureyev, especially, was loath to relinquish.

In consultation with Willy Rozenbaum, Canesi decided to treat Nureyev with the same experimental drug that had drawn Hudson to Paris earlier that fall. Known as HPA-23, the drug was thought to halt replication of the virus and had to be given intravenously every day. (Researchers had yet to learn that viral replication began again the minute the patient went off the drug.) Hudson had responded so well to the drug that after a brief round of treatments he had returned to the United States convinced he was cured. Rudolf, too, responded well, prompting Canesi to reduce the number of injections to three or four a week. When Rudolf went on tour with the Ballet de Nancy, Canesi went with him, rushing back to Paris in between dates to look after his growing AIDS caseload.

Maintaining his professional distance proved increasingly difficult, however, as Rudolf distrusted formality and preferred to view Canesi as a friend. He invited him on holidays, shopped for antiques with him, and telephoned him from all over the world. The house calls Canesi paid to his Quai Voltaire apartment were hardly routine. Rudolf would want to know what films and plays had he seen and for the next two hours they would discuss everything but Rudolf's health. And yet Rudolf knew precisely where to draw the line. On tour with him, Canesi once offered to carry his suitcase. Rudolf stopped him. "Please don't, because if you start to do that, I'm going to get used to it."

Rudolf was treated with HPA-23 for several months, and even today, Canesi has no idea whether Nureyev's improved health was due to the experimental drug (which was later discontinued) or was simply a by-product of his own remarkable constitution. When Rudolf saw that he could still dance, and dance vigorously and often, he, like Hudson, decided he was cured. "And for a long time," said Robert Tracy, "it seemed as if he were." He had always drawn strength from adversity, and AIDS was simply one more obstacle he felt certain he could overcome. "They're not going to scare me with this," he told Tracy.

His cure-all remained work. He still believed that dancing was the only thing in the world that kept him going, perhaps because it was the only thing in the world that made him feel complete. As long as he sold tickets, he would dance, he told friends, knowing full well that he would always be able to do so, somewhere. Still, his notices of late had grown harsher, for he continued to dance roles that begged comparison with his younger self. In August 1984, when he appeared in New York with his Friends troupe at the Uris Theater,* the critics were downright hostile. "It is pathetic to watch this man . . . driving himself through an exhausting evening of performances that he just can't pull off," wrote Burt Supree in *The Village Voice*. His "stiff, earthbound jumps were painful to see," concurred Jennifer Dunning of *The New York Times*. And yet, at forty-six, Nureyev could still excite an audience. Increasingly his performances were becoming acts of defiance, against aging, against gravity and, finally, against illness. "I would tell him please go and dance," says Canesi. "I wanted him to work. I could see it was very good for him." The doctor would come to believe that dancing was prolonging his life more than medicine ever could.

But his health proved erratic. In the spring of 1985, he developed pneumonia while starring in his *Romeo and Juliet* at the Palais des Congrès. Conductor John Lanchbery went backstage to find Nureyev wrapped in blankets, shaking, the sweat "pouring" down his face.

"My dear, you ought to be in bed!"

---

*In what would be his final Friends season on Broadway.

"If I were home," Rudolf replied, "my mother would cure me. She'd put goose fat on my chest." And then he went on and finished the performance.

When shortly thereafter he had to drop out of a performance of *Giselle* at the Opéra, he asked Baryshnikov to take his place. "Rudolf could dance with a hundred-degree temperature over and over again. I wouldn't be able to walk ten feet," recalls Baryshnikov, who suspected that Rudolf had AIDS but never asked him. "I used to take class with him when he was so hot I thought he would explode. I never saw anything like it. He always thought no matter what, you can always drink hot tea with lemon and honey and that could cure everything."

For all his jealousy and put-downs, Nureyev had enormous regard for his younger rival. He felt sure Baryshnikov's example would inspire the Paris dancers. "We thought it very strange," says Monique Loudières, Baryshnikov's Giselle that night, "because Rudolf always danced, even when he was very sick." Rudolf attended the performance and afterward took Baryshnikov and several dancers out to dinner near the Opéra. "Rudolf was so happy that Misha had come," says Loudières. "I was surprised because usually when he wasn't dancing, he seemed almost jealous of the one who was."

Two weeks later, when Rudolf returned to the role of Albrecht, Loudières was distressed to see him looking "gaunt and cadaverous," rather more like one of the spectral wilis in the ballet's second act than the cocky, playful Count. Minutes before curtain time, he warned her that if he fell to the ground and couldn't get up, she was to continue, alone. "It was horrible. Usually when he was in pain, he was so willful that he never showed anything, but this time you could see that he was really not well."

He needed to get out of Paris, he told Jane Hermann, who took him off for a few days to Stavros Niarchos's compound in Lyford Cay. Rudolf spent four days in bed. "He was terribly sick, running an awful fever," recalls Hermann. "I said to him, 'Have you had the test?' and he said, 'Yes.' That's all he ever said. I had vaguely heard about AIDS and somehow I suspected. I remember going out to the car and sitting there crying because I knew what was coming. I just didn't know how long it would be." Rudolf's rapid recovery, however, convinced her to put aside her worries and hope for the best. When Baryshnikov asked her about the rumors, she denied them "vehemently," not only because she knew Rudolf would want her to but because, for a long while, she convinced herself that they weren't true.

Other friends also had trouble reconciling the rumors with Rudolf's capacity for strenuous, unrelenting work. Ballet de Nancy director Hélène Traïline was not alone in thinking, "It's a lie. You can't have such vitality, expend such strength." Clive Barnes apparently agreed; in June

1985, he reported in the *New York Post* that rumors of Nureyev's "imminent death" had been, like Mark Twain's, "vastly exaggerated."*

His closest friends, the cluster he called family, detected small, incremental changes. "He's so unpredictable these days," Maude Gosling lamented to Rudi van Dantzig that summer. Rudolf was in London at the time, staying with Maude during his appearances with Japan's Matsuyama Ballet at the Coliseum. During the two-week season, he appeared in every performance of *Swan Lake*, and his costumes were strewn about her house, "still wet with perspiration and he doesn't clean or dry them, he just piles them up."

It pained him to be in London, Rudolf confided to van Dantzig. There were too many ghosts. He continued to feel slighted by the Royal Ballet, and he missed Nigel Gosling. With Nigel's death, he had drawn closer to Maude. He regularly invited her on tour and holiday, paying her expenses. As a tribute to her dearest friend, Antony Tudor, he presented the first all-Tudor program at the Paris Opéra, and when, after several tries, he failed to convince the choreographer to come and supervise, he called on Maude to take his place. Maude had danced in Tudor's earliest creations and was the original Caroline in his *Lilac Garden*, a signature work that Tudor approved for the Paris program. "That boy of yours was the first one who gave me a whole evening," he told Maude. Despite Tudor's notoriously prickly temperament and forbidding aura, he and Rudolf had grown fond of each other over the years, having spent many evenings together in New York with the Goslings and Tudor's lover, Hugh Laing.† On many of these occasions, Rudolf had tried to coax a new ballet from Tudor without success.

Ironically, the first major production to follow the Tudor program was Nureyev's *Washington Square*, a treatment of the Henry James novella about a young New York heiress stifled by her father and betrayed by the opportunistic suitor with whom she falls in love. In the 1970s, Tudor had been asked to turn this story into a ballet for Nureyev and Cynthia Gregory. The request had come from Oliver Smith, then codirector of American Ballet Theatre. When Tudor declined, Smith took the idea to Nureyev, who initially balked at tackling a script so ideally suited to Tudor, in the psychological complexity of its characters and the probing subtlety of its drama. In truth, though, Nureyev's abiding interest in exploring the psychology of his characters was not far removed from Tudor's own. And once an idea grabbed hold of him, he could not let it go. When he finally returned to the James story many years later, he

*Without naming the illness of which he was reputed to be dying.
†Tudor's affection remained constant. When, in the 1980s, Tudor was awarded the prestigious Kennedy Center Honor, he chose Nureyev to make the presentation. A scheduling problem made it necessary for Margot Fonteyn to replace him.

chose Charles Ives's *Holidays* Symphony as his score. His first attempt at an all-American ballet was replete with such well-worn images of American life as cowboys, marching bands, Union and Confederate sol diers, black minstrels and a corps of Statues of Liberty. Where Tudor's dance dramas used gesture and movement to delineate states of mind, Nureyev overloaded dramatic moments with too many steps, the ballet's theatricality and ideas simply overwhelming his choreography. When the ballet premiered in New York in July 1986, Nureyev, in the role of the father, was booed. "Seventy minutes of bombastic step-ridden choreography," charged Martha Duffy of *Time* magazine. Tudor attended the premiere and pronounced it "a rave," but Nureyev was never convinced that he meant it.

NOW THAT NUREYEV lived most of the year in Paris, his Quai Voltaire apartment was the closest he came to having a real home. At his London house he had merely "perched," said Lynn Seymour; in Paris, "he really dug in." But as Violette Verdy saw him, he was "never really at home anywhere. . . . As surrounded as he was by talented, fascinating, and important people, he was profoundly alone, and he knew it." He had grown reconciled to his solitude, he told a reporter. "A thing happens with age or experience: you learn to live with yourself. You can concentrate, you can read, you can do without this constant dialogue with the world outside." He continued to seek out casual sex, in parks, in bars, from ads in gay porn magazines. The prospect of an enduring attachment seemed less and less likely. At forty-seven, he was no longer the beautiful creature Margot Fonteyn had once described as a "a young lion." His face was drawn and weathered, his trademark shaggy hair thinning and combed far forward over his forehead to hide his receding hairline. When Princess Firyal begged him to comb it back, telling him he looked "like Napoleon with your hair like that," he replied, only partly in jest, "And what's wrong with that?" Increasingly, he felt old and overlooked; for the first time in his life his sexual allure began to fail him. "No one's interested in me anymore," he lamented one day to van Dantzig. "Even in love. I'm too old. They all walk past me. It's so degrading. With women, I can get what I want, but I don't want them. They drive me crazy."

For all his professed love of isolation, Nureyev was rarely alone. That autumn he took Maude with him on a tour to China, and he often had friends come to stay in Paris. Jane Hermann arrived that Christmas, Fonteyn soon after, and Maude and Lynn Seymour after her. Douce was a constant presence, ministering to his every need ("I'm there daily. One hundred and ten per cent for Rudolf"), disregarding the slights. She brought order to his life and "took care of money, meetings, everything," said Genya Polyakov. "Rudolf wanted her to be paid for the job, but she refused. So he could never be free from her. It was a dependency." And because she had "no other life," as Charles Jude puts it, she was free to go wherever Rudolf asked. She not only ran his Paris household but oversaw the renovation of his farm in Virginia, just as she had his Quai Voltaire apartment. "I ask him what he wants and he never gives me an answer," she grumbled one day. "When he finally sees what I've done, he's furious. If I don't do anything, he's also furious. He tells everyone that I've failed him, so you can't win." Rudolf "treated her awfully," says Rudi van Dantzig. But she was "afraid that someone else would take her place." When someone else briefly did—namely, Rudolf's new secretary, Marie-Suzanne Soubie—Douce was overcome with jealousy, her animosity toward Soubie palpable. She kept on hoping that Rudolf might marry her, undeterred by his homosexuality, even as she paid for the hustlers who came to his apartment. On formal occasions, such as the Rothschilds' annual Christmas fête and Opéra premieres, she would appear as his date. According to her friend Gilles Dufour, creative director for Chanel Studio, "she liked the idea that people were seeing her with him." His friends became her friends, and for the duration of Rudolf's life, she never had a steady boyfriend. As Michel Canesi saw her, Douce was "living under an illusion. It was a relationship that never existed except in her mind." The music publisher Mario Bois, who handled Rudolf's choreographic rights, brought along a friend to a dinner party Rudolf was hosting one night. Seeing that there were thirteen at the table, the superstitious Rudolf forced Douce to move to a small table by herself.

Rudolf continued to have many male friends. But his most devoted circle was composed almost entirely of women, a situation that increasingly baffled him, especially since he considered them inferior to men. Looking around him one day, he exclaimed to Seymour with mock despair, "Here I am, I'm supposed to *loathe* these fucking women and I'm surrounded by them." Women he looked to for comfort and understanding, men for sex and guidance. His intellectual mentors had always been male: Pushkin and Bruhn in dance, Gosling in culture, Nicholas Georgiadis and Jacob Rothschild in art and finance. "I am probably a male chauvinst pig," he acknowledged, "but I consider men to have a better organized brain and better able to separate themselves from nature and their own nature. Men respond to music better. They are the leaders in all the visual arts and in architecture. Men are better at the military; men are better cooks; men are better at everything. They also have the highest level of sensibility and sensitivity. And so it has to be. . . ."

His closest male friend in Paris was Charles Jude, who had been on the verge of leaving for American Ballet Theatre when Rudolf was named the Opéra's director. Bored at the Paris Opéra, he had yearned to travel. "With me, you will go abroad. Stay!" Rudolf ordered Jude, fifteen years his junior. Jude would not only travel extensively with

Rudolf but go on to dance the leading role in virtually every Nureyev ballet, his long-limbed elegance and silken technique recalling those of Erik Bruhn. While Rudolf set exacting standards for him, regularly studying him from the wings, privately he was affectingly gentle and shy with him. Whenever he wanted to invite Jude somewhere, he would never approach him directly, but would ask Jude's wife, Florence Clerc, to invite him.

Over the next several years, they got together regularly, sometimes at Rudolf's apartment, sometimes at the Judes' house near the Bastille, where they lived with their two young daughters, Caroline and Johanna, and two dogs. The warmth and vitality of the Jude home gave Rudolf something he never imagined he could have wanted, something he couldn't get from "his women" or from his young male lovers: a domestic family life with children. The scenario had always struck him as alien and daunting. But the more enmeshed he became in the Judes' life, the more convinced he became that he wanted to adopt the entire family. "He loved men and was always seeking them," recalls Clerc, "but there came a time when he seemed less and less interested in that lifestyle and more interested in ours."

When Rudolf invited them to live with him and asked Jude which region he preferred, Jude assumed he was joking and proposed Bordeaux. "Fine, we'll buy a château and all go and live there, you, me, Florence, the children and the dogs," Rudolf startled him by saying. A week later, Rudolf produced a brochure listing all the châteaus for sale in Bordeaux and asked Jude to choose one. Did the children want a swimming pool? he asked Florence. "He wanted Charles and me to become his family," she says, "but I wanted my family life to be a little apart. I don't think he understood why it was not possible."

Rudolf hoped to make it possible by having a child with them. "He said to me, 'We have to put our sperm together in a tube, mix it and then put it in Florence.'" The fantasy gripped him. Having accepted that Jude would never become his lover, he had come to view him as his spiritual son, the chief beneficiary of his artistic legacy. (Not long before his death, he made Jude a custodian of his ballets.) But with the sense of his mortality weighing on him, he also longed to pass on himself, to father his ideal self, as his choice of Jude suggests. In his fantasy, the product of their union is the perfect dancer, an ideal blend of the attributes he considered to be his and Jude's finest. "He wanted to have a boy, with my body and his head," Jude says.

Thoughts of posterity had nagged at him since the early 1980s, when he first began to seriously think of having a child. Leaning down to a friend's pregnant belly one night, he whispered, "Baby, will you remember me when I'm old and everybody's forgotten me?" As he grew older, he considered other candidates. Enamored of Nastassja Kinski's beauty, he told friends that he'd "love to have a child with her." Tessa Kennedy, he surmised, having had four handsome blond sons, would no doubt give him a beautiful blond son of his own. And then there was Douce, always there was Douce, who he knew longed to carry his child.

In 1987, his urge was serious enough that he took up the subject with his doctor. "Would it be a good idea for me to have babies?" he wondered. Canesi told him it was "impossible" because the risk of his passing on the AIDS virus was too great. "Okay, forget it," he said, though the regret lingered all the same.

RUDOLF TURNED forty-eight on March 17, 1986. He was hardly in a festive mood as he rallied from another bout of pneumonia to dance Béjart's *Songs of a Wayfarer* at the Vienna State Opera. Michael Birkmeyer, who saw him earlier in the day, thought he looked "terrible" and refused to attend the performance, a decision many of Rudolf's other colleagues had privately begun to make as well. Birkmeyer didn't know that Rudolf had just received some devastating news: Erik Bruhn was dying of lung cancer in a Toronto hospital. Bruhn was then fifty-eight and the director of the National Ballet of Canada, a post he had assumed the same year Rudolf became director in Paris. He had for many years lived with the dancer and choreographer Constantin Patsalas. He and Rudolf retained their hold on each other, though, despite the barbed comments that often flew between them. Bruhn had grown increasingly caustic with age. At dinner in Toronto one night with dancer Linda Maybarduk and her husband, a clearly inebriated Bruhn began listing the famous people he knew and the properties he owned. "It was embarrassing," says Maybarduk, recalling how Rudolf cut him short: "All your properties I could put in my apartment at the Dakota."

Bruhn had always suffered from poor health and ulcers and had long been a chain smoker; only a few months earlier, he and Glen Tetley had vowed to kick the habit together. In recent weeks he had been troubled by coughing. His friends were alarmed at how thin he'd become. Still, he had refused to call his doctor, just as his mother had done in her last days. By the time he went for X rays in early March, the cancer in his lungs had metastasized. He was hospitalized immediately.

The news that Bruhn was ill made Rudolf determined to see him as soon as he could. That night of his forty-eighth birthday, Rudolf joined a few old friends for dinner, among them Birkmeyer; Wilhelm Hübner, the president of the Vienna Philharmonic; and Hübner's Russian-speaking wife, Lydia, who with their children, "Vaxy" and Elisabeth, constituted Rudolf's Viennese "family." Ardent ballet fans, the Hübners had first befriended Rudolf in the early 1970s, during his frequent guest appearances with the Vienna Opera Ballet. By now, it was one of the few major European companies that still invited him to dance on a regular basis. (Four years earlier, he had been granted Austrian citizenship, helped by the company's director and the mayor of Vienna.) Concerned about Rudolf's health, having heard the AIDS rumors, Birkmeyer pulled him aside at one point to ask if they were true. "I am Tatar," Rudolf reminded him peremptorily. "AIDS is not going to fuck me, I'm going to fuck AIDS."

He had more immediate battles at hand. At the Paris Opéra the following week, he was forced into a showdown with guest choreographer Maurice Béjart. To thunderous approval of his two new ballets for the Opéra, Béjart walked onstage and, "hushing the house with a royal gesture," announced he was promoting Manuel Legris and Eric Vu An to the Opéra's highest rank. Only Nureyev had the authority to grant such honors, and no sooner had the curtain come down than Nureyev strode out and yelled, "Poisson d'Avril! [April Fool!]," making it clear to the dancers that he had not approved Béjart's power play. Manuel Legris was in tears at the confusion. "It was a big scandal," he says. "Béjart was a little bit in love with Eric [Vu An] and he wanted to do something special for him. He knew that Rudolf liked me as a dancer, so he figured 'perhaps if I make both étoiles . . .'" He had badly miscalculated. Immediately, a meeting of ministry officials was convened in André Larquié's office. Béjart failed to show. "Rudolf was there looking very pale," said Igor Eisner, the Ministry of Culture's Inspector general of dance. "Paul Piot, the former Opéra president, asked him how he was and Rudolf answered, 'Still alive.' It was an unbelievable trial for him, an affront."

This latest challenge to Nureyev's regime was rooted in personal grievance. Relations between him and Béjart had never been easy; "they had too much personality together," as one observer put it. According to Eisner, Béjart felt passed over when Nureyev became the new director in Paris. While Béjart headed the Brussels-based Ballet of the 20th Century, one of Europe's most popular troupes, Brussels was not Paris. Furthermore, he considered Nureyev an inferior choreographer and thought that the Opéra should be run by a French choreographer such as himself. Nureyev respected Béjart's ballets and wanted them for Paris. In 1985, over dinner at the Quai Voltaire, he invited Béjart to work with the company. Béjart promised a world premiere, The Miraculous Mandarin, to music by Béla Bartók, with Nureyev in the starring role. "It's a real present," a delighted Nureyev told Eisner. Two days later, Béjart changed his mind and decided on a comic homage to the Paris Opéra Ballet called Arépo, "opéra" spelled backward, which did not include Nureyev. By the time rehearsals were under way, Rudolf was on tour, and the atmosphere inside the Palais Garnier was, as Eisner recalled, "anti-Rudolf," which Béjart exploited. He chose Guillem to star in *Arépo* and told her that if she came to Brussels, he would make another ballet for her, "knowing that Rudolf would be annoyed if she left," recalls Elizabeth Cooper, Béjart's longtime principal pianist and a member of the *Arépo* cast. "Paris likes cabals and there was a desire in the company to see Béjart rise to the head of the ballet," said Eisner, recalling how Nureyev's productions and manner had at first been unpopular with many of the dancers. "Rehearsals had gone well and the dancers liked Béjart's choreography. They felt that Nureyev was too much of a dictator. 'Czar Rudolf,' they called him." Béjart went further, dubbing him "the Phantom of the Opéra."

The day of the premiere, Béjart hinted to Nureyev that he planned to nominate Vu An and Legris as étoiles. What Rudolf said is disputed by Béjart, but according to one well-placed source, a visibly irritated Rudolf told Béjart to do as he wished, by which he meant, "See if I care, don't bother me." Emboldened by the success of *Arépo*, Béjart claimed he had Nureyev's tacit approval.

Feeling betrayed, his professional life on the line, Nureyev called a press conference the next day to announce that he had not approved the two dancers' promotions. Béjart's response was to denounce him on French television and call for his resignation. In an attempt to whip up nationalistic fervor, he said: "I accuse Mr. Nureyev of having lied, of having deliberately organized this affair so that his name, absent from the evening, would be quoted in the press. . . . I am asking that an intruder get out. Au revoir, Mr. Nureyev." It was au revoir, Mr. Béjart, instead. Opéra officials stood by Nureyev and declared Béjart's action "an abuse of power," noting that the choreographer "appears to be going through a psychologically difficult period, where he mistakes desire for reality. . . ." Nureyev emerged with a surge of loyalty even from the dancers who had opposed him.

In the midst of what Eisner came to call "the little revolution that failed," Rudolf learned that Bruhn was rapidly deteriorating. "Once Erik knew he had cancer, he didn't seem to have any desire to live," recalls Valerie Wilder, a close associate in Toronto. He was always telling friends, "I'm going to die young and quick." "He was a controlling person and it seemed to me that he engineered his own death," says Wilder. "There were so many people who wanted to come to visit him, but Erik was private about his death and didn't want a lot of people around. He wanted to see Rudolf, though. And Rudolf seemed driven to come here."

Rudolf called Erik daily, frustrated at being detained in Paris. He vowed to fly over the minute he could get away. Bruhn was still well enough to "get a giggle out of the intrigues at the Opéra." But then he felt himself weakening, and still Rudolf hadn't come. "I hope he does get here," he said anxiously one day, convincing Wilder that he was "staying alive for him."

On Thursday, March 27, Rudolf took the Concorde to New York, flew to Toronto, and went immediately to Bruhn's bedside. The sight of Bruhn linked to tubes, his face wan and thin, must have been a cruel forecast. They talked late into the evening and Rudolf held him. Erik was visibly weak, and by the time Rudolf returned the next morning, Erik could no longer speak. He could only follow "Rudik" with his eyes. It was devastating to see Erik that way, Rudolf said afterward. He returned to New York later that day and Erik slipped into a coma. He died three days later, on April 1, April Fools' Day.*

Rudolf grieved privately and spoke little of Erik's death. It was a blow from which he never fully recovered. "It was awful," was all he could say to Baryshnikov the day he returned to New York. "It was a sad story, Erik's career," Baryshnikov observes today. "He was a much better dancer than Rudolf and he didn't have one-tenth the career.... He deserved much more credit. Ask any young dancer now, 'Who is Erik Bruhn?' and they will say, 'Yes, he was a dancer, but with whom? Where? Danish or American?'"

AT A PRESS CONFERENCE the day before Bruhn died, Nureyev and Baryshnikov announced their intention to appear together, along with their respective companies, in a joint gala at the Metropolitan Opera House to be held that July. The Paris Opéra had last performed in New York in 1948 to disastrous reviews. Nureyev's renown and leadership were to bring the thirty-eight-year hiatus to an end, an ironic turn of events considering that the company's 1980 tour had been canceled on his account.

The 1986 American tour was a personal triumph for Nureyev and a critical and commercial triumph for the Paris Opéra Ballet. It was now widely acknowledged that the Russian had infused vitality into the moribund company and restored it to international significance. Clive Barnes called the company "simply amazing.... Such brilliance and finesse is all the more remarkable because it is not so long ago that the Paris Opéra

*The fact that Bruhn died so quickly and under such secretive circumstances prompted speculation as to whether his death might have been AIDS-related. The death of his lover, Patsalas Constantin, from AIDS a couple of years later confirmed the rumor in the minds of many. Bruhn's close friends remain unconvinced. His X rays revealed lung cancer, they say, and his doctors looked no further. Not long after Bruhn's death, Patsalas developed dementia, an AIDS-related symptom, and grew increasingly paranoid. He was then living in Bruhn's apartment, and on several occasions Bruhn's friend Joanne Nisbet, his neighbor and the ballet mistress of the National Ballet of Canada, saw Patsalas at the building's incinerator, disposing of Bruhn's possessions. Many of his papers and costumes are thought to have disappeared in this way.

Ballet was, despite its occasional good dancer, virtually the laughing stock of the civilized dance world."

The dancing was given a far more enthusiastic reception than the dances, which, when choreographed by Nureyev, were pretty much dismissed by the critics. "A choreographer of staggering incompetence," sniped Arlene Croce of his *Raymonda*, *Swan Lake* and *Washington Square*. But audiences were captivated by the Paris dancers, especially by the glamorous Guillem, the revelation of the season, and even Nureyev came in for some admiring reviews for his dancing. Still, in Rudolf's view, balletgoing had lost the excitement it had known in the days when he and Fonteyn had made every performance an occasion. Ensemble unity had taken precedence over star power, he lamented in *The New York Times*. The public still filled the seats, he said, "but you don't have an event."

A celebrity-packed Franco-American gala launched the Parisians' return to the Met. Steven Spielberg, Liza Minnelli and First Lady Nancy Reagan were among the black-tie patrons who paid a thousand dollars for their tickets. Gene Kelly served as host, while Guillem and Patrick Dupond brought the house down with their pas de deux from *Le Corsaire*, just as Fonteyn and Nureyev had twenty-four years earlier. Nureyev and Baryshnikov also put in appearances, in one number escorting Leslie Caron through a nostalgic medley of her movie musicals, including *An American in Paris*. But perhaps the most symbolic event for Nureyev occurred on the first night of his *Raymonda* when, after all the drama of the Béjart affair, he came onstage to announce Manuel Legris's promotion to *étoile*, the first time the honor had been bestowed outside Paris.

During the company's stopover in Washington, D.C., Nureyev invited a number of the dancers to his two-hundred-year-old farm in nearby Woodburn, in the famous Hunt Country of Virginia. He took childlike pleasure in playing gentleman farmer, hosting a barbecue, and showing off his 421-acre property, with its pine grove, pond, stream, brick barn, smokehouse, stables and thirteen-room red-brick Georgian manor house, built in 1790. One afternoon he gave Sylvie Guillem a tour on the back of his new three-wheel, all-terrain motorbike. The farm was his American arcadia. He spoke of plans to restore its historic gristmill and waterwheel and to create a lily pond. In the nineteenth-century barn, he planned one day to teach master classes to gifted dance students. The main house had barely any furniture, but already he had purchased a massive pipe organ from a local church. The organ filled an entire room and Douce's brother had to knock down a wall to install it. Nightly, the music of Bach could be heard along this isolated stretch of country road, Harmony Church Road, as it happened to be called.

In August, Rudolf chartered his own boat for the first time and brought together friends from disparate parts of his life for a two-week cruise off the southern coast of Turkey. Maude came from London, Wallace Potts from Los Angeles, Douce, Robert Tracy and Michel Canesi from Paris. Only the men were aware of his HIV status. Canesi was nervous about spending two weeks in close quarters with such a mix of personalities. But he knew that Rudolf needed to be surrounded by friends and knew, too, that he enjoyed a certain amount of friction, creative and otherwise. Rudolf and Wallace had remained close, though they rarely saw each other. Everywhere they went, Rudolf looked for a house to buy. Turkey reminded him of Ufa, Maude told Canesi: "the colors, the designs, the way people lived."

RUDOLF HAD COME to believe that he would never again see his mother. "It is one of the greatest disappointments in my life," he told a reporter the following summer. "I have tried many times to convince the authorities that it is only humane to allow a mother to be with her son. . . . If maybe she were Jewish they would gain some political advantage in allowing her to leave. But that is not the case, so she must stay."

Since she could not come to him, he would try to go to her. He pressed every French official he knew into helping him secure a visa. Culture Minister Jack Lang and Opéra president André Larquié had taken steps to arrange such a visit through talks with the Soviet embassy in Paris and the French embassy in Moscow. But under Kremlin leaders Yuri Andropov and Konstantin Chernenko, the authorities were not inclined to show consideration to traitors who needed to return home for family emergencies. Just how resistant they still were to his presence was reinforced when Jamie Wyeth was instructed to remove his paintings of Nureyev from a major Wyeth family exhibition scheduled to tour Moscow and Leningrad in March 1987.

But in November 1987, Rudolf received a call from his sister Razida and knew that he had to return home immediately. His mother was gravely ill. With no time for diplomatic wrangling, he telephoned Roch-Olivier Maistre, a French cultural official, at home. Encouraged by Mikhail Gorbachev's new policy of glasnost, the Ministry of Culture was then engaged in talks with the Soviets about a visit by the Paris Opéra Ballet. Delighted by the company's great success in America under Nureyev, Culture Minister François Léotard (Lang's successor) saw enormous public relations value in sending the company to the Soviet Union — particularly with Nureyev returning to his homeland for the first time since his defection in 1961.* He "absolutely had to go at once,"

---

*Ironically, the Soviets had also seen his public relations value prior to the historic Kirov tour to Paris in 1961.

Rudolf now informed Maistre. "So we put this trip together rather quickly," Maistre recalls, "in incredible circumstances."

Those circumstances were unprecedented: The Soviets granted Nureyev a forty-eight-hour visa, allowing him just one night in Ufa with his mother. And yet now that he had finally won permission to return home, after an absence of twenty-six years, he was terrified that once in, he would never be allowed out. The seven-year prison term to which he had been sentenced following his defection was still standing. Although he knew of Gorbachev's reforms, his view of Soviet politics remained fixed in 1961. "He could see things only as they were when he left," says Maistre. "He was afraid they would grab him."* "I might end up in Siberia," he told Maistre one day.

To ensure his protection, Maistre, in his role as government chaperon, was to accompany him to Ufa, as was Jeanine Ringuit, a Russian-speaking impresario whom Rudolf had met in his first days in Paris with the Kirov. Rudolf was not about to take any chances, however, and not only announced his trip to the press but called Jacqueline Onassis before he left Paris. Would she rescue him if he were arrested? She assured him that she would.

Despite all his years of travel, he had never lost his terror of flying, and during takeoff, he curled up in a ball in his seat, clutching a pillow. As the plane approached Moscow, he was equally fearful of what awaited him there. "He had a lot of anxiety," recalls Maistre, who sat next to him. "He had left the country with certain memories and he knew he was about to confront a new reality. There were also fears about his family. How would a reunion with them come off? What kind of welcome would he get in Russia?"†

A fleet of reporters and autograph seekers were on hand to greet him inside Sheremyetevo Airport on Saturday, November 14. As the snow fell outside, he stood backlit by television lights, dapper in a green beret, herringbone overcoat and patterned Missoni scarf. No mention of his return had been made in the Soviet press, but word had leaked out.

What was his opinion of Gorbachev? he was asked. The decidedly apolitical Nureyev gave an uncharacteristically measured reply. "I would rather have him at the head of government than someone else," he said, paraphrasing Joseph Brodsky, the émigré Soviet poet and Nobel laureate.

*In February 1986, Baryshnikov had been invited to come to a conference and gala at the Bolshoi Theater and to dance there. But he declined after his proposal to bring ABT to the Bolshoi Theater was rejected.

†The day he flew to Moscow, Luigi Pignotti ran into Rostropovich in a restaurant in Milan. "How's Rudinka?" he asked Pignotti, one of the few people to know about Rudolf's trip. "He's on his way to Ufa," Luigi told him, though Rostropovich refused to believe it. "It's not possible. No, no, no, no! Not possible."

Would he dance again at the Kirov? "Whatever is left in me of dancing, yes, I would love to show it here."

Standing among the well-wishers, avoiding the flashing bulbs, was Liuba Romankova,* one of only two faces familiar to Rudolf. He had alerted her to his arrival and she had promised to come from Leningrad, bringing along her twin brother, Leonid. True, they were all older now, and Liuba wore glasses that pinched her nose and gave her a studious, birdlike air. But to her, Rudolf had not changed, "except that he walked more slowly and looked more stately. He even boasted, saying, 'Look, I still have all my teeth and I don't wear glasses.' " Fearful as ever of the KGB, she made sure to drop her gloves whenever a reporter's camera lens was pointed in her direction. "Don't you want to share in my glory?" Rudolf asked her. "No, Rudik," she answered, "this glory will cost me a lot. The KGB has a vigilant eye." She worried that she might be fired from the esteemed Ioffe Physics Institute were it discovered that she had left work to greet Nureyev's plane.

His flight to Ufa wasn't to leave until later that night, so Rudolf went into Moscow for a walk around Red Square. There he exuded a sense of "deep happiness," recalls Maistre. Ironically, it was only the American and European tourists, not the Soviets, who recognized him. Before heading off to dinner at the French embassy, Rudolf visited with Liuba and Leonid at the apartment of a friend of theirs, in the outskirts of the city. For Liuba it was an afternoon of animated conversation between old friends. But Roch-Olivier Maistre was struck by how out of place Rudolf seemed. "Of course Rudolf was very happy to see his friends and there was such warmth. But there was something paradoxical about seeing an incredible personality like Nureyev, with the kind of lifestyle he could afford, in a cheap, tiny Muscovite apartment which barely had electricity and running water."

Aeroflot Flight BL 339 to Ufa was crowded and choppy. The seats were tattered, many of them crammed with suitcases and cartons. Unlatched tray tables flapped disconcertingly during takeoff. Rudolf was "dumbfounded" at the state of the plane and fretted for most of the 105-minute flight. When the plane touched down at 2:05 A.M., Ufa was blanketed in snow and Rudolf was remembering his past. He used to wear homemade skates to school, he told Maistre and Ringuit. "I would hang on to passing cars for a ride on the ice." Maistre saw at once that he was "apprehensive, but at the same time expressed a certain excitement that something marvelous was happening."

To Rudolf's surprise, his family had gathered inside the Intourist VIP lounge to meet him. Smiling broadly, he rushed to embrace his sister Razida, who held out a tiny bouquet of red carnations. The expen-

*Her married name was Liuba Myasnikova.

sive roses she had purchased earlier in the day had perished in the sub-zero temperatures. The others were virtual strangers, as Rudolf and Razida had been to their father when Hamet returned home from the war. He was introduced to Razida's sons, Viktor, twenty-five, and Yuri, eighteen, and to his niece Alfia, Lilya's daughter. She had been barely a year old when he had brought her a wagon from East Germany on his last visit home in 1961. Now Alfia had a child of her own, a six-year-old son named Ruslan. While she had imagined what her famous uncle might look like, based on the childhood photographs she'd seen, she felt awkward and tongue-tied once they were face-to-face. Nervous about his visit, she had scoured Ufa for the butter she was sure he would want for his toast and had rewallpapered her living room with Razida's help.

At fifty-two, Razida was just three years older than Rudolf but looked at least a decade older, with graying hair, lined brow and harsh, rasping voice. Given the late hour, Razida drove Rudolf and his escorts to the Rossiya (Russian) Hotel, a cheerless building in downtown Ufa facing a giant statue of Lenin. As in the old days, a key matron kept watch on each floor.

At 9 A.M. Razida came to take Rudolf to see their mother, who, following a stroke, was paralyzed, bedridden and nearly blind. Farida lived in a four-story white-brick apartment block near October Prospect, a five-minute drive from his hotel, in the same cramped tenement flat that Hamet had proudly written to Rudolf about the year Rudolf defected. Now she shared the two rooms with her daughter Lilya, her granddaughter Alfia, Alfia's husband, Oleg, and their young son. Farida and Lilya occupied the only bedroom. With Lilya virtually paralyzed as well, having failed to recover from her hit-and-run accident, Alfia was burdened with the care of her mother, a deaf-mute, and her grandmother. Razida had her own family to care for.

Alfia led Rudolf into Farida's room, where she lay in a semiconscious state. Rudolf was shocked at how ill and frail she looked, so far from the daunting figure he remembered. She had lost her voice, and though she could sometimes muster a faint whisper, they had learned to read her lips. She stared at Rudolf, trying to place him. Rudolf saw her lips move, but she did not make a sound. "Is he real?" she asked Alfia. Rudolf wanted to know what she had said, so Alfia told him. "She thought she was hallucinating," Alfia recalls. Rudolf was devastated. He had never expected that they would not be able to speak to each other. Alfia left him alone with her. When he emerged one hour later, he was disconsolate. "Can you believe it? She didn't recognize me."

Razida rushed to Farida's bedside. "Do you know who that was, Mama? Did you recognize him?" "Yes, it was Rudik," she whispered. "I could recognize the movement of her lips," recalls Razida, "but he was so distressed, he didn't believe me when I told him what she said."

Lilya was also gravely ill and disoriented, but she knew her brother at once. The moment he patted her on the shoulder, she turned to Alfia and, beaming, mouthed, "Rudik, Rudik." Seeing how enraptured she was, Rudolf kissed her. A pall hung over their reunion nonetheless, and Rudolf stayed only to share a glass of vodka and eat buttered toast, forgoing the banquet Alfia had prepared. Despite their joy at being reunited, "we all felt a bit awkward," admits Razida, who introduced him to her husband, Boris. "It was difficult to start a conversation. We didn't know what to say."

Rudolf went off to visit the places of his childhood, but the tour did little to relieve his despair. A photographer from the Russian news agency Tass had been hired to record his visit. Since Rudolf did not allow him inside his mother's flat, the photographer offered to take him around to his old haunts. Rudolf agreed, and Razida, his nephew Yuri, and his great-nephew, Ruslan, joined them. He wanted to visit his father's grave, but the Muslim cemetery was buried beneath four feet of snow and his way was blocked. His first stop was the Ufa Opera House. Because it was Sunday, the artists had the day off and no one there recognized him. He tried calling Zaitouna Nazretdinova, the ballerina who had so captivated him on his first outing to the ballet. But since the Soviets had insisted that his trip happen quietly, none of his former colleagues knew he was there, and he failed to find any of them. His old home on Zentsov Street had been knocked down and replaced by another soulless apartment block, and he barely recognized the landscape, much of it overtaken by industrial sprawl. Passing a row of old wooden houses, he remarked, "Yes, that's the Ufa I remember," but there was little else that remained. The school that he and Albert had attended was now a dance school and also closed; at the Nesterov Museum, the security guard shouted when the photographer tried to take Nureyev's picture. She, like most of Ufa's citizens, attached no special meaning to the name Rudolf Nureyev.

On the flight back to Moscow, Rudolf was withdrawn, his disappointment palpable to his French escorts. Liuba and Leonid were waiting for him at Domodedovo Airport, Moscow's domestic airport, a grim, backward place that Rudolf deplored. He needed a stiff drink, he told them as they drove into Moscow, and then talked to them for hours, with a degree of candor that took them both by surprise. Liuba was "amazed at all the emotion he had kept hidden from us all these years. He told us how he'd been afraid to open his mouth for fear of exhibiting his provinciality and how he had desperately tried to make up for his lack of a proper education. . . ." Despite all that he had read and seen and learned in the West, he lamented, he would "never have anything more than individual snippets of information. I'll never have a complete education."

* * *

FARIDA DIED of a stroke three months after their reunion, on February 5, 1988.* Unaware of her death, Rudolf lunched with Wallace Potts and Natasha Harley at La Côte Basque, one of New York's most elegant restaurants. Before dropping Rudolf off at the Dakota, Harley shopped for antiques with him along Madison Avenue. She arrived home to an urgent call from his niece Gouzel in Paris, informing her of Farida's death. She immediately invited Rudolf to dinner at her apartment on East Sixty-eighth Street. But when the bell rang one hour later, it was Baryshnikov who stood at her door. Rudolf had just called him, he said. Could he help her prepare dinner? The two men reminisced late into the night, about Pushkin and Xenia and their lives in Leningrad. Harley kept bringing bottles of champagne, pleased to see Rudolf "laughing at memories." At Rudolf's invitation, the Bolshoi dancers Nina Ananiashvili and Andris Liepa also stopped in. The pair were preparing to make their debut with the New York City Ballet, having long wanted to dance Balanchine. They were among the first Russian dancers given leave to appear with a Western company. With glasnost easing Cold War tensions, Soviet dancers no longer had to renounce their homeland to expand their creative horizons.

*His sister Lilya died of a brain hemorrhage soon after.

29

Songs of a Wayfarer

NUREYEV'S VICTORY over Béjart, coupled with the Paris Opéra's acclaimed 1986 American tour, ushered in the first, and only, period of détente with his dancers. Nureyev solidified that relationship with his lavish new production of *Cinderella*, which premiered on October 24, 1986. A vehicle for Sylvie Guillem and Nureyev's first major hit with French audiences, the ballet was considered, as René Sirvin wrote in *Le Figaro*, "a triumph—the word is not too strong." It showed off the company's strengths, its panache, precision and attack, and confirmed the star power of Guillem, to whom all of Paris was in thrall.

Nureyev had at first resisted designer Petrika Ionesco's suggestion to set the ballet in a movie studio but found that he "couldn't think to do it any other way." He would later say that he had tailored his conception to French tastes ("I gave them what they wanted"), although his half-million-dollar production clearly reflects his own love affair with Hollywood glamour and American pop culture. Based on the popular nineteenth-century French version of the fairy tale, Nureyev's *Cinderella*, to Prokofiev's music, reset the scene to the Hollywood dream factory of the 1930s.

In Nureyev's version, Cinderella is the mistreated stepdaughter of an ambitious stage mother, who has big plans to push her own two daughters into the movies. The Prince is the studio's matinee idol, while the fairy godmother is a cigar-chomping producer mogul, the star maker of the scenario and, fittingly, the role Nureyev assigned himself.* His ballet is replete with the film lore he had gleaned over many years,

*Michael Denard danced the role on opening night.

beginning with his "Roxy nights" at the Goslings'. Cinderella dances dreamily with a hatstand, emulating Fred Astaire's famous dance with a broom. Instead of a ball, she attends a screen test, making her entrance under the glare of the paparazzi's flashing bulbs. The sound stage of Act 2 brings references to Betty Grable, Buster Keaton, King Kong and, in the comic solo Nureyev devised for himself, Groucho Marx, complete with mustache and glasses. (Some contend that he danced the role as a parody of Sander Gorlinsky.) He also inserted slapstick Chaplinesque routines, a tribute to his favorite film star. (There are "three things that cheer me up," he once said: Bach "in any form," Shakespeare, and Charlie Chaplin, "any time day or night.") Naturally the ballet ends happily ever after, which, in Nureyev's terms, means that Cinderella and her Prince have their final pas de deux perfectly recorded for posterity by an onstage film crew. This Cinderella wins not only her leading man, but a film contract and, with it, the promise of stardom and immortal fame.

HOWEVER WILLING Nureyev was to play a supporting character role in his own creations, he was hardly willing to cede the spotlight altogether. From 1987 to 1989, he bowed to pressures from the Opéra not to dance as often as he wanted. He continued to nourish his unique appetite for performance, however, and sold out other theaters despite largely unflattering reviews. "The only critic is a full house," he liked to say, having revised his earlier statement that "the only critic is yourself." Despite what many mistook for denial, Nureyev was never less than clear-eyed about his capabilities. That didn't stop him from striving to exceed them or from growing testy when praise was not forthcoming. After performances, there were always well-wishers backstage, telling him how wonderful he had been. "But sometimes he was asking me, 'How was it?' " said Luigi Pignotti. "A few times I didn't answer because I have to say truth. I cannot lie to Rudolf. So I shut up. So he said . . . 'So the performance was no good.' I said, 'It was a performance, Rudolf, but you've done better.' And he said, 'Fine, okay. That's it.' But many people lied to him until the end. . . ."

It was because his youth had once blazed so irresistibly that audiences were loath to acknowledge his physical decline. For in his, of course, lay their own. He could still turn in an astonishingly theatrical performance, at once profound and poetic, but his line, jump and speed were gone. And yet, having ignored the laws of retirement for men, the best of whom rarely went on past the age of forty, Nureyev, at forty-nine, felt he still had much to offer. "Even if there was egg on his face, he wasn't going to get off while he had breath," says Lynn Seymour. Rather than compete with their former selves, many older dancers chose to bypass the traditional full-length classics in favor of more dramatic, less technically exacting roles. Nureyev, however, had always danced against crippling odds, drawing strength from challenge. He continued to dance his most arduous classical roles, as Dudinskaya and Fonteyn had done well into their fifties. But women generally have longer careers in dance, in part because their spines don't suffer the stress that comes from lifting another body. Rudolf couldn't help being aware that ballet belonged to the young. After all, it was because Sergeyev had insisted on performing past his prime that the twenty-three-year-old Nureyev had been invited to replace him on the tour to Paris. Yet as late as 1989, when he was fifty-one, the same age Sergeyev had been on that first Kirov tour, Nureyev's repertory still included *Giselle, Swan Lake* and *La Sylphide*. Trusted colleagues like Genya Polyakov begged him to change his repertory, to ease into more mature character roles. "We spoke about *The Brothers Karamazov, King Lear* and *Richard III*, perhaps some Chekhov pieces. He wouldn't listen. I tried to get him not to always do double pirouettes like the young men, but he would say, 'If I don't do it, I will lose it.' He had a desire; he realized his desire. No weakness. Crippled or wrapped in bandages, he went onstage. It was the spirit before the body."

Nowhere was this more evident than during a February 1987 performance of his *Don Quixote* at La Scala Opera House. Patricia Neary, the newly installed director, had invited him to dance with Sylvie Guillem. He could barely make it through rehearsal, she says; a series of pirouettes would leave him so winded that he would have to sit down. "How are you going to do this?" she asked. "Don't worry how I'm going to do this!" came his indignant reply. For the first two acts, Guillem was pretty much on her own. But somehow, in the last act, Nureyev tapped some hidden reserve and brought the house down. "People went insane," says Neary. "He was fighting everything, but still he was doing it."

He was also still doing his Nijinsky roles with the Ballet de Nancy in August 1987, prompting Clive Barnes to write of his *Spectre de la Rose* that "his appearance has by now become an embarrassment." The ballet disappeared from his repertory soon after. For those who knew, or suspected, that he was HIV-positive, it was, as Baryshnikov later said, "perfectly understandable" why he needed to be onstage: "It was a death to be offstage. No matter how he was dancing. . . ." Nureyev's silence about his illness would later inflame controversy in gay circles. However, Nureyev had never been a political warrior and, in any event, believed that he could overcome his illness if he fought hard enough. To talk about it would be to indulge in self-pity and court defeat.

Nevertheless, the AIDS rumors shadowed him in America, where journalists pursued a more aggressive line of inquiry. His privacy violated, Nureyev was quick to resort to his Tatar armor, his ready defense to keep the world at bay. "Obviously it's wrong so why do we have to chew it?"

he snapped at Lewis Segal of the *Los Angeles Times.* "I'm alive. I'm very well. I don't have any AIDS . . . they say this has AIDS, that has AIDS — now it's in fashion to have AIDS."

However impolitic his reply, in truth, he was anxious about his health by the winter of 1987. When Wallace Potts told him about a new antiviral drug called AZT, introduced in America in May of that year, Rudolf demanded that Michel Canesi prescribe it for him. Canesi hesitated. AZT was just begining to be used in France and given the high doses then being administered (twelve hundred milligrams compared to the five hundred generally given today), he worried that the side effects would interfere with Rudolf's dancing. While its merits remain controversial, AZT was shown to slow the replication of the AIDS virus. In America, Rudolf knew of people who were put on the drug when their T cell counts fell below 500.* In France, however, doctors were starting their HIV patients on AZT only after their counts fell below 250. As Rudolf's counts were not yet that low, Canesi thought it imprudent to give him a drug about which he knew so little. "He was furious at me when I said no. This was the first of two fights we had." Eventually, Canesi gave in because "I was afraid that people would reproach me someday for not having given it to him." Nureyev's pill taking, though, was haphazard at best. "He went off every time with tons of drugs, and every time I went to see him I found unused packets all over the place."

He was fastidious, however, where his Opéra colleagues were concerned. Once during rehearsal, a ballerina's hairpin pricked his cheek and ballet mistress Patricia Ruanne instinctively wiped the drop of blood from his face. "Can you come to my dressing room?" he asked her. "I presumed he wanted me to do something for him. When I got there, he said, 'Pat, wash your hands, please.' I started to say something, and he just said, 'Don't talk.'" His insistence struck her as odd at the time.

AS HE GREW OLDER, Nureyev found it harder to shake the indignities visited on him. Every slight, whether real or imagined, only served to deepen his abiding suspicion and fierce code of loyalty. In October 1987, he joined Baryshnikov in a benefit performance for the Martha Graham Company at New York's City Center. The gala also included the legendary Bolshoi prima Maya Plisetskaya, who made a historic appearance with the two defectors, a further sign of the changing climate. Nureyev and Baryshnikov both danced in *Appalachian Spring*, with Nureyev cast as the mercurial Revivalist and Baryshnikov as the husbandman. Rudolf had long wanted *Appalachian Spring* for the Paris Opéra Ballet and had

*T cells are white blood cells that are key components of the immune system. A normal count runs anywhere from 500 to 1,000.

pressed Graham to give it to the company, but she resisted. Of all her works, it was the one closest to her heart: Aaron Copland had composed the music for her and she had first danced it with her then husband, Erick Hawkins. Furthermore, she wasn't convinced the French could dance it with the appropriate American accent.

A gala supper followed at the Hotel Pierre, where Nureyev and Baryshnikov were seated on either side of Graham. Shortly into the dinner, however, Graham was moved to Halston's table, and Rudolf found himself sandwiched between the arts patron Alice Tully and Lee Traub, whose husband was chairman of Bloomingdale's. Rudolf sat there simmering. Not only was he angry at the delays over *Appalachian Spring*, he resented what appeared to him to be the company's courting of Baryshnikov. During his twelve-year association with the Graham troupe he had never asked for a fee, and he now felt neglected, slighted and unappreciated.

According to Graham's then associate director, Ron Protas, Graham had intended to surprise him that night by giving him *Appalachian Spring*. She felt torn about the decision but had decided that Rudolf should have it as thanks for all he had done for her company. "Martha asked me to move her," claims Protas. "She said, 'Darling, could I sit next to Halston? Rudolf doesn't talk to me.' So I moved her and then all hell broke loose." Marching over to Protas's table, Rudolf emptied a glass of water on his head. "You are an ungrateful hypocrite," he scoffed, and then retrieved his guests Jessye Norman, Judy Peabody and Robert Tracy. As Rudolf led them out, Protas shouted after Tracy, "I'll never give Rudolf *Appalachian Spring*!"

Nureyev never would win *Appalachian Spring* for the Paris Opéra Ballet. Graham was so chagrined by his outburst, with its implication of disloyalty and dishonesty, that she, or possibly she and Protas,* dispatched a letter the next day to the society writer Aileen Mehle (aka Suzy), in whose *New York Post* column it ran. Nureyev was "facing a tragic moment for a dancer," Graham wrote, "for he, as I did, only wanted to dance. The turmoil he expressed by striking out at me during the supper and at Ron came from this, more than anything."[†]

Whatever Graham's role in the events and what followed, Rudolf blamed Protas for having engineered them; it was widely known that she didn't make a move without conferring with him. In time she came to miss Rudolf, and would speak of him "with great fondness," says Protas,

---

*"I do remember thinking at the time, 'Is this a Ron Protas creation, a Martha, or is it a joint effort?'" recalls Aileen Mehle. "My thought now would be that it was a joint effort."
†Graham was apparently so distressed by his treatment of Protas that in her letter, she denied that she had ever intended to give him the ballet, which, according to Protas, she knew wasn't true.

recounting how two years before her death, the arthritic Graham struggled to write Rudolf a personal note. Her hands had become so gnarled that she could hold a pen only by forcing it under her right knuckle with her left hand. Still, according to Protas, she doggedly struggled through five drafts, fearing "that Rudolf wouldn't think it came from her unless she did." Graham never received a reply to her letter, though it is not known whether Rudolf ever saw it. The two never spoke again.

NUREYEV TURNED FIFTY in 1988 and the world's leading ballet companies rushed to honor him, finally tendering once again the invitations they had long withheld. The ballet world was looking back, wanting to honor him for all that he had achieved. Rudolf, however, continued to look ahead at all he wanted to do. When the Royal Ballet invited him to perform *Giselle* in London in January, he was asked which of its ballerinas he wanted to partner. Still hurt by what he saw as his banishment from the Royal once Fonteyn retired, he determined to show London what he had accomplished in Paris and decided to present Sylvie Guillem in her Covent Garden debut.* *Giselle* was the first ballet he and Fonteyn had danced together in 1962. Now he was seven years older than Fonteyn had been at their debut, while the twenty-three-year-old Guillem was the same age Rudolf had been at the time.

With the exception of Clement Crisp's calling him "an icon of romantic fervour," Nureyev's reviews were far from adulatory, and the night belonged chiefly to Guillem, whose virtuosity charmed the house. At their curtain call, Rudolf nudged her forward like a proud parent and afterward stood alongside her at the stage door, signing autographs.

To celebrate his birthday on March 17, Baryshnikov invited him to dance *Giselle* with American Ballet Theatre in Los Angeles. Though still mourning the death of his mother the previous month, Rudolf appeared in high spirits. That evening Herbert Ross and Lee Radziwill gave a candlelit dinner party for him at Ross's home.† The guests, all old friends, included Baryshnikov, Douce, Wallace, Armen Bali's daughter Jeannette Etheredge and John Taras, who gave Rudolf the new biography of Balanchine he had written with Richard Buckle. After dinner Rudolf mugged for Taras's camera, playfully sticking a floral wreath on his head as he struck a Dionysian pose.

---

*In 1986, Anthony Dowell, one of the Royal Ballet's greatest stars, had been named artistic director of the company.

†The pair would marry quietly in September at Radziwill's apartment, with Rudolf, the bride's sister, Jacqueline Onassis and a handful of friends and family members in attendance, including Caroline Kennedy Schlossberg, John F. Kennedy Jr., Steve Martin, Bernadette Peters and John Taras. After the ceremony, Jacqueline Onassis hosted a dinner party for the couple at her Fifth Avenue apartment.

In a year rife with tributes, the most unlikely came from the one company that had rejected Nureyev all his days in the West. Coincidentally, on the twenty-seventh anniversary of his defection, Nureyev made his debut with the New York City Ballet at the New York State Theater, the house that Balanchine built. At the invitation of Peter Martins, now Balanchine's successor as director, Nureyev danced with Merrill Ashley in the Balanchine-Stravinsky masterwork *Orpheus*, a role he had never performed. Marked by its subtlety and sculptural movement style, the ballet recounts the Greek myth in which the poet-musician Orpheus tries to retrieve his wife, Eurydice, from Hades. Knowing how badly Rudolf had wanted to dance with the company, Martins hoped not only to give him "that experience" but to give the students of the company-affiliated School of American Ballet the chance to experience Nureyev's artistry up close in a Balanchine ballet. The role of Orpheus demanded more stage presence than dancing, which proved something of a sticking point when Martins tendered his invitation. Nureyev wanted to dance Apollo, one of Martins's signature roles. Martins said no, although he was aware that Nureyev was still dancing the role with his Friends group. "I'm not good enough for Apollo? Not as good as you?" Rudolf challenged him. "That's not the problem," replied Martins, who had retired from dancing at the age of thirty-seven. "I think you're too old. But I think you'd be beautiful in *Orpheus*." Rudolf kept insisting on *Apollo* but in the end relented. Coached by Martins and John Taras, Rudolf "worked very hard," says Martins, "and was very good in it."

That same month the most glamorous names in ballet saluted him in a lavish birthday gala at the Metropolitan Opera House, timed to coincide with the Paris Opéra Ballet's third consecutive New York season. Devised by Jane Hermann, "Nureyev: A Celebration" was, as Clive Barnes wrote afterward, "a lovely, heart-warming occasion: an outpouring of affection for the world's favorite dancer" that was not without its share of pomp and ceremony. Michelle Rocard, the wife of France's Prime Minister, bowed to Nureyev from a center box while New York Mayor Ed Koch presented him with a Tiffany Crystal Apple, an honor reserved for distinguished guests of the city. And the entire Paris Opéra Ballet, together with students from its school, marched in the grand défilé, a regal processional never before presented outside the Paris Opéra. The French dancers advanced to center stage according to rank, beginning with the youngest pupils of the Paris Opéra Ballet school and ending with the stars of the company. They were followed by an august parade of Nureyev's peers, partners and choreographers, among them Mikhail Baryshnikov, Peter Martins, Peter Schaufuss, Maria Tallchief, Carla Fracci, Yvette Chauviré, Karen Kain, Cynthia Gregory, John Taras, Violette Verdy, Rudi van Dantzig, Murray Louis and, surprisingly, Lincoln Kirstein. The entire audience jumped to its feet, screaming, when Margot Fonteyn arrived to crown the processional. Seen on a New York stage for the first time in seven years, her hair now gray, she looked regally elegant in a multicolored gown. As Nureyev kissed her and led her to center stage, red, white and blue confetti and balloons rained down on them. During his solo bow, a huge banner emblazoned with "Nureyev" unfurled from the ceiling, prompting a surge of approval from the audience and a boyish, exultant smile from Rudolf.

Although the Paris dancers performed three of the four works that evening, Nureyev struck the most poignant note with his richly nuanced performance of a man railing against his destiny in *Songs of a Wayfarer*, the duet Maurice Béjart had created for him seventeen years earlier. To songs by Mahler, sung on this occasion by Jessye Norman, Nureyev danced opposite Charles Jude's figure of fate, echoing his protégé's steps as fate leads the wayfarer toward death. The ballet was singularly important to Rudolf, Jude recalls. "The wanderer wants everything to be perfect, to be great, but there is always this shadow behind him, holding him back. This was Rudolf." In the ballet's final moment, Nureyev disappears into the darkness, a man reconciled to his fate. Or so it appeared to the audience. When Jane Hermann congratulated him backstage afterward and remarked on how wonderful the evening had been, Rudolf looked at her slyly and, without thanking her, said, "You're just trying to get me to retire."

30

Like Nikiya in Bayadère

ON FEBRUARY 21, 1989, Sylvie Guillem defected from the Paris Opéra Ballet, the opening blow in what would prove Nureyev's *annus horribilis*. The news that Guillem had been lured to London to lend some glamour to the ranks of the Royal Ballet led *Le Monde* to call her loss "a national catastrophe." Only Fonteyn, Nureyev and Natalia Makarova had won lengthy guest-artist positions with the Royal Ballet. But Guillem was the first to be given a long-term contract that allowed her control over her repertoire and choice of partners, performances and even costume. Rudolf had clearly taught her well. Outside of her twenty-five annual appearances with the Royal, she was free to dance wherever she chose,* something she had been prevented from doing in Paris. She had felt encumbered by the rules and hierarchy of the Paris Opéra. "The walls were starting to close in," she explained, sounding rather like her *patron* Nureyev. "I wanted to know my schedule six months in advance and I wanted to decide [with the company's artistic staff] what I would dance and they said to me, 'If we give you this, everyone will ask for it.' Later they said, 'We're sure you won't leave because this is your home, we made you.'"

No one had been more instrumental in the making of Guillem than Nureyev, who was deeply wounded by her abrupt departure. That it was for the Royal Ballet only sharpened his sense of betrayal. Guillem had begun fashioning a more glamorous persona, trading in her ballerina-with-

*One year later, Guillem would make her debut with the Kirov Ballet in *Swan Lake* and *Don Quixote*.

the-chignon look for red, stylishly bobbed hair à la Louise Brooks. "Rudolf was angry at me when I left," Guillem acknowledged, at the time, "but I didn't understand why he didn't want to help me. Rudolf doesn't like it when people don't agree with him and very often I didn't agree with him and would tell him. Often it was about ballets—either he wanted me to dance something and I didn't want to, or I wanted to dance something that he didn't want me to. . . . We fought a lot." Apart from her talent and beauty, it was Guillem's nerve and strength that attracted Rudolf to her. So much so, in fact, that he confided in one friend, "Doesn't she know I would have married her?" "He had never met any dancer who challenged him that way," says Jane Hermann. According to Luigi Pignotti, Guillem hurt him by not seeking his counsel before making her decision. But as the director of a large company, he could not single her out any more than he already had, just as Ashton had been unable to do more for Nureyev. "She was very much like Rudolf," observed Genya Polyakov, who was close to both. "He left his house, she left hers."

Guillem's departure presented Nureyev with a pressing problem. Guillem was the linchpin of *The Rules of the Game*, Twyla Tharp's first ballet for the Paris Opéra. Nureyev had enticed Tharp to Paris by promising her Guillem; Tharp in fact had it written into her contract that the ballet could not premiere without her. The choreographer, however, gamely agreed to rework the entire ballet and championed her other dancers to the press. "When reporters asked me about '*le désastre*,' the defection of Sylvie—who, it would seem all of Paris was mourning—I replied, 'No, the Paris Opéra is stronger than any one element. . . .'" Chanel's Gilles Dufour, the ballet's costume designer, was at Nureyev's apartment one night when he happened to express his regret at Guillem's leaving. Annoyed, Rudolf jabbed his finger at a photograph of her. "Look, she will never, never be Margot Fonteyn, whatever she does."

Grateful for the way Tharp had navigated what could have been another disaster for him, Rudolf hosted a small dinner party for her at Les Halles following her successful opening night. She was struck by the way he kept ordering oysters and champagne, "going far beyond the boundaries of reason into excess to finally reach his comfort zone." He became fairly drunk and, in a gesture of affection, bit down on Tharp's arm as he once had Noël Coward's and Arnold Schwarzenegger's, "hard enough," she wrote, "to leave teeth marks for a day."

Rudolf faced more problems a few weeks later: The Paris dancers again threatened to strike the night his production of *The Sleeping Beauty* was due to have its Opéra premiere. This time around they were upset by a proposed plan to force dancers to become certified before they could teach. Marie-Hélène de Rothschild was chairing the benefit gala, a highlight of the social season timed to coincide with Nureyev's fifty-first birthday. When, at the eleventh hour, the dancers refused to dance, La Baronne insisted that the party would go on even if the show did not. With characteristic aplomb, she directed the caterers to serve the dinner as quickly as possible. The ballet opened the following night to enthusiastic reviews, with regular ticket holders finding themselves at its premiere.

The challenges to Nureyev's leadership were just beginning. In June, he caused an uproar among the *étoiles* after he invited twenty-year-old Kenneth Greve to dance the role of the Prince in *Swan Lake*. The son of a Danish golf champion and a hairdresser, Rudolf's new protégé was a member of the corps of American Ballet Theatre and a former apprentice at the New York City Ballet. Standing six feet, five inches, with curly blond hair, gray-blue eyes and a long-limbed, boyish physique, he had the noble, Apollonian good looks of the young Erik Bruhn. Indeed, Bruhn had been Greve's role model as a student at the Royal Danish Ballet School. Rudolf met Greve in 1988, when he was preparing to dance *Orpheus* with the New York City Ballet. At the time, Greve had been in need of a work permit and had approached Rudolf for a recommendation. After watching him in class and learning that Greve had studied with Bruhn in Denmark, Rudolf signed the note of recommendation. Nearly a year passed before he ran into Greve, again in class at American Ballet Theatre. Proposing that Greve work with him after class, he asked him to peform some combinations. Ten days later, Greve was awakened at 4 A.M. by a call from Paris. Would he like to come to Paris to become a *danseur étoile* at the Paris Opéra? "I was shocked by his offer. I was in the corps de ballet at ABT, I had been out of school for three years, I was twenty years old. The Paris Opéra was totally closed; if you do enter, you start at the bottom—and anyway, I didn't know him very well. I had just talked to him a bit and that was it. I said, 'Sure, I'd love to, but don't you think you're taking a big chance?' "

"It's *my* decision," Rudolf replied, and proposed that Greve dance *Don Quixote* in twelve days' time. He would try, Greve answered. "I don't want you to try, I want you to do." Soon Rudolf changed his mind, deciding on his version of *Swan Lake*, "the most difficult ballet he could have chosen," Greve insists.

It was a "mad idea," Baryshnikov told Greve, when asked for his advice. Confiding that he would soon vacate his post as ABT's director, Baryshnikov urged the young dancer to go to Paris. "You're going to have a lot of trouble with the Opéra," he said, "but it's a fantastic opportunity." For the next six months, Greve's life would become inextricably bound up with Rudolf's. He traveled with him, received daily coaching, dined with him. Rudolf felt it essential to educate his young charge. He showed him religious paintings in the Louvre and bought him books: *Moby-Dick*,

Madame Bovary, Hamlet, Nabokov's *Lectures on Literature.* "He always gave me paperbacks. He said the book didn't need to look beautiful."

In short order, Greve had become the object of Rudolf's desire. "People were saying that's why he had so much respect for me, a young boy with so little life experience." Greve had a girlfriend in New York and considered himself heterosexual, but was anxious to spare Rudolf's feelings. He did see that he had much to learn from Rudolf, and possibly much to gain, and wondered whether he harbored any sexual attraction for him. "We had a long discussion about it and I told him I couldn't find any. He kept trying to convince me that I would like it somehow, that I was gay and just didn't know it. I said to him that maybe I would find that out, but that I didn't feel it now. He told me I was stupid. He said, 'Soon I will be old fart and no more beautiful body!' At times, he was very nice; at other times, he was very pushy. I always rejected him. I told him that I loved him as a father, as an artist, even as a person, 'but I cannot love you in that way. I'm sorry. I wish I could.'" Though he stayed with Rudolf in Paris ("Forget the hotel, I need to have you around twenty-four hours"), he slept across the hall, in the apartment Rudolf kept for guests. Still, he sometimes sent mixed messages, whether resting his hand on Rudolf's knee or agreeing to scrub his back during Rudolf's ritual daily baths. To the young dancer, however, "it was like washing my father's back. He loved it when I squeezed his head and would ask me to squeeze harder and harder. But he never provoked me into a nasty situation, never."

Greve's spell at the Opéra was decidedly short-lived. Greve danced just two performances of *Swan Lake,* with Rudolf playing the magician Rothbart, before the company's *étoiles* balked at performing with him, citing his inexperience and status as an outsider. His partner, Elisabeth Platel, flat out refused to dance with Greve. Furious, Rudolf berated her in her dressing room one night between acts of *Swan Lake* and told her he didn't want her to dance his ballets anymore. Platel cried her way through the entire Black Swan pas de deux.

Staunchly defending his right to install Greve as a guest star, he told a reporter, "If you give in, you are completely ruled by unions." The more obvious explanation was that Rudolf was completely ruled by his infatuation with Greve, whose name, ironically, means "strike" in French. Faced with widespread opposition, Rudolf was forced to back down. But he refused to admit he'd made a mistake—even though, according to Genya Polyakov, "he knew he was wrong." It was the first time that he had allowed his personal cravings to mar his professional judgment. His contract as ballet director was about to expire and Rudolf was enmeshed in negotiations with his old friend Pierre Bergé, the Opéra's new President. A small, strong-willed, pugnacious man who was, as one colleague recalls, "not one to easily share power," Bergé had already fired Daniel Barenboim as musical and artistic director of the new Bastille Opera. He was charged with renewing Nureyev's contract but intended to keep Rudolf "more firmly on a leash," according to Igor Eisner. Bergé insisted that Rudolf meet three conditions. He had to spend six months a year in Paris; he could choose only the first, not the subsequent, cast of any ballet he mounted; and he had to work in concert with Jean-Albert Cartier, an administrator Rudolf disliked. Rudolf insisted on artistic autonomy and the freedom to tour; he called Igor Eisner and André Larquié at all hours of the night to complain about Bergé's demands and enlisted Mario Bois, who handled his choreographic royalties, to negotiate. They were all convinced that Bergé did want Rudolf for the job. "He wasn't going to call in the police if Rudolf was in Paris five months instead of six," said Eisner. Yet while Rudolf clearly wished to continue, he showed a "near-suicidal" impulse during the negotiations. According to Eisner, there was a shared feeling among Bergé and his supporters at the Opéra and the Ministry of Culture that " 'If he signs, we keep him; if he doesn't, what a relief!' "

As the negotiations dragged on, Nureyev continued without a contract. That summer, ignoring complaints from Bergé that his frequent absences had demoralized the company, Rudolf toured to Mexico City with a new group of Friends, among them Kenneth Greve. There they gave four performances at a fifteen-hundred-seat supper club, with Greve dancing *Flower Festival at Genzano*, a Bruhn staple. Rudolf took Greve to Venice and on to his new home on the Isole dei Galli, his trio of rocky islands off the Amalfi coast of Italy. Nureyev had always wanted a house by the sea, and after years of searching near Capri, he fell in love with the Isole dei Galli the moment he first saw it in 1988. "It's perfect," he told Luigi, who negotiated its purchase on his behalf. "It's like boat in the middle of the sea." The islands had no running water but the ideal provenance: They had belonged to Léonide Massine, the Diaghilev protégé and legendary Ballets Russes dancer and choreographer, from whose family Nureyev bought them for $1.4 million.* The islands of Lunga, Brigante and Rotunda had been immortalized by Homer as the home of the Sirens, whose tantalizing song drove men insane and then to their death. Odysseus had resisted the lure of their song only by having himself lashed to the mast of his ship as it sailed past. Later they had served as a prison and, in the seventeenth century, as a pirate's lair. Massine had poured enormous energy and the bulk of his earnings into cultivating his deserted islands; the locals referred to him as "the mad Russian who has bought a rocky island where only rabbits could live." In time, Massine built himself not only a villa (its design guided by Le

*He spent an additional $700,000 on improvements.

Corbusier) but four terraced gardens planted with fruits, a boathouse, four beaches, guest quarters, a lighthouse and a restored fourteenth-century tower, complete with Carrara marble pillars and a dance studio, its floor made of Siberian pine. The open-air theater Massine built had been destroyed in a storm, and one of Rudolf's goals on assuming ownership was to rebuild it, with the hope of one day turning the islands into the cultural center Massine had envisioned.

A thirty-minute boat ride from Positano and difficult to reach when the seas were choppy, Galli was nevertheless close enough to the coastline that guests often awoke to the sound of tourist boats and a woman's voice describing, in assorted languages, the island of the famous Russian dancer Rudolf Nureyev. In August, they were pestered by mosquitoes. Still, sitting on his terrace, the chairs and tables designed by Massine, Nureyev could gaze out at his own expanse of sea and experience what Massine had felt when he wrote of being "overcome by the beauty of the view across the sea, with the Gulf of Salerno spreading out in the distance. . . . I knew that I would find the solitude I had been seeking, a refuge from the exhausting pressures of my chosen career."

In the adjoining room, antique tiles spelled out his mother's name in Arabic. Within the next two years, Nureyev would have all the interior walls covered with tiles, many shipped from Seville, and import a desalination plant from Japan to produce his own water supply. He astonished his Ravello neighbor Gore Vidal with his industry.

Here on the island, Rudolf and Kenneth passed their days simply: swimming, riding on Rudolf's jet ski, and working in his studio. Greve couldn't please him physically, but "I could please him in another way. It was very satisfying for him to see me perform the steps the way he wanted. He rarely said that it was good, and once when he did, I got excited, but then he qualified it. 'Next time better.' He would jab me in the chest with his finger, saying, 'You must do more, more!' He'd leave marks on my chest." Rudolf also found it satisfying to listen to Greve. "That sounds like Erik," he would say, and then launch into stories of their first days in Denmark when he thought Bruhn was "gorgeous, a god" and he was "willing to give up everything for him."

Unlike Bruhn, Greve was playful and affectionate, with an open manner and ready laugh. He was not only attractive but an easy, sympathetic companion, someone capable of making Rudolf happy. "We would do crazy things together, like play the piano and go ice skating in Central Park. He laughed so much. He was excited by the whole situation, it thrilled him. I think I made him very sad sometimes, but most of the time I made him laugh a lot. He was full of complications and when he laughed, it was a release." Over dinner one night, Rudolf confided that he had a fatal disease without naming it. Did he have cancer? Greve asked. "No, I have special disease," Rudolf said. Greve could see

NUREYEV: HIS LIFE] 502

that Rudolf was ailing and distressed by his aging body. But whether out of naïveté or genuine concern, he was convinced that his presence in Rudolf's life brought him more pleasure than pain.

Rudolf was more consumed by unfulfilled longing than Greve realized. To mark Kenneth's twenty-first birthday on August 11, Rudolf hosted a birthday party for him at his Dakota apartment and gave him a blue Armani suit.* But fearing competition from younger men, Rudolf invited his own, not Kenneth's, contemporaries. As much as he pushed Greve to pursue his own independent career, he kept a vigilant eye on his activities, anxiously brooding whenever he couldn't reach him. According to Mario Bois, "he went absolutely crazy over him to the point that he was calling me in Paris in the middle of the night, saying, 'Where is this young stupid boy?' "

RUDOLF HAD RETURNED to New York to rehearse *The King and I.* He had agreed to play the King, Yul Brynner's signature role, in a stage revival of the Rodgers and Hammerstein musical. "I was always game to try something new, something different," he explained. "Now I'm into musicals." His decision infuriated Pierre Bergé, who could not fathom how the director of the Paris Opéra could agree to tour North America in a musical comedy. "I thought it was ridiculous. It was not his métier." As Nureyev saw it, he was not needed in Paris as much as Bergé assumed. He had planned his seasons in advance and was content to leave the company's day-to-day concerns to his handpicked lieutenants, returning only for rehearsals of new productions. To comply with his obligations in Paris, he had accepted the tour on condition that it was booked in stretches of a couple of months at a time. Still, knowing that the United States forbade foreigners with HIV from entering the country, he was terrified when the play's American insurance agents asked him to take a blood test. He refused and the tour went ahead anyway, without insurance.

For Nureyev, the principal lure of *The King and I* was money: he was guaranteed $1,000,000 plus expenses, and a percentage of the profits for twenty-four weeks' work. The show also gave him the chance to try his hand at yet another medium that might prolong his life on the stage. Earlier that spring, he had been bowled over by Baryshnikov's kinetic performance on Broadway in *Metamorphosis*, adapted from the Kafka novel. (Baryshnikov, ten years younger, had moved into modern dance, theater and film.) And Rudolf had always loved American musicals, ever since he had seen Lola Fisher in *My Fair Lady* all those years ago in Leningrad. The role of the King had first been offered to him ten years

*Ironically, Greve would wear the suit to his wedding five years later.

earlier in Australia, but he had turned it down, thinking it would cut into his dancing. Now there were fewer calls for his dancing, or as he aptly phrased it, "the offers . . . disincrease." Compared to the record 299 performances he gave in 1975, Nureyev danced 81 times in 1988, hardly retirement, but a lighter load all the same. If Bergé wanted him to dance less, Rudolf implied, he would have to make up the lost income and time onstage elsewhere. At the Opéra, his director's salary came to $6,000 a month, with an extra $6,000 each time he danced a full-length ballet and $3,000 for short works. Elsewhere his performance fee was higher, anywhere from $5,000 at the Royal Ballet to approximately $20,000 in Japan. When Rudi van Dantzig warned him that the Opéra might "kick him out" over *The King and I*, Rudolf insisted he needed money. The Opéra wasn't paying him enough and he had lots of French taxes to pay, despite his best efforts to avoid them. But did he really need money? In addition to the millions accrued from his performances, which averaged more than two hundred annually in the 1970s, he received royalties from the many ballets he had staged. Nearly every week a Nureyev ballet was performed somewhere in the world. And he had always invested his money wisely through Gorlinsky, who still maintained bank accounts for him in Liechtenstein. He had homes in Paris, Monte Carlo, New York, a farm in Virginia and an island in Italy. He owned valuable antiques, an impressive collection of textiles, scores of kilims and several fine paintings. Among these was Sir Joshua Reynolds's handsome *Portrait of George Townshend, Lord de Ferrars*, purchased from the dealer Richard Feigen for $850,000, and Johann Heinrich Fuseli's dramatic *Satan Starting from the Touch of Ithuriel's Lance*, inspired by Milton's *Paradise Lost*, which he bought at auction that June for $1,160,000.

From August to November, while Bergé and Nureyev traded insults via the international press and Bergé and Bois haggled over his contract, Rudolf took up his duties as Siam's haughty king. He found the character entirely sympathetic. "Basically the king is supposed to be a bad character, with unlimited power, and all the problems arising from it. But I love absolute power. . . . He is inquisitive, he wants to learn, he has many positive qualities." If behaving like a king was not a problem, *sounding* like one was another matter. His body was by far his most eloquent instrument. Though he approached his first musical theater role with trepidation, Donald Pippin, the show's musical director, gave him scales to sing and, as Nureyev explained, "redirected the croaking." He disarmed his costar, Liz Robertson, by singing his difficult solo "A Puzzlement" for her at their first meeting. A pert, pretty woman with short blond hair and a winsome manner, Robertson, who had married composer Alan Jay Lerner as his eighth wife, arrived expecting a big ego and was taken aback when Rudolf "sold himself to me, instead of the other way around."

The play had just two previews before opening in Toronto on August 21, 1989. Douce, Kenneth Greve and Robert Tracy flew in especially for Rudolf's theatrical debut. Though his reviews were mixed and grew increasingly less flattering as the tour headed west, his drawing power kept the houses full. (Two fanatical admirers saw the show sixty-one times.) In twenty-four weeks on the road, the show would gross approximately $13 million, at the time a box-office record for a touring musical.

The first weeks of the tour did not go smoothly. Rudolf was surprised at how hard it was to remember his lines and to make them "intelligible," as Robertson recalls. "We couldn't understand what he was saying half the time." But he was not willing to work on his performance. His voice was "sweet but small," and after hearing Rudolf nightly struggle through his songs, Robertson suggested that he might want to speak them, Rex Harrison–style. "He went bananas and marched off in a huff because he felt I was criticizing his voice. To him, being in a musical meant singing."

Anxious about his health, he dreaded catching a chill and would not allow any theater on the tour to use its air conditioning during performances. He was still unaccustomed to his body microphone the night he unintentionally broke character during "Shall We Dance?" to inform Robertson—and the entire house: "Liz! Air conditioning on!"

But the root problem was that he wanted to be dancing. Standing in the wings, he was rarely focused on the action onstage. Instead, he was on the phone to Paris shouting about his contract, or setting up dance dates, or coaching Greve in one of his ballets. In Toronto, he and Greve stayed in adjoining rooms at the Four Seasons Hotel. Having arranged for Greve to dance his *Don Quixote* in Florence, Rudolf worked with him each day before and during performances of *The King and I.* He even enlisted Karen Kain to rehearse Greve in a studio at the O'Keefe Centre so that Greve wouldn't lose precious minutes while Rudolf was onstage playing the King. "He was planning for Kenneth's future and was angry with me when I said I couldn't go to Florence to dance with him," remembers Kain, who had never seen Rudolf "so smitten." Greve, she says, "wasn't bad, but he was too young to pull off the role and he wasn't experienced as a partner."

Other Toronto friends, such as Linda Maybarduk, worried that Greve was using Rudolf. The night they came to her home for dinner and stayed up late watching Rudolf in *Valentino*, Greve was, to her mind, "playing with Rudolf's affections, touching him and holding him and doing all the things that lovers do." Yet another evening, Greve pulled Maybarduk's husband aside to complain of Rudolf's unwanted advances when they were alone. Although Rudolf would regularly have young hustlers to his suite, his craving for Greve had grown desperate.

"Look, you can save me so much money," he joked with him. But one night in a fury, he threw a clock radio at him, just missing his leg. In an instant, Greve shoved an armoire, not realizing there was a television set inside. The TV fell out, grazing Rudolf's leg. "He told me I had 'destroyed' his career, so I told him how ridiculous the situation was. We ended up laughing like crazy."

Still, Greve was concerned enough about the changing tenor of their relationship that he appealed to Liz Robertson for help. "I've got a girlfriend and Rudolf won't accept this," he moaned. When Robertson tried reasoning with Rudolf over dinner in Boston, he called her "all the names under the sun. He was besotted by Kenneth and didn't want to hear it."

While his fights with Kenneth resulted in some "appalling performances" and made Robertson feel as if she were carrying the show, she could also see what a vulnerable, lonely time it was for Rudolf. One night at a restaurant a stranger insisted he must be "that Baryshnikov guy" and asked for his autograph. When the stranger refused to believe otherwise, Rudolf signed Baryshnikov's name. Robertson was struck by the way he managed to elicit from her "the most maternal feelings" and she found herself running to get him food and protecting him because "he made you want to look after him."

But in Boston in mid-September, she began to pull away. Finding him in his dressing room before a performance rehearsing Greve and Marie-Christine Mouis, a ballerina with the Boston Ballet, she told him she couldn't carry the show alone. That same night, midway through the performance, he and Kenneth had a terrific row after Rudolf discovered him kissing Mouis. Furious, Rudolf slapped him hard with his whole hand, and Kenneth fell to the floor. The two launched into a shouting match behind the scenery that could be heard by the actors onstage. Rudolf was hardly in the mood for the love scene with Robertson that followed. "If he had turned his career around and had a real success in *The King and I*, it would have been a wonderful triumph for him," suggests Jane Hermann. "But when he didn't get good reviews, he just lived through the tour to get paid. It was a lot of money, which he loved, but it did toll the death knell." Rudolf would concede as much to Robertson a few years later. "Tell me, I recollect I was very bad in *The King and I*." And she agreed.

Greve left Rudolf in Boston and refused to rejoin him. Soon he went to Florence to dance Rudolf's *Don Quixote* and there met the ballerina who would become his wife. While he and Rudolf saw each other occasionally after that and kept in touch by phone, the relationship was over. Rudolf continued to offer him advice, but when Greve proposed a visit a year later, Rudolf told him not to come. "I don't want to stir the soup," he said.

* * *

THE ANGUISHED LOVE of an older man for a young boy was the subject of the last full ballet made for Nureyev. *Death in Venice*, Flemming Flindt's adaptation of the Thomas Mann novella, premiered in Verona in May 1991. Set to music by Bach, the ballet held obvious personal resonance. Rudolf could identify with the middle-aged writer Gustav von Aschenbach and his obsession with the beautiful Polish schoolboy Tadzio; he understood firsthand the power of sexual love to overwhelm reason. The ballet proved a chilling metaphor for Nureyev's offstage situation: As a mysterious plague spreads through Venice, the older man sits by the sea, watching the blond youth at play while his own life ebbs away. His was "a great acting performance," wrote John Percival, one of the few critics to see it, "dominating the stage as much in his stillness as in his movements."

Nureyev had by then appeared in one other new work by Flindt, *The Overcoat*, made to measure for him shortly before he went into *The King and I*. Based on Gogol's tale of an impoverished clerk who believes that a magnificent coat will change his life, Flindt's *Overcoat* showed Rudolf as the fifty-one-year-old man that he was. His role drew more on dramatic skill than virtuosity. While the structure is Flindt's, "the details are really his," acknowledges the choreographer. He welcomed Nureyev's input, particularly the way he gave the clerk, Akaky Akakievich, a "wonderful, slapstick" Chaplinesque touch. His performance was uniformly well received. For once, concurred the critics, he was not competing with younger dancers or, worse, with his younger self.

MEMORIES OF vintage Nureyev were very much in the air, however, when in November 1989 the dancer returned to the Kirov stage for the first time since 1961. He had been invited by the Kirov Ballet's director, former classmate Oleg Vinogradov. Thirty-two years had passed since Nureyev's dazzling debut opposite Dudinskaya. Nevertheless, he accepted Vinogradov's offer, for he longed to dance once more on the Kirov stage. To show the Russians something of the dancer he had become in the West, he chose the role of James in *La Sylphide*, one of the first roles Erik had taught him. But he arrived in Leningrad with a bad foot and then tore the calf muscle in his other leg during a rehearsal with his twenty-year-old Kirov partner, Zhanna Ayupova. In a rare show of prudence, Nureyev thought it best to dance *The Overcoat* instead. Vinogradov refused to accommodate him. His rehearsals for *Sylphide*, led by old partner and friend Ninel Kurgapkina, proved grueling; he often had to stop in order to rest. According to Kurgapkina, "he kept asking me, 'Do I have to dance? Or is it better that I don't?' " He was convinced that Vinogradov intended to humiliate him. "I don't know why I did it. It's probably a very childish thing . . . but I'm of the school of Margot Fonteyn. . . . If you could stand, you could dance." Later he would tell friends that Vinogradov "buried" him.

On the night of November 17, the lights dimmed once again in the blue-and-gold jeweled Maryinsky Theater, and when the curtain rose, a familiar figure sat in an armchair, pretending to be asleep. It was a curious evening. Though his big solo in the first act earned little applause, he improved in the second, and his interpretive power and clarity came as a revelation to his fans of long ago. For this, and for their excitement at seeing him again, the audience gave him a standing ovation that went on for thirty minutes. One reviewer concluded that "the tragedy for the Leningrad audience was that its encounter with Nureyev came too late. We were removed from him in space and now we are removed from him in time." Another wrote sadly, "We tried to look through time to see the dance as it would have been thirty, or even twenty years ago. Our ovations were addressed to the past. . . ." His former partners all sat abreast in the front row, Dudinskaya, Osipenko, Kurgapkina, Kolpakova, Ter-Stepanova. His Leningrad friends Tamara and Liuba were also there, as were his sister Razida and niece Alfia, neither of whom had ever seen him dance. And in the company box sat Anna Udeltsova, his first teacher in Ufa, now one hundred years old.

"My dear boy. My little boy!" she had cried the day he paid her a special visit, bringing her an Yves Saint Laurent silk scarf. "Remember how they used to call me your second mother?" Yes, of course, he replied, happy to indulge her memories. She told him how Pushkin had called her once from Leningrad to beg her to use her influence with Rudik. "Tell him not to work so hard. He doesn't listen to any of us, maybe he'll listen to you."

"Thank God I didn't listen to you or to him," Rudolf replied. "And I still don't listen to anybody."

Like many of Rudolf's Leningrad friends, Udeltsova had trouble reconciling the boy she knew with the star he had become. "Just imagine! This small dirty Tatar now sits next to Jacqueline Kennedy," she said, insulting Rudolf profoundly.

He had arrived in Leningrad on November 12, accompanied by an entourage that included Douce, Luigi, Phyllis Wyeth, the pop composer Tony Venice, an Italian physiotherapist, an American television crew from *CBS Sunday Morning* and assorted reporters from around the globe. Tamara was waiting for him inside the terminal, where twenty-eight years before she had seen his flight off to Paris; next to her was Alla Osipenko, the last Kirov ballerina to see him at Le Bourget the day he defected. Tamara had been prepared for Rudik to "dance badly," but not for him to have "no energy whatsoever." When she called him at the Hotel

Leningrad, he complained to her that Vinogradov hadn't invited him to stage one of his own ballets at the Kirov. At the dress rehearsal, he became annoyed with her after she questioned his choice of costume, a knee-baring kilt that, in her view, "made him look ugly and underlined his shortcomings." When she had known him in Leningrad, he had spent hours reviewing the smallest details of his costumes. He had never been lax about his standards. "He was a different Rudik. I became very sad."

His reunion with Liuba and Leonid, the Romankov twins, was a happier affair. He dined at Liuba's home, invited her to Phyllis Wyeth's birthday party, and enlisted her and Douce to buy a special present for Dudinskaya, whom he greeted warmly, as he did Sergeyev, when he visited the Vaganova School. Trailed by reporters, he stood in fifth position in Pushkin's former classroom and toured the school's museum, stopping to savor the newly unveiled photographs of himself, Baryshnikov and Makarova on the "wall of defectors," as this recent installation was informally dubbed.

And yet the trip was uncomfortable and the food scarce, except at the Italian consulate, where Luigi had arranged a dinner of risotto and Chianti for Rudolf. In their hotel lobby the next morning, Luigi spied Rudolf looking at pictures of the Isole dei Galli. "Why don't we go back to Italy?" Rudolf asked. "What are we doing here?"

"But this is your country," Luigi insisted.

"No," Rudolf answered. "It's not my country anymore."

For Rudolf, it was an emotionally muted homecoming. "Though we spoke and laughed and hugged each other, there wasn't real communication," he said afterward. The people who came to see him, his fans, "looked like people who came out of the Gulag. Strange, worn, shabby old people. . . . Depressing . . ." And the Kirov was artistically stunted. "They go to the West," he said, "but they don't *see*."

Rudolf danced a second time on November 19 and promptly returned to Paris. There he spoke "sadly" about the visit to Genya Polyakov. "I didn't show them how I was but how I am," he lamented.

NUREYEV AND Pierre Bergé had reached an impasse. Hours after returning to Paris, Rudolf met with him to resolve their conflict once and for all. "He said he wanted to remain at the Opéra, but asked me to give him time to go to the States to perform in *The King and I*," recalls Bergé. "I said he would have to make a choice." The next day, November 22, Rudolf resigned his post as the Opéra's *directeur de la danse*. He assumed the less demanding role of chief choreographer, with the understanding that he would both produce a new work and personally rehearse two of his productions each year. He had pushed as far as he could go and in the end refused to bow to Bergé's authority. Though Bergé denies to this day that they ever fought or that Nureyev was ever forced out, Nureyev spoke as if he had been fired, dramatically telling reporters, "I have been betrayed like Nikiya, in *Bayadère.*"

He regretted the loss keenly, calling Charles Jude each night to inquire about the company. He felt unappreciated for all he had done there and became incensed when he learned that his replacement was to be thirty-one-year-old Patrick Dupond. While it's unlikely any choice would have pleased him, to his mind Dupond was "a very nice boy . . . charming at the dinner. But he doesn't know classical dance." At dinner with Michel Canesi and Bergé's predecessor, André Larquié, Rudolf kept saying to Larquié, 'When we go back to the Opéra . . ." He half expected the Opéra to ask him back. "He wanted it with all his heart," said Canesi.

In the meantime, he rejoined *The King and I* in California and concurrently toured with Nureyev and Friends, visiting cities in the United States, Canada and Mexico. Both tours had been arranged by Andrew Grossman of Columbia Artists Management, whom Rudolf's friends took to calling "the undertaker" because of his dolorous manner and dark clothing. Grossman had met Rudolf through Sander Gorlinsky in 1984 and and had arranged a number of his U.S. tours. He had recently taken over Rudolf's bookings. After twenty-seven years, Rudolf had fired Gorlinsky as his agent and manager. He was angry that Gorlinsky had urged him not to buy the Isole dei Galli and the apartment adjoining his on the Quai Voltaire. He also accused him of not doing enough to keep him dancing, refusing to listen when Gorlinsky advised him against exhausting himself on endless one-night-stand tours. "The reviews were getting worse and worse," notes Jane Hermann, "and Gorlinsky was the one saying to him, 'Slow down, don't lose Paris.'"

Where Gorlinsky was an old-world, gentlemanly agent who nevertheless drove a hard bargain, Andrew Grossman was, as Hermann describes him, "a phenomenal booker," though one who "knew nothing of the ballet business." But he fully understood the value of Rudolf's celebrity and was more than happy to trade on his brand name recognition. He kept Rudolf dancing, getting him twenty thousand dollars per performance in the twilight of his career and making a handsome profit for himself in the process. Though Rudolf transferred his management to Grossman, he still let Gorlinsky's office manage his European bank accounts and taxes, despite his claims that Gorlinsky had been stealing his money for years.* Still, as Grossman quickly learned, where Rudolf's money was concerned, "he didn't trust anybody. He hated paying commissions and hated paying anybody for anything." Rudolf regularly insisted on being paid in cash and, upon arriving in New York, would present Grossman with "a satchel of money"—a hundred thousand dol-

*Gorlinsky died on May 12, 1990.

lars in small bills was not uncommon—to take to the bank. While he and Rudolf never had a formal contract, Grossman handled all of his financial transactions to the end of his life, with the exception of those relating to the Paris Opéra. Theirs was a partnership "made in heaven," says Hermann. "How many agents could have provided Rudolf with the kind of work Grossman engendered—or the money?"

Grossman had already booked *The King and I* for the coming year, with Rudolf guaranteed $1.5 million. Then, in February 1990, only three months after Rudolf lost his post at the Opéra, the Rodgers and Hammerstein office pulled the rights. "They hated him in it," Grossman says. "They said, 'We'd love you to tour the show, just get us another star.' But the presenters wanted Nureyev."

Rudolf quickly turned his eye to the American Ballet Theatre, where Jane Hermann had taken over as director in September 1989 following Baryshnikov's departure. He expected Hermann to invite him to become director or to stage one of his ballets. But she didn't. Nor did she ask him to participate in ABT's fiftieth anniversary gala in San Francisco, where he happened to be performing in *The King and I* at the time. At the dinner given by Hermann following the gala, Rudolf bridled listening to the columnist Herb Caen rave about the evening. Nureyev looked glum, Caen reported in his column the next day. "The more people raved about the . . . gala, the glummer he looked."

There was certainly much to distract him during his two-week stay in the city where he and Fonteyn had once spent an infamous night in jail: There were dinners with Armen Bali and Jeannette Etheredge, a visit to Makarova's Napa estate and an opening night party in his honor, attended by local celebrities Makarova, oil heir Gordon Getty and writer Danielle Steel. But eventually his frustration erupted and in a nasty public scene at Jeremiah Tower's restaurant, Stars, one night, he lashed out at Hermann, calling her "a Jewish cunt."*

Hermann knew that Rudolf wanted her to make him director. "It would have been lovely to say to Bergé, 'Screw you, I'm joining Ballet Theatre.' I can't blame Rudolf for that." But as she saw it, she had no job to offer him. Designer Oliver Smith, the company's former codirector with founder Lucia Chase, had already asked to return as codirector.† The company was "devastatingly in debt," and it was Hermann's job to reduce it. "The board would not have agreed to Rudolf. His productions

---

*The remark was also meant for Pamela Harlech, who had been recently named board chairman of the English National Ballet, as the London Festival Ballet was now called. Peter Schaufuss had been fired as director, and Rudolf assumed that Harlech would at the very least sound him out.

†Smith joined Chase as codirector of the five-year-old Ballet Theatre in 1945. He and Hermann ran the company from 1990 to 1992.

were huge and there was no money for new sets and costumes." She also recognized that he was "on the brink, healthwise."

Hermann quickly learned that it was difficult to maintain his friendship when she couldn't accommodate him professionally. "Because he had faith in me, he felt that I betrayed him." Lillian Libman, the liaison for his Friends seasons, had warned her once not to confuse her value to Rudolf with friendship. "She told me, 'Suddenly he won't call you for six months because you haven't planned a season for him.'" As Rudolf saw it, however, Hermann didn't value him as she had when he was nightly filling the Metropolitan Opera House for her.

Friends passed off his epithets, such as the one thrown at Hermann, as characteristic outbursts, however crude. For many, though, they raised a deeper question: Was Rudolf anti-Semitic? Around the time of his fight with Hermann, Herbert Ross stopped speaking to him after Rudolf made several anti-Semitic remarks about her. "I'm the last person to defend her, but I told him, 'Six million people died because of remarks like that,' and he just got this sheepish look." In private, he referred to *The New York Times* dance critic Anna Kisselgoff as "the Yiddish bitch" and most of the press as "Jewish leftist liberals." Lillian Libman would later regret that she hadn't taken a stronger stand against these remarks, although Jane Hermann and even Herbert Ross were not convinced that he was truly anti-Semitic. "I was never sure that it was anything more than using foul language," says Hermann. Rudolf had always had numerous Jewish friends and minders, among them Genya Polyakov, Jacob Rothschild, Eva Evdokimova, Valery Panov, Lillian Libman, Sol Hurok, Gorlinsky and Grossman. According to Polyakov, he said things, but he didn't really mean them. "In Russia, if you're really anti-Semitic, you don't have anything to do with Jews, and a lot of Rudolf's friends were Jewish. If he said something against Jane Hermann, it's not because of her religion. It's because he didn't like her."

Andrew Grossman, however, was convinced that Rudolf "hated the Jews. He had this obsession that the Jews controlled the money in the banks. We were in Atlanta once and Princess Firyal asked him to do a fund-raiser for the Palestinians. Rudolf wanted to do it and I told him, 'If you do it, your career will be finished in the free world.' And he didn't do it. He grew up at a time when the Jews were scapegoats in Russia. It was deeply entrenched in the culture and he couldn't rise above it on certain levels. And yet he accepted me. You might say, 'Yeah, he used you because you're a smart Jew. You're a Shylock.' But I never felt that from him."

He teasingly addressed Misha Baryshnikov as Moishe, a Jewish name. This had nothing to do with anti-Semitism, according to Baryshnikov, though for many others it reflected Rudolf's belief that it was "the ultimate put-down." As Baryshnikov understood him, Rudolf "was not prejudiced, not racially. Everything was *personal* about him. Yes, he changed his mind sometimes about people and yes, he could turn on people if people—from his point of view—were not loyal. But this non-sense about Moishe and Misha . . . we called each other different names. . . . You know Rudy had a big mouth. And he was just barking sometimes at some people, especially when he was excited."

THE KING AND I closed in February 1990, and one month later, the Rudolf Nureyev Farewell Tour opened in Mexico. At least that's what the promoters were calling it. Nureyev, however, hotly denied that he had any intention of quitting the stage at fifty-two. Of the original Friends, only Charles Jude remained, and for the second year in a row, Nureyev danced only character roles. Few choreographers were willing to grant him the rights to their ballets, and just months earlier the Balanchine Trust had refused him *Apollo.** The trust's director advised Grossman that Rudolf's performance was by then "detrimental to the image of Balanchine." Grossman pleaded with her, knowing how Rudolf would react to such news.

But Rudolf danced on, seventy-eight times that year, ignoring the critics and defying the powers who would see him stop. On tour with him in Jacksonville, Florida, in the spring of 1990, the Danish ballerina Vivi Flindt† marveled at how he could appear exhausted and nearly crip-pled, hobbling on bandaged feet, and yet somehow, as performance time neared, spring slowly and completely to life. "In my life now, there are two alternatives," he told the writer Luke Jennings in Jacksonville. "Do nothing and age in bitterness. Or I can dance. Keep in good health, physically and spiritually. And I feel useful. Adequate. And I *can* do it. . . . I know I'm like Sarah Bernhardt with her wooden leg, but . . ."

To the critics who savaged him, he had indeed become a sorry sight. *The Miami Herald* wrote of his "grotesque, pathetic . . . self-delusion." That he had compromised his artistic integrity was a view he did not share. His repertoire now consisted only of interpretative, largely char-acter roles in works such as *The Overcoat, The Lesson, The Moor's Pavane* and *Songs of a Wayfarer*, and he was still capable of giving a performance that could win over the most skeptical of critics. Dancing *The Overcoat* at the Edinburgh Festival in August 1990, he earned his last good review.

*The ballet is owned by three people. The American performing rights are held by Ta-naquil LeClerq, Balanchine's third wife, and the foreign and media rights are held by Karin von Aroldingen and Barbara Horgan. According to Horgan, the trio at first ignored complaints about Rudolf's performance, but finally decided to act when the criticism was directed at the trust itself, for allowing Rudolf "to make an ass out of himself."
†Flindt is married to the choreographer Flemming Flindt.

The ballet "extracts from him a performance of unquestionable greatness—utterly unfaked in its characterisation . . . ," wrote Judith Mackrell in the *Independent*.

> Far from trying to gloss over the decline of his technique it is out of the ruin of Nureyev the dancer that he creates the character of Akakievich the social misfit. . . . Painfully exposed, Nureyev thus reveals how hard these moves now come to him, allowing the shakiness of the pirouette, the fumbled finish of the tours en l'air, the gravity-bound jumps to convey the absurd and pitiful extremes of Akakievich's aspirations and ineptitude. . . . What is crucial to the role is that gleaming through Nureyev's most effortful movement are the still luxuriant stretch of a foot, the perfect placing of a tendu. For it is these points of reference which create the ballet's pathos— not only concerning the fragility of Akakievich's illusions but of Nureyev's own mortality as a dancer as well.

While Martha Graham and Merce Cunningham danced well into their seventies (frequently choreographing roles for themselves that took their own aging into account), ballet is much less forgiving than modern dance. The domain of princes and fairy tale, its language celebrates youth and beauty. There were many who did not want to see their favorite stage lover as a doddering old man. For them, Nureyev's dancing was no longer the potent aphrodisiac it once had been, so they reacted with mockery and scorn.

His fans and devoted friends like Maude Gosling supported him utterly in his decision to continue. "He still gets an audience, he still gets paid, he's still happy doing it. . . . Look at Callas. They dragged her down, they killed that woman. Nobody tells a writer or a painter to stop. Whereas everybody keeps asking Rudolf, 'When are you going to stop?' and it drives him *frantic* . . . he's still got something to give—look at the fans at the stage door. Why should he stop?"

What did it matter if the venues weren't what they once were? When the journalist Lynn Barber met him that July in Orta, a resort on the Italian lakes, he was dancing to less than full houses. The next day, he was to drive one hour to Milan, fly ninety minutes to Naples, and drive for three hours to perform outdoors in the small ancient town of Paestum that same evening. His gypsy life was as it had always been except that now his Italian manager was his longtime masseur, Luigi, who, to Barber's chagrin, spoke of his attempts to book a tour for Nureyev in Bangkok "as if he were some bottom-of-the-bill conjuror instead of one of the greatest dancers of the century." It was Pignotti and Jude who took care of Rudolf on these tours around the provinces and provided him with the sense of family he craved. He felt happy eating spaghetti in Luigi's big kitchen in Milan and felt "safe" knowing Jude was along on the tour, often inviting him back to his suite to watch television late into the night. "Charles told me a few times that it was not so easy for him with Rudolf clinging so much," says Vivi Flindt, recalling how Jude often put Rudolf to bed after a show when Rudolf was especially tired.

FOR NUREYEV as for Fonteyn, "real life is onstage," a line he claimed Fonteyn often repeated to him. Fonteyn's name came up frequently in his conversation. He spoke of his debt to her, his affection for her, their shared commitment to dancing. "She's such great company but now she won't let us play with her," he told Luke Jennings. "I'd like to spoil her, oh, take her here, there. We don't have to be in the theatre or see the theatre ever ever again."

But such time together was never to be recaptured, for Fonteyn was dying of ovarian cancer. When she ventured beyond her farm in Panama, it was usually to visit M. D. Anderson Hospital in Houston, Texas. Devastated by Tito Arias's death following an operation for colon cancer in November 1989, the seventy-one-year-old Fonteyn had been characteristically private about her own illness and Rudolf was among the few friends to know. After twenty-five years of caring for a paraplegic husband, she dreaded being infirm herself, not wanting to trouble anyone else with worry. Tito's round-the-clock nursing had drained her savings; with no pension to show for her forty-five years of service to British ballet, she was living in the now-run-down farmhouse she and Tito had built on a ranch near El Higo, fifty miles west of Panama City. Here, tended by Tito's longtime manservant, Buenaventura Medina, and surrounded by her five dogs and herd of four hundred cattle, she lived a Spartan existence far removed from her glamorous life as the Royal Ballet's prima ballerina assoluta. Her portable phone reached only as far as Panama City, and it habitually went dead when the weather was windy. For long-distance calls, she had to drive down the road to a small hotel run by a neighbor.

Still, Rudolf managed to speak to her several times a week by phone and visited her regularly in Houston, forgoing his dread of hospitals to bring her comfort and colorful shawls. "He would come any time we thought she was sad," says her stepdaughter, Querube Arias, who oversaw her care. Once, en route from New York to Los Angeles, he arranged a layover in Houston, and had a taxi wait for him while he stopped in to see her. By 1990 Fonteyn had already endured three operations and was pretty much confined to her bed. "I used to tour theaters, now I tour hospitals," she joked to Luigi Pignotti without a trace of self-pity. Rudolf was "heartbroken" to see how frail she looked. Nevertheless, where Querube and others "were so careful with her," he refused to treat her as an invalid and pushed her to "do things with her body that she didn't want to do." The doctors wanted her to use a cane, she complained to him one day. "So what?" he replied, as if this latest indignity were simply a bothersome inconvenience. And so, then as earlier, she rose to the challenge he set for her, secure in the knowledge that he knew her body's strengths better than she did herself.

Though Fonteyn was never to know it, Rudolf anonymously paid a number of her medical bills. But her stays were expensive and she ran out of money. She was forced to sell several pieces of jewelry at Christie's. On May 30, 1990, a gala benefit held in her honor at Covent Garden raised £250,000 ($420,000) toward a trust fund to support her for the rest of her life. The night before the gala, Jacob Rothschild hosted a dinner at his home for Rudolf, Margot, Querube Arias and Maude Gosling. When it came time to descend the stairs to dinner, Rudolf simply hoisted Margot aloft as he had countless times onstage.

Sylvie Guillem and Jonathan Cope starred in MacMillan's *Romeo and Juliet*, appearing in the roles Fonteyn and Nureyev had danced both at the ballet's premiere twenty-five years earlier and in their last appearance together at Covent Garden in 1976. On this occasion, Rudolf danced Mercutio and shared the stage with Guillem for the first time since their rift. The organizers, however, had not intended for him to dance at all, but, rather, to *sit* with Fonteyn. "He took it for granted that we wanted him to dance," recalls committee member Anya Sainsbury, the former Royal Ballet dancer Anya Linden. "It was his idea to dance Mercutio. We couldn't very well say, 'Well, actually no, we had somebody else in mind.' "

Roused by their enormous affection for Fonteyn, more than two thousand people, among them Princess Margaret, Princess Diana and ninety-two-year-old Dame Ninette de Valois, jammed the Royal Opera House to pay tribute to her. The fact that Rudolf was dancing for Fonteyn and that "she was there to see it was wonderful," says Monica Mason, one of his many partners in the audience that night. "But in terms of his dancing, it was heartbreaking. Because of course it was a reminder of what happens to us." Though terribly frail, Fonteyn "willed herself not to show a moment of flagging," says Anya Sainsbury. But at the party afterward in the Crush Bar, she looked suddenly despairing when she asked Sainsbury to find Rudolf. "He was here a minute ago. Now he's gone." Sainsbury caught up with him at the stage door, where he was waiting for a cab. "He was upset about something and in one of his moods and I had to beg him to stay. I just went on and on and when I told him how distressed Margot was that he was unhappy, he said, 'She doesn't need me.' Finally, he relented."

*   *   *

FONTEYN DIED on February 21, 1991, twenty-nine years to the day she and Rudolf first danced together in *Giselle*. In the interim, he had partnered her nearly seven hundred times. "She was suffering a lot," he said after her death. "So, in a way, it was good for her, I think . . . a release." When she realized that the doctors could do no more for her, she asked to return to Panama, where she wanted to be cremated and buried on top of Tito.

Rudolf had visited her there one month earlier. He was in Chicago, on tour with Nureyev and Friends, when the news came. Refusing to answer even Jude's knock at the door, he spent three hours on the phone to Querube Arias, questioning her for details about Margot's last moments. "He wanted to know everything, how she died, how she dealt with the pain, what she wanted." Neither she nor Fonteyn had known that Rudolf was sick and only in hindsight did Querube understand that he was thinking of his own death.

Fonteyn had planned her funeral with the same deliberate care that she had planned everything else. She insisted on the same church, priest and mass as Tito. Rudolf did not attend her funeral or the memorial service that followed in London. "I'd like to but I can't," he explained when Querube invited him. He could not mourn her publicly. Instead, he flew to his new house on the West Indian island of Saint Barthélemy, and there consoled himself by playing Bach, lying in the sun, and swimming in the sea.

31

Diminuendo

FOR THOSE WHO CONSIDERED the Fonteyn years the zenith of Nureyev's career, his farewell tour of Britain two months after her death was certainly its low point. The tour was managed not by Andrew Grossman or Luigi Pignotti but by a decidedly small-time promoter from Hove, near Brighton, whose headliners included Bill Haley and the Comets and Pat Boone, their best years far behind them. While Grossman had a few projects in the works for Rudolf, among them the role of Dracula in a new stage production and a revival of *Tovarich*, opposite Leslie Caron, he could do "nothing more for him," and begged Rudolf not to take on the English tour. "That's your sacred ground. Don't do it," he told him.

The tour began in April at the Sunderland Empire in northeast England and finished on the south coast at Brighton, with stops in between at such provincial venues as the Cambridge Corn Exchange and the Portsmouth Guildhall. Night after night, hobbled by a painful ingrown toenail, Rudolf lumbered through *The Lesson* and *The Moor's Pavane* to taped music on Spartan stages, prompting Clement Crisp to deem the enterprise "unworthy of him." Others were far harsher. The *Daily Mail* called it "almost as garish as a sideshow," while the British columnist Anthony Gardner, mocking Nureyev's refusal to retire, branded him "the latest star to join the ranks of the going, going, not quite gone."

Though his roles were well within his range, he was booed. In Sunderland, fifty patrons demanded their money back, while one mother and daughter sued the theater for "emotional distress and disappointment." His appalling reception put the critic Nicholas Dromgoole in mind of jackals and hyenas tearing at the carcass of a once-regal panther.

His supporting cast, led by Vivi Flindt and Evelyne Desutter, avoided any mention of reviews. Rudolf kept to himself more than usual and for the first time in memory, Flindt saw that he was mentally fatigued. "He wanted the show to go on, out it wasn't with the same commitment." His health was declining rapidly and from then on, recalled Michel Canesi, "you couldn't mention AIDS, and it all accelerated."

Rudolf lashed out at the critics, believing their attacks to be personally motivated. "You are only interested in character assassination . . ." he snapped at a reporter from the *Times* (London). And yet increasingly, he seemed to invite their ire. One month before the English tour, he tried to bar Anna Kisselgoff from attending a Nureyev and Friends performance at the Tilles Center for the Arts at Long Island University, an hour's drive from New York City. "If she comes, I will get a bucket of shit and throw it on her head," he vowed. After he called and threatened her, Andrew Grossman agreed to seat Kisselgoff way up in the balcony where Rudolf couldn't see her from the stage. During the first ballet, the theater's main exit door flung open and there stood Rudolf in his Moor costume, "looking for Anna." He slammed the door and opened others, but never found her. Kisselgoff made no mention of the episode in her review, which even Rudolf begrudgingly admitted was "fair."

His last ever appearance in London was in May at the three-thousand-seat Wembley Conference Center and sold out. ("Wembley! I didn't know that," he later claimed. "Honestly. . . . The agreement was in a theater.") Tessa Kennedy was one of his few friends to brave the performance, the majority feeling, as Monica Mason did, that "there was so little left of what he had been." Afterward Kennedy came to agree, recalling it as "tragic . . . horrible . . . there were these rows of nasty chairs covered in hideous material, and fluorescent strip lighting. The audiences were often ghastly, too. . . ."

It was a far cry from the height of Rudimania when fans would wait days in line for tickets, and royalty and movie stars thronged the great opera houses to see him. Then he regularly needed a police escort to leave a theater, and audiences screamed themselves hoarse and refused to let him go, not the other way around.

FONTEYN'S DEATH, coupled with his professional demise, was enough to cripple his serenity altogether. "Everybody's dropping off the tree. There's less and less friends and so you just wait till you drop off the tree. Meanwhile you enjoy life to the full, deny nothing." Hard work and struggle were as necessary to Nureyev as sex, and it was not surprising that he should embark on a new performing career, one that harnessed his passion for music and physical eloquence. So he began to prepare for what he called his "solitude" by teaching himself the piano in earnest and studying to become a conductor. The role of maestro was in many ways the perfect segue, the commanding midway point between stage and spectator.

In his roles as coach, producer and director, Nureyev had already demonstrated the kinds of strengths Leonard Bernstein considered the hallmarks of a great conductor. As Bernstein told viewers of his *Omnibus* program, the conductor "must not only make his orchestra play, he must make them want to play. He must exalt them, lift them, start their adrenaline pouring, either through cajoling or demanding or raging. But however he does it, he must make the orchestra love the music as he loves it. It is not so much imposing his will on them like a dictator; it is more like projecting his feelings around him so that they reach the last man in the second violin section. And when this happens—when one hundred men share his feelings, exactly, simultaneously, responding as one to each rise and fall of the music, to each point of arrival and departure, to each little inner pulse—then there is a human identity of feeling that has no equal elsewhere. It is the closest thing I know to love itself. On this current of love the conductor can communicate at the deepest levels with his players, and ultimately with his audience." Exchange the words "play" for "perform," "music" for "dance" and "orchestra" for "dancers," and Bernstein could have been describing Nureyev.

When he was a boy, Nureyev's first love had been music and he had since gained a near-encyclopedic knowledge of the classical repertory. For years he had expressed his interest in conducting. But it wasn't until the late 1970s, when conductor Karl Böhm encouraged him, that Nureyev began to consider the idea seriously. Böhm urged Nureyev to study for *at least* one year. To Rudolf, however, that meant staying in one place, something he wasn't convinced he could ever do. Soon after, he ran into Herbert von Karajan in the Palais Garnier and complimented the maestro on his youthful mien. "You should become a conductor," Karajan told him. "Conductors live a long time. Come to me, I will teach you all my tricks." Needing "a third blessing" before he could be convinced, he appealed to his New York neighbor Leonard Bernstein in 1988. The night they met, Bernstein was agitated over U.S.-Israeli relations and alternated between dispensing advice and airing his views on Israel, all the while taking drags on his cigarette and punctuating his remarks with arpeggios on the piano. "What do you think about my trying to conduct at this stage of life?" Rudolf asked him. "You're so enormously talented, why not?" replied Bernstein, who advised him to enroll in the conductors' course at New York's renowned Juilliard School.

Rudolf investigated the possibility, but was soon on the road in *The King and I*, studying music on his own instead. Insisting on access to a piano, both in his hotel suite and backstage, he practiced whenever he could, slowly and painstakingly teaching himself to read and deconstruct Bach's *The Well-Tempered Clavier*. He also bought a Ruckers harpsichord, one of only three in the world, and an electric Cassio keyboard, his salvation during airport layovers.

Knowing that Rudolf would want to be "the greatest [conductor] in the world," Bernstein had instructed him to "find an old maestro and drag all the information from him." By the time Nureyev got around to serious study in the winter of 1990, Bernstein was dead. So he turned instead to an old friend, Varujan Kojian, the music director of the Santa Barbara Symphony and a former concertmaster of the Los Angeles Philharmonic. The two had met in the 1970s when Kojian conducted for Nureyev's Friends tours. Though Rudolf could read music, he had never tackled a conductor's score. After just three weeks, Kojian pushed him to conduct a student ensemble, which he did, albeit reluctantly. "Imagine this supremely graceful man nearly stumbling on to the podium," Kojian recalled. Without advance fanfare, Rudolf also conducted excerpts from *The Sleeping Beauty* for three ballet performances during the U.S. tour with his Friends group. Despite a life immersed in music and his dancer's instinctive feel for tempi, he suddenly understood "how those bastard conductors feel. You have this fantastic struggle with the orchestra to keep the tempi up. The brass is heavy, the contrabasses are heavy: to keep them together with the violins, you have to goose them all the time."

Invigorated by the possibilities of a fulfilling second career, he soon put in a call to his old friend Wilhelm "Papa" Hübner, a professor at the Vienna Academy of Music. During his decade-long presidency of the Vienna Philharmonic, Hübner had made numerous connections in the world's music capital, which he was only too happy to put at Rudolf's disposal. A respected figure, he would not have wasted his time had he not seen promise in Rudolf, knowing all the same that a good conductor was at least five years in the making.

He first instructed Rudolf himself, the two of them poring over Haydn's *La Chasse* Symphony in the Hübners' modest Vienna flat, its walls decorated, simply, with portraits of the Mozarts, father and son. With Lydia Hübner and her daughter, Elisabeth, preparing his meals and tending to him, Rudolf could apply himself fully to his lessons. Day and night, as he listened to recordings, he studied their scores. One week later, Hübner brought in a professor of conducting from the Vienna Music Academy to teach him how to hold a baton, and within a day Rudolf was standing in the Hübners' living room conducting recorded scores.

The speed with which Rudolf absorbed the subtleties of conducting amazed Hübner. Some conductors took a year to learn a new piece;

Rudolf spent a total of three weeks preparing for his conducting debut. As he saw it, Rudolf was "living *in* the music, not for it." The next step was to get him before an orchestra, so Hübner sent him on to Dr. Franz Moser, the director of the Vienna Residenz Orchestra, the well-regarded young troupe Hübner had founded two years earlier. "Children," he told them at their first rehearsal, "this is a man who's just starting, but help him because you will see that he's good." It is surely a testament to Nureyev's passion and dedication that the musicians accepted him when they might easily have dismissed him as a dilettante, or worse, as some celebrity-for-hire. Once again, his determination made up for his late start, just as it had in Leningrad decades earlier.

Though Hübner had planned for Rudolf to make his debut in September, the professor decided his pupil was ready after just eleven rehearsals with the musicians. On June 25, seven months after his first lesson, a visibly nervous Nureyev took the podium at Vienna's elegant Palais Auersperg and before a select audience of three hundred led the Residenz Orchestra in an evening of Haydn's *La Chasse*, Mozart's Violin Concerto K. 218 and Tchaikovsky's Serenade for String Orchestra. "Everyone was very impressed, including the musicians, who are not so easily impressed," Franz Moser said afterward.

Five days later, looking happier and more at ease, he conducted a second evening of works that included Stravinsky's *Apollon Musagète*. Nureyev's love for the music and the Balanchine ballet it inspired* was both "visible and audible" to those who recalled his debut in *Apollo* twenty-four years earlier. Michael Birkmeyer, one of several Nureyev protégés in the audience, was moved at seeing Rudolf's sheer joy. "He looked like he was in another realm. He could hardly walk to the podium, but when he got there, he posed like Karajan and the moment the music started, you felt there was another power."

Rudolf quickly found his own movement style. While most conductors make what Hübner described as "a big, overly dramatic flourish — wump!" at the end of a piece and "dance" on the podium, Rudolf used his body sparingly because he didn't want audiences to view him as a dancer. When Hübner advised him not to look at the score as he conducted ("You know it by heart, put it away"), Rudolf replied that he needed to show that he could read the music, that he wasn't simply moving in time to music but was actually conducting what was written on the page. Still, he knew he was just a novice and needed reassurance that the audience wasn't simply applauding his effort. "Are you sure it was good?" he repeatedly asked Hübner.

In July he wielded the baton at concerts in Ravello and Athens.†

---

*Which Nureyev had first danced in Vienna.
†After viewing the videotape Hübner showed him of Rudolf at Athens's Herodes Atticus

Returning to Vienna for further study that summer, Rudolf traveled an hour outside the city to Feistritz, a castle where Hübner held annual chamber music seminars. Once there, however, he was beset by fevers that left him soaked through with sweat. When Lydia Hübner took him his breakfast tray one morning, she was distressed to find him shivering beneath layers of woolen blankets in the summer heat. Despite her protests, he insisted on seeing out the day's rehearsal with the student orchestra Hübner had assigned to him and went on to practice Beethoven's *Eroica* Symphony and Strauss's *Delirium Waltz*, reputedly Karajan's favorite waltz.

But at the end of September, after traveling to Budapest to conduct at the opera house, Rudolf experienced severe kidney pains. The Hübners' son, Vaxy, a urologist, urged his parents to return Rudolf to Vienna, where he was diagnosed with an obstructed kidney. Rudolf confided in him that he was HIV-positive, and Hübner took precautions not to have the news leaked. He even kept it from his parents after inserting a stent to drain Rudolf's kidney.

Douce came for nearly a week and sat by his hospital bed day and night. She and Lydia Hübner were there when he awoke from the anesthesia and angrily insisted on getting up, against his doctor's orders. He resisted strenuously when Lydia Hübner had to hold him down at one point. "Finally he gave up, because I was much stronger than he was." Once recovered, he would complain that the procedure had cost him a fortune.

ALTHOUGH HIS conducting career was gaining momentum, the furies that drove him to dance could not be appeased. Three weeks after his kidney attack, against the advice of everyone he knew, he went on an exhausting month-long tour of Australia. It was to be his last tour as a dancer and it was another disaster. Thin and depleted, he could barely walk, let alone get through a rehearsal. For the first time in his career, he changed a program at the last minute because he simply could not muster the strength to dance it. In place of *Songs of a Wayfarer* and *The Lesson*, he opted for his Nijinsky stand-by, *L'Après-midi d'un Faune*, and *The Moor's Pavane*.

The audiences were "furious," remembers Charles Jude. Not only had they paid a lot of money to see him, but because Nureyev hadn't performed in Australia in fourteen years, audiences came expecting the Nureyev of *Le Corsaire* and *Don Quixote*. "They wanted to see him jump and turn and when they saw [what he did], they wanted their money

Theater, an impressed Riccardo Muti pronounced him "better than some professional conductors."

back." No one waited for him at the stage door. When an old friend came backstage to greet him and asked about his health, Rudolf replied, "Look at me. I'm fine!" But he didn't look fine, and many suspected that he was unaware of his actual appearance onstage.

Back in Europe three weeks later, he traveled eight hours by car from Vienna to Czestochowa, a small town in Poland, to give a concert and practice conducting on the local orchestra there. It was December, and gray snow covered the ground. Rudolf stayed three days in the bleak Motel Orbis, subsisting on sausages and sweet wine. "It could be worse," he would say stoically when asked how he was. Other times he would say simply, "Surviving." On his return trip to Vienna by overnight train, he took a rare glance back at an earlier train ride—the three days spent on that endless stretch from Ufa to Leningrad. "My mother packed a suitcase of bread, tortes, eggs. Those eggs were marvelous. I just looked out the window the whole way. . . ."

The Christmas Eve he spent at the Château de Ferrières with the Rothschilds a few nights later must have seemed as distant from Czesto-chowa as Rudolf now felt from the Ufa of his childhood. Knowing that he was angry with Douce, Marie-Hélène de Rothschild hoped to broker peace between them yet again. So she encouraged Douce to come in disguise as a man and introduced her to Rudolf as a musician friend of Jerome Robbins. "He was very nice," she recalled. "Only after while did he realize it was Douce and then there was a big reconciliation."

He was soon back in Vienna to conduct the Residenz Orchestra on New Year's Eve. At a black-tie dinner concert at the Palais Auersperg, he conducted a program of Strauss waltzes. The next morning he rose early to take part in a live international telecast, appearing as the sultan in the ballet *Thousand and One Nights*. Dressed in a turban, harem pants and robe, recalling that other Rudolph in *The Sheik*, he performed a role that required more presence than dancing.

A few days later, he left for the Caribbean island of St.-Bart's. One year earlier, he had purchased a beach house on a rocky promontory, convinced that sea and sun were his best medicine. The house was simply furnished and completely open to the sea on one side, which made Rudolf feel as if he were riding on the coast's dashing waves. Situated on the island's less fashionable side, the house struck Jacqueline Onassis as too remote and uncomfortable. "If Rudolf invites you to visit, say no," she advised Querube Arias. "My houses are all strange, isolated places that would not appeal to society people," Rudolf acknowledged. "They are not presentable."

In St.-Bart's, he practiced the piano and read orchestral scores, even taking them with him to the beach when he went for a swim. Feeling invigorated, in late February he flew to Berlin to stage his version of *The Sleeping Beauty* at the Deutsche Oper, assisted by Patricia Ruanne, the former London Festival Ballet dancer he had installed at the Paris Opéra as ballet mistress.* Some days he looked robust; on others, he tired easily and had trouble walking. But not once did Ruanne hear him complain. Any difficulties were masked by banter. Demonstrating a jump to the dancer playing the Prince, he stopped suddenly and joked, "Carcass not working. I hope I haven't displaced the plumbing," referring to his recent kidney surgery.

Though rehearsals went smoothly, neither Rudolf nor Ruanne was pleased with the young German ballerina cast as the witch Carabosse. Her approach was "a bit too Bette Davis," so Ruanne urged Rudolf to take on the role himself. "Oh, shit," came the reply, "I'll have to learn it all." But he quickly consented to dance it opening night after Ruanne agreed to "cut out some of the running around" and arranged a few rehearsals for him with the witch's goons. "Well," he said after his first run-through, "at least boys are pretty."

Rudolf was everything he never wanted any other Carabosse to be, recalls Ruanne, but "absolutely riveting—an extraordinary performance." Where he had always demanded that Carabosse be elegant and extremely icy, "with a volcano seething inside," Rudolf put his own spin on the role and came on, as Ruanne describes it, "like a bat out of hell."

Nevertheless, it was in the role of an angel that Rudolf danced for the last time. The ballet, presented in Budapest on February 28, 1992, was Gábor Keveházi's *Cristoforo*.† Rudolf could never have imagined that he would not dance again.

IN MARCH, three weeks before his fifty-fourth birthday, Rudolf returned to Russia with Douce François and Neil Boyd, an affable young Australian who had become his new valet. Rudolf had been studying with the Muscovite conductor Vladimir Vais, who had arranged for him to rehearse with orchestras in Kazan, Yalta and St. Petersburg, as it was once again being called. Rudolf flew first to Kazan, the Tatar capital and his mother's childhood home. The poor accommodation and winter temperatures were hardly good for his health. Yet Rudolf would not be deterred. "I have to go for my mother," he insisted to Lydia Hübner, who years earlier had taken jeans and chocolates to her in Leningrad at Rudolf's request. "In her memory, I have to do it." His sister Razida traveled the 250 miles from Ufa to see him.

During the day, Rudolf rehearsed Prokofiev's *Romeo and Juliet*, music he knew by heart. At night, he unwound with the musicians. To

*Ruanne had been his first Juliet in the *Romeo and Juliet* he had staged for the Festival Ballet in 1976.
†An ode to Christopher Columbus, another wayfarer.

Douce, he seemed unusually contented. "He was with his own people," she explained. One night they went to a sauna with the musicians and then out into the bitter cold, an old Russian prescriptive for robust health. The next day, Rudolf came down with what he thought was pneumonia. His father had died of lung cancer and he feared that the illness would overwhelm his own lungs, which he believed had been weakened in childhood. "Like my father, like my father," he kept repeating to Douce, who knew only too well that "when he's afraid like that, he's hard to calm."

Nevertheless, he went on to St. Petersburg, where he stayed with Ninel Kurgapkina and celebrated his fifty-fourth birthday at the home of his old friend Liuba. His friends quickly saw that he was ill and took him for tests at the Military Medical Academy, though he continued to stay on in Kurgapkina's flat. For more than a week, he was treated for pneumonia, but he failed to improve and his temperature hovered at 104 degrees. A panicked Douce called Michel Canesi in Paris. Rudolf insisted he was fine and told Canesi that he intended to go on to Yalta. Canesi urged him to come home. Rudolf relented, but not before going to the Maryinsky Theater with Liuba to see the Kirov dancers perform their first Jerome Robbins's ballet, *In the Night*. Liuba was worried when she said goodbye to him at the airport because he could barely walk on his own to the plane. Douce had already left for Paris, having decided not to upgrade her discounted ticket, leaving Rudolf to travel alone.

Back in Paris, he was diagnosed with pericarditis, an inflammation of the heart's outer membrane, a serious condition often seen in people with AIDS. He was rushed to the Ambroise-Paré clinic at Neuilly, where he was operated on immediately. He survived the surgery, but Canesi felt sure he was shortly going to die. Jane Hermann flew to Paris and rushed to the hospital. She, too, doubted Rudolf would make it and, in an effort to buoy his spirits, invited him to conduct a performance of *Romeo and Juliet* at the Metropolitan Opera House one month later. Though she suspected that he might never have the strength, she knew that a performance at the Met was the best prescription anyone could give him, and she wanted to be the one to deliver it. Following their contretemps over the directorship of ABT, they hadn't spoken in nearly a year, and she longed to say yes to him again. "You really mean it?" he said when she told him. Rudolf somehow pulled through and was soon sitting up in bed, headphones in place, poring over the Prokofiev score.

While he refused to go public with his disease, he was under no illusions about the gravity of his situation. "I'm afraid there will be no more dancing. It's finished," he told Marika Besobrasova. Robert Tracy, who hadn't seen him in over a year, was struck by how much weight he had lost. The day Tracy visited him in Hôpital Notre-Dame du Perpétuel Secours, where he had been transferred, Rudolf asked him to call his

New York friends and inform them that he was ill. He never used the word "AIDS," although Tracy did in his conversations with Lincoln Kirstein, Jacqueline Onassis, Tessa Kennedy, Lillian Libman and Jamie Wyeth. Rudolf was furious when he learned that Tracy had described him as having AIDS. To name his disease was to give in to it, and Rudolf still believed he could defeat it.

He and Canesi had made a pact that the doctor would tell him when it was time to put his affairs in order. That time had come, the doctor advised him the day he returned home to the Quai Voltaire. It had taken him the whole afternoon to broach the subject. "I expected him to be terribly shocked. Not at all. It was one of those moments of great quietness, calm and friendship between us." Rudolf's lawyers, Jeannette Thurnherr from Liechtenstein and Barry Weinstein from Chicago, were soon summoned to Paris, to map out the provisions of his will.

Rudolf arrived in New York on April 21, eleven days before the performance. He rehearsed each morning with ABT's principal conductor, Charles Barker, and a pianist and after lunch reviewed the score at home for several hours, without speaking to anyone. Then he would rest before supper. Canesi had agreed to his going on one condition: that he take a nurse with him. But Rudolf reneged when he learned the cost: four thousand dollars for the two weeks. Rudolf also told Canesi that he didn't need his services any longer. Three days later he called to apologize, astonishing the doctor. "Is that really Mr. Nureyev who is apologizing?"

Despite daily two-hour infusions of ganciclovir and though visibly depleted, Rudolf had no intention of slowing his customary pace. The night Susan Hendl came to dinner at the Dakota, Rudolf insisted on going to a midnight screening of *Raise the Red Lantern*, a film about the Chinese Cultural Revolution. Hendl had assisted Balanchine with the staging of *Le Bourgeois Gentilhomme* and had remained a friend of Rudolf's ever since. As they left the movie theater, Hendl took his arm, but Rudolf protested, 'Susie, you can't, I'm too weak." Yet once he was back in his apartment, his energy revived. It was the middle of the night before Hendl was able to leave.

On the way to Lincoln Center a few days later, he ran into Peter Martins and stood with him for over an hour on a street corner discussing the tempi of *The Sleeping Beauty*. "We agreed on certain sections and disagreed on others," Martins recalls. "I would dance and he would dance. People walked by and some of them recognized him and there we were discussing *Sleeping Beauty*. He had become very serious. He was not looking at tricks walking by or giving me nasty remarks about Balanchine or calling me Danish Princess. What really mattered was the Tchaikovsky music."

Rudolf rehearsed hard for his American conducting debut and won the admiration of Charles Barker, who, knowing that Rudolf was gravely ill, apprised the musicians beforehand. With its changing meters and quick transitions, Prokofiev's *Romeo and Juliet* is one of the most challenging ballet scores for even the most experienced conductors. "It has every possible trial," concedes Barker, "especially in the third act, when rarely does the entire orchestra play together. It's forty minutes of dealing with small groups of instruments. Most often it's only two or three instrument groups playing together and only for a bar or two and then it changes to another instrument group. It's very difficult to keep your concentration and focus." Rudolf rehearsed just once with the ABT orchestra; his effort alone impressed the musicians.

Since Rudolf had never formally retired from dancing, Hermann decided to turn Ballet Theatre's spring gala into a kind of "farewell New York" performance. Jacqueline Onassis agreed to be honorary chairman of the evening and attended a dress rehearsal, as did Jessye Norman, which cheered Rudolf immensely. His protégés Sylvie Guillem and Laurent Hilaire were invited to reprise the roles Fonteyn and Nureyev had danced at *Romeo and Juliet*'s world premiere twenty-seven years earlier. "The company needed Guillem in that performance like a hole in the head," recalls Hermann. "I moved heaven and earth to get her in there because I had promised Rudolf I wouldn't tell her how sick he was. She didn't want to do it. She said, 'This is going to be a circus for Rudolf to conduct. This isn't about my performance.' She kept jacking up her price and I paid her what she asked for, which shocked her. I told her, 'You'd better do this or you're going to be sorry.' She came in, and when she saw him at his apartment, she realized he was sick. I left around three A.M. and she was still there."

As Guillem predicted, a glittering crowd turned out the night of May 6, principally to see Rudolf. But it wasn't his conducting they had come to applaud as much as it was a life fully dedicated to the dance, a commitment that had touched them all. In the audience were his first Giselle, Irina Kolpakova, and his last, Alessandra Ferri. There were Natalia Makarova, Violette Verdy, Darci Kistler and a sprinkling of New York socialites, Anne Bass, Blaine Trump and Pat Buckley among them. And there was Monique van Vooren. Maude Gosling had flown in from London, Michel Canesi from Paris, Wallace Potts from Los Angeles, Jeannette Etheredge from San Francisco.

Rudolf stepped up to the podium wearing white tie and tails looking wan. But as soon as the audience greeted him, he came to life, galvanized by their affection. Steadying himself with his left hand, he raised his baton with his right. Canesi worried that Rudolf might falter and then said to himself that even if he died on the stage, "That's what Rudolf wants."

Peter Martins studied only Nureyev the entire performance, intrigued by his involvement and moved by his humility. "I never had so much respect for him as I did that night. That's when he became the person that I always thought was there, but [he] had never allowed to show. . . . Now he knew there was no time to fool around." Although Clive Barnes praised the performance, others complained of sluggish tempi. However for Martins, as for ABT conductor Charles Barker and many others, *how* he conducted was less significant than that he conducted at all.

Elated by his performance, Rudolf was also wiped out by it. At the party Hermann threw for him at the Dakota afterward, he had to retire to his bedroom, where his friends and former ballerinas took turns going in to see him. "Thank you for supporting me all these years," he told some of them. The next day he left for his farm in Virginia, accompanied by Jeannette and Wallace, and there walked his many acres. His bedside reading included a *New York Times* review of Anatole Broyard's *Intoxicated by My Illness: And Other Writings on Life and Death.*

Soon after, he returned to Vienna to conduct a program of Rossini and Mozart arias at the Palais Auersperg. Though plainly not up to the task, he willed himself through it. He could move only his fingers, not his arms, and "everyone saw that he was really ill. His skin was white; in his face, only his eyes moved."

Each day drained him further and from then on, "he went like a candle, little by little," as Luigi Pignotti recalled. In July, he flew to San Francisco to give what would be his last concert, leading an orchestra of students at the University of California in Prokofiev's *Romeo and Juliet* and Beethoven's *Eroica*. To gather strength for the concert, he spent five days in the Napa Valley, California's wine country, with Jeannette, Armen Bali and Jeremiah Tower, the celebrated American chef he had met decades earlier when Tower was a student at Harvard. The friends cooked and relaxed at the home of Natalia Makarova, who had offered it to them in her absence. The recent addition of a chapel on her property greatly amused Rudolf, who joked that "it would take more than a chapel to save her soul." Though they never spoke of AIDS or illness, it was clear something was, as Tower recalls, "very, very wrong." It wasn't so much the way Rudolf looked as the way he shuffled when he walked. When people asked, as they increasingly did, what was wrong with him, Jeannette told them his shoes were too tight. It was an absurd line, she knew. However, because Rudolf had conducting engagements lined up, one in Japan, another in Australia, she, like her mother, hoped to protect his opportunities, if not his privacy. They were both devoted to him, says Tower, recalling how they would tuck him into bed at night and stay with him until he fell asleep because "Rudolf loved the attention." When Bali's son, Arthur, died in a car accident in 1983, Rudolf had dropped everything to be with her. She now considered him her second son.

* * *

RETURNING TO Paris in July, Rudolf immediately set to work on staging *La Bayadère*. With *Bayadère*, his career in the West came full circle. This was the ballet in which he had first dazzled Paris during the Kirov's debut tour to the West in 1961, and the first ballet he had produced for the Royal Ballet in 1963. At the Kirov, his debut in the role of Solor announced his charismatic nobility, and led, inevitably, to his debuts as Albrecht, Désiré and Siegfried. *La Bayadère* was the only major Petipa ballet Nureyev had not staged in its entirety.

While he had staged its phantasmal Shades scene, he had long hoped to mount the entire four-act ballet. He had a champion in Igor Eisner, the Inspector general of dance, who periodically sent him postcards with only "*Bayadère*" scrawled across them.

The ballet had been proposed for an earlier Paris Opéra season and then postponed. "At last, *Bayadère*," Rudolf said on learning that its premiere was firmly set for October 8, 1992, perhaps sensing that *Bayadère* was the last ballet he was likely to produce.

To summon onstage the fantasy world he imagined, he called on his friends Ezio Frigerio and Franca Squarciapino. The husband-and-wife team envisioned a reverie of the Orient, its forms, colors and architecture drawn from the monuments and paintings of the Indian and Ottoman empires. Rudolf savored the ballet's excesses, "its colors, exuberance, voluptuousness and brilliant vicissitudes recalling *The Thousand and One Nights*," he told a reporter. Together with Patricia Ruanne, he studied the Kirov's production on videotape and invited his ex–Kirov partner Ninel Kurgapkina to come over from St. Petersburg to supervise rehearsals. His major amendements centered naturally enough on the male dancers, to whom he gave a more prominent role.

While work on the ballet proceeded easily, Rudolf's cardiac exam showed renewed signs of pericarditis. Over Canesi's objections, Rudolf forswore further treatment and decamped for his home on Galli for his standard curative: sun and sea. He was joined there by friends from the different parts of his life. Liuba Romankova came from St. Petersburg with her husband, Marika Besobrasova from Monte Carlo and Wallace Potts from Los Angeles. Wallace, who was HIV-positive, grew more involved in Rudolf's care and called Canesi almost daily with bulletins on his health, though it was often difficult to get a clear connection. Rudolf swam, studied orchestral scores, and, for the first time in his life, conserved his energy. On an afternoon visit to Gore Vidal in nearby Ravello, he languished "exhausted, on a sofa, drinking white wine, not speaking, until we got on to the latest ballet gossip." The story then making the rounds was Darci Kistler's call to the police after her husband, Peter

Martins, hit her during an argument.* "Peter Martins—he kill wife, no? No. Sad," Rudolf said quietly, recalling how he had hoped to put the moves on the sixteen-year-old Martins in Denmark when Erik warned him, "No, Too young. Go to jail." To Vidal, Rudolf's face was "ravaged but beautiful, still very much Tatar king. The upper body has begun to waste away, but the lower is still unaffected, legs powerful, and the feet— for a dancer—not too misshapen, no hammertoes."

By the time Marika Besobrasova arrived at the Isole dei Galli in late August, however, Rudolf had grown so weak and undernourished that he had to be airlifted off the island by helicopter and flown back to Paris. Canesi was waiting for him at Charles de Gaulle Airport on September 3, never believing that Rudolf would ever make it back from Galli alive. He was beginning to think that Rudolf was, perhaps, indestructable, though his first glimpse of the "ghostly" figure tottering toward him told him otherwise. Rudolf finally saw his deterioration reflected in the doctor's eyes. "Now," he asked plainly, "is it the end?"

There were only three weeks to go before the premiere, and much of Bayadère had still to be set. The day Rudolf returned to rehearsal in the Petipa studio, the dancers were shocked to see their once-feral director looking enfeebled, try though they did to carry on as if nothing had changed. He could barely speak above a whisper and could not demonstrate movements without losing his balance. "It was very, very hard," says Isabelle Guérin, whom he cast in the leading role of Nikiya. "Even when I knew he was really tired, I tried to joke with him. He was sick and dying, but he still had an aura and something in his eyes was shining." The dancers knew what the ballet meant to him and worked in an atmosphere of "absolute fervor," recalls Hélène Traïline, then the Opéra's director of programming. The entire company, "even those who had been against him," responded with uncharacteristic generosity. "They wanted to make him forget all the hurt feelings and conflicts from before." That might have been the case had the corps de ballet not reminded him of old times by threatening an ecostrike on being asked to wear stuffed parrots on the sleeves of their costumes.

With Bayadère, Rudolf intended to pay homage both to Petipa and to the traditions that had governed his career. While he followed the Kirov's production closely, he and Ninel Kurgapkina were not always in agreement. According to Ruanne, who assisted them both, "his eyebrows would go up, the eyes would widen and he would say something to her in Russian that invited no further discussion." He decided, for example, to restore the more complicated original version of the variation danced by Gamzatti, Kurgapkina's signature role, and began to make changes to

*Kistler dropped the charges and the couple soon reconciled.

Solor's solo at the beginning of the third act Shades scene, which he had first staged for the Opéra in 1974. On his good days, he conveyed an air of intensity and managed to indicate the movements, although too weak to perform them himself. On his bad days, he supervised rehearsals reclining from a divan.* "You would ask how he was and he would say, 'Still alive,'" recalls Ruanne. "Then came a point when you didn't ask anymore." When he lost strength, Charles Jude, Laurent Hilaire and Manuel Legris, chosen to alternate in the role of Solor, choreographed Solor's solos in his stead, "mixing all the difficult steps he liked" to please and excite him. "Yes," Legris recalls him saying. "That's perfect." Though he was not to dance in his ballet, Rudolf planned to conduct on opening night.

When the rigors of rehearsal became too onerous, he began spending less and less time in the studio, and more and more time at home and at the Hôpital Notre Dame du Perpétual Secours in Levallois, a suburb northwest of Paris. His female friends took turns nursing him at the Quai Voltaire. The first to arrive was seventy-three-year-old Marika Besobrasova, then seventy-three and the kind of strong-minded, elegant, maternal figure Rudolf implicitly trusted. They were soon joined by the black Rotweiler Rudolf brought home one day after spying it in a pet store near the Palais Garnier. He named the dog Solor for *Bayadère*'s warrior hero, changing it to Soloria when "he" turned out to be female. But not only was the dog not housebroken, it was fearful and sick, with bronchitis, eye and knee problems and a fever. Regardless, Rudolf grew so attached to Soloria that he felt hurt whenever she refused to sleep with him in his overheated bedroom. Marika quickly discovered that the best way to get Rudolf's attention was to address him as Solaria Rudolfovna.

The premiere was one week away when Pierre Bergé decided that Rudolf was too ill to conduct opening night. The problem was, no one wanted to be the messenger, "an excruciating task," as Hélène Traïline thought of it. Finally, she called Canesi, having concluded that medical intervention was the only authority he might accept. Rudolf was in Perpétuel Secours Hospital the day Canesi recommended that he not conduct the premiere. "It will exhaust you," the doctor said, "and perhaps your ballet will suffer as a result." Rudolf became furious. "Don't shit on my brain!" he lashed out at the doctor from his bed.

The next day Rudolf returned to the opera house, hell-bent on showing his colleagues that he indeed had the necessary vigor to conduct the premiere. When Hélène Traïline went to greet him near a backstage

---

*As a new production of *Swan Lake* was also in rehearsal, time constraints prevented Rudolf from mounting the ballet's fourth and final act.

staircase, he glared at her and pushed away the arm of the young man assigned to assist him. As he started to descend, he faltered badly and nearly toppled down the stairs before the young man caught his arm again. Still, he persisted. Entering the rehearsal studio, he curtly refused any assistance. "No divan," he said, and for the rest of the day insisted on sitting upright in a chair, although the effort clearly exhausted him.

It was Nureyev's last battle.

32

Curtain Call

ON OCTOBER 8, 1992, Nureyev watched the premiere of La Bayadère from a box in the Palais Garnier. Decades earlier, his own performance in the ballet had prompted comparisons to Nijinsky. This time, Laurent Hilaire was Solor; Isabelle Guérin his beloved temple dancer, Nikiya; and Elisabeth Platel her rival, the rajah's daughter, Gamzatti. Guérin knew it was the last time Rudolf would see her dance. She danced for him, she recalls, but all that night she worried that he would be overcome with emotion and "leave us during the performance." Hurt that Rudolf had decided to give opening night to Laurent Hilaire (Nureyev's professionalism having overridden sentiment), Charles Jude did not attend the premiere.

Earlier that evening, Luigi had hastened to the Quai Voltaire to help Rudolf bathe and dress. The sinewy dancer's body that had trained daily and that Luigi knew so well had lost all trace of muscle tone. "He had no hips, there was just skin. He could not stand straight and he was shuffling along on bent knees, so I took him by the hand to hold him up. I tried everything because I was so embarrassed." Rudolf, however, barely took notice of the openmouthed stares that met him at the opera house. "It looked like he had the plague and nobody came close to him. I kept asking him, 'Rudolf, are you sure you want to do this? Are you happy?' And he said, 'Very.'"

Too weak to sit upright, Rudolf lay stretched out on a divan, propped up by pillows. He had wanted to sit in the orchestra, and when Canesi forbade him, arguing that he would not be able to leave if he needed to, Rudolf countered, "But I won't see everything in the loge."

Friends from around the world had converged on Paris for the occasion. In the loge with him were Canesi, Luigi, Marika and Jeannette Etheredge, and elsewhere in the theater, Sylvie Guillem, Rosella Hightowcr, Pierre Lacotte, Roland Petit, Zizi Jeanmaire, Violette Verdy, John Taras, John Lanchbery, the Rothschilds. At the first interval, many of them lined up to pay their compliments, unaware that although his body was supine, Rudolf's mind was keenly immersed in his ballet.

"Jack, you change orchestration in any of that act?" he demanded of John Lanchbery, who had orchestrated the score.

"No," Lanchbery answered, "I haven't changed anything."

"The trombones sounded heavier than usual at the end of the act," Rudolf continued.

"But, Rudolf," Lanchbery reminded him, "this is the Paris Opéra. The trombone players always play too loudly."

"Oh, yes," Rudolf answered quietly. "I forgot that."

When the curtain came down on the final act, Rudolf decided to take a bow. As Canesi and Luigi led him toward the stage, they reminded him that he needn't go through with it. "I must do it, but let it be quick," he said, knowing full well the impact his appearance would have.

When the curtain rose again, Rudolf was standing center stage, supported by Isabelle Guérin and Laurent Hilaire. He was greeted with stunned silence, then thunderous applause as the crowd rose to its feet. The emotion in the house was palpable as cries of "Bravo" mingled with the more urgent cries of "Au revoir" for the gaunt figure in evening clothes, a luxuriant red shawl draped over his left shoulder. For a split second, Rudolf let go of the hands supporting him and took command of the stage, the only place he had ever felt at home. Smiling, drawing strength from the adulation, he raised his arm weakly in salute and in farewell.

No sooner had the curtain come down than French officialdom rushed in to honor him. In a private ceremony on the stage, with Rudolf seated on the rajah's throne, first Pierre Bergé and then Culture Minister Jack Lang paid tribute to him in speeches. Lang then decorated Nureyev with the insignia of the Commander of Arts and Letters, one of France's highest honors for lifetime achievement. Photographers pushed dancers aside to get a better shot of Nureyev. To John Taras, it was a distressing scene. "[Rudolf] couldn't stand, and his eyes were haunted."

Still, he insisted on going on to the gala supper, where, seated between Maude and Marie-Hélène de Rothschild, he made a point of speaking to Bergé about the next year's program. Midway through the meal, he asked Canesi and Luigi to take him home. On their way out, they were stopped by Bergé, who asked that Rudolf sit for a portrait for *Paris Match*. A room had been draped in blue fabric for this purpose. Marika tried to prevent it, but Rudolf wanted to have his picture taken. The photographs, published instantly around the world, made it clear just how ill he was. Soon the English papers were reporting that Nureyev had AIDS despite denials from the Opéra and Nureyev's friends.

The fact that he was dying was never discussed openly among those closest him. When answering his telephone, they learned not to refer to illness, for Rudolf was often listening on the extension in his bedroom, refusing to be sidelined.

It was a losing battle. When Rudi van Dantzig and Toer van Schayk came to visit him the day after the premiere, Douce met them in the hallway with specific directions. "Don't tell him that you came specially for him, it will make him suspicious. And don't mention his disease, he absolutely doesn't want that. The best is just to talk about the future as if nothing were wrong." She was gathering reviews of the premiere for him, careful to remove the ones that mentioned AIDS. Few passed her censorship. "Is that all?" Rudolf asked when she handed him just three newspapers.

Van Dantzig had skipped the premiere and flown in for the second performance. He thought that if Rudolf had the energy to mount a three-act ballet, he couldn't possibly be all that ill. But once in Rudolf's apartment, he was overcome by a sense of gloom. The rooms suggested neglect, and in one of them, "boxes and bottles of medicine and capsules were lying and standing about in nonchalant disorder." The objects, he later wrote, "looked shorn of warmth and lustre, it was evident that for a long time no one had taken care of them: all attention was focused on one room, Rudolf's bedroom." On a table, a bouquet of lilies sent by Madonna was still wrapped in cellophane; in the kitchen, Jacqueline Onassis's red roses had been stuck haphazardly into a plastic bottle.

As bid, van Dantzig attempted to mask his distress as he sat on Rudolf's bed and laid his hand on his thin leg, knowing how much he relished human touch. Rudolf was lying in bed in his darkened room, a small lamp by his side the only available light. "His eyes and mouth seem more pronounced, burning and almost swallowing his other features, as if all his senses reach out for the world through his face, starving for the merest fragment of his surroundings." With great effort, Rudolf recounted the previous night's success and how marvelously the dancers performed his ballet. From time to time, Marika, Jeannette and Douce came in to check on him. "My women," he would remind van Dantzig. "See? Always my women." He hoped to go out that night to see Roland Petit's company, but on hearing this, Douce suggested he wait a few days and then they would go antiquing together. So many lovely things had been put aside for him, she said. Her words struck van Dantzig "like promises to a child who needs to be mollified."

The next day, John Taras arrived to find an apartment full of people speaking in hushed tones. "Rudolf is asleep," they whispered, and then suddenly Rudolf walked into the salon, unsupported, and joined Taras on the sofa. He spoke eagerly of the ballet company he hoped to establish in Leningrad, in a small theater at the Hermitage. Would Taras like to participate? he asked. Rudolf laid out his plans. He and Taras would take a gastronomic tour of Europe. But first Rudolf was to conduct *Coppélia* for Roland Petit and the Kirov Ballet orchestra and *Petrouchka* at the Dutch National Ballet.

Two days after the premiere, Rudolf left for St.-Bart's with Charles Jude, Florence Clerc, Jeannette Etheredge and Soloria. Though Jude was supposed to dance *Bayadère*, he bowed out to accompany Rudolf, who he was certain hoped to die by the sea. Like Fonteyn, Rudolf had chosen a cherished, if remote, part of the world to live out his final days. John Taras ran into Rudolf at the airport and couldn't believe that in his condition, Rudolf had the strength to go anywhere. Canesi decided it was unfair to stop him but arranged for the local hospital to check on him daily.

For twelve days, they stayed at Rudolf's beach house, where work had just been completed on Nureyev's bedroom and terrace overlooking the sea. One morning after Florence climbed down a rocky incline for a swim in the waves, Rudolf set off after her, only to be restrained by Jude, who insisted he go to the sandy beach instead. Florence was stunned that Rudolf should think to follow her into such rough waters. "He still wanted to experience everything, but he was so weak, it was very sad." Rudolf returned to the house and refused to speak to Jude for the rest of the day.

Rudolf spent his days studying the great conductors on videotape and worked with Jude on a new ballet, *The Prince of the Pagodas*. One afternoon the Canadian dancer Frank Augustyn came to visit. Augustyn, yet another Nureyev alumnus, had become director of the Ottawa Ballet and wanted Rudolf to conduct the new work he was choreographing. Rudolf had invited him to St.-Bart's, and when Augustyn accepted, Rudolf replied, "Good, just don't be too late." What a strange thing to say, thought Augustyn, unaware that Rudolf was dying. He had seen the photographs in *Paris Match*, but assumed that Rudolf was still recovering from heart surgery until he arrived on the island and saw "this thin waif of a man . . . lying on his bed staring up at the ceiling." On Rudolf's recommendation, Augustyn had agreed to set his ballet to Beethoven's *Eroica* Symphony, which Rudolf had already conducted.

"Which movement did you choose?" Rudolf now asked him.

"The second," said Augustyn.

"Ah," Rudolf replied without missing a beat, "the funeral march."

Augustyn was speechless. "He got me and was making a joke of it. He still had his sense of humor."

Reinvigorated by the heat, sunshine and sandy beaches, Rudolf seemed content on St.-Bart's, though there were moments when his memory lapsed and he didn't know where he was. His friends were exhausted by the responsibility of caring for him around the clock and, not least, by the fear that he might die in this isolated place. After Jeannette left, only the Judes remained with Rudolf. But Rudolf did not want to leave. "Why don't we stay here?" he asked them. Needing to resume their own lives, they soon returned him to Paris, the winter, and more rounds of tests.

With the publication of the *Paris Match* photos, Michel Canesi had been besieged by calls from reporters demanding to know if Nureyev had AIDS. "I'm a close friend of Rudolf's," they would say. "How is he, *really?*" Two British journalists had even booked seats on Rudolf's flight to St.-Bart's and pestered Jude all the way there to introduce them. Jude refused to comment, as did Canesi, fearing the press might show up at the airport the day Rudolf returned to Paris. Instead, Canesi informed them that Rudolf was returning two days later. Rudolf looked disappointed when only Canesi was there to greet him at Roissy Airport. "When I told him about the trick I had played on the photographers, he was a little irritated about it. He was not afraid of the press, even at the end."

In the last months of his life, Nureyev's universe grew ever more circumscribed. He moved only between Notre-Dame du Perpétuel Secours Hospital and his Quai Voltaire apartment. At home, Maude, Marika, Douce, Wallace, Jeannette and Jane Hermann cared for him in alternating shifts, cooking, washing, feeding, waiting. They were assisted by Rudolf's thirty-three-year-old live-in nurse, François "Frank" Lousassa, a hip, quiet-spoken black man, who had emigrated to Paris from his native Guadeloupe several years earlier. Tall and muscular, his hair cut short on the sides, a mop of curls on top, he was always fashionably turned out, favoring colorful patterned sweaters, black leather pants and funky black combat boots. Rudolf's name was only vaguely familiar to him; he knew he was a star, but knew nothing of the ballet, or of Rudolf's "financially privileged" milieu. Rudolf took to him at once, perhaps responding to a male presence and to Frank's refusal to coddle him as "his women" did. Frank challenged Rudolf just as Rudolf had Margot: not allowing him to play the invalid.

Rudolf began asking for Frank whenever he was absent. "All these women loved him so much and were so eager to please him," Frank recalls. "But they tried to do too much for him. I wasn't fussing over him every five minutes. I wanted to make him work a little, to make him feel as if he were still part of life." Where everyone else kept the drapes in Rudolf's bedroom drawn, Frank opened them to let the sunlight in, to put him in rhythm with the day. And where the others brought Rudolf breakfast in bed and helped him to eat, Frank insisted that he sit up in a chair and feed himself. Even in Rudolf's depleted state, Frank took the measure of the man immediately. "I wanted to let him have his autonomy, to finish his journey himself."

As Rudolf lay dying, Douce became "overly obsessive" in her concern, and at times Rudolf simply refused to see her. He had no choice, however, but to see the lawyers who came to Paris in November, to take his deposition in the palimony lawsuit Robert Tracy now brought against him. Tracy was HIV-positive and, after developing a bad case of shingles earlier that June, had begun to worry about his own future. He had not realized it at the time, but his having been asked to the signing of Rudolf's American will in April meant he was not a beneficiary.* With no steady income, he hired the famous palimony expert Marvin Mitchelson "to protect me," he later explained, "because I wasn't being protected." Tracy was still living at the Dakota apartment, which had recently been turned over to Nureyev's American foundation. Tracy's lawsuit alienated him from most of Nureyev's friends, who were incensed that he should seek compensation when Rudolf was near death. They were sure he meant to suggest that Rudolf had given him the AIDS virus and they suspected he was after the Dakota apartment, which was worth millions.†

Rudolf had been trying for two years to get Robert out of his apartment but, not wanting to confront him directly, had enlisted various friends to ask Robert to leave. Yet at the same time, he continued to use Tracy as "his New York Douce," as Jude thought of him, relying on him to look after his apartment, make dinner dates, and keep track of his New York affairs. According to Michel Canesi, Rudolf took Tracy's lawsuit in stride. "He wasn't angry with Robert. He didn't mind, he was so detached from everything." Only two pressing matters concerned him: He added a codicil to his will, making Canesi a special adviser on his European foundation's medical activities.‡ He told Canesi, "When the moment comes, you'll know what to do." And he asked Jude to be the custodian of his ballets. "It was very awkward for me, so I said, 'No, Rudolf, in one month you'll be better and you can look after them yourself again.' "

As his health declined, Rudolf spent more and more time at the hospital. In mid-November, despite a severely compromised immune system and severe bouts of thrush, a yeast infection of the mouth, Rudolf went home for a few days and immediately set up meetings to discuss the coming year's Paris Opéra season. But now Rudi van Dantzig sensed

*Two wills signed in April 1992 covered Nureyev's European and American assets. His holdings were to be turned over to two foundations, one based in Liechtenstein, the other in Chicago.
†In 1993, it was sold for $1.85 million.
‡Neither the codicil nor the foundation's follow-up board minutes used the word "AIDS." Instead, the trustees resolved to help "dancers or artists suffering from illness or decease [sic] for which Dr. M. F. Canesi is a specialized doctor."

an air of resignation. With his mouth and throat infected, Rudolf winced when he swallowed, and Marika had to spoon-feed him her homemade vegetable broth. "I can't eat," he murmured sadly, but without reproach. "I can't do anything anymore. . . ."

On November 20, he was readmitted to Perpétuel Secours Hospital and there spent the last six weeks of his life. He was unable to eat, leaving Canesi no choice but to put him on an intravenous drip, even though he knew there was a huge risk of infection, as with all patients whose immune systems have broken down. Beyond that, there was nothing more Canesi could do for him. Never once complaining, Rudolf passed the time with headphones on his ears, preparing to conduct *Coppélia* in Marseilles. "You felt he was living in this music," says Frank Lousassa. For a change of pace, Frank played him tapes of Afro-Caribbean music and danced around the room for Rudolf, telling him, "This is the way we do it back home."

Among the many friends who visited him was Marie-Hélène de Rothschild. Having suffered for years from debilitating arthritis,* she knew firsthand how stark hospitals could feel, so she dressed up "especially to go see him," making sure to wear "pretty clothes and bright colors."

On another occasion, Marika and Wallace smuggled Solaria into his room, hoping to cheer him. But according to Marika, "Rudolf was away a little bit already and didn't pay much attention to her." He was fully reconciled to his situation the afternoon Patricia Ruanne came by to talk about some of the problems in *La Bayadère* that needed resolving. Rudolf was reading newspapers in bed, swathed in shawls, a Missoni knit cap on his head, "looking like an Eastern potentate." The television was on, as it was almost steadily, but the picture was scrambled, so Rudolf asked Ruanne to get the nurse to fix it. He was trying to get Canal Plus, a pay TV channel he watched at home, but of course the hospital didn't carry it. When Ruanne relayed the news, Rudolf suddenly sighed and said, "I'm tired of this, let's hope it will soon be over."

Thinking he might benefit from a psychiatrist, Michel Canesi sent a colleague in to see him. No sooner had the doctor introduced himself than Rudolf ordered him out of his room. The psychiatrist had the same surname as a lawyer in Austria who Rudolf believed had taken him for a large sum of money. Their session barely lasted thirty seconds.

Nureyev's family and Leningrad friends had their own remedies in mind. His sister Rosa and thirty-one-year-old niece Gouzel came regularly to the hospital, even though Rudolf was not often in the mood to see them. Rudolf's nephew Yuri was also in Paris, taking music lessons and living in the flat Rudolf owned across the hall. Jude considered their

*She died on March 1, 1996.

relations "strange" and could never tell "why he wanted to see them or why he didn't." Gouzel, a now strikingly pretty young woman, disliked many of Rudolf's friends and was not shy about saying so. Rosa had come from La Turbie and was staying in the other studio flat that Rudolf owned and Gouzel lived in, one floor up from his own. Michel Canesi was certain that Rosa disapproved of him, thinking him too young and cheerful to be a doctor. Suspicious of the foods Rudolf was being given, she annoyed Marika by throwing out her special broth and replacing it with one of her own, "some strange soup with grease that made him sick," was how Marika described it. When Canesi tried to convey to Rosa the gravity of Rudolf's condition, she brushed him off by saying in her Russianized French, "Oh, don't worry, a little bouillon and he will improve." Like most of Rudolf's friends, Canesi found it "impossible" to communicate with her. Still, as Marika recalls, experiencing "the power of these Mongol people" gave her a keener understanding of Rudolf. "That mixture of great power, great presence and then some things that are absolutely out of our habits."

Meanwhile, in St. Petersburg, where AIDS barely went acknowledged and was little understood, Liuba Myanikova received a phone call one day from a medical student she had never met. Kirov director Oleg Vinogradov had urged him to get in touch with her, he said, because he had discovered a potential cure for the dying Nureyev, one improbably called WN7: White Nights Number Seven. She was so desperate to help Rudolf that without knowing much about the mysterious WN7, she rushed a sample of it to the airport and persuaded a Paris-bound passenger to deliver it to Nureyev. Since it was illegal to take medicine out of the country, she poured it into a Chanel perfume bottle. The "cure" amused but little relieved Nureyev's doctor, who had no intention of administering an unknown drug to his famous patient. "It was supposed to be steeped in hot water and inhaled. It was very Gothic and ridiculous and if Rudolf's condition had not been so bad, I'm sure he would have found it very funny."

By mid-December Rudolf had difficulty recognizing friends and was drifting in and out of consciousness. At Gouzel's insistence, a security guard was hired to keep visitors, journalists and crazy fans away. Only Rudolf's closest friends and family members were admitted into his room and even they at well-spaced intervals, given the friction among some of them. His family in Ufa was summoned to Paris. Razida brought with her the herbal remedy that a member of the Bashkirian Writers' Union had given to her for Rudolf and was upset when his doctors refused to give it to him. She arrived in Paris on Christmas Day, followed by her niece Alfia and Alfia's infant daughter, Genya. Rosa and Gouzel met them at the airport, though relations among them all were decidedly cool and little helped by Alfia's feeling that her cousin Gouzel treated them disdainfully as "simple folk from Ufa." Rosa, as the eldest Nureyev child, insisted on taking charge, which led to frequent quarrels between them, especially when she and Razida cooked meals for Rudolf. According to Razida, "Rosa insisted that he should have chicken broth and no one could argue with her."

Not wanting Rudolf disturbed, Rosa also tried to prevent his friends from going in to see him. This struck many of them as a gross irony, given that Rudolf had spent most of his life keeping *her* at a distance. Never in his life had he ceded control to anyone, nor did he designate anyone to take over in his final weeks before he slipped, progressively, into unconsciousness. In their grief, his friends and family scrambled to lay claim to their Rudolf, each certain they knew him best. The truth was, his life was comprised of as many strands, colors and patterns as the tapestries crowding his apartments. And of the people who had mattered to him most—his mother, Pushkin, Erik, Nigel, Maude, Margot and Jude—only Maude and Jude remained.

With Jude standing by his side and Frank Lousassa holding his hand, Rudolf slipped away peacefully at 3:30 P.M. on January 6, 1993, Russian Christmas Eve. He was fifty-four years old. Rosa had stepped outside for a moment and returned to find her brother dead. The news spread quickly to the friends and relatives in the hallway outside, throughout Paris and around the world.

"I ALWAYS SAID he would be there to hold my hand when I went, and was quite sure that he would." It was January 11, 1993, the day before Rudolf's funeral and Maude Gosling was still coming to grips with his death. She had flown to Paris that afternoon with Jane Hermann and Tessa Kennedy and checked into the Hôtel Voltaire, where Jeannette, Wallace, Marika, Rudi van Dantzig and scores of dancers had converged. Down the street, police cars were posted outside Number 23 Quai Voltaire, in advance of the car conveying Rudolf's body home. His friends had decided that his final journey should take him from his Paris apartment to the opera house. Michel Canesi engaged Frank Lousassa to stay with the body until morning. Rosa, Gouzel, Razida, Alfia, Yuri and a handful of Rudolf's closest friends joined him inside Rudolf's apartment, but when Jeannette and Marika came by, Gouzel started screaming and refused to let them in. Though discomfited by the angry scene that erupted, Frank felt he had no choice but to abide by the family's wishes.

He was surprised, however, when the family finally trooped off to bed, leaving him, a virtual stranger, alone with the body. Driving rains and thunder rattled the windows of the grand salon, making him nervous. To calm himself, he sipped a glass of white wine and talked to Rudolf, all night long reassuring him that he had not been abandoned.

Rudolf's friends arrived the next morning to accompany his casket to the Palais Garnier. His coffin was set on the low table at which Rudolf took his morning tea, and following his instructions, he had been dressed for burial in his tuxedo and colored Missoni cap. While Douce paced nervously from room to room, Tessa Kennedy knelt by the coffin and André Larquié surveyed the honors adorning it. At Larquié's suggestion a death mask had been made, following the grand, if obsolete, tradition reserved for Europe's greatest artists. It was also Larquié who had organized Rudolf's funeral, an affair befitting a state dignitary. Admission to the funeral was by invitation only and the invitations had been color-coded to designate where the mourners should stand.

The roads leading to the Palais Garnier were cordoned off, and hundreds of ballet fans pressed against police barriers in the Place de l'Opéra, straining for a view. Outside the nineteenth-century opera house, the steps were banked with lavish wreaths, pots and bouquets from, among others, Yves Saint Laurent, the Niarchos family, the Capezio "family," Roland Petit and Zizi Jeanmaire, and Princess Firyal, whose wreath bore the message "Nunu dance in peace." "Merci Rudolph," read the sash on Pierre Bergé's red roses, while the bouquet sent by Jack Lang and the Ministry of Culture came dressed in the colors of the republic.

The Palais Garnier was where Rudolf's career in the West had begun in 1961. It was also where he had spent six remarkably productive years as dance director in the 1980s, and where he had made his last appearance on a stage three months earlier, in October 1992. At 10 A.M. six male dancers, led by Charles Jude, carried Rudolf's plain oak coffin into the opera house and to the top of the grand staircase. Lining their way were ballet students, Rudolf's honor guard. The civil ceremony was held not on the stage but in the foyer, the simplicity of the wooden casket standing out starkly against the cold, white marble. A small velvet cushion, bearing the insignia of a Commander of Arts and Letters, was placed two steps below. Clustered at the foot of the stairs were a chamber group and, directly across, the mourners. For thirty minutes, the disparate elements of Nureyev's nomadic life were drawn together in a single room. There were Rudolf's weeping sisters in black wool coats, scarves tied around their heads, consoled by international socialites in mink and sable. There were his nieces and nephews, Gouzel, Alfia, Yuri and Victor, his old Kirov partner Ninel Kurgapkina, his English friends and colleagues, Maude, Lynn Seymour, Joan Thring, Antoinette Sibley, Anthony Dowell, Merle Park, John Tooley as well as his American friends, including Wallace, Jeannette, Jane, Lee Radziwill, Phyllis Wyeth, John Taras, Monique van Vooren. Not surprisingly, Robert Tracy stayed away. There were also prominent Parisians such as Leslie Caron, Marie-Hélène and Guy de Rothschild, Douce, Baron Alexis de Redé,

Roland Petit, Yvette Chauviré, Pierre Lacotte, Igor Eisner, Jean Babilée, Patrick Dupond and an Italian contingent led by Carla Fracci, Luigi, Vittoria Ottolenghi and Franco Zeffirelli.

Some of them stood on the steps; hundreds more peered down from balconies. The pomp and ceremony amused Lynn Seymour. Rudolf, she recalled, "would have had a good old laugh at all the assholes suddenly paying tribute."

As the musicians played selections from Bach and Tchaikovsky, friends read extracts from Rudolf's five favorite artists: Pushkin, Byron, Michelangelo, Goethe and Rimbaud, each in his original language. It fell to Jack Lang to speak of Nureyev himself and in his extravagant and florid eulogy he described how the gods had bestowed on Nureyev remarkable gifts: "Beauty, power and a taste for the absolute. . . . He attained a mythical dimension. Like the phoenix, he is reborn each morning after having spent himself each night." Quoting Baryshnikov, he added, "He had the charisma and the simplicity of a man of the earth and the untouchable arrogance of the gods."

To the mournful strains of Mahler's *Songs of a Wayfarer*, sung on a recording by Jessye Norman, Jude and the other pallbearers carried the casket to a waiting hearse. From there, a cortege of Renault minibuses conveyed the hundred or so selected mourners to the Russian Orthodox cemetry at Sainte-Geneviève-des-Bois. In late November, Rudolf had selected this burial ground of White Russian émigrés over the more famous Père Lachaise, Nijinsky's final resting place. The site he chose was an hour's ride from the opera house that had welcomed him to the West and whose movement to modernize he had choreographed. Even here the perpetual outsider felt he must push for position. For among the ornate gravestones of exiled dukes and countesses, Serge Lifar was also buried. "Make sure I'm not too close to Lifar," Rudolf had instructed his American lawyer. When he was head of the Opéra, exorcising the spirit of Lifar had been one of his most difficult tasks, Rudolf told Gore Vidal. "We name rooms after this one, after that one. *They* make me name Lifar Room. Always evil in that room. . . . Bad ghost."

As Rudolf's coffin was lowered into the ground, his friends tossed in ballet slippers. And white roses rained down on the dancer one last time.

Epilogue

EVEN IN DEATH, Nureyev provoked controversy. Dr. Canesi initially announced that Nureyev had died from a cardiac complication following "a grievous illness." The word "AIDS" was never uttered, igniting a firestorm of protest from AIDS activists. "Following Mr. Nureyev's wishes," the doctor added, "I can't say any more." But say more he did, nine days later, in an interview with *Le Figaro*, France's most widely read newspaper. In a long account of Nureyev's illness, Canesi confirmed that Nureyev had indeed died from AIDS. He maintained that contrary to his earlier statement, Nureyev had given him authority to divulge the true cause of his death. "If I clarify things now, it is because there is no such thing as a shameful disease. I am thinking of all the anonymous patients who are suffering from being ostracized. Rudolf lived for 13 or 14 years with this virus, thanks to his force, his combativeness. People should know that. He was too famous to be able to hide the truth."*

Canesi was right: Nureyev's fame made him once more an international symbol, this time of the politics surrounding the disease with which he had long feared being identified. Twelve days after his death, he graced the cover of *Newsweek*, the first time since his heydey in 1965. But now the story was not "NUREYEV: The New Nijinsky," but "AIDS and the Arts: A Lost Generation." And sadly for novelist and AIDS activist Paul Monette, as for many gay men, Nureyev was no longer "a great hero" of the age or of the arts. "I consider him a coward," Monette told

---

*About the only place where the truth remained hidden was Ufa. Local press reports noted only that Nureyev had died, making no mention of AIDS. Though barely talked about, the disease was irrevocably linked to homosexuality and regarded as a terrible shame.

Newsweek. "I don't care how great a dancer he was." Nureyev had a responsibility to the gay community, Monette insisted, to leverage his fame to raise public consciousness of the disease. Striking a more personal note, Edward Albee recalled feeling "dismayed that Rudolf refused to admit he was sick. He would have gotten so much more affection and acceptance had he."

Mikhail Baryshnikov was also unhappy, but for a different reason. A front-page obituary in *The New York Times* characterized Nureyev as anti-Semitic. Two days after Nureyev's death, Baryshnikov sent a letter to the *Times*, protesting what he saw as an unfamiliar view of the man he had known. But the paper didn't print it. The decision was made "reluctantly," cultural editor Paul Goldberger explained. "We felt strongly that [Baryshnikov's] allegations . . . were without merit. . . . We looked into it, and we felt there was sufficient evidence to support what we said. . . ." Baryshnikov found an outlet for his displeasure, instead, in *The New Yorker,* in a brief interview that appeared the following month. "The question about anti-Semitic remarks was absolutely unfair and not right," said Baryshnikov. He was outraged that the *Times* expressed such views in its appraisal of the life and achievements of a major artist.

"AFTER I DIE," Nureyev told Charles Jude, "it will be a long time before they finish with the business of my money." It was almost as if Nureyev had made sure of that. For years friends had urged him to hire a good estates lawyer, but Nureyev had resisted, balking at the fees and suspicious of those who would mind his money. More significantly, perhaps, he had not wanted to be encumbered by the thought, let alone the business, of dying. So he let his lawyers handle the fine points of his will. Nevertheless, he dearly wanted to ensure that his hard-won earnings would not disappear into the state coffers.

His estate was complicated by his transborder status: Nureyev was an Austrian citizen, who died in Paris. He left assets in Liechtenstein, Italy, France, Monaco, the Caribbean and the United States. Just how much Nureyev was worth may never be known, though estimates put his total net worth at approximately twenty-five to thirty million dollars.

In a will signed in Paris on April 14, 1992, Nureyev bequeathed all of his European assets, plus his house in St.-Bart's, his farm in Virginia, the rights to his ballets and all of his bank accounts, to the Ballet Promotion Foundation. Created by Nureyev in 1975, the foundation is managed from Zurich, though situated in Liechtenstein, a tax haven famous for its secrecy laws. In another, supplemental will, signed in New York on April 28, 1992, Nureyev named the newly incorporated Chicago-based Rudolf Nureyev Dance Foundation the sole recipient of his American assets. Nureyev's American tax lawyer, Barry Weinstein, set up the new foundation specifically to segregate Nureyev's remaining American assets from those that fell under European jurisdiction.

The two foundations were founded to forward Nureyev's two principal concerns: to avoid paying estate taxes and to perpetuate his name and legacy. Precisely what the latter entailed, however, soon became a matter of dispute. As outlined by Nureyev in his wills and follow-up letters of instruction to his executors, both were to underwrite ballet performances, commission new works and give grants to companies and young dancers.

In addition, the European foundation was to fund AIDS-related research and medical care for sick dancers. It was also to provide scholarships to promising Russian dancers intent on studying ballet in the West, with the understanding that they would later "contribute to the development of dance in my country of origin where I commenced my career as a dancer." That life's work was to be commemorated by setting aside Nureyev's art, costumes, textiles and musical instruments for public exhibition. "It is my wish and I give binding instructions to the trustees to provide with the capital and the properties or the proceeds, therefrom, for the perpetuity of my name in museum or gallery exhibition form as a memory of my life style [sic] and carrier [sic]* as a person and as a dancer and in which I have engaged myself in the field of choreographique art and music. . . ." Nureyev hoped that the exhibit would be located in Paris. His will first described the city as "the center of my life," and was then amended by hand to read "an important part of my life," most likely to avoid potential tax claims by the French government.

To the European foundation also fell the task of overseeing the bequests Nureyev made to his family. He left two hundred thousand dollars each to Rosa, Razida and Lilya's daughter, Alfia, and fifty thousand dollars each to Gouzel, Alfia's son, Ruslan, and to his two nephews, Yuri and Victor. In addition, Nureyev gave his sister Rosa and niece Gouzel the lifetime right to live free of charge in smaller apartments he owned, and his sister Razida and niece Alfia the right to each live in one of the houses on his farm in Virginia. The European foundation was to bear any expenses incurred by his Ufa relatives in emigrating to the United States as well as education costs for his nieces, nephews and great-nephew, provided that their studies were of a serious nature.

Upon Nureyev's death, his foundations moved quickly to liquidate his assets, in particular the contents of his Paris and New York homes. Along with his paintings, furniture, carpets and costumes, they included personal effects, such as family photo albums and framed pictures of Erik Bruhn, Margot Fonteyn and his mother. Christie's soon announced that Nureyev's belongings and ballet memorabilia would be sold at two auc-

*Presumably "career."

tions, one in New York in December 1993, the other in London in January 1994.

But no sooner had Christie's begun cataloging and photographing the contents of Nureyev's Quai Voltaire apartment than Gouzel Nureyeva arrived with a lawyer and sheriff in tow. They promptly sealed the apartment. Gouzel and Rosa initiated a lawsuit against the European foundation, charging that it was violating Nureyev's wishes. Rudolf had wanted a museum with *all* of his collections, they maintained, and would not have wished to see them dispersed at auction. And they questioned whether Nureyev had really intended for the bulk of his estate to go to a foundation and not to his family. His lawyers, they said, had taken advantage of Nureyev's weakened condition to mislead him for their own gain — at his relatives' expense.

Both auctions were postponed until a compromise was struck: The foundations would either withhold or buy back at auction a number of costumes and family photographs if Rosa and Gouzel agreed not to block them. The New York sale earned $7.9 million, the London sale $2.79 million. Rosa and Gouzel, however, did not drop their lawsuit.

Nureyev's Ufa relatives accepted his bequests though they were never fully apprised of the details of their legacy. They looked askance at Gouzel and Rosa's litigation, thinking that Rudolf had treated them fairly. They themselves felt, however, that they were being kept in the dark by a foundation that had little regard for them. Though Nureyev had given both Alfia's and Razida's families the right to live in one of the houses on his Viriginia estate, they had never seen it and had no idea what kind of life they might lead there, not to mention what such a rent-free arrangment might be worth. To visit the farm, they needed an invitation to secure a visa. But when Alfia and Razida looked to the foundation for help, nothing came of it. They were told that the European foundation had paid seventy-five thousand dollars to an immigration lawyer, but no answers were forthcoming. At one point, the foundation's secretary, an arrogant young Swiss lawyer named Marc Richter, offered Razida thirty thousand dollars to renounce her living right to the Virginia home, telling her it was impractical to move to a country where she didn't speak the language. She replied that she could hardly buy an apartment in St. Petersburg or Moscow for that small sum. Within minutes, he had raised the offer to a hundred thousand dollars.

Armen Bali then took up their cause, fulfilling her promise to Rudolf to look after his relatives. Visas were procured. Bali actively discouraged them from visiting the house, or living in Virginia's Hunt Country; too isolated, she decreed. Instead, they were financially compensated and she helped them and their families to relocate to her hometown of San Francisco, advising them on everything from which houses they should buy to schools for their children.

In the meantime, Gouzel and Rosa brought a second lawsuit, this time against Nureyev's American foundation. Nureyev's tax lawyer, Barry Weinstein, had named himself president of the Rudolf Nureyev Dance Foundation, and his wife, a daughter and a law partner as the four members of its board. Gouzel and Rosa charged that Weinstein had set up the foundation to benefit himself and his family and challenged the very premise that Rudolf had even wanted a foundation in the United States. Rudolf had never intended, they asserted, to put his tax lawyer in charge of an organization with whose artistic mission he had no expertise. They also claimed that Weinstein, too, had taken advantage of Rudolf when he was too ill and confused to understand what he was doing. Weinstein denied any wrongdoing. At the trial in Manhattan in the fall of 1997, Charles Jude testified that Nureyev, at the time he signed his wills in 1992, "was in full possession of his mental faculties." In June 1998, a Federal District Court judge in Manhattan confirmed this view by upholding that the American foundation was legitimately established.

Weinstein did recognize that he needed someone with dance world credentials to guide artistic policy. He had invited Jane Hermann to replace his daughter on the board in 1994. She resigned a short time later, however, saying that Weinstein refused to give her full access to foundation documents. At Hermann's suggestion, Armen Bali's daughter, Jeannette Etheredge, a ballet fan, though not a professional, replaced her. But Weinstein was still reluctant to talk openly about the foundation's activities, even to the dance press. Nevertheless, records filed with the state of Illinois attorney general's office show that in its first six years of operation, it awarded approximately one million of its seven million dollars in assets to a number of ballet schools and companies that were associated with Nureyev during his career, including the Paul Taylor Dance Company, the Martha Graham Center for Contemporary Dance and the School of American Ballet.

THE FOUNDATION also made an out-of-court settlement with Robert Tracy, fearing that the publicity of a trial might lead other ex-lovers to come forward. Tracy was to receive an amount estimated to be about six hundred thousand dollars, to be paid in regular installments until the year 2000. This was granted with the proviso that he neither grant interviews nor write about his life with Rudolf. Apart from the total value of the settlement, the American foundation's largest single expenditure in time and money has been the legal defense of its right to exist.*

*According to Crain's Chicago Business, the foundation's legal fees during 1996 totaled $220,000; its charitable grants for the same period totaled $250,453.

At the heart of the litigation was the question of how Nureyev wanted his assets apportioned among his family, his foundations and a museum or exhibition in his name. Through her lawyer, Gouzel has claimed that she and her uncle were close. She had been his "eyes and ears in the ballet world," her lawyer said, nursing Nureyev when he became ill. But according to Charles Jude, who spent many hours at Nureyev's bedside during those final months, Nureyev "wanted everything to go to his foundations. I asked him how he was going to decide [who was to be on its board]* and he said that the most important thing was his money, and he wanted people who could make his money go furthest. He said if he wanted his name to remain, he needed money. If all the money was given away [to his relatives], then the name is given away. For him, money was power." In 1997, the European foundation made an out-of-court settlement with Rosa and Gouzel for $1.8 million.

Still, five years after Nureyev's death, neither foundation had made the kind of bold artistic statement that its creator was famous for making, nor done much to perpetuate his name. Rather than honor Nureyev's forward-looking spirit, perhaps through major commissions to new choreographers, the American foundation chose in 1997 to underwrite a Bolshoi Ballet production of the full-length version of *Le Corsaire* by the Boston Ballet. The European foundation, however, has honored some of Nureyev's wishes by providing grants in his name to a number of leading European ballet schools as well as by supporting the participation of promising Russian dancers in the prestigious Prix de Lausanne, the sole world-class ballet competition open only to preprofessional dancers. It also sponsored an exhibition at the historic Carnavalet Museum in Paris in 1997. A selection of Nureyev's remaining possessions, including costumes, ballet memorabilia, musical instruments and annotated scores, went on view. The museum announced plans to establish a permanent room to Nureyev as it has to other notable Parisians, Proust among them.

Nureyev had also made provisions for a hundred thousand dollars in annual grants to go to AIDS-related research and to artists living with the disease. Yet even as late as April 1998 Michel Canesi felt stymied in his efforts to act as Nureyev's representative in this mission; he had been given dispensation by the Liechtenstein foundation to award only thirty thousand dollars in medical grants in total since Nureyev's death. The American foundation proved no more enthusiastic. Shortly before the 1995 Christie's New York sale, Canesi wrote to Weinstein asking him to reserve a percentage of the auction proceeds for AIDS research in

---

*While the U.S. board is dominated by Nureyev's lawyer, the European board includes Jacob Rothschild, John Tooley, former general administrator of the Royal Opera House, Hugues Gall, director of the Paris Opéra, and Douce François.

Rudolf's name. He hoped the initiative might enhance the sale and attract additional funds. Weinstein never acknowledged his letter.

Despite the infighting and legal battles, Nureyev's real legacy lives in the generations of dancers he molded, the companies he inspired, the audiences he shocked and dazzled, the public he brought to the dance.

MANY OF THEM still seek him out in the Sainte-Geneviève-des-Bois cemetery.* There they find his monument, commissioned by the European foundation from Ezio Frigerio, Nureyev's designer for his final *Bayadère*. Unveiled three years after his death to replace the makeshift cross over his grave, Nureyev's tombstone is in the form of an elaborate traveling trunk, covered by a loosely draped Oriental carpet. The carpet is woven from thousands of brilliantly hued Murano glass mosaics and bordered by a fringe worked in bronze. The effect is of stilled motion, as if this were but a moment of repose in an ongoing journey.

*Ironically, many who come for Nureyev also stop and visit Lifar.

SOURCE NOTES

SELECTED BIBLIOGRAPHY

INDEX

SOURCE NOTES

Because Rudolf Nureyev died at the age of fifty-four, most of the people who had populated his life were still alive when I began my research. As a result, this book is based primarily on interviews, in many cases with those who had yet to speak openly about him, if at all. Since I interviewed some sources repeatedly during the five years I spent researching and writing this book, I have not dated each quotation. I have, however, listed my sources for key facts and quotations. All unattributed quotes are from my interviews with those who requested anonymity.

I also consulted various archives and personal collections for letters, diaries, drawings, photographs, press clippings and government documents. All quoted Soviet documents from the Archive of the Central Committee of the CPSU were declassified by the author, as was Hamet Nureyev's military file from the Russian State Military Archive. Nearly all the quotations from Cecil Beaton's diaries come from his unpublished diaries. While portions of Beaton's diaries were published during his lifetime, many of these were heavily edited. In citing periodicals, I have listed the title of a particular article only when it is a major feature; otherwise I have cited only the author, publication and date of publication.

ABBREVIATIONS

RN   Rudolf Nureyev, *Nureyev* (New York: E. P. Dutton & Co., 1963).

MF   Margot Fonteyn, *Autobiography* (New York: Warner Books, 1977).

EB   John Gruen, *Erik Bruhn: Danseur Noble* (New York: Viking Press, 1979).

LS   Lynn Seymour with Paul Gardner, *Lynn: The Autobiography of Lynn Seymour* (London: Granada Publishing, 1984).

MG   Maude Gosling, "Nureyev in the West," *Ballet Review*, Spring 1994.

RVD   Rudi van Dantzig, *Het spoor van een komeet [The Trail of a Comet]* (Zutphen: Gaillarde Pers, 1993).

BR   *Ballet Review.*

PF   Patricia Foy, producer and director, *Rudolf Nureyev*, documentary, Antelope Films in association with Orfeo Films, Radio Telefis Eireann and Reiner Mortiz Associates, 1991.

Prologue

A record crowd of fifty thousand: *The Art Newspaper*, No. 45, February 1995.
"Everything I have . . .": Interview with Simon Robinson.
The snakeskin Nehru jacket . . . much talked-of: Nureyev wore this outfit for his appearance on *The Dick Cavett Show*, July 25, 1975.
"Dance home with something . . .": *New York Times*, January 6, 1993.
"Never look back . . .": MG.
"It's finished": Interview with Pierre Lacotte.
Don't put things . . .": Interviews with Rudi van Dantzig.
The mood was high: Author's observations.
"After I die . . .": Interviews with Charles Jude.
he intended for his possessions: Interview with Gouzel Nureyeva.
In his will: Rudolf Nureyev's will.
agreed to a compromise: Interviews with Gouzel Nureyeva and David Lewellyn.
Hours before the New York auction: Interview with Gouzel Nureyeva.
"He was serious . . .": Interview with Mikhail Baryshnikov.

1 / *The Season of Bad Roads*

For the details of the Nureyevs' family life, I relied primarily on private family documents as well as on numerous interviews and conversations with Rudolf Nureyev's sister Razida Yevgrafova, his niece Alfia Rafikova, his boyhood friend Albert Arslanov and several neighbors and family friends in Ufa.

All information on Hamet Nureyev's military background comes from the Russian State Military Archive and from the Archive of the Ministry of Defense in Moscow.

For background information on the Red Army, on Hamet Nureyev's military profile and on life in Soviet Russia during the Second World War, I drew on a variety of published sources, listed below, as well as on interviews with Professor Mark von Hagen, director of the Harriman Institute at Columbia University and author of *Soldiers in the Proletarian Dictatorship: The Red Army and the Soviet Socialist State 1917–1930*. For historical details on Soviet life in the Urals, I also drew on my interview with Professor Vladimir Brovkin of the Davis Center for Russian Studies at Harvard University.

All quotes from Razida Yevgrafova, Alfia Rafikova and Albert Arslanov are from the author's interviews, unless otherwise noted, and translated from the Russian by Natasha Gerasimova.

Farida had only reluctantly: Interview with Alfia Rafikova.
After her neighbors: Interview with Razida Yevgrafova.
In the new social order: Interviews with Mark von Hagen.
clean white sheets: Interview with Razida Yevgrafova, who recalled that an Ufa neighbor, who was traveling with the Nureyevs, recounted this episode to her many years afterward.
"it seems to me . . . stateless . . .": RN, p.26; Nureyev would remain stateless until 1982, when he eventually gained Austrian citizenship.
"might still show some initiative . . .": Mikhail Heller and Aleksandr Nekrich, *Utopia in Power: The History of the Soviet Union from 1917 to the Present* (New York: Touchstone, 1992), p. 307.
"Everywhere and in everything [Stalin] . . .": Brian Moynahan, *The Russian Century: A History of the Last Hundred Years* (New York: Random House, 1994), p. 139.
"save Stalin himself . . .": Geoffrey Hosking, *The First Socialist Society* (Cambridge, Mass.: Harvard University Press, 1993), pp. 195–196.
"If I had the vast . . .": Heller and Nekrich, *Utopia in Power*, p. 307.
"Such a good prince . . .": Ibid., p.297.
"slightly unbalanced mentally . . .": Moynahan, *The Russian Century*, p. 140.

"I know of no other . . .": Heller and Nekrich, *Utopia in Power*, p. 308.

At birth, Rudolf's father: Hamet Nureyev's birth certificate.

"inured to the Siberian cold": John Lawrence, *A History of Russia* (New York: Meridian, 1993), p. 57.

"Our Tatar blood runs faster . . .": *RN*, p. 28.

dreamed of becoming a priest: Interview with Gouzel Nureyeva.

attended the village *mekteb*: Dzhamalyutdin Validi, *Ocherk istorii obrazovannosti i literatury tatar: do revolyutsii 1917: fragmenty knigi (Sketch of the History of Education and Literature of the Tatars: Before the Revolution of 1917: Fragments of a Book)* (Kazan: Biblioteka zhurnala "Kazan," 1992), reprint of a book originally published in 1925.; also Kh. Alishev and R. U. Amirkhanov, eds., *Narodnoye prosveshcheniye u tatar v dooktyabrskiy period (Public Education Among the Tatars in the pre-October Period)* (Kazan: Institut yazyka, literatury i istorii, 1992).

Neighbors and even members of the same: Interview with Vladimir Brovkin.

Where the Whites urged solidarity: Richard Pipes, *The Formation of the Soviet Union: Communism and Nationalism 1917–1923* (Cambridge, Mass.: Harvard University Press, 1964).

At the time, nine out of ten: Moynahan, *The Russian Century*, p. 23.

In an early version: Interview with Mark von Hagen.

At the age of seven: Interview with Alfia Rafikova.

"Do you know why . . .": Interview with Razida Yevgrafova.

"backwardness up to superpower . . .": Hedrick Smith, *The New Russians* (New York: Avon Books, 1991), p. 234.

*the Communist Party had 1,360,000 members: Robert Conquest, *The Harvest of Sorrow* (New York: Oxford University Press, 1986), p. 104.

"For them the Revolution was . . .": *RN*, p. 27.

Hamet had told his new wife: Interview with Alfia Rafikova.

"He finished his schooling . . .": Ibid.

*By 1932, 62 percent of peasant households: These statistics drawn from Sheila Fitzpatrick, *The Russian Revolution* (Oxford, Eng.: Oxford University Press, 1994), p. 138.

Hamet's granddaughter recalls: Interview with Alfia Rafikova.

"as if she were a little . . .": Interview with Alfia Rafikova.

2 / A Friend, a Religion, a Way to Good Fortune

"the bible of High Stalinism . . .": Robert Conquest, *Stalin: Breaker of Nations* (New York: Penguin Books, 1992), p. 212.

"Anyone who . . . restored or deleted 'facts . . .' ": Heller and Nekrich, *Utopia in Power*, p. 293.

"I have fired . . .": Dmitiri Volkogonov, *Stalin: Triumph and Tragedy* (Rocklin, Calif.: Prima Publishing, 1992), p. 324.

Between 1937 to 1938: By the start of the war, just three years later, 70 percent of its commanders had less than one year's experience in the positions they then held.

Stalin, in fact, murdered: Moynahan, *The Russian Century*, p. 145.

"everything of value . . .": *RN*, p. 29.

"stood no chance . . .": Ibid., p. 30.

"Icy, dark, and, above all, hungry . . .": Ibid., p. 29.

"ice months . . .": Moynahan, *The Russian Century*, p. 25.

"like dirty mountains . . .": *RN*, p. 29.

"in the middle of a green . . .": Ibid., p. 28.

"cried all the time . . .": Interview with Razida Yevgrafova.

"strange words . . .": *RN*, p. 29.

"without raising her . . .": Ibid., p. 32.

*Religious practice: Heller and Nekrich, *Utopia in Power*, p. 407.

"That feeling of doctors . . .": *RN*, p. 32.

"adored . . . which still makes me . . .": Ibid., p. 31.
"I looked upon music . . .": Ibid., p. 35.

3 / Epiphany

the Devil's Inkpot . . . : Victor and Jennifer Louis, *The Complete Guide to the Soviet Union* (New York: St. Martin's Press, 1991), p. 584.
"The town was somehow . . .": Ibid., p. 586.
"I can't find words . . .": *RN*, p. 32.
"Hello, my beloved son . . .": Hamet Nureyev to Nureyev family, August 1942.
"Ballsy lady!": *PF*.
"Why do I always have to . . .": Interview with Aza Kuchumova.
"We were all poor then . . .": Interview with Inna Guskova.
"It was on that first day . . .": *RN*, p. 37.
"But I never . . .": Interview with Albert Arslanov.
"But when the shot appeared . . .": Alexander Bland, *The Nureyev Valentino: Portrait of a Film* (Don Mills, Ont.: Collier Macmillan Canada, Ltd., 1977), p. 34.
"Hey, Adolf!": Interview with Albert Arslanov.
"had difficulty . . .": Interview with Inna Guskova.
"I spent all my leisure time . . .": *RN*, p. 38.
"In my mind . . .": *PF*.
"his mother had purchased only one ticket . . .": Nureyev gave two different accounts of his first visit to the Ufa Opera House. This was the version he recounted in his autobiography and most frequently. In an interview with director Lindsay Anderson for BBC-TV in 1974, however, he recalled that his mother purchased tickets for his sisters only; however, after he complained about being left at home, his mother took him to look at the theater and by chance, they managed to sneak inside.
a place "you could only . . .": *RN*, p. 42.
"Something was happening . . .": Ibid.
The Song of the Cranes . . . created to honor: Choreographed by Nina Anisimova, the ballet actually had two premieres. On March 23, 1944, only its first act was performed; one year later, the entire three-act ballet was danced.
Zaitouna Nazretdinova: Nazretdinova would eventually be named People's Artist of the Soviet Union, the third dancer to be accorded this high honor, after Olga Lepeshinskaya and Galina Ulanova, who received the honor simultaneously.

4 / Hamet

"a shadow appeared . . . this great big man . . .": Interviews with John Lanchbery.
"all very uncomfortable . . .": *PF*.
"To go to the toilet . . .": Transcript of "A Tribute to Rudolf Nureyev," Presented at the American Film Institute Theater, Kennedy Center for the Arts, *BR*, Winter 1993.
Hamet taught Rudolf how to grind: Interviews with Albert Arslanov.
"reserved and solitary . . .": Interview with Aza Kuchumova.
"a severe, very powerful . . .": *RN*, p. 26.
"I suddenly saw . . .": *PF*.
he would tell Kenneth Greve: Interviews with Kenneth Greve.
"useful for making yourself popular . . .": *RN*, p. 44.
"That, to me, was heaven . . .": Ibid.
"He was not like the other . . .": Interview with Marat Hismatullin.
"At the lesson . . .": *PF*.
"fall down and start crying . . .": Interview with Marat Hismatullin.
"Folk dancing is a fiery dance . . .": *PF*.

"like a sponge . . .": Interview with Pamira Suleimanova.
"Because nothing connected with . . .": *RN*, p. 45.
"There was that typical . . .": Interview with Inna Guskova.
"just a little Tatar boy . . . help him with the social . . .": *PF*.
Udeltsova looked a decade older . . ."very old woman . . .": Interview with Albert Arslanov.
"the daughter of petty bourgeois parents . . .": *Materials on the History of Russian Ballet*, vol. 2
    (Leningrad: Leningrad Choreographic School, 1939), p. 240.
"She was so kind . . .": Interview with Pamira Suleimanova.
"live inside the dance . . . He didn't have . . .": Interview with Irina Klimova.
A warm, maternal figure: Interviews with Albert Arslanov, Pamira Suleimanova, Inna Guskova.
"ally . . .": *PF*.
his obstinate pride prevented: Interviews with Alfia Rafikova and Razida Yevgrafova.
"He beat me up . . .": *PF*.
"would be looking all the time . . .": Interview with Pamira Suleimanova.
"There's no hope for you": Interview with Razida Yevgrafova.
"black despair . . .": *RN*, p. 49.
his father was too proud to admit: Ibid.; also Lindsay Anderson interview with Nureyev, BBC-
    TV, January 27, 1974.

5 / The Road to Leningrad

they took to calling him: Interview with Albert Arslanov.
Johnny Weissmuller's yodeling hero: Ibid.
"Sometimes we drove her to tears . . .": Interview with Marat Hismatullin.
"Hamet came to see me . . .": *PF*.
"Even if he did . . .": Interview with Irina Klimova.
"He never seemed to care . . .": Interview with Pamira Suleimanova.
"We were all amazed . . .": S. Juravlev, "Out of Childhood," *Russian Seasons*, no. 2, vol. 13,
    1993.
"improvised traveling theater": *RN*, p. 53.
"He felt there was . . . only tough on those . . .": Interview with Pamira Suleimanova.
"He wanted someone to . . .": Interview with Pamira Suleimanova.
"dying to get to work . . .": Interview with Magaphura Saligaskarova.
"I didn't care . . .": Interview with John Lanchbery.
"When I discovered . . .": Lindsay Anderson interview, BBC-TV.
"A man from our Ministry . . .": Interview with Zaitoung Nazretdinova.
"like a madman": *RN*, p. 57.
"My dear, you are still young . . .": Interview with Magaphura Saligaskarova.
"Dancing for me in those . . .": *RN*, p. 61.
"as if he belonged . . ." and subsequent quotation: Interview with Pamira Suleimanova.
"He approached me . . .": Interview with Eldus Habirov.
he joined the Ufa Ballet on a tour to Penza: Ufa Ballet program, July 1954.
a former company member: Maguera Yamaieva quoted in "Rudka of Ufa," *Danser Magazine*,
    January 1994.
"there were huge black clouds . . .": *RN*, p.63.
"a consecrated ground . . .": Tamara Karsavina, *Theatre Street* (New York: E. P. Dutton &
    Company, 1961), p. 118.
"During the time of the . . .": Request from V. P. Shelkov to Comrade Gumerov, Minister of
    Culture of the Bashkirian ASSR, July 2, 1955, reprinted in "The Personal Matter of Rudolf
    Nureyev," *St. Petersburg News*, March 17, 1993.

6 / A Window on the West

All quotes from Menia Martinez and Sergiu Stefanschi are from the author's interviews, unless otherwise specified.

"a city blessed by God": Luke Jennings, "The Dance of Time," *Sunday Correspondent*, May 27, 1990.

"We copied, borrowed . . .": *The Dance Encyclopedia*, Anatole Chujoy and P.W. Manchester, eds. (New York: Simon & Schuster, 1967), p. 789.

* "The great, the outstanding feature of the new ballet . . .": Lynn Garafola, *Diaghilev's Ballets Russes* (New York: Oxford University Press, 1989), p. 36.

"a Napoleon of the arts . . .": Ibid., p. ix.

"transformed ballet into . . .": Ibid., p. vii.

"The question of whether the ballet . . .": Elizabeth Souritz, *Soviet Choreographers in the 1920s* (Durham, N.C.: Duke University Press, 1990), p. 44.

"the time of Stravinsky . . . the most shameful . . .": Solomon Volkov, *St. Petersburg: A Cultural History* (New York: Free Press, 1995), p. xv.

"hoped to destroy . . .": Ibid., p. xvi.

"mandatory nationwide optimism": Nina Alovert, "Ballet and Moral Life in Soviet Society," *BR*, Summer 1994.

"an oasis of Russian culture . . .": Natalia Makarova, *A Dance Autobiography* (New York: Alfred A. Knopf, 1979), p. 22.

"soft and fluid": *RN*, pp. 65–66.

"Young man, you'll either become . . .": Ibid.

"ogled this feral . . . glittered defiantly": Elena Tchernichova, "Young Nureyev," *BR*, Spring 1994.

"He had only a small . . .": Interview with Elena Tchernichova.

"Ghengis Khan . . ." Tchernichova, *BR*, Spring 1994.

"like mice": Interview with Elena Tchernichova.

*A ballet school "is the most . . .": John Russell, *New York Times Magazine*, June 20, 1982.

three different uniforms: Richard Buckle, *Nijinsky* (New York: Simon & Schuster, 1971), p. 13.

"We were all subliminally taught . . .": Valery Panov, *To Dance* (New York: Alfred A. Knopf, 1978), p. 82.

"everyone who was waiting . . .": Ibid., p. 41.

"lifeless forms . . .": Ibid., p. 84.

"It's not too much to say . . .": David Daniel, "Nureyev Observed," *Christopher Street*, August 1976.

"Don't forget that . . .": *RN*, p. 71.

"He's a boss . . .": Interviews with Sergiu Stefanschi.

"We'd stand straight . . .": Interview with Marina Cherednichenko.

"obstinate little idiot . . .": *RN*, p. 73.

7 / Pushkin

All quotes from Liuba Romankova (now Myasnikova) are from the author's interviews, unless otherwise specified.

"He had patience . . .": Interview with Mikhail Baryshnikov.

"exceedingly calm . . .": Interview with Alla Sizova.

" 'That youngster . . .' ": Buckle, *Nijinsky*, p. 9.

"like runners their wands . . .": Lincoln Kirstein, *Dance: A Short History of Classic Theatrical Dancing* (New York: Dance Horizons, Inc., 1969), p. 253.

"people in his classes . . .": Arsen Degen, "The Creation of an Image: Our Interlocutor—
Honored Artist of RSFSR Mikhail Baryshnikov," *Smena*, December 8, 1973, reprinted in
Nina Alovert, *Baryshnikov in Russia* (New York: Holt, Rinehart and Winston, 1984),
p. 200.
"horribly difficult . . .": Interview with Tatiana Legat.
"He knew very well . . .": Interview with Mikhail Baryshnikov.
"Look at yourself, Nureyev . . .": *RN*, p. 76.
"Cabrioles, for instance . . .": John Percival, *Nureyev: Aspects of the Dancer* (New York: G. P.
Putnam's Sons, 1975), p. 28.
"We heard he was . . .": Interview with Marina Cherednichenko.
"I suffered a lot . . .": Interviews with Tamara Zakrzhevskaya.
"To my dear friend . . .": Interview with Albert Arslanov.
"You can imagine . . .": Percival, *Nureyev*, p. 52.
"played on the occasion . . .": *RN*, p. 78.
"the extent to which . . .": Ibid.
"smelled of Russian sarafans": Interviews with Tamara Zakrzhevskaya.
"She would demonstrate . . .": Interview with Tatiana Legat.
"I'm a good listener . . .": Taped interview with Walter Terry, April 25, 1978. Oral History
Project, Dance Collection, New York Public Library at Lincoln Center.
"your own life . . .": Ibid.
a small, plump: For background on Elisaveta Paji, I relied on interviews with Tamara Zakrzhevskaya and Liuba Myasnikova, who is identified in the text as Liuba Romankova, her
name before marriage.
"My mother was . . .": Interviews with Razida Yevgrafova.
"at home with his parents . . . Denied": Hamet Nureyev to Valentin Shelkov, January 1956,
kindly made available by the Vaganova Choreographic Institute, St. Petersburg.
"Dear Papa . . .": Rudolf Nureyev to Hamet Nureyev, February 19, 1956, kindly made available
by the Rudolf Nureyev Museum, Ufa.
"a Tatar boy, whose headpiece . . .": Leonard Lyons, "The Dance Factory," *New York Post*,
January 10, 1956.
"They seemed to us . . .": Makarova, *A Dance Autobiography*, p. 25.
"we would stand . . .": Interview with Marina Cherednichenko.
"it was like being awarded . . .": *RN*, p. 77.
"no strings . . .": Interview with Albert Arslanov.
"one could feel his . . .": Ibid.
"He was very glad . . .": Ibid.
"you couldn't buy anything . . .": Interviews with Nikita Dolgushin.
"to give them a foreign . . .": Ibid.
"The way they were described . . .": Interview with Elena Tchernichova.
"Rudolf wasn't dancing very well . . .": Interview with Marina Cherednichenko.
"Leave me alone . . .": Interviews with Nikita Dolgushin.
"His combinations provoked . . .": *PF*.
"the picture of a typical Russian peasant . . .": Panov, p. 175.
"big, slow pliés . . .": Interview with Vladimir Vasiliev.
"One day it was my turn . . .": Elena Tchernichova, *BR*, Spring 1994.
"She has to help me . . .": Ibid.
"Don't forget . . .": Interview with Alla Sizova.
"still considered the final arbiter . . .": Panov, *To Dance*, p. 215.
"made changes in our coda . . .": Interview with Alla Sizova.
"astounded the hall . . .": Interview with Silva Lon.
"[It] was something you did not . . .": Daniel, "Nureyev Observed."
"Nureyev amazed everyone . . .": Interview with Vladimir Vasiliev.
"Nureyev was the first male dancer . . .": Ibid.

"How did you like us? . . .": Interview with Silva Lon.
"little boy lost": *MF*, p. 243.
"this very sympathetic boy . . .": Bob Colacello, "The Last Days of Nureyev," *Vanity Fair*, March 1993.
his admission, thirty years later: Liuba Myasnikova, "Some of My Memories," in *Rudolf Nureyev: Three Years in the Kirov Theatre* (St. Petersburg: Pushkinsky Fond., 1995), p. 112.
"The *sportivniks* . . .": Interviews with Menia Martinez.
"was like a bomb . . .": Interview with Sergei Sorokin.
"I can say with confidence . . .": T. Vecheslova, "The Young Stars of Our Ballet," *Vecherny Leningrad (Evening Leningrad)*, July 3, 1958.
"What's the matter, Rudik . . ." and subsequent anecdote: Interview with Natalia Dudinskaya.

8 / The Kirov

All quotes from Menia Martinez, Tamara Zakrzhevskaya, Nikita Dolgushin, Alla Osipenko and Liuba Romankova (now Myasnikova) are from the author's interviews unless otherwise noted.

"Remember how . . .": Interview with Albert Arslanov.
"There was never any . . .": *RN*, p. 92.
according to the current director of the Ufa Ballet: Interview with Radic Gareev, 1994. His official title is director, the Bashkirian State Opera and Ballet Theater.
"He was doing . . .": Interview with Tatiana Legat.
"He learned the role . . .": Interview with Natalia Dudinskaya.
"Because of his temperament . . .": Ibid.
"It was like an eruption . . .": Daniel, "Nureyev Observed."
"A dancer with excellent . . .": "The Youth of the Leningrad Ballet," *Teatralni Leningrad (Theater Leningrad)*, vol. 42, 1958.
"he got everything . . .": Interview with Tatiana Legat.
"utter astonishment . . . How do you like . . .": Interviews with Tamara Zakrzhevskaya.
"never missed . . .": *RN*, p. 79.
"They're giving me a flat . . .": Ninel Kurgapkina, "I'll Tell You About My Friend," in *Rudolf Nureyev: Three Years in the Kirov Theatre*, p. 38.
"couldn't stand": Interviews with Tamara Zakrzhevskaya.
"a bearskin rug . . .": Interview with Silva Lon.
"you had to push things . . .": Ibid.
"Rosa didn't stand . . .": Interview with Alla Sizova.
"calm of domestic life . . . not only the traditions . . .": Nikita Dolgushin, "Portrait in Retrospect," in *Rudolf Nureyev: Three Years in the Kirov Theatre*, p. 56.
"All conversations were about . . .": Interview with Mikhail Baryshnikov.
"Rudolf is playing": E. Shadrina, "The Partner. A Conversation with A. Shelest," *Kultura*, March 20, 1993.
"was a pretty woman . . .": *RN*, p. 94.
"She indulged . . .": Interview with Silva Lon.
"despotic . . . She wouldn't take her eagle . . .": Myasnikova, "Some of My Memories," p. 124.
"She really twisted him round . . .": Interview with Liuba Myasnikova.
"Don't listen to the assholes . . .": Mikhail Baryshnikov with Joan Acocella, "Memories of Nureyev," *Vogue*, March 1993.
"a great artist should . . .": Myasnikova, "Some of My Memories," p. 126.
"He would say something and . . .": Interview with Liuba Myasnikova.
"It caused a sensation": Interview with Alla Sizova.
"There's no shortage . . .": Kurgapkina, "I'll Tell You About My Friend," p. 29.
"Even here . . . Who do you think . . .": Interview with Vladilen Semenov.

"It's not difficult . . .": Interview with Askold Makarov.
"very rough . . . They did not believe . . .": Clive Barnes, *Nureyev* (New York: Helene Obolensky Enterprises, Inc., 1982), p. 42.
"He was an odd bird . . .": Gennady Smakov, *The Great Russian Dancers* (New York: Alfred A. Knopf, 1984), p. 227.
"We were both . . . a fanatic like him": Interview with Ninel Kurgapkina.
"when he raises me up over him . . .": Kurgapkina, "I'll Tell You About My Friend," p. 29.
"Just help me to hold on . . . Don't mess": Interview with Ninel Kurgapkina.
"Once cannot but recognize . . .": Vera Chistyakova, "R. Nureyev-Armen," *Teatralni Leningrad (Theater Leningrad)*, vol. no. 23, 1959.
"Please see to it . . .": Interviews with Menia Martinez.
"like a crazy man . . . I'll never see you . . .": Ibid.
"stunned by the revelation . . .": *MF*, p. 183.
"A million items . . .": Panov, *To Dance*, p. 120.
"treacherous temptation . . . To help us avoid . . .": Ibid., p. 119.
"all these Shavrovchiki": Interviews with Irina Kolpakova.
"he was born to play": Interview with Sergiu Stefanschi.
"We were all . . .": Interviews with Irina Kolpakova.
"do the complete opposite . . .": Kurgapkina, "Let Me Tell You About My Friend," p. 36.
"so very new and strange . . .": Allan Kriegsman, *Washington Post*, May 1, 1983.
Petit told the organizer . . . "shy and yet . . .": Interview with Roland Petit.
"He is never with our delegation . . .": Interviews with Menia Martinez.
"tumultuous applause . . . young ambassadors . . .": *Izvestiya [News]*, August 16, 1959.
"I don't need . . .": Interview with Alla Sizova.
"He didn't like it . . .": Interview with Vladimir Vasiliev.
"Young Nureyev is unique . . .": *Rabotnicheskoye Delo*, August 29, 1959, reprinted in *Teatralnaya Zhizn (Theatre Life)*, issue no. 8, 1960.
"Bach": Interview with Val Golovitser.
"Oh, how I'd love" . . . "No problem . . .": Interview with Silva Lon.
"Today I've been told . . .": Anna Udeltsova to Rosa Nureyeva, September 10, 1959, kindly made available by the Rudolf Nureyev Museum, Ufa.
"were like bullfights . . . irresistible peculiarities . . . His dancing is not perfection": Smakov, *The Great Russian Dancers*, pp. 228–229.
"an aura of mystery . . .": Interview with Valentina Mironova.
a disgruntled fan threw an old broom: Interview with Tanya Tarasova.
"has turned out to be . . .": Rudolf Nureyev to Silva Lon, October 1959.
"people were going crazy about" . . . "Well, of course . . .": John Lombardi, "Nureyev's Fight Against Time," *New York Times Magazine*, December 13, 1981.
"Death as a setting . . .": Arlene Croce, *Going to the Dance* (New York: Alfred A. Knopf, 1982), p. 280.
"did not have a big jump . . .": Percival, *Nureyev*, p.39.
"Why do you walk" . . . . "And you, Askold . . .": Interview with Askold Makarov.
"laced with a touch of . . .": Smakov, *The Great Russian Dancers*, p. 228.
"I've never so much . . ."; "it went like a dream . . .": Olga Moiseyeva, "Worthy of Admiration," *Rudolf Nureyev: Three Years in the Kirov Theatre*, p. 76.
"The first act went well . . .": Rudolf Nureyev to Silva Lon.
"Go to a restaurant . . .": Interviews with Irina Kolpakova.
"both prince and peasant . . .": Richard Buckle, *Nijinsky* (New York: Simon & Schuster, 1971), p. 142.
"were much more aware . . .": Alovert, *Baryshnikov in Russia*, p. 96.
"I first played . . .": *Ballet News*, July/August 1979, p. 22.
"This is the beginnning of a new era!": Interviews with Irina Kolpakova.

"He came . . . and he conquered": Krasovskaya, "A Time for Searching, a Time for New Faces," *Neva*, Issue No. 10, 1960.
"doesn't so much depart . . .": "The Search for New Paths in Art," *Smena (Young Guard)*, February 27, 1960.
"unlike anyone's we have ever . . .": Yuri Slonimsky, "Talent and the Ballet," *Atlantic Monthly*, June 1960.
"His style is both . . .": Vera Chistyakova, *Smena*, August 3, 1960.
"like an old country . . .": Interview with Silva Lon.
She had never expected such success: Interviews with Alfia Rafikova.
"When he and my mother . . .": Interviews with Razida Yevgrafova.
"Good afternoon, my dear Rudolf . . .": Hamet Nureyev to Rudolf Nureyev and Rosa Nureyeva, May 1960, kindly made available by Razida Yevgrafova and Alfia Rafikova.

9 / Distant Stages

"No sleep for you . . .": Tamara Zakrzhevskaya, "I'll Never Forget That Day," *Rudolf Nureyev: Three Years in the Kirov Theatre*, p. 178.
"with us and yet" . . . "There were moments . . .": Myasnikova, "Some of My Memories," p. 118.
"So where do you sleep" and subsequent anecdote: Kurgapkina, "I'll Tell You About My Friend," p. 38.
"no idea about homosexuality . . .": *RVD*, p. 138.
he also told a male lover in London: Interview with Keith Baxter.
secret crush on Liuba's twin: Myasnikova, "Some of My Memories," p. 113.
‡Truman Capote anecdote: Gerald Clarke, *Capote* (New York: Ballantine Books, 1988), p. 292.
"like a woman . . .": Shadrina, "The Partner, A Conversation with A. Shelest."
"My *Bayadère* . . .": RN to Silva Lon, March 3, 1960.
struck up a friendship with Lola Fisher: Interview with Lola Fisher.
"leggy, beguiling blond": *New York Post*, June 19, 1960.
"I left my heart . . .": Ibid.
"bored stiff": Myasnikova, "Some of My Memories," p. 130.
traveled with the cast . . . on their chartered bus: Interview with Lola Fisher.
"I whish you a very happy . . .": Lola Fisher's souvenir program of the Kirov's *Don Quixote*, May 27, 1960.
"I saw with what hunger . . .": *RN*, p. 101.
"we didn't have anything to say . . .": Interview with Ninel Kurgapkina.
"thrilling bass . . .": *RN*, p. 101.
"Go and bug them . . .": Interview with Tatiana Legat.
"All these Pihal . . .": Interviews with Tamara Zakrzhevskaya.
"How stupid and simpleminded . . .": Inscription on photograph, Rudolf to Tamara, June 23, 1960.
"I'm a dancer, not a mime . . ." and subsequent anecdote: Interview with Elena Tchernichova, also interviews with Tamara Zakrzhevskaya.
"How dare you" . . . "Leave Tatyana . . .": T. Satyr, "Korolevskiy Podarok [A Royal Gift]," undated clipping.
"Not exile . . .": *RN*, p. 99.
asked a Moscow acquaintance: Val Golovitser.
"Hope that the tour of the Americans in my absence . . .": Inscription on photograph, RN to Tamara Zakrzhevskaya, September 1960. In a book about Nureyev, Peter Watson reports that Nureyev went to see ABT perform in Moscow, hoping to meet Bruhn. However, Rudolf had already left for Berlin by the time ABT arrived in Moscow.
"sideshows": Kurgapkina, "I'll Tell You About My Friend," p. 32.
"I met a gentle boy . . .": *RVD*, p. 138.
"No one else at the Kirov . . .": Interview with Valentina Mironova.

"It was a sensation for me . . .": Percival, *Nureyev*, p. 36.
"painter with a long name . . .": Interview with Inna Guskova.
"It's better not to . . .": Interviews with Razida Yevgrafova.
A few weeks before the premiere: In *Perpetual Motion*, a biography of Nureyev, Otis Stuart gives an erroneous account of this episode. He claims that Rudolf preferred rehearsing *Laurencia* and *La Bayadère* with Dudinskaya to working on the new ballet. In fact he very much wanted to dance in *Legend* and was caught by the conflict. Stuart claims that Nureyev came late for rehearsal deliberately, which is incorrect. And it was Shelest and not Dudinskaya with whom he was due to rehearse. Rudolf had no performances with Dudinskaya during all of 1961.
"I am going to rehearse the *real thing* . . .": Interviews with Irina Kolpakova.
"Replacing him became . . .": Ibid.
"I don't know whether someone planned . . .": Percival, *Nureyev*, p. 37.
"It couldn't have been . . .": RN, p. 104.
"He understood everything . . .": Shadrina, "The Partner: A Conversation with A. Shelest."

10 / *Coup de Théâtre*

All quotes from Clara Saint, Pierre Lacotte, Alla Osipenko, Irina Kolpakova, Alla Sizova, Tamara Zakrzhevskaya, Liuba Romankova and Razida Yevgrafova are from the author's interviews, unless otherwise noted. Quotes attributed to Rudolf Nureyev also come from these interviews, unless otherwise indicated.

For the background material on the events leading to Nureyev's defection, I drew on the interviews listed above as well as on a telephone conversation with Jean-Pierre Bonnefous and on an interview with Gregory Alexinsky, the chief of border control for Le Bourget Airport at the time of Nureyev's defection. Additional sources are listed in the notes.

I have also drawn on information contained in official Soviet documents secured from the Center for Storing Contemporary Documentation (formerly the Archive of the Central Committee of the CPSU) in Moscow. All excerpts from Soviet documents come from these formerly secret files, which were declassified at the author's request.

"For so long, more than . . .": Bronislava Nijinsky, *Early Memoirs*, translated and edited by Irina Nijinska and Jean Rawlinson (New York: Holt, Rinehart and Winston, 1981), p. 266.
*Bernard Taper, *Balanchine: A Biography* (New York: Times Books, 1984), p. 76.
"this Russian who was slowly . . .": Interview with Pierre Lacotte.
"Well, the dancers are very tired . . .": Ibid.
"It's been such a wonderful . . .": Ibid.
"dreamed of finding it" and subsequent quotation: RN, p.105.
Strizhevski, a large, brawny man . . . : Interviews with Irina Kolpakova and Alla Osipenko.
"How dare you come in . . .": Interview with Alla Osipenko.
"Yura felt they got along well . . .": Interview with Tatiana Legat.
"he stunned the audience . . .": PF.
"rank after rank . . .": Alexander Bland, *The Royal Ballet: The First Fifty Years* (Garden City, N.Y.: Doubleday & Co., Inc., 1981), p. 140.
"The name Nureyev . . .": Interviews with Igor Eisner.
"mercurial": Interview with Michael Wishart.
The likes of which one viewer had heard . . . : Michael Wishart, *High Diver* (London: Blond & Briggs, 1977), p. 178.
"the strangest, and uncontestably the most . . .": *The New Yorker*, February 3, 1962.
"Since the Romantic period . . .": Richard Buckle, *Nijinsky*, p. 95.
"chilling excitement of a high-wire act . . ." Wishart, *High Diver*, p. 178.
"stir up the subconscious . . .": Smakov, *The Great Russian Dancers*, p. 226.
"We will not soon forget . . .": Olivier Merlin, *Le Monde*, May 25, 1961.

"*l'aérien* Rudolf Noureev": Claude Baignères, *Le Figaro*, May 22, 1961.
"*Les Ballets de Leningrad* . . .": René Sirvin, *L'Aurore*, May 17, 1961.
"from the point of view of music . . .": Richard Buckle, *In the Wake of Diaghilev* (New York: Holt, Rinehart and Winston, 1983), p. 274.
"young, free, rich girl": Interview with Jacqueline de Ribes.
"amazed by the sexual mores": *Independent*, January 10, 1993.
His flamboyance was the talk of: Information about the Marquis de Cuevas is drawn from Dominick Dunne, "Danse Macabre," *Vanity Fair*, February 1987, *Town & Country*, May 1994, and interviews with Jacqueline de Ribes, Violette Verdy, Clara Saint, Rosella Hightower and John Taras.
"The marquis got taken with . . .": Interviews with John Taras.
"like a bird": Interviews with Violette Verdy.
"his stepping-stone . . .": Dunne, "Danse Macabre."
"He's a mujik": Interview with Pierre Lacotte.
"His fans drove . . .": Interview with Marina Cherednichenko.
"Why don't you lecture them? . . .": Interviews with Irina Kolpakova.
"called to mind an extraordinary . . .": Smakov, *The Great Russian Dancers*, p. 200.
"He's a very strange . . .": Interview with Alla Osipenko.
Soloviev and Nureyev were the focus of gossip: Interviews with Alla Osipenko, Irina Kolpakova, Alla Sizova.
*"Sergeyev had enough power . . .": Lombardi, "Nureyev's Fight Against Time."
"Variations entre Danseurs . . .": *L'Humanité*, June 3, 1961.
"Don't worry" . . . "I can handle it.": Interview with Michael Wishart.
"haunted": Ibid.
It was the strength of the collective: *RN*, p. 14.
"a great dancer with . . .": *Observer*, June 18, 1961.
"still needed discipline": Lombardi, "Nureyev's Fight Against Time."
*Arkady N. Shevchenko, *Breaking with Moscow* (New York: Alfred A. Knopf), p. 45.
"Look what a marvelous success"; "There's nothing . . .": Interview with Alla Osipenko.
"the most marvelous interpretation . . .": Olivier Merlin, *Le Monde*, June 16, 1961.
"Absolutely not" and subsequent quotations pertaining to this account: Interview with Alla Osipenko.
Pierre Lacotte's account of seeing Rudolf off at Le Bourget: Otis Stuart, in his biography of Nureyev, claims that Rudolf "begged Lacotte to come to the hotel so that they could drive to the airport in Lacotte's car." Lacotte, however, says that Stuart got it backwards and that it was he who called Rudolf and offered to meet him at the airport.
"You won't be coming with us . . .": *RN*, p. 18.
"Khrushchev wants you . . .": Lombardi, "Nureyev's Fight Against Time."
"I know exactly what kind . . ."; "No, no . . ."; "He's not being . . .": Interview with Pierre Lacotte.
"They're sending me back . . .": Interviews with Irina Kolpakova and Alla Osipenko.
"I did everything . . .": Interview with Alla Osipenko.
"Tell Rudolf I can . . .": Interview with Pierre Lacotte.
"You must come right away . . .": Telephone conversation with Jean-Pierre Bonnefous.
"We told him there . . .": Interview with Gregory Alexinsky.
"a kind of second . . .": *RN*, p. 22.
"What would your reaction be . . .": Colacello, "The Last Days of Nureyev."
"I am sustained only . . .": Inscription to Tamara on a photograph of Nureyev, 1961.
"severed his lifeline . . . knew himself only . . .": Lombardi, "Nureyev's Fight Against Time."
"I cannot imagine him being . . .": *Daily Express*, June 17, 1961.
"No, we are not engaged . . .": *Daily Mail*, June 17, 1961.
"*Bonnes nouvelles!*" "*Tu avais dansé* . . .": Janet Flanner, *Paris Was Yesterday*, ed. Irving Drutman (New York: Harcourt Brace Jovanovich, 1988), p. 27.

"through the barrier": *Evening Standard*, June 16, 1961.
"*Coup de théâtre*": *Le Figaro*, June 17–18, 1961.
"Red dancer": *Evening Standard*, June 16, 1961.
"leaping like Nijinsky himself . . .": *Daily Express*, June 17, 1961.
"It is good . . .": Arlene Croce, *The New Yorker*, January 18, 1993.
"Rudolf's defection was the most . . .": Mikhail Baryshnikov, "Memories of Nureyev."

11 / *Fallout*

"in the depths . . .": Interviews with Sir John Tooley.
"There is nothing mysterious . . .": *Daily Mail*, June 17, 1961.
"There is none missing": Ibid.
"left us in the lurch . . . it was another of": Interview with Marina Cherednichenko.
"the Odette of the Leningrad . . .": *Times* (London), June 17, 1961.
"nothing was said . . . shyly . . . appeared no more . . . the one he had . . .": MF, p. 231.
"destroyed any idea . . .": Shadrina, "The Partner. A Conversation with A. Shelest."
$8,000 a month salary: *New York Times*, June 20, 1961.
"Here, in the West . . .": Ibid.
"the glare of the new media . . . culminate almost . . .": David Halberstam, *October 1964* (New York: Ballantine Books, 1995), p. 164.
"It's very strange . . .": RN, 14.
"So I'd been told . . .": PF.
"dropped into London . . .": *Time*, June 23, 1961.
"was not scheduled to dance . . .": *New York Times*, June 19, 1961.
Time ran a photo of Yuri Soloviev: *Time*, June 23, 1961.
"rob . . . of the chance to see . . .": *The Observer*, June 18, 1961.
"unethical and irresponsible": *Daily Telegraph*, June 22, 1961.
"is conquering London . . .": Andrew Porter, *Financial Times*, June 24, 1961.
"the unquestionable star . . .": *Observer*, June 18, 1961.
"I am well protected . . .": *Daily Mail*, June 22, 1961.
"I shall never return . . .": *New York Times*, June 24, 1961.
"like a Christmas tree": Franz Spelman, "Nureyev: The Defecting Soviet Ballet Star Talks," *Show Business Illustrated*, October 31, 1961.
*Harold Schonberg concurred: *New York Times*, June 24, 1961.
"I could not get over . . ." and rest of quote from author interview with Violette Verdy except the sentences that begin "He had conceived the part of the prince . . ." and "I had never seen such a vulnerable . . ." which are from "Violette Verdy: Speaking of Nureyev," BR, vol. 5, no. 2, 1975–76.
"a brilliant executant . . .": *New York Times*, June 24, 1961.
"I didn't like the way . . .": Spelman, "Nureyev."
"made a hopeless mistake": RN, p. 113.
"seemed earthbound": Smakov, *The Great Russian Dancers*, p. 228.
"tempted by a mysterious . . .": RN, p. 114.
"traitor" . . . "Go back to Moscow": *Sunday Times*, July 2, 1961.
"It was just the kind . . .": Interview with Violette Verdy.
"Oh, not again . . .": Bronislava Nijinska, *Early Memoirs*, p. 470.
"pleased to be serenely . . .": RN, p. 115.
"He was in such . . .": Interview with Rosella Hightower.
"He is the reincarnation . . .": Spelman, "Nureyev."
"So we said . . .": Interview with Pierre Bergé.
"crazy mixed up dancer": Arnold Haskell, "A Sorry Affair," *Dancing Times*, August 1961.
"Thank God! . . .": Interviews with Tamara Zakrzhevskaya.
Sizova's mother had become: Interview with Alla Sizova.

"For me it was . . .": *PF.*
"cursed him as much . . .": Interview with Inna Guskova.
"no one called him . . .": Interviews with Alfia Rafikova.
"Mama . . . You forgot to ask . . .": *PF.*
"There was a shrine . . .": Interview with Mikhail Baryshnikov.
"Yura had a lot of . . .": Interview with Tatiana Legat.
"Yes, of course . . .": Interview with Elena Tchernichova.
"only the wrong . . .": Panov, *To Dance*, p. 150.

12 / New Horizons

"He felt it wasn't . . .": Interview with Rosella Hightower.
"He threw it . . .": Monique van Vooren, *Viva*, September 1977.
"Raymundo and Rudolf . . .": Dunne, "Danse Macabre."
"never let me . . .": Interviews with Sonia Arova.
"Pushkin's sign . . .": Interview with Rosella Hightower.
"The integrity was . . .": Interviews with Violette Verdy.
"the Soviet dancer . . .": Jean Fayard, *Le Figaro*, July 15, 1961.
because they "have . . .": *Newsweek*, October 16, 1978.
"he had understood . . .": *RN*, p. 120.
"There is a Russian . . .": *EB*, p. 107.
"fell in love . . .": Interview with Rosella Hightower.
Tallchief, for her part: Telephone conversation with Maria Tallchief.
"so very attractive . . .": Maria Tallchief with Larry Kaplan, *Maria Tallchief: America's Prima Ballerina* (New York: Henry Holt and Co., 1997), p. 276.
"whether friend or enemy . . .": *PF.*
"almost neurotically antagonistic . . .": Spelman, "Nureyev."
"He practices . . .": Ibid.
"only the secret . . .": Ibid.
"There's someone . . .": Colacello, "The Last Days of Nureyev."

13 / Rudik and Erik

All quotes attributed to Erik Bruhn are from *EB*, unless otherwise noted. All quotes attributed to Margot Fonteyn are from *MF* unless otherwise noted. All quotes from Sonia Arova are from the author's interviews, unless otherwise noted.

Information on Bruhn's background comes from *EB* as well as from interviews with Sonia Arova, Flemming Flindt, Ingrid Glindemann, Susse Wold, John Lanchbery, Glen Tetley and Violette Verdy.

"For two or three . . .": John Gruen, *The Private World of Ballet* (New York: Penguin Books, 1976), p. 273.
"He dances to please . . .": Clive Barnes, *New York Times*, May 22, 1967.
"There seemed to be . . .": Gruen, *The Private World of Ballet*, p. 275.
"He was always . . .": Interview with Glen Tetley.
"a great attraction . . .": Tallchief, *Maria Tallchief*, p. 283.
"an instrument of it . . .": "Violette Verdy: Speaking of Nureyev," *BR*, vol. 5, no. 2, 1975–76.
"a dirty dancer": Interview with Peter Martins.
"That's wrong . . .": *EB*, p. 112.
"Erik had it . . .": Interview with Rosella Hightower.
"quit": Gruen, *Private World of Ballet*, p. 275.
"I became frightened . . .": Ibid., p. 270.
"amazing": Interview with Flemming Flindt.

"He was disrespectful . . .": Interview with Peter Martins.
"Why don't the . . .": EB, p. 110.
"enormous hostility . . .": Interview with Glen Tetley.
"puzzling time": Tallchief, *Maria Tallchief*, p. 285.
"I doubt Rudolf . . .": Interview with John Taras.
"it masturbated my . . .": Interview with Kenneth Greve.
"the only dancer . . .": *Time*, April 16, 1965.
"Rudolf took Erik . . .": Interview with Glen Tetley.
"Greek-god face": EB, p. 105.
"Well, we all knew . . .": Interviews with John Lanchbery.
"a different Erik": EB, p. 60.
"There was a conservative . . .": Interview with Marit Gruson. Note: Identified in the text as Gentele, her surname at the time.
"It may well be . . .": John Martin, *New York Times*, May 2, 1955.
"Teach it . . . If Erik . . .": Interview with Rosella Hightower.
"Pure Strindberg": Interview with Marit Gruson.
"When she did . . .": Gruen, *The Private World of Ballet*, p. 272.
"She just assumed . . .": Ibid.
"At the time his English . . .": Ibid., pp. 274–75.
"Pull God's beard!": Julie Kavanagh, *Secret Muses: The Life of Frederick Ashton* (London: Faber & Faber, 1996), p. 301.
"Head is like you . . .": MF, p. 107.
". . . but, of course, name . . .": Keith Money, *Fonteyn & Nureyev: The Great Years* (London: Harvill, 1994) p. 10.
"cheerful, friendly . . .": RN, p. 127.
"I hear that . . ." and subsequent quotes relating to this account: MF, pp. 236–38.
"very sweet, chummy . . .": Telephone conversation with Colette Clark.
"an amazing vital . . .": RN, p. 128.
"She liked sweet, good . . .": Telephone conversation with Colette Clark. English biographer John Percival would claim that Nureyev "delighted Rambert" with his compliments about her leading ballerina Lucette Aldous, which seems highly doubtful given Clark's eyewitness account.
"old narrow picturesque . . .": RN, p. 128.
"The fact is that Mr. Haskell . . .": Alexander Bland, "A Sorry Affair—Indeed!," *Dancing Times*, September 1961.
"gypsy" . . . "slim, smooth . . .": Alexander Bland, *Dance Magazine*, March 1962.
"Tell me about this man . . .": Maude Gosling and Joseph Houseal, "Nureyev in the West," BR, Spring 1994.
"I forget quickly": "Table Talk," *Observer*, October 1961.
"the best young Russian": Money, *Fonteyn & Nureyev*, p. 9.
she had determined to keep track: Bland, *The Royal Ballet*, p. 130.
"You're that Russian fellow . . .": Money, *Fonteyn & Nureyev*, pp. 9–10.
"You're dealing with . . .": Interview with Sonia Arova.
"unusually generous . . .": Interview with Rosella Hightower.
"like a hawk": Interview with Sonia Arova.
"Erik was this protected . . .": Interview with Glen Tetley.
"kept the child in Erik . . .": Interview with Susse Wold.
"turn in a second . . .": EB, p. 159.
"Erik's alcoholism . . .": Interviews with Violette Verdy.
"In her, Ashton has . . .": Haskell, *Dancing Times*, June 1936.
"like a ringmaster . . .": Percival, *Nureyev*, pp. 161–62.
"looking nervous, solemn . . .": Interviews with John Lanchbery.

14 / "Actually, I Am Romantic Kind of Dancer"

"He is a guest in my house . . .": Editor's log, *Ballet Today*, December 1961.
"I'm here": *Times* (London), October 27, 1961.
"That boy doesn't need . . .": PF.
"a wall of animosity": Richard Buckle, *In the Wake of Diaghilev* (New York: Holt, Rinehart and Winston, 1982), p. 286.
"very blood stream was . . .": Cecil Beaton, unpublished diaries.
"He's better than Nijinsky!": Ibid.
"savage intensity . . .": Alexander Bland, *Observer*, November 5, 1961.
"dancing for himself . . .": from Peter Williams, *Dance and Dancers*, December 1961.
"We all clapped and cheered . . .": Money, *Fonteyn & Nureyev*, p. 10.
"there could be no question . . .": Mary Clarke, *Dance News*, December 1961.
"a dance of despair . . .": Richard Buckle, *Sunday Times*, November 5, 1961.
"too many ingredients": Kavanagh, *Secret Muses*, p. 460.
"exactly the image . . .": "Clement Crisp on Nureyev," BR, Spring 1995.
"boyish grace than masculine . . .": Clive Barnes, *Dance Magazine*, December 1961.
"Babilée with a Soloviev . . .": Bland, *Observer*, November 5, 1961.
"no paragon like Bruhn": unsigned, *Dance and Dancers*, December 1961.
"a strange, haunted artist . . .": Bland, *Observer*, November 5, 1961.
"I kissed him . . .": Hugo Vickers, *Cecil Beaton* (London: Weidenfeld & Nicolson, 1993), p. 446.
"What were you doing . . .": MF, p. 240.
He had been deeply embarrassed: Interview with Susse Wold.
"I saw an arm raised . . .": Ninette de Valois, *Step by Step* (London: W. H. Allen, 1977), p. 104.
"hostile stage hands": Harold Hobson, *The Christian Science Monitor*, November 14, 1961.
"a pure ballet without any story line": Interview with Nikita Dolgushin.
"full of inspiration . . .": RN, p. 134.
"The boys were so thrilled . . .": Interview with Rosella Hightower.
"Rudolf had never met . . .": Interviews with Marika Besobrasova.
"we were used to . . .": Interview with Rosella Hightower.
"It was like a dream . . .": RN, p. 135.
"was vibrant with the kind . . .": Janet Flanner (Genêt), *The New Yorker*, February 3, 1962.
"Everyone in Paris was trying . . .": Interview with Zizi Jeanmaire.
"circus" . . . "may have been of . . .": Marie-François Christout, *Ballet Today*, March 1962.
"the-man-in-the-living-room": Ann Barzel, "Looking at Television," *Dance Magazine*, March 1962.
"exactly where we are . . .": Money, *Fonteyn & Nureyev*, p. 120.
"nightmare world of immense . . .": RN, p. 139.
"is as exhilarating . . .": Taper, *Balanchine*, p. 260.
"how strange, how weird . . ." Francis Mason, *I Remember Balanchine* (New York: Doubleday, 1991), p. 490.
"It was very cloak . . .": Interview with Barbara Horgan.
told "a story . . .": Walter Terry, *Theater Arts*, July 1962.
"He wanted to see . . .": Mason, *I Remember Balanchine*, p. 490.
"We had all just . . .": Interview with Barbara Horgan.
"made George nostalgic . . .": Interview with Betty Cage.
"a contemporary classicism . . .": Taper, *Balanchine*, p. 251.
"a one-man show . . .": Leon Harris, "Nureyev Uptight," *Esquire*, July 1968.
"My ballets are dry . . .": Mason, *I Remember Balanchine*, p. 490.
"He wasn't simply . . .": Interview with Barbara Horgan.
the great classical and romantic ballets defined him: "Mr. Nureyev on His Future," *Times* (London), October 27, 1961.
"People don't seem to understand . . .": Walter Terry, *Theater Arts*, July 1962.

"came as something of a . . .": Margot Fonteyn, *The Magic of Dance* (London: British Broadcasting Corporation, 1979), p. 64.
"Don't you think . . .": *MF*, p.242.
"She had steel . . .": *MG*.
"but from time to time . . .": Interviews with John Lanchbery.
"We entered into . . .": *MF*, p. 242.
"Who is that little Chinese girl . . .": Joseph Houseal, "Dame Ninette de Valois: Remembering Rudolf Nureyev," *BR*, Summer 1994.
"Elegance . . . was discernible . . .": Ninette de Valois, *Come Dance with Me* (New York: The World Publishing Co., 1957), p. 123.
"Her word . . .": *MF*, p. 79.
"from national adoration . . .": Bland, *The Royal Ballet*, p. 97.
"asked indignantly . . .": *MF*, p. 108.
"long the reigning . . .": *Time*, April 16, 1965.
"What British ballet . . .": Lincoln Kirstein, *Ballet: Bias & Belief* (New York: Dance Horizons, 1983), pp. 412–13.
"She was deeply . . .": Interviews with Keith Money.
"I faltered . . .": *MF*, p. 243.
*"Actually, I am romantic . . ." BBC interview with Clive Barnes, February 25, 1962.
"There seems to be . . .": Interview with Theodora Christon.
"Make sure you don't . . .": Interview with Michael Wishart.
"a terrific rage . . ." and subsequent quotation: Cecil Beaton, unpublished diaries.
"the epitome of Edwardian . . .": Vickers, *Cecil Beaton*, p. 502.
"with ever more suspicion . . .": Cecil Beaton, unpublished diaries.
"It was like we were . . .": Interview with Princess Margaret.
TONY GETS PAGE ONE: UPI story, paper unknown, February 18, 1962.
"it would have been absurd . . .": *Sunday Times*, February 18, 1962.
"We have had . . .": Alexander Bland, *Observer Weekend Review*, February 25, 1962.
"We can imagine . . .": Mary Clarke, *Sunday Times*, February 25, 1962.
"from mere petulance . . .": *Times* (London), February 22, 1962.
"one of his great . . .": Alexander Bland, *Observer Weekend Review*, February 25, 1962.
"played the whole second . . .": Clive Barnes, *Nureyev*, p. 102.
"He threw Margot's game . . .": Interviews with Lord Snowdon.
"The emotions of the audience . . .": Interviews with John Lanchbery.
"a well rehearsed piece of corn . . .": Editorial in *Dance and Dancers*, April 1962.
"There has been so much . . .": Arnold Haskell and Mary Clarke, eds., *The Ballet Annual, 1963* (London: Adam & Charles Black, 1963), p. 19.
"deeply intriguing but . . .": A.V. Coton, *Daily Telegraph*, February 22, 1962.
"too unmanly . . .": Andrew Porter, *Financial Times*, February 22, 1962.
"And I was running after him . . .": Elizabeth Kaye, "Nureyev: Dancing in His Own Shadow," *Esquire*, March 1991.
"If one person . . .": *MG*.
"he jumped very . . .": Interview with Melissa Hayden.
"went on and on . . ." *Dancing Times*, April 1962.
"It would have been . . .": Irving Kolodin, *Saturday Review*, March 24, 1962.
"as immediately and decisively . . .": P.W. Manchester, *Christian Science Monitor*, March 17, 1962.
"novelty . . .": Walter Terry, *New York Herald Tribune*, March 12, 1962.
"no matter how strongly . . .": John Martin, *New York Times*, March 25, 1962.
"His ballets are . . .": Anatole Chujoy, *Dance News*, April 1962.
"First time he danced . . .": Harris, "Nureyev Uptight."

15 / The Trial

Information and all quotes in this chapter were drawn from interviews with eyewitnesses Tamara
Zakrzhevskaya and Alla Osipenko.

16 / The Beatnik and the Prince

All quotes attributed to Erik Bruhn are from *EB*, unless otherwise noted. All quotes from Sonia
Arova are from the author's interviews, unless otherwise noted.

"Charlik, Erik say . . .": Charles Gordon, "Net Assets, Gross Behaviour," *Spectator*, January 16,
  1993.
"a nose for stars . . .": Interview with Anthony Russell-Roberts.
"If you're going to get big . . .": Ibid.
"In those days . . .": Gordon, "Net Assets, Gross Behavior."
"If he is not . . .": *Times* (London), March 23, 1962.
"He could prove . . .": *Topic*, March 31, 1962.
"I wonder what . . .": Interview with Valerie Wilder.
"Someone recognized . . .": Interview with Ingrid Glindemann.
"singing Erik's praises . . .": Interview with Monica Mason.
"We were in love . . .": Interviews with Antoinette Sibley.
"You could see . . .": Interview with Anya Sainsbury.
"telling him what was . . .": *EB*, p. 121.
"This is what . . .": Fernau Hall, *Ballet Today*, June 1962.
"talk of whose . . .": A. H. Franks, *Dancing Times*, May 1962.
"it seems likely to overshadow . . .": Peter Williams, *Dance and Dancers*, May 1962.
"pyrotechnic display . . .": Gordon, "Net Assets, Gross Behavior."
"complete solitude . . .": Peter Williams, *Dance and Dancers*, June 1962.
"so abstracted as to be . . .": Lillian Moore, *Dancing Times*, June 1962.
"a strangely disturbing . . .": Ibid.
"treated a young man . . .": Franks, *Dancing Times*, July 1962.
"He was not only free . . .": Interview with Princess Margaret.
"You have helped . . .": Interviews with Sir John Tooley.
"A beatnik and a prince . . .": Walter Terry, *New York Herald Tribune*, June 10, 1962.
"His grand manner . . .": Richard Buckle, *Buckle at the Ballet* (New York: Atheneum, 1980),
  p. 258.
"Erik Bruhn is certainly . . .": *Sunday Times*, November 12, 1961.
"this extraordinary quality . . .": Interviews with Lord Snowdon.
"when centuries of conformity . . .": Harris, "Nureyev Uptight."
"the only field still . . .": John Lahr, *Prick Up Your Ears: The Biography of Joe Orton* (New
  York: Limelight Editions, 1986), p. 154.
"The sixties had a term . . .": Arlene Croce, *The New Yorker*, January 18, 1993.
"Admittedly, ballet had a public . . .": Buckle, *Sunday Times*, May 20, 1962.
"not a classical dancer": *EB*, p.121.
"the devoutness of a . . .": John Martin, "The Royal Ballet's Most Uncommon Commoner,"
  Saturday Review, April 27, 1963.
"totally dominant woman": Interview with Christopher Gable.
"Madam kept her . . .": Interview with Monica Mason.
"Madam very much loved . . .": Interview with Michael Somes.
"He would do all . . .": Interview with Christopher Gable.
"He had all of them . . .": Interviews with Georgina Parkinson.
"there was absolutely nothing . . .": Interview with Dame Ninette de Valois.
"The lights were never on . . .": Interviews with Antoinette Sibley.

"I hate saying this, Madam . . .": Interviews with John Lanchbery.
"chop and change . . .": Clive Barnes, *Dance and Dancers*, August 1962.
"It was dressed with . . .": Fernau Hall, *Ballet Today*, August to September 1962.
"a critic's nightmare": Clive Barnes, *Dance and Dancers*, August 1962.
"the greatest male dancer . . .": Oleg Kerensky, *Daily Mail*, July 3, 1962.
"found it hard to take . . .": Money, *Fonteyn & Nureyev*, p. 17.
"minority cult to . . .": Croce, *The New Yorker*, January 18, 1993.
"The legend of Nijinsky . . .": *Dance and Dancers*, August 1962.
"We were after his past . . .": Margaret Willis, "Dame Ninette de Valois: The Mother of British Ballet," *Dance Magazine*, February 1994.
"was the obvious one . . .": Interviews with Sir John Tooley.
"I had never seen him . . .": EB, p. 124.
"Appearance of RUDOLF . . .": Money, *Fonteyn & Nureyev*, p. 104.
"Erik couldn't dance . . .": Interview with Alexander Grant.
"completely withdrew . . .": Interviews with Georgina Parkinson.

17 / "So You Are Great Ballerina"

"get a pas de deux . . .": Interview with Lupe Serrano.
"Barnum of the Arts": *New York Times*, March 10, 1974.
"It's in the nature . . .": *New York Times*, March 6, 1974.
"Ten minutes . . .": MF, p. 251.
"looked not in the least . . .": Mary Clarke, *Dancing Times*, December 1962.
"worth going a thousand miles . . .": Alexander Bland, *Observer*, November 4, 1962.
"shed half her years . . .": Noel Goodwin, *Daily Express*, November 1962.
"So you are Great Ballerina . . .": Money, *Fonteyn & Nureyev*, p. 104.
"peaked and was on the way . . .": Interviews with Georgina Parkinson.
"flick of the whip": Money, *Fonteyn & Nureyev*, p. 104.
"When I am dancing . . .": *Daily Mail*, November 5, 1962.
"God! I've never . . .": Interviews with Sir John Tooley.
"suddenly improved . . ." and subsequent quote: *The Roy Strong Diaries* (London: Weidenfeld & Nicolson, 1997).
"biting remarks": Kavanagh, *Secret Muses*, p. 467.
"Margot had always . . .": Interviews with Georgina Parkinson.
"People were always terribly . . .": Interview with Christopher Gable.
"She is disgustingly . . .": Richard Buckle, *Sunday Times*, March 30, 1969.
"malleability and humility": Kavanagh, *Secret Muses*, p. 233.
"[I] bullied and bullied . . .": Foy documentary, *Margot Fonteyn*, 1989.
"never to respond . . .": Interview with Keith Money.
"he was desperately . . .": *TV Times*, December 17, 1970.
"she had been trained . . .": Interview with Keith Money.
"work herself up to . . .": MG.
"She gives maternal dignity . . .": Cecil Beaton, unpublished diaries.
"that reluctant laugh . . .": Martha Graham, *Blood Memory* (Garden City, N.Y.: Doubleday, 1991), p. 244.
"If I hadn't found Margot . . .": Interviews with Keith Money.
"caught up in the music . . .": *Times* (London), November 8, 1962.
Rudolf's interpretation brought the ballet into focus: John Gunstone, "Man with a New Career," publication unknown, 1966.
"In *Giselle* . . .": editorial, *Dance and Dancers*, December 1962.
"I don't know why . . .": Interviews with John Lanchbery.
Blair had taken himself off to Copenhagen: "Curtain Up," *Dance and Dancers*, November 1962.

"waiting for Margot to . . .": Interviews with Georgina Parkinson.
"the whole thing": David Vaughan, *Frederick Ashton and His Ballets* (London: A&C Black Ltd., 1977), p. 330.
"People now think it's camp . . .": Kavanagh, *Secret Muses*, p. 469.
"into a kind of tabloid . . .": Alexander Bland, *Observer*, March 10, 1963.
"gave Fred the idea . . .": Interviews with Keith Money.
"Mystery grows around . . .": *Daily Mail*, November 1962.
"troubled Tartar": *Time*, November 30, 1962.
"always close enough . . .": Interviews with Joan Thring.
after his doctor warned: Note from the doctor to Michael Wood, Director of the Royal Ballet School, November 9, 1962, Royal Ballet Archives.
"Erik is driving . . .": Interview with Joy Brown.
"Erik couldn't be intimate . . .": Interview with Susse Wold.
during a stopover at Cairo Airport: Interview with Keith Money.
"Things were . . . taken from . . .": Luke Jennings, "The Dance of Time," *Sunday Correspondent*, May 27, 1990.
FALSE NAME FOR SCARED . . . : *Daily Telegraph* (Sydney), December 3, 1962.
wished to be released: Ballet Sub-committee minutes, December 1962, Royal Ballet archives.
"I have lost any sense . . .": *Adelaide News*, December 18, 1962.
"in a crabby . . .": Interview with Lupe Serrano.
"dying of shyness" and subsequent quotes: Mason, *I Remember Balanchine*, p. 490.

18 / From the Nureyev Front

"enough publicity to . . .": Clive Barnes, *Dance and Dancers*, April 1963.
"Does anybody remember . . .": *PF.*
"spent a great deal . . .": Interview with Michael Somes.
Ashton's reenactment of a reception in Lima, Peru: Kavanagh, *Secret Muses*, p. 469.
"Fred would be running . . .": Interview with Michael Somes.
"feminine woman": *MF*, p. 249.
"the same revolution . . .": Clive Barnes, *Dance and Dancers*, April 1963.
"Michael . . . was standing . . .": Alexander Bland, *Observer*, March 10, 1963.
"not partners, they were . . .": Interview with Michael Somes.
"Oh, Jack, you . . .": Interviews with John Lanchbery.
"I could have kicked . . .": Vickers, *Cecil Beaton*, p. 459.
"What a day of . . .": Bill Beresford to Cecil Beaton, undated but, given the events described, is March 8, 1963.
"arrive pleading . . .": Money, *Fonteyn & Nureyev*, p. 41.
"a ruse" and subsequent quotations on this page and next: Cecil Beaton's unpublished diaries.
"I don't understand about . . .": Truman Capote to Cecil Beaton, February 4, 1963.
"Fonteyn's entire career": Dale Harris, quoted in Vaughan, *Frederick Ashton and His Ballets*, p. 335.
"[His] half-mocking smile . . .": Clive Barnes, *Dance and Dancers*, April 1963.
"Extraordinary actors . . .": Peter Brook, *Observer*, March 17, 1963.
"whether Ashton could . . .": Haskell and Clarke, eds., *The Ballet Annual*, p. 14.
"My Danish friend . . .": *Daily Mail*, April 1, 1963.
"a new kind of expressiveness . . .": Barnes, *Nureyev*, p. 120.
"a crucifier": Joseph Houseal, "Donald MacLeary on Nureyev," *BR*, Spring 1996.
"He could only be Rudolf . . .": Interview with Michael Somes.
"those sinuous . . .": James Monahan, *Dancing Times*, May 1963.
"matching gesture to beat . . .": Percival, *Nureyev*, p. 69.
"Unimaginable success!": *MF*, p. 133.

This time around, all eyes were focused on her young partner: In her autobiography Fonteyn reports that *Time* and *Newsweek* gave Rudolf simultaneous cover stories in 1963, an error that has been repeated in a number of subsequent accounts of the 1963 season. Nureyev did in fact grace the covers of both magazines simultaneously, but not until the spring of 1965.

"ballet's most celebrated . . .": *Newsweek*, March 25, 1963.
"attention he received . . .": Lillian Moore, *Dancing Times*, July 1963.
"fairly shaking the Met . . .": Walter Terry, *New York Herald Tribune*, April 26, 1963.
"Margot's greatest . . .": Interview with Alexander Grant.
"an easy moment . . .": Interviews with Keith Money.
"Like all performers . . .": Harris, "Nureyev Uptight."
"Nothing less than a . . .": *Chicago American*, April 27, 1963.
"the hottest little team . . .": *New York Herald Tribune*, April 30, 1963.
"We weren't used . . .": Interviews with Antoinette Sibley.
"The international glamor . . .": John Martin, *Saturday Review*, May 25, 1963.
"an unhealthy interest . . ." and subsequent quotes and information drawn from Soviet documents secured from the Center for Storing Contemporary Documentation (formerly the Archive of the Central Committee of the CPSU) in Moscow.
HE LOVES NO ONE . . . : article reprinted in *Rudolf Nureyev: Three Years in the Kirov Theatre*, pp. 247–48. Also *New York Times*, April 10, 1963; *New York Herald Tribune*, April 10, 1963; and *Variety*, February 6, 1963.
"Nureyev Coiffure": *Dance Magazine*, June 1963.
"It looked like something . . .": *Newsweek*, April 1963.
"Those poor fellows . . .": Paris, *Garbo*, p. 466 footnote.
she and Rudolf hit it off: Beaton letter to Mercedes de Acosta, July 3, 1963, quoted in Hugo Vickers, *Loving Garbo* (London: Jonathan Cape, 1994), p. 217.
"extraordinary . . .": John Lombardi, "Nureyev's Fight Against Time."
[Hurok] wasn't about to broker: Harlow Robinson, *The Last Impresario: The Life, Times, and Legacy of Sol Hurok* (New York: Penguin Books, 1995), p. 395.
"for a generation . . .": Lombardi, "Nureyev's Fight Against Time."
"I said, 'You poor baby . . .' ": Interview with Lynn Seymour.
"this old barnstormer" and subsequent quotes: Cecil Beaton unpublished diaries.
"the greatest": Jean-Claude Carrière, *Studio Magazine*, 1987.
"Fonteyn Follies": Money, *Fonteyn & Nureyev*, p. 53.
"We didn't really . . .": Interviews with Joan Thring.
"I am sure you realize . . .": Royal Ballet memo from John Tooley to Rudolf Nureyev, June 21, 1963, unsigned.
"a kind of crossroads . . .": Interview with Hélène Traïline.
"It's really the house . . .": *Realités*, January 1966.
"How Much Bullion . . .": *Daily Mail*, August 1, 1963.
"Well that's for you . . ." and subsequent quotes regarding this episode: Money, *Fonteyn & Nureyev*, p. 57.
"due to the fact . . .": Document signed by Brezhnev and secured from Center for Storing Contemporary Documentation in Moscow.
"The Russian jumps . . .": Nancy Mitford to Cecil Beaton, August 25, 1963.
"was like Bach . . .": Taped interview with Walter Terry, April 25, 1978. Oral History Project, The Dance Collection, New York Public Library at Lincoln Center.
"true"; "a poet's dream . . .": Erik Bruhn, "Beyond Technique," *Dance Perspectives* 36 (New York: Dance Perspectives Foundation, 1968), p. 44.
"against some resistance . . .": Kavanagh, *Secret Muses*, p. 477.
"When I change . . .": Olga Maynard, *Dance Magazine*, May 1973.
"if one partner is dumb?": *Newsweek*, April 19, 1965.
"the highest I could . . .": Interview with Monica Mason.

"Rudi dear . . .": Interviews with John Lanchbery.
"very, *very* hard . . .": Interviews with Georgina Parkinson.
"and precisely how . . .": Interview with Monica Mason.
"you could hear around . . .": Interviews with Georgina Parkinson.
"Cabriole better . . .": Interview with Monica Mason.
NUREYEV ON "WHY I RAN OFF . . .": *Daily Express*, November 29, 1963.
"a major new resource . . .": Clive Barnes, *Dance and Dancers*, January 1964.
"the truly remarkable . . .": Croce, *The New Yorker*, January 18, 1993.
"Now with *La Bayadère* . . .": *Dance and Dancers*, January 1964.
Ashton's decision to give: Kavanagh, *Secret Muses*, p. 482.
number of boys enrolled at the Royal Ballet School: *Dancing Times*, June 1964.
"had forfeited his . . .": *Times* (London), December 27, 1964.
"There was a tradition . . .": Interview with Christopher Gable.
"steadily rising . . .": *New York Times*, October 7, 1963.
"struggled for possession . . .": *LS*, p. 236.
"You've got . . .": Interview with Christopher Gable.
"drinking a lot . . .": Interview with Pierre Bergé.
"the same shy . . .": Interviews with Clara Saint.
"to protect [Yves] . . .": Alice Rawsthorn, *Yves Saint Laurent: A Biography* (Garden City, N.Y.: Doubleday, 1996), p. 63.
"Erik was very domineering . . .": Interview with Pierre Bergé.
"seemed somewhat down . . .": *EB*, p. 142.
"We have perhaps . . .": Vittoria Ottolenghi, *Rudolf Nureyev: Confessioni, Una conversazione lunga trent'anni* (Roma: Editoriale Pantheon, 1995), p.35; also Vittoria Ottolenghi to author, September 16, 1997.

19 / A God, a Man, a Bird, Himself

All quotes from Joan Thring and Lynn Seymour are from the author's interviews, unless otherwise noted. All quotes attributed to Margot Fonteyn are from MF, unless otherwise noted.

"being on top . . .": Interview with Marianne Faithfull.
"absolutely gung ho": Interview with Lynn Seymour.
"it's like the way . . .": *Newsweek*, April 19, 1965.
"generosity of mind . . .": David Astor's Foreword to Nigel Gosling, *Prowling the Pavements: Selected Art Writings 1950–1980*, ed. Robert Tracy (United States: A Lives Examined Book, 1986), p. xiii.
"never miss reading . . .": *MG*.
"shrewed, tough, easily hurt . . .": Bland, *The Nureyev Image*, p. 44.
"He knew that in his . . .": Interview with Jane Hermann.
"They were both at . . .": Interview with Rudi van Dantzig.
"Nigel and Maude were like my . . .": Elizabeth Grice, "How Rudi Leapt into Our Lives," *Observer*, January 19, 1993.
"Although we came to . . .": Ibid.
"a quiet, peaceful place . . .": *MG*.
"when he wanted to . . .": Ibid.
"My mother was so very happy . . .": Interview, ITV London, June 17, 1981.
"filled the house . . .": Grice, "How Rudi Leapt into Our Lives."
"Protean complication . . .": Bland, *The Nureyev Image*, p. 58.
Kabuki Lil: Interview with Lynn Seymour.
"flower child": Buckle, *In the Wake of Diaghilev*, p. 280.
"Oh, hi": Interviews with Joan Thring.
"She was mad about him" and subsequent quote: Ibid.

"I've never known a vainer . . .": Marlene Dietrich, *My Life* (London: Weidenfeld & Nicolson, 1989), p. 150.
"women were simply . . .": Interview with Herbert Ross.
"He was cold . . .": Colacello, "The Last Days of Nureyev."
"fascinating" . . . "Here was. . . .": Interview with Edward Albee.
"He saw himself as a sexual . . .": Interview with Querube Arias.
"With women, you have to . . .": Interviews with Violette Verdy.
"Rudi used to go . . .": Gerard Raymond interview on author's behalf with Derek Jarman, unpublished transcript.
"rough-trade pickups . . .": Interview with Michael Wishart.
"horrified by Rudi's . . .": Interview with Glen Tetley.
"He certainly loved . . .": Interviews with Antoinette Sibley.
"would enter confidently . . .": Ned Sherrin, quoted in the program for the Nureyev Gala Tribute, London Coliseum, March 13, 1994.
"frequently discussed . . .": H. Montgomery Hyde, *The Other Love* (Boston: Little, Brown and Company, 1970), p. 3.
"He never denied . . .": Interview with Edward Albee.
"the gay world knew . . .": Interviews with John Lanchbery.
"constantly surrounded . . .": Interview with Christopher Gable.
"A Royal Gala . . .": Michael Wishart to Stephen Tennant, December 8, 1963.
"when he leaves the theater . . .": *Time*, April 16, 1965.
"No, no . . .": Don Short, *Daily Mirror*, December 12, 1963.
"women are silly . . .": *Time*, April 16, 1965.
"It is a big prison . . .": Harris, "Nureyev Uptight."
"Sporadic . . .": Sally Quinn, *The Washington Post*, June 1, 1974.
"To know what it is . . .": Kaye, "Nureyev: Dancing in His Own Shadow."
MARGOT, MY PERFECT . . . : *Daily Mirror*, December 12, 1963.
"It was as though the audience . . .": Violette Verdy, BR, 1975–76.
"Margot's best-case . . .": Interviews with Keith Money.
"She would never . . .": Richard Buckle, *Sunday Times*, March 30, 1969.
"recklessly passionate": Kavanagh, *Secret Muses*, p. 342.
"gold bracelets . . .": Ibid., p. 411.
"We were all so jealous . . .": Interview with Princess Margaret.
"talking away . . .": Interview with Querube Arias.
"Until I married Tito . . .": Margot Fonteyn documentary, *Margot Fonteyn*, 1989, directed by Patricia Foy.
"she knew what it . . .": Interview with Theodora Christon.
Tito made passes at other women: Interviews with Joy Williams Brown, Sonia Arova, Joan Thring, Keith Money, Georgina Parkinson, John Taras.
"this girlfriend whom he would have . . .": Colacello, "The Last Days of Nureyev."
"oh, that's one of Tito's ladies . . .": Interview with Theodora Christon.
"Margot's way of getting . . .": Interviews with Keith Money.
"didn't know how much more . . .": Interview with Joy Williams Brown.
"hated" the way Tito . . .: Interviews with Joan Thring.
"that crazy Russian . . .": Interview with Querube Arias.
"There was a real connection . . .": Interview with Joy Williams Brown.
"a lady with two great loves . . .": Colacello, "The Last Days of Nureyev."
"less generous in her praise . . .": Kavanagh, *Secret Muses*, p. 471.
"a love affair without scars . . .": Diane Solway, "Ballet Partners: Why the Magic Faded," *New York Times*, September 1, 1985.
"Number one . . .": Interview with Theodora Christon.
"We all suspected . . .": Interviews with Georgina Parkinson.
"Knowing the people . . .": Interview with Jane Hermann.

"He said that Margot . . .": Interview with Eugene Polyakov.
"I've got to push . . .": Interview with Michael Wishart.
According to one biographer's undocumented and highly speculative account: Peter Watson, *Nureyev* (London: Hodder and Stoughton, 1995), p. 274
"something of an amateur's . . ." *MF*, p. 258.
"beat the record . . .": Diana Mann, "Melbourne," *Ballet Today*, July 1964.
"point of interest . . .": Howard Palmer, *Sun*, May 6, 1964.
"one of the loveliest . . .": Mann, "Melbourne."
"a girl met . . .": *Evening Standard*, May 19, 1964.

20 / *Nureyev and Fonteyn*

All quotes from Michael Birkmeyer, Lord Snowdon and Joan Thring are from the author's interviews, unless otherwise noted.

"mythical creatures . . .": Money, *Fonteyn & Nureyev*, p. 136.
"all those traffic directions": Interview with Thor Sutowski.
she liked movement she could "attack": Interview with Joy Williams Brown.
"Oh! They not do that . . .": Money, *Fonteyn & Nureyev*, p. 162.
* "His rehearsal had just ended . . .": Interview with Paul Taylor.
"Petipa seen through the mind . . .": *Newsweek*, April 19, 1965.
"had left no dramatic element . . .": Royal Ballet board minutes, July 28, 1964.
"threw . . . like she was a bag . . .": Interviews with Joan Thring.
* "He knows that Spoletini adore temperament . . .": Paul Taylor, *Private Domain* (New York: Alfred A. Knopf, 1987), p. 210.
"it showed more promise . . .": Bland, *The Nureyev Image*, p. 92.
"she was exquisite . . .": Noël Coward, *The Nöel Coward Diaries*, ed. Graham Payne and Sheridan Morley, (Boston: Little, Brown and Company, 1982), pp.569–70.
"just so amused by Noël": Interviews with Joan Thring.
"a curious wild animal . . .": Coward, *The Nöel Coward Diaries*, p. 570.
"Real life often seemed so much more unreal than the stage . . .": Margot Fonteyn documentary, directed by Patricia Foy.
"Margotito": Interview with Joy Williams Brown.
"She never allowed him . . .": Interview with Theodora Christon.
"He sits on his ass . . .": Martin Bernheimer, *Los Angeles Times*, September 4, 1977.
"a projection of his own mind": Alexander Bland, *Dancing Times*, December 1964.
"It's a story very particular . . .": *Dance and Dancers*, January 1972.
"an unusual man ready for . . .": Derek Prouse, *Sunday Times*, December 27, 1964.
"Water, for example . . .": René Sirvin, program for *Swan Lake*, Opéra de Paris Garnier, December 1984.
"Well, everybody, including Rudik . . .": *EB*, pp. 149–50.
"from something deep inside him . . .": James Neufeld, *Power to Rise: The Story of the National Ballet of Canada* (Toronto: University of Toronto Press, 1996), p. 105.
"I use my own choreography . . .": Bernheimer, *Los Angeles Times*, September 4, 1977.
"If I'm just a good dancer . . .": Interview with Michael Birkmeyer.
"Stick to your profession . . .": Interview with Wilhelm Hübner.
"fuck off" . . . and subsequent quote: Interviews with Joan Thring.
"He always gave everything he had . . .": Interview with Princess Margaret.
"We died with laughter . . .": Ibid.
"Everyone was a Rudolf fan": Interview with Wilhelm Hübner.
"creative talent": Horst Koegler, *Opernwelt*, December 1964.
"provides intriguing glimpses . . .": Linda Zamponi, *Dance Magazine*, December 1964.
"In sleek boots . . .": *LS*, p. 237.

"He didn't have that gloomy Russian . . .": Interview with Lynn Seymour.
"I don't care if it's broken": LS, p. 238.
"I had the strong feeling . . .": Interview with Betty Oliphant.
"It was the most beautiful James . . .": EB, p. 145.
"It's Bournonville. You don't change": Neufeld, *The Power to Rise*, p. 101.
"Very foolishly . . .": Ibid.
Ralph Hicklin, *The Globe and Mail*, January 6, 1965.
information on the gala: *Time*, January 29, 1965; also *New York Times*, January 19, 1965.
"Excellent, wonderful . . .": *Newsweek*, April 19, 1965.
"the most breathtaking moments . . .": *New York Times*, January 19, 1965.

21 / *Rudimania*

All quotes from Lynn Seymour, Georgina Parkinson, Christopher Gable, Keith Baxter, Roland Petit and Joan Thring are from the author's interviews, unless otherwise noted.

"our ballet": LS, p. 181
"I told him that if he wants . . .": Kavanagh, *Secret Muses*, p. 485.
the culmination of all my . . .": LS, p. 182.
"Romeo is a nice, normal . . .": Ibid, p. 184.
"neither as an abstract . . .": Barnes, *Nureyev*, p. 120.
"a seminervous breakdown . . .": Interviews with Georgina Parkinson.
"Sorry, honey . . .": Interview with Christopher Gable.
"triumphant success . . .": Andrew Porter, *Financial Times*, February 10, 1965.
"[He] specializes in a kind . . .": Richard Buckle, *Sunday Times*, February 14, 1965.
"better on half a foot . . .": *Times* (London), February 10, 1965.
"the Man of the Hour": *Time*, April 16, 1965.
"the Russian Revolution": *Newsweek*, April 19, 1965.
"the New Boy in Town": Gay Talese, *New York Times*, April 22, 1965.
"money grabber who is pushing back . . .": Program Guide, *Washington Post*, Gaslight Review, September 1965.
"Nureyev Show": Allen Hughes, *New York Times*, April 18, 1965.
"Everywhere [he] walked . . .": Talese, *New York Times*, April 22, 1965.
"today only personality . . .": Diana Vreeland letter to Cecil Beaton, quoted in Vickers, *Cecil Beaton*, p. 497.
"champion Mod Dresser": *Sun*, December 31, 1965.
"No Adam, no Eve . . .": *Daily Express*, November 1965.
"catch of the season . . .": *Newsweek*, May 31, 1965.
"the Pope of Pop Art": Bob Colacello, *Holy Terror: Andy Warhol Close Up*, (New York: Harper-Collins, 1990), p. 5.
The idea for their "Fifty Most Beautiful People" party: Interview with Lester Persky.
"spaced-out heiresses . . .": Colacello, *Holy Terror*, p. 5.
Sedgwick stood high up on a rafter: Victor Bokris, *The Life and Death of Andy Warhol* (New York: Bantam Books, 1989), p. 170.
"Rudi! You filthy Communist . . .": Andy Warhol and Pat Hackett, *Popism: The Warhol Sixties* (New York: Harcourt Brace & Company, 1980), p. 104.
"You name them . . .": Interview with Sybil Christopher.
"favorite American woman": Ainslie Dinwiddie, *Newsweek*, May 31, 1965.
"enormously self-aware . . .": Interview with Edward Albee.
"he picked the thing up . . .": Interview with Theodora Christon.
"rushed them back . . .": *The Ed Sullivan Show*, CBS, May 23, 1965.
"How much longer . . .": Interviews with Sir John Tooley.
Annette Page complained to Ashton: Interviews with John Lanchbery.

"Because of their presence . . .": Interviews with Antoinette Sibley.
"for the benefit . . .": Kavanagh, *Secret Muses*, p. 480.
"I admire your spirit . . .": Interviews with John Lanchbery.
"he has a great deal of knowledge . . .": Gunstone, "Man With a New Career."
"For me a country is just a place to dance . . .": *Newsweek*, April 19, 1965.
"Celtic good looks": Telephone conversation with Patrick Garland.
"somebody very beautiful" and subsequent quotes for this anecdote: Interview with Keith Baxter.
"friendship overlaid with eroticism": Keith Baxter, letter to author, March 21, 1997.
"happily splashing the oars . . .": Ibid.
"two bottles one night . . .": Ibid.
"though it was only a pretense . . .": Ibid.
"I thrive on differences . . .": EB, p. 147.
Fracci kept calling Rudolf Erik . . .": Interview with Carla Fracci.
"to show what I learned . . .": *Time*, July 1, 1966.
"one of the wildest . . .": *New York Times*, May 21, 1966.
"deliberately designed . . .": *Observer*, May 29, 1966.
"what you've got" and subsequent quote: Interview with Thor Sutowski.
"my obsession for religious props . . .": Harris, "Nureyev Uptight."
"He didn't partner his ballerina . . .": Interview with Carla Fracci.
Rudolf thought her "lazy": Interview with Martin Kamer.
"he saw that I didn't have . . .": Interview with Carla Fracci.
For background on Nureyev's *Sleeping Beauty*, see Percival, *Nureyev* and Bland, *The Nureyev Image.*
"an apparent desire to match . . .": Clive Barnes, *New York Times*, September 18, 1970.
"pseudo-Spanish Russian ballet": Richard Buckle, *Sunday Times*, October 7, 1973.
"I wanted the story . . .": Laura Bell, *Show*, April 1971.
"clowning like a tipsy money": Buckle, *Sunday Times.*
"nobody else brings . . .": Percival, *Nureyev*, pp. 202-3.
"You cannot fly around the world . . .": Interview with Peter Martins.
"You don't put yourself . . .": Kavanagh, *Secret Muses*, p. 479.
"no formal knowledge" and subsequent quote: Ibid.
"He was too strong . . .": Interview with Anthony Dowell.
"utterly exhausting . . .": Interview with Anthony Russell-Roberts.
"fond": Ibid.
"demanded upon . . .": Interview with Alexander Grant.
"So what more was there . . .": Interview with Michael Somes.
"being totally perceived . . .": Donna Perlmutter, *Shadowplay: The Life of Antony Tudor* (New York: Limelight Editions, 1995), p. 291.
"incremental changes in . . .": Sali Ann Kriegsman, BR, Winter 1993.
"Gentleman, I expect you have all . . .": MF, p. 281.
"I saw the patriarch of mankind . . .": Buckle, *Buckle at the Ballet*, p. 193.
"That may have been the moment . . .": Interview with Marianne Faithfull.
"And whatever you do . . .": RVD, p. 78.
"absolutely out of their brains": Interviews with Joan Thring.
"freak-out": MF, p. 287.
"What children you . . .": *New York Daily News*, July 12, 1967.
"the ballet battlefield": Walter Terry, *Saturday Review*, May 27, 1967.
"Bruhn's dancing . . .": *The New Yorker*, May 27, 1967.
"the man whom Nureyev considers . . .": *Time*, May 19, 1967.
"mock Rudolf for caring . . .": Interview with Marit Gruson.
"Rudik has always claimed . . .": EB, p. 124.
"This is a hell of a way . . .": MF, p. 281.
"I was trying to raise money . . .": Interview with John Taras.

"peacock . . .": Interview with Sybil Christopher.
"the kind of character . . .": Colacello, *Holy Terror*, p. 147.
Keller would have a brief affair with Talitha Getty: Interview with Hiram Keller.
"He expected me . . .": Ibid.
"just flabbergasted by . . .": Interview with Jeremiah Tower.

22 / *"Nothing Tomorrow, Now, at Once!"*

All quotes from Joan Thring and Michael Brown are from the author's interviews, unless otherwise indicated.

"He told me what Balanchine . . .": Mason, *I Remember Balanchine*, p. 491.
"He was very strict about that . . .": Interview with John Taras.
"was less of a game . . .": George Jackson, *Ballet Today*, November 1967.
"individual way of phrasing . . .": Horst Koegler, *Dance and Dancers*, February 1968.
"Balanchine's Apollo does not . . .": Interview with John Taras.
"Nureyev beats the lot . . .": Buckle, *Buckle at the Ballet*, p. 330.
"overriding sin . . .": Arlene Croce, *Afterimages* (New York: Alfred A. Knopf, 1977), p. 112.
"there is more than one way . . .": David Vaughan, *Dance Magazine*, August 1974.
"It was very interesting . . .": Interview with Peter Martins.
at a cost of forty-five thousand pounds: William Hickey, *Daily Express*, November 1, 1967.
"very Novosibirsk . . .": Interview with Martin Kamer.
"I want that . . .": Interviews with Sir John Tooley.
"medieval, baronial . . .": Buckle, *In the Wake of Diaghilev*, p. 286.
She appeared at one dinner party: Interview with Rudi van Dantzig.
"the child" and subsequent quotes this page: Source withheld.
"half-hearted": "Dance Diary," *Dance and Dancers*, December 1967.
"they had even called in . . .": EB, p. 157.
"One could almost sense . . .": Marian Laurell, *Ballet Today*, January/February 1968.
"If you listen to the music . . .": MG.
"there is a feeling of . . .": Bland, *The Nureyev Image*, p. 120.
"Oh, don't bother . . .": Interview with Marit Gruson.
"Take care of the princess . . .": Ibid.
"I come here to dance with you . . .": Interview with Gerd Andersson.
"knitting": Interview with Merle Park.
"in the real sense of the word" and subsequent quote: Joseph Houseal, "Dame Ninette de Valois: Remembering Nureyev," BR, Summer 1994.
"splendid dancing can disguise . . .": Fernau Hall, *Daily Telegraph*, December 17, 1968.
"run of the mill stuff . . .": Nicholas Dromgoole, *Sunday Telegraph*, March 10, 1968.
"never less than efficient . . .": Clive Barnes, *New York Times*, May 12, 1968.
"No version of *The Nutcracker* . . .": Barnes, *Nureyev*, p. 195.
"full of in-jokes . . .": Kavanagh, *Secret Muses*, p. 498.
"classical-erotic-acrobatic idiom": Ibid.
"absolute bliss" and subsequent quote: Interviews with Antoinette Sibley.
ASHTON OUT OF DATE: Mary Clarke, *Dancing Times*, February, 1968.
"Yes and it's having a very grand . . ." and subsequent quote: Buckle, *Buckle at the Ballet*, p. 294.
"I can't control . . .": Gerard Raymond interview on author's behalf with Derek Jarman, 1994.
"his doggy": Interview with Merle Park.
"Can you come straight over here?" and subsequent quotes relating to this episode: Keith Money's deposition to the police, spring 1968, which he kindly read to the author.
Hamet had died of lung cancer on February 25: Interviews with Alfia Rafikova.
"Boy wants to be beautiful . . .": Harris, "Nureyev Uptight."

"I learn from you . . .": *MF*, p. 284.
"the almost stylized . . .": Clive Barnes, *New York Times*, April 24, 1968.
"exotic intruder": P.W. Manchester, *Dancing Times*, June 1968.
"Jackie, Ari, Rudi . . .": *New York Times*, April 22, 1968.
"Don't tell Rudi" and subsequent quotes relating to this episode: Interview with Glen Tetley.
"It's a kind of new language . . .": *Newsweek*, May 25, 1970.
van Dantzig scarcely believed: Interview with Rudi van Dantzig.
"I know what I am doing . . .": John Percival, *Times* (London), February 13, 1971.
"You can do all those things . . .": Lindsay Anderson interview with Nureyev, BBC-TV, January 27, 1974.
"work on new pieces . . .": Baryshnikov, "Memories of Nureyev."
"What do you mean: rehearse tomorrow . . .": *RVD*, p. 17.
"Tell me, what is the ballet . . .": Ibid., p. 23.
"who is very shy . . .": Interview with Rudi van Dantzig.
"I have to think about my reputation.": *RVD*, p. 31.
"pretentious and tiresome . . ." and subsequent Beaton quotes: Beaton's unpublished diaries.
"the odd, essentially unbelievable . . .": Clive Barnes, *New York Times*, May 1, 1969.
Keller told van Vooren: Interviews with Hiram Keller and Monique van Vooren.
"Ed always hung out . . .": Interview with Hiram Keller.
"How is boy . . .": Interview with Monique van Vooren.
"He was mad for Wallace . . .": Interviews with John Lanchbery.
"It was awe at first . . .": Colacello, "The Last Days of Nureyev."
"big, friendly, shy . . .": Interview with Rudi van Dantzig.
"Rudolf thought [van Dantzig] . . .": Interview with Lynn Seymour.
"That upset him a lot . . .": Interview with Rudi van Dantzig.
"He wants me to travel with him . . .": *RVD*, p. 41.

23 / I Want, You Must

All quotes from Rudi van Danzig, Glen Tetley, Paul Taylor and Senta Driver are from the author's interviews, unless otherwise noted.

"moved lightly but somewhat . . ." and subsequent quote: *RVD*, pp. 56–57.
"is what makes ballet . . .": Peter Williams, *Dance and Dancers*, April 1970.
"la croqueuse des diamants . . .": *RVD*, p. 59.
"He never tells one . . .": MG.
"This was a huge break to do . . .": Interview with Antoinette Sibley.
"ideal . . .": Interview with Monica Mason.
"completely 'honest' dancer . . .": *LS*, p. 235.
"the most exacting . . .": *Claire Motte: Ballerine* (Paris: Editions Henri Vayrier, 1981), pp. 199–200. Motte recalled that their rehearsals took place in September 1969; however, since their performances took place in mid-October 1969, it seems more likely that they rehearsed at that time.
"push you to the edge . . .": Interview with Monica Mason.
"awkward choreography": Interviews with John Lanchbery.
"I ran to one corner . . .": Interview with Merle Park.
PIQUED NUREYEV STALKS . . . : Anna Kisselgoff, *New York Times*, May 17, 1970.
"in perfect form . . .": Clive Barnes, *New York Times*, April 22, 1970.
"a new grandeur . . .": Croce, *Afterimages*, p. 377.
"the technical side . . .": *Newsweek*, May 25, 1970.
"Because I feel so alien . . .": John Gruen, *New York Times*, June 21, 1970.
Ashton had broken down in his dressing room: Kavanagh, *Secret Muses*, p. 501.
"I can never thank Fred . . .": Interview with Princess Margaret.

"He said he was dancing at the Met . . .": Colacello, "The Last Days of Nureyev."

"There was no side . . .": Interview with Lynn Seymour.

"They were very happy . . .": Interview with Princess Firyal.

"could be silly together . . .": Interview with Jamie Wyeth.

"loved to have fun . . .": Interview with Querube Arias.

"Rudolf must have thought . . .": Interviews with John Lanchbery.

"Wallace was totally . . .": Interview with Glen Tetley.

"Rudolf's willpower ran . . .": Interview with Jane Hermann.

"He was very proud . . .": Interview with Herbert Ross.

"he never wanted to keep . . .": Interview with John Taras.

"was the only person . . .": Colacello, "The Last Days of Nureyev."

"always felt compassion . . .": Sasha Anawalt, *The Joffrey Ballet: Robert Joffrey and the Making of an American Dance Company* (New York: Scribner, 1996), p. 319.

"the story of this ballet . . .": Lincoln Kirstein, *Nijinsky Dancing* (New York: Alfred A. Knopf, 1975), p. 137.

"there was no more money . . .": Interview with Edward Albee.

"He was furious . . .": Interview with Lucette Aldous.

"pas de defectors": *Newsweek*, quoting the *Daily Mail*, November 9, 1970.

"We don't do that . . .": Interview with Lucette Aldous.

"You dance like them . . .": John Percival, *Times* (London), February 13, 1971.

"I have not my Russian . . .": Interview with Lucette Aldous.

"Tell Rudolf not to . . .": Monique van Vooren letter to Nureyev about her trip to Leningrad in March 1971, read to the author by van Vooren.

Pushkin had written to say that Rudolf had done well: *Washington Post*, June 9, 1974.

"He never fully understood . . .": Interview with Mikhail Baryshnikov.

"there was the obligatory . . ." and subsequent quote: RVD, p. 72.

"with his blessing": Interview with Mikhail Baryshnikov.

she was dressed for the occasion: Interview with Rudi van Dantzig.

Gouzel was completely spellbound: Interview with Gouzel Nureyeva.

"She was really something . . .": Ibid.

"I have some sausages . . .": Interview with Alla Osipenko.

"Tell her how I am . . ." and subsequent quotes this page: Interviews with Marika Besobrasova.

"I believe there is something . . .": John Percival, *Times* (London), February 13, 1971.

"There's no story . . .": LS, p.247.

"terrifying perfectionist": Ibid, p. 246.

"moody, demanding . . .": Humphrey Burton, *Leonard Bernstein* (Garden City, N.Y.: Doubleday, 1994), p. 270.

"desperate to be . . .": Interviews with Antoinette Sibley.

"would fight . . .": Interview with Monica Mason.

"Nureyev conforms . . .": Mary Clarke, *Dancing Times*, December 1970.

"A few years ago, I could still manage . . .": Laura Bell, *Show*, April 1971.

"He'd call and say . . .": Interviews with Natasha Harley.

For background on Armen Bali, I drew on Carol Purroy, "Armen Bali," *55-plus!*, vol. II, no. 1, January 1997; Anita Clay Kornfeld, "Conversation with a Survivor," *San Francisco Sunday Examiner & Chronicle*, October 3, 1976; and Blake Green, "The Queen of the Ballet Groupies," *San Francisco Chronicle*, March 1, 1979.

Rudolf called her his *druk*: Telephone conversation with Armen Bali.

"because it was very hard . . .": Ibid.

"they have never given me . . .": Green, "The Queen of the Ballet Groupies."

Maggy "loved" having Rudolf: Interview with Loretta Young.

"When I came in . . .": Ibid.

NUREYEV'S BACK IN TOWN–SOCIALLY: Enid Nemy, *New York Times*, December 16, 1970.

"all the Beautiful people . . .": "Suzy Says," *Daily News*, February 5, 1971.

"all beautiful smiles . . .": Ibid.
"The most famous dancer in the world": Percival, *Nureyev*, p. 102.
The dancers were unable to continue: Interview with Eva Evdokimova.
"Never again": Percival, *Nureyev*, p. 104.
all the preparation he needed for future work: "Nureyev Talks to D&D," *Dance & Dancers*, January 1972.
"One is as difficult . . .": Interview with Theodora Christon.
"believed in the fame game . . .": Colacello, *Holy Terror*, p. 10.
"adored": Interview with Jamie Wyeth.
Rudolf thought Warhol "ugly": Ibid.
"What color are your . . .": Colacello, *Holy Terror*, p. 107.
"dancedom's most famous crotch": "Royal Rip: Andy Warhol Interviews Rudolf Nureyev, Sort Of," *Interview*, No. 22, 1972.
"a nuclear look": Colacello, *Holy Terror*, p. 107.
"He's so great . . .": "Royal Rip," 1972.
"You'd best ask . . .": *LS*, p. 255.
"He believed in you . . .": Interview with Lynn Seymour.
"I screamed, I yelled . . .": Terry Coleman, *Guardian*, July 24, 1972.
reportedly out of deference to Fonteyn: Percival, *Nureyev*, p. 107.
"the animal quality . . .": Anna Kisselgoff, *New York Times*, March 29, 1973.
"the pic is timid . . .": *Variety*, August 16, 1972.
"took the plunge . . .": Murray Louis, *Inside Dance* (New York: St. Martin's Press, 1980), p. 98.
"the kind of dancer who . . .": Croce, *Afterimages*, p. 91.
Taylor . . . had agreed to the experiment mainly out of . . . : Interview with Paul Taylor.
"from the waist down . . .": Sally Banes, *Connoisseur*, March 1986.
"how far Paul and I . . .": Bell, *Show*, April 1971.
"extraordinarily calm . . .": Jean Battey Lewis, *Washington Post*, June 9, 1974.
"ballet freaks and the curiosity-seeking chic . . .": George Gelles, *Boston Sunday Globe*, July 9, 1972.
"which is where all the jumping . . .": Interview with Senta Driver.

24 / No Nureyev, No Job

All quotes from Mikhail Baryshnikov and Karen Kain are from the author's interviews unless otherwise noted.

"If Covent Garden can't . . .": ITV interview, June 17, 1981.
*Bruhn had instructed his agent . . . : *EB*, p. 173.
Celia Franca weighed in private notes: Neufeld, *Power to Rise*, p. 142.
"Rudi kept saying . . .": Interview with Betty Oliphant.
"enormous, mammoth . . .": Ibid., 143.
"as he had got it . . .": Ibid., p. 151.
"we had to listen . . .": Interview with David Scott.
"great lessons in theatricality . . .": Interview with Veronica Tennant.
"to sparkle": Interview with Karen Kain.
"She kept away . . .": Neufeld, *Power to Rise*, p. 146.
"Your arms *not* too short . . .": Karen Kain, with Stephen Godfrey and Penelope Reed Doob, *Movement Never Lies: An Autobiography* (Toronto: McClelland & Stewart, 1994), p. 105.
"Do like Margot . . .": Ibid.
"the hardest thing he could . . .": Ibid., p. 103.
"spin like a top": Interview with Karen Kain.
"I called Margot . . .": Interview with Veronica Tennant.
"verbal vulgarity": Interview with Jeremiah Tower.

"He saw me as a kind of . . .": Interview with Betty Oliphant.
"wears its $350,000 price tag . . .": William Littler, *Toronto Star*, September 2, 1972.
"That was quite a kiss . . .": Vanessa Harwood's personal diary, 1972.
"raging . . .": Ann Barzel, *Dance News*, June 1973.
"He prided himself . . .": Neufeld, *Power to Rise*, pp. 151–152.
"You and Margot have guts . . .": Kain, *Autobiography*, p. 105.
"was castrated . . .": *Globe and Mail*, February 9, 1974.
"reach towns all over the world . . .": Elizabeth Salter, *Helpmann: The Authorised Biography* (Brighton: Angus & Robertson, 1978), p. 235.
" 'Ah Red Shoes!' . . .": Ibid.
" a minor European princess . . .": Kavanagh, *Secret Muses*, p. 237.
"Bobby was passionate . . .": Interview with Lucette Aldous.
"The majority of the masses . . .": *New York Times*, January 16, 1973.
"finish the phrase" and subsequent quote: Interview with Martin Kamer.
Richard Attenborough . . . admitted to being "amazed": Peter Williams, "The Power Behind the Cheshire Cat Smile," *Dance and Dancers*, March 1974.
"I set all the camera . . .": Lindsay Anderson interview with Nureyev, BBC-TV, January 27, 1974.
"done so well . . .": Anna Kisselgoff, *New York Times*, November 3, 1973.
"So now I know . . .": John Fraser, *Globe and Mail*, February 9, 1974.
"You don't see anything . . .": Interviews with Luigi Pignotti.
"You have everything! . . .": Kain, *Autobiography*, p. 107.
"The way she does Aurora . . .": *Time*, March 18, 1974.
"papa": Interviews with Linda Maybarduk.
"You shit-fuckers . . .": Vanessa Harwood, personal diary, 1972.
"the roar of the audience . . .": Interview with Veronica Tennant.
"So what is a nice company . . .": Clive Barnes, *New York Times*, May 6, 1973.
"mess with the classics": Nancy Goldner, *Nation*, May 14, 1973.
"are not feats . . .": Ibid.
"If all the [company's] Auroras . . .": Anna Kisselgoff, *New York Times*, April 27, 1973.
"one of the most talented . . .": Clive Barnes, *New York Times*, April 24, 1974.
"gasp of appreciation": Kain, *Autobiography*, p. 70.
"they loved the way we did . . .": Neufeld, *Power to Rise*, p. 153.
"You gave her muskrat?": Kain, *Autobiography*, p. 76.
"[I]is she stone deaf . . .": John Percival, *Dance Magazine*, September 1973.
"with an intricate Renaissance hairdo . . .": Makarova, *Autobiography*, p. 144.
"very little patience . . .": Interviews with Georgina Parkinson.
"she was so angry . . .": Interviews with Linda Maybarduk.
"that man . . .": *Newsweek*, August 13, 1973.
"Paris was a try-out . . .": Fraser, *Globe and Mail*, February 9, 1974.
Privately he dubbed her: Interviews with John Lanchbery.
"they started booing . . .": Diane Solway, *New York Times*, December 18, 1983.
Newsweek was reporting rumors: *Newsweek*, February 1, 1974.
"I once asked him . . .": Interview with Merle Park.
"Don't forget that I am one . . .": John Gruen, *New York Times*, May 5, 1974.
"He gave himself no . . .": Interview with Lynn Seymour.
"All my days are about . . .": John Gruen, *After Dark*, May 1976.
"What, do you want me . . .": Telephone conversation with Armen Bali.
"When I stop . . .": Martin Bernheimer, *Los Angeles Times*, September 4, 1977.
"So I want to be onstage . . .": *Toronto Star*, August 26, 1972.
"the savage young creature . . .": Cecil Beaton's unpublished diaries.
"It's hard to believe . . .": *Newsweek*, May 20, 1974.
"I'm staying put . . .": Fraser, *Globe and Mail*, Feb. 9, 1974.

"Never have I seen . . .": John Percival, *Dance and Dancers*, September 1974.
". . . in those days [Bruhn's] . . .": Clive Barnes, *New York Times*, May 27, 1974.
"about teachers and technique . . .": Baryshnikov, "Memories of Nureyev."
"now I do . . .": Ibid.
"Don't let them . . .": Interviews with Linda Maybarduk.
"Rudolf was so excited . . .": Ibid.
"Are you all right?": Interview with Joanne Nisbet.
"People were used to seeing me . . .": *EB*, p. 190.
"sick with nerves": Interviews with Linda Maybarduk.
"If I had continued . . .": *EB*, p. 191.
"When he walks out onto the stage . . .": Croce, *Afterimages*, p. 68.
"competing for his spot": Baryshnikov, "Memories of Nureyev."
"How was he?": Interview with Princess Firyal.

25 / *Tyger! Tyger!*

All quotes from Jamie Wyeth, Phyllis Wyeth and Patricia Ruanne are from the author's interviews, unless otherwise noted.

"Always I intrude . . .": Gruen, *New York Times*, May 5, 1974.
"Why are you . . .": Interviews with Charles Jude.
"I was lying on . . .": Ibid.
"He was mostly attracted to . . .": Interview with Elizabeth Cooper.
"He was very protective . . .": Patricia Boccadoro, "Nureyev Exposed," *Observer*, January 20, 1997.
"We didn't have an argument . . .": *EB*, p. 206.
"I asked him how much . . .": Interview with Barbara Horgan.
"Generally I'm not fond . . .": *New York Times*, January 10, 1975.
"the Nureyev of sport . . .": *New York Times*, May 7, 1982.
"kill himself with . . .": Olga Maynard, *Dance Magazine*, March 1975.
"the Promethean figure . . .": Anna Kisselgoff, *New York Times*, June 15, 1975.
"Not since the lion . . .": Clive Barnes, *New York Times*, June 21, 1975.
"No matter what words may say . . .": *Time*, May 14, 1973.
"the temple of pelvic truths": Interview with Peter Sparling.
"All my life I have been a devotee of sex . . .": Graham, *Blood Memory*, p. 160.
"lost my will . . ." Ibid., p. 237.
"rebirth": *Time*, May 14, 1973.
"she needed stars . . .": Agnes de Mille, *Martha: The Life and Work of Martha Graham* (New York: Vintage Books, 1992), p. 399.
"This is the only time . . .": Kisselgoff, June 15, 1975.
"someone she could instill . . .": Interview with Peter Sparling.
"I had never seen anything . . .": Gruen, *After Dark*, May 1976.
"stopped in amazement": de Mille, *Martha*, p. 398.
"pre-eminent coquette" and subsequent quoted description: Ibid., pp. 397–98.
"was just like Martha . . .": Interview with Ron Protas.
"let him have it": Graham, *Blood Memory*, p. 244.
"I told him . . .": Ibid.
"I didn't approach Rudolf . . .": Kisselgoff, June 15, 1975.
"the bringer of light": Graham, *Blood Memory*, p. 241.
"balletic": Interview with Janet Eilber.
"Is it really Graham . . ." Kisselgoff, June 15, 1975.
"feed on": Gruen, *After Dark*, May 1976.

"try to reshape himself": Interview with Peter Sparling.
"retiring to modern dance": Robert Tracy, *Goddess* (New York: Limelight Editions, 1997),
 p. 318.
"If I hadn't done *Raymonda* . . .": Carol Lawson, *New York Times*, November 30, 1975.
"Halston wanted to stitch . . .": Tracy, *Goddess*, p. 321.
without even mentioning the scene: Interview with Joy Williams Brown.
"I will never . . .": Ibid.
"like an MGM promotion": Tracy, *Goddess*, p. 321.
"was not ridiculous . . .": Croce, *Afterimages*, p. 161.
"I always thought . . .": Interview with Mikhail Baryshnikov.
"ninety-nine percent sex . . .": de Mille, *Martha*, p. 261.
"personal incantational . . .": Walter Terry, *Saturday Review*, February 7, 1976.
"looked dazed and mortified . . .": Interviews with Nancy Sifton.
"You men have to learn . . .": Interview with Peter Sparling.
"I don't claim . . .": Hubert Saal, *Newsweek*, December 22, 1975.
"Now we're seeing . . .": *New York Post*, July 19, 1975.
"But of course when the time . . .": Kavanagh, *Secret Muses*, p. 567.
"transformed steps into fire": Gelsey Kirkland, *Dancing on My Grave* (New York: Doubleday
 & Co., Inc., 1986), p. 162.
"rehearsal queen": Interview with Charles France.
"Rudi seemed to be genuinely proud of me . . .": Kirkland, *Dancing on My Grave*, p. 162.
"the world's greatest *Corsaire* hero . . .": Croce, *New Yorker*, August 11, 1975.
"by sheer good will . . .": Alan M. Kriegsman, *Washington Post*, August 6, 1978.
". . . she has such total self-annihilation . . .": Joan Juliet Buck, British *Vogue*, December
 1978.
"greatest": Interview with Karen Kain.
"a large, regal bird . . .": Kain, *Autobiography*, pp. 116–17.
"of a little soldier . . .": Ibid.
"He got a little pouty . . .": Interview with Karen Kain.
"Any second now . . .": Ibid.
"in the air . . .": Neufeld, *Power to Rise*, p. 170.
"You're absolutely mad . . .": Interview with Michael Brown.
"schlep across . . .": Interview with Eva Evdokimova.
"Everyone who cares about him . . .": Louis, *Inside Dance*, p. 101.
"hanging on for dear . . .": Interview with Herbert Ross.
"It was an outrageous . . .": Ibid.
"Poor Rudolf, he's so sick . . .": Interview with Loretta Young.
"Why not?": Interviews with Alfia Rafikova.
Lilya had been struck down: Information on Lilya's accident is drawn from interviews with her
 daughter and her sister Razida.
"My mother would like to see me . . .": Julie Kavanagh, *Cosmopolitan*, May 1977.
"desperate": Robert D. McFadden, *New York Times*, May 14, 1977.
107,000 signatures: Marcia Kramer, *New York Daily News*, November 11, 1977.
"I had some very rough . . .": Carol Lawson, *New York Times*, May 9, 1976.
"Suddenly, even violently . . .": Anna Kisselgoff, *New York Times*, April 22, 1976.
"an orgy of exhibitionism": James Monahan, *Dancing Times*, September 1976.
"However dumb one is . . .": Alexander Bland, *The Nureyev Valentino*, p. 29.
"I thought, 'Three months . . .' ": Walter Terry, *Saturday Review*, April 30, 1977.
"You can't pretend . . .": Alexander Bland, *Horizon*, September 1977.
"Me and my women . . .": RVD, p. 91.
"probably not very active . . .": Bland, *Horizon*, September 1977.
"gave them fantasies . . .": John Gruen, *Vogue*, August 1977.
"very slowly and with great . . .": Bland, *Horizon*, September 1977.

"Fuck you, you can't do . . .": Interview with Glen Tetley.

"I told him . . .": Interview with Loretta Young.

"In my case . . .": Bland, *The Nureyev Valentino*, p. 32.

"no interest in women" and subsequent quote: Otis Stuart, *Perpetual Motion: The Public and Private Lives of Rudolf Nureyev* (New York: Simon & Schuster, 1995), p. 213.

VITAL NUREYEV . . . : *New York Times*, October 6, 1977.

"Seen up close . . .": Pauline Kael, *The New Yorker*, November 7, 1977.

"show us the way" and subsequent description of Ashton: RVD, p. 93.

"Holy maracas! . . .": *The Muppet Show*, January 20, 1978 (first aired in London).

"just wanted to make . . .": Interview with Glen Tetley.

"I need them to be there . . .": Interviews with Linda Maybarduk.

"Sometimes I don't even know . . .": RVD, p. 80.

"Probably became better . . .": Colacello, "The Last Days of Nureyev."

"there was something compellingly . . .": Interview with Glen Tetley.

"Jamie was having a meeting . . .": Pat Hackett, ed., *The Andy Warhol Diaries* (New York: Warner Books, Inc., 1989), p. 28.

"the terribly nervous": Interview with Jamie Wyeth.

"How do you taste?": Interview with Phyllis Wyeth.

"got totally into it": Interview with Jamie Wyeth.

"there's nothing to do . . .": Kriegsman, *Washington Post*, Ausugt 6, 1978.

"highly theatrical . . .": Anna Kisselgoff, *New York Times*, July 19, 1978.

"all traces of Victorian . . .": Alexander Bland, *Observer Review*, June 5, 1977.

"racing not only toward . . .": Kriegsman, *Washington Post*, August 6, 1978.

As John Taras saw it: Interviews with John Taras.

"Sorry the Easter bunny . . .": Interviews with Patricia Ruanne.

"Luigi took everything off . . .": Interview with Peter Martins.

hoped to smuggle Rudolf into Makarova's wedding: Telephone conversation with Armen Bali.

"very seldom suggested . . .": James Monahan, *Dancing Times*, August 1977.

"Does she really want to . . .": Telephone conversation with Armen Bali.

26 / Nomad de Luxe

"In the middle of lunch . . .": Interview with Luigi Pignotti.

"*mes pieds dans l'eau*": Interview with Princess Firyal.

"coming out of Russia . . .": Ibid.

"Stavros was always competing . . .": Interview with Rosemarie Kanzler.

"act like a prima donna": Interview with Princess Firyal.

"Rudolf's Rich Groupie Set": Julie Kavanagh, "Nureyev Dances On," *Vanity Fair*, July 1986.

"He much preferred . . .": Interview with Phyllis Wyeth.

"the undisputed queen . . .": Natasha Fraser, "The Last Queen," *W Magazine*, May 1996.

"felt nervous about . . .": Dinah Hall, "Nureyev's Curtain Call," *The World of Interiors*, November 1995.

"He was very clever . . .": Telephone conversation with Marie-Hélène de Rothschild.

"She loved Rudolf . . .": Fraser, "The Last Queen," May 1996.

"He always noticed . . .": Telephone conversation with Marie-Hélène de Rothschild.

"she didn't like the obvious . . .": Interview with Jacqueline de Ribes.

"The Rothschild style . . .": Fraser, "The Last Queen."

"Rudi Nureyev and his wickedness": Melvyn Bragg, *Richard Burton: A Life* (New York: Warner Books, 1988), p. 472.

"was so luxurious . . .": Fraser, "The Last Queen."

"if Marie-Hélène didn't like . . .": Ibid.

"Rudolf loved it that I . . .": Telephone conversation with Marie-Hélène de Rothschild.

"You're the only Russian Bedouin . . .": Interview with Princess Firyal.

"It's another facet . . .": Kavanagh, "Nureyev Dances On."

"I took him up . . ." quoted in Christie's promotional videotape for Nureyev auction.

"He liked to feast . . .": Hall, "Nureyev's Curtain Call."

"a brother . . .": Kavanagh, "Nureyev Dances On."

"He'd call the Met and say . . .": Interview with Jane Hermann.

"his small Versailles": Henry Channon, *Chips: The Diaries of Sir Henry Channon*, ed. Robert Rhodes James (London: Weidenfeld & Nicolson, 1967), p. 459.

"She was madly in love . . .": Interview with Jacqueline de Ribes.

Clara Saint remembers: Interviews with Clara Saint.

"Rudolf brought excitement . . .": Interview with Princess Firyal.

"There wasn't any question . . .": Interview with Jane Hermann.

"Douce, she eats my air": Interview with Jamie Wyeth.

"She never understood Rudolf . . .": Interviews with Luigi Pignotti.

"Douce could be too much . . .": Interview with Alexis de Redé.

"Douce finished": Interview with Jacqueline de Ribes.

She was once driving Rudolf: Interviews with Natasha Harley.

"From the word 'go' . . .": Interviews with John Lanchbery.

"He knew the difference . . .": Interview with Princess Firyal.

"He didn't want to belong . . .": Interviews with Luigi Pignotti.

"a lot of women are terribly . . .": Kavanagh, "Nureyev Dances On."

"he loved setting up this battle . . .": Interview with Jane Hermann.

"tall, imposing man . . .": *LS*, p. 296.

"You must dance in the . . .": Ibid.

"If I interrupt my dancing career . . .": Interviews with John Tooley.

"The constant cry . . .": Ibid.

"mend fences . . ." John Tooley memo to Norman Morrice, December 12, 1977.

"If you didn't want to talk to Rudi . . .": Nigel Gosling to John Tooley, April 1981.

"The moment [Margot] ceased . . .": ITV-TV, interview with Mavis Nicholson, June 17, 1981.

"cruised": Interview with Robert La Fosse.

"He stared at me . . .": Ibid.

"virtual convenience stores": Randy Shilts, *And the Band Played On: Politics, People, and the AIDS Epidemic* (New York: Penguin Books, 1988), p. 89.

"in awe": Interview with Robert La Fosse.

"It's very democratic . . .": Gerald Clarke, *Capote*, pp. 510–511.

"I have to go get . . .": Interview with Robert La Fosse.

"Don't you think Frank is a spy? . . .": Interview with Rudi van Dantzig.

27 / *Balanchine*

"I was thinking . . .": Interview with Barbara Horgan.

"For ages I've wanted . . .": *New York Times*, April 8, 1979.

"He is just like anyone else. . . .": Ibid.

"It should be simple . . .": *RVD*, p. 143.

"I would love to be the instrument . . .": Taper, *Balanchine*, p. 354.

"He was always making remarks . . .": Interview with Peter Martins.

"was like a father to me": Richard Buckle with John Taras, *George Balanchine: Balletmaster* (New York: Random House, 1988), p. 298.

"Balanchine knew he was very serious . . .": Interview with Peter Martins.

"Are you going to go home . . .": Mason, *I Remember Balanchine*, p. 491.

"He learns so slowly": Interview with Barbara Horgan.

"because I'm so used to thinking . . .": *New York Times*, April 8, 1979.

"Then he would figure out . . .": Mason, *I Remember Balanchine*, p. 491.

"edgy": Interview with Susan Hendl.

"Rudolf expects you . . .": Interview with Peter Martins.
"a pretentious bore . . .": Arlene Croce, *The New Yorker*, May 7, 1979.
"Yes, good. It'll get . . .": Interview with Susan Hendl.
". . . had changed it so much . . .": Ibid.
"suddenly thought Rudolf . . .": Interview with Jamie Wyeth.
"bright young man": Interview with Melissa Hayden.
"That's when everything . . .": Colacello, "The Last Days of Nureyev."
"There were one or two other . . .": Interview with Phyllis Wyeth.
"a childlike quality . . .": Interviews with Violette Verdy.
"seeing if I would . . .": Colacello, "The Last Days of Nureyev."
"always doing things": Interview with Melissa Hayden.
"Rudi was never going . . .": Interviews with Violette Verdy.
"as the next best thing . . .": Anawalt, *The Joffrey Ballet*, p. 319.
"a strange being, half human, half animal . . .": Cyril Beaumont quoted in Kirstein, *Nijinsky Dancing*.
". . . the manner in which he caressed . . .": Lydia Sokolova, *Dancing for Diaghilev: The Memoirs of Lydia Sokolova* (London: Columbus Books Ltd., 1989), p. 41.
"completely annihilated himself . . .": *Skyline*, PBS-TV, interview with Emile Ardolino, March 20, 1979.
"what would be the most natural thing . . .": Ibid.
"you have to try to say it . . .": *New York Times*, March 4, 1979.
"the personification of the spiritual . . .": Buckle, *Nijinsky*, p. 159.
"Petrouchka must live . . .": Olga Maynard, "Petrouchka," *Dance Magazine*, February 1970.
"What is interesting to me . . .": *Skyline*, PBS-TV, March 20, 1979.
"Now, however, I can afford . . .": Walter Terry, "Nureyev at Forty," *Saturday Review*, November 11, 1978.
"threw a little laugh . . .": RVD, p. 117.
"wrongheaded": Anna Kisselgoff, *New York Times*, March 8, 1979.
"an exquisitely judged performance": Clive Barnes, *New York Post*, March 8, 1979.
"that bleakness of soul . . .": Ibid.
"truly terrible Petrushka . . .": Arlene Croce, *The New Yorker*, March 25, 1979.
"Nureyev in the title role . . .": Anna Kisselgoff, *New York Times*, March 25, 1979.
"marvelously caught all those . . .": Barnes, *New York Post*, March 8, 1979.
"luxuriate in the movement . . .": Croce, *The New Yorker* , March 25, 1979.
"The intangible bond . . .": Alexander Bland, "Nureyev and Nijinsky," *Observer*, June 24, 1979.
"seemed really happy . . .": Interview with Princess Firyal.
"enormous": Interview with Alexander Grant.
"He's gone offstage!" and subsequent quotes this page: Interview with Karen Kain.
"This smells like home . . .": RVD, p. 129.
"a very intuitive man . . .": Interview with George Weidenfeld.
"didn't get the impression . . .": Interview with Mica Ertegün.
"I climbed over . . .": Interview with Jane Hermann.
"crack about Rudolf": Ibid.
"wonderful new role": Flora Lewis, *New York Times*, November 21, 1979.
"like manna from heaven": Ibid.
"about what has been dubbed . . .": John Percival, *Dance and Dancers*, January 1980.
"whose gift to humanity . . .": Phyllis Grosskurth, *Byron: The Flawed Angel* (New York: Houghton Mifflin Company 1997), p. 312.
"The thing about Byron . . .": Flora Lewis, *New York Times*, November 21, 1979.
"is forever divided between . . .": Marie-Françoise Christout, *Dance and Dancers*, January 1980.
"Does it shock you? . . .": Lewis, *New York Times*, November 21, 1979.
"warmed up to me . . .": Interview with Florence Clerc.
"torn and scorched . . .": Interview with Jean Guizerix.

"It was a paradox...": Interview with Wilfride Piollet.

"A monstrosity...": Lewis, *New York Times*, November 21, 1979.

"confused, disorderly...": Irène Lidova, *Dance News*, January 1980.

"inspired Nureyev to his best...": Percival, *Dance & Dancers*, January 1980.

"was always there for him...": Interview with Susan Hendl.

"We'll start out with caviar...": Interview with Patricia Neary.

"Anyone who was willing...": Ibid.

"Douce wanted to keep...": Interviews with Charles Jude.

"went over now and then...": Telephone interview with Marie-Hélène de Rothschild.

"build": Dinah Hall, "Nureyev's Curtain Call."

"instinctive taste": Ibid.

"Rudolf's fantasy of things...": Interview with Pierre Bergé.

"one on top of the other...": Hall, "Nureyev's Curtain Call."

"and everywhere you look...": Interviews with Antoinette Sibley.

"didn't want to spend money...": Interviews with Natasha Harley.

"resigned...": *Daily Telegraph*, March 17, 1979.

"All I wanted was...": New York *Daily News*, April 24, 1980.

"I have a big favor...": Interviews with Natasha Harley.

"They kissed each other...": Ibid.

"She didn't know how to...": Telephone conversation with Armen Bali.

"I tried, but it was...": Interviews with Marika Besobrasova.

"Explain to her...": Interviews with Natasha Harley.

"Gouzela gave him nothing but...": Telephone conversation with Armen Bali.

"mother him": Interview with Eva Evdokimova.

"very emotional about seeing...": Interviews with Charles Jude.

"shocked": Telephone conversation with Armen Bali.

"If *she* stays here...": Interviews with Luigi Pignotti.

"There was a time when it was easier...": John Lombardi, "Nureyev's Fight Against Time."

"window-dressing for the over-the-hill...": *Ballet News*, April 1980.

"Now the boys feel...": Ibid.

"All this may sound terribly French...": Anna Kisselgoff, *New York Times*, February 24, 1980.

"fiend for working...": *New York Times*, April 25, 1980.

"A dancer must learn...": *Dance Magazine*, July 1980.

"terrible, he just doesn't know...": Andy Warhol, *The Andy Warhol Diaries*, p. 283.

"you must think of something...": Lombardi, "Nureyev's Fight Against Time."

"Where once he dazzled...": David Dougill, *Sunday Times*, June 15, 1980.

"He looks wonderfully slim...": Mary Clarke, *Dancing Times*, August 1980.

"for some time...": Arlene Croce, *The New Yorker*, August 4, 1980.

"...had enough excitement...": Anna Kisselgoff, *New York Times*, November 7, 1980.

"There are a few friendlies...": Lombardi, "Nureyev's Fight Against Time."

"Why were Rudolf Nureyev...": Tobi Tobias, *New York*, August 17, 1981.

"When he dances Romeo's...": Deborah Jowitt, *Village Voice*, July 22, 1981.

"I stopped expecting perfection...": Lombardi, "Nureyev's Fight Against Time."

"Probably I've danced...": Interview with Patricia Neary.

"Did you say...": Ibid.

"Where other dancers would...": Interview with Eva Evdokimova.

"...doing it much easier...": MG.

"You mean, you don't...": Interview with Monica Mason.

"Yes, stop while you are still...": Interview with Michael Birkmeyer.

"It's my life...": Lombardi, "Nureyev's Fight Against Time."

"awestruck...": Interview with Jane Hermann.

"I think he's heroic...": Lombardi, "Nureyev's Fight Against Time."

"could have been twins": Interview with James Toback.

"Nastassia's movie . . .": Ibid.
"Sex was very liberating . . .": Lombardi, "Nureyev's Fight Against Time."
"real romantic notions": Interview with James Toback.
"Tell her to sew . . .": Ibid.
"They had this mercurial . . .": Interview with Jamie Wyeth.
"When someone close to him . . .": Interviews with Charles Jude.
"It's like losing . . .": *RVD*, p. 145.
"When I die . . .": Mason, *I Remember Balanchine*, p. 493.
"Has Lincoln seen *Manfred*?": Interview with Jamie Wyeth.
"his company": Interview with Patricia Neary.
"I really don't want . . .": Ibid.
"That's like prostitution": Ibid.
"Nureyev and George Balanchine's . . .": *Dance Magazine*, May 1983.

28 / "Ritorna Vincitor!"

"the only place in the world . . .": "A Conversation with Jean Babilée," *BR*, Summer 1994.
"Jane the Sherman tank": Interviews with Linda Maybarduk.
"reduced to a mass of jelly . . .": Kavanagh, "Nureyev Dances On."
Eisner . . . proposed Nureyev: Interviews with Igor Eisner.
"He had been courting the company . . .": Ibid.
"*Ritorna vincitor!*": Ibid.
"Maybe it's finally time . . .": Alan M. Kriegsman, *Washington Post*, May 1, 1983.
"Rudolf and Natasha hadn't had a good . . .": Interview with Jane Hermann.
"I'm going to bash his head . . .": Interview with Zizi Jeanmaire.
"I don't want your fucking ballets . . .": Ibid.
"My body has Petipa . . .": Interview with Jean Guizerix.
"The entire world of dance . . .": de Mille, *Martha*, p. 403.
"Before Rudolf . . .": Interview with Manuel Legris.
"He wanted to have . . .": Interview with Monique Loudières.
NUREYEV LAUNCHES STAR WARS: *Le Quotidien de Paris*, January 26, 1984.
"at just the right moment . . .": Interview with Yvette Chauviré.
"frou-frou . . .": Interview with Isabelle Guérin.
"It was a shock . . .": Interview with Laurent Hilaire.
"He really managed . . .": Interview with Patrice Bart.
"I said, 'My God . . .' ": Interview with Manuel Legris.
"who first astounded us . . .": Clement Crisp, *Financial Times*, February 13, 1984.
"It was difficult for him . . .": Interview with Eugene "Genya" Polyakov.
"acts of provocation": Interview with André Larquié.
"He just stayed in a corner . . .": Interview with Monique Loudières.
"He was always right . . .": Interview with Isabelle Guérin.
"a lot about the way to be . . .": Diane Solway, "Sylvie Guillem," *European Travel & Life*, April 1990.
"took the light": Interview with Manuel Legris.
"Look, there's the world": Interviews with Michel Canesi.
"Freddie went crazy . . .": Interview with Alexander Grant.
"a big row": Ibid.
"aggressive . . .": Interview with Anthony Russell-Roberts.
"They'll call it English . . .": Interview with Alexander Grant.
"airborne quality": Interview with Glen Tetley.
"so desperate": Interview with Rudi van Dantzig.
"It's impossible for me . . .": *RVD*, p. 181.

"I didn't even ring him . . .": Luke Jennings, "Nureyev's Coda," *New Yorker*, December 28, 1992–January 4, 1993.
IMPOSSIBLE NOUREEV!: *Le Quotidien de Paris*, July 22, 1984.
"In the beginning . . .": Interview with Genya Polyakov.
"You do all the other *Swan Lakes* . . .": Interview with Manuel Legris.
"for some very straightforward . . .": Michel Canesi and René Sirvin, *Le Figaro*, January 15, 1993.
"drenched in the morning": Colacello, "The Last Days of Nureyev."
But also preoccupying him: Interviews with Michel Canesi.
"EPIDEMIC: The Mysterious and Deadly Disease . . .": *Newsweek*, April 11, 1983.
Canesi believed that only about 10 percent: Interviews with Michel Canesi.
"I thought, 'What if I make . . .' ": Ibid.
"I will be dead very . . .": Interview with Genya Polyakov.
"about my condition": Interview with André Larquié.
"the time had come": Interviews with Michel Canesi.
"Please don't . . .": Ibid.
"And for a long time . . .": Colacello, "The Last Days of Nureyev."
"It is pathetic . . .": Burt Supree, *Village Voice*, September 11, 1984.
"stiff, earthbound jumps . . .": Jennifer Dunning, *New York Times*, August 17, 1984.
"I would tell him . . .": Interviews with Michel Canesi.
"pouring": Interviews with John Lanchbery.
"Rudolf could dance with a hundred-degree . . .": Interview with Mikhail Baryshnikov.
"We thought it very strange . . .": Interview with Monique Loudières.
"He was terribly sick . . .": Interview with Jane Hermann.
"vehemently": Ibid.
"It's a lie . . .": Interview with Hélène Traïline.
"imminent death": Clive Barnes, *New York Post*, June 29, 1985.
"He's so unpredictable . . .": *RVD*, p. 177.
"That boy of yours . . .": MG.
"70 minutes of bombastic . . .": Martha Duffy, *Time*, July 28, 1986.
"a rave": Perlmutter, *Shadowplay*, p. 293.
"perched": Hall, "Nureyev's Curtain Call."
"never really at home anywhere . . .": Colacello, "The Last Days of Nureyev."
"A thing happens with age . . .": Kavanagh, "Nureyev Dances On."
"a young lion . . .": MF, p. 251.
"like Napoleon with your . . .": Interview with Princess Firyal.
"No one's interested in me . . .": *RVD*, p. 200.
"I'm there daily . . .": Jennings, "Nureyev's Coda."
"took care of money . . .": Interview with Genya Polyakov.
"no other life": Interviews with Charles Jude.
"I ask him what he wants . . .": *RVD*, p. 160.
"treated her awfully . . .": Interview with Rudi van Dantzig.
"she liked the idea . . .": Interview with Gilles Dufour.
"living under an illusion . . .": Interviews with Michel Canesi.
Seeing that there were 13 at the table: Interviews with Mario Bois.
"Here I am . . .": Kavanagh, "Nureyev Dances On."
"I am probably a male chauvinist . . .": Michael Pye, GEO, August 1983.
"With me, you will go abroad . . .": Martine Planells, "Charles Jude: le fils prodige," *Danser*, November 1993.
"He loved men . . .": Interview with Florence Clerc.
"Fine, we'll buy a chateau . . .": Interviews with Charles Jude.
"He wanted Charles and me . . .": Interview with Florence Clerc.
"He said to me, 'We have to . . .' ": Interviews with Charles Jude.

"Baby, will you remember me . . .": Interviews with Linda Maybarduk.
"Would it be a good idea . . .": Interviews with Michel Canesi.
"terrible": Interview with Michael Birkmeyer.
"It was embarrassing . . .": Interviews with Linda Maybarduk.
"I am Tatar . . .": Interview with Michael Birkmeyer.
"hushing the house with . . .": Interviews with Igor Eisner.
"*Poisson d'Avril!*": Interview with Elizabeth Cooper.
"It was a big scandal . . .": Interview with Manuel Legris.
"Rudolf was there looking . . .": Interviews with Igor Eisner.
"they had too much personality . . .": Interview with Elizabeth Cooper.
"It's a real present . . .": Interviews with Igor Eisner.
"knowing that Rudolf would be annoyed . . .": Interview with Elizabeth Cooper.
"Paris likes cabals . . .": Interviews with Igor Eisner.
"I accuse Mr. Nureyev . . .": *Philadelphia Inquirer*, March 27, 1986.
"abuse of power . . .": *Sunday Times*, March 30, 1986.
"appears to be going through . . .": *Philadelphia Inquirer*, March 27, 1986.
"Once Erik knew . . .": Interview with Valerie Wilder.
"get a giggle out of . . .": Ibid.
"It was awful . . .": Interview with Mikhail Baryshnikov.
"It was a sad story . . .": Ibid.
"simply amazing . . .": Clive Barnes, *New York Post*, July 9, 1986.
"A choreographer of staggering . . .": Arlene Croce, *Sight Lines*, p. 310.
"but you don't have an event": *New York Times*, July 8, 1986.
plans to restore: Interview with Sam Welsh.
"The colors, the designs . . .": Interviews with Michel Canesi.
"It is one of the greatest disappointments . . .": *Daily Mail*, August 25, 1987.
"absolutely had to go . . .": Interview with Roch-Olivier Maistre.
"He could see things only . . .": Ibid.
called Jacqueline Onassis before he left Paris: Interview with Liuba Myasnikova.
"He had a lot of anxiety . . .": Interview with Roch-Olivier Maistre.
"I would rather have him . . .": *New York Times*, November 15, 1987.
"except that he walked . . .": Interview with Liuba Myasnikova.
"deep happiness": Interview with Roch-Olivier Maistre.
"dumbfounded": Ibid.
The expensive roses she had purchased, and other details of Nureyev's visit with his family come from the author's interviews with Razida Yevgrafova and Alfia Rafikova, who were present.
"Is he real?": Interview with Alfia Rafikova.
"amazed at all . . .": Myasnikova, "Some of My Memories," p. 116.
"laughing at memories": Interviews with Natasha Harley.

29 / Songs of a Wayfarer

"a triumph . . .": René Sirvin, *Le Figaro*, October 27, 1986.
"couldn't think to do it . . .": *New York Times*, June 14, 1987.
"three things that cheer me up . . .": Ibid.
"But sometimes he was asking me, 'How . . .' ": BBC Radio, January 1994.
"Even if there was egg . . .": Interview with Lynn Seymour.
"We spoke about . . .": Interview with Genya Polyakov.
"How are you doing to do this?": Interview with Patricia Neary.
"his appearance has by now become . . .": Clive Barnes, *New York Post*, September 1987.
"perfectly understandable . . .": *The New Yorker*, February 8, 1993.
"Obviously it's wrong so why do . . .": Lewis Segal, *Los Angeles Times*, March 22, 1987.

"He was furious at me . . .": Interviews with Michel Canesi.
"He went off every time . . .": Canesi and Sirvin, *Le Figaro*, January 15, 1993.
"Can you come to my . . .": Interviews with Patricia Ruanne.
"Martha asked me . . .": Interview with Ron Protas.
"You are an ungrateful hypocrite": "Suzy," *New York Post*, October 8, 1987.
"I'll *never* give Rudolf . . .": Colacello, "The Last Days of Nureyev."
"facing a tragic moment . . .": "Suzy," *New York Post*, October 9, 1987.
"with great fondness": Interview with Ron Protas.
"an icon of romantic fervour": Clement Crisp, *Financial Times*, January 7, 1988.
"that experience": Interview with Peter Martins.
"I'm not good enough . . .": Ibid.
"a lovely, heart-warming . . .": Clive Barnes, *New York Post*, June 29, 1988.
"The wanderer wants everything . . .": Interviews with Charles Jude.
"You're just trying to get me . . .": Interview with Jane Hermann.

30 / *Like Nikiya, in* Bayadère

All quotes from Kenneth Greve and Liz Robertson are from the author's interviews, unless otherwise indicated.

"a national catastrophe": Solway, "Sylvie Guillem."
"The walls were starting . . .": Solway, ibid.
"Rudolf was angry . . .": Ibid.
"Doesn't she know . . .": Interview with Jane Hermann.
"She was very much like . . .": Interview with Genya Polyakov.
"When reporters asked me . . .": Twyla Tharp, *Push Comes to Shove* (New York: Bantam, 1992), p. 325.
"Look, she will never . . .": Interview with Gilles Dufour.
"going far beyond the boundaries . . .": Tharp, *Push Comes to Shove*, p. 327.
"You're going to have a lot of trouble . . .": Interview with Kenneth Greve.
Platel cried her way through: Interview with Elisabeth Platel.
"If you give in . . .": *New York Times*, November 2, 1989.
"he knew he was wrong": Interview with Genya Polyakov.
"not one to easily share . . .": Interview with Roch-Olivier Maistre.
"more firmly on a leash": Interviews with Igor Eisner.
"near-suicidal": Ibid.
"It's perfect": Interviews with Luigi Pignotti.
"the mad Russian who has bought . . .": Vicente Garcia-Marquez, *Massine* (New York: Alfred A. Knopf, 1996), p. 186.
"overcome by the beauty . . .": Ibid., p. 97.
He astonished his neighbor Gore Vidal: Lynn Barber, *Independent on Sunday*, January 10, 1993.
"He went absolutely crazy . . .": Interviews with Mario Bois.
"I thought it was ridiculous . . .": Interview with Pierre Bergé.
"the offers . . . disincrease": *Toronto Star*, August 22, 1989.
"Basically the king . . .": Ibid.
"redirected the croaking": Jennifer Dunning, "Rudolf Nureyev: Actor and King," *New York Times*, August 16, 1989.
"He was planning for Kenneth's future . . .": Interview with Karen Kain.
"playing with Rudolf's affections . . .": Interviews with Linda Maybarduk.
"Look, you can save me . . .": Interviews with Kenneth Greve.
"I've got a girlfriend . . .": Interview with Liz Robertson.
"If he had turned his career around . . .": Interview with Jane Hermann.
"a great acting performance . . .": John Percival, *Times* (London), June 4, 1991.

"the details are really his . . .": Interview with Flemming Flindt.
"he kept asking me . . .": Interview with Ninel Kurgapkina.
"I don't know why I did it . . .": Luke Jennings, *The New Yorker*, December 28, 1992–January 4, 1993.
"buried": Telephone conversation with Armen Bali.
"the tragedy for the Leningrad audience . . .": Veronica Strizhak, *Smena*, November 30, 1989.
"My dear boy . . .": Videotape of Nureyev's visit with Anna Udeltsova, courtesy of Luigi Pignotti.
"Just imagine! This small dirty . . .": Interview with Liuba Myasnikova.
"dance badly": Interviews with Tamara Zakrzhevskaya.
"made him look ugly . . .": Ibid.
"wall of defectors": Interview with Marina Vivien.
"Why don't we . . .": Interviews with Luigi Pignotti.
"Though we spoke and laughed . . .": *Observer*, April 21, 1991.
"looked like people who came out of . . .": Charles Bremner, "Out of Steppe," *Times Saturday Review*, March 30, 1991.
"sadly": Interview with Genya Polyakov.
"He said he wanted to remain . . .": Interview with Pierre Bergé.
"I have been betrayed . . .": Interviews with Igor Eisner.
"a very nice boy . . .": Elizabeth Kaye, *Esquire*, March 1991.
"When we go back to the Opéra . . .": Canesi and Sirvin, *Le Figaro*, January 15, 1993.
"He wanted it with all his heart": Ibid.
"The reviews were getting . . .": Interview with Jane Hermann.
"he didn't trust anybody . . .": Interview with Andrew Grossman.
"a satchel of money": Ibid.
"They hated him in it . . .": Ibid.
"The more people raved . . .": Herb Caen, *San Francisco Chronicle*, February 22, 1990.
"a Jewish cunt": Interviews with Jane Hermann and Jeremiah Tower.
"It would have been lovely . . .": Interview with Jane Hermann.
"I'm the last person to defend . . .": Interview with Herbert Ross.
"the Yiddish bitch"; "Jewish leftist liberals": Interview with Andrew Grossman.
"I was never sure . . .": Interview with Jane Hermann.
"In Russia, if you're really anti-Semitic . . .": Interview with Genya Polyakov.
"hated the Jews . . .": Interview with Andrew Grossman.
"the ultimate put-down": Interview with Herbert Ross.
"was not prejudiced, not racially . . .": *The New Yorker*, February 8, 1993.
"detrimental to the image": Interview with Barbara Horgan.
Vivi Flindt marvelled at how: Interview with Vivi Flindt.
"In my life now . . .": Luke Jennings, "The Dance of Time," *Sunday Correspondent*, May 27, 1990.
"grotesque, pathetic . . .": Laurie Horn, *Miami Herald*, undated review, 1990.
"extracts from him a performance . . .": Judith Mackrell, *Independent*, August 31, 1990.
"He still gets an audience . . .": Lynn Barber, "A Dance to Defy Time," *Independent on Sunday*, August 19, 1990.
"safe": Interview with Vivi Flindt.
"Charles told me a few times . . .": Ibid.
"She's such great company . . .": Jennings, "The Dance of Time."
"He would come any time we thought . . .": Interview with Querube Arias.
"I used to tour theaters . . .": Interviews with Luigi Pignotti.
"heartbroken": Interview with Querube Arias.
"were so careful with her . . .": Ibid.
"So what?": Ibid.
"He took it for granted . . .": Interview with Anya Sainsbury.
"she was there to see it . . .": Interview with Monica Mason.

"willed herself not to show . . .": Interview with Anya Sainsbury.
"She was suffering a lot . . .": Luke Jennings, "Nureyev's Coda," *The New Yorker*, December 28, 1992–January 4, 1993.
"He wanted to know everything . . .": Interview with Querube Arias.
"I'd like to . . .": Ibid.

31 / *Diminuendo*

"nothing more for him": Interview with Andrew Grossman.
"unworthy of him": Clement Crisp, *Financial Times*, May 5, 1991.
"almost as garish as . . .": *Daily Mail*, May 7, 1991.
"the latest star to join the ranks . . .": Anthony Gardner, *Evening Standard*, April 3, 1991.
"emotional distress . . .": *Daily Mail*, October 25, 1991.
jackals and hyenas: Nicholas Dromgoole, *Sunday Telegraph*, May 12, 1991.
"He wanted the show . . .": Interview with Vivi Flindt.
"you couldn't mention AIDS . . .": Canesi and Sirvin, *Le Figaro*, January 15, 1993.
"You are only interested in character . . .": *Times* (London), May 3, 1991.
"If she comes . . .": Interview with Andrew Grossman.
"looking for Anna": Ibid.
"fair": Ibid.
"Wembley! I didn't . . .": Bremner, "Out of Steppe."
"there was so little left . . .": Interview with Monica Mason.
"tragic . . . horrible . . .": Jennings, "Nureyev's Coda."
"Everybody's dropping off the tree . . .": Bremner, "Out of Steppe."
"must not only make his orchestra . . .": Humphrey Burton, *Bernstein*, p. 253.
"You should become . . .": Donna Perlmutter, "From Barre to Baton," *Los Angeles Times*, July 18, 1991.
"You're so enormously talented . . .": Interview with Jane Hermann, who was also present.
"the greatest [conductor] in the world": Jann Parry, "The Dancing Years Are Not Over Yet," *Observer*, April 21, 1991.
"find an old maestro . . .": Perlmutter, "From Barre to Baton."
"Imagine this supremely . . .": Ibid.
"how those bastard conductors . . .": Parry, "The Dancing Years Are Not Over Yet."
"living *in* the music . . .": Interview with Wilhelm Hübner.
"Children . . .": Ibid.
"Everyone was impressed . . .": Jennings, "Nureyev's Coda."
"visible and audible": Susi Fleischmann to Nancy Sifton, July 3, 1991.
"He looked like he was . . .": Interview with Michael Birkmeyer.
"a big, overly dramatic . . .": Interview with Wilhelm Hübner.
"better than some . . .": Ibid.
she was distressed to find him: Interview with Lydia Hübner.
Rudolf confided in him: Interview with Vaxy Hübner.
"Finally he gave up . . .": Interview with Lydia Hübner.
"furious": Interviews with Charles Jude.
"Look at me . . .": Interview with Lucette Aldous.
"It could be worse . . .": Interview with Elizabeth Kendall.
"My mother packed a suitcase . . .": Elizabeth Kendall, *HG*, August 1992.
"He was very nice . . .": Telephone interview with Marie-Hélène de Rothschild.
"If Rudolf invites you to visit . . .": Interview with Querube Arias.
"My houses are all strange . . .": Linda Lee-Potter, *Daily Mail*, March 2, 1991.
"Carcass not working . . .": Interviews with Patricia Ruanne.
"a bit too Bette Davis": Ibid.
"with a volcano seething inside": Ibid.

"I have to go for my mother . . .": Interview with Lydia Hübner.
"He was with his own . . .": Jennings, "Nureyev's Coda."
"Like my father . . .": Ibid.
"You really mean it?": Interview with Jane Hermann.
"I'm afraid there will be no more . . .": Interviews with Marika Besobrasova.
"I expected him to be terribly . . .": Interviews with Michel Canesi.
"Is that really Mr. Nureyev . . .": Canesi and Sirvin, *Le Figaro*, January 15, 1993.
"Susie, you can't . . .": Interview with Susan Hendl.
"We agreed on certain sections . . .": Interview with Peter Martins.
"It has every possible trial . . .": Interview with Charles Barker.
"The company needed Guillem like . . .": Interview with Jane Hermann.
"That's what Rudolf wants": Interviews with Michel Canesi.
"I never had so much respect . . .": Interview with Peter Martins.
"Thank you for supporting me . . .": Interview with Susan Hendl.
his bedside reading: Interview with Sandy Perry, former manager of Woodburn Estates, Nureyev's Virginia home.
"everyone saw that he was really ill . . .": Jennings, "Nureyev's Coda."
"he went like a candle . . .": Interviews with Luigi Pignotti.
"it would take more than a chapel . . .": Interview with Jeremiah Tower.
"At last, *Bayadère*": Interviews with Patricia Ruanne.
"its colors, exuberance . . .": *L'Événement du Jeudi*, October 1992.
"exhausted, on a sofa . . .": Gore Vidal, *Palimpsest* (New York: Random House, 1995), p. 130.
"ghostly": Interviews with Michel Canesi.
"And so, is it the end?:" Canesi and Sirvin, *Le Figaro*, January 15, 1993.
"It was very, very hard . . .": Interview with Isabelle Guérin.
"absolute fervor": Interview with Hélène Traïline.
"even those who had been against . . .": Ibid.
"his eyebrows would go . . .": Interviews with Patricia Ruanne.
"You would ask . . .": Ibid.
"mixing all the difficult steps . . .": Interview with Manuel Legris.
Solaria Rudolfovna: Interviews with Marika Besobrasova.
"an excruciating task": Interview with Hélène Traïline.
"Don't shit on my brain!": Interviews with Michel Canesi.
"No divan": Interview with Hélène Traïline.

32 / *Curtain Call*

All quotes from Charles Jude and Marika Besobrasova are from the author's interviews, unless otherwise noted.

"leave us during the . . .": Interview with Isabelle Guérin.
"He had no hips . . .": Interviews with Luigi Pignotti.
"But I won't see everything . . .": Interviews with Michel Canesi.
"Jack, you change orchestration . . .": Interviews with John Lanchbery.
"I must do it . . .": Interviews with Michel Canesi.
"[Rudolf] couldn't stand . . .": Jennings, "Nureyev's Coda."
"Don't tell him that you . . ." and subsequent van Dantzig quotes these pages: *RVD*, pp. 244–49.
He and Taras would take: Interview with John Taras.
"He still wanted to . . .": Interview with Florence Clerc.
refused to speak to Jude: Interviews with Charles Jude.
"Good, just don't be too late": Interview with Frank Augustyn.
"I'm a close friend . . .": Interviews with Michel Canesi.

"financially privileged": Interviews with François "Frank" Lousassa.
"All these women . . .": Ibid.
"overly obsessive": Interviews with Marika Besobrasova.
"to protect me . . .": Colacello, "The Last Days of Nureyev."
"He wasn't angry with Robert . . .": Interviews with Michel Canesi.
He added a codicil to his will: Codicil to Rudolf Nureyev's will, signed October 30, 1992.
"when the moment comes . . .": Ibid.
"I can't eat . . .": *RVD*, p. 251.
"You felt he was living . . .": Interviews with François Lousassa.
"especially to go see him . . .": Telephone interview with Marie-Hélène de Rothschild.
"looking like an Eastern potentate": Interviews with Patricia Ruanne.
Gouzel . . . disliked many of Rudolf's friends: Interviews with Gouzel Nureyeva.
"Oh, don't worry . . .": Interviews with Michel Canesi.
Liuba Romankova received a phone call: Interview with Liuba Myasnikova.
"It was supposed to be steeped . . .": Interviews with Michel Canesi.
"simple folk from Ufa": Interviews with Alfia Rafikova.
"Rosa insisted that he should . . .": Interviews with Razida Yevgrafova.
"I always said he would be . . .": Colacello, "The Last Days of Nureyev."
the simplicity of the wooden casket: Author's observations.
"would have had a good old laugh . . .": Interview with Lynn Seymour.
"Make sure I'm not too close . . .": Interviews with Michel Canesi.
"We name rooms after this . . .": Vidal, *Palimpsest*, p. 128.

Epilogue

"a grievous illness": *New York Times*, January 7, 1993.
"If I clarify things now . . .": Canesi and Sirvin, *Le Figaro*, January 15, 1993.
"AIDS and the Arts . . .": *Newsweek*, January 18, 1993.
"a great hero": Ibid.
"dismayed that Rudolf refused . . .": Interview with Edward Albee.
"reluctantly . . .": *The New Yorker*, February 8, 1993.
"After I die . . .": Interviews with Charles Jude.
"contribute to the development of dance . . .": Rudolf Nureyev's will, dated and signed, Paris, April 14, 1992.
"It is my wish . . .": Ibid.
gave them the right to live in one of the houses on his Virginia estate: Letter of Instruction to the Trustees of Ballet Promotion Foundation, dated and signed, Paris, April 15, 1992.
challenged the very premise that Rudolf even wanted a foundation: Telephone interview with Gerald Rosenberg.
"was in full possession . . .": Brigitte Hernandez, "Le ballet des héritiers," *Le Point*, March 14, 1998.
"a Federal District Court judge in Manhattan confirmed . . .": United States District Court, Southern District of New York. Judge Denny Chin's Opinion: 94 Civ. 7701 (DC), June 25, 1998.
She resigned . . . saying . . . : Interview with Jane Hermann.
"eyes and ears in the ballet world": Terry Pristin, "Nureyev's Jetés vs. Estate Sharks," *New York Observer*, January 23, 1995.
records filed with the state of Illinois: Forms AG990 from July 1992 to June 30, 1996; also: Registration Statement of the Rudolf Nureyev Dance Foundation, May 15, 1992.
"wanted everything to go . . .": Interviews with Charles Jude.
Canesi wrote to Weinstein: Michel Canesi to Barry Weinstein, October 17, 1994.

SELECTED BIBLIOGRAPHY

Alexandrova, Vera. *A History of Soviet Literature*. Garden City, N.Y.: Doubleday & Company, Inc., 1963.

Alovert, Nina. *Baryshnikov in Russia*. New York: Holt, Rinehart and Winston, 1984.

Anawalt, Sasha. *The Joffrey Ballet: Robert Joffrey and the Making of an American Dance Company*. New York: Scribner, 1996.

Austin, Richard. *Lynn Seymour: An Authorised Biography*. London: Angus and Robertson Publishers, 1980.

Barnes, Clive. *Nureyev*. New York: Helene Obolensky Enterprises, Inc., 1982.

Barnes, Patricia. *The Children of Theatre Street*. New York: Penguin Books, 1979.

Bland, Alexander. *The Nureyev Image*. London: Studio Visa, 1977.

———. *The Nureyev Valentino: Portrait of a Film*. Ontario: Collier Macmillan Ltd., 1977.

———. *The Royal Ballet: The First Fifty Years*. Garden City, N.Y.: Doubleday & Company, Inc., 1981.

Bosworth, Patricia. *Diane Arbus: A Biography*. New York: W. W. Norton & Company, 1984.

Bragg, Melvyn. *Richard Burton: A Life*. New York: Warner Books, 1990.

Buckle, Richard. *Nijinsky*. New York: Simon & Schuster, 1971.

———. *Buckle at the Ballet*. New York: Atheneum, 1980.

———. *In the Wake of Diaghilev*. New York: Holt, Rinehart and Winston, 1983.

———, in collaboration with John Taras. *George Balanchine: Ballet Master*. New York: Random House, 1988.

———. *Diaghilev*. London: Weidenfeld & Nicolson, 1993.

Conquest, Robert. *The Harvest of Sorrow: Soviet Collectivization and the Terror Famine*. New York: Oxford University Press, 1986.

———. *Stalin: Breaker of Nations*. New York: Penguin Books, 1991.

Coward, Noël. *The Noël Coward Diaries*. Edited by Graham Payne and Sheridan Morley. Boston: Little, Brown and Company, 1982.

Croce, Arlene. *Afterimages*. New York: Alfred A. Knopf, 1977.

———. *Going to the Dance*. New York: Alfred A. Knopf, 1982.

———. *Sight Lines*. New York: Alfred A. Knopf, 1987.

De Mille, Agnes. *Martha: The Life and Work of Martha Graham*. New York: Vintage Books, 1992.

Faithfull, Marianne, with David Dalton. *Faithfull: An Autobiography*. Boston: Little, Brown and Company, 1994.

Fitzpatrick, Sheila. *The Russian Revolution*. Oxford, England: Oxford University Press, 1994.

Flanner, Janet (Genêt). *Paris Was Yesterday: 1925–1939*. Edited by Irving Drutman. New York: Harcourt Brace Jovanovich, 1988.

Fonteyn, Margot. *The Magic of Dance*. London: British Broadcasting Company, 1979.

———. *Autobiography*. New York: Warner Books, 1977.

Fraser, John. *Private View: Inside Baryshnikov's American Ballet Theatre*. Toronto: Bantam Books, 1988.

Garafola, Lynn. *Diaghilev's Ballets Russes*. New York: Oxford University Press, 1989.

Garciá-Márquez, Vicente. *Massine: A Biography*. New York: Alfred A. Knopf, 1995.

Gosling, Nigel. *Prowling the Pavements: Selected Art Writings, 1950–1980*. New York: A Lives Examined Book, 1986.

Graham, Martha. *Blood Memory*. Garden City, N.Y.: Doubleday, 1991.

Gruen, John. *Erik Bruhn: Danseur Noble*. New York: Viking Press, 1979.

———. *The Private World of Ballet*. New York: Penguin Books, 1976.

Hackett, Pat, ed. *The Andy Warhol Diaries*. New York: Warner Books, Inc., 1989

Heller, Mikhail and Nekrich, Aleksandr. *Utopia in Power: The History of the Soviet Union from 1917 to the Present*. New York: Simon & Schuster, 1992.

Hixson, Walter L. *Witness to Disintegration: Provincial Life in the Last Year of the USSR*. Hanover, N.H.: University Press of New England, 1993.

Hosking, Geoffrey. *The First Socialist Society: A History of the Soviet Union from Within*. Cambridge, Mass.: Harvard University Press, 1993.

Huckenpahler, Victoria. *Ballerina: A Biography of Violette Verdy*. New York: Marcel Dekker, Inc., 1978.

Kain, Karen, with Stephen Godfrey and Penelope Reed Doob. *Movement Never Lies: An Autobiography*. Toronto: McClelland and Stewart, Inc., 1994.

Karsavina, Tamara. *Theatre Street*. New York: E. P. Dutton & Co., Inc., 1961.

Kavanagh, Julie. *Secret Muses: The Life of Frederick Ashton*. London: Faber & Faber, 1996.

Kirkland, Gelsey, with Greg Lawrence. *Dancing on My Grave*. Garden City, N.Y.: Doubleday & Company, Inc., 1986.

Kirstein, Lincoln *Nijinsky Dancing*. New York: Alfred A. Knopf, 1975.

———. *Ballet: Bias & Belief*. New York: Dance Horizons, 1983.

———. *Four Centuries of Ballet*. New York: Dover Publications, Inc., 1984.

Klose, Kevin. *Russia and the Russians: Inside the Closed Society*. New York: W. W. Norton & Company, 1984.

Lahr, John. *Prick Up Your Ears: The Biography of Joe Orton*. New York: Limelight Editions, 1986.

Lawrence, John. *A History of Russia*. New York: Meridian Books, 1993.

Leonard, Richard Anthony. *A History of Russian Music*. New York: The Macmillan Company, 1957.

Levin, Bernard. *The Pendulum Years: Britain and the Sixties*. London: Pan Books, 1972.

Louis, Murray. *Inside Dance*. New York: St. Martin's Press, 1980.

Louis, Victor and Jennifer. *The Complete Guide to the Soviet Union*. New York: St. Martin's Press, 1991.

Makarova, Natalia. *A Dance Autobiography*. New York: Alfred A. Knopf, 1979.

Martins, Peter, with Robert Cornfield. *Far from Denmark*. Boston: Little, Brown and Company, 1982.

Mason, Francis. *I Remember Balanchine: Recollections of the Ballet Master by Those Who Knew Him*. New York: Doubleday & Company, 1991.

Money, Keith. *Fonteyn: The Making of a Legend*. New York: Reynal & Company, 1974

———. *Fonteyn & Nureyev: The Great Years*. London: Harvill, 1994.

Moynahan, Brian. *The Russian Century: A History of the Last Hundred Years*. New York: Random House, 1994.

Neufeld, James. *Power to Rise: The Story of the National Ballet of Canada.* Toronto: University of Toronto Press, 1996.

Nijinska, Bronislava. *Early Memoirs.* Translated and edited by Irina Nijinska and Jean Rawlinson. New York: Holt, Rinehart and Winston, 1981.

Nureyev, Rudolf. *Nureyev.* New York: E. P. Dutton & Co., Inc., 1963.

Oliphant, Betty. *Miss O: My Life in Dance.* Winnipeg, Can.: Turnstone Press, 1996.

Ottolenghi, Vittoria. *Rudolf Nureyev: Confessioni.* Rome: Editoriale Pantheon, 1995.

Panov, Valery, with George Feifer. *To Dance.* New York: Alfred A. Knopf, 1978.

Pasi, Mario, and Luigi Pignotti. *Nureyev: La Sua Arte la Sua Vita.* Milan: Sperling Kupfer Editori, 1993.

Percival, John. *Nureyev: Aspects of the Dancer.* New York: G. P. Putnam's Sons, 1975.

Perlmutter, Donna. *Shadowplay: The Life of Antony Tudor.* New York: Limelight Editions, 1995.

Petit, Roland. *J'ai Dansé sur les Flots.* Paris: Bernard Grasset, 1993.

Robinson, Harlow. *The Last Impresario: The Life, Times, and Legacy of Sol Hurok.* New York: Penguin Books, 1994.

Roslavleva, Natalia. *Era of the Russian Ballet.* New York: E. P. Dutton & Co., Inc., 1966.

Scott, John. *Behind the Urals: An American Worker in Russia's City of Steel.* Bloomington, Ind.: Indiana University Press, 1989.

Seymour, Lynn, with Paul Gardner. *Lynn: The Autobiography of Lynn Seymour.* London: Granada Publishing Limited, 1984.

Shervchenko, Arkady N. *Breaking with Moscow.* New York: Alfred A. Knopf, 1985.

Shilts, Randy. *And the Band Played On: Politics, People, and the AIDS Epidemic.* New York: Penguin Books, 1988.

Smakov, Gennady. *The Great Russian Dancers.* New York: Alfred A. Knopf, 1984.

Smith, Hedrick. *The Russians.* New York: Ballantine Books, 1977.

———. *The New Russians.* New York: Avon Press, 1991.

Snowdon. *A Photographic Autobiography.* New York: Times Books, 1979.

Sokolova, Lydia. *Dancing for Diaghilev: The Memoirs of Lydia Sokolova.* London: Columbus Books Ltd., 1989.

Souritz, Elizabeth. *Soviet Choreographers in the 1920s.* Durham, N.C.: Duke University Press, 1990.

Steegmuller, Francis. *Cocteau: A Biography.* London: Constable and Company Ltd., 1986.

Strauss, Robert. *The Trans-Siberian Rail Guide.* Edison, N.J.: Compass Publications, 1993.

Stuart, Otis. *Perpetual Motion: The Public and Private Lives of Rudolf Nureyev.* New York: Simon & Schuster, 1995.

Tallchief, Maria, with Larry Kaplan. *Maria Tallchief: America's Prima Ballerina.* New York: Henry Holt and Company, 1997.

Taper, Bernard. *Balanchine: A Biography.* New York: Times Books, 1984.

Taylor, Paul. *Private Domain.* New York: Alfred A. Knopf, 1987.

Tharp, Twyla. *Push Comes to Shove.* New York: Bantam Books, 1992.

Valois, Ninette de. *Come Dance with Me.* London: The World Publishing Co., 1957.

Vickers, Hugo. *Cecil Beaton.* London: Weidenfeld & Nicolson, 1993.

Volkogonov, Dmitri. *Stalin: Triumph and Tragedy.* Rocklin, Calif.: Prima Publishing, 1992.

Volkov, Solomon. *St. Petersburg: A Cultural History.* New York: The Free Press, 1995.

von Hagen, Mark. *Soldiers in the Proletarian Dictatorship: The Red Army and the Soviet Socialist State, 1917–1930.* Ithaca, N.Y.: Cornell University Press, 1990.

Warhol, Andy, and Pat Hackett. *POPism: The Warhol '60s.* New York: Harvest Books, 1990.

Watson, Peter. *Nureyev: A Biography.* London: Hodder & Stoughton, 1994.

Wishart, Michael. *High Diver.* London: Blond & Briggs, 1977.

Zakrzhevskaya, T. I.; L. P. Myasnikova; et al. *Rudolf Nureyev: Three Years in the Kirov Theatre.* St. Petersburg, Russia: Pushkinsky Fond, 1995.

INDEX

PERMISSIONS